贵州2015统计年鉴

GUIZHOU STATISTICAL YEARBOOK

GUIZHOU STATISTICAL YEARBOOK

贵州省统计局 国家统计局贵州调查总队 编

Compiled by Guizhou Provincial Bureau of Statistics NBS Survey Office in Guizhou

中国统计出版社
China Statistics Press

图书在版编目(CIP)数据

贵州统计年鉴. 2015 : 汉英对照 / 贵州省统计局,
国家统计局贵州调查总队编. -- 北京 : 中国统计出版社,
2015.10
ISBN 978-7-5037-7649-6

Ⅰ. ①贵… Ⅱ. ①贵… ②国… Ⅲ. ①统计资料-贵
州省-2015-年鉴-汉、英 Ⅳ. ①C832.73-54

中国版本图书馆 CIP 数据核字(2015)第 223604 号

贵州统计年鉴-2015

作　　者/ 贵州省统计局　国家统计局贵州调查总队
英文翻译/ 贵州统计应用研究院
责任编辑/ 佘竞雄
出版发行/ 中国统计出版社
地　　址/ 北京市丰台区西三环南路甲 6 号　邮政编码/100073
电　　话/ 邮购(010)63376909　书店(010)68783171
网　　址/ http://www.zgtjcbs.com
印　　刷/ 贵州新华印务有限公司
经　　销/ 新华书店
开　　本/ 890mm×1240mm　1/16
字　　数/ 1558 千字
印　　张/ 35
版　　别/ 2015 年 10 月第 1 版
版　　次/ 2015 年 10 月第 1 次印刷
定　　价/ 330.00 元

本书附同版本 CD-ROM 一张,光盘内容以书面文字为准。
如有印装差错,由本社发行部调换。

编 者 说 明

一、《贵州统计年鉴 -2015》系统收录了 2014 年贵州省国民经济和社会发展等各方面的统计数据，改革开放以来特别是 2010 年以来的主要统计数据，以及 2014 年全国、各省（区、市）主要统计数据，是反映贵州省情的重要工具书。

二、本年鉴包括 29 个部分：综合；国民经济核算；人口；就业人员和职工工资；固定资产投资；对外经济贸易；能源；财政税收；价格；人民生活；城市概况；资源和环境；农业；工业；建筑业；运输和邮电；批发和零售业；住宿、餐饮业和旅游业；金融业；教育和科技；文化、体育和卫生；社会服务及其他；民营经济；民族自治地方；经济强县；扶贫与开发；市（州）、县（市、区、特区）资料；全国及各省（区、市）资料；历年资料。为便于读者使用统计数据，在每部分之后附有主要统计指标解释。

三、本年鉴中，凡由有关部门（单位）提供的数据都在表式注释中说明了数据来源；部分指标统计范围、口径发生变化在表下均有注释，使用时请读者注意。

四、本年鉴中部分数据合计数或相对数由于计算单位或取舍不同而产生的计算误差，均未作机械调整。

五、本年鉴表中符号使用说明："…"表示数据不足最小计量单位；"空格"表示该统计指标数据不详或无数据；"#"表示该指标的其中项。

本年鉴在编辑、出版、发行过程中，得到了有关部门（单位）的大力支持和帮助，在此谨致衷心感谢！

Editor' s Notes

I. Guizhou Statistical Yearbook 2015 is an annual statistical publication, it system induded the statistical data, which reflects comprehensively the economic and social development of Guizhou Province. It covers data for 2014, key statistical data for the years since Reform and Opening-up especially the year 2010, and Main Statistics of Province (autonomous regions, municipalities) as well as the whole country. It is a useful reference book to thoroughly know Guizhou.

II. The Yearbook contains 29 chapters: General Survey; National Accounts; Population; Employment and Wages; Investment in Fixed Assets; Foreign Trade and Economic Cooperation; Energy; Government Finance and Taxation; Price Indices; People' s Living Conditions; General Survey of Cities; Resources and Environment; Agriculture; Industry; Construction; Transport, Postal and Telecommunication Services; Wholesale and Retail Trades; Hotel, Catering Services and Tourism; Financial Intermediation; Education, Science and Technology; Culture, Sports and Public Health; Social Services and Others; Private Economy; Minority Nationality Autonomous Areas; Economically Strong Counties; Anti-poverty and Development; Main Statistics of Prefectures and Counties; Main Statistics of Provinces (autonomous regions, municipalities) and the Whole Country; Historical Statistics. Explanatory Notes on Main Statistical Indicators is attached to the end of each chapter to help the readers to use the statistical data in this book.

III. Notes are taken under the data tables in which the data are provided by relative departments (unit) In part of the statistical divisions or the caliber of the changes in table are all noted. Please pay attention when you use it.

IV. Statistical discrepancies on totals and relative figures due to rounding are not adjusted in the yearbook.

V. Notations used in the yearbook: " …" indicates that the figure is not large enough to be measured with the smallest unit in the table; " blank space" indicates that data are unknown or are not available; " #" indicates a major breakdown of the total.

Thanks for enthusiastic of many relational departments and individuals to the editing, publication and distribution of the Yearbook!

《贵州统计年鉴-2015》 编辑委员会

李尚宽（省安全监管局局长）
傅迎春（省旅游局局长）
沈　健（省粮食局局长）
叶　韬（省扶贫办主任）
宋宇峰（省食品药品监管局局长）
薛建英（省国税局局长）
赵广忠（省气象局局长）
李德明（省通信管理局局长）
戴季宁（人民银行贵阳中心支行行长）
张卫民（贵阳海关关长）
刘文新（贵阳市市长）
周　荣（六盘水市市长）
魏树旺（遵义市代市长）
曾永涛（安顺市市长）
陈　晏（铜仁市代市长）
陈昌旭（毕节市市长）
杨永英（黔西南州州长）
冯仕文（黔东南州州长）
向红琼（黔南州州长）

Editorial Board

Ye Tao: Director ofthe Provincial Anti-poverty Office

Song Yufeng: Director of Guizhou province food and drug supervision bureau

Xue Jianying: Director of the Provincial National Taxation Administration

Zhao Guangzhong: Director of Guizhou Meteorological Bureau

Li Deming: Director of Guizhou Communication

Dai Jining: Director of the People´s Bank of China Guiyang Branch

Zhang Weimin: Director of Guiyang Customs of the People´s Republic of China

Liu Wenxin: Mayor of Guiyang City

Zhou Rong: Mayor of Liupanshui City

Wei Shuwang: Mayor of Zunyi City

Zeng Yongtao: Deputy Mayor of Anshun City

Chen Yan: Mayor of Tongren City

Chen Changxu: Mayor of Bijie City

Yang Yongying: Chief Executive of Qianxinan Autonomous prefectare.

Feng Shiwen: Chief Executive of Qiandongnan Autonomous prefectare.

Xiang Hongqiong: Chief Executive of Qiannan Autonomous prefectare.

《贵州统计年鉴-2015》编辑人员

Gui Zhou Statistical rearbook-2015 Editorial staff

目 录

CONTENTS

一 综 合
General Survey

1-1 行政区划(2014) …… 2
Divisions of Administrative Areas

1-2 各市(州)、县(市、区、特区)名称(2014) …… 3
Name of Each City (State, Prefecture) and County (City, District, Special Region)

1-3 法人单位数 …… 4
Namber of legal person units

1-4 按行业分法人单位数 …… 5
Number of legal person units Grouped by sector

1-5 社会经济主要指标 …… 6
Major Social and Economic Indicators

1-6 社会经济主要指标结构 …… 14
Composition Indicators on National Economic and Social Development

1-7 社会经济主要指标比例、效益 …… 17
Major Indicators on Proportions and Efficiency in Economic Social Development

1-8 贵州社会经济主要指标占全国比重 …… 20
Proportion of Guizhou´s Main Economic and Social Indicators to the Whole Country

主要统计指标解释 …… 22
Explanatory Notes on Main Statistical Indicators

二 国民经济核算
National Accounts

2-1 地区生产总值 …… 27
Gross Domestic Product

2-2 地区生产总值构成 …… 28
Composition of Gross Domestic Product

2-3 地区生产总值(按支出法计算) …… 29
Gross Domestic Product(Accounted by Expenditure Approach)

2-4 三次产业对地区生产总值增长的拉动 …… 30
Contribution of the Three Strata of Industry to GDP Growth

2-5 三次产业贡献率 …… 30
Share of the Contributions of the Three Strata of Industry to the Increase of the GDP

主要统计指标解释 …… 31
Explanatory Notes on Main Statistical Indicators

三 人 口
Population

3-1 全省历次人口普查主要指标 …… 37
Main Indicators on National Population Census in 1953,1964,1982,1990,2000 and 2010
3-2 第六次人口普查全省世居民族人口数 …… 38
Population of all ethnic groups on the Sixth National Population Census
3-3 年末常住人口(半年口径) …… 39
Permanent Resident Population(at least half a year)
3-4 户籍人口 …… 40
Household Registered Population
3-5 计划生育 …… 40
Family Planning
主要统计指标解释 …… 41
Explanatory Notes on Main Statistical Indicators

四 就业人员和职工工资
Employment and Wages

4-1 就业人员及劳动报酬 …… 45
Number of Employed Personnels and Wages
4-2 非私营单位就业人员年末人数(2014) …… 46
Number of Employed Persons in Non-private Units at Year-end
4-3 非私营单位女性就业人员年末人数(2014) …… 47
Number of Employed Female in Non-private Units at the Year-end
4-4 非私营单位各行业在岗职工年末人数(2014) …… 48
Working Staff and Workers in Non-private units at the Year-end by Sector
4-5 非私营单位在岗职工工资总额(2014) …… 49
Total Wages Bill of Working Staff and Workers in Non-private units
4-6 非私营单位各行业在岗职工平均工资(2014) …… 50
Average Wages of Working Staff and Workers in Non-private units by Sector
4-7 非私营单位各行业从业人员平均工资(2014) …… 51
Average Wages of Working Staff and Workers in Non-private units by Sector
4-8 城乡私营企业户数和就业人员(2014) …… 52
Number of Private Enterprises and Employed Persons in Urban and Rural Areas by Sector
4-9 城乡个体工商户数和就业人员(2014) …… 53
Number of Household and Self-Employed Individuals in Urban and Rural Areas
4-10 城镇新就业人数和失业人数 …… 54
Number of Newly Employed Persons and Unemployed Persons in Urban Areas
4-11 下岗失业人员享受再就业优惠政策情况 …… 54
Statistics of Re-employment Preferential Policies for Laid-off Workers
4-12 职业技能鉴定 …… 54
Occupation Skill Appraisal
4-13 劳动力市场需求人员、求职人员及构成 …… 55
Persons Required by Labor Market, Job Seckers and Ies Composition
主要统计指标解释 …… 56
Explanatory Notes on Main Statistical Indicators

五　固定资产投资
Investment in Fixed Assets

5-1　全社会固定资产投资 …… 60
Total Investment in Fixed Assets in the whole Province
5-2　全社会工业投资 …… 61
Industry Investment in the Whole Province
5-3　按行业、隶属关系和注册类型分固定资产投资(2014) …… 62
Investment in Fixed Assets by Sector, Jurisdiction of Management and Registration Status
5-4　按行业分 500 万元以上固定资产投资施工项目(2014) …… 64
Number of Construction Projects over 5 Million Yuan under Construction by Sector
5-5　房地产开发企业基本情况(2014) …… 66
Basic Conditions of Real Estate Development Enterprises
5-6　房地产开发投资主要指标 …… 68
Main Indicator on Real Estate Development
5-7　房地产开发企业商品房屋销售面积(2014) …… 69
Floor Space of Commercialized Buildings
5-8　房地产开发企业商品房屋销售额(2014) …… 69
Total Sale of Commercialized Buildings
主要统计指标解释 …… 70
Explanatory Notes on Main Statistical Indicators

六　对外经济贸易
Foreign Trade and Economic Cooperation

6-1　进出口总额 …… 79
Total Value of Imports and Exports
6-2　按地区分的出口商品总额 …… 79
Total Value of Export by Region
6-3　按地区分的进口商品总额 …… 79
Total Value of Import by Region
6-4　海关出口商品分类 …… 80
Value of Export Commodities by Category
6-5　海关进口商品分类 …… 82
Value of Import Commodities by Category
6-6　利用外资 …… 84
Foreign Capital Absorbed
6-7　外商直接投资按行业分项目个数 …… 85
Number of Projects for Contracted Foreign Direct Investment by Sector
6-8　按行业分外商直接投资协议金额 …… 85
Agreement Value of Foreign Direct Investment by Sector
6-9　按行业分外商实际直接投资额 …… 86
Actually Used Amount of Foreign Direct Investment by Sector
6-10　对外经济合作 …… 86
Economic Cooperation with Foreign Countries or Regions
主要统计指标解释 …… 87
Explanatory Notes on Main Statistical Indicators

七 能　源
Energy

7-1　能源生产、消费总量及构成 …… 91
Total Production and Consumption of Energy and Its Composition
7-2　综合能源平衡表 …… 92
Overall Energy Balance sheet
7-3　煤炭平衡表 …… 93
Coal Balance Sheet
7-4　电力平衡表 …… 94
Electricity Balance Sheet
7-5　分行业能源消费总量(2010-2011) …… 95
Total Energy Consumption by Sector
7-6　分行业能源消费总量(2012-2014) …… 97
Total Energy Consumption by Sector
7-7　能源生产消费弹性系数 …… 99
Elasticity Ratio of Energy Production and Consumption
7-8　生活能源消费量 …… 99
Energy Consumption for Non-Production Purpose
7-9　人均生活能源消费量 …… 100
Annual Average Per Capita Energy Consumption of Households
7-10　能源利用效率 …… 100
Using Efficiency of Energy
主要统计指标解释 …… 101
Explanatory Notes on Main Statistical Indicators

八 财政税收
Government Finance and Taxation

8-1　财政收入 …… 107
Financial Revenue
8-2　财政支出 …… 107
Financial Expenditure
8-3　分级一般公共预算收入(2014) …… 108
General Public Financial Budget Revenue by Level
8-4　分级一般公共预算支出(2014) …… 108
General Public Financial Budget Expenditure by Level
8-5　税收收入(按产业分) …… 109
Tax Revenue(by Industry)
8-6　税收收入(按企业类型分) …… 109
Taxation Revenue(by Business Entities)
8-7　国税税收收入(按产业分) …… 110
National Tax Revenue(by Industry)
8-8　地方系统税收收入(按产业分) …… 110
Local Tax Revenue(by Industry)
8-9　国税税收收入(按企业类型分) …… 111
National Taxation Revenue(by Business Entities)
8-10　地方系统税收收入(按企业类型分) …… 111
Local Taxation Revenue(by Business Entities)

8-11 国家税收收入(分行业、分税种)(2014) …… 112
Taxation Revenue of the Central Government(By Industrial Sector and Taxation Category)
8-12 地方系统税收收入(分行业、分税种)(2014) …… 114
Taxation Revenue of the Local Government(By Industrial Sector and Taxation Category)
主要统计指标解释 …… 116
Explanatory Notes on Main Statistical Indicators

九 价格指数
Price Indices

9-1 居民消费价格分类指数 …… 121
Consumer Price Indices by Category
9-2 商品零售价格分类指数 …… 124
Retail Price Indices by Category
9-3 工业生产者出厂价格分类指数 …… 125
Ex-Factory Price Indices of Industrial Products by Gategory
9-4 工业生产者购进价格指数 …… 127
Purchasing Price Index of Industrial Producer
9-5 农业生产资料价格分类指数 …… 127
Price Indices of Means of Agricultural Production by Category
9-6 固定资产投资和房地产销售价格指数 …… 128
Price Indices of Investment in Fixed Assets and Real Estate
主要统计指标解释 …… 129
Explanatory Notes on Main Statistical Indicators

十 人民生活
People´s Living Conditions

10-1 城乡人民生活水平 …… 133
People´s Livelihood in Urban and Rural Areas
10-2 城镇居民家庭生活基本情况 …… 135
Basic Conditions of Urban Households Life
10-3 城镇居民家庭人均现金收支 …… 136
Per Capita Annual Cash Income and Expenditure of Urban Households
10-4 城镇居民家庭人均消费性支出 …… 137
Per Capita Annual Consumption Expenditure of Urban Household
10-5 城镇居民家庭人均购买主要商品数量 …… 138
Per Capita Annual Purchases of Major Commodities of Urban Househoulds
10-6 每百户城镇居民家庭耐用消费品拥有量 …… 138
Number of Major Durable Consumer Goods Owned Per 100 Urban Households
10-7 按收入等级分城镇居民家庭收入、消费情况(2014) …… 139
Statistics of Income and Consumption of Urban Househoulds by Level of Income
10-8 农村居民家庭生活基本情况 …… 140
Basic Conditions of Rural Households Life
10-9 农村居民家庭人均可支配收入 …… 141
Per Capita Annual Net Income of Rural Households
10-10 农村居民家庭人均年总支出 …… 142
Per Capita Annual Gross Expenditures of Rural Households
10-11 农村居民家庭人均年现金收支 …… 143
Per Capita Annual Cash Income and Expenditure of Rural Households

10-12 农村居民家庭每人主要消费品消费量 …… 144
Per Capita Annual Consumption of Major Consumer Goods in Rural Households
10-13 每百户农村居民家庭年末耐用消费品拥有量 …… 144
Number of Durable Consumer Goods Owned By Per 100 Rural Households at the Year-end
10-14 按收入五等份分农村居民家庭收入、消费情况(2014) …… 145
Income and Consumption of Rural Househoulds by Income Quintile
10-15 农村居民家庭人均经营费用和生产性固定资产购置 …… 146
Per Capita Expenditure for Household Operations and Expenditure for Purchasing Productive Fixed Assets of Rural Households
主要统计指标解释 …… 147
Explanatory Notes on Main Statistical Indicators

十一 城市概况
General Survey of Cities

11-1 城市公用事业 …… 153
City Public Utilities
11-2 城市气象(2014) …… 155
Climate of Major Cities
11-3 城市平均气温(2014) …… 155
Monthly Average Temperature of Major Cities
11-4 城市建设(2014) …… 156
City Construction
11-5 城市设施水平(2014) …… 156
Level of Public Facilities in Cities
11-6 城市供水(2014) …… 157
Tap Water Supply in Cities
11-7 城市燃气(2014) …… 158
Supply of Gas in Cities
11-8 城市市政设施(2014) …… 159
Municipal Infrastructure in Cities
11-9 城市绿地和园林(2014) …… 160
Parks and Green Areas in Cities
11-10 城市市容环境卫生(2014) …… 160
Urban Sanitation in Cities
主要统计指标解释 …… 161
Explanatory Notes on Main Statistical Indicators

十二 资源和环境
Resources and Environment

12-1 主要河流(省内部分)主要特征值(2014) …… 167
Major Feature of Some Part of The Main River
12-2 主要矿产资源(2014) …… 168
Major Mineral Resources
12-3 森林资源 …… 169
Forest Resources
12-4 自然保护区 …… 170
Natural Reserves
12-5 森林公园 …… 170
Forest Parks

12-6 水资源和水质监测 …… 171
Water Resource and Monitoring of Water Quality
12-7 环保系统机构、人员数 …… 172
Number of Enviornmental Protection Agencies and Persons Engaged
12-8 环境保护资金投入 …… 172
Investment in Environmental Protection
12-9 废水治理 …… 173
Waste Water Treatment
12-10 空气质量及污染治理 …… 174
Air Quality and Treatment of Industrial Waste Gas
12-11 固体废物生产及处理 …… 175
Production and Treatment of Industrial Solid Wastes
12-12 环境污染事故 …… 176
Accident of Environment Pollution
12-13 自然灾害 …… 176
Natural Disasters
主要统计指标解释 …… 177
Explanatory Notes on Main Statistical Indicators

十三 农 业
Agriculture

13-1 农村基本情况及农业生产条件 …… 185
Basic Conditions of Rural Areas and Agricultural Production
13-2 年末主要农业机械拥有量 …… 186
Major Agricultural Machinery at the Year-end
13-3 灌溉、除涝治水 …… 186
Irrigation, Flood Prevention, Water and Soil Conservation
13-4 农林牧渔业增加值 …… 187
Value-Added of Farming,Forestry, Animal Husbandry, Fishery and Their Services
13-5 农林牧渔业总产值 …… 188
Gross Output Value of Farming,Forestry,Animal Husbandry, Fishery and Their Services
13-6 主要农作物播种面积 …… 189
Sown Areas of Major Farm Crops
13-7 主要农作物产品产量 …… 190
Yields of Major Farm Crops
13-8 主要农作物单产 …… 190
Yields of Major Farm Crops Per Mu
13-9 茶叶、水果面积及产量 …… 191
Total Sown Areas and Yields of Tea,Fruit
13-10 造林及林产品产量 …… 191
Areas of Forestation and Output of Forest Products
13-11 畜牧业生产及水产品 …… 192
Livestock and Aquatic Products
主要统计指标解释 …… 193
Explanatory Notes on Main Statistical Indicators

十四 工 业
Industry

14-1 规模以上工业企业单位数 …… 198
Number of Industrial Enterprises above Designated Size

14-2 按行业分规模以上工业企业单位数 …… 199
Number of Industrial Enterprises above Designated Size by Sector
14-3 规模以上工业增加值 …… 201
Value added of Industry above Designated Size
14-4 按行业分规模以上工业增加值 …… 202
Value added of Industry above Designated Size by Sector
14-5 规模以上工业总产值 …… 204
Gross Output Value of Industry above Designated Size
14-6 按行业分规模以上工业总产值 …… 205
Gross Output Value of Industry above Designated Size by Sector
14-7 规模以上工业企业主要经济指标 …… 207
Major Economic Indicators of Industrial Enterprises above Designated Size
14-8 大中型工业企业主要经济指标 …… 207
Major Economic Indicators of Large and Medium-sized Industrial Enterprises
14-9 规模以上工业主要产品产量 …… 208
Output of Major Industrial Products above Designated Size
14-10 规模以上工业企业主要经济指标(2014) …… 209
Main Economic Indicators of Industrial Enterprises above Designated Size
14-11 规模以上工业企业分行业主要经济指标(2014) …… 210
Main Economic Indicators of Industrial Enterprises above Designated Size by Sector
14-12 规模以上国有控股工业企业主要经济指标(2014) …… 212
Major Economic Indicators of State-controlled Industrial Enterprises above Designated Size
14-13 规模以上集体工业企业主要经济指标(2014) …… 214
Main Economic Indicators of All Collective-owned Industrial Enterprises above Designated Size
14-14 规模以上外商投资和港澳台投资工业企业主要经济指标(2014) …… 215
Major Economic Indicators of all above Designated Size Industrial Enterprises Funded by Foreigners and Hong kong, Macao and Taiwan
14-15 规模以上工业企业主要经济效益指标(2014) …… 216
Main Indicators on Economic Efficiency of all Industrial Enterprises above Designated Size
14-16 规模以上国有控股工业企业主要经济效益指标(2014) …… 218
Major Indicators on Economic Efficiency of State-controlled Industrial Enterprises above Designated Size
14-17 规模以上集体工业企业主要经济效益指标(2014) …… 220
Main Indicators on Economic Benefit of Collective-owned Industrial Enterprises above Designated Size
14-18 大中型工业企业主要经济指标占全省规模以上工业比重(2014) …… 221
Percentages of Main Indicators of Large and Medium Industrial Enterprises as the whole Industrial Enterprises above Designated Size
14-19 规模以上大中型工业企业分行业主要经济指标(2014) …… 222
Main Indicators on Economic of Large and Medium Industrial Enterprises by Sector
14-20 规模以上工业销售产值(2014) …… 224
Output Value of Industrial mdustrial Sales above Designated Size
14-21 规模以上工业主要产品产量、销售量和产销率(2014) …… 225
Output, Sales Volume, Ratio of Produots Sold of major Industrial Produots above Designated Size
14-22 高技术产业基本情况 …… 227
Basic Statistics on High-tech Industry
主要统计指标解释 …… 228
Explanatory Notes on Main Statistical Indicators

十五 建筑业
Construction

15-1 建筑业主要指标 …… 235
Main Economic Indicators on Construction Enterprises

15-2 建筑业主要生产指标(2014) …… 236
Main Production Indicators on Construction Enterprises
15-3 建筑业企业房屋建筑(2014) …… 238
House Buildings by Construction Enterprises
主要统计指标解释 …… 240
Explanatory Notes on Main Statistical Indicators

十六 运输和邮电
Transport, Postal and Telecommunication Services

16-1 境内运输线路长度 …… 245
Length of Domestic Transport Routes
16-2 民用航空运输 …… 246
Civil Aviation Transportation
16-3 民用汽车拥有量 …… 246
Possession of Civil Vehicles
16-4 快递业务量 …… 247
Express Delivery Services
16-5 旅客运量及周转量 …… 247
Passenger Traffic and Passenger-Kilometers
16-6 货物运输量及周转量 …… 247
Freight Traffic and Ton-Kilometers
16-7 电信主要指标 …… 248
Major Indicators of Telecommunications
16-8 邮政、电信主要指标 …… 249
Major Indicators of Post
主要统计指标解释 …… 250
Explanatory Notes on Main Statistical Indicators

十七 批发和零售业
Wholesale and Retail Trades

17-1 社会消费品零售总额 …… 255
Total Retail Sales of Consumer Goods
17-2 限额以上批发业和零售业 …… 255
Basic Conditions of Enterprises above Designated Size in Wholesale and Retail Trade
17-3 限额以上批发业企业(2014) …… 256
Basic Conditions of Enterprises above Designated Size in Wholesale Trade
17-4 限额以上批发业企业主要财务指标(2014) …… 260
Main Financial Indicators of Enterprises above Designated Size in Wholesale Trade
17-5 限额以上零售业企业(2014) …… 262
Basic Conditions of Enterprises above Designated Size in Retail Trade
17-6 限额以上零售业企业主要财务指标(2014) …… 266
Main Financial Indicators of Enterprises above Designated Size in Retail Trade
17-7 商品交易市场 …… 268
Commodity Exchange Markets
主要统计指标解释 …… 269
Explanatory Notes on Main Statistical Indicators

十八　住宿、餐饮业和旅游业
Hotel, Catering Services and Tourism

18-1　限额以上住宿业和餐饮业 …… 275
Basic Conditions of Enterprises above Designated Size in Hotels and Catering Services
18-2　限额以上住宿业企业(2014) …… 276
Basic Conditions of Enterprises above Designated Size in Hotel Services
18-3　限额以上餐饮业企业(2014) …… 278
Basic Conditions of Enterprises above Designated Size in Catering Services
18-4　旅游业 …… 280
Tourism
18-5　来黔境外旅游人数及人均消费支出 …… 281
Number of Overseas Tourists Visiting Guizhou and Average Per Capita Spending
18-6　接待外国旅游人数(按地区分) …… 281
Number of Overseas Tourists Visiting Guizhou(by Country/Territory)
18-7　旅游外汇收入 …… 282
Foreign Exchange Earnings from Tourism
18-8　旅馆业接待经营 …… 283
Operation of Hotels
18-9　星级饭店 …… 283
Star-rated Hotels
18-10　风景名胜区 …… 284
National Parks
18-11　全国重点文物保护单位 …… 286
Historical and Cultrual Relics under Key Protection
18-12　星级饭店 …… 288
Star-rated Hotels
主要统计指标解释 …… 295
Explanatory Notes on Main Statistical Indicators

十九　金融业
Financial Intermediation

19-1　金融机构人民币存贷款余额 …… 301
Total Deposits and Total Loans of Financial Institutions
19-2　保险 …… 301
Insurance
19-3　财产保险 …… 302
Property Insurance
19-4　财产保险主要指标(2014) …… 303
Major Indicators on Property Insurance
19-5　人寿保险 …… 304
Life Insurance
19-6　人寿保险主要指标(2014) …… 305
Major Indicators on Life Insurance
19-7　贵州上市公司股票发行情况(A 股)(2014) …… 306
Summary List of Stocks Publicly Issued by Guizhou Enterprises(A Shares)
主要统计指标解释 …… 307
Explanatory Notes on Main Statistical Indicators

二十　教育和科技
Education, Science and Technology

20-1　各级各类学校数 …… 311
Number of Schools by Level and Type
20-2　各级各类学校专任教师数 …… 312
Number of Full-time Teachers by Level and Type of School
20-3　各级各类学校招生数 …… 313
Number of New Students Enrollment by Level and Type of School
20-4　各级各类学校在校生数 …… 314
Number of Students Enrollment by Level and Type of School
20-5　各级各类学校毕业生数 …… 315
Number of Graduates by Level and Type of School
20-6　教师职称 …… 316
Technical Rank of Teachers
20-7　各级各类学校女学生和女教师数 …… 317
Female Students and Teachers by Level and Type of School
20-8　各级各类学校师生比 …… 318
Student-Teacher Ratio by Level of School
20-9　各级各类学校学生入学率 …… 318
Enrollment Rate by Level and Type of School
20-10　普通高等学校(2014) …… 319
Regular Institutions of Higher Education
20-11　普通高等学校分科专任教师数(2014) …… 319
Number of Full-time Teachers in Institutions of Higher Education by Field of Study
20-12　研究生数 …… 320
Number of Postgraduates
20-13　技工学校 …… 320
Technical Schools
20-14　中等职业学校(机构)数(2014) …… 321
Number of Secondary Vocational Schools
20-15　中等职业学校(2014) …… 321
Secondary Vocational Schools
20-16　中等职业学校(机构)学生分科类情况(2014) …… 322
Students in Secondary Vocational Schools by Field of Study
20-17　民族教育 …… 323
Minority Nationality Education
20-18　民办教育 …… 324
Private Education
20-19　成人教育 …… 325
Adult Education
20-20　科技活动 …… 326
Scientific and Technological Activities
20-21　研究与试验发展(R&D)活动 …… 327
Scientific Research and Development
20-22　规模以上工业企业科技活动 …… 328
Scientific and Technology Activities above Designated Size
20-23　规模以上工业企业新产品开发及生产情况(2014) …… 329
New product Development and production above Designated Size
20-24　政府属独立研究与开发机构科技活动 …… 330
Scientific and Technological Activities of Government-affiliated Independent Research Institutions

20-25 省部级以上成果登记(完成人员) ······ 332
Staffs Personnel of Provincial or Ministerial Level and above
20-26 省部级以上成果登记(数量及投资额) ······ 333
Number of Achievements and Investment of Projects at Provincial or Ministerial Level and above(number & investment)
20-27 事业、企业单位各类专业技术人员 ······ 334
Specialized Technical Personnel in Enterprises and institutions
20-28 专利申请受理及授权 ······ 335
Patent Application Accepted and Granted
20-29 科协系统科学技术普及情况 ······ 336
Popularization of Science and Technology
主要统计指标解释 ······ 337
Explanatory Notes on Main Statistical Indicators

二十一 文化、体育和卫生
Culture, Sports, and Public Health

21-1 文化事业机构和人员 ······ 345
Number of Institutions and Personnel in Cultural Industry
21-2 文化事业单位数 ······ 346
Basic Statistics on Culture Establishment
21-3 文化娱乐业(2014) ······ 346
Culture and Entertainment Industry
21-4 艺术表演场所(2014) ······ 346
Art Preformances Places
21-5 文化部门艺术表演团体(2014) ······ 347
Art Troupes of Culture Sector
21-6 群众文化馆(站)(2014) ······ 347
Mass Culture Centers(Stations)
21-7 广播、电视 ······ 348
Radio and Television Industry
21-8 广播、电视节目播出时间(2014) ······ 349
Broadcasting Hours of Radio and Television Programs
21-9 图书出版 ······ 349
Books Published
21-10 杂志出版 ······ 350
Magazines Published
21-11 报纸出版 ······ 350
Newspaper Published
21-12 报纸分类出版数量(2014) ······ 350
Number of Newspaper Published by Category
21-13 体育运动员 ······ 351
Athletes
21-14 体育运动获奖 ······ 351
Medals Won by Guizhou Athletes in Domestic and International Competitions
21-15 公共体育场地 ······ 352
Number of Public Stadiums and Gymnasiums
21-16 群众体育活动 ······ 352
Activities of Mass Sports
21-17 卫生事业 ······ 353
Health Care

21-18 卫生机构、床位、人员数(2014) …… 354
Number of Health Institutions, Beds and Personnels
21-19 卫生防疫防治和妇幼卫生事业 …… 355
Sanitation and Epidemic Prevention, Maternity and Child Care
21-20 县及县以上医院、卫生院(2014) …… 356
Hospitals and Health Centers at County Level and above
21-21 县、乡、村三级医疗、预防、保健 …… 357
Health Organization at County, Town and Village Level
21-22 28 种传染病报告发病及死亡人数(2014) …… 358
List of 28 Infectious Diseases Reported and Number of Death
21-23 28 种传染病报告发病率、死亡率及病死率(2014) …… 359
List of Incidence, Death and Mortality Rates of 28 Infectious Disease Reported
21-24 5 岁以下儿童和孕产妇死亡率 …… 360
Mortality Rate of the Maternal and Children Aged under 5
21-25 新型农村合作医疗 …… 360
Conditions of New Cooperative Medical System
主要统计指标解释 …… 361
Explanatory Notes on Main Statistical Indicators

二十二 社会服务及其他
Social Services and Others

22-1 律师、公证、调解工作 …… 367
Lawyers, Notarization and Mediation
22-2 国内公证文书分类 …… 368
Domestic Notarial Documents by Type
22-3 消费者协会受理投诉 …… 369
Cases Accepted and Heard by Consumer Association
22-4 检察院主要业务 …… 370
Cases of Procuratorate
22-5 人民法院刑事一审案件收案 …… 370
First Trail Criminal Cases Accepted by Courts
22-6 人民法院刑事一审案件结案 …… 371
First Trail Criminal Cases Settled by Courts
22-7 人民法院刑事案件中青少年犯罪 …… 371
Juvenile Delinquency Among Criminal Cases
22-8 生产安全 …… 372
Production Safety
22-9 火灾 …… 373
Fire Accidents
22-10 交通事故(2014) …… 373
Traffic Accidents
22-11 社会保险 …… 374
Social Insurance
22-12 社会福利机构 …… 375
Social Welfare Institutions and Enterprises
22-13 社会福利机构工作人员 …… 375
Staff Employed by Social welfare Institutions and Enterprises
22-14 社会服务及设施和民政事业发展主要指标 …… 376
Main Indicators of Social Services & Facilities and Civil Administration Career Development

22-15 社会福利救济主要支出 …… 376
Major Expenditures of Welfare Relief Funds
22-16 享受补助、救济人员 …… 377
Persons Receiving Subsidies and Relief Funds
22-17 享受国家定期抚恤、补助、救济人员数 …… 377
Persons Receiving Regular Subsidy and Commiseration of Country
22-18 残疾人事业基本情况 …… 378
Basic Information of Person with Disablility
22-19 婚姻 …… 380
Marriages and Divorces
22-20 殡葬服务情况 …… 380
Funeral and Interment Services
主要统计指标解释 …… 381
Explanatory Notes on Main Statistical Indicators

二十三 民营经济
Private Economy

23-1 民营经济基本情况(2014) …… 386
Basic Information of Private Economy
23-2 民营经济增加值 …… 387
Value-added of Private Economy
23-3 民营经济分产业增加值占该产业增加值比重 …… 387
Value-added of Private Economy Unit as Percentage to GDP
23-4 民营经济固定资产投资(2014) …… 388
Private Economic Investment in Fixed Assets
23-5 规模以上民营经济工业企业主要经济指标(2014) …… 389
Main Economic Indicators of Industrial Enterprises above Designated Size of Private Economy
23-6 限额以上民营经济批发零售企业主要经济指标(2014) …… 392
Main Economic Indicators of Wholesale and Retail Trade Enterprises above Designated Size of Private Economy
23-7 限额以上民营经济住宿餐饮企业主要经济指标(2014) …… 394
Main Economic Indicators of Accommododation and Catering Enterprises above Designated Size of Private Economy
23-8 资质以上民营经济建筑企业主要经济指标(2014) …… 396
Main Economic Indicators of Construction Enterprises above Qualification of Private Economy

二十四 民族自治地方
Minority Nationality Autonomous Areas

24-1 民族自治地方行政区划 …… 399
Administrative Division of Minority Nationality Autonomous Areas
24-2 少数民族分布 …… 399
Geographic Distribution of Minority Nationalities
24-3 民族自治地方经济社会主要指标 …… 400
Major Social and Economic Indicators of Minority Nationality Autonomous Areas
24-4 民族自治地方经济社会主要指标(2014) …… 401
Major Economic Indicators of Minority Nationality Autonomous Areas
24-5 民族自治地方一般公共预算收入(2014) …… 403
General Public Financial Budget Revenue of Minority Nationality Autonomous Areas
24-6 民族自治地方一般公共预算支出(2014) …… 403
General Public Financial Budget Expenditure of Minority Nationality Autonomous Areas

二十五　经济强县
Economically Strong Counties

25-1　经济强县主要指标(一)(2014) …… 407
Major Indicators of Economically Strong County(1)
25-2　经济强县主要指标(二)(2014) …… 408
Major Indicators of Economically Strong County(2)

二十六　扶贫与开发
Anti-poverty and Development

26-1　扶贫开发重点县主要指标占全省比重(2014) …… 411
Major Indicators of Basilic County of Anti-poverty and Development and Its Percentage to Provincial Total
26-2　贫困人口及发生率(2014) …… 412
Number of Poverty Population and It′s Arisen Rate
26-3　扶贫开发重点县主要指标(2014) …… 414
Major Indicators on Basilic County of Anti-poverty and Development

二十七　市(州)、县(市、区、特区)资料
Main Statistics of City(State, Prefecture) and County(City, District, Special Region)

27-1　各市(州)生产总值及增速(2014) …… 420
Gross Domestic Product and Its Composition by Region
27-2　各市(州)年末常住人口 …… 421
Permanent Population at the year-end by Region
27-3　各市(州)户籍人口 …… 422
Household Registered Population by Region
27-4　各市(州)非私营单位在岗职工年平均人数、年平均工资(2014) …… 423
Number of Staff and Workers and Their Annual Average Wages in Non-private units by Region
27-5　各市(州)投资、消费(2014) …… 424
Investment in Fixed Assets by Region
27-6　各市(州)能源利用效率(2014) …… 424
Energy using Effutency by Region
27-7　各市(州)一般公共预算收入(2014) …… 425
General Public Financial Budget Revenue by Region
27-8　各市(州)一般公共预算支出(2014) …… 425
General Public Financia Budget Expenditure by Region
27-9　各市(州)金融机构人民币存贷款余额(2014) …… 426
Saving Deposits and Loans Balance of Financial Institutions by Region
27-10　各市(州)所在城市城镇居民家庭人均年收支(2014) …… 426
Per Capital Annual Disposable Income and Expenditure of Urban Households of Major Cities
27-11　各市(州)农村居民家庭人均年收支(2014) …… 427
Per Capita Net Income and Living Expenditure of Rural Households by Region
27-12　各市(州)所在城市分类价格指数 …… 427
Urban Residents Consumer Price Indices of Major Cities by Region
27-13　各市(州)乡村从业人员数(2014) …… 428
Rural Employment by Region
27-14　各市(州)农业机械总动力及拥有量(2014) …… 428
Total Power and Possession of Agricultural Machinery by Region

27-15 各市(州)农林牧渔业总产值(2014) …… 429
Gross Output Value of Farming, Forestry, Animal Husbandary, Fishery and Their Services by Region
27-16 各市(州)农用化肥施用量(2014) …… 429
Consumption of Chemical Fertilizers for Agricultural Use by Region
27-17 各市(州)主要农作物播种面积(2014) …… 430
Sown Areas of Major Farm Crops by Region
27-18 各市(州)主要农产品产量(2014) …… 430
Output of Major Farm Crops by Region
27-19 各市(州)牲畜出、存栏量(2014) …… 431
Amount of Livestocks in Hand and Slaughtered by Region
27-20 各市(州)主要畜产品、水产品产量(2014) …… 431
Output of Major Livestock Products and Aquatic Products by Region
27-21 各市(州)规模以上工业增加值(2014) …… 432
Total Gross Industrial Value-added above Designated Size by Region
27-22 各市(州)规模以上工业企业主要工业产品产量(2014) …… 432
Ouput of Major Industrial Products above Designated Size by Region
27-23 各市(州)公路里程(2014) …… 433
Length of Highways by Region
27-24 各市(州)邮政、电信主要指标(2014) …… 433
Major Indicators of Telecommunications and Post by Region
27-25 各市(州)教育事业主要指标(2014) …… 434
Major Indicators of Education by Region
27-26 各市(州)卫生人员数(2014) …… 434
Number of Employed Persons in Health Care Institutions by Region
27-27 各市(州)每千人口拥有卫生技术人员数(2014) …… 435
Medical Technical Personnel in Health Care Institutions Per 1000 Persons by Region
27-28 各市(州)社区卫生服务中心(站)医疗服务情况(2014) …… 435
Medical Services of Community Health Service Centers(Stations) by Region
27-29 各市(州)医疗卫生机构服务情况(2014) …… 436
Services in Hospitals by Region
27-30 各市(州)火灾(2014) …… 437
Fires by Region
27-31 各县(市、区、特区)地区生产总值(2014) …… 438
Gross Domestic Product by County(City, District, Special region)
27-32 各县(市、区、特区)人均地区生产总值(2014) …… 440
Per Capita Gross Domestic Product by County(City, District, Special region)
27-33 各县(市、区、特区)年末常住人口 …… 441
Permanent Population at Year-end by County(City, District, Special region)
27-34 各县(市、区、特区)户籍人口(2014) …… 443
Household Registered Population by County(City, District, Special region)
27-35 各县(市、区、特区)固定资产投资 …… 444
Investment in Fixed Assets by County(City, District, Special region)
27-36 各县(市、区、特区)一般公共预算收入(2014) …… 446
General Public Financial Budget Revenue by County(City, District, Special region)
27-37 各县(市、区、特区)一般公共预算支出(2014) …… 448
General Public Financial Budget Expenditure by County(City, District, Special region)
27-38 各县(市、区、特区)城镇常住居民人均可支配收入(2014) …… 450
Per Capita Disposable in come of urban Households by County(City, District, Special region)
27-39 各县(市、区、特区)农民人均纯收入(2014) …… 451
Per Capita Net Income of Rural Households by County(City, District, Special region)

27-40 各县(市、区、特区)乡村从业人员(2014) …… 452
Number of Rural Employment by County(City, District, Special region)
27-41 各县(市、区、特区)农林牧渔业总产值(2014) …… 454
Gross Output Value of Farming, Forestry, Animal Husbandry and Fishery and Its Order by County(City, District, Special region)
27-42 各县(市、区、特区)粮食、肉类产量(2014) …… 456
Output of Grain, Meat and Its Order by County(City, Section, Special region)
27-43 各县(市、区、特区)油菜籽、烤烟产量(2014) …… 458
Output of Rapeseed and Flue-cured Tobacco and Its Order by County(City, District, Special region)
27-44 各县(市、区、特区)规模以上工业增加值(2014) …… 460
Value-added of Industry above Designated Size and Its Order by County(City, District, Special region)
27-45 各县(市、区、特区)社会消费品零售总额(2014) …… 462
Total Retail Sales of Consumer Goods by County(City, District, Special Region)
27-46 各县(市、区、特区)金融机构人民币存贷款余额(2014) …… 464
Urban and Rural Resident Savings Deposit Balance and Its Order by County(City, District, Special region)
27-47 各县(市、区、特区)普通中学(2014) …… 466
Regular Secondary Schools by County(City, District, Special region)
27-48 各县(市、区、特区)小学(2014) …… 470
Primary Schools by County(City, District, Special region)

二十八 全国及各省(区、市)资料
Main Statistics of Provinces(autonomous regions, municipalities) in the Whole Country

28-1 全国及各省(区、市)人口、生产总值(2014) …… 474
The Population and GDP of the Whole Country and All Provinces
28-2 全国及各省(区、市)固定资产投资(不含农户)、房地产开发情况(2014) …… 476
The Investment in Fixed Assets(Excluding Farmer) and Real Estate Development of the Whole Country and All Province
28-3 全国及各省(区、市)内外贸易(2014) …… 478
Imports and Exports of the Whole Country and All Provinces
28-4 全国及各省(区、市)主要农产品产量(2014) …… 479
The Output of Main Agricultural Products of the Whole Country and All Provinces
28-5 全国及各省(区、市)主要工业产品产量(2014) …… 480
The Output of Main Industrial Products of the Whole Country and All Provinces

二十九 历年资料
Historical Statistics

29-1 全省地区生产总值 …… 485
Gross Domestic Product
29-2 全省地区生产总值增长速度 …… 486
Indices of Gross Domestic Product
29-3 全省地区生产总值指数(1978 年=100) …… 487
Indices of Gross Domestic Product(year of 1978=100)
29-4 年末常住人口 …… 488
Permanent Population at the Year-end
29-5 人口自然变动 …… 489
Natural Change of Population
29-6 户籍人口 …… 490
Household Registered Population
29-7 就业人员 …… 491
Employed Persons

29-8 非私营单位在岗职工人数 …… 492
Number of Staff and Workers in Non-private Units
29-9 非私营单位在岗职工平均工资 …… 493
Average Wages of Staff and Workers in Non-private Units
29-10 全社会固定资产投资 …… 494
Total Investment in Fixed Assets in the Whole Province
29-11 财政收支 …… 495
Financial Revenue and Expenditure
29-12 人民生活 …… 496
People´s Living Conditions
29-13 农林牧渔业总产值 …… 498
Gross Output Value of Farming, Forestry, Animal Husbandry and Fishery
29-14 农林牧渔业总产值增长速度 …… 499
Indices of Gross Output Value of Farming, Forestry, Animal Husbandry and Fishery
29-15 农林牧渔业总产值指数(1978 年=100) …… 500
Indices of Gross Output Value of Farming, Forestry, Animal Husbandry and Fishery(year of 1978=100)
29-16 主要农产品产量 …… 501
Output of Major Farm Crops
29-17 工业总产值 …… 502
Gross Output Value of Industry
29-18 工业增加值 …… 503
Value-added of Industry
29-19 工业增加值增长速度 …… 504
Indices of Value-added of Industry
29-20 规模以上工业主要经济指标 …… 505
Major Economic Indicators of Industrial Enterprises above Designated Size
29-21 主要工业产品产量 …… 507
Output of Major Industrial Products
29-22 建筑业总产值和房屋建筑面积 …… 508
Gross Output Value of Construction and Floor Space of Building
29-23 交通运输 …… 509
Transportation
29-24 旅客周转量和货物周转量 …… 510
Passenger-kilometers and Freight Ton-kilometers
29-25 内外贸易 …… 511
Domestic Trade, Foreign Trade and Economic Cooperation
29-26 旅游 …… 512
Tourism
29-27 金融机构人民币各项存贷款余额 …… 513
Saving Deposits and Loans Balance of Financial Institutions
29-28 教育 …… 514
Education
29-29 卫生 …… 516
Health Care

贵州2015
统计年鉴
GUIZHOU
STATISTICAL YEARBOOK

1 综合
General Survey

1-1 行政区划(2014)

Divisions of Administrative Areas

单位:个 (unit)

市(州)名称	City (Autonomous Prefecture)	地级单位 Units at Prefectural Level	#市 Cities	县级单位 Units at County Level	县 Counties	自治县 Autonomous Counties	县级市 Cities at County Level	市辖区 Districts under the Jurisdiction of City
全省合计	**Total**	**9**	**6**	**88**	**55**	**11**	**7**	**14**
贵阳市	Guiyang	1	1	10	3		1	6
六盘水市	Liupanshui	1	1	4	2			1
遵义市	Zunyi	1	1	14	8	2	2	2
安顺市	Anshun	1	1	6	1	3		2
毕节市	Bijie	1	1	8	6	1		1
铜仁市	Tongren	1	1	10	4	4		2
黔西南布依族苗族自治州	Qianxinan	1		8	7		1	
黔东南苗族侗族自治州	Qiandongnan	1		16	15		1	
黔南布依族苗族自治州	Qiannan	1		12	9	1	2	

注：资料来源于省民政厅(下表同)。
Note:Date in the table are obtained from the department of civil affairs(the same applies to the next table).

1-1 续表 continued

市(州)名称	City (Autonomous Prefecture)	特区 Special District	镇 Town	街道办事处 Street Communities	乡 Township	#民族乡 Ethnic Community Township	城市社区居民委员会 Neighbourhood Committees	村民委员会 Village Committees
全省合计	**Total**	**1**	**762**	**134**	**500**	**208**	**2016**	**16747**
贵阳市	Guiyang		45		32	18	539	996
六盘水市	Liupanshui	1	44	11	48	40	153	1019
遵义市	Zunyi		177	20	48	8	330	1679
安顺市	Anshun		45	11	32	10	140	1007
毕节市	Bijie		104	35	124	72	208	3451
铜仁市	Tongren		81	14	77	38	207	2748
黔西南布依族苗族自治州	Qianxinan		78	18	43	3	125	1083
黔东南苗族侗族自治州	Qiandongnan		108	9	88	15	168	3307
黔南布依族苗族自治州	Qiannan		80	16	8	4	146	1457

1—2 各市(州)、县(市、区、特区)名称(2014)

Name of Each City(State,Prefecture) and County(City,District,Special Region)

市(州)名称 City(Autonomous Prefecture)	县(市、区、特区)名称 County(City,District,Special Region)
贵阳市 Guiyang	南明区 云岩区 花溪区 乌当区 白云区 观山湖区 清镇市 开阳县 息烽县 修文县 Nanming Yunyan Huaxi Wudang Baiyun Guanshanhu Qingzhen Kaiyang Xifeng Xiuwen
六盘水市 Liupanshui	钟山区 六枝特区 盘县 水城县 Zhongshan Liuzhi Panxian Shuicheng
遵义市 Zunyi	红花岗区 汇川区 赤水市 仁怀市 遵义县 桐梓县 绥阳县 正安县 Honghuagang Huichuan Chishui Renhuai Zunyi Tongzi Suiyang Zhengan 凤岗县 湄潭县 余庆县 习水县 道真仡佬族苗族自治县 务川仡佬族苗族自治县 Fenggang Meitan Yuqing Xishui Daozhen Wuchuan
安顺市 Anshun	西秀区 平坝区 普定县 关岭布依族苗族自治县 镇宁布依族苗族自治县 Xixiu Pingba Puding Guanling Zhenning 紫云苗族布依族自治县 Ziyun
毕节市 Bijie	七星关区 大方县 黔西县 金沙县 织金县 纳雍县 赫章县 威宁彝族回族苗族自治县 Qixingguan Dafang Qianxi Jinsha Zhijin Nayong Hezhang Weining
铜仁市 Tongren	碧江区 万山区 江口县 石阡县 思南县 德江县 沿河土家族自治县 松桃苗族自治县 Bijiang Wanshan Jiangkou Shiqian Sinan Dejiang Yanhe Songtao 玉屏侗族自治县 印江土家族苗族自治县 Yuping Yinjiang
黔西南布依族苗族自治州 Qianxinan	兴义市 兴仁县 普安县 晴隆县 安龙县 望谟县 贞丰县 册亨县 Xingyi Xingren Puan Qinglong Anlong Wangmo Zhenfeng Ceheng
黔东南苗族侗族自治州 Qiandongnan	凯里市 黄平县 施秉县 三穗县 镇远县 岑巩县 天柱县 锦屏县 Kaili Huangping Shibing Sansui Zhenyuan Cengong Tianzhu Jinping 剑河县 台江县 黎平县 榕江县 从江县 雷山县 麻江县 丹寨县 Jianhe Taijiang Liping Rongjiang Congjiang Leishan Majiang Danzhai
黔南布依族苗族自治州 Qiannan	都匀市 福泉市 荔波县 贵定县 瓮安县 平塘县 罗甸县 长顺县 龙里县 惠水县 Duyun Fuquan Libo Cuiding Wengan Pingtang Luodian Changshun Longli Huishui 独山县 三都水族自治县 Dushan Sandu

1-3 法人单位数

Number of legal person units

单位：个 (unit)

指　标	Item	2010年	2011年	2012年	2013年	2014年
法人单位数	**Number of juridical entity**	110274	116423	133420	174739	209858
按三次产业分	**Grouped by three strata Industry**					
第一产业	Primary industry	3140	4120	9842	26764	30956
第二产业	Secondary industry	18814	20457	24323	32330	40673
#工业	Industry	16670	18020	21480	28717	35521
第三产业	Tertiary industry	88320	91846	99255	115645	138229
按经济类型分	**Grouped by Registration Status**					
国有经济	State-owned Units	33776	33592	34105	28242	32066
集体经济	Collective-owned Units	3526	3541	3558	2762	3590
私营经济	Self-employed Units	30345	33243	44773	67985	88523
联营经济	Joint Ownership Units	274	299	302	609	668
股份制经济	Share Holding Units	1653	1840	1945	1920	2360
外商投资经济	Foreign Funded Units	225	218	225	158	218
港澳台商投资经济	Units with Funds from Hong Kong, Macao and Taiwan	187	201	194	168	218
其他经济	Others	40288	43489	48318	72895	82215
按机构类型分	**By Enterprises,Institutions and Agencies**					
企业	Enterprises	54865	60595	76029	118290	147401
事业单位	Institutions	21653	21404	21702	18610	20901
机关	Agencies	7265	7216	7211	6851	7190
社会团体	Social groups	3525	3589	3785	4643	5546
民办非企业单位	Private non-enterprise unit	1921	2056	2300	2295	2701
其他组织机构	Others	21045	21563	22393	24050	26119

注:2013年为第三次经济普查数据(下表同）。
Note:Data in 2013 is provided by the third economy census.

1-4 按行业分法人单位数

Number of legal person units Grouped by sector

单位：个 (unit)

行业门类	Item	2010年	2011年	2012年	2013年	2014年
全省总计	**Total**	**110274**	**116423**	**133420**	**174739**	**209858**
农、林、牧、渔业	Total Agriculture、Forestry、Animal Hasbandry 、Fishery	3365	4422	10235	27662	32131
采矿业	Mining and Quarrying	4926	5269	5630	5575	6917
制造业	Manufacturing	10490	11444	14525	21696	26912
电力、燃气及水的生产和供应业	Production and supply of Electricity, Gasand water	1254	1307	1404	1606	1877
建筑业	Construction	2144	2437	2843	3613	4967
批发和零售业	Wholesale and Retail Trades	15592	17073	19844	28354	36267
交通运输、仓储和邮政业	Transportation, storage and past	1586	1740	1971	2679	3300
住宿和餐饮业	Hotel and Catering services	1542	1664	2144	4060	5043
信息传输、软件和信息技术服务业	Information Transmit, Computer serrices and soflware trade	2051	2136	1195	1401	1907
金融业	Financial Intermediation	759	894	1159	1378	1761
房地产业	Real Estate	4614	5126	5660	5542	7367
租赁和商务服务业	Leasing and Commerce services	5001	5622	6385	9068	12131
科学研究和技术服务业	Scientific Research, Technic Services and Geological prospecting	3213	3194	3532	4240	4756
水利、环境和公共设施管理业		1119	1167	1262	1223	1510
居民服务、修理和其他服务业	Services to Households repairs and other Services	1623	1770	2414	3404	4451
教育	Education	9592	9650	9869	9925	11290
卫生和社会工作	Healthcare and Social work	3988	4049	3926	4027	4537
文化、体育和娱乐业	Culture, Sports and Entertainment	1480	1515	2896	2854	3476
公共管理、社会保障和社会组织	Public Administration Social Security	35935	35944	36526	36432	39258

注：行业分类2011年及以前按照《国民经济行业分类》(GB/T4754—2002)执行，2012年及以后按照《国民经济行业分类》(GB/T4754—2011)执行。

Note:《classification of national economy industry》(GB/T4754-2002) was used before 2011,and 《classification of national economy industry》(GB/T4754-2011) was used after 2012.

1-5 社会经济主要指标

指标	Item	总量指标 1978	2000	2005
人口	**Population**			
年末常住人口(万人)	Total Population at the Year-end (10000 persons)	2686.40	3755.72	3730
#城镇人口	Urban Population	323.97	896.49	1002.25
乡村人口	Rural Population	2362.43	2859.23	2727.75
#男性人口	Male	1364.82	1968.00	1920.55
女性人口	Female	1321.58	1787.72	1809.45
年平均人口(万人)	Annual Average Population(10000 persons)	2663.27	3732.89	3718
就业	**Employment**			
就业人员(万人)	Year-end Employees (10000 persons)	1053.67	1866.28	1944.29
#非私营单位职工人数	Staff and Workers	171.19	193.96	202.02
城镇登记失业人数（万人）	Urban Registeration Unemployment (10000 persons)		10.23	12.13
国民经济核算	**National Accounting**			
地区生产总值(亿元)	Gross Domestic Product (100 million yuan)	46.62	1029.92	2005.42
第一产业	Primary Industry	19.42	271.20	368.94
第二产业	Secondary Industry	18.73	391.20	821.16
工　业	Industry	15.24	328.73	707.35
建筑业	Construction	3.49	62.47	113.81
第三产业	Tertiary Industry	8.47	367.52	815.32
人均地区生产总值(元)	Per capita GDP(yuan)	175	2759	5394
固定资产投资	**Investment in Fixed Assets**			
全社会固定资产投资(亿元)	Total Investment in Fixed Assets in the Whole Province (100 million yuan)	10.93	402.50	1018.25
消费	**Consumption**			
社会消费品零售总额	Total Retail Sales of Consumer Goods(100 million yuan)	21.23	355.58	615.75
对外贸易	**Foreign Trade**			
进出口总额（亿美元）	Total Value of Imports and Exports(USD 100 million)	0.16	6.60	14.04
#出口额	Total Exports	0.03	4.21	8.59
利用外资	**Utilization of Foreign Capital**			
签订合同项目(个)	Projects of Agreements and Contracts(unit)		59	61
实际利用外资金额(万美元)	Foreign Capital Actually Absorbed(USD 10000)	※148	19545	19568
财政	**Government Finance**			
财政总收入(亿元)	Total Financial Revenue(100 million yuan)	14.20	153.04	366.16
#一般公共预算收入(亿元)	Local Financial Revenue (100 million yuan)	6.26	85.23	182.50
一般公共财政支出(亿元)	Financial Expenditure (100 million yuan)	12.30	201.57	520.73
价格指数(上年=100)	**Price Indices(preceding year=100)**			
居民消费价格总指数	Consumer Price Index	100.3	99.5	101.0
商品零售价格总指数	Retail Price Index	100.3	97.3	101.3
农业生产资料价格总指数	General Price Index of Means of Agricultural Production	△102.1	100.6	110.2
工业生产者出厂价格指数	Ex-Factory Price Index of Industrial Producer		100.4	107.2
工业生产者购进价格指数	Purchasing Price Index of Industrial Producer		102.9	107.4

Major Social and Economic Indicators

Aggregate Indicators					增长速度（%） Indices and Growth Rates (%)								
					2014比以上各年增长 Increase Rate in 2014 over the Following years						平均增长速度 Average Annual Growth Rate		
2010	2011	2012	2013	2014	1978	2000	2010	2011	2012	2013	1979–2014	2001–2014	2011–2014
3479	3469	3484	3502.22	3508.04	30.6	-6.6	0.8	1.1	0.7	0.2	0.7	-0.5	0.2
1176.25	1212.76	1268.52	1324.89	1403.57	333.2	56.6	19.3	15.7	10.6	5.9	4.2	3.3	4.5
2302.75	2256.24	2215.48	2177.33	2104.47	-10.9	-26.4	-8.6	-6.7	-5.0	-3.3	-0.3	-2.2	-2.2
1797.43	1801.21	1818.61	1822.50	1817.91	33.2	-7.6	1.1	0.9	0.0	-0.3	0.8	-0.6	0.3
1681.57	1667.79	1665.39	1679.72	1690.13	27.9	-5.5	0.5	1.3	1.5	0.6	0.7	-0.4	0.1
3508	3474	3477	3493	3505	31.6	-6.1	-0.1	0.9	0.8	0.3	0.8	-0.4	-0.02
1770.90	1792.80	1825.82	1864.21	1909.69	81.2	2.3	7.8	6.5	4.6	2.4	1.7	0.2	1.9
210.67	225.91	249.67	273.27	278.63	62.8	43.7	32.3	23.3	11.6	2.0	1.4	2.6	7.2
12.18	12.51	12.56	13.66	14.09	-100.0	37.7	15.7	12.6	12.2	3.1		2.3	3.7
4602.16	5701.84	6852.20	8086.86	9266.39	3108.9	383.5	62.8	41.6	24.7	10.8	10.1	11.9	13.0
625.03	726.22	891.91	998.47	1280.45	443.0	87.1	24.0	22.5	12.8	6.6	4.8	4.6	5.5
1800.06	2194.33	2677.54	3276.24	3857.44	5378.5	474.6	76.5	49.7	28.1	12.3	11.8	13.3	15.3
1516.87	1829.20	2217.06	2686.52	3140.88	5711.0	452.6	71.1	45.3	25.7	11.1	11.9	13.0	14.4
283.19	365.13	460.48	590.69	717.69	3616.5	607.8	105.5	73.7	40.9	18.2	10.6	15.0	19.7
2177.07	2781.29	3282.75	3812.15	4128.50	6632.7	502.5	62.2	39.2	24.2	10.4	12.4	13.7	12.9
13119	16413	19710	23151	26437	2384.3	415.6	62.8	40.2	23.5	10.4	9.3	12.4	13.0
3186.28	4234.44	5717.80	7373.60	9025.75					57.9	22.4			
1531.64	1899.92	2266.27	2601.20	2936.85	13733.5	725.9	91.7	54.6	29.6	12.9	14.7	16.3	17.7
31.47	48.88	66.32	82.90	107.71	65377.2	1531.9	242.3	120.4	62.4	29.9	19.7	22.1	36.0
19.20	29.85	49.52	68.86	93.97	329619.3	2134.2	389.4	214.8	89.8	36.5	25.2	24.8	48.7
42	70	53	149	172		191.5	309.5	145.7	224.5	15.4		7.9	42.3
34026	71674	109805	157415	213053		990.1	526.1	197.3	94.0	35.3		18.6	58.2
969.57	1329.99	1644.48	1918.23	2130.90	14906.3	1292.4	119.8	60.2	29.6	11.1	14.9	20.7	21.8
533.73	773.08	1014.05	1206.41	1366.67	21731.8	1503.5	156.1	76.8	34.8	13.3	16.1	21.9	26.5
1631.48	2249.40	2755.68	3082.66	3542.80	28703.3	1657.6	117.2	57.5	28.6	14.9	17.0	22.7	21.4
102.9	105.1	102.7	102.5	102.4									
103.0	105.5	102.0	101.5	101.2									
101.1	111.1	100.7	99.0	99.0									
104.7	105.4	101.0	97.4	98.3									
109.8	115.0	102.3	96.4	98.6									

1-5 续表1

指　　标	Item	总量指标		
		1978	2000	2005
能源生产与消费	**Total Production and Consumption of Energy**			
一次能源生产总量（万吨标准煤）	Total Production of Primary Energy(10000 tons of SCE)	1204.51	3288.83	7957.07
能源消费总量(万吨标准煤)	Total Energy Consumption(10000 tons of SCE)	674.50	4278.60	5641.25
农业	**Agriculture**			
主要农产品产量(万吨)	Output of Major Farm Products(10000 tons)			
粮　　食	Grain	643.36	1161.30	1152.06
油　　料	Oil-bearing Crops	9.89	74.34	84.89
#油菜籽	Rapeseed	7.34	66.20	76.51
烤　　烟	Flue-cured Tobacco	8.11	31.09	34.45
肉类总产量	Meat	12.80	124.06	187.01
水 产 品	Aquatic Products	0.37	6.24	9.46
工业	**Industry**			
规模以上工业企业	Industrial Enterprises above Designated Size			
增加值（亿元）	Added Value(100 million yuan)		216.99	585.85
#轻工业	Light Industry		82.16	177.19
重工业	Heavy Industry		134.83	408.66
主营业务收入(亿元)	Revenue from Principal Business(100 million yuan)		593.80	1577.16
利税总额(亿元)	Total Profits(100 million yuan)		87.44	232.49
主要工业产品产量	Output of Major Industrial Products			
发电量(亿千瓦小时)	Electricity(100 million kwh)	41.43	404.70	786.78
电解铝(万吨)	Aluminum(10000 tons)	2.32	27.19	41.99
成品钢材(万吨)	Rolled Steel(10000 tons)	4.95	150.93	214.85
水泥(万吨)	Cement(10000 tons)	130.93	783.88	1557.97
磷矿石(万吨)	Phosphorite(10000 tons)	169.02	588.70	878.79
茅台酒(吨)	Mao-Tai Chiew(ton)	1067	5397	8885
卷烟(万箱)	Cigarettes(10000 cases)	31.60	187.40	208.21
建筑业	**Construction**			
建筑业总产值(亿元)	Gross Output Value of Construction(100 million yuan)	4.40	109.06	271.23
房屋建筑施工面积(万平方米)	Floor Space of Buildings under Construction(10000 sq.m)	313	1792	3153
房屋建筑竣工面积(万平方米)	Floor Space of Buildings Completed(10000 sq.m)	164	824	1150
交通运输业	**Transportation**			
运输线路长度(公里)	Length of Transportation Routes(km)			
铁路营业里程	Length of Railways	1365	1641	1986
公路线路里程	Length of Highways in Operation	25954	34643	46893
客运量(万人)	Passenger Traffic(10000 persons)	3294	53032	64450
旅客周转量(亿人公里)	Passenger-Kilometers(100 million passenger-km)	25.50	238.36	312.40
货运量(万吨)	Freight Traffic(10000 tons)	3467	15615	21771
货物周转量(亿吨公里)	Freight Ton-Kilometers(100 million ton-km)	79.60	404.07	646.55

continued

Aggregate Indicators					增长速度 (%) Indices and Growth Rates (%)								
2010	2011	2012	2013	2014	2014比以下各年增长 Increase Rate in 2014 over the Following years						平均增长速度 Average Annual Growth Rate		
					1978	2000	2010	2011	2012	2013	1979–2014	2001–2014	2011–2014
13100.00	12739.97	14932.17	14404.15	15136.11	1156.6	360.2	15.5	18.8	1.4	5.1	7.3	11.5	3.7
8175.43	9067.85	9878.38	9298.54	9708.78	1339.4	126.9	18.8	7.1	-1.7	4.4	7.7	6.0	4.4
1112.30	876.90	1079.50	1029.99	1138.50	77.0	-2.0	2.4	29.8	5.5	10.5	1.6	-0.1	0.6
60.34	78.85	87.38	91.53	98.05	891.4	31.9	62.5	24.3	12.2	7.1	6.6	2.0	12.9
51.62	71.81	78.18	81.78	86.69	1081.1	31.0	67.9	20.7	10.9	6.0	7.1	1.9	13.8
37.02	32.50	37.31	41.79	35.34	335.8	13.7	-4.5	8.7	-5.3	-15.4	4.2	0.9	-1.2
179.09	179.97	190.27	199.74	201.80	1476.6	62.7	12.7	12.1	6.1	1.0	8.0	3.5	3.0
8.79	10.88	13.47	16.70	20.99	5573.0	236.4	138.8	92.9	55.8	25.7	11.9	9.1	24.3
1227.17	1638.71	2055.46	2531.92	3117.60		639.4	77.8	46.9	26.4	11.3		15.4	15.5
413.99	545.78	773.04	969.29	1185.13		598.1	81.3	47.8	25.7	11.5		14.9	16.0
813.18	1092.93	1282.42	1562.63	1932.47		646.4	76.0	46.5	26.9	11.2		15.4	15.2
3926.01	5022.11	5966.52	7357.43	8655.87		1357.7	120.5	72.4	45.1	17.6		21.1	21.9
671.39	901.37	1172.15	1268.68	1310.38		1398.6	95.2	45.4	11.8	3.3		21.3	18.2
1358.69	1359.01	1548.44	1620.08	1682.27	3960.5	315.7	23.8	23.8	8.6	3.8	10.8	10.7	5.5
88.79	90.36	104.35	112.28	65.21	2710.8	139.8	-26.6	-27.8	-37.5	-41.9	9.7	6.4	-7.4
391.04	462.77	560.22	573.28	552.39	11059.4	266.0	41.3	19.4	-1.4	-3.6	14.0	9.7	9.0
3694.84	5250.89	6100.45	8352.95	9386.89	7069.4	1097.5	154.1	78.8	53.9	12.4	12.6	19.4	26.3
1579.21	2084.18	2281.95	2905.44	3397.42	1910.1	477.1	115.1	63.0	48.9	16.9	8.7	13.3	21.1
12911	13815	14272	15729	18319	1616.9	239.4	41.9	32.6	28.4	16.5	8.2	9.1	9.1
239.24	245.23	249.35	254.29	258.36	717.6	37.9	8.0	5.4	3.6	1.6	6.0	2.3	1.9
622.96	824.72	1039.95	1365.00	1640.24									
5756	6779	8254	12174	13890	4343.2	674.9	141.3	104.9	68.3	14.1	11.1	15.7	24.6
1350	1530	1863	2450	2801	1608.6	239.9	107.5	83.1	50.3	14.3	8.2	9.1	20.0
2002	2070	2058	2093	2373	73.8	44.6	18.5	14.6	15.3	13.4	1.5	2.7	4.3
151644	157820	164542	172564	179079	590.0	416.9	18.1	13.5	8.8	3.8	5.5	12.4	4.2
97793	120554	142809	83435	86572									
514.41	631.74	718.22	593.62	635.50									
40310	44890	52765	72700	85673									
1012.20	1060.69	1177.78	1292.11	1442.24									

1-5 续表2

指　　标	Item	总量指标		
		1978	2000	2005
邮电通信业	**Post and Telecommunication**			
邮路总长度(公里)	Number of Postal Routes(km)		63538	64926
函件(万件)	Number of Letters(10000 pcs)	3880	6943	5728
交换机容量(万门)	Capacity of Telephone Exchanges(10000 lines)	8.95	260.46	1369.55
年末固定电话用户(万户)	Number of Telephones Subscribers at the Year-end (10000 subscribers)	3.80	153.70	466.49
移动电话用户(万户)	Number of Mobile Telephones Subscribers(10000 subscribers)		79.70	509.42
互联网宽带接入端口(万个)	Number of Subscribers of Internet Service(10000 subscribers)			51.21
旅游业	**Tourism**			
旅游总人数(万人次)	Total Number of Visitors(10000 persons)		1980	3099
#入境旅游人数	Number of International Tourists Inbound		18.39	27.62
旅游总收入(亿元)	Total Tourism Income(100 million yuan)		57.95	242.83
#国际旅游外汇收入(万美元)	International Earnings from Tourism (USD 10000)		6092	10141
金融业	**Financial Intermediatio**			
全部金融机构人民币各项存款余额(亿元)	Total Savings Deposit Balancen(100 million yuan)	18.05	1106.64	2777.54
#个人储蓄存款	Savings Deposit	1.84	539.49	1350.90
全部金融机构人民币各项贷款余额(亿元)	Total Loan Balance (100 million yuan)	21.62	1064.82	2303.93
教育	**Education**			
专任教师数	Full-time Teachers			
普通高等学校(万人)	Regular Institutions of Higher Education (10000 persons)	0.28	0.72	1.44
普通中学(万人)	Regular Secondary Schools (10000 persons)	5.42	8.12	12.27
小学(万人)	Primary Schools(10000 persons)	15.59	17.48	18.37
在校学生数	Students Enrollmen			
普通高等学校(万人)	Regular Institutions of Higher Education (10000 persons)	1.33	7.55	20.68
普通中学(万人)	Regular Secondary Schools(10000 persons)	137.17	157.20	254.96
小学(万人)	Primary Schools(10000 persons)	423.60	500.21	473.76
小学学龄儿童入学率(%)	Enrollment Rate of School-age Children (%)	89.5	98.5	98.3
文化	**Culture**			
图书总印数(万册)	Number of Books Printed Copies (10000 copies)	5842	10289	9993
杂志总印数(万册)	Number of Magazines Printed Copies(10000 copies)	69	994	1349
报纸总印数(万份)	Number of Newspapers Printed Copies(10000 copies)	11930	28799	35172
家庭	**Household**			
城镇居民平均每户常住家庭人口(人)	Average Persons Per Urban Household(person)	5.41	3.11	3.06
农村居民平均每户常住人口(人)	Average Persons Per Rural Household(person)	5.80	4.52	4.40
婚姻	**Marital**			
准予登记结婚(万对)	Marriage Registration Permitted(10000 households)	△7.02	28.02	21.13
离婚人数(万人)	Divorce(10000 persons)	△0.38	1.54	8.21
居住	**Residence**			
城镇人均住宅建筑面积(平方米)	Per Capita Building Space in Urban Areas(sq.m)	5.45	17.60	26.40
农村居民人均年末使用房屋面积(平方米)	Per Capita Living Space in Rural Areas(sq.m)		19.75	23.50
生活	**Per Capita Standard of Living**			
城镇常住居民人均可支配收入(元)	Per Capita Annual Disposable Income of Urban Households (yuan)	261	5121	8147
农村常住居民人均可支配收入(元)	Per Capita Annual Net Income of Rural Residents(yuan)	109	1374	1877

continued

Aggregate Indicators					增长速度 (%) Indices and Growth Rates (%)								
					2014比以下各年增长 Increase Rate in 2014 over the Following years						平均增长速度 Average Annual Growth Rate		
2010	2011	2012	2013	2014	1978	2000	2010	2011	2012	2013	1979–2014	2001–2014	2011–2014
96174	99155	136429	154810	407046		540.6	323.2	310.5	198.4			14.2	
5939	5041	6036	5192	3809.37	33.8	-45.1	-35.9	-24.4	-36.9	-26.6	-0.1	-4.2	-10.5
3673.01	4838.00	5026.53	5870.04	5671.60	65487.0	2077.5	54.4	17.2	12.8	-3.4	19.6	24.6	11.5
432.61	403.96	380.00	362.99	339.10	9452.4	120.6	-21.6	-16.1	-10.8	-6.6	13.3	5.8	-5.9
1964.40	2175.22	2515.00	2871.75	3059.85		3739.2	55.8	40.7	21.7	6.6		29.8	11.7
231.69	437.87	435.79	575.95	668.40			188.5	52.6	53.4	16.1			30.3
12913.02	17019.36	21401.18	26761.28	32134.94		1508.0	148.9	88.8	50.2	20.1		21.9	25.6
50.01	58.51	70.50	77.70	85.50		364.9	71.0	46.1	21.3	10.0		11.6	14.3
1061.23	1429.48	1860.16	2370.65	2895.98		4501.2	172.9	102.6	55.7	22.2		31.5	28.5
12958	13507	16894	20143	21671		255.7	67.2	60.4	28.3	7.6		9.5	13.7
7363.92	8742.79	10540.06	13265.01	15263.26	73390.4	1279.2	107.3	74.6	44.8	15.1	20.6	20.6	20.0
3244.99	3934.48	4806.09	5919.05	6620.56	321587.5	1127.2	104.0	68.3	37.8	11.9	25.5	19.6	19.5
5747.53	6841.92	8274.78	10104.30	12368.30	46635.9	1061.5	115.2	80.8	49.5	22.4	19.3	19.1	21.1
2.04	2.19	2.28	2.54	2.81	822.6	288.1	38.1	28.6	23.2	10.6	6.7	10.2	8.4
14.31	14.74	15.63	16.23	17.20	199.3	111.9	20.2	16.7	10.0	6.0	3.3	5.5	4.7
19.79	19.71	19.80	19.30	19.29	23.8	10.3	-2.5	-2.1	-2.6	-0.1	0.6	0.7	-0.6
32.33	34.41	38.38	41.90	46.04	3050.4	509.8	42.4	33.8	20.0	9.9	10.3	13.8	9.2
276.75	282.71	287.38	296.01	301.10	115.8	91.5	8.8	6.5	4.8	1.7	2.2	4.8	2.1
433.50	408.74	380.08	355.53	346.31	-16.1	-30.8	-20.1	-15.3	-8.9	-2.6	-0.6	-2.6	-5.5
97.9	98.6	99.3	99.3	99.1	11.0	0.7	1.2	0.5	-0.2	-0.2	0.3	0.0	0.3
8069	8492	7304	6278	10099	7.5	-1.8	25.2	18.9	38.3	60.9	1.5	-0.1	5.8
1300	1413	1485	1575	1523	2182.6	53.2	17.2	7.8	2.6	-3.3	9.0	3.1	4.0
37004	44931	41704	38954	36409	226.5	26.4	-1.6	-19.0	-12.7	-6.5	3.1	1.7	-0.4
3.03	2.98	3.01	3.01	3.01	-44.4								
4.34	4.32	4.31	4.68	3.49	-19.3								
37.51	37.34	41.78	42.98	43.72		56.0	16.6	17.1	4.6	1.7		3.2	3.9
12.79	14.44	16.25	17.15	19.14		1140.9	49.6	32.5	17.8	11.6		19.7	10.6
27.42	27.83	27.86	34.84	36.58	539.3	107.8	33.4	31.4	31.3	5.0	5.4	5.4	7.5
27.26	29.63	29.75	27.08	31.61		60.1	16.0	6.7	6.3	16.7		3.4	3.8
14143	16495	18701	20667	22548	1141.1	211.1	40.6	26.9	14.9	7.0	7.3	8.4	8.9
3472	4145	4753	5434	6671	867.5	211.4	57.6	38.3	24.0	10.3	6.5	8.4	12.0

1-5 续表3

指标	Item	总量指标 1978	2000	2005
社会保险	**Social Insurance**			
社会保险基金收入(亿元)	Revenue of Social Insurance Fund (100 million yuan)		22.87	57.34
社会保险基金支出(亿元)	Expenses of Social Insurance Fund (100 million yuan)		23.41	53.78
卫生	**Health Care**			
医院、卫生院(个)	Number of Hospitals and Health Centers(unit)	4510	1878	1843
执业(助理)医师(万人)	Number of Licensed (Assistant) Doctors (10000 persons)	2.12	4.57	3.55
医院、卫生院床位数(万张)	Number of Beds(10000 beds)	3.75	5.51	5.84
城市市政建设	**City Construction**			
供水总量(万立方米)	Volume of Tap Water Supply(10000 cu.m)	5389	45693	63705
城市排水管道长度(公里)	Length of Sewer Pipelines(km)	214	1665	4313
人工煤气供应量(万立方米)	Volume of Coal Gas Supply(10000 cu.m)			19209
出租汽车(辆)	Taxi(unit)	☆33	7352	12386
年末公共交通运营车辆数(辆)	Number of Public Vehicles under Operation at Year-end (Buses and Trolley Buses, etc.)(unit)	●326	●4144	5814
年末实有道路长度(公里)	Length of Paved Roads at Year-end(km)	184	1679	3518
城市园林绿地面积(公顷)	Area of Parks and Green Land (hectare)	1037	9939	31161
环境	**Environment**			
环保资金投入(亿元)	Environment Protection Investment(100 million yuan)	☆0.17	10.98	33.26
环境污染事故(起)	Accident of Environment Pollution(unit)			28
火灾、交通事故	**Basic Statistics on Fires and Traffic Accidents**			
火灾发生数(起)	Number of Fires(case)	2501	1608	2299
直接财产损失(万元)	Losses Converted into Cash(10000 yuan)	1734.21	2814.70	1078.50
交通事故发生数(起)	Number of Traffic Accidents(case)	3104	2593	3315
损失折款(万元)	Losses Converted into Cash(10000 yuan)	236.07	1899.62	2507.06

注：1.年末总人口及分项指标1978、2000年为常住一年口径。2.规模以上工业统计口径2000—2010年为年主营业务收入500万元及以上的工业企业，2011年起为年主营业务收入2000万元及以上工业企业(以下相关表同)。茅台酒产量从2005年起按包装量统计。3.全社会固定资产投资统计口径2010年为计划总投资50万元及以上固定资产项目投资、房地产开发投资及农村农户投资，2011年起为计划总投资500万元及以上固定资产项目投资、房地产开发投资及农村农户投资(以下相关表同)。4.由于交通运输部对公路、水运运输量统计方案进行调整，2013年相关数据统计口径发生变化，相同指标数据与以往年份不可比(下表同)。5.本表速度指标中，地区生产总值、工业增加值和城乡居民收入及分项指标均按可比价格计算。6.工业生产者出厂价格指数2010年及以前为全部工业品出厂价格指数，工业生产者购进价格指数2010年及以前为全部原材料、燃料、动力价格指数，统计口径不变。7.储蓄存款2010年及以前为城乡居民储蓄存款(以下相关表同)。8.农村常住居民人均可支配收入2013年及以前为农民人均纯收入。9.“△”为1979年数据；“☆”为1981年数据；“●”为“标台”。

continued

Aggregate Indicators					增长速度(%) Indices and Growth Rates (%)								
					2014比以下各年增长 Increase Rate in 2014 over the Following years						平均增长速度 Average Annual Growth Rate		
2010	2011	2012	2013	2014	1978	2000	2010	2011	2012	2013	1979–2014	2001–2014	2010–2014
201.56	256.94	310.85	351.06	386.81		1591.6	91.9	50.5	24.4	10.2		22.4	17.7
151.41	181.74	229.08	279.25	319.42		1264.3	111.0	75.8	39.4	14.4		20.5	20.5
2005	2071	2210	2429	2612	-42.1	39.1	30.3	26.1	18.2	7.5	-1.5	2.4	6.8
4.22	4.40	4.92	5.59	5.78	172.3	26.6	37.1	31.3	17.5	3.4	2.8	1.7	8.2
9.75	10.80	12.97	15.58	17.84	375.3	223.5	83.0	65.1	37.6	14.5	4.4	8.7	16.3
63572	67766	71168	74730	79789	1380.6	74.6	25.5	17.7	12.1	6.8	7.8	4.1	5.8
5507	5977	6148	8146	8856	4038.3	431.9	60.8	48.2	44.0	8.7	10.9	12.7	12.6
26963	30515	34167	23788	16034			-40.5	-47.5	-53.1	-32.6			-12.2
15087	17196	20600	22946	24394		231.8	61.7	41.9	18.4	6.3		8.9	12.8
4984	5364	5429	6484	7355			47.6	37.1	35.5	13.4			10.2
4081	4487	4875	5787	6325	3337.5	276.7	55.0	41.0	29.7	9.3	10.3	9.9	11.6
45500	48024	51081	67029	71048	6751.3	614.8	56.1	47.9	39.1	6.0	12.5	15.1	11.8
89.52	106.70	97.35	133.70	175.25	-100.0	1496.1	95.8	64.2	80.0	31.1		21.9	18.3
4	7	4	9	3			-25.0	-57.1	-25.0	-66.7			-6.9
1630	1170	959	2915	4221	68.8	162.5	159.0	260.8	340.1	44.8	1.5	7.1	26.9
4416.80	6625.40	5147.20	11203.00	17667.00	918.7	527.7	300.0	166.7	243.2	57.7	6.7	14.0	41.4
1764	1566	1361	1241	1145	-63.1	-55.8	-35.1	-26.9	-15.9	-7.7	-2.7	-5.7	-10.2
1208.00	1611.39	1698.58	1477.91	1282.45	443.2	-32.5	6.2	-20.4	-24.5	-13.2	4.8	-2.8	1.5

Note:1.As to total population at the year-end and subitems in this table,the year 1978 and 2000 refer to permanent population in one year scope. 2.The scale above ind ustrial enterprises statistics was the industrial of main business income of 5 million yuan and above in 2000 to 2010. And from 2011, it is the industrial of main business income of 20 million yuan and above(The relative tables in this chapter are the same). 3.In 2010, data in the table referred to those projects that planned to invest 500,000 yuan at least in investment in fixed assets, real estate development and rural household investment. From 2011,the statistical coverage has referred to those projects that planned to invest 5000,000 yuan at least in investment in fixed assets, real estate development and rural household investment(The relative tables in the chapter are the same). 4.Because the statistics schemes of highway, waterway transport volume are adjusted by the Ministry of Transport of the People's Republic of China, the correlation data statistics caliber changes for 2013, the same indicators can not compare with previous years (the same applies to the next table). 5.As to growth rates in the table,GDP, value-added of industry, per capita annual disposable income of urban households and per capita annual net income of rural residents and their sub items were calculated at constant price. The average annual growth rate of total inve stment in fixed assets in the whole province and its sub items were calculated by accumulation method. 6.The year 2010 and before, Ex-Factory price index of industrial product refere to the ex-factory price index of the whole industrial products and purchasing price index of industrial producer refer to the price index of the whole raw materials, fuels and power. The statistics caliber isn't changed. 7.The year 2010 and before,savings deposit refer to resident savings deposit of urban and rural(The relative tables in this chapter are the same). 8.Ruralpermanent residents's disposable income in 2013 and before was per capita net income of farms. 9.Data with "△" refer to the year 1979, with "☆" refer to the year 1981, with "※" refer to the year 1985, and with "●" refer to standard unit.

1-6 社会经济主要指标结构

Composition Indicators on National Economic and Social Development

单位：% (%)

指 标	Item	2010	2011	2012	2013	2014
人口	**Population**					
城镇、乡村	Grouped by Urban and Rural Area					
城 镇	Urban Population	33.8	35.0	36.4	37.8	40.0
乡 村	Rural Population	66.2	65.0	63.6	62.2	60.0
性别	Grouped by Sex					
男性人口	Male	51.7	51.9	52.2	52.0	51.8
女性人口	Female	48.3	48.1	47.8	48.0	48.2
就业人员	**Employment**					
第一产业	Primary Industry	68.3	66.6	65.1	63.3	61.3
第二产业	Secondary Industry	11.5	12.0	13.0	14.2	15.3
第三产业	Tertiary Industry	20.2	21.3	21.8	22.5	23.4
国民经济核算	**National Accounting**					
地区生产总值	In GDP					
第一产业	Primary Industry	13.6	12.7	13.0	12.3	13.8
第二产业	Secondary Industry	39.1	38.5	39.1	40.5	41.6
第三产业	Tertiary Industry	47.3	48.8	47.9	47.2	44.6
投资	**Investment in Fixed Assets**					
全社会固定资产投资	Structure of Total Investment in Fixed Assets in the Whole Province					
#中央	Central	10.2	8.2	6.8	6.7	6.7
地方	Local	89.8	91.8	93.2	93.3	93.2
#国有经济	State-owned Economic Unit	50.4	47.0	44.3	44.5	46.2
非国有经济	Non-State-owned Economic Unit	49.6	53.0	55.7	55.5	53.8
资金来源结构	Grouped by Source of Funds					
国家预算内资金	State Budgetary Appropriation	8.7	10.7	8.6	6.8	6.5
国内贷款	Domestic Loans	20.8	16.1	15.3	11.9	11.9
利用外资	Foreign Investment	0.3	0.3	0.2	0.2	0.3
自筹资金	Self-raising Funds	45.5	49.6	52.5	55.8	57.3
其他资金	Others	24.8	23.4	23.4	25.4	24.1
对外贸易	**Foreign Trade**					
出 口	Total Exports	61.0	61.1	74.7	83.1	87.2
进 口	Total Imports	39.0	38.9	25.3	16.9	12.8
财政	**Government Finance and Tax**					
一般公共预算收入	General Public Financial Budget Revenue					
省 级	Provincial Level	20.3	21.4	17.7	17.5	18.3
市 级	Prefectural Level	23.3	21.9	20.2	20.6	20.9
县 级	County level	44.0	45.7	51.2	52.2	50.1
乡 级	Township Level	12.4	11.0	10.9	9.8	10.7

1-6 续表1 continued

单位：% (%)

指 标	Item	2010	2011	2012	2013	2014
能源	**Energy**					
一次能源生产总量	Structure of Total Energy Production					
原 煤	Coal	89.9	91.4	88.8	89.4	85.5
水 电	Hydro-power	10.1	8.6	11.2	10.6	14.4
能源终端消费总量	Structure of Total Energy Consumption					
#原 煤	Coal	48.0	48.8	48.0	38.2	37.9
天然气	Natural Gas	0.8	0.6	0.7	1.3	1.3
电 力	Electricity	33.3	33.2	33.1	37.4	37.1
农业	**Agriculture**					
农林牧渔业增加值	Structure of Value-added of FFAFS					
农 业	Farming	61.7	59.3	62.9	62.6	64.7
林 业	Forestry	4.5	4.4	4.2	4.6	5.2
畜牧业	Animal Husbandry	28.7	30.7	27.5	27.2	25.2
渔 业	Fishery	1.4	1.8	2.0	2.3	2.2
农林牧渔服务业	FFAF Seryices	3.7	3.8	3.4	3.2	2.7
工业	**Industry**					
规模以上工业增加值	In the Industrial Enterprises above Designated Size					
#轻工业	Light Industry	33.7	32.7	37.6	38.3	38.0
重工业	Heavy Industry	66.3	67.3	62.4	61.7	62.0
#大型企业	Large Industry	38.0	37.2	44.0	43.8	38.7
中型企业	Medium-sized Industry	24.6	23.9	26.2	29.9	29.3
小型企业	Small Industry	37.4	36.6	29.2	26.0	31.5
建筑业	**Construction**					
建筑业总产值	Structure of Gross Output Value of Construction					
国有经济及国有控股	State-owned	79.6	79.9	82.7	80.8	77.1
非国有经济	Non-state-owned	20.4	20.1	17.3	19.2	22.9
交通运输业	**Transportation**					
货运量	Structure of Freight Traffic					
铁 路	Railways	19.8	16.1	12.6	8.9	7.4
公 路	Highways	77.9	81.7	85.3	89.5	91.0
水 运	Waterways	2.3	2.2	2.1	1.6	1.6
客运量	Structure of Passenger Traffic					
铁 路	Railways	3.5	3.3	2.7	5.2	5.1
公 路	Highways	94.5	94.9	95.6	92.7	92.7
水 运	Waterways	2.0	1.8	1.7	2.1	2.2
旅游业	**Tourism**					
来黔涉外旅游人数	Structure of Tourists Visiting Guizhou					
外 国 人	Foreigners	37.2	40.4	43.1	41.1	42.0
港澳同胞	Compatriots from Hong Kong and Macao	27.3	28.9	29.6	29.5	28.7
台湾同胞	Compatriots from Taiwan	35.5	30.7	27.3	29.3	29.3
金融业	**Financial Intermediation**					
金融机构人民币各项存款余额	Structure of Total Savings Deposit Balance					
#财政存款	Treasury Deposit	4.9	5.1	3.9	3.2	3.5
个人储蓄存款	Personal Savings Deposit	44.1	45.0	45.6	44.6	43.4

1-6 续表2 continued

单位：% (%)

指标	Item	2010	2011	2012	2013	2014
金融机构人民币各项贷款余额	Structure of Total Loan Balance					
#短期贷款	Short-Term Loan	17.7	18.9	21.1	22.2	22.7
中长期贷款	Middle-Term & Long-Term Loan	79.7	79.5	77.4	76.8	76.0
教育(学历教育口径)	**Education**					
在校学生	Structure of Students Enrollment					
#高等教育阶段	Higher Education	5.3	5.6	6.4	7.1	7.8
高中阶段	Senior Secondary Schools	12.6	13.8	15.3	17.7	19.5
初中阶段	Junior Secondary Schools	27.2	27.7	27.9	27.9	27.2
小学阶段	Primary Schools	54.9	52.9	50.4	47.2	45.5
专任教师	Structure of Full-time Teachers					
#高等教育阶段	Higher Education	5.5	5.9	5.9	6.5	7.0
高中阶段	Senior Secondary Schools	11.9	12.7	13.9	15.5	16.8
初中阶段	Junior Secondary Schools	29.5	29.4	29.4	29.2	29.2
小学阶段	Primary Schools	53.1	52.1	50.8	48.8	47.1
人民生活	**People's Living Conditions**					
城镇居民消费性支出	Consumption Structure of Urban Residents					
#食品类	Food	39.9	40.2	39.7	35.9	34.9
衣着类	Clothing	11.0	10.7	11.1	10.2	8.2
居　住	Residence	8.9	9.7	8.1	10.9	15.9
家庭设备用品及服务	Household Facilities,Articles and Services	6.7	7.6	6.8	7.9	7.1
医疗保健	Medicines and Medical Services	5.4	5.1	5.2	4.6	6.1
交通和通信	Transport and Communications	12.6	12.3	15.0	13.6	12.3
教育文化娱乐服务	Education, Cultural and Recreation Services	12.5	11.7	11.1	14.2	13.6
农村居民生活消费支出	Consumption Structure of Rural Residents					
#食品类	Food	46.3	47.6	44.6	43.0	41.7
衣着类	Clothing	4.8	5.4	5.8	5.4	5.7
居　住	Residence	21.8	18.5	19.4	20.7	20.1
家庭设备、用品及服务	Household Facilities,Articles and Services	4.8	5.6	5.4	5.7	5.9
医疗保健	Medicines and Medical Services	6.2	7.1	7.2	6.4	6.2
交通和通信	Transport and Communications	8.1	8.8	9.5	10.3	10.7
文教、娱乐、用品及服务	Recreation,Education and Cultural Articles and Services	6.5	5.3	5.8	6.4	8.1
卫生	**Health Care**					
卫生机构床位	Structure of Beds of Health Care Institutions					
#医院、卫生院	Hospitals and Health Centers	92.6	91.9	95.0	95.4	95.8
卫生技术人员结构	Structure of Medical Technical Personnels					
#执业(助理)医师	Licensed(Assistant) Doctors	41.1	39.2	37.9	35.7	34.0
环境	**Environment**					
环境保护投入资金	Structure of Environment Protection Investment					
#老工业污染源治理资金	Old Industry Pollute Fountain Treatment	7.6	13.2	12.8	14.1	10.5
城市环境基础设施建设	Urban Environment Infrastructure Investment	32.3	35.6	36.7	43.5	48.0

1—7 社会经济主要指标比例、效益

Major Indicators on Proportions and Efficiency in Economic Social Development

指 标	Item	2010	2011	2012	2013	2014
人口与就业	**Population and Employment**					
城镇人口比重	Proportion of Urban Population	33.8	35.0	36.4	37.8	40.01
人口出生率(‰)	Birth Rate(‰)	13.96	13.31	13.27	13.05	12.98
人口死亡率(‰)	Death Rate(‰)	6.55	6.93	6.96	7.15	7.18
人口自然增长率(‰)	Natural Growth Rate(‰)	7.41	6.38	6.31	5.90	5.80
城镇登记失业率(%)	Registered Unemployment Rate in Urban Areas(%)	3.63	3.63	3.29	3.26	3.27
国民经济核算	**National Accounting**					
县域经济增加值占GDP比重(%)	Add Value in County Economy Share of GDP(%)	66.4	65.9	66.3	67.0	68.0
民营经济增加值占GDP比重(%)	Add Value in Non-public-owned Economic Share of GDP(%)	35.0	36.9	40.3	43.2	46.1
人均地区生产总值(元)	Per Capita Gross Domestic Product(yuan)	13119	16413	19710	23151	26437
固定资产投资	**Investment in Fixed Assets**					
固定资产交付使用率(%)	Rate of projects fixed assets completed and put into use	57.5	54.0	53.6	50.2	58.1
项目投产竣工率(%)	Rate of projects completed and put into use	71.1	68.9	73.8	68.8	74.1
消费	**Consumption**					
社会消费品零售总额相当于地区生产总值比例(%)	Proportion of Retail Sales of Consumer Goods to GDP(%)	32.2	30.7	29.6	29.6	31.7
人均社会消费品零售额(元)	Per Capita Ratail Sales of Consumer Goods(yuan)	4227	5042	5832	6774	8379
对外贸易	**Foreign Trade**					
进出口总额相当于地区生产总值比例(%)	Proportion of Total Value of Imports and Exports as Percentage to GDP(%)	4.6	5.6	6.1	6.4	6.2
财政	**Government Finance**					
财政总收入相当于地区生产总值比例(%)	Proportion of Total Financial Revenues to GDP(%)	21.1	23.3	24.0	24.0	23.0
一般公共预算支出相当于地区生产总值比例(%)	Proportion of General Budget Expenditure to GDP (%)	35.5	39.5	40.2	38.5	14.7
能源	**Energy**					
能源生产弹性系数	Elasticity Ratio of Energy Production	1.43		1.26	0.37	0.47
电力生产弹性系数	Elasticity Ratio of Electricity Production	0.03		1.27	0.33	0.41
能源消费弹性系数	Elasticity Ratio of Energy Consumption	0.63	0.73	0.65	0.65	0.38
电力消费弹性系数	Elasticity Ratio of Electricity Consumption	0.89	0.87	0.80	0.61	0.39
每万元地区生产总值能耗(吨标准煤/万元)(可比价)	Energy Consumption Per Unit of GDP (ton of SCE/10000 yuan) (equivalent value)	2.2480	1.7140	1.6444	1.5801	1.2967
农业	**Agriculture**					
每亩播种面积农产品产量	Output of Farm Crops Per Mu of Sowning Area					
粮 食(公斤)	Grain(kg)	244	191	236	220	242
油 料(公斤)	Oil-bearing Crops(kg)	76	98	106	109	112

注：县域经济增加值占GDP比重，是除贵阳市南明区、云岩区、花溪区、乌当区、白云区、观山湖区，六盘水市钟山区，遵义市红花岗区、汇川区，安顺市西秀区，毕节市七星关区，铜仁市碧江区、万山区等13个区之外的75个县(市、特区)经济总量占88个县(市、区、特区)GDP合计数的比重。

Note:The add value in county economy share of GDP is the proportion of 75 counties economy the 13 districts such as Nanming,Yunyan,Huaxi,Wudang,Baiyun,Guan shanhu,Zhongshan,Honghuagang,Huichuan,Xixiu,Qixingguan,Bijiang,Wanshan,etc to total GDP of 88 counties.

1-7 续表1 continued

指 标	Item	2010	2011	2012	2013	2014
工业（规模以上）	**Industry(above Designated Size)**					
总资产贡献率(%)	Ratio of Total Assets to Industrial Output Value(%)	12.84	14.13	15.97	19.11	13.00
资本保值增值率(%)	Capital Maintenance and Appreciation Rate (%)	125.32	118.66	121.72	117.66	115.87
流动资产周转次数(次/年)	Number of Times of Turnover of Circulating Fund (times/year)	1.75	1.95	1.89	1.72	1.86
成本费用利润率(%)	Ratio of Profits to Industrial Cost(%)	9.04	9.98	11.89	14.53	8.03
建筑业	**Construction**					
建筑业劳动生产率(元/人)(按增加值计算)	Overall Labour Productivity in Construction(yuan/person) (account by value-added)	89177	98494	141459	155658	160881
技术装备率(元/人)	Value of Machinery Per Laborer (yuan/person)	8232	9982	8148		
产值利税率(%)	Ratio of Per-tax Profits to Gross Output Value(%)	5.9	5.9	5.5		5.9
交通运输业	**Transportation**					
铁路网密度(公里/万平方公里)	Railway Density(km/10000 sq.km)	113.64	117.50	116.82	118.83	134.70
公路网密度(公里/万平方公里)	Highway Density(km/10000 sq.km)	8608.12	8958.70	9340.26	9797.13	10165.30
邮电通信业	**Postal and Telecommunication Services**					
电话普及率(包括移动电话)(部/百人)	Popularization Rate of Telephone (set/100 persons)	68.90	74.35	83.27	93.25	97.98
移动电话普及率(部/百人)	Popularization Rate of Mobile Telephone (set/100 persons)	56.46	62.71	72.34	82.78	88.21
旅游业	**Tourism**					
每一来黔境外旅游者消费支出(美元/人天)	Daily Expenditure of Per Tourists Visiting Guizhou(USD/preson and day)	171.76	168.68	167.13	181.05	180.65
金融	**Finance**					
金融机构人民币各项存款余额相当于地区生产总值比例(%)	Deposit of Financial Institutions as Percentage of GDP(%)	160.0	153.3	153.8	164.0	164.7
金融机构人民币各项贷款余额相当于地区生产总值比例(%)	Loans of Financial Institutions as Percentage of GDP(%)	124.9	120.0	120.8	124.9	133.5

1-7 续表2 continued

指　　标	Item	2010	2011	2012	2013	2014
教育	**Education**					
学龄儿童入学率(%)	Enrollment Rate of School-age Children(%)	97.9	98.6	99.3	99.3	99.1
初中阶段毛入学率(%)	Enrollment Rate of Primary School Graduates Entering into Junior Secondary Schools(%)	97.6	94.2	97.4	101.1	102.5
高中阶段毛入学率(%)	Enrollment Rate of Junior secondary School Graduates Entering into Senior secondary Schools(%)	55.0	58.9	62.2	68.0	78.0
高等教育毛入学率(%)	Enrollment Rate of Senior secondary School Graduates Entering into Institution of Higher Learning(%)	20.0	23.2	25.5	27.4	29.4
教师负担学生系数(学生/教师)	Student-Teacher Ratio (student/teacher)					
普通高校	Regular Institution of Higher Education	15.89	15.74	16.83	16.53	15.36
普通高中	Regular Senior Secondary Schools	18.75	19.02	18.59	18.25	18.00
普通初中	Regular Junior Secondary Schools	19.52	19.23	18.31	18.23	17.29
小　学	Primary Schools	21.90	20.74	19.20	18.43	17.96
城乡收入比例	**Urban-rural income ratio**					
城乡居民收入比(以农村常住居民人均可支配收入=1)	Ratio of Annual Income of Urban Residents to Rural(rural resident=1)	4.07	3.98	3.93	3.80	3.38
卫生	**Health Care**					
每万人拥有执业(助理)医师数(人)	Number of Licensed(Assistant) Doctors Per 10000 Persons(person)	12.0	10.4	11.2	13.0	13.4
每万人拥有床位数(张)	Number of Beds in Hospitals and Health Centers Per 10000 Persons(bed)	30.0	27.7	32.1	38.1	42.0
城市建设	**City Construction**					
人均公园绿地面积(平方米)	Per Capita Area of Parks and Green Land (sq.m)	5.33	5.50	6.68	7.98	8.66
用水普及率(%)	Percentage of Population with Access to Tap Water(%)	86.5	86.9	87.6	88.5	90.2
燃气普及率(%)	Percentage of Households with Access to Tap Gas(%)	54.5	55.0	55.2	58.7	60.3
环境、灾害	**Environment and Disaster**					
环保投入相当于地区生产总值比例(%)	Environment Protection Investment as Percentage to GDP(%)	1.9	1.9	1.4	1.7	1.9
亿元地区生产总值生产安全事故死亡人数(人/亿元)	Deaths of Industrial Accidents per Unit of GDP(person/100 million yuan)	0.42	0.29	0.19	0.14	0.11
平均每起火灾损失(万元)	Average Loss of Per Fire(10000 yuan)	2.71	5.66	5.37	3.84	4.19
平均每起交通事故损失(万元)	Average Loss of Per Traffic Accident (10000 yuan)	0.68	1.03	1.25	1.19	1.12

1-8 贵州社会经济主要指标占全国比重

Proportion of Guizhou's Main Economic and Social Indicators to the Whole Country

指标	Item	全国 China		贵州 Guizhou		贵州占全国比重(%) Proportion of Guizhou to China(%)	
		2010	2014	2010	2014	2010	2014
土地面积(万平方公里)	**Area of Territory(10000 sq.km)**	**960**	**960**	**17.62**	**17.62**	**1.8**	**1.8**
人口	**Population**						
年末总人口(万人)	Total Population at the Year-end (10000 persons)	134091	136782	3479	3508	2.6	2.6
就业	**Employment**						
就业人员(万人)	Employees(10000 persons)	76105	77253	1770.9	1909.69	2.3	2.5
非私营单位职工平均工资(元)	Average Wage of Staff and Workers(yuan)	36539	56339	31458	54685	86.1	97.1
国民经济核算	**National Accounting**						
地区生产总值(亿元)	Gross Domestic Product(100 million yuan)	408903.0	636462.7	4602.16	9266.39	1.1	1.5
第一产业	Primary Industry	39354.6	58332	625.03	1280.45	1.6	2.2
第二产业	Secondary Industry	188804.9	271392.4	1800.06	3857.44	1.0	1.4
第三产业	Tertiary Industry	180743	306739	2177.07	4128.50	1.2	1.3
人均地区生产总值(元)	Per Capita Gross Domestic Product(yuan)	30567	46652	13119	26437	42.9	56.7
固定资产投资	**Investment in Fixed Assets**						
全社会固定资产投资(亿元)	Total Investment in Fixed Assets (100 million yuan)	278121.9	512760.7	3186.28	9025.75	1.1	1.8
消费	**Consumption**						
社会消费品零售总额(亿元)	Total Retail Sales of Consumer Goods (100 million yuan)	156998	271896	1531.64	2936.85	1.0	1.1
对外贸易	**Foreign Trade**						
进出口总额(亿美元)	Total Value of Imports and Exports (USD 100 million)	29740	43030	31.47	107.71	0.1	0.3
#出口	Total Exports	15778	23428	19.20	93.97	0.1	0.4
财政	**Government Finance**						
一般公共预算收入(亿元)	General Public Financial Budget Revenue (100 million yuan)	83102	140350	533.73	1366.67	0.6	1.0
一般公共预算支出(亿元)	General Public Financial Budget Expenditure (100 million yuan)	89874	151662	1631.48	3542.80	1.8	2.3
能源	**Energy**						
一次能源生产总量(万吨标准煤)	Total Production of Primary Energy(10000 tons of SCE)	312125	360000	13100.00	15136.11	4.2	4.2
能源终端消费总量(万吨标准煤)	Consumption of Energy (10000 tons of SCE)	360648	426000	7373.10	9015.18	2.0	2.1
农业	**Agriculture**						
粮食产量(万吨)	Output of Grain(10000 tons)	54648	60703	1112	1139	2.0	1.9
油料产量(万吨)	Output of Oil-bearing Crops (10000 tons)	3230	3507	60.34	98.05	1.9	2.8
工业	**Industry**						
发电量(亿千瓦小时)	Output of Electricity (100 million kwh)	42072	56496	1359	1682	3.2	3.0
卷　烟(万箱)	Output of Cigarettes(10000 cases)	23753	26099	239	258	1.0	1.0

1-8 续表 continued

指 标	Item	全 国 China 2010	全 国 China 2014	贵 州 Guizhou 2010	贵 州 Guizhou 2014	贵州占全国比重(%) Proportion of Guizhou to China(%) 2010	贵州占全国比重(%) Proportion of Guizhou to China(%) 2014
交通运输业	**Transportation**						
铁路营业里程(万公里)	Length of Railways(10000 km)	9.12	11.18	0.20	0.24	2.2	2.1
公路里程(万公里)	Length of Highways(10000 km)	400.82	446.39	15.16	17.91	3.8	4.0
旅客周转量(亿人公里)	Passenger-Kilometers(100 million passenger-km)	27894	30096	514.41	635.50	1.8	2.1
货物周转量(亿吨公里)	Freight Ton-Kilometers(100 million ton-km)	141837	185398	1012.20	1442.24	0.7	0.8
邮电通信业	**Post and Telecommunication**						
电信业务总量(亿元)	Business Revenue of Telecommunications (100 million yuan)	29993	18150	566.40	353.98	1.9	2.0
邮政业务总量(亿元)	Business Volume of Post (100 million yuan)	1985	3696	15.50	27.75	0.8	0.8
旅游业	**Tourism**						
国际旅游外汇收入(亿美元)	International Earnings from Tourism (USD 100 million)	458	569	1.30	2.17	0.3	0.4
国内旅游收入(亿元)	Domestic Earnings from Tourism (100 million yuan)	12580	30312	1052.64	2882.66	8.4	9.5
金融业	**Finance**						
金融机构人民币各项存款余额(亿元)	Total Savings Deposit Balance(100 million yuan)	718238	1138645	7363.92	15263.26	1.0	1.3
金融机构人民币各项贷款余额(亿元)	Total Loan Balance(100 million yuan)	479196	816770	9250.26	18888.19	1.9	2.3
教育	**Education**						
普通高等学校(所)	Regular Institutions of Higher Education(unit)	2358	2529	47	55	2.0	2.2
普通高等学校专任教师(万人)	Full-time Teachers of Regular Institutions of Higher Education(10000 persons)	134.3	153.5	2.04	2.81	1.5	1.8
普通高校在校大学生(万人)	Students Enrollment of Regular Institutions of Higher Education(10000 persons)	2231.8	2547.7	32.33	46.04	1.4	1.8
文化	**Culture**						
图书总印数(亿册)	Number of Books Printed Copies (100 million copies)	71.7	84.0	0.81	1.01	1.1	1.2
期刊总印数(亿册)	Number of Magazines Printed Copies (100 million copies)	32.2	32.0	0.13	0.15	0.4	0.5
报纸总印数(亿份)	Number of Newspapers Printed Copies (100million copies)	451.2	465.0	3.70	3.64	0.8	0.8
卫生	**Health Care**						
医院(个)	Number of Hospitals(unit)	21000	25861	2005	2612	9.5	10.1
执业(助理)医师(万人)	Number of Licensed(Assistant) Doctors (10000 persons)	241.3	289.3	4.22	5.78	1.7	2.0
医院床位(万张)	Number of Beds in Hospitals(10000 beds)	338.7	496.1	9.75	17.84	2.9	3.6
人民生活	**People's Livelihood**						
城镇常住居民人均可支配收入(元)	Per Capita Annual Disposable Income of Urban Households(yuan)	19109	28844	14143	22548	74.0	78.2
农村常住居民人均纯收入(元)	Annual Per Capita Net Income of Rural Residents(yuan)	5919	10489	3472	6671	58.7	63.6

注：贵州占全国比重中，非私营单位职工平均工资、人均地区生产总值、人民生活占比表示贵州相当于全国的比例。
Note: The ratio in proportion of people's livelihood shows the proportion of Guizhou to China.

主要统计指标解释

行政区划 指国家对行政区域的划分。根据有关法规规定，我国的行政区域划分如下：(1)全国分为省、自治区、直辖市；(2)省、自治区分为自治州、县、自治县、市；(3)自治州分为县、自治县、市；(4)县、自治县分为乡、民族乡、镇；(5)直辖市和较大的市分为区、县；(6)国家在必要时设立的特别行政区。

国民经济行业分类 2012年起统计定期报表使用《国民经济行业分类》（GB/T4754-2011）。该分类是由国家统计局组织修订，经国家质检总局和国家标准化委员会批准，于2011年4月29日发布实施。该次修订是在2002年分类标准的基础上，参照联合国《国际标准产业分类》修订第四版（ISIC/Rev.4）进行的。修订后的《国民经济行业分类》（GB/T4754-2011）共有门类20个，大类96个，中类432个，小类1094个。

可比价格 指计算各种总量指标所采用的扣除了价格变动因素的价格，可进行不同时期总量指标的对比。按可比价格计算总量指标有两种方法：一种是直接用产品产量乘某一年的不变价格计算；另一种是用价格指数进行缩减。

平均增长速度 我国计算平均增长速度有两种方法：一种是“水平法”，又称几何平均法，是以间隔期最后一年的水平同基期水平对比来计算平均每年增长（或下降）速度；另一种是“累计法”，又称代数平均法或方程法，是以间隔期内各年水平的总和同基期水平对比来计算平均每年增长（或下降）速度。在一般正常情况下，两种方法计算的平均每年增长速度比较接近；但在经济发展不平衡、出现大起大落时，两种方法计算的结果差别较大。

本《年鉴》内所列的平均增长速度，除固定资产投资用“累计法”计算外，其余均用“水平法”计算。从某年到某年平均增长速度的年份，均不包括基期年在内。如改革开放三十六年的平均增长速度是以 1978 年为基期计算的，则写为 1979-2014 年平均增长速度。

Explanatory Notes on Main Statistical Indicators

Divisions of Administrative Areas refers to the division of administrative areas by the state. The relative laws stipulate that: 1) The whole country is divided into provinces, autonomous regions and municipalities directly under the central government; 2) Provinces and autonomous regions are divided into autonomous prefectures, counties, autonomous counties and cities; 3) Autonomous prefectures are divided into counties, autonomous counties and cities; 4) Counties and autonomous counties are divided into townships, nationality townships and towns; 5) Municipalities and large cities are divided into districts and counties, 6) The state shall, when necessary, establish special administrative regions.

Industrial Classification of the National Economy The Industrial Classification of the National Economy (GB/T 4754-2011) is introduced starting from the compilation of 2012 annual statistics. The revision, based on the 2002 classification, was organized by the National Bureau of Statistics taking into consideration of the International Standards of the Industrial Classification of All Economic Activities (ISIC/Rev.4) of the United Nations. The new Classification was promulgated by the National Administration of Quality Supervision, Inspection and Quarantine and State Committee for Standardization on April 29, 2011. The revised version of the Industrial Classification of the National Economy (GB/T 4754-2002) is composed of 20 major divisions, 96 divisions, 432 major groups and 1094 groups.

Comparable Price Refers to the calculation of the total amount of indicators used to deduct the price changes in the price, can be carried out in different periods of the total index contrast. There are two ways to calculate the total amount of the total index: one is that the output of the product is directly used for one year. The other is to reduce the price by the price index.

Average Annual Growth Rate There are two methods of method for calculating the average growth rate of our country: one is "horizontal", also known as the geometric mean method is to last year's levels of interval compared with the base period level to calculate the average annual growth (or decline) speed; another is the "cumulative method", also known as algebraic average method and equation method is combined with a interval in each level compared with the base period level to calculate average annual growth (or decline) speed. In the normal case, two methods for calculating the average annual growth rate is close to; but when the unbalanced economic development, the emergence of big ups and downs, two methods to calculate the results vary greatly.

The average annual growth rates listed in Yearbook are calculated by the level approach except for the growth rates are computed. For instance, the average annual growth rate of the 36 years since 1978 is shown as the average annual growth rate of 1979-2014 without showing the base year 1978.

2 国民经济核算

National Accounts

2-1 地区生产总值

Gross Domestic Product

单位：亿元 (100 million yuan)

指　标	Item	2010	2011	2012	2013	2014	2014年比2013年增长(%) Increase Rate in 2014 over 2013(%)
地区生产总值	**Gross Domestic product**	**4602.16**	**5701.84**	**6852.20**	**8086.86**	**9266.39**	**10.8**
按产业分	**By Three Strata of Industry**						
第一产业	Primary Industry	625.03	726.22	891.91	998.47	1280.45	6.6
第二产业	Secondary Industry	1800.06	2194.33	2677.54	3276.24	3857.44	12.3
第三产业	Tertiary Industry	2177.07	2781.29	3282.75	3812.15	4128.50	10.4
按国民经济行业分	**By Sector**						
农　业	Agriculture	625.03	726.22	891.91	1031.70	1316.08	6.5
#农林牧渔服务业	Agriculture Forestry, Animal Husbandry and Fishery Services				33.23	35.63	3.3
工　业	Industry	1516.87	1829.20	2217.06	2686.52	3140.88	11.1
#金属制品、机械和设备修理业	Repair Serivice of Metal Products, Machinery and Equipment				0.97	1.13	11.8
建筑业	Construction	283.19	365.13	460.48	590.69	717.69	18.2
批发和零售业	Wholesale and Retail Trade	367.52	448.77	514.49	582.05	624.17	9.4
交通运输、仓储和邮政业	Transport, Storage and Post	480.32	590.91	687.45	772.44	828.69	9.3
住宿和餐饮业	Hotel and Catering Services	180.73	224.40	266.58	294.86	322.71	6.8
金融业	Financial Intermediation	231.51	297.27	365.87	444.53	491.65	14.2
房地产业	Real Estate	139.64	160.30	176.75	202.94	220.48	6.0
其他服务业	Other Services	777.35	1059.64	1271.61	1481.13	1604.04	11.8
营利性服务业	For-profit Services	283.45	398.09	467.57	546.11	591.36	11.4
非营利性服务业	Non-profit Services	493.90	661.55	804.04	935.02	1012.68	12.0
人均地区生产总值(元)	**Per Capita Gross Domestic Product(yuan)**	**13119**	**16413**	**19710**	**23151**	**26437**	**10.4**

注：1、2013年数据根据第三次经济普查资料进行修订；2、2013年和2014年国民经济核算数据按照国家统计局统一要求，采用《国民经济行业分类》（GB/T4754－2011）和《三次产业划分规定》（国统字〔2012〕108号）。2013年起第一产业增加值等于农业、林业、畜牧业、渔业增加值之和，不包含农林牧渔服务业；第二产业增加值等于工业与建筑业增加值之和再扣除工业中开采辅助活动增加值、金属制品机械和设备修理业增加值。农林牧渔服务业，开采辅助活动，金属制品机械和设备修理业归入第三产业。（以下相关表同）

Note: 1.Data of 2013 is revised according to third time econimic census;2 Data of national economy account has to adapt to 《National economy industrial classification》 and 《Three industry division rule》 according to national statistical department.From 2013,the first industry added value has included added value of agriculture, forestry,graziery and fishery excepet service of those industries;(the related tables in the chapter are the same).the second industry added value equals to the sum of industry's added value and construction's added value, then deduct the added value of exploit activities, metal product machinery and equipment repair. the third industry includes service in agriculture, forestry,graziery ,fishery, exploit activities, metal product machinery and equipment repair.

2-2 地区生产总值构成

Compostion of Gross Domestic Product

单位：%　　　　　　　　　　　　　　　　　　　　　　　　　　　　　　　　(%)

指　标	Item	2010	2011	2012	2013	2014
地区生产总值	**Gross Domestic product**	**100.0**	**100.0**	**100.0**	**100.0**	**100.0**
按产业分	**By Three Strata of Industry**					
第一产业	Primary Industry	13.6	12.7	13.0	12.3	13.8
第二产业	Secondary Industry	39.1	38.5	39.1	40.5	41.6
第三产业	Tertiary Industry	47.3	48.8	47.9	47.2	44.6
按国民经济行业分	**By Sector**					
农　业	Agriculture	13.6	12.7	13.0	12.7	14.2
#农林牧渔服务业	Agriculture Forestry, Animal Husbandry and Fishery Services				0.4	0.4
工　业	Industry	33.0	32.1	32.4	33.2	33.9
#金属制品、机械和设备修理业	Repair Serivice of Metal Products, Machinery and Equipment					
建筑业	Construction	6.1	6.4	6.7	7.3	7.7
批发和零售业	Wholesale and Retail Trade	8.0	7.9	7.5	7.2	6.7
交通运输、仓储和邮政业	Transport Storage and Post	10.4	10.4	10.0	9.6	9.0
住宿和餐饮业	Hotel and Catering Services	3.9	3.9	3.9	3.6	3.5
金融业	Financial Intermediation	5.0	5.2	5.3	5.5	5.3
房地产业	Real Estate	3.0	2.8	2.6	2.5	2.4
其他服务业	Other services	17.0	18.6	18.6	18.4	17.3
营利性服务业	For-profit Services	6.2	7.0	6.8	6.8	6.4
非营利性服务业	Non-profit Services	10.8	11.6	11.8	11.6	10.9

2-3 地区生产总值(按支出法计算)

Gross Domestic Product（Accounted by Expenditure）

指 标	Item	2010	2011	2012	2013	2014	2014年比2013年增长(%) Increase Rate in 2014 over 2013(%)
地区生产总值(亿元)	**Gross Domestic Product**	**4602.16**	**5701.84**	**6852.20**	**8086.86**	**9266.39**	**10.8**
最终消费	Final Consumption Expenditure	2931.13	3438.71	3950.64	4535.82	5288.50	11.5
居民消费	Household Consumption	2181.37	2566.78	2910.93	3332.70	3982.27	13.5
农村居民	Rural Household	770.06	908.51	994.67	1182.14	1417.43	9.2
城镇居民	Urban Household	1411.31	1658.27	1916.26	2150.56	2564.84	15.9
政府消费	Government Consumption	749.76	871.93	1039.71	1203.12	1306.23	6.2
资本形成总额	Gross Capital Formation	2575.27	3229.30	4164.37	5261.41	6114.31	26.9
固定资本形成总额	Gross Fixed Capital Formation	2510.39	3147.46	4067.26	5141.75	5928.80	26.0
库存增加	Changes in Inventories	64.88	81.84	97.11	119.66	185.51	62.6
货物和服务净出口	Net Outflow of Goods and Services	-904.24	-966.17	-1262.81	-1710.37	-2136.42	
构成(%)	**Composition(%)**						
以最终消费为100	Final Consumption Expenditures=100						
居民消费	Household Consumption	74.4	74.6	73.7	73.5	75.3	
政府消费	Government Consumption	25.6	25.4	26.3	26.5	24.7	
以居民消费为100	Household Consumption Expenditures=100						
农村居民	Rural Household	35.3	35.4	34.2	35.5	35.6	
城镇居民	Urban Household	64.7	64.6	65.8	64.5	64.4	
最终消费率(%)	**Final Consumption Rate(%)**	**63.7**	**60.3**	**57.7**	**56.1**	**57.1**	
资本形成率(%)	**Capital Formation Rate(%)**	**56.0**	**56.6**	**60.8**	**65.1**	**66.0**	
城乡居民人均消费水平比(农村居民=1)	**Urban/Rural Consumption Ratio (rural households=1)**	**3.92**	**3.49**	**3.47**	**3.08**	**2.84**	

注：表中居民消费按常住半年人口计算，城乡居民人均消费水平比根据第六次人口普查数据进行修订，2010年居民消费数据根据新农合数据进行修订。

Note:The Data of Household Consumption in the table are calculated based on permanent population in half a year scope.Urban/Rural Consumption ratio is adjusted according to the result of the sixth National population census.In the year 2010,the data of household consumption were adjusted according to the data of New cooperatrie Medical.

2-4 三次产业对地区生产总值增长的拉动

Contribution of the Three Strata of Industry to GDP Growth

单位：百分点 (percentage points)

指 标	Item	2010	2011	2012	2013	2014
地区生产总值	**Gross Domestic Product**	**12.8**	**15.0**	**13.6**	**12.5**	**10.8**
第一产业	Primary Industry	0.6	0.2	1.1	0.6	0.7
第二产业	Secondary Industry	6.6	7.0	6.7	5.9	5.1
#工 业	Industry	5.3	5.9	5.3	4.5	3.8
第三产业	Tertiary Industry	5.6	7.8	5.8	6.0	5.0

2-5 三次产业贡献率

Share of the Contributions of the Three Strata of Industry to the Increase of the GDP

单位：% (%)

指 标	Item	2010	2011	2012	2013	2014
地区生产总值	**Gross Domestic Product**	**100.0**	**100.0**	**100.0**	**100.0**	**100.0**
第一产业	Primary Industry	5.0	1.1	7.6	5.1	6.4
第二产业	Secondary Industry	51.1	46.8	49.6	46.8	47.7
#工 业	Industry	41.6	39.2	38.7	36.2	35.4
第三产业	Tertiary Industry	43.9	52.1	42.8	48.1	45.9

主要统计指标解释

国内生产总值(GDP) 指一个国家所有常住单位在一定时期内生产的全部最终产品和服务的价值总和。国内生产总值有三种表现形态，即价值形态、收入形态和产品形态。从价值形态看，它是所有常住单位在一定时期内生产的全部产品和服务价值减去同期投入的全部产品和服务价值的差额，即所有常住单位的增加值之和；从收入形态看，它是所有常住单位在一定时期内的生产活动所形成的原始收入之和；从产品形态看，它是所有常住单位在一定时期内最终使用的产品和服务减去进口的产品和服务的价值总和。在实际核算中，国内生产总值有三种计算方法，即生产法、收入法和支出法。三种方法分别从不同的方面反映国内生产总值及其构成。

对于一个地区来说，称为地区生产总值。

三次产业 三次产业的划分是世界上较为常用的产业结构分类，但各国的划分不尽一致。我国的三次产业划分是：

第一产业指农业、林业、畜牧业、渔业（不含农林牧渔服务业）。

第二产业指采矿业（不含开采辅助活动），制造业（不含金属制品、机械和设备修理业），电力、热力、燃气及水的生产和供应业，建筑业。

第三产业指除第一、二产业以外的其他行业。

支出法国内（地区）生产总值 是从最终使用的角度反映一个国家(或地区)一定时期内生产活动最终成果的一种方法，包括最终消费支出、资本形成总额及货物和服务净出口三部分。计算公式为：

支出法国内（地区）生产总值=最终消费支出+资本形成总额+货物和服务净出口

最终消费支出 指常住单位为满足物质、文化和精神生活的需要，从本国经济领土和国外购买的货物和服务的支出。它不包括非常住单位在本国经济领土内的消费支出。最终消费支出分为居民消费支出和政府消费支出。

居民消费支出 指常住住户在一定时期内对于货物和服务的全部最终消费支出。居民消费支出除了直接以货币形式购买的货物和服务的消费支出外，还包括以其他方式获得的货物和服务的消费支出，即所谓的虚拟消费支出。居民虚拟消费支出包括如下几种类型：单位以实物报酬及实物转移的形式提供给居民的货物和服务；住户生产并由本住户消费了的货物和服务，其中的服务仅指住户的自有住房服务和付酬的家庭雇员提供的家庭和个人服务；金融机构提供的金融中介服务；保险机构提供的保险服务。

政府消费支出 指政府部门为全社会提供的公共服务的消费支出和免费或以较低的价格向居民住户提供的货物和服务的净支出，主要包括行政管理、卫生文教、国防支出等。

资本形成总额 指常住单位在一定时期内新形成的固定资产和增加的库存存货的价值，包括固定资本形成总额和存货增加两部分。

固定资本形成总额 指常住单位在一定时期内获得的固定资产减处置的固定资产的价值总额。固定资产是通过生产活动生产出来的，且其使用年限在一年以上、单位价值在规定标准以上的资产，不包括自然资产。可分为有形固定资本形成总额和无形固定资本形成总额。有形固定资本形成总额主要包括住宅、非住宅建筑物、机器设备的购置价值、土地改良支出、大牲畜和新增经济林价值。无形固定资本形成总额包括矿藏的勘探、计算机软件等获得减处置。

存货增加 指常住单位在一定时期内存货实物量变动的市场价值，即期末价值减期初价值的差额，再扣除当期由于价格变动而产生的持有收益。存货增加可以是正值，也可以是负值，正值表示存货比基期上升，负值表示存货比基期下降。存货包括生产单位购进的原材料、燃料和储备物资等存货，以及生产单位生产的产成品、在制品和半成品等存货。

货物和服务净出口　指货物和服务出口减货物和服务进口的差额。出口包括常住单位向非常住单位出售或无偿转让的各种货物和服务的价值；进口包括常住单位从非常住单位购买或无偿得到的各种货物和服务的价值。由于服务活动的提供与使用同时发生，一般把常住单位从非常住单位得到的服务作为进口，非常住单位从常住单位得到的服务作为出口。货物的出口和进口价值都按离岸价格计算，服务业出口和进口价值按交易发生时的市场价格计算。

Explanatory Notes on Main Statistical Indicators

Gross Domestic Product (GDP) refers to the final products and services produced by all resident units in a country (or a region) during a certain period of time. Gross domestic product is expressed in three different perspectives, namely value, income, and products respectively. GDP in its value perspective refers to the total value of all goods and services produced by all resident units during a certain period of time, minus the total value of input of goods and services of the nature of non-fixed assets; in other words, it is the sum of the value-added of all resident units. GDP from the perspective of income includes the primary income created by all resident units and distributed to resident and non-resident units. GDP from the perspective of products refers to the value of all goods and services for final demand by all resident units plus the net exports of goods and services during a given period of time. In the practice of national accounting, gross domestic product is calculated from three approaches, namely production approach, income approach and expenditure approach, which reflect gross domestic product and its composition from different angles.

For a region, it is called as Gross Regional Product.

Three Strata of Industry Classification of economic activities into three strata of industry is a common practice in the world, although the grouping varies to some extent from country to country. In China economic activities are categorized into the following three strata of industry:

Primary industry refers to agriculture, forestry, animal husbandry and fishery.（excluding services in support of these industries）

Secondary industry refers to mining and quarrying(excluding support activities for mining), manufacturing (excluding Repair Services of metal Products, Machinery and Equipment), production and supply of electricity, heat, gas and water, and construction.

Tertiary industry refers to all other economic activities not included in the primary or secondary industries.

GDP by Expenditure Approach refers to the method of measuring the final results of production activities of a country (region) during a given period from the perspective of final uses. It includes final consumption expenditure, gross capital formation and net export of goods and services. The formula for computation is.:

GDP by expenditure approach = final consumption expenditure + gross capital formation +

net export of goods and services

Final Consumption Expenditure refers to the total expenditure of resident units for purchases of goods and services from both the domestic economic territory and abroad to meet the needs of material, cultural and spiritual life. It does not include the expenditure of non-resident units on consumption in the economic territory of the country. The final consumption expenditure is broken down into household consumption expenditure and government consumption expenditure.

Household Consumption Expenditure refers to the total expenditure of resident households on the final consumption of goods and services. In addition to the consumption of goods and services bought by the households directly with money, the household consumption expenditure also includes expenditure on goods and services obtained by the households in other ways, i.e. the so-called imputed consumption expenditure, which includes the following: (a) the goods and services provided to households by employers in the form of payment in kind and transfer in kind; (b) goods and services produced and consumed by the households themselves, in which the services refer to the owner-occupied housing and services offered by payed family employees; (c) financial intermediate services provided by financial institution;(d) insurance services provided by the insurance institution.

Government Consumption Expenditure refers to the consumption expenditure spent for the provision of public services provided by the government to the whole country and the net expenditure on the goods and services provided by the government to households free of charge or at reduced prices, including administration, health and education, expenditure on national defense, etc.

Gross Capital Formation refers to the newly formed fixed assets and increased the net value of inventory during a given period, thus including gross fixed capital formation and changes in inventories.

Gross Fixed Capital Formation refers to the value of acquisitions less those disposals of fixed assets during a given period. Fixed assets are the assets produced through production activities with unit value above a specified amount and which could be used for over one year. Natural assets are not included.Gross fixed capital formation can be categorized into total tangible fixed capital formation and total intangible fixed capital formation. Total tangible fixed capital formation includes the value of the construction projects and installation projects completed and the equipment, apparatus and instruments purchased (less those disposed) as well as the value of land improved, the value of draught animals, breeding stock and animals for milk, for wool and for recreational purposes and the newly increased forest with economic value. Total intangible fixed capital formation includes the prospecting of minerals and the acquisition of computer software minus the disposal of them.

Changes in Inventories refers to the market value of the change in the physical volume of inventory of resident units during a given period, i.e. the difference between the values at the beginning and at the end of the period minus the gains due to the change in prices. The changes in inventories can have a positive or a negative value. A positive value indicates an increase in inventory while a negative value indicates a decrease in inventory. The inventory includes raw materials, fuels and reserve materials purchased by the production units as well as the inventory of finished products, semi-finished products and work-in-progress.

Net Export of Goods and Services refers to the exports of goods and services subtracting the imports of goods and services. Exports include the value of various goods and services sold or gratuitously transferred by resident units to non-resident units. Imports include the value of various goods and services purchased or gratuitously acquired resident units from non-resident units. Because the provision of services and the use of them happen simultaneously, the acquisition of services by resident units from abroad is usually treated as import while the acquisition of services by non-resident units in this country is usually treated as export. The exports and imports of goods are calculated at FOB. Export and cmport value of service industry are calculated at the markee price when transaction occurs

人 口

3

Population

3-1 全省历次人口普查主要指标

Main Indicators on National Population Census in 1953,1964,1982,1990,2000 and 2010

单位：万人 (10000 persons)

指 标	Item	第一次 (1953年) The First	第二次 (1964年) The Second	第三次 (1982年) The Third	第四次 (1990年) The Forth	第五次 (2000年) The Fifth	第六次 (2010年) The Sixth
总人口	**Total Population**	**1503.73**	**1714.05**	**2855.29**	**3239.11**	**3524.77**	**3474.65**
按城镇、乡村分	**Grouped by Residence**						
城镇人口	Urban population	109.91	203.55	540.22	623.17	844.51	1174.78
乡村人口	Rural population	1393.82	1510.51	2315.07	2615.94	2680.25	2299.87
城镇人口比重（%）	The proportion of urban population(%)	7.31	11.88	18.92	19.24	23.96	33.81
按性别分	**Grouped by Male and Female**						
男	Male	759.80	868.48	1464.08	1676.88	1846.45	1795.15
女	Female	743.93	845.57	1391.21	1562.22	1678.32	1679.50
性别比(以女性为100)	Sex Ratio(female=100)	102.13	102.71	105.24	107.34	110.02	106.89
人口年平均增长率（%）	The growth rate of Annual Average Population(%)		1.32	2.89	1.59	0.82	-0.14
家庭总户数（万户）	Total Number of Household (10000 households)	340.15	390.96	565.93	721.04	923.94	1038.96
户均规模（人/户）	Average Family Size(person/household)	4.42	4.38	4.93	4.41	3.74	3.24
人口自然变动（‰）	**Natural Change of Population(‰)**						
出生率	Birth Rate	38.43	52.62	24.81	23.09	20.59	13.96
死亡率	Death Rate	17.61	20.66	7.60	7.90	7.53	6.55
自然增长率	Natural Growth Rate	20.82	31.96	17.21	15.19	13.06	7.41
年龄结构（%）	**Age Composition (%)**						
0-14岁	Aged 0-14	37.88	38.82	40.88	32.68	30.17	25.22
15-64岁	Aged 15-64	58.52	58.42	54.45	62.71	63.87	66.21
65岁及以上	Aged 65 and Over	3.59	2.76	4.66	4.61	5.97	8.57
民族	**Population by Ethnicity**						
汉族	Han	1109.84	1312.89	2112.95	2114.88	2191.17	2219.85
占总人口比重（%）	Percentage to Total Population(%)	73.81	76.61	74.00	65.29	62.16	63.89
年均增长率（%）	Annual average growth rate(%)		0.37	-0.35	-1.24	-0.49	0.27
少数民族	Ethnic Minorities(10 000 persons)	393.89	401.16	742.35	1124.23	1333.60	1254.80
占总人口比重（%）	Percentage to Total Population(%)	26.19	23.39	26.00	34.71	37.84	36.11
年均增长率（%）	Annual average growth rate(%)		-1.12	1.06	2.93	0.87	-0.46
受教育程度	**Education Attainments**						
小 学	Primary School		352.71	822.65	1210.75	1535.30	1368.07
初 中	Junior Secondary School		53.80	325.86	475.78	727.48	1035.07
高 中	Senior Secondary School		13.38	84.72	127.50	199.67	253.02
大专以上	Junior College and Above		3.96	11.09	25.06	67.49	183.88
文盲人口	Illiterate Population			1202.24	969.11	598.58	303.85
文盲率（%）	Illiterate Rate(%)			42.11	29.92	16.98	8.74
每十万人口拥有的各种受教育程度人口（人）	**Population with Various Education Attainments Per 100000 Persons (person)**						
小 学	Primary School				37379	43557	39373
初 中	Junior Secondary School				14688	20639	29789
高中/中专	Senior Secondary School and Technical Secondary School				3973	5665	7282
大专及以上	Junior College and Above				774	1915	5292

注：表中数据来源于历次人口普查公报。

Note:Data in this table come from the communique of the six national population censuses.

3-2 第六次人口普查全省世居民族人口数

Population of all ethnic groups on the Sixth National Population Census

单位：万人 (10000 persons)

指 标	Item	第六次人口普查(2010年)
总人口	Total Population	3474.86
男	Male	1790.55
女	Female	1684.31
汉族	Han	2234.42
男	Male	1151.79
女	Female	1082.63
蒙古族	Mongolian	4.16
男	Male	2.32
女	Female	1.84
回族	Hui	18.48
男	Male	9.50
女	Female	8.98
苗族	Miao	396.84
男	Male	204.09
女	Female	192.75
彝族	Yi	83.45
男	Male	42.96
女	Female	40.49
壮族	Zhuang	5.26
男	Male	2.65
女	Female	2.61
布依族	Bouyei	251.06
男	Male	127.11
女	Female	123.95
满族	Manchu	2.31
男	Male	1.19
女	Female	1.12
侗族	Dong	143.19
男	Male	75.02
女	Female	68.17
瑶族	Yao	4.09
男	Male	2.14
女	Female	1.95
白族	Bai	17.95
男	Male	9.59
女	Female	8.36
土家族	Tujia	143.70
男	Male	73.65
女	Female	70.05
畲族	She	3.66
男	Male	1.91
女	Female	1.75
水族	Shui	34.87
男	Male	18.03
女	Female	16.84
仫佬族	Mulam	2.50
男	Male	1.33
女	Female	1.17
羌族	Qiang	0.16
男	Male	0.09
女	Female	0.07
毛南族	Maonan	2.73
男	Male	1.42
女	Female	1.31
仡佬族	Gelao	49.52
男	Male	25.89
女	Female	23.62
未定族称人们共同体	Undetermined called People Community	61.28
男	Male	32.01
女	Female	29.27

注：表中数据来源于第六次人口普查机器汇总数。

Note:Data in this table are obtained from machine summany number of the Sixth Population Census.

3-3　年末常住人口(半年口径)

Permanent Resident Population (at least half a year)

单位：万人 (10000 persons)

指　标	Item	2010	2011	2012	2013	2014
年末总人口	**Total Population at the Year-end**	**3479**	**3469**	**3484**	**3502.22**	**3508.04**
按城镇、乡村分	Grouped by Residence					
城　镇	Urban	1176.25	1212.76	1268.52	1324.89	1403.57
乡　村	Rural	2302.75	2256.24	2215.48	2177.33	2104.47
按性别分	Grouped by Sex					
男	Male	1797.43	1801.21	1818.61	1822.50	1817.91
女	Female	1681.57	1667.79	1665.39	1679.72	1690.13
性别比(以女性为100)	Sex Ratio(female=100)	106.89	108.00	109.20	108.50	107.56
年平均人口	Annual Average Population	3508	3474	3477	3493	3505
家庭年末总户数(万户)	Total Number of Household (10000 households)	1038.96	1066.13	1103.77	1125.07	1133.00
家庭户规模(人/户)	Average Family Size(person/household)	3.24	3.16	3.10	3.11	3.08
人口自然变动	**Natural Change of Population**					
出生人数	Number of Birth	48.52	46.24	46.13	45.58	45.50
出生率(‰)	Birth Rate(‰)	13.96	13.31	13.27	13.05	12.98
死亡人数	Number of Death	22.76	24.07	24.20	24.97	25.17
死亡率(‰)	Death Rate(‰)	6.55	6.93	6.96	7.15	7.18
自然增长人数	Natural Increase of Population	25.76	22.17	21.93	20.61	20.33
自然增长率(‰)	Natural Growth Rate(‰)	7.41	6.38	6.31	5.90	5.80

3-4 户籍人口

Household Registered Population

单位：万人 (10000 persons)

指　标	Item	2010	2011	2012	2013	2014
年末总人口	**Total Population at the Year-end**	**4189.00**	**4238.44**	**4249.48**	**4286.15**	**4325.49**
农　业	Agriculture	3512.92	3551.18	3557.14	3584.17	3616.27
非农业	Non-agriculture	676.07	687.26	692.34	701.98	709.22
构成(以年末总人口=100)(%)	**Composition (total population at the year-end=100)(%)**					
农　业	Agriculture	83.9	83.8	83.7	83.6	83.6
非农业	Non-agriculture	16.1	16.2	16.3	16.4	16.4

注：资料来源于省公安厅。
Note:Data in the table above are obtained from the Public Security Department of Guizhou Province.

3-5 计划生育

Family Planning

单位：万人 (10000 persons)

指　标	Item	2010	2011	2012	2013	2014
生育政策符合率(%)	Family Planning Rates(%)	92.8	93.9	94.7	95.0	95.2
采取节育措施人数	Number of Contraception Users	563.07	572.94	611.10	622.72	610.26
避孕率(含复合使用药具)(%)	Contraception Rates(Including Using contraceptives)(%)	88.2	88.1	89.0	89.0	89.1

注：资料来源于省卫生计生委。
Note:Data in the table are provided from the Health and Family Planning of Guizhou Provincial.

主要统计指标解释

总人口 指一定时点、一定地区范围内的有生命的个人的总和。年度统计的年末人口数指每年 12 月 31 日 24 时的人口数。

城镇人口和乡村人口 城镇人口是指居住在城镇范围内的全部常住人口；乡村人口是除上述人口以外的全部人口。

出生率(又称粗出生率) 指在一定时期内(通常为一年)一定地区的出生人数与同期内平均人数之比，用千分率表示。本资料中的出生率指年出生率，其计算公式为：

$$\text{出生率} = \frac{\text{年出生人数}}{\text{年平均人数}} \times 1000\ ‰$$

公式中：出生人数指活产婴儿，即胎儿脱离母体时(不管怀孕月数)，有过呼吸或其他生命现象。年平均人数指年初、年底人口数的平均数，也可用年中人口数代替。

死亡率(又称粗死亡率) 指在一定时期内(通常为一年)一定地区的死亡人数与同期内平均人数之比，用千分率表示。本资料中的死亡率指年死亡率，其计算公式为：

$$\text{死亡率} = \frac{\text{年死亡人数}}{\text{年平均人数}} \times 1000\ ‰$$

人口自然增长率 指在一定时期内(通常为一年)人口自然增加数(出生人数减死亡人数)与该时期内平均人数之比，用千分率表示。计算公式为：

$$\text{人口自然增长率} = \frac{\text{本年出生人数} - \text{本年死亡人数}}{\text{年平均人数}} \times 1000\ ‰$$

$$= \text{人口出生率} - \text{人口死亡率}$$

Explanatory Notes on Main Statistical Indicators

Total Population refers to the total number of people alive at a certain point of time within a given area. The annual statistics on total population is taken at midnight, the 3lst of December.

Urban Population and Rural Population Urban population refers to all people residing in cities and towns, while rural population refers to population other than urban population.

Birth Rate (or Crude Birth Rate) refers to the ratio of the number of births to the average population during a certain period of time (usually a year), expressed in ‰. Birth rate in the chapter refers to annual birth rate. The following formula is used:

$$\text{Birth Rato} = \frac{\text{Number of Births}}{\text{Annual Average Population}} \times 1000‰$$

Number of births in the formula refers to live births, i.e. when a baby has breathed or showed any vital phenomena regardless of the length of pregnancy.

Annual average population is the average of the number of population at the beginning of the year and that at the end of the year. Sometimes it is substituted by the mid-year population.

Death Rate(or Crude Death Rate) refers to the ratio of the number of deaths to the average population during a certain period of time (usually a year), expressed in ‰. Death rate in the chapter refers to annual death rate. The following formula is used:

$$\text{Death Rato} = \frac{\text{Number of Death}}{\text{Annual Average Population}} \times 1000‰$$

Natural Growth Rate of Population refers to the ratio of natural increase in population (number of births minus number of deaths) in a certain period of time (usually a year) to the average population of the same period, expressed in ‰. The following formula is applied:

$$\text{Natural Growth Rate of Population} = \frac{\text{Number of Births} - \text{Number of Death}}{\text{Annual Average Population}} \times 1000‰$$

$$= \text{Birth Rate} - \text{Death Rate}$$

4 就业人员和职工工资

Employment and Wages

4-1 就业人员及劳动报酬

Number of Employed Personnels and Wages

指 标	Item	2010	2011	2012	2013	2014	2014年比2013年增长(%) Increase Rate in 2014over 2013(%)
就业人员(万人)	**Number of Employed Persons (10000 persons)**	**1770.90**	**1792.80**	**1825.82**	**1864.21**	**1909.69**	**2.4**
按产业分	**Grouped by Three Strata of Industry**						
第一产业	Primary Industry	1209.55	1194.39	1189.04	1179.76	1171.02	-0.7
第二产业	Secondary Industry	203.52	215.86	238.10	264.32	291.42	10.3
第三产业	Tertiary Industry	357.82	382.55	398.68	420.13	447.25	6.5
按城乡分	**Grouped by Urban and Rural**						
城镇	Urban Area	525.76	554.14	596.06	639.67	690.28	7.9
乡村	Rural Area	1245.14	1238.66	1229.76	1224.54	1219.41	-0.4
非私营单位在岗职工人数(万人)	**Total Number of Staff and Workers of Non-privately-owned unit (10000 persons)**	**210.67**	**225.91**	**249.67**	**273.27**	**278.63**	**2.0**
国有单位	State-owned Unit	146.81	158.26	161.19	152.41	153.29	0.6
集体单位	Collective-owned Unit	6.41	7.17	6.16	5.49	5.27	-4.0
其他单位	Others	57.45	60.47	82.32	115.37	120.07	4.1
非私营单位在岗职工工资总额(亿元)	**Total Wage of Staff and Workers of Non-privately-owned unit (100 million yuan)**	**649.55**	**830.11**	**1050.68**	**1322.82**	**1508.25**	**14.0**
国有单位	State-owned Unit	470.49	606.80	729.04	780.07	862.93	10.6
集体单位	Collective-owned Unit	15.72	22.12	24.29	27.27	31.43	15.3
其他单位	Others	163.34	201.19	297.36	515.48	613.89	19.1
非私营单位在岗职工平均工资(元)	**Average Wage of Staff and Workers of Non-privately-owned unit (yuan)**	**31458**	**37331**	**42733**	**49087**	**54685**	**11.4**
国有单位	State-owned Unit	32718	38914	45825	52327	56918	8.8
集体单位	Collective-owned Unit	24703	31601	40420	50545	59458	17.6
其他单位	Others	29006	33851	36816	44819	51627	15.2

注：在岗职工包含劳务派遣人员(以下相关表同)。

Note:The working staff at work include labor dispatching personnel (the related tables in the chapter are the same).

4-2 非私营单位就业人员年末人数(2014)

Number of Employed Persons in Non-private Units at Year-end

单位：人 (person)

指 标	Item	就业人员 Number of Employed	国有单位 State-owned Unit	集体单位 Collective-owned Unit	其他单位 Unit of Other Type of Ownership
总 计	**Total**	**3047470**	**1692304**	**60709**	**1294457**
按企事业、机关分	**By Enterprises,Institutions and Agencies**				
企 业	Enterprises	1780402	430187	60304	1289911
事 业	Institutions	874725	869862	397	4466
机 关	Agencies	392343	392255	8	80
按产业分	**By Three Strata of Industry**				
第一产业	Primary Industry	15362	11656	147	3559
第二产业	Secondary Industry	1173796	291816	34119	847861
第三产业	Tertiary Industry	1858312	1388832	26443	443037
按国民经济行业分	**By Sector**				
农、林、牧、渔业	Agriculture,Forestry,Animal Husbandry and Fishery	15362	11656	147	3559
采矿业	Mining	175868	12381	1724	161763
制造业	Manufacturing	440806	41282	6036	393488
电力、热力、燃气及水生产和供应业	Production and Supply of Electricity Heat, Gas and Water	129544	101476	405	27663
建筑业	Construction	427578	136677	25954	264947
批发和零售业	Wholesale and Retail Trades	139426	30070	4734	104622
批发业	Wholesale	71022	27278	2857	40887
零售业	Retail Trades	68404	2792	1877	63735
交通运输、仓储和邮政业	Transport,Storage and Post	112030	59568	1406	51056
住宿和餐饮业	Hotels and Catering Services	38379	4958	679	32742
信息传输、软件和信息技术服务业	Information Transmission, Software and Information Technology	32921	3045	33	29843
金融业	Financial Intermediation	83538	17562	12665	53311
房地产业	Real Estate	78813	5081	1089	72643
租赁和商务服务业	Leasing and Commerce Services	45021	7350	3405	34266
租赁业	Leasing Services	1487	176	39	1272
商务服务业	Commerce Services	43534	7174	3366	32994
科学研究、技术服务业	Scientific Research,Technic Services and Geological Prospecting	76551	57009	293	19249
水利、环境和公共设施管理业	Management of Water Conservancy, Environment and Public Facilities	49535	45079	197	4259
居民服务、修理和其他服务业	Services to Households,Repair and Other Services	12916	4449	290	8177
教 育	Education	510505	494815	694	14996
卫生和社会工作	Health and Social Service	181393	169431	854	11108
卫 生	Health	177808	166066	838	10904
社会工作	Social Service	3585	3365	16	204
文化、体育和娱乐业	Culture,Sports and Entertainment	19921	13798		6123
#新闻和出版业	News Publishing Company	4135	1958		2177
广播、电视、电影和影视录音制作业	Broadcasting,Television,Film and Video Trade	6045	5220		825
体 育	Sports	1485	828		657
公共管理、社会保障和社会组织	Public Administration Social Securities and Social Organization	477363	476617	104	642

4-3 非私营单位女性就业人员年末人数(2014)

Number of Employed Female in Non-private Units at the Year-end

单位：人 (person)

行 业	Sector	女性就业人员数 Number of Female Employed	国有单位 State-owned Unit	集体单位 Collective-owned Unit	其他单位 Unit of Other Type of Ownership
总 计	**Total**	**1017184**	**632715**	**16612**	**367857**
农、林、牧、渔业	Agriculture,Forestry,Animal Husbandry and Fishery	4382	3198	11	1173
采矿业	Mining and Quarrying	21136	1447	98	19591
制造业	Manufacturing	146145	13805	2295	130045
电力、热力、燃气及水生产和供应业	Production and Supply of Electricity,Heat,Gas and Water	34208	26763	86	7359
建筑业	Construction	52470	24569	3860	24041
批发和零售业	Wholesale and Retail Trades	59872	8859	1592	49421
批发业	Wholesale	23405	7718	880	14807
零售业	Retail Trades	36467	1141	712	34614
交通运输、仓储和邮政业	Transport,Storage and Post	31100	16566	638	13896
住宿和餐饮业	Hotels and Catering Services	22684	2863	421	19400
信息传输、软件和信息技术服务业	Information Transmission,Software and Information Technology	12697	901	19	11777
金融业	Financial Intermediation	39680	7647	5580	26453
房地产业	Real Estate	29179	2159	421	26599
租赁和商务服务业	Leasing and Commerce Services	13623	2605	498	10520
租赁业	Leasing Services	395	57	12	326
商务服务业	Commerce Services	13228	2548	486	10194
科学研究、技术服务业	Scientific Research,Technic Services	20714	16520	70	4124
水利、环境和公共设施管理业	Management of Water Conservancy, Environment and Public Facilities	25703	23832	20	1851
居民服务、修理和其他服务业	Services to Households Repair and Other Services	5790	2072	67	3651
教 育	Education	236193	228087	396	7710
卫生和社会工作	Health and Social Service	107662	100238	486	6938
卫 生	Health	105914	98627	476	6811
社会工作	Social Service	1748	1611	10	127
文化、体育和娱乐业	Culture,Sports and Entertainment	8417	5434		2983
#新闻和出版业	News Publishing Company	1761	796		965
广播、电视、电影和影视录音制作业	Broadcasting,Television,Film and Video Trade	2288	1945		343
体 育	Sports	542	243		299
公共管理、社会保障和社会组织	Public Administration Social Securities and Social Organization	145529	145150	54	325

4-4　非私营单位各行业在岗职工年末人数(2014)

Working Staff and Workers in Non-private units at the Year-end by Sector

单位：人　　　　(person)

指　标	Item	职工人数 Number of Staff and Workers	国有单位 State-owned Unit	集体单位 Collective-owned Unit	其他单位 Unit of Other Type of Ownership
总　　计	**Total**	**2786286**	**1532950**	**52683**	**1200653**
按企事业、机关分	**By Enterprises,Institutions and Agencies**				
企　业	Enterprises	1624258	375806	52301	1196151
事　业	Institutions	807663	802867	374	4422
机　关	Agencies	354365	354277	8	80
按产业分	**By Three Strata of Industry**				
第一产业	Primary Industry	13705	10174	121	3410
第二产业	Secondary Industry	1049040	246284	27702	775054
第三产业	Tertiary Industry	1723541	1276492	24860	422189
按国民经济行业分	**By Sector**				
农、林、牧、渔业	Agriculture,Forestry,Animal Husbandry and Fishery	13705	10174	121	3410
采矿业	Mining and Quarrying	171202	11579	1709	157914
制造业	Manufacturing	429033	39021	5763	384249
电力、热力、燃气及水生产和供应业	Production and Supply of Electricity,Heat, Gas and Water	118269	90701	403	27165
建筑业	Construction	330536	104983	19827	205726
批发和零售业	Wholesale and Retail Trades	132682	26812	3671	102199
批发业	Wholesale	66047	24241	1966	39840
零售业	Retail Trades	66635	2571	1705	62359
交通运输、仓储和邮政业	Transport,Storage and Post	106416	57269	1371	47776
住宿和餐饮业	Hotels and Catering Services	37419	4765	678	31976
信息传输、软件和信息技术服务业	Information Transmission,Software and Information Technology	31818	2910	33	28875
金融业	Financial Intermediation	76773	16669	12363	47741
房地产业	Real Estate	75248	4816	1051	69381
租赁和商务服务业	Leasing and Commerce Services	43928	7041	3297	33590
租赁业	Leasing Services	1475	172	35	1268
商务服务业	Commerce Services	42453	6869	3262	32322
科学研究、技术服务业	Scientific Research,Technic Services and Geological Prospecting	71981	54434	292	17255
水利、环境和公共设施管理业	Management of Water Conservancy, Environment and Public Facilities	40142	35914	187	4041
居民服务、修理和其他服务业	Services to Households Repair and Other Services	11646	3564	287	7795
教　育	Education	477275	462355	692	14228
卫生和社会工作	Health and Social Service	167299	155629	834	10836
卫　生	Health	163758	152304	818	10636
社会工作	Social Service	3541	3325	16	200
文化、体育和娱乐业	Culture,Sports and Entertainment	19044	13178		5866
#新闻和出版业	News Publishing Company	4084	1933		2151
广播、电视、电影和影视录音制作业	Broadcasting,Television,Film and Video Trade	5803	5042		761
体　育	Sports	1383	727		656
公共管理、社会保障和社会组织	Public Administration Social Securities and Social Organization	431870	431136	104	630

4-5 非私营单位在岗职工工资总额(2014)

Total Wages Bill of Working Staff and Workers in Non-private units

单位：亿元 (100 million yuan)

指 标	Item	工资总额 Total Wage Bill	国有单位 State-owned Unit	集体单位 Collective-owned Unit	其他单位 Unit of Other Type of Ownership
总 计	**Total**	**1508.25**	**862.92**	**31.43**	**613.89**
按企事业、机关分	**By Enterprises,Institutions and Agencies**				
企 业	Enterprises	878.99	235.68	31.26	612.06
事 业	Institutions	435.39	433.42	0.17	1.80
机 关	Agencies	193.87	193.83		0.03
按产业分	**By Three Strata of Industry**				
第一产业	Primary Industry	5.75	4.86	0.01	0.88
第二产业	Secondary Industry	526.35	138.86	9.06	378.43
第三产业	Tertiary Industry	976.15	719.21	22.36	234.59
按国民经济行业分	**By Sector**				
农、林、牧、渔业	Agriculture,Forestry,Animal Husbandry and Fishery	5.75	4.86	0.01	0.88
采矿业	Mining and Quarrying	87.80	5.86	0.60	81.35
制造业	Manufacturing	207.10	20.95	1.91	184.24
电力、热力、燃气及水生产和供应业	Production and Supply of Electricity,Heat,Gas and Water	88.53	70.08	0.12	18.33
建筑业	Construction	142.92	41.97	6.44	94.51
批发和零售业	Wholesale and Retail Trades	67.52	26.53	0.94	40.05
批发业	Wholesale	43.24	25.38	0.54	17.32
零售业	Retail Trades	24.28	1.15	0.40	22.72
交通运输、仓储和邮政业	Transport,Storage and Post	64.20	38.23	0.65	25.31
住宿和餐饮业	Hotels and Catering Services	12.63	1.76	0.19	10.68
信息传输、软件和信息技术服务业	Information Transmission,Software and Information Technology	24.41	1.48	0.01	22.92
金融业	Financial Intermediation	94.44	14.10	18.26	62.08
房地产业	Real Estate	33.34	1.75	0.33	31.26
租赁和商务服务业	Leasing and Commerce Services	19.95	3.26	1.04	15.64
租赁业	Leasing Services	0.61	0.07	0.02	0.52
商务服务业	Commerce Services	19.34	3.19	1.02	15.12
科学研究、技术服务业	Scientific Research,Technic Services and Geological Prospecting	41.54	32.36	0.13	9.05
水利、环境和公共设施管理业	Management of Water Conservancy, Environment and Public Facilities	13.70	12.20	0.04	1.46
居民服务、修理和其他服务业	Services to Households Repair and Other Services	4.11	1.35	0.10	2.65
教 育	Education	258.70	252.67	0.35	5.68
卫生和社会工作	Health and Social Service	100.75	95.52	0.28	4.95
卫 生	Health	99.31	94.18	0.26	4.87
社会工作	Social Service	1.43	1.34	0.01	0.08
文化、体育和娱乐业	Culture,Sports and Entertainment	9.53	7.04		2.49
#新闻和出版业	News Publishing Company	2.12	1.15		0.96
广播、电视、电影和影视录音制作业	Broadcasting,Television,Film and Video Trade	2.94	2.63		0.31
体 育	Sports	0.80	0.39		0.41
公共管理、社会保障和社会组织	Public Administration Social Securities and Social Organization	231.34	230.94	0.05	0.35

4-6 非私营单位各行业在岗职工平均工资(2014)

Average Wages of Working Staff and Workers in Non-private units by Sector

单位：元 (yuan)

指　标	Item	平均工资 Average Wage	国有单位 State-owned Unit	集体单位 Collective-owned Unit	其他单位 Unit of Other Type of Ownership
总　计	**Total**	**54685**	**56918**	**59458**	**51627**
按企事业、机关分	**By Enterprises,Institutions and Agencies**				
企　业	Enterprises	54578	63124	59555	51665
事　业	Institutions	54634	54711	45841	41517
机　关	Agencies	55293	55297	54875	37675
按产业分	**By Three Industries**				
第一产业	Primary Industry	42114	47799	12149	26036
第二产业	Secondary Industry	50492	56701	31914	49201
第三产业	Tertiary Industry	57354	57034	91777	56312
按国民经济行业分	**By Sector**				
农、林、牧、渔业	Agriculture,Forestry,Animal Husbandry and Fishery	42114	47799	12149	26036
采矿业	Mining and Quarrying	50830	52566	34932	50878
制造业	Manufacturing	48127	52866	32965	47866
电力、热力、燃气及水生产和供应业	Production and Supply of Electricity,Heat,Gas and Water	73030	74833	29425	67459
建筑业	Construction	44922	41774	31415	47930
批发和零售业	Wholesale and Retail Trades	51500	99127	25559	39785
批发业	Wholesale	64804	104781	27217	42741
零售业	Retail Trades	37714	45329	23652	37792
交通运输、仓储和邮政业	Transport,Storage and Post	60222	67058	47487	52504
住宿和餐饮业	Hotels and Catering Services	34017	37297	28249	33653
信息传输、软件和信息技术服务业	Information Transmission,Software and Information Technology	76047	50886	28879	78608
金融业	Financial Intermediation	125750	86706	151474	132692
房地产业	Real Estate	45334	36618	31058	46171
租赁和商务服务业	Leasing and Commerce Services	46583	46761	33211	47824
租赁业	Leasing Services	41632	42512	46824	41373
商务服务业	Commerce Services	46758	46868	33061	48083
科学研究、技术服务业	Scientific Research,Technic Services and Geological Prospecting	58753	59633	43630	56066
水利、环境和公共设施管理业	Management of Water Conservancy,Environment and Public Facilities	34248	34195	21342	35291
居民服务、修理和其他服务业	Services to Households Repair and Other Services	35656	38438	35391	34396
教　育	Education	54966	55450	51291	39715
卫生和社会工作	Health and Social Service	61597	62825	33577	46282
卫　生	Health	62044	63308	32413	46405
社会工作	Social Service	41085	40917	92313	39714
文化、体育和娱乐业	Culture,Sports and Entertainment	50017	53947		41476
#新闻和出版业	News Publishing Company	52924	62498		44714
广播、电视、电影和影视录音制作业	Broadcasting,Television,Film and Video Trade	50896	52377		41117
体　育	Sports	54664	52907		56413
公共管理、社会保障和社会组织	Public Administration Social Securities and Social Organization	54043	54040	50298	56458

4-7 非私营单位各行业从业人员平均工资(2014)

Average Wages of Working Staff and Workers in Non-private units by Sector

单位：元 (yuan)

指 标	Item	平均工资 Average Wage	国有单位 State-owned Unit	集体单位 Collective-owned Unit	其他单位 Unit of Other Type of Ownership
总 计	**Total**	**52772**	**54083**	**55520**	**50927**
按企事业、机关分	**By Enterprises,Institutions and Agencies**				
企 业	Enterprises	53299	59940	55601	50961
事 业	Institutions	52108	52167	43172	41381
机 关	Agencies	51853	51856	54875	37675
按产业分	**By Three Industries**				
第一产业	Primary Industry	38873	43165	11456	25684
第二产业	Secondary Industry	49608	54148	31444	48771
第三产业	Tertiary Industry	54892	54162	87210	55264
按国民经济行业分	**By Sector**				
农、林、牧、渔业	Agriculture,Forestry,Animal Husbandry and Fishery	38873	43165	11456	25684
采矿业	Mining and Quarrying	50309	50877	34895	50429
制造业	Manufacturing	47606	51327	32107	47451
电力、热力、燃气及水生产和供应业	Production and Supply of Electricity,Heat, Gas and Water	68675	69206	29368	67209
建筑业	Construction	45192	43057	31088	47731
批发和零售业	Wholesale and Retail Trades	49887	90191	22187	39402
批发业	Wholesale	61593	94858	21676	42484
零售业	Retail Trades	37194	44031	22964	37318
交通运输、仓储和邮政业	Transport,Storage and Post	58807	65702	46999	51156
住宿和餐饮业	Hotels and Catering Services	33813	37032	28219	33443
信息传输、软件和信息技术服务业	Information Transmission,Software and Information Technology	75068	49846	28879	77662
金融业	Financial Intermediation	118477	83996	148654	122601
房地产业	Real Estate	44867	35708	31197	45730
租赁和商务服务业	Leasing and Commerce Services	46156	45870	32237	47566
租赁业	Leasing Services	41463	42017	44421	41298
商务服务业	Commerce Services	46319	45965	32092	47812
科学研究、技术服务业	Scientific Research,Technic Services and Geological Prospecting	57290	58055	43562	54972
水利、环境和公共设施管理业	Management of Water Conservancy, Environment and Public Facilities	31706	31466	20868	34646
居民服务、修理和其他服务业	Services to Households Repair and Other Services	34214	34961	34848	33789
教 育	Education	52706	53134	50964	38892
卫生和社会工作	Health and Social Service	59127	60147	33351	45711
卫 生	Health	59498	60543	32211	45833
社会工作	Social Service	40873	40725	92313	39219
文化、体育和娱乐业	Culture,Sports and Entertainment	48944	52697		40704
#新闻和出版业	News Publishing Company	52426	61696		44401
广播、电视、电影和影视录音制作业	Broadcasting,Television,Film and Video Trade	50003	51689		39362
体 育	Sports	52879	49782		56382
公共管理、社会保障和社会组织	Public Administration Social Securities and Social Organization	50699	50692	50298	55838

4-8 城乡私营企业户数和就业人员(2014)

Number of Private Enterprises and Employed Persons in Urban and Rural Areas by Sector

指 标	Item	私营企业户数(户) Number of Private Enterprises (Household)	城 镇 Urban Areas	乡 村 Rural Areas	就业人员(人) Number of Employees (Person)	城 镇 Urban Areas	乡 村 Rural Areas
总 计	**Total**	**262477**	**102057**	**160420**	**2078228**	**903119**	**1175109**
农、林、牧、渔业	Agriculture,Forestry,Animal Husbandry and Fishery	34927	4715	30212	249031	39766	209265
采掘业	Mining and Quarrying	6651	2415	4236	71104	27247	43857
制造业	Manufacturing	30927	8931	21996	328073	112983	215090
电力、热力、燃气及水的生产和供应业	Production and Supply of Electricity Heat Gas and Water	1360	505	855	16508	6291	10217
建筑业	Construction	13972	6056	7916	120450	60141	60309
批发和零售业	Wholesale and Retail Trades	73656	32415	41241	592769	318405	274364
交通运输、仓储和邮政业	Transport,Storage and Post	5845	2228	3617	48484	20563	27921
住宿和餐饮业	Hotels and Catering Services	18948	10936	8012	75328	27196	48132
信息传输、软件和信息技术服务业	Information Transmission,Software and Information Technology	7850	3038	4812	51920	26684	25236
房地产业	Real Estate	10106	5306	4800	95785	56330	39455
租赁和商务服务业	Leasing and Commerce Services	32163	14490	17673	215931	113144	102787
居民服务、修理和其他服务业	Services to Households Repair and Other Services	11764	4848	6916	83605	37545	46060
卫生和社会工作	Health and Social Service	774	331	443	12307	5837	6470
文化、体育和娱乐业	Culture,Sports and Entertainment	2135	965	1170	17324	8267	9057
其他行业	Others	11399	4878	6521	99609	42720	56889

注：资料来源于省工商局(下表同)。

Note: Data in the table are obtained from Guizhou Provincial Industrial and Commercial Bureau(the same applies to the next table).

4-9 城乡个体工商户数和就业人员(2014)

Number of Household and Self-Employed Individuals in Urban and Rural Areas

指　标	Item	个体工商户数(户) Number of individual industrial and commercial households(Household)	城镇 Urban Areas	乡村 Rural Areas	就业人员(人) Number of Employed (Person)	城镇 Urban Areas	乡村 Rural Areas
总　计	**Total**	**1280048**	**558179**	**721869**	**2208110**	**951387**	**1256723**
农、林、牧、渔业	Agriculture,Forestry,Animal Husbandry and Fishery	25686	4517	21169	53349	8767	44582
采掘业	Mining and Quarrying	3744	902	2842	19063	7618	11445
制造业	Manufacturing	61403	26917	34486	143698	55017	88681
电力、热力、燃气及水的生产和供应业	Production and Supply of Electricity Heat Gas and Water	508	165	343	1283	347	936
建筑业	Construction	3789	653	3136	19615	1440	18175
批发和零售业	Wholesale and Retail Trades	847044	367427	479617	1290235	552022	738213
交通运输、仓储和邮政业	Transport,Storage and Post	24223	9866	14357	39180	15947	23233
住宿和餐饮业	Hotels and Catering Services	157170	79093	78077	337647	171709	165938
信息传输、软件和信息技术服务业	Information Transmission,Software and Information Technology	9260	4391	4869	16663	8402	8261
房地产业	Real Estate	182	121	61	584	321	263
租赁和商务服务业	Leasing and Commerce Services	18861	7251	11610	35582	12691	22891
居民服务、修理和其他服务业	Services to Households Repair and Other Services	100855	44656	56199	197832	90986	106846
卫生和社会工作	Health and Social Service	4020	1998	2022	11594	7176	4418
文化、体育和娱乐业	Culture,Sports and Entertainment	5331	2969	2362	15966	9777	6189
其他行业	Others	17972	7253	10719	25819	9167	16652

4-10 城镇新就业人数和失业人数

Number of Newly Employed Persons and Unemployed Persons in Urban Areas

单位：万人 (10000 persons)

指 标	Item	2010	2011	2012	2013	2014	2014年比2013年增长(%) Increase Rate in 2014 over 2013(%)
新就业人数总计	Total Incremental Employed Personnels	27.71	35.94	50.63	63.39	75.03	18.4
#新增就业人数	Number of Newly Incremental employed persons	21.89	28.37	42.23	55.49	68.37	23.2
城镇登记失业人数	Number of Registered Unemployed Persons in Urban Areas	12.18	12.51	12.56	13.66	14.09	3.1
城镇登记失业率(%)	Registered Unemployment Rate in Urban Areas(%)	3.63	3.63	3.29	3.26	3.27	0.01

注：资料来源于省人力资源社会保障厅(以下相关表同)。
Note: Data in the table are obtained from Guizhou Department of Human Resources and Social Security(the related tables in the chapter are the same).

4-11 下岗失业人员享受再就业优惠政策情况

Statistics of Re-employment Preferential Policies for Laid-off Workers

单位：人 (person)

指 标	Item	2013	2014	2014年比2013年增 长(%) Increase Rate in 2014 over 2013(%)
下岗失业人员实现再就业	Laid-off Workers	141833	152902	7.8
#就业困难对象实现就业	Residents Experiencing Employment Difficulty	70397	74902	6.4
消除零就业家庭(户)	Number of Househoulds rased Zero-employment Families (househould)	256	171	-33.2
促进零就业家庭成员就业	Promoting Zero-employment Families Employed	318	191	-39.9
从事公益性岗位人数	Number of Persons Engaged in Public-service Jobs	89620	74430	-16.9
享受职业培训补贴人数	Number of Persons Receiving Professional Training Subsidies	149368	80310	-46.2
享受职业介绍补贴人数	Number of Persons Receiving Job Services Subsidies	4084	1957	-52.1
享受技能鉴定补贴人数	Number of Persons Receiving Skill Identification Subsidies	39108	28656	-26.7
享受社会保险补贴人数	Number of Persons Receiving Social Insurance Subsidies	84683	62512	-26.2
使用就业再就业资金(万元)	Using Employment and Re-employment Fund(10000 yuan)	214296	187105	-12.7
#社会保险补贴	Social Insurance Subsidies	55450	41625	-24.9
岗位补贴	Post Subsidies	84805	69639	-17.9
职业培训补贴	Professional Training	35622	33897	-4.8
职业介绍补贴	Job Services	257	234	-8.9
扶持公共就业服务	Supporting Public Employment Service	1122	2888	157.4

4-12 职业技能鉴定

Occupation Skill Appraisal

单位:人 (person)

指 标	Item	2010	2011	2012	2013	2014
参加职业技能鉴定	Number of Persons Joining in Occupation Skill Appraisal	82135	114691	135948	132382	188815
获取证书人数	Number of Persons With Qualification Certificates	73717	105141	125959	123983	175487
#高级技工	Advanced Mechanic	5989	11322	13454	11463	20346
#技 师	Technician	372	615	364	837	1116
#高级技师	Advanced Technician	163	138	115	375	333

4-13 劳动力市场需求人员、求职人员及构成

Persons Required by Labor Market, Job Seckers and Ies Composition

单位：人 (person)

指 标	Item	2013 绝对数 Absolute-Figure	2013 构成(%) Composition	2014 绝对数 Absolute-Figure	2014 构成(%) Composition	2014年比2013年增长(%) Increase Rate in 2014 over 2013(%)
劳动力市场需求人员合计	**Number of Persons Required by Labor Market**	**271138**	**100.0**	**291293**	**100.0**	**7.4**
农林牧渔业	Agriculture,Forestry,Animal Husbandry and Fishery	4043	1.5	4943	1.7	22.3
采矿业	Mining	3909	1.4	3465	1.2	-11.4
制造业	Manufacturing	49289	18.2	58426	20.1	18.5
电力、热力、燃气和水的生产和供应业	Production and Supply of Electricity Heat Gas and Water	4286	1.6	5294	1.8	23.5
建筑业	Construction	10820	4.0	10554	3.6	-2.5
交通运输、仓储和邮政业	Transport,Storage and Post	9020	3.3	7096	2.4	-21.3
信息传输、软件和信息技术服务业	Information Transmission, Software and Information Technology	8439	3.1	9518	3.3	12.8
批发和零售业	Wholesale and Retail Trades	62979	23.2	65267	22.4	3.6
住宿和餐饮业	Hotels and Catering Services	47007	17.3	55569	19.1	18.2
金融业	Financial Intermediation	3056	1.1	3483	1.2	14.0
房地产业	Real Estate	4308	1.6	7549	2.6	75.2
租赁和商务服务业	Leasing and Business Services	9507	3.5	7674	2.6	-19.3
科学研究、技术服务和地质勘查业	Scientific Research,Technic Services and Geological Prospecting	437	0.2	343	0.1	-21.5
水利、环境和公共设施管理业	Management of Water Conservancy, Environment and Public Facilities	232	0.1	139	0.05	-40.1
居民服务、修理和其他服务业	Services to Households Repair and Other Services	35040	12.9	37070	12.7	5.8
教 育	Education	2122	0.8	2663	0.9	25.5
卫生和社会工作	Health and Social Service	1503	0.6	700	0.2	-53.4
文化、体育和娱乐业	Culture,Sports and Entertainment	13959	5.1	10365	3.6	-25.7
公共管理、社会保障与社会组织	Publie Administration,Social Securities and Social Organization	1182	0.4	1175	0.4	-0.6
劳动力市场求职人员合计	**Number of Person Applying for A Job**	**211708**	**100.0**	**226626**	**100.0**	**7.0**
新成长的失业青年	New grown Unemployed Youngth	32042	15.1	34111	15.1	6.5
#应届高校毕业生	Graduating Students from higer School	15429	7.3	18734	8.3	21.4
就业转失业人员	Working Staff Transmiting into Unemploye	52229	24.7	53061	23.4	1.6
其他失业人员	Other Unempolyed	14185	6.7	10777	4.8	-24.0
在业人员	Working Staff	16079	7.6	25092	11.1	56.1
下岗职工	Laid-off Workers	6392	3.0	6133	2.7	-4.1
退休人员	Retired	315	0.1	462	0.2	46.7
在学人员	Enrollment	7960	3.8	14224	6.3	78.7
本地农村人员	Persons of Domesitc Country	47644	22.5	52964	23.4	11.2
外埠人员	Outside	34862	16.5	29802	13.2	-14.5

主要统计指标解释

就业人员 指在16周岁及以上，从事一定社会劳动并取得劳动报酬或经营收入的人员。这一指标反映了一定时期内全部劳动力资源的实际利用情况，是研究我国基本国情国力的重要指标。

单位就业人员 指在各级国家机关、政党机关、社会团体及企业、事业单位中工作，取得工资或其他形式的劳动报酬的全部人员。包括在岗职工、再就业的离退休人员、民办教师以及在各单位中工作的外方人员和港澳台方人员、兼职人员、借用的外单位人员和第二职业者。不包括离开本单位仍保留劳动关系的职工。各单位的就业人员反映了各单位实际参加生产或工作的全部劳动力。

在岗职工 指在本单位工作并由单位支付工资的人员，以及有工作岗位，但由于学习、病伤产假等原因暂未工作，仍由单位支付工资的人员。

国有单位职工指在国有经济单位及其附属机构工作，并由其支付工资的各类人员。

城镇集体单位职工指在城镇集体经济单位及其管理部门工作，并由其支付工资的各类人员。

其他单位职工指在联营经济、股份制经济、外商投资经济、港、澳、台投资经济单位工作，并由其支付工资的各类人员。

工资总额 指各单位在一定时期内直接支付给本单位全部就业人员的劳动报酬总额。工资总额的计算原则应以直接支付给就业人员的全部劳动报酬为根据。各单位支付给就业人员的劳动报酬以及其他根据有关规定支付的工资，不论是计入成本的还是不计入成本的，不论是按国家规定列入计征奖金税项目的，还是未列入计征奖金税项目的，不论是以货币形式支付的还是以实物形式支付的，均包括在工资总额内。

平均工资 指企业、事业、机关单位的就业人员在一定时期内平均每人所得的货币工资额。它表明一定时期职工工资收入的高低程度，是反映就业人员工资水平的主要指标。计算公式为：

$$平均工资=\frac{报告期实际支付的全部就业人员工资总额}{报告期全部就业人员平均人数}$$

城镇登记失业人员 指有非农业户口，在一定的劳动年龄内(16周岁至退休年龄)，有劳动能力，无业而要求就业，并在当地劳动保障部门进行失业登记的人员。

城镇登记失业率 城镇登记失业人员与城镇单位就业人员(扣除使用的农村劳动力、聘用的离退休人员、港澳台及外方人员)、城镇单位中的不在岗职工、城镇私营业主、个体户主、城镇私营企业和个体就业人员、城镇登记失业人员之和的比。计算公式为：

$$城镇登记失业率=\frac{城镇登记失业人数}{(城镇单位就业人员-使用的农村劳动力-聘用的离退休人员-聘用的港澳台及外方人员)+不在岗职工+城镇私营业主+城镇个体户主+城镇私营企业及个体就业人员+城镇登记失业人数}\times 100\%$$

Explanatory Notes on Main Statistical Indicators

Employed Persons refer to persons aged 16 and over who are engaged in gainful employment and thus receive remuneration payment or earn business income. This indicator reflects the actual utilization of total labour force during a certain period of time and is often used for the research on China's economic situation and national power.

Persons Employed in Various Units refer to all the persons working in government agencies of various levels, political and party organizations, social organizations, enterprises and institutions, and receiving wages or other forms of payment. They include fully-employed staff and workers, re-employed retirees, teachers in the schools run by the local people, foreigners and Chinese compatriots from Hong Kong, Macao, and Taiwan working in various units, part-time employees, employees of other units working temporarily at current posts, and employees holding the second job, but do not include persons who have left their working units while keeping their labour contract (employment relation) unchanged. This indicator reflects the total number of laborers actually engaged in production or other operations in various units.

Employed Staff and Workers refer to persons who work in, and receive wages from their working units, including persons who have their work posts but are temporarily absent from work for reasons of study or on sick, injury or maternal leave and still receive wages from their working units.

State Owned Unit Staff refer to the staff of the state-owned units refers to the work of the state-owned economic units and their subsidiary bodies, and all kinds of personnel to pay wages.

The workers of the collective unit of the town refers to the work of the collective economic units and the management department of the urban and towns.

Other unit staff refers to the joint venture, the joint stock economy, foreign investment in the economy, Hong Kong, Macao, Taiwan investment economic units, and by the payment of all kinds of personnel.

Total Wage Bill refers to the total remuneration payment to employed persons in various units during a certain period of time. The calculation of total wage bill is based on the total remuneration payment to employed persons . Therefore, all the wages and salaries and other payments to employed persons are included in the total wage bill regardless of sources, reckoning the cost of production or not, category, listing as items of premium taxation or not, and forms, paying in cash or in kind.

Average Wage refers to the average wage in money terms per person during a certain period of time for employed persons in enterprises, institutions, and government agencies, which reflects the general level of wage income during a certain period of time and is calculated as follows:

$$\text{Average Wage} = \frac{\text{Total Wage Bill of Employed Personsat Reference Time}}{\text{Average Number of Persons Employed at Reference Time}}$$

Registered Unemployed Persons in Urban Areas refer to the persons with non-agricultural household registration at certain working ages (16 years old to retirement age), who are capable of working, unemployed and willing to work, and have been registered at the local employment service agencies to apply for a job.

Registered Unemployment Rate in Urban Areas refers to the ratio of the number of the registered unemployed persons to the sum of the number of persons employed in various units (minus the employed rural labour force, re-employed retirees, and Hong Kong, Macao, Taiwan or foreign employees), laid-off staff and workers in urban units, owners of private enterprises in urban areas, owners of self-employed individuals in urban areas, employees of private enterprises in urban areas, employee of self-employed individuals in urban areas, and the registered unemployed persons in urban areas. The formula is as follows:

$$\text{Registered unemployment rete in urban areas} = \frac{\text{number of registered urban unemployed persons}}{\begin{array}{l}\text{(number of persons employed in urban units}-\text{employed rural labour forcere}-\text{employed}\\ \text{retirees}-\text{Hong Kong, Macan, Taiwan of foreign employees) +laid}-\text{off staff and workers+}\\ \text{owners of urban private enterprises+owners of urban self}-\text{employed individuals+employ-}\\ \text{ees of urban private enterprises+employees of urban self}-\text{employed individuals+regis-}\\ \text{tered unemployed persons in urban areas}\end{array}} \times 100\%$$

固定资产投资

5

Investment in Fixed Assets

5-1 全社会固定资产投资

Total Investment in Fixed Assets in the whole Province

单位：亿元 (100 million yuan)

指　标	Item	2010	2011	2012	2013	2014	2014年比2013年增长(%) Increase Rate in 2014 over 2013(%)
全社会固定资产投资	**Total Investment in Fixed Assets in theWhole Province**	**3186.28**	**4234.44**	**5717.80**	**7373.60**	**9025.75**	**22.4**
#房地产开发	Real Estate Development	556.69	873.48	1467.60	1942.54	2187.67	12.6
按隶属关系分	Grouped by Jurisdiction of Management						
中　央	Central	324.62	343.59	389.96	492.80	605.60	22.9
地　方	Local	2861.66	3890.85	5327.85	6880.80	8420.15	22.4
按经济类型分	Grouped by Registration Status						
国有经济	State-owned Units	1605.82	1989.06	2530.97	3284.11	4167.03	26.9
集体经济	Collective-owned Units	29.01	42.61	42.55	27.33	21.97	-19.6
个体经济	Self-employed Units	172.91	879.44	1141.36	1706.29	2121.21	24.3
联营经济	Joint Ownership Units	2.16	3.69	6.71	2.80	6.54	133.2
股份制经济	Share holding Units	774.14	174.15	205.34	2062.31	2399.36	16.3
外商投资经济	Foreign Funded Units	35.85	29.78	29.45	28.83	36.65	27.1
港澳台商投资经济	Units with Funds from Hong Kong,Macao and Taiwan	34.18	72.49	117.60	77.70	100.49	29.3
其他经济	Others	532.21	1043.22	1643.81	184.23	172.51	-6.4
按构成分	Grouped by Structure						
建筑安装工程	Construction and Installation	2010.16	3047.70	4150.18	5707.82	7272.65	27.4
设备工具器具购置	Purchase of Equipment and Instruments	494.07	520.42	531.71	581.84	654.88	12.6
其他费用	Others	682.04	666.32	1035.91	1083.94	1098.21	1.3
按三次产业分	Grouped by Three Strata of Industry						
第一产业	Primary Industry	80.71	126.48	150.58	185.69	210.37	13.3
第二产业	Secondary Industry	1087.87	1357.21	1636.25	1953.90	2328.31	19.2
#建筑业	Construction	13.32	24.15	22.26	12.36	15.90	28.7
第三产业	Tertiary Industry	2017.70	2750.75	3930.97	5234.01	6487.07	23.9
资金来源合计	**Total Sources of Funds**	**4108.87**	**5150.89**	**6219.71**	**8199.43**	**9955.33**	**21.4**
国家预算资金	State Budget	355.96	548.98	537.04	559.21	644.40	15.2
国内贷款	Domestic Loans	852.62	827.08	950.02	975.43	1183.18	21.3
利用外资	Foreign Investment	10.71	14.72	11.49	14.19	27.76	95.6
自筹资金	Self-raising Funds	1869.01	2555.43	3263.76	4571.70	5704.03	24.8
其他资金	Others	1020.58	1204.69	1457.41	2078.89	2395.96	15.3
房屋建筑面积(万平方米)	**Floor Space of Buildings(10000 sq.m)**						
施工面积	Floor Space under Construction	14456	13959	18510	27642	34043	23.2
#住　宅	Residential Buildings	10123	8875	11045	16775	17256	2.9
竣工面积	Floor Space Completed	5325	2988	3496	7299	8143	11.6
#住　宅	Residential Buildings	4054	1671	1880	5032	4730	-6.0

注：固定资产投资统计口径2010年为计划总投资50万元及以上固定资产项目投资，房地产开发项目投资及农村农户投资；2011年起为计划总投资500万元及以上固定资产项目投资，房地产开发项目投资及农村农户投资(以下相关表同)。

Note: According to 2010, data in the table referred to those projects that planned to invest 500000 yuan at least in investment in fixed assets, real estate development and rural household investment. From 2011,the statistical coverage has referred to those projects that planned to invest 5 million yuan at least in investment in fixed assets, real estate development and rural household investment(The relative tables in the chapter are the same).

5-2 全社会工业投资

Industry Investment in the Whole Province

单位：亿元 (100 million yuan)

指 标	Item	2010	2011	2012	2013	2014	2014年比2013年增长(%) Increase Rate in 2014 over 2013(%)
工业投资	**Industry Investment**	**1074.55**	**1333.06**	**1614.00**	**1950.07**	**2338.02**	**19.9**
按隶属关系分	**Grouped by Jurisdiction of Morenagement**						
中 央	Central Investment	152.19	141.13	115.55	157.01	191.81	22.2
地 方	Local Investment	922.36	1191.93	1498.45	1793.06	2146.21	19.7
按国民经济行业分	**By Sector**						
采矿业	Mining	374.61	404.25	408.35	400.25	446.00	11.4
#煤炭开采和洗选业	Mining and Washing of Coal	337.39	347.88	308.38	273.49	289.01	5.7
黑色金属矿采选业	Mining and Processing of Ferrous Metal Ores	1.68	4.25	12.44	8.02	9.35	16.7
有色金属矿采选业	Mining and Processing of Non-Ferrous Metal Ores	9.92	17.84	26.64	35.14	24.16	-31.3
制造业	Manufacturing	428.33	687.42	951.83	1218.19	1517.05	24.5
#化学原料和化学制品制造业	Manufacture of Raw Chemical Materials and Chemical Products	65.09	64.58	75.76	114.38	131.10	14.6
黑色金属冶炼和压延加工业	Smelting and Pressing of Ferrous Metals	32.89	60.27	85.21	49.23	48.88	-0.7
有色金属冶炼和压延加工业	Smelting and Pressing of Non-ferrous Metals	49.90	58.49	55.41	60.30	71.09	17.9
电力、热力、燃气及水生产和供应业	Production and Supply of Electricity, Heat, Gas and Water	271.61	241.39	253.81	331.64	374.97	13.1
#电力、热力生产和供应业	Production and Supply of Electric Power and Heat Power	254.12	215.20	219.16	271.31	308.61	13.7

注：行业划分2010年按国民经济行业分类(GB/T 4754—2002)，2011年起按国民经济行业分类(GB/T 4754—2011)(以下相关表同)。
Note: According to 2010, industry was classified by industrial classification (GB / T 4754-2002). Since 2011,it has been classified by Sector Classification (GB / T 4754-2011) (The relative tables in the chapter are the same).

5-3 按行业、隶属关系和注册类型分固定资产投资(2014)

单位：亿元

指　标	Item	固定资产投资 Investment in Fixed Assets
固定资产投资	**Investment in Fixed Assets**	**8778.40**
农、林、牧、渔业	Agriculture, Forestry, Animal Husbandry and Fishery	259.97
#农　业	Farming	102.28
畜牧业	Animal Husbandry	46.91
农、林、牧、渔服务业	Services in Support of Agriculture	86.12
采矿业	Mining	446.00
#煤炭开采和洗选业	Mining and Washing of Coal	289.01
制造业	Manufacturing	1516.84
#酒、饮料和精制茶制造业	Manufacture of Liquor, Beverages and Refined Tea	21.59
烟草制品业	Manufacture of Tobacco	4.12
造纸和纸制品业	Manufacture of Paper and Paper Products	14.27
石油加工、炼焦和核燃料加工业	Processing of Petroleum, Coking, Processing of Nuclear Fuel	16.12
化学原料和化学制品制造业	Manufacture of Raw Chemical Materials and Chemical Products	131.10
医药制造业	Manufacture of Medicines	69.26
非金属矿物制品业	Manufacture of Non-metallic Mineral Products	287.99
黑色金属冶炼和压延加工业	Smelting and Pressing of Ferrous Metals	48.88
有色金属冶炼和压延加工业	Smelting and Pressing of Non-ferrous Metals	71.09
电力、热力、燃气及水生产和供应业	Production and Supply of Electricity, Hear, Gas and Water	374.97
#电力、热力生产和供应业	Production and Supply of Electric Power and Heat Power	308.61
建筑业	Construction	9.25
交通运输、仓储和邮政业	Transport, Storage and Post	1725.64
#铁路运输业	Railway Transport	390.89
道路运输业	Road Transport	1263.11
仓储业	Storage	41.83
信息传输、软件和信息技术服务业	Information Transmission, Software and Information Technology	54.73
#电信、广播电视和卫星传输服务业	Telecommunication Radio and Television and Satellite Transmission Services	45.36
批发和零售业	Wholesale and Retail Trades	102.36
住宿和餐饮业	Hotels and Catering Services	85.11
金融业	Financial Intermediation	5.45
房地产业	Real Estate	2580.40
租赁和商务服务业	Leasing and Business Services	48.67
租赁业	Leasing	1.57
商务服务业	Business Services	47.10
科学研究和技术服务业	Scientific Research and Technical Service	21.04
#研究和试验发展	Research and Experimental Development	4.63
水利、环境和公共设施管理业	Management of Water Conservancy, Environment and Public Facilities	1236.21
#水利管理业	Management of Water Conservancy	90.60
居民服务、修理和其他服务业	Services to Households, Repair and Other Services	29.69
教　育	Education	139.37
卫生和社会工作	Health and Social Service	38.37
#卫　生	Health	32.99
文化、体育和娱乐业	Culture, Sports and Entertainment	59.99
#文化艺术业	Cultural and Art Activities	21.97
公共管理、社会保障和社会组织	Public Management, Social security and Social Organization	44.32

注：本表统计口径为计划总投资500万元及以上的固定资产项目投资，房地产开发项目投资。

Investment in Fixed Assets by Sector, Jurisdiction of Management and Registration Status

(100 million yuan)

按隶属关系分 Grouped by Jurisdiction of Management		按注册类型分 Grouped by Registration Status			
中央 Central Investment	地方 Local Investment	内资企业 Domestic Funds	港、澳、台商投资企业 Funds from Hong Kong, Macao and Taiwan	外商投资企业 Foreign Funded	个体经营 Self-employed Individual
605.60	**8172.80**	**8607.85**	**100.49**	**36.65**	**33.41**
0.33	259.65	249.66	1.14	1.24	7.94
0.09	102.19	98.01	0.26		4.01
	46.91	43.52	0.07	0.24	3.08
0.03	86.09	83.94	0.77	1.00	0.41
5.61	440.39	435.57	5.74	1.34	3.35
3.90	285.11	282.79	5.74		0.48
37.92	1478.92	1485.75	13.24	10.29	7.56
	21.59	19.49		1.99	0.12
0.18	3.94	4.12			
	14.27	14.11			0.16
	16.12	16.12			0.01
1.67	129.43	131.07			0.03
	69.26	68.05	0.03	1.18	
7.29	280.71	276.31	4.40	5.04	2.25
	48.88	48.36		0.52	
9.23	61.86	71.08			0.01
148.28	226.69	343.30	30.44	1.07	0.16
145.03	163.58	276.94	30.44	1.07	0.16
	9.25	9.19			0.07
364.98	1360.66	1725.03	0.05	0.45	0.11
364.16	26.73	390.89			
0.53	1262.59	1263.11	0.00		
0.03	41.80	41.22	0.05	0.45	0.11
34.13	20.60	38.29	0.49	15.95	
33.19	12.17	29.41		15.95	
0.70	101.67	101.12	0.27	0.14	0.84
0.65	84.45	77.25	0.05	2.26	5.55
	5.45	5.45			
3.15	2577.25	2528.47	43.54	3.24	5.14
	48.67	48.47			0.20
	1.57	1.53			0.04
	47.10	46.94			0.16
2.25	18.79	20.60	0.17	0.15	0.13
1.96	2.67	4.63			
5.55	1230.66	1232.43	3.00	0.47	0.31
0.59	90.00	90.60			
0.11	29.58	28.94			0.76
1.01	138.36	137.07	2.16		0.14
0.52	37.86	37.94		0.05	0.38
0.50	32.49	32.64			0.35
	59.99	59.43			0.56
	21.97	21.97			
0.40	43.92	43.90	0.19		0.24

Note: This table's statistical criteria is total investment plan of 5 Million yuan and above the fixed assets investment projects, investment in real estate development project.

5-4 按行业分500万元以上固定资产投资施工项目(2014)

Number of Construction Projects over 5 Million Yuan under Construction by Sector

指 标	Item	施工项目(个) Number of Projects under Construction This Year (unit)	#新开工项目 Started This Year	本年投产项目(个) Number of Projects Put into Use (unit)	项目建成投产率(%) Rate of Projects Completed and Put into Use(%)
总计	**Total**	**9622**	**6958**	**7113**	**73.9**
农、林、牧、渔业	Agriculture, Forestry, Animal Husbandry and Fishery	973	812	805	82.8
#农、林、牧、渔服务业	Service in Support of Agriculture	179	145	142	79.4
采矿业	Mining	678	487	536	79.0
#煤炭开采和洗选业	Mining and Washing of Coal	344	226	261	75.9
制造业	Manufacturing	1811	1246	1310	72.3
#酒、饮料和精制茶制造业	Manufacture of Liquor, Beverages and Refined Tea	47	32	38	80.7
烟草制品业	Manufacture of Tobacco	10	8	6	63.3
造纸和纸制品业	Manufacture of Paper and Paper Products	20	14	17	82.0
石油加工、炼焦和核燃料加工业	Processing of Petroleum, Coking and Processing of Nuclear Fuel	12	7	6	50.0
化学原料和化学制品制造业	Manufacture of Raw Chemical Materials and Chemical Products	136	90	98	71.6
医药制造业	Manufacture of Medicines	64	38	41	64.6
非金属矿物制品业	Manufacture of Non-metallic Mineral Products	426	322	337	79.1
黑色金属冶炼和压延加工业	Smelting and Pressing of Ferrous Metals	44	22	29	66.4
有色金属冶炼和压延加工业	Smelting and Pressing of Non-ferrous Metals	40	26	24	59.1
电力、热力、燃气及水的生产和供应业	Production and Supply of Electricity,Heat,Gas and Water	473	288	314	66.5
#电力、热力生产和供应业	Production and Supply of Electric Power and Heat Power	299	170	190	63.5
建筑业	Construction	71	68	47	66.0
交通运输、仓储和邮政业	Transport, Storage and Post	1527	1225	1255	82.2
#铁路运输业	Railway Transport	31	11	4	13.0
道路运输业	Road Transport	1415	1164	1204	85.1
仓 储 业	Storage	53	34	35	65.6

5-4 续表 continued

指 标	Item	施 工 项 目 (个) Number of Projects under Construction This Year (unit)	#新开工 项 目 Started This Year	本年投产 项 目 (个) Number of Projects Put into Use (unit)	项目建成 投 产 率 (%) Rate of Projects Completed and Put into Use(%)
信息传输、软件和信息技术服务业	Information Transmission, Software and Information Technology	92	75	78	85.1
#电信、广播电视和卫星传输服务业	Telecommunication Radio and Television and Satellite Transmission Services	73	60	63	87.2
批发和零售业	Wholesale and Retail Trades	225	166	168	75.0
住宿和餐饮业	Hotels and Catering Services	196	143	148	75.9
金 融 业	Financial Intermediation	16	11	13	79.2
房地产业	Real Estate	683	462	434	63.5
租赁和商务服务业	Leasing and Business Services	73	61	48	65.3
租 赁 业	Leasing	4	4	4	92.3
商务服务业	Business Services	69	57	44	63.6
科学研究和技术服务业	Scientific Research, Technical Service	44	35	32	73.3
#研究和试验发展	Research and Experimental Development	3	1	1	44.4
水利、环境和公共设施管理业	Management of Water Conservancy, Environment and Public Facilities	1916	1329	1326	69.2
#水利管理业	Management of Water Conservancy	383	235	278	72.6
居民服务、修理和其他服务业	Services to Households, Repair and Other Services	90	68	71	79.6
教 育	Education	326	219	228	70.0
卫生和社会工作	Health and Social Service	134	86	86	64.2
#卫 生	Health	96	59	58	60.8
文化、体育和娱乐业	Culture, Sports and Entertainment	113	76	83	73.2
#文化艺术业	Cultural and Art Activities	47	29	36	76.4
公共管理、社会保障和社会组织	Public Management, Social security and Social Organization	183	101	131	71.6

5-5 房地产开发企业基本情况(2014)

单位：亿元

指　标	Item	总 计 Total
企业个数(个)	**Number of Enterprises(unit)**	**2591**
年末从业人员总计(人)	**Number of Employed Persons at the Year-end (person)**	**55992**
本年完成投资	**Investment Completed This Year**	**2187.67**
按工程用途分	By Use of Project	
#商品住宅	Residential Buildings	1350.34
办公楼	Office Buildings	151.97
商业营业用房	Houses for Business Use	443.98
其　他	Others	241.38
按构成分	By Type of Construction	
建筑工程	Construction	1709.55
安装工程	Installation	122.91
设备工器具购置	Purchase of Equitment and Instruments	19.15
其他费用	Others	336.05
资金来源合计	**Total Source of Funds This Year**	**2807.78**
#国内贷款	Domestic Loans	242.62
利用外资	Foreign Investment	3.41
自筹资金	Self-raising Fund	964.86
其他资金来源	Others	1125.72
#个人按揭贷款	Personal Housing Mortgage Loans	370.66
土地购置费	Land Acquisition Costs	140.33
待开发土地面积(万平方米)	Land Space to Be Developed (10000 sq.m)	1243.70
购置土地面积(万平方米)	Land Space Purchased This Year(10000 sq.m)	936.36
施工房屋面积(万平方米)	Floor Space Under Construction(10000 sq.m)	20369.36
竣工房屋面积(万平方米)	Floor Space Completed(10000 sq.m)	2842.32
房屋建筑面积竣工率(%)	Rate of Floor Space of Buildings Completed(%)	13.95
新开工房屋面积(万平方米)	**Floor Space Started This Year(10000 sq.m)**	**4616.49**
住　宅	Residential Buildings	2829.30
办公楼	Office Buildings	187.80
商业营业用房	Houses for Business Use	849.88
其　他	Others	749.51

Basic Conditions of Real Estate Development Enterprises

(100 million yuan)

内资企业 Domestic Funded	#国有企业 State-owned Enterprises	#私营有限责任公司 Private Limited Liability Company	#私营股份有限公司 Private Share-holding Corporations Limited	港澳台商投资企业 Enterprises with Funds from HongKong, Macao and TaiWan	外商投资企业 Foreign Funded Enterprises
2550	**27**	**983**	**104**	**31**	**10**
54704	**746**	**17717**	**1979**	**1134**	**154**
2141.12	**10.07**	**531.09**	**56.22**	**43.48**	**3.07**
1313.41	7.59	322.62	37.50	34.70	2.23
149.31	0.00	16.04	2.88	2.41	0.25
440.65	1.03	123.71	10.03	2.85	0.48
237.74	1.44	68.72	5.80	3.53	0.11
1670.68	8.55	407.80	44.26	36.28	2.60
120.01	0.09	36.08	4.39	2.80	0.10
19.11		6.37	0.50	0.01	0.03
331.31	1.43	80.85	7.07	4.39	0.35
2747.47	**15.74**	**691.46**	**69.65**	**55.99**	**4.32**
236.17	1.25	61.16	7.45	6.45	
				3.05	0.36
948.63	1.32	324.31	34.08	15.93	0.30
1100.92	6.53	205.54	25.62	21.60	3.21
364.10	1.94	72.44	9.54	4.69	1.87
138.81	0.26	41.53	4.25	1.49	0.03
1127.58	1.03	203.52	13.93	116.12	
928.05		331.56	9.89	8.32	
20033.21	132.51	5587.04	757.60	247.94	88.21
2758.32	16.67	725.40	102.48	79.33	4.67
13.77	12.58	12.98	13.53	32.00	5.29
4532.95	**33.22**	**1536.13**	**202.09**	**73.16**	**10.37**
2783.52	26.55	994.26	109.25	44.52	1.25
178.12	0.01	30.35	16.55	7.45	2.23
837.12	1.81	291.95	29.62	8.92	3.85
734.19	4.85	219.58	46.67	12.28	3.04

5-6 房地产开发投资主要指标

Main Indicator on Real Estate Development

指　标	Item	2010	2011	2012	2013	2014	2014年比2013年增长(%) Increase Rate in 2014 over 2013(%)
本年土地购置面积（万平方米）	**Land Space Purchased This Year (10000 sq.m)**	**1027**	**883**	**708**	**1210**	**936**	**-22.6**
本年完成投资(亿元)	**Investment Completed This Year (100 million yuan)**	**556.69**	**873.48**	**1467.60**	**1942.54**	**2187.67**	**12.6**
#住　宅	Residential Buildings	328.63	576.44	930.31	1224.23	1350.34	10.3
资金来源合计(亿元)	**Source of Funds(100 million yuan)**	**1135.61**	**1533.83**	**1696.00**	**2500.55**	**2807.78**	**12.3**
#国内贷款	Domestic Loans	160.10	172.78	230.61	226.82	242.62	7.0
利用外资	Foreign Investment	0.72	4.47	4.29		3.41	
自筹资金	Self-raising Funds	268.68	526.09	518.44	877.20	964.86	10.0
房屋建筑面积(万平方米)	**Floor Space of Buildings(10000 sq.m)**						
施工面积	Floor Space under Construction	7906	10261	13245	17357	20369	17.4
#本年新开工面积	Floor Space Started This Year	2871	2885	3788	5628	4616	-18.0
#住　宅	Residential Buildings	5971	7689	9654	12316	13793	12.0
竣工面积	Floor Space Completed	1048	1455	1417	1765	2842	61.1
#住　宅	Residential Buildings	826	1102	1120	1352	2046	51.3

5-7 房地产开发企业商品房屋销售面积(2014)

Floor Space of Commercialized Buildings

单位：万平方米 (10000 sq.m)

指 标	Item	商品房屋销售面积 Floor Space of Commercialized Buildings Sold	#住 宅 Residential Buildings
总计	**Total**	**3178.12**	**2707.09**
现房	Existing House	475.95	384.21
期房	Forward House	2702.17	2322.88
按登记注册类型分	**Grouped by status of Registration**		
#内资企业	Domestic Funded Enterprises	3140.89	2675.63
#国有企业	State-owned Enterprises	18.43	14.77
集体企业	Collective-owned Enterprises		
其他有限责任公司	Other Limited Liability Corporations	1862.44	1553.99
股份有限公司	Share-holding Corporations Ltd.	109.46	96.85
私营独资企业	Private-funded Enterprises	19.76	19.64
私营有限责任公司	Private Limited Liability Corporations	973.54	845.09
私营股份有限公司	Private Share-holding Corporations Ltd.	114.57	105.47
港澳台商投资企业	Enterprises with Funds from Hong Kong,Macao and Taiwan	30.94	25.54
#与港澳台商合资经营企业	Joint-venture Enterprises	8.43	6.89
港澳台商独资经营企业	Enterprises with Sole Fund	22.51	18.65
外商投资企业	Foreign Funded Enterprises	6.29	5.93

5-8 房地产开发企业商品房屋销售额(2014)

Total Sale of Commercialized Buildings

单位：亿元 (100 million yuan)

指 标	Item	商品房屋销售额 Total Sale of Commercialized Buildings Sold	#住 宅 Residential Buildings
总计	**Total**	**1370.31**	**1000.01**
现房	Existing House	190.62	124.03
期房	Forward House	1179.70	875.98
按登记注册类型分	**Grouped by status of Registration**		
#内资企业	Domestic Funded Enterprises	1345.57	980.54
#国有企业	State-owned Enterprises	7.00	4.97
集体企业	Collective-owned Enterprises		
其他有限责任公司	Other Limited Liability Corporations	828.57	588.49
股份有限公司	Share-holding Corporations Ltd.	41.91	30.57
私营独资企业	Private-funded Enterprises	6.85	6.64
私营有限责任公司	Private Limited Liability Corporations	395.28	298.62
私营股份有限公司	Private Share-holding Corporations Ltd.	47.30	39.11
港澳台商投资企业	Enterprises with Funds from Hong Kong,Macao and Taiwan	21.75	16.91
#与港澳台商合资经营企业	Joint-venture Enterprises	7.59	6.08
港澳台商独资经营企业	Enterprises with Sole Fund	14.17	10.83
外商投资企业	Foreign Funded Enterprises	2.99	2.55

主要统计指标解释

全社会固定资产投资 是以货币形式表现的在一定时期内全社会建造和购置固定资产的工作量以及与此有关的费用的总称。该指标是反映固定资产投资规模、结构和发展速度的综合性指标，又是观察工程进度和考核投资效果的重要依据。全社会固定资产投资包括固定资产项目投资、房地产开发投资和农户投资。全社会固定资产投资按登记注册类型可分为国有、集体、个体、联营、股份制、外商、港澳台商、其他等。

房地产开发投资 指各种登记注册类型的房地产开发公司、商品房建设公司及其他房地产开发法人单位和附属于其他法人单位实际从事房地产开发或经营活动的单位统一开发的包括统代建、拆迁还建的住宅、厂房、仓库、饭店、宾馆、度假村、写字楼、办公楼等房屋建筑物和配套的服务设施，土地开发工程（如道路、给水、排水、供电、供热、通讯、平整场地等基础设施工程）的投资；不包括单纯的土地交易活动。

固定资产投资的资金来源 根据固定资产投资的资金来源不同，分为国家预算资金、国内贷款、债券、利用外资、自筹资金和其他资金。

(1)国家预算资金 自2011年起，按照全国人大和国务院的要求，各级财政的所有资金，包括税收和非税收入，均必须纳入预算管理，我国已不存在预算外资金的概念，因此各级政府用于固定资产投资的财政资金均为预算资金。由于已经没有预算外资金，因此名称改为国家预算资金，包括中央预算资金和地方预算资金，旧的国家预算内资金的内容和现中央预算资金的内容基本一致。

国家预算包括一般预算、政府性基金预算、国有资本经营预算和社保基金预算。各类预算中用于固定资产投资的资金全部作为国家预算资金填报，其中一般预算中用于固定资产投资的部分包括基建投资、车购税、灾后恢复重建基金和其他财政投资。各级政府债券也应归入国家预算资金。

根据《2011年政府收支分类科目》确定的收支范围，目前纳入政府性基金预算的资金主要包括：农网还贷资金、山西省煤炭可持续发展基金、铁路建设基金、民航基础设施建设基金、民航机场管理建设费、海南省高等级公路车辆通行附加费、转让政府还贷道路收费权、港口建设费、散装水泥专项资金、新型墙体材料专项基金、旅游发展基金、文化事业建设费、地方教育附加、江苏省地方教育基金、国家电影事业发展专项资金、新菜地开发建设基金、新增建设用地土地有偿使用费、育林基金、森林植被恢复费、中央水利建设基金、地方水利建设基金、南水北调工程基金、残疾人就业保障金、政府住房基金、城市公用事业附加、国有土地使用权出让金、国有土地收益基金、农业土地开发资金、大中型水库移民后期扶持基金、大中型水库库区基金、三峡水库库区基金、中央特别国债经营基金、中央特别国债经营基金财务收支、彩票公益金、城市基础设施配套费、小型水库移民扶助基金、国家重大水利工程建设基金、车辆通行费、船舶港务费、体育部门收费、司法部门的涉外涉港澳台公证书工本费、贸促会收费、长江口航道维护费、电力改革预留资产变现资金、铁路资产变现资金、其他政府性基金。

(2)国内贷款 指报告期固定资产投资项目单位向银行及非银行金融机构借入用于固定资产投资的各种国内借款，包括银行利用自有资金及吸收存款发放的贷款、上级主管部门拨入的国内贷款、国家专项贷款（包括煤代油贷款、劳改煤矿专项贷款等），地方财政专项资金安排的贷款、国内储备贷款、周转贷款等。

(3)利用外资 指报告期收到的境外（包括外国及港澳台地区）资金(包括设备、材料、技术在内)。包括对外借款(外国政府贷款、国际金融组织贷款、出口信贷、外国银行商业贷款、对外发行债券和股票)、外商直接投资、外商其他投资(包括利用外商投资收益在国内进行固定资产再投资活动的资金)。不包括我国自有外汇资金(国家外汇、地方外汇、留成外汇、调济外汇和国内银行自有资金发放的外汇贷款等)。各类外资按报告期末的外汇牌价（中间价）折成人民币计算。

(4)自筹资金 指固定资产投资单位在报告期收到的，由各企事业单位筹集用于固定资产投资的资金，包括各类企事业单位的自有资金和从其他单位筹集的用于固定资产投资的资金，但不包括各类财政性资金、从各类金融机构借入资金和国外资金。与原有的自筹资金概念相比，最大的变化是地方财政资金全部归为国家预算资金，自筹资金中不再含有财政资金。

(5)其他资金来源 指在报告期收到的除以上各种资金之外的用于固定资产投资的资金。包括社会集资、个人资金、无偿捐赠的资金及其他单位拨入的资金等。

固定资产投资按国民经济行业分 根据建设项目建成投产后的主要产品或主要用途及社会经济活动性质来确定国民经济行业。一般情况下，一个建设项目或一个企业、事业单位只能属于一种国民经济行业。

固定资产投资按隶属关系分 是按照建设单位或企业、事业、行政单位的主管上级机关确定的。

(1) 中央 是由中共中央、人大常委会和国务院各部、委、局、总公司以及直属机构直接领导的建设项目和企业、事业、行政单位。这些单位的固定资产投资计划由国务院各部门直接编制和下达，统一组织或委托下级实施。

(2) 地方 是由省（自治区、直辖市）、地区（州、盟、省辖市）、县（旗、县级市）三级政府及业务主管部门直接领导和管理的建设项目、企业、事业、行政单位。地方项目还包括不隶属以上各级政府及主管部门的建设项目和企业、事业单位，如外商投资企业和无主管部门的企业等。

固定资产投资按构成分 固定资产投资活动按其工作内容和实现方式分为建筑安装工程，设备、工具、器具购置，其他费用三个部分。

(1)建筑安装工程(建筑安装工作量)：指各种房屋、建筑物的建造工程和各种设备、装置的安装工程。包括各种房屋建造工程；各种用途设备基础和各种工业窑炉的砌筑工程及金属结构工程；为施工而进行的各种准备工作和临时工程以及完工后的清理工作等；铁路、道路的铺设，矿井的开凿及石油管道的架设等；水利工程；防空地下建筑等特殊工程；列入房屋工程预算内的暖气、卫生、通风、照明、煤气等设备的价值及装设油饰工程；列入建筑工程预算内的各种管道(蒸汽、压缩空气、石油、给排水等管道)、电力、电讯、电缆、导线等的敷设工程；以及各种机械设备的安装工程；为测定安装工程质量，对设备进行的试运工作；房地产开发单位进行的商品房屋开发建设工程、土地开发工程。

在安装工程中，不包括被安装设备本身的价值。

(2)设备、工具、器具购置：指建设单位或企、事业单位购置或自制的，达到固定资产标准的设备、工具、器具的价值。新建单位及扩建单位的新建车间，按照设计或计划要求购置或自制的全部设备、工具、器具，不论是否达到固定资产标准均计入"设备、工具、器具购置"中。

(3)其他费用：指在固定资产建造和购置过程中发生的，除建筑安装工程和设备、工器具购置投资完成额以外的应当分摊计入固定资产投资的费用，不指经营中财务上的其他费用。

施工项目个数、本年投产项目个数和本年新开工项目个数：每一个建设项目只计算为一个项目个数。

施工项目个数 指本年正式进行过建筑或安装施工活动的建设项目个数。包括本年新开工项目，以前年度开工跨入本年继续施工项目，本年全部建成投产项目、以前年度全部停缓建在本年恢复施工的项目，本年进行过施工又在本年内全部停缓建的项目。

本年投产项目个数 指报告期内按设计文件规定建成主体工程和相应配套的辅助设施，形成生产能力或工程效益，经过验收合格，并且已正式投入生产或交付使用的建设项目。建成投产项目个数是反映报告期建设成果和考核投资效果的重要依据。

全部建成投入生产或交付使用的工业项目是指设计文件规定形成生产能力的主体工程及其相应配套的辅助设施全部建成，经负荷试运转，证明具备生产设计规定合格产品的条件，并经过验收鉴定合格或达到竣工验收标准，与生产性工程配套的生活福利设施可以满足近期正常生产的需要，正式移交生产的建设项目；非工业项目是指设计文件规定的主体工程和相应配套工程全部建成，能够发挥设计规定的工程效益，经验收鉴定合格或达到竣工验收标准，正式移交使用的建设项目。

凡对环境有污染的建设项目，要按照有关部门规定，在“三废”治理工程按设计规定建成，并经环保部门验收鉴定合格，交付使用后，整个项目才能作为全投项目。达不到要求的则不能作为全投项目统计。

本年新开工项目个数 指报告期内新开工的建设项目。包括新开工的新建项目、扩建项目、改建项目、单纯建造生活设施项目、迁建项目和恢复项目。新开工项目的确定以总体设计或计划文件中所规定的永久性工程正式开工为准。本年新开工项目个数是反映全年新开工的固定资产投资规模的指标。

房屋施工面积　指报告期内施工的全部房屋建筑面积。包括本期新开工的面积、上期跨入本期继续施工的房屋面积、上期停缓建在本期恢复施工的房屋面积、本期竣工的房屋面积以及本期施工后又停缓建的房屋面积。多层建筑应填各层建筑面积之和。

房屋竣工面积　指报告期内房屋建筑按照设计要求已全部完工，达到住人和使用条件，经验收鉴定合格或达到竣工验收标准，可正式移交使用的各栋房屋建筑面积的总和。

竣工面积以房屋单位工程（栋）为核算对象，在整栋房屋符合竣工条件后按其全部建筑面积一次性计算，而不是按各栋施工房屋中已完成的部分或层次分割计算。

计算本年房屋竣工面积，要求严格执行房屋竣工验收标准。民用建筑一般应按设计要求在土建工程和房屋本身附属的水、电、卫（包括设计中有的煤气、暖气）工程已经完工，通风、电梯等设备已经安装完毕，做到水通、灯亮，经验收鉴定合格，并正式交付给使用单位后，才能计算竣工面积。工业及科研等生产性房屋建筑一般应按设计要求在土建工程（包括水、暖、电、卫、通风）及属于房屋组成部分的生活间、操作间等已经完成（不包括安装设备的基础工程），可以进行工艺设备和管线安装时，方可计算本年房屋竣工面积。

房屋建筑面积竣工率　指一定时期内房屋竣工面积占同期房屋施工面积的比率。

商品房销售面积　指报告期内出售商品房屋的合同总面积(即双方签署的正式买卖合同中所确定的建筑面积)。由现房销售建筑面积和期房销售建筑面积两部分组成。

商品房销售额　指报告期内出售商品房屋的合同总价款(即双方签署的正式买卖合同中所确定的合同总价)。该指标与商品房销售面积同口径，由现房销售额和期房销售额两部分组成。

Explanatory Notes on Main Statistical Indicators

Total Investment in Fixed Assets in the Whole Country refers to the volume of activities in construction and purchases of fixed assets of the whole province and related fees, expressed in monetary terms during the reference period. It is a comprehensive indicator which shows the size, structure and growth of the investment in fixed assets, providing a basis for observing the progress of construction projects and evaluating results of investment. Total investment in fixed assets in the whole province includes investment in fixed assets , investment in real estate development and rural household investment. Total investment in fixed assets in the whole province includes, by type of ownership, the investment by State-owned units, collective-owned units, individuals, joint ownership units, share-holding units, as well as investments by entrepreneurs from foreign countries and from Hong Kong, Macao and Taiwan, and by other units.

Investment in Real Estate Development refers to investment by real estate development companies, commercialized buildings construction companies and other real estate development units of various types of ownership in the construction of buildings, such as residential buildings, factory buildings, warehouses, hotels, guesthouses, holiday villages, office buildings, and the complementary service facilities and land development projects, such as roads, water supply, water drainage, power supply, heating supply, telecommunications, land leveling and other infrastructural projects. It does not include activities in pure land transactions.

Sources of Funds for Investment in Fixed Assets are categorized as funds from the State budget, domestic loans, bonds , foreign investment, self-raised funds, and others, depending on the sources of investment.

(1) Fund from the State budget From 2011, in accordance with the requirements of the NPC and the State Council, all levels of financial funds included tax and non-tax revenue that both of them must be included in the budget management. And our country has no concept of extra-budgetary funds. So the financial funds of all levels of government that is using for investment in fixed assets are budget funds. Because they have no extra-budgetary funds, the name was changed to state budget funds, including the central budget and local budget funds. The original contents of the state budget funds and the central budget funds are basically the same.

State budget includes the general budget, the government fund budget, the state capital budget and the social security fund budget. All kinds of budget funds for investment in fixed assets are as fill for state budget funds. Among them, the section of general budget which is for investment in fixed assets are including infrastructure investment portion, vehicle purchase, post-disaster restoration and reconstruction funds and other financial investments. All levels of government bonds should also be included in state budget funds.

According to "2011 Government revenue and expenditure classification of subjects" to determine the scope of revenue and expenditure, the current government funds into the capital budget include: rural loan funds, coal Sustainable Development Funds in Shanxi province, railway construction funds, CAAC Infrastructure Development funds, aviation airport management and construction fees, highway vehicle traffic surcharge in Hainan province, transfer government loan road pricing right, port construction fees, bulk cement special funds, new wall materials special funds, tourism development funds, culture construction fees, additional local education, local education funds in Jiangsu province, National Film career development funds, new vegetable field development and construction funds, new construction land use fees, silviculture funds, Forest vegetation restoration fees, central water conservancy construction funds, local water conservancy construction funds, North Water Transfer Project funds, disabled employment security funds, government housing funds, additional city utilities, State-owned land use right transfer fee, State-owned Land Income funds, agricultural land development funds, medium-sized reservoir resettlement support funds, medium-sized reservoir funds, Three Gorges Reservoir funds, central special treasury management funds, central special treasury fund financial revenue and expenditure operations, lottery, urban infrastructure fee, small reservoir resettlement support funds, major national water conservancy construction funds, vehicle tolls, harbor dues, sports department charges, the judiciary involving Hong Kong, Macao and Taiwan foreign notary fees, CCPIT charges, Yangtze Estuary

Waterway maintenance fees, electricity reform realization of assets set aside funds, railway assets realized capital, other government funds.

(2) Domestic loans refer to loans of various forms borrowed by investing units from banks and non-bank financial institutions during the reference period for the purpose of investment in fixed assets, including loans issued by banks from their self-owned funds and deposit, loans appropriated by higher authorities, special loans by government(Including coal oil loans, special loans by correctional mine and so on), loans arranged by local government from special funds, domestic reserve loan, and working loan.

(3) Foreign investment refers to foreign funds received abroad (including foreign and Hong Kong, Macao and Taiwan regions) funds (covering equipment, materials and technology)during the reference period, including foreign borrowings (loans from foreign governments and international financial institutions, export credit, commercial loans from foreign banks, issue of bonds and stocks overseas), foreign direct investment and other foreign investments. Excluded from this category is capital in foreign exchanges owned by China (foreign exchanges owned by the central and local governments, foreign exchanges retained by enterprises, foreign exchanges by enterprises through the regulating mechanism, loans in foreign exchanges issued by the Bank of China with its own fund, etc.). Various types of foreign investment in accordance with the reporting period, the exchange rates (mid-point) converted into Renminbi.

(4) Self-raised funds refer to funds for investment in fixed assets received during the reference period by investing units, including investment in fixed assets using own funds of various enterprises and institutions or funds raised from other units other than financial funds, funds borrowed from financial institutions and overseas funds. Compared with the original concept of self-raised funds, the biggest change is all owned by funds for the state budget funds, self-raised funds in the longer contain financial funds.

(5) Others refer to funds for investment in fixed assets received from sources other than those listed above, including capital raised through issuing bonds by enterprises or financial institutions, funds raised from individuals and through donations, and funds transferred from other units.

Investment in Fixed Assets by Sector The classification of construction projects by sector is determined by the major products or the purpose of the projects when they are put into production or use, and by the nature of their social economic activities. In general, one project or one enterprise or institution can only be classified into one sector.

Investment in Fixed Assets by Jurisdiction of Management refers to the classification of investment by the competent authorities under which investment is made by construction units, enterprises, institutions or administrative units.

(1) Central investment refers to the investment in projects or by enterprises, institutions or administrative units which are under the direct leadership and management of the State Council and of the national commissions, ministries, agencies and State-owned large corporations. Various ministries and departments of the State Council prepare and implement plans for investment in fixed assets by those departments, and arrange and ensure the supply of materials and key equipment required for the projects.

(2) Local investment refers to the investment in projects or by enterprises, institutions or administrative units which are under the direct leadership and management of departments under the provincial, prefecture and county governments. Also included are projects by foreign-invested enterprises and enterprises without competent managing authorities.

Investment in Fixed Assets by Structure By their contents and the mode of implementation, investment activities are classified into 3 categories, i.e. construction and installation, purchase of equipment and instrument, and other expenses.

(1) Construction and installation (work volume of construction and installation): refers to the construction of houses and buildings and the installation of various kinds of equipment and instruments. They include construction of houses; equipment foundations, industrial kilns and stoves, and metal structure work; preparation works and temporary works for project construction, and clearing up works post project construction; pavement of railways and roads, drilling of mines and putting up of oil pipes; construction of water conservancy; construction of underground air-raid shelters and construction of other special projects; value of equipment for heating, sanitation, ventilation, lighting, gas, painting, etc. that are covered by the budget of housing projects; laying out of various pipelines (for steam, compressed air, petroleum, tap water and sewage) and wiring and cabling for electric power and for communications; installation of various machinery and equipment; testing operation for pre-testing the quality of installation projects, and land and other development work conducted by real estate developers for commercialized housing. The value of equipment installed is itself not included in the value of installation projects.

(2) Purchase of equipment and instruments: refers to the total value of equipment, tools, and instruments purchased or self-produced which come up to the cut-off point for fixed assets by the construction units or investing enterprises or institutions. Equipment, tools and instruments purchased or self-produced for new workshops by newly established or expanded units are categorized as "purchase of equipment and instruments" no matter whether they come up to the cut-off point for fixed assets.

(3) Other expenses: refer to expenses arising during the construction or purchase of fixed assets other than those mentioned above.

Number of Projects under Construction, projects put into use and new projects: Every construction project is only counted as a number of projects.

Number of Projects under Construction refer to number of all projects with actual construction or installation activities in current year, including newly started projects, projects started previously and extended into the current year, projects completed and put into operation in current year, projects suspended previously and resumed in current year, and projects started this year but suspended or postponed in current year.

Number of Projects Put into Use refer to projects have completed the main construction and correspondent auxiliary facilities in accordance with the design documents, resulting in forming production capacity (efficiency) and have been checked and accepted after relevant tests, and have been formally delivered for use. Number of projects put into use is an important basis that reflects the results of the report and assessment phase of construction investment results.

All of the industrial projects which completed and put into production or delivery referred to the design document form a production capacity of the main project and its corresponding supporting ancillary facilities completed. After commissioning overloaded, prove that it has the conditions for production design which provide qualified products, And go through acceptance of accreditation or reach completion and acceptance criteria, and supporting productive projects and welfare facilities to meet the needs of normal production recently, formally handed over the production of construction projects; Non-industrial project is the main project design by documents and the corresponding ancillary works are completed, and be able to play the design requirements of the project benefits, go through acceptance of accreditation or reach completion and acceptance criteria, formally handed over to use for construction projects.

All of the construction projects which pollute the environment, in accordance with relevant regulations, in the "three wastes" treatment works built according to the design requirements, and accredited by the environmental protection department, after delivery and use, the entire project can be used as a all of investment projects. Below standard of projects can not be used as all of investment projects to count.

Number of new projects this year refers to newly started construction projects during the reporting period. It includes a newly started new projects and expansion projects, renovation projects, simple living facilities construction projects, relocation projects and restoration projects. New projects in order to determine the overall design or plan to file the required permanent project started prevail. The number of new projects this year is a reflection of newly started investment in fixed assets indicators.

Floor Space under Construction refers to the total floor space of all the buildings in the reference period,, including floor space of newly started buildings during the reference period, floor space of construction extended form the previous period to the reference period, floor space of construction suspended or postponed in the previous period and resumed in the reference period, floor space of construction completed in the reference period, and floor space of construction started and then suspended or postponed in the reference period.

Floor Space Completed refers to the floor space of all buildings completed in the reference period, which have been appraised and accepted or come up to the designed standards and have been put into use.

The accounting object of the completion of the area is unit of housing project (building), the entire houses meet the completed conditions, in accordance with all construction area to disposable calculated, rather than divisional calculated in accordance with the construction of the building house which finished part or hierarchical.

In calculating the size of houses completed this year is demanded strictly enforced housing completion and acceptance criteria. Civil construction should generally be in accordance with the design requirements of civil works and the house itself attached water, electricity, health (including the design of some gas, heating) project has been completed, Ventilation, elevators and other equipment has been installed, to water and lights, through acceptance accreditation, and formally delivered to the use of the unit, in order to calculate the completion of the area. Industry and research and other production of housing construction general design requirements should be in the civil works (including water, heating, electricity, health, ventilation) and are an integral part of life, housing, the operating room, etc. have been completed (not including the installation of foundation engineering equipment), process equipment and piping can be installed, be counted this year housing area.

Housing construction area completion rate refers to the total gross floor area of completed housing area accounted for the same period the rate of housing construction area during the reference period.

Area of Commercialized Housing Sold refers to total contracted area of commercialized housing (i.e. area of floor space as designated in the formal contracts signed by both sides) during the reference time. It constitutes floor space of completed housing and floor space of future housing.

Value of Commercialized Housing Sold refers to the total contracted value (i.e. value of sales/purchase for selling/purchase of commercialized housing as designated in the contract signed by both sides) during the reference time. This indicator has the same coverage as the area of commercialized housing sold, which constitutes floor space of completed housing and floor space of housing yet to be completed.

6

对外经济贸易

Foreign Trade and Economic Cooperation

6-1 进出口总额
Total Value of Imports and Exports

指　标	Item	2010	2011	2012	2013	2014	2014年比2013年增长(%) Increase Rate in 2014 over 2013(%)
进出口总额(万元)	**Total Value of Imports and Exports(RMB 10000 yuan)**	**2132280**	**3172193**	**4189987**	**5136541**	**6623074**	**28.9**
出口总额	Total Exports	1299881	1936946	3129409	4265712	5778924	35.5
进口总额	Total Imports	832399	1235246	1060578	870829	844150	-3.1
进出口差额	Balance	467482	701700	2068831	3394883	4934774	45.4
进出口总额(万美元)	**Total Value of Imports and Exports(USD 10000)**	**314680**	**488758**	**663156**	**829009**	**1077133**	**29.9**
出口总额	Total Exports	192018	298509	495223	688598	939726	36.5
进口总额	Total Imports	122662	190249	167933	140411	137407	-2.1
进出口差额	Balance	69356	108260	327290	548187	802319	46.4

注：资料来源于贵阳海关(以下相关表同)。
Note: Data in the table are obtained from Guiyang Customhouse(the same applies to the relative tables below) .

6-2 按地区分的出口商品总额
Total Value of Exports by Region

单位：万美元　　(USD 10000)

地　区	Country (Territory)	2010	2011	2012	2013	2014
总　计	**Total**	**192018**	**298509**	**495223**	**688598**	**939726**
亚　洲	Asia	120024	186317	299176	373558	510734
非　洲	Africa	5307	8296	33260	45552	105979
欧　洲	Europe	18937	23746	57520	110395	116378
拉丁美洲	Latin America	8998	29284	23704	30960	42967
北 美 洲	North America	22826	35270	61443	107210	120804
大 洋 洲	Oceania	15926	15596	20120	20923	42864

6-3 按地区分的进口商品总额
Total Value of Imports by Region

单位：万美元　　(USD 10000)

地　区	Country (Territory)	2010	2011	2012	2013	2014
总　计	**Total**	**122662**	**190249**	**167933**	**140411**	**137407**
亚　洲	Asia	64064	79069	54464	46860	45111
非　洲	Africa	8595	22188	16509	20491	21483
欧　洲	Europe	7770	9946	8317	16465	16475
拉丁美洲	Latin America	14950	22722	23920	7005	10634
北 美 洲	North America	11670	18644	25409	16705	11065
大 洋 洲	Oceania	15613	37680	39314	32885	32639

6-4 海关出口商品分类

单位：万美元

指　标	Item
总　计	**Total**
#活动物；动物产品	Live Animals;Animal Products
植物产品	Vegetable Products
动、植物油、脂及其分解产品；精制的食用油脂；动、植物蜡	Animal or Vegetable Fats and Oils and their Cleavage Products;Prepared Edible Fats; Animal or Vegetable Waxes
食品；饮料、酒及醋；烟草及烟草代用品的制品	Prepared Foodstuffs; Beverages, Spirits And Vinegar; Tobacco and Manufactured Tobacco Substitutes
矿产品	Mineral Products
化学工业及其相关工业的产品	Products of The Chemical or Industries Allied
塑料及其产品；橡胶及其产品	Plastics and Articles Thereof Rubber and Articles Thereof
生皮、皮革、毛皮及其制品；鞍具及挽具；旅行用品、手提包及类似品；动物肠线(蚕胶丝除外)制品	Raw Hides and Skins, Leather, Fur Skins and Articles Thereof; Saddlery and Harness; Travel Goods, Handbags and Similar Containers; Articles of Animal Gut (Other Than Silk-Worm Gut)
木及木制品；木炭；软木及软木制品；稻草、秸秆、针茅或其他编结材料制品；篮筐及柳条编结品	Wood and Articles of Wood; Wood Charcoal; Cork and Articles of Cork; Manufactures of Straw, of Esparto or of Other Plaiting Materials; Basket Ware and Wickerwork
木浆及其他纤维状纤维素浆；纸及纸板的废碎品；纸、纸板及其制品	Pulp of Wood or of Other Fibrous Cellulosic Material; Waste and Scrap of Paper or Paperboard; Paper and Paperboard and Articles Thereof
纺织原料及纺织制品	Textiles and Textile Articles Silk
鞋、帽、伞、杖、鞭及其零件；已加工的羽毛及其制品；人造花；人发制品	Footwear, Headgear, Umbrellas, Sun Umbrellas, Walking-Sticks, Seat-Sticks, Whips, Riding-Crops and Parts Thereof; Prepared Feathers and Articles Made Therewith; Artificial Flowers; Articles of Human Hair
石料、石膏、水泥、石棉、云母及类似材料的制品；陶瓷产品；玻璃及其制品	Gypsum, Cement, Asbestos,Mica or Similar Materials;Ceramic Products; Glass and Glassware
天然或养殖珍珠、宝石或半宝石、贵金属、包贵金属及其制品；仿首饰；硬币	Natural or Cultured Pearls, Precious or Semi-Precious Stones, Precious Metals, Metals Clad With Precious Metal and Stones, Precious Metals, Metals Clad With Metal and Articles Thereof; Imitation Jewellery; Coin
贱金属及其制品	Base Metals and Related Products
机器、机械器具、电气设备机器及其零件、录音机及放声机、电视图象、声音的录制和重放设备及其零件、附件	Machinery and Mechanical Appliances; Electrical Equipment; Parts Thereof; Sound Recorders and Reproducers, Television Image and Sound Recorders and Reproducers; and Parts and Accessories of Recorders and Reproducers; and Parts and Accessories of Such Artic
车辆、航空器、船舶及有关运输设备	Vehicles, Aircraft, Vessels And Associated Transport Equipment
光学、照相、电影、计量、检验、医疗或外科用仪器及设备、精密仪器及设备；钟表；乐器及上述物品的零件、附件	Optical, Photographic, Cinematographic, Measuring, Checking, Precision, Medical or Surgical Instruments and Apparatus; Clocks And Watches; Musical Instruments; Parts and Accessories Thereof
杂项制品	Miscellaneous Manrfactured Articles
艺术品、收藏品及古物	Works of Art, Collector's Pieces and Antiques

Value of Expert Commodities by Category

(USD 10000)

2010	2011	2012	2013	2014	2014年比2013年增长(%) Increase Rate in 2014 over 2013(%)
192018	**298509**	**495223**	**688598**	**939726**	**36.5**
97	116	120	109	147	34.9
457	721	1620	1786	2971	66.3
413	335	295	321	195	-39.3
17476	20772	26934	23871	25174	5.5
12790	11185	13313	14074	14690	4.4
100049	171897	129288	81290	134626	65.6
19117	28879	53324	77174	84378	9.3
44	419	17137	31400	29758	-5.2
52	3	206	607	2072	241.4
107	144	5403	15830	21127	33.5
994	1635	45892	67867	144816	113.4
128	164	17649	30953	43120	39.3
2201	5906	24899	62294	63551	2.0
4	5	44	1238	5701	360.5
6415	10858	38193	67344	87861	30.5
28060	37541	50648	72093	118467	64.3
2137	2451	8196	10997	15290	39.0
333	577	4872	8997	11582	28.7
1144	4796	56868	119590	131642	10.1
	105	322	763	710	-6.9

6-5 海关进口商品分类

Value of Import Commodities by category

单位：万美元 (USD 10000)

指 标	Item	2010	2011	2012	2013	2014	2014年比2013年增长(%) Increase Rate in 2014over 2013(%)
总 计	**Total**	**122662**	**190249**	**167933**	**140411**	137407	**-2.1**
#活动物；动物产品	Live Animals;Animal Products		0.36	282	140	1	-99.3
植物产品	Vegetable Products	30	21	96	365	1756	381.1
动、植物油、脂及分解品；精制的食用油脂；动、植物蜡	Animal or Vegetable Fats and Oils and their Cleavage Products; Prepared Edible Fats; Animal or Vegetable Waxes		0.01	1			
食品；饮料、酒及醋；烟草及烟草代用品的制品	Prepared Foodstuffs; Beverages,Spirits And Vinegar;Tobacco and Manufactured Tobacco Substitutes	13	18	54	38	60	57.9
矿产品	Mineral Products	73337	135384	118523	94334	84089	-10.9
化学工业及其相关工业的产品	Products of The Chemical or Industries Allied	1712	1471	1713	1682	2975	76.9
塑料及其产品；橡胶及其产品	Plastics and Articles Thereof Rubber and Articles Thereof	25366	28578	22983	17508	15789	-9.8
生皮、皮革、毛皮及其制品；鞍具及挽具；旅行用品、手提包及类似品；动物肠线（蚕胶丝除外）制品	Raw Hides and Skins, Leather, Fur Skins and Articles Thereof; Saddlery and Harness; Travel Goods, Handbags and Similar Containers; Articles of Animal Gut (Other Than Silk-Worm Gut)		4	9	26	24	-7.7
木及木制品；木炭；软木及软木制品；稻草、秸秆、针茅或其他编结材料制品；篮筐及柳条编结品	Wood and Articles of Wood; Wood Charcoal; Cork and Articles of Cork; Manufactures of Straw, of Esparto or of Other Plaiting aterials; Basket Ware and Wickerwork		15	5		441	
木浆及其他纤维状纤维素浆；纸及纸板的废碎品；纸、纸板及其制品	Pulp of Wood or of Other Fibrous Cellulosic Material; Waste and Scrap of Paper or perboard; Paper and Paperboard and Articles Thereof	382	849	412	402	487	21.1
纺织原料及纺织制品	Textiles and Textile Articles Silk	19	65	328	761	443	-41.8
鞋、帽、伞、杖、鞭及其零件；已加工的羽毛及其制品；人造花；人发制品	Footwear, Headgear, Umbrellas, Sun Umbrellas, Walking-Sticks, Seat-Sticks, Whips, Riding-Crops and Parts Thereof; Prepared Feathers and Articles Made Therewith; Artificial Flowers; Articles of Human Hair		8		33	2	-93.9

6-5 续表 continued

单位：万美元 (USD 10000)

指 标	Item	2010	2011	2012	2013	2014	2014年比2013年增长(%) Increase Rate in 2014 over 2013(%)
石料、石膏、水泥、石棉、云母及类似材料的制品；陶瓷产品；玻璃及其制品	Articles of Stone, Plaster, Cement,Asbestos, Mica or Similar Materials;Ceramic Products; Glass and Glassware	210	62	50	33	15	-54.5
天然或养殖珍珠、宝石或半宝石、贵金属、包贵金属及其制品；仿首饰；硬币	Natural or Cultured Pearls,Precious or Semi-Precious Stones,Precious Metals,Metals Clad With Precious Metal and Stones, Precious Metals,Metals Clad With Precious Metal and Articles Thereof;Imitation Jewellery;Coin		2	38	20	2	-90.0
贱金属及其制品	Base Metals and Articles of Base Metal	6079	7308	2870	2748	1361	-50.5
机器、机械器具、电气设备及其零件；录音机及放声机、电视图象、声音的录制和重放设备及其零件、附件	Machinery and Mechanical Appliances; Electrical Equipment; Parts Thereof; Sound Recorders and Reproducers, Television Image and Sound Recorders and Reproducers; and Parts and Accessories of Recorders and Reproducers; and Parts and Accessories of Such Artic	10629	10552	15409	16938	23888	41.0
车辆、航空器、船舶及有关运输设备	Vehicles, Aircraft, Vessels And Associated Transport Equipment	2311	1769	642	947	305	-67.8
光学、照相、电影、计量、检验、医疗或外科用仪器及设备、精密仪品及设备；钟表；乐器；上述物品的零件、附件	Optical, Photographic, Cinematographic, Measuring, Checking, Precision, Medical or Surgical Instruments and Apparatus; Clocks And Watches; Musical Instruments; Parts and Accessories Thereof	2550	3904	4496	4393	3705	-15.7
杂项制品	Miscellaneous Manufactured Articles	24	239	22	41	27	-34.1
艺术品、收藏品及古物	Works of Art, Collectors' Pieces and Antiques					1	

6-6 利用外资
Foreign Capital Absorbed

指 标	Item	2010	2011	2012	2013	2014
项目数(个)	**Number of Signed Contracts(unit)**	**42**	**70**	**53**	**149**	**172**
#直接利用外资	Direct Foreign Investment	37	66	53	75	67
合资企业	Joint Venture	4	26	22	20	26
合作经营企业	Cooperative Venture	7	6		4	2
独资企业	Sole-foreign Enterprise	26	34	31	51	39
签订合同金额(万美元)	**Contracted Foreign Capital(USD 10000)**	**45024**	**170785**	**57383**	**118021**	**338663**
#直接利用外资	Direct Foreign Investment	45024	170785	57383	118021	338663
合资企业	Joint Venture	8591	73566	37868	22423	71500
合作经营企业	Cooperative Venture	5486	9922	240	6163	17972
独资企业	Sole-foreign Enterprise	30947	87297	19275	89435	249191
实际利用外资额(万美元)	**Foreign Capital Actually Absorbed(USD 10000)**	**34026**	**71674**	**109805**	**157415**	**213053**
#直接利用外资	Direct Foreign Investment	29546	51541	49116	57673	46565
合资企业	Joint Venture	8885	23856	17845	14979	8800
合作经营企业	Cooperative Venture	73	657	320		817
独资企业	Sole-Foreign Enterprise	20588	27028	30951	42694	36948
外商投资企业基本情况	**Registered Foreign-funded Enterprise**					
年末实有外商投资法人企业(户)	Number of Foreign-funded Enterprises at the year-end(unit)	603	644	686	740	594
#本年登记户数(户)	Number of Registered Enterprises at the year-end(unit)	31	46	46	77	60
投资总额(万美元)	Total Investment(USD 10000)	413189	568345	766967	969886	1547158
注册资本(万美元)	Registered Capital(USD 10000)	250964	321179	419657	523496	775630
#外 方	Capital from Foreign Partners	186005	255181	329321	423032	612198

注：1.资料来源于省发展改革委、省商务厅。2.2011年起实际利用外资统计口径变化，除直接利用外资外，还包括外商投资企业投注差外债实际到位资金和外商投资企业境内投资实际到位资金两部分(以下相关表同)。

Note:1.Data in this table are obtained from the Provincial Development and Reform Commission and the Provincial Department of Commerce.

2.From 2011, the statistical caliber of actual utilization of foreign capital has changed, which in addition to the direct use of foreign capital, including FIEs bets poor external debt actual funds and foreign-invested enterprises in the territory of actual funds invested in two parts as well (the same applies to the relative tables below).

6−7 外商直接投资按行业分项目个数

Number of Projects for Contracted Foreign Direct Investment by Sector

单位：个 (unit)

行 业	Sector	2010	2011	2012	2013	2014
总 计	**Total**	**37**	**66**	**53**	**75**	**67**
#农、林、牧、渔业	Agriculture,Forestry,Animal Husbandry and Fishery	6	6	11	9	11
采矿业	Mining	2	2	3	1	1
制造业	Manufacturing	8	16	20	28	17
电力、热力、燃气及水生产和供应业	Production and Supply of Electricity, Hear, Gas and Water	1	7	3	8	4
建筑业	Construction	1	2	1	1	
交通运输、仓储和邮政业	Transport, Storage and Post	3		1	1	1
信息传输、软件和信息服务业	Information Transmission, Software and Information Technology	1	1		1	
批发和零售业	Wholesale and Retail Trades	7	7	3	9	8
住宿和餐饮业	Hotels and Catering Services	2		2		2
金融业	Financial Intermediation	1	2			4
房地产业	Real Estate		5	1	3	4
租赁和商务服务业	Leasing and Business Services	3	10	6	8	6
科学研究和技术服务业	Scientific Research and Technical Service	1	3		1	1
水利、环境和公共设施管理业	Management of Water Conservancy, Environment and Public Facilities	1	3	1	3	6
居民服务、修理和其他服务业	Services to Households, Repair and Other Services		1		2	1
文化、体育和娱乐业	Culture, Sports and Entertainment		1			1
公共管理、社会保障和社会组织	Public Management, Social security and Social Organization			1		

6−8 按行业分外商直接投资协议金额

Agreement Value of Foreign Direct Investment by Sector

单位：万美元 (USD 10000)

行 业	Sector	2010	2011	2012	2013	2014
总 计	**Total**	**45024**	**170785**	**57383**	**118021**	**338663**
农、林、牧、渔业	Agriculture,Forestry,Animal Husbandry and Fishery	12736	8666	5783	11277	8296
采矿业	Mining	1235	1875	3677	-530	58434.7
制造业	Manufacturing	16014	55293	23779	67099	94074
电力、热力、燃气及水的生产和供应业	Production and Supply of Electricity, Hear, Gas and Water	500	15492	3068	15072	52284
建筑业	Construction	20	12083	142	-1952	3740
交通运输、仓储和邮政业	Transport, Storage and Post	3857		8053	350	2966
信息传输、软件和信息技术服务业	Information Transmission, Software and Information Technology	100	500		-68	11800
批发和零售业	Wholesale and Retail Trades	1808	6512	-1160	1576	15155
住宿和餐饮业	Hotels and Catering Services	1720	-8	155		248
金融业	Financial Intermediation	1000	5142	510		55894
房地产业	Real Estate	697	24520	483	7510	13036
租赁和商务服务业	Leasing and Business Services	2103	27913	12314	3517	5316
科学研究和技术服务业	Scientific Research and Technical Service	1951	7118		500	-2020
水利、环境和公共设施管理业	Management of Water Conservancy, Environment and Public Facilities	500	3993	64	13183	19425
居民服务、修理和其他服务业	Services to Households, Repair and Other Services		304		487	4
文化、体育和娱乐业	Culture, Sports and Entertainment	783	1382			10
公共管理、社会保障和社会组织	Public Management, Social security and Social Organization			515		

6-9 按行业分外商实际直接投资额

Actually Used Amount of Foreign Direct Investment by Sector

单位：万美元 (USD 10000)

指　标	Item	2010	2011	2012	2013	2014
总　计	**Total**	**29546**	**51541**	**49116**	**57673**	**46565**
#农、林、牧、渔业	Agriculture,Forestry,Animal Husbandry and Fishery	4300	8200	755	2009	3266
采矿业	Mining	905	737	450	4	1644
制造业	Manufacturing	14318	20078	5179	24528	17000
电力、热力、燃气及水的生产和供应业	Production and Supply of Electricity, Hear, Gas and Water		7330	8188	10173	5809
建筑业	Construction		21	5328	9	
交通运输、仓储和邮政业	Transport, Storage and Post		3006			
信息传输、软件和信息技术服务业	Information Transmission, Software and Information Technology			500	32	
批发和零售业	Wholesale and Retail Trades	368	1172	2526	1342	1447
住宿和餐饮业	Hotels and Catering Services	15		103	50	
金融业	Financial Intermediation	1000				
房地产业	Real Estate	3125	2272	22484	4218	12701
租赁和商务服务业	Leasing and Business Services	3385	6327	548	7554	1743
科学研究和技术服务业	Scientific Research and Technical Service	2120	1985	2991		
水利、环境和公共设施管理业	Management of Water Conservancy, Environment and Public Facilities			64	7485	2955
居民服务、修理和其他服务业	Services to Households, Repair and Other Services	10	313		163	
教育	Culture, Sports and Entertainment				16	
文化、体育和娱乐业	Public Management, Social security and Social Organization		100		90	

6-10 对外经济合作

Economic Cooperation with Foreign Countries or Regions

指　标	Item	2010	2011	2012	2013	2014
境外经济合作	**Economic Cooperation with Foreign Countries or Territories**					
签订合同项目(个)	Number of Contracts(unit)	24	25	22	23	43
#对外承包工程	Contracted Projects	24	25	22	23	43
签订合同金额(万美元)	Value of Contracts(USD 10000)	32431	29649	21430	16897	61792
#对外承包工程	Contracted Projects	32431	29649	21430	16897	61792
实际营业额(万美元)	Actual Turnover(USD 10000)	22003	30015	40007	45940	60166
#对外承包工程	Contracted Projects	22003	30015	40007	45940	50129
年末在外人员(人)	Persons in Abroad(year-end)(person)	1789	1938	2442	1615	2114
#对外承包工程	Contracted Projects	1789	1926	2442	1615	2114
省外经济合作	**Economic Cooperation with Other Provinces**					
引进省外项目(个)	Number of Contracted Projects(unit)	2640	4637	2368	2325	2341
引进省外资金(亿元)	Contracted Value(100 million yuan)	992	2580	3857	5017	6271

注：表中数据不含铝镁设计院及国内国际标的项目。

Note: Data in the table don't contain bidding projects of the Magnesium and Design Institute and the domestic and international.

主要统计指标解释

进出口总额 指实际进出我国国境并引起我国物质资源存量增加或者减少的货物金额。包括我国国境内法人和其他组织、个人进出口的一般贸易、易货贸易、加工贸易、补偿贸易、保税区和保税仓库进出境货物、国际援助物资或捐赠品。我国规定出口货物按离岸价格统计，进口货物按到岸价格统计。

外商直接投资 指外国企业和经济组织或个人（包括华侨、港澳台胞以及我国在境外注册的企业）按我国有关政策、法规，用现汇、实物、技术等在我国境内开办外商独资企业、与我国境内的企业或经济组织共同举办中外合资经营企业、合作经营企业或合作开发资源的投资（包括外商投资收益的再投资），以及经政府有关部门批准的项目投资总额内企业从境外借入的资金。

对外承包工程 指各对外承包公司以招标议标承包方式承揽的下列业务：(1)承包国外工程建设项目，(2)承包我国对外经援项目，(3)承包我国驻外机构的工程建设项目，(4)承包我国境内利用外资进行建设的工程项目，(5)与外国承包公司合营或联合承包工程项目时我国公司分包部分，(6)对外承包兼营的房屋开发业务。对外承包工程的营业额是以货币表现的本期内完成的对外承包工程的工作量，包括以前年度签订的合同和本年度新签订的合同在报告期内完成的工作量。

Explanatory Notes on Main Statistical Indicators

Total imports and exports refer to the actual cause of out of our borders and the stock of material resources to increase or decrease the amount of goods, including my own country legal persons and other organizations, individuals, import and export of general trade, barter trade, processing trade, compensation trade, bonded and bonded warehouse entry and exit of goods, international aid or donations. China provides export goods at FOB, CIF value of imported goods according to statistics.

Foreign Direct Investment refers to the investments inside China by foreign enterprises and economic organizations or individuals (including overseas Chinese, compatriots from Hong Kong, Macao and Taiwan, and Chinese enterprises registered abroad), following the relevant policies and laws of China, for the establishment of ventures exclusively with foreign own investment, Sino-foreign joint ventures and cooperative enterprises or for co-operative exploration of resources with enterprises or economic organizations in China. It includes the re- investment of the foreign entrepreneurs with the profits gained from the investment and the funds that enterprises borrow from abroad in the total investment of projects which are approved by the relevant department of the government.

Overseas Contracted Project refers to projects undertaken by Chinese contractors (project contracting companies) through bidding process. They include: (1) overseas civil engineering construction projects financed by foreign investors; (2) overseas projects financed by the Chinese government through its foreign aid programs; (3) construction projects of Chinese diplomatic missions, trade offices and other institutions stationed abroad; (4) construction projects in China financed by foreign investment; (5) sub-contracted projects to be taken by Chinese contractors through a joint umbrella project with foreign contractor(s); (6) housing development projects. The business income from international contracted projects is the work volume of contracted projects completed during the reference period, expressed in monetary terms, including completed work on projects signed in previous years.

7 能源

Energy

7-1 能源生产、消费总量及构成
Total Production and Consumption of Energy and Its Composition

单位：万吨标准煤 (10000 tons of SCE)

指 标	Item	2010	2011	2012	2013	2014
一、绝对数	**Absolute Figure**					
一次能源生产总量	Total Production of Primary Energy	13100.00	12739.97	14932.17	14404.15	15136.11
#原 煤	Coal	11778.54	11642.93	13264.62	12881.58	12933.72
水 电	Hydro-power	1321.46	1097.04	1667.56	1522.57	2181.11
能源终端消费总量	Final Consumption of Energy	7373.10	8359.80	9156.04	8715.49	9015.18
#原 煤	Coal	3538.23	4079.55	4390.45	3332.22	3417.21
天然气	Natural Gas	55.71	53.05	62.08	109.99	118.10
电 力	Electricity	2457.22	2777.89	3031.64	3257.13	3346.96
二、构成(%)	**Composition(%)**					
一次能源生产总量	Total Production of Primary Energy	100.0	100.0	100.0	100.0	100.0
#原 煤	Coal	89.9	91.4	88.8	89.4	85.5
水 电	Hydro-power	10.1	8.6	11.2	10.6	14.4
能源终端消费总量	Final Consumption of Energy	100.0	100.0	100.0	100.0	100.0
#原 煤	Coal	48.0	48.8	48.0	38.2	37.9
天然气	Natural Gas	0.8	0.6	0.7	1.3	1.3
电 力	Electricity	33.3	33.2	33.1	37.4	37.1

注：1.电力、热力按等价热值折算。2.2013—2014年数据根据第三次经济普查资料进行修订(以下各表同)。

Note: 1.Electric power and heating pouer are converted on the basic of equal caloric value. 2.The data for 2013 to 2014 has been adjusted according to the third economy census (The same as in the following tables).

7−2 综合能源平衡表
Overall Energy Balance Sheet

单位：万吨标准煤 (10000 tons of SCE)

指　标	Item	2010	2011	2012	2013	2014
可供消费的能源总量	**Total Energy Available for Consumption**	**8237.33**	**9551.40**	**10082.26**	**9405.14**	**9802.02**
一次能源生产量	Primary Energy Output	13100.00	12739.97	14932.17	14404.15	15136.11
省外调入	Inflow from Other Provinces	769.65	1040.78	1000.35	1339.15	1302.67
调出省外(一)	Outflow from Guizhou Province(一)	5827.75	4028.72	5729.88	6344.93	6120.25
年初年末库存差额	Stock Changes in the Year	48.17	-200.62	-121.04	6.78	-519.35
能源消费总量	**Total Energy Consumption**	**8175.43**	**9067.85**	**9878.38**	**9298.54**	**9708.78**
在总量中：	Consumption by Sector					
农、林、牧、渔、水利业	Agriculture Forestry,Animal Husbandry, Fishery and Water Conservancy	141.96	129.52	127.17	136.16	146.86
工　业	Industry	5289.48	5895.88	6431.08	5452.49	5529.57
建筑业	Construction	82.51	76.13	85.00	113.37	138.49
交通运输、仓储和邮政业	Transport,Storage and Post	538.48	597.73	706.39	665.41	711.87
批发、零售业和住宿、餐饮业	Wholesale and Retail Trades, Hotels and Catering Services	513.29	554.60	662.18	831.99	816.29
其　他	Others	614.04	675.13	581.22	957.24	1102.53
生活消费	Household Consumption	995.67	1138.87	1285.34	1141.89	1263.19
在总量中：	Consumption by Usage					
终端消费	End-use Consumption	7373.10	8359.80	9156.04	8715.49	9015.18
#工　业	Industry	4487.15	5187.82	5708.78	4869.44	4835.96
加工转换损失量	Losses During the Process of Energy Conversion	577.64	484.95	465.90	354.31	386.07
#炼　焦	Coking	80.12	67.93	106.40	86.22	76.81
损失量	Energy Losses	224.69	223.10	256.44	228.74	307.53
平衡差额	**Balance**	**61.90**	**483.55**	**203.88**	**106.60**	**93.25**

7-3 煤炭平衡表
Coal Balance Sheet

单位：万吨 (10000 tons)

指 标	Item	2010	2011	2012	2013	2014
可供量	**Total Energy Available for Consumption**	**11230.30**	**12738.14**	**13568.87**	**13717.84**	**13279.50**
生产量	Output	15954.02	15601.02	18107.05	18517.78	18508.29
调出省外(一)	Outflow from Guizhou Province(一)	4993.21	2812.84	4221.14	5137.04	4816.78
年初年末库存差额	Stock Changes in the Year	269.49	-217.46	-485.23	-11.36	-701.08
消费量	**Total Energy Consumption**	**11177.47**	**12084.97**	**13327.63**	**13650.74**	**13117.60**
在消费量中:	Consumption by Sector					
农、林、牧、渔、水利业	Agriculture Forestry,Animal Husbandry, Fishery and Water Conservancy	132.66	115.69	131.04	152.84	164.00
工 业	Industry	9415.02	10145.51	11057.47	10802.63	10118.51
建筑业	Construction	24.67	20.26	20.00	27.69	26.83
交通运输、仓储和邮政业	Transport,Storage and Post	14.06	15.16	42.76	80.86	68.00
批发、零售业和住宿、餐饮业	Wholesale and Retail Trades, Hotels and Catering Services	463.13	510.90	695.00	976.06	945.42
其 他	Others	503.30	563.10	504.14	928.36	1033.87
生活消费	Household Consumption	624.63	714.36	877.22	682.30	760.97
在消费量中:	Consumption by Usage					
终端消费	End-use Consumption	3976.62	4779.70	5808.55	5211.62	5710.81
#工 业	Industry	2214.17	2840.74	3538.39	2363.51	2711.72
中间消费(用于加工转换)	Intermediate Consumption (Consumed in Conversion)	7165.85	7265.27	7464.08	8439.12	7406.79
#发 电	Power Generation	4913.10	5557.29	5391.75	5714.04	4931.64
炼 焦	Coking	1005.61	948.43	1034.10	1198.30	1028.31
损失量	Losses in Coal Washing and Dressing	35.00	40.00	55.00		
平衡差额	**Balance**	**52.83**	**653.17**	**241.24**	**67.10**	**161.90**

7-4 电力平衡表
Electricity Balance Sheet

单位：亿千瓦小时 (100 million kwh)

指 标	Item	2010	2011	2012	2013	2014
可供量	**Total Energy Available for Consumption**	**835.52**	**944.13**	**1046.72**	**1128.02**	**1173.73**
生产量	Output	1385.64	1372.87	1610.89	1678.10	1747.71
水 电	Hydropower	416.58	348.88	537.30	492.70	700.52
火 电	Thermal Power	969.06	1023.99	1073.59	1185.40	1047.19
调出省外(一)	Outflow from Guizhou Province(一)	550.40	428.74	564.17	550.08	573.98
消费量	**Total Energy Consumption**	**835.52**	**944.13**	**1046.72**	**1128.02**	**1173.73**
在消费量中：	Consumption by Sector					
农、林、牧、渔、水利业	Agriculture Forestry,Animal Husbandry, Fishery and Water Conservancy	4.22	3.89	3.95	4.51	4.83
工 业	Industry	639.64	715.53	782.96	851.90	864.37
建筑业	Construction	11.10	10.33	13.33	16.87	20.36
交通运输、仓储和邮政业	Transport,Storage and Post	22.71	25.94	26.26	21.89	24.35
批发、零售业和住宿、餐饮业	Wholesale and Retail Trades, Hotels and Catering Services	12.42	14.80	18.72	21.48	25.09
其 他	Others	23.26	28.58	31.53	36.65	43.35
生活消费	Household Consumption	122.17	145.06	169.98	174.72	191.38
在消费量中：	Consumption by Usage					
终端消费	End-use Consumption	774.62	883.42	976.82	1054	1074.96
#工 业	Industry	578.74	654.82	713.06	777.88	765.60
输配损失量	Losses in Transmission	60.90	60.71	69.90	74.02	98.77

7-5 分行业能源消费总量(2010-2011)

Total Energy Consumption by Sector

单位：万吨标准煤 (10000 tons of SCE)

行业	Sector	2010	2011
工业	Industry	5289.48	5895.87
采掘业	Mining	751.50	685.36
#煤炭采选业	Mining and Washing of Coal	682.81	606.00
黑色金属矿采选业	Mining and Processing of Ferrous Metal Ores	9.58	9.85
有色金属矿采选业	Mining and Processing of Non-Ferrous Metal Ores	14.08	16.91
非金属矿采选业	Mining and Processing of Non-metal Ores	22.03	27.37
制造业	Manufacturing	4028.50	4733.39
农副食品加工业	Processing of Food from Agricultural Products	12.76	14.23
食品制造业	Manufacture of Foods	9.41	13.13
饮料制造业	Manufacture of Beverages	50.43	73.72
烟草加工业	Manufacture of Tobacco	22.07	20.51
纺织业	Manufacture of Textile	2.60	2.73
服装及其他纤维制品制造业	Manufacture of Garments and Other Fiber Products	1.12	1.43
皮革、毛皮、羽绒及其制品业	Manufacture of Leather, Fur, Feather and Related Products	0.16	0.21
木材加工及竹、藤、棕、草制品业	Processing of Timber, Manufacture of Wood, Bamboo, Rattan, Palm and Straw Products	6.43	7.50
家具制造业	Manufacture of Furniture	0.33	0.42
造纸及纸制品业	Manufacture of Paper and Paper Products	10.69	25.27
印刷业,记录媒介的复制	Printing, Reproduction of Recording Media	1.75	1.66
文教体育用品制造业	Cultural,Educational and Sports Articles	0.31	0.49
石油加工及炼焦业	Processing of Petroleum, Coking	127.21	207.44
化学原料及化学制品制造业	Manufacture of Raw Chemical Materials and Chemical Products	1000.00	1189.63
医药制造业	Manufacture of Medicines	13.94	18.56

注：表中数据按国民经济行业分类(GB/T4754-2002)分。

Note:Data in this table is classified by sector of the National Economy (GB/T4754-2002).

7−5 续表 continued

行　业	Sector	2010	2011
化学纤维制造业	Manufacture of Chemical Fibres	22.27	14.06
橡胶制品业	Manufacture of Rubber	51.82	54.92
塑料制品业	Manufacture of Plastics	9.87	9.17
非金属矿物制品业	Manufacture of Non-metallic Mineral Products	870.29	945.45
黑色金属冶炼及压延加工业	Smelting and Pressing of Ferrous Metals	955.29	1066.28
有色金属冶炼及压延加工业	Smelting and Pressing of Non-ferrous Metals	759.11	943.84
金属制品业	Manufacture of Metal Products	28.22	36.74
普通机械制造业	Manufacture of Ordinary Machinery	17.00	17.34
专用设备制造业	Manufacture of Special Purpose Machinery	7.72	7.71
交通运输设备制造业	Manufacture of Transport Equipment	16.74	17.54
电气机械及器材制造业	Manufacture of Electrical Machinery and Equipment	2.35	3.75
电子及通信设备制造业	Manufacture of Electronic and Telecommunications Equipment	1.69	2.64
仪器仪表及文化、办公用机械制造业	Manufacture of Measuring Instruments and Machinery for Cultural Activity	0.27	0.27
其他制造业	Others	26.65	36.74
电力、煤气及水的生产和供应业	Electric Power, Gas and Water Production and Supply	509.49	477.12
电力、蒸汽、热水的生产和供应业	Production and Supply of Electric Power and Heat Power	471.33	437.02
煤气生产和供应业	Production and Supply of Gas	26.14	26.59
自来水的生产和供应业	Production and Supply of Water	12.02	13.51
建筑业	**Construction**	**82.51**	**76.13**
交通运输、仓储和邮政业	Transport,Storage and Post	538.48	597.73
批发、零售业和住宿、餐饮业	Wholesale and Retail Trades, Hotels and Catering Services	513.29	554.60
其他行业	Others	614.04	675.13
生活消费	Household Consumption	995.67	1138.87

7-6 分行业能源消费总量(2012-2014)
Total Energy Consumption by Sector

单位：万吨标准煤 (10000 tons of SCE)

行 业	Sector	2012	2013	2014
工业	**Industrial**	**6431.08**	**5452.49**	**5529.57**
采矿业	Mining	565.37	616.66	613.17
#煤炭开采和洗选业	Mining and Washing of Coal	536.75	520.68	517.93
黑色金属矿采选业	Mining and Processing of Ferrous Metal Ores	13.89	11.65	9.53
有色金属矿采选业	Mining and Processing of Non-Ferrous Metal Ores	5.85	16.52	16.28
非金属矿采选业	Mining and Processing of Non-metal Ores	8.88	38.13	39.09
制造业	Manufacturing	5209.02	4168.82	4313.53
#农副食品加工业	Processing of Food from Agricultural Products	18.13	20.97	21.83
食品制造业	Manufacture of Foods	10.48	16.24	18.47
酒、饮料和精制茶制造业	Manufacture of Beverages	66.06	42.98	46.27
烟草制品业	Manufacture of Tobacco	18.18	18.29	20.10
纺织业	Manufacture of Textile	0.95	1.98	4.18
纺织服装、服饰业	Manufacture of Textile Wearing Apparel, Footware and Caps	0.67	1.50	0.99
皮革、毛皮、羽毛及其制品和制鞋业	Manufacture of Leather,Furs,Feather and Related Products	1.45	1.24	0.58
木材加工和木、竹、藤、棕、草制品业	Timber Processing,Manufacture of Wood, Bamboo, Rattan,Palm and Straw Products	5.98	11.17	13.81
家具制造业	Manufacture of Furniture	0.26	2.30	3.32
造纸和纸制品业	Manufacture of Paper and Paper Products	29.23	28.85	27.33
印刷业和记录媒介复制业	Printing,Reproduction of Recording Media	0.70	3.93	5.19
文教、工美、体育和娱乐用品制造业	Manufacture of Culture and ducation,Industrial, Sports,and Entertainment Products	0.58	0.92	0.98

注：表中数据按国民经济行业分类(GB/T4754-2011)分。
Note:Data in this table is classified by sector of the National Economy Industry(GB/T4754-2011).

7-6 续表 continued

单位：万吨标准煤 (10000 tons of SCE)

行 业	Sector	2012	2013	2014
石油加工、炼焦和核燃料加工业	Processing of Petroleum,Coking,Processing of Nuclear Fuel	335.63	229.98	253.35
化学原料和化学制品制造业	Manufacture of Raw Chemical Materials and Chemical Products	1349.97	771.43	773.68
医药制造业	Manufacture of Medicines	15.88	17.48	17.34
化学纤维制造业	Manufacture of Chemical fiber	7.69	6.01	6.24
橡胶和塑料制品业	Manufacture of Rubber and Plastics	251.57	29.55	23.43
非金属矿物制品业	Manufacture of Non-metallic Mineral Products	1249.33	701.30	713.99
黑色金属冶炼和压延加工业	Smelting and Pressing of Ferrous Metals	1283.58	1068.62	1089.57
有色金属冶炼和压延加工业	Smelting and Pressing of Non-ferrous Metals	500.51	1008.61	1025.73
金属制品业	Manufacture of Metal Products	4.44	88.33	117.41
通用设备制造业	Manufacture of General Purpose Machinery	19.91	12.93	13.58
专用设备制造业	Manufacture of Special Purpose Machinery	5.18	9.34	11.08
汽车制造业	Manufacture of Automotive	11.87	9.94	15.63
铁路、船舶、航空航天和其他运输设备制造业	Manufacture of Railroad, Marine, Aerospace and Other Transportation Equipment	9.34	17.44	12.01
电气机械和器材制造业	Manufacture of Electrical Machinery and Equipment	3.74	3.84	3.05
计算机、通信和其他电子设备制造业	Manufacture of Communication Equipment, Computers and Other Electronic Equipment	0.90	2.47	1.78
仪器仪表制造业	Manufacture of Measuring Instruments and Machinery	0.96	0.88	2.15
其他制造业	Others	1.15	13.86	20.96
废弃资源综合利用业	Recycling and Disposal of Waste	4.72	10.99	18.37
金属制品、机械和设备修理业	Manufacture of Metal products, Machinery and Equipment Repair		15.45	31.14
电力、热力、燃气及水生产和供应业	Electric Power, Heat, Gas and Water Production and Supply	656.69	667.00	602.87
电力、热力生产和供应业	Production and Supply of Electric Power and Heat Power	630.71	615.82	563.37
燃气生产和供应业	Production and Supply of Gas	19.62	30.98	18.18
水的生产和供应业	Production and Supply of Water	6.35	20.20	21.32
建筑业	**Construction**	**85.00**	**113.37**	**138.48**
交通运输、仓储及邮政	Transportation,Storage,Postal & Telecommunications Services	706.39	665.41	711.87
批发、零售业和住宿、餐饮业	Wholesale,Retail Trade and Catering Services	662.18	831.99	816.29
其他行业	Others	581.22	957.24	1102.53
生活消费	Household Consumption	1285.34	1141.89	1263.19

7-7 能源生产消费弹性系数

Elasticity Ratio of Energy Production and Consumption

指 标	Item	2010	2011	2012	2013	2014
地区生产总值比上年增长(%)	Growth Rate of Gross Domestic Product (GDP) over Preceding Year	12.8	15.0	13.6	12.5	10.8
能源生产比上年增长(%)	Growth Rate of Energy Production over Preceding Year	18.3	-2.8	17.2	-3.5	5.1
能源消费总量比上年增长(%)	Growth Rate of Energy Consumption over Preceding Year	8.1	10.9	8.9	8.1	4.4
电力生产比上年增长(%)	Growth Rate of Electricity Production over Preceding Year	0.4	-0.9	17.3	4.2	4.1
电力消费比上年增长(%)	Growth Rate of Electricity Consumption over Preceding Year	11.4	13.0	10.9	7.6	4.2
能源生产弹性系数	Elasticity Ratio of Energy Production	1.43		1.26		0.47
能源消费弹性系数	Elasticity Ratio of Energy Consumption	0.63	0.73	0.65	0.65	0.41
电力生产弹性系数	Elasticity Ratio of Electricity Production	0.03		1.27	0.33	0.38
电力消费弹性系数	Elasticity Ratio of Electricity Consumption	0.89	0.87	0.80	0.61	0.39

注：地区生产总值增长速度按可比价格计算。

Note:The growth rates of GDP are calculated at comparable prices.

7-8 生活能源消费量

Energy Consumption for Non-Production Purpose

能源品种	Item	2010	2011	2012	2013	2014
生活能源消费量(万吨标准煤)	**Energy Consumption for Non-Production Purpose (10000 tons of SCE)**	**995.67**	**1138.87**	**1285.34**	**1141.89**	**1263.19**
煤炭(万吨)	Coal (10000 tons)	624.63	714.36	877.22	682.30	760.97
煤油(万吨)	Kerosene (10000 tons)	0.04	0.04	0.05	0.06	…
液化石油气(万吨)	Liquefied Petroleum Gas (10000 tons)	8.82	9.55	8.49	6.57	10.84
天然气(亿立方米)	Natural Gas(100 million cu.m)	0.12	0.13	0.99	1.90	2.24
煤气(亿立方米)	Gas (100 million cu.m)	1.14	1.28	1.43	3.75	3.41
电力(亿千瓦小时)	Electricity (100 million kwh)	122.17	145.06	169.98	174.72	191.38

7－9 人均生活能源消费量
Annual Average per Capita Energy Consumption of Households

指 标	Item	2010	2011	2012	2013	2014
平均每人生活消费能源（千克标准煤／人）	**Annual Average Non-Productive Consumption Per Capita(kg of SCE/person)**	**287.26**	**327.83**	**369.73**	**326.89**	**360.38**
煤炭(千克)	Coal(kg)	180.21	205.63	252.33	195.32	217.10
电力(千瓦小时)	Electricity(kwh)	352.48	417.56	488.94	500.18	546.00
液化石油气(千克)	Liquefied Petroleum Gas(kg)	2.54	2.75	2.44	1.88	3.09
煤气(立方米)	Gas(cu.m)	3.29	3.68	4.11	10.74	9.73

7－10 能源利用效率
Using Efficiency of Energy

指标	Item	2010	2011	2012	2013	2014
每万元地区生产总值能源消费量(吨标准煤／万元)(可比价)	**Energy Consumption Per Unit of GDP (ton of SCE/10000 yuan) (at comparable prices)**	**2.2480**	**1.7140**	**1.6444**	**1.3762**	**1.2967**
每万元地区生产总值能耗上升或下降(%)	**Energy Consumption Rise or Fall Per Unit of GDP(%)**	**-4.25**	**-3.51**	**-4.06**	**-3.91**	**-5.78**
每万元地区生产总值电力消费量（千瓦小时／万元）	**Electricity Consumption Per Unit of GDP(kwh/10000 yuan)**	**2297.45**	**1784.56**	**1742.36**	**1666.57**	**1567.84**
每万元地区生产总值煤炭消费量(吨／万元)	**Coal Consumption Per Unit of GDP (ton/10000 yuan)**	**3.07**	**2.28**	**2.22**	**2.02**	**1.75**
能源消费总量(万吨标准煤)	Total Energy Consumption (10000 tons of SCE)	8175.43	9067.85	9878.38	9298.54	9708.78
每吨能源生产的地区生产总值(万元／吨标准煤)	GDP Produced by Per Unit of Energy (10000 yuan/ton)	0.44	0.58	0.61	0.47	0.49
规模以上工业能源消费量(万吨标准煤)	Energy Consumption of Industry above Designated Size(10000 tons of SCE)	4373.38	4803.14	5142.00	5759.90	5549.08
规模以上工业万元增加值能耗上升或下降(%)	Million yuan added value Energy Consumption Rise or Fall of Industry above Designated Size(%)	-10.00	-8.02	-8.52	-4.75	-13.39

注：2011年起，地区生产总值按2010年可比价格计算，2010年按2005年可比价格计算。

Note: From 2011, GDP has been calculated at 2010 comparable prices, and in the year of 2010 they were calculated at 2005 comparable prices.

主要统计指标解释

能源生产总量 指一定时期内全省一次能源生产量的总和。一次能源生产量包括原煤、原油、天然气、水电、核能及其他动力能(如风能、地热能等)发电量，不包括低热值燃料生产量、生物质能、太阳能等的利用和由一次能源加工转换而成的二次能源产量。

能源消费总量 指一定时期内全省各行业和居民生活消费的各种能源的核算能源消费总量指标。能源消费总量分为终端能源消费量、能源加工转换损失量和损失量三部分。

终端能源消费量：指一定时期内全省各行业和居民生活消费的各种能源在扣除了用于加工转换二次能源消费量和损失量以后的数量。

能源加工转换损失量：指一定时期内全省投入加工转换的各种能源数量之和与产出各种能源产品之和的差额，是观察能源在加工转换过程中损失量变化的指标。

能源损失量：指一定时期内能源在输送、分配、储存过程中发生的损失和由客观原因造成的各种损失量，不包括各种气体能源放空、放散量。

能源生产弹性系数 是能源生产量的增长与国民经济增长速度之间的比值。计算公式为：

$$\text{能源生产弹性系数}=\frac{\text{能源生产总量年平均增长速度}}{\text{地区生产总值年平均增长速度}}$$

电力生产弹性系数 是电力生产量的增长与国民经济增长速度之间的比值。计算公式为：

$$\text{电力生产弹性系数}=\frac{\text{电力生产量年平均增长速度}}{\text{地区生产总值年平均增长速度}}$$

能源消费弹性系数 是能源消费增长速度与国民经济增长速度之间的比值。计算公式为：

$$\text{能源消费弹性系数}=\frac{\text{能源消费量年平均增长速度}}{\text{地区生产总值年平均增长速度}}$$

电力消费弹性系数 是电力消费增长速度与国民经济增长速度之间的比值。计算公式为：

$$\text{电力消费弹性系数}=\frac{\text{电力消费量年平均增长速度}}{\text{地区生产总值年平均增长速度}}$$

每万元地区生产总值能源消耗量 指一定时期内，每生产一个计量单位的生产总值所消耗的能源。计算公式为：

$$\text{每万元地区生产总值能源消耗量}=\frac{\text{能源消费总量}}{\text{地区生产总值}}$$

每万元地区生产总值电力消耗量 指一定时期内，每生产一个计量单位的生产总值所消耗的电力。计算公式为：

$$\text{每万元地区生产总值电力消耗量}=\frac{\text{全社会用电量}}{\text{地区生产总值}}$$

Explanatory Notes on Main Statistical Indicators

Total Energy Production refers to the total production of primary energy by all energy producing enterprises in the country in a given period of time. The production of primary energy includes that of coal, crude oil, natural gas, hydro-power and electricity generated by nuclear energy and other means such as wind power and geothermal power. However, it excludes the production of fuels of low calorific value, bio-energy, solar energy and the secondary energy converted from the primary energy.

Total Energy Consumption refers to the total consumption of energy of various kinds by the production sectors and the households in our province in a given period of time. Total energy consumption can be divided into three parts: end-use energy consumption; loss during the process of energy conversion; and energy loss.

End-use Energy Consumption: It refers to the total energy consumption by material production sectors, non material production sectors and households in the country(region)in a given period of time, but excludes the consumption in conversion of the primary energy into the secondary energy and the loss in the process of energy conversion.

Loss During the Process of Energy Conversion: It refers to the total input of various kinds of energy for conversion, minus the total output of various kinds of energy in the country in a given period of time. It is an indicator to show the loss that occurs during the process of energy conversion.

Loss: It refers to the total of the loss of energy during the course of energy transport, distribution and storage and the loss caused by any objective reason in a given period of time. The loss of various kinds of gas due to gas discharges and stocktaking is excluded.

Elasticity Ratio of Energy Production is an indicator to show the relationship between the growth rate of energy production and the growth rate of the national economy. The formula is:

$$\text{Elasticity Ratio of Energy Production} = \frac{\text{Average Annual Growth Rate of Energy Production}}{\text{Average Annual Growth Rate of National Economy}}$$

Elasticity Ratio of Electricity Production is an indicator to show the relationship between the growth rate of electricity production and the growth rate of the national economy. Its formula is:

$$\text{Elasticity Ratio of Electricity Production} = \frac{\text{Average Annual Growth Rate of Electricity Production}}{\text{Average Annual Growth Rate of National Economy}}$$

Elasticity Ratio of Energy Consumption is an indicator to show the relationship between the growth rate of energy consumption and the growth rate of the national economy. The formula is:

$$\text{Elasticity Ratio of Energy Consumption} = \frac{\text{Average Annual Growth Rate of Energy Consumption}}{\text{Average Annual Growth Rate of National Economy}}$$

Elasticity Ratio of Electricity Consumption is an indicator to show the relationship between the growth rate of electricity consumption and the growth rate of the national economy. The formula is:

$$\text{Elasticity Ratio of Electricity Consumption} = \frac{\text{Average Annual Growth Rate of Electricity Consumption}}{\text{Average Annual Growth Rate of National Economy}}$$

Energy Consumption per Unit of GDP(ton of SCE/10000 yuan) refers to the energy consumption per unit of Gross Domestic Product in a country or the Gross Regional Product in a region in the same reference period. The formula is:

$$\text{Energy Consumption per Unit of GDP} = \frac{\text{Total Energy Consumption}}{\text{Gross Domestic Product}}$$

Electricity Consumption per Unit of GDP(KWh/10000 yuan) refers to the electricity consumption per unit of Gross Domestic Product in a country or the Gross Regional Product in a region in the same reference period. The formula is:

$$\text{Electricity Consumption per Unit of GDP} = \frac{\text{Total Electricity Consumption}}{\text{Gross Domestic Product}}$$

贵州2015
统计年鉴
GUIZHOU
STATISTICAL YEARBOOK

财政税收

8

Government Finance and Taxation

8-1 财政收入
Financial Revenue

单位：亿元 (100 million yuan)

指　　标	Item	2010	2011	2012	2013	2014	2014年比2013年增长(%) Increase Rate in 2014 over 2013(%)
财政总收入	**Total Government Revenue**	**969.57**	**1329.99**	**1644.48**	**1918.23**	**2130.90**	**11.1**
#一般公共预算收入	General Public Financial Budget Revenue	533.73	773.08	1014.05	1206.41	1366.67	13.3
#增值税(含改征增值税)	Value Added Tax	66.00	76.41	85.74	96.06	117.03	21.8
营业税	Business Tax	136.73	181.73	241.53	300.78	344.49	14.5
企业所得税	Company Income Tax	51.14	70.69	86.53	103.15	123.84	20.1
个人所得税	Individual Income Tax	27.42	33.24	32.29	34.65	32.52	-6.1
资源税	Resource Tax	11.01	11.95	12.72	15.33	17.05	11.2
城市维护建设税	City Maintenance and Construction Tax	29.18	37.82	45.79	53.71	57.64	7.3
房产税	House Property Tax	8.41	9.73	11.60	17.13	23.43	36.8
契　税	Deed Tax	13.98	23.91	33.00	41.42	66.93	61.6
土地增值税	Land Appreciation Tax	11.98	13.76	19.07	29.41	64.64	119.8
国有资本经营收入	State-owned Capital Operating Income	4.88	6.38	7.21	10.97	12.91	17.7
罚没收入	Penalty Receipts	16.66	23.50	25.14	31.15	33.29	6.9
行政事业性收费	Charge of administrative and Institutional vnits	30.06	45.98	65.71	76.71	70.73	-7.8
专项收入	Special Program Receipts	59.07	85.91	84.85	73.84	65.08	-11.9

注：资料来源于省财政厅(以下相关表同)。
Note:Data in the table are provided by the Provincial Department of Finance(The relative tables in this chapter are the same).

8-2 财政支出
Financial Expenditure

单位：亿元 (100 million yuan)

指　　标	Item	2010	2011	2012	2013	2014	2014年比2013年增长(%) Increase Rate in 2014over 2013(%)
一般公共预算支出	**General Public Financial Budget Expenditure**	**1631.48**	**2249.40**	**2755.68**	**3082.66**	**3542.80**	**14.9**
#一般公共服务	Expenditure for General Public Services	212.69	307.21	430.16	488.78	422.49	-13.6
国　防	Expenditure for National Defense	3.66	4.15	4.58	4.74	5.25	10.7
公共安全	Expenditure for Public Security	101.46	117.31	146.21	168.22	187.97	11.7
教　育	Expenditure for Education	292.06	376.86	500.51	560.67	637.03	13.6
科学技术	Expenditure for Science and Technology	16.66	21.68	28.98	34.27	44.34	29.4
文化体育与传媒	Expenditure for Culture, Sport and Media	23.98	35.31	49.85	48.68	54.69	12.3
社会保障和就业	Expenditure for Social Safety Net and Employment Effort	140.76	194.78	235.40	264.52	299.72	13.3
医疗卫生与计划生育	Expenditure for Medical and health care and Family Planning	127.68	173.26	201.05	228.71	303.25	32.6
节能环保	Expenditure for Environment Protection	54.32	55.45	65.73	66.44	85.34	28.4
城乡社区	Expenditure for Urban and Rural Community Affairs	53.00	65.52	100.65	109.46	101.29	-7.5
农林水	Expenditure for Agriculture, Forestry and Water Conservancy	246.76	278.47	361.87	400.31	447.19	11.7
交通运输	Expenditure for Transportation	109.61	305.16	288.56	299.79	432.01	44.1

注：节能环保2010—2011年为环境保护数据。
Note:Data of energy saving refer to the data of environmental protection in 2010 to 2011.

8-3 分级一般公共预算收入(2014)

General Public Financial Budget Revenue by Level

单位：亿元 (100 million yuan)

指标	Item	总计 Provincial Total	省级 Province	地级 Prefecture	县级 County	乡镇级 Villages and Towns
一般公共预算收入	**General Public Financial Budget Revenue**	**1366.67**	**250.32**	**285.06**	**685.20**	**146.09**
税收收入	**Tax revenue**	**1026.70**	**190.18**	**221.40**	**478.69**	**136.43**
#增值税	Value Added Tax	117.03	24.97	33.90	46.54	11.62
营业税	Business Tax	344.49	89.46	77.72	136.29	41.03
企业所得税	Company Income Tax	123.84	61.82	21.87	32.04	8.12
个人所得税	Individual Income Tax	32.52	6.51	7.99	13.61	4.41
资源税	Resource Tax	17.05	3.41	3.56	5.57	4.51
城市维护建设税	City Maintenance and Construction Tax	57.64	0.34	23.00	28.64	5.66
房产税	House Property Tax	23.43		0.04	19.81	3.58
契税	Deed Tax	66.93		17.42	39.11	10.40
土地增值税	Land Appreciation Tax	64.64		4.62	52.04	7.98
非税收入	**Non-tax revenue**	**339.97**	**60.14**	**63.66**	**206.51**	**9.66**
#专项收入	Special Program Receipts	65.08	17.33	21.08	25.09	1.59
行政事业性收费	Charge of administrative and Institutional vnits	70.73	14.92	13.20	38.11	4.50
罚没收入	Penalty Receipts	33.29	5.75	8.50	18.42	0.62
国有资本经营收入	State-owned Capital Operating Income	12.91	0.01	2.14	10.76	

8-4 分级一般公共预算支出(2014)

General Public Financial Budget Expenditure by Level

单位：亿元 (100 million yuan)

指标	Item	总计 Total	省级 Province	地级 Prefecture	县级 County	乡镇级 Villages and Towns
一般公共预算支出	**General Public Financial Budget Expenditure**	**3542.80**	**874.84**	**393.47**	**2043.67**	**230.83**
#一般公共服务	Expenditure for General Public Services	422.49	43.66	49.46	248.44	80.93
国防	Expenditure for National Defense	5.25	0.71	2.80	1.72	0.02
公共安全	Expenditure for Public Security	187.97	47.47	34.44	104.30	1.76
教育	Expenditure for Education	637.03	75.74	54.82	487.18	19.29
科学技术	Expenditure for Science and Technology	44.34	15.41	6.83	21.65	0.44
文化体育与传媒	Expenditure for Culture, Sport and Media	54.69	14.62	11.18	26.61	2.29
社会保障和就业	Expenditure for Social Safety Net and Employment Effort	299.72	60.80	50.28	174.60	14.04
医疗卫生	Expenditure for Medical and health care and Family Planning	303.25	22.37	30.64	232.08	18.16
节能环保	Expenditure for Environment Protection	85.34	8.31	13.61	58.80	4.62
城乡社区事务	Expenditure for Urban and Rural Community Affairs	101.29	0.65	20.48	68.26	11.89
农林水事务	Expenditure for Agriculture, Forestry and Water Conservancy	447.19	69.78	24.74	292.31	60.36
交通运输	Expenditure for Transportation	432.01	385.73	16.20	29.38	0.70

8-5 税收收入(按产业分)

Tax Revenue(by Industry)

单位：亿元 (100million yuan)

指　　标	Item	2010	2011	2012	2013	2014
税收收入合计	**Total Tax Revenue**	**831.97**	**1072.87**	**1308.63**	**1546.50**	**1787.08**
第一产业	Primary Industry	1.26	1.20	1.63	2.42	3.07
第二产业	Secondary Industry	448.88	574.26	684.06	776.41	835.11
采矿业	Mining	118.05	142.59	152.21	130.72	115.92
制造业	Manufacturing	226.09	293.84	330.55	380.35	406.62
电力、燃气及水的生产和供应业	Production and supply of Electricity, gas and Water	60.65	59.42	70.72	74.70	71.86
建筑业	Construction	44.09	78.41	130.58	190.63	240.73
第三产业	Tertiary Industry	381.83	497.40	622.92	767.67	948.89
交通运输、仓储及邮政业	Transport,Storage and Post	16.10	19.04	19.13	20.31	19.35
信息传输、计算机服务和软件业	Information Transmission,Computer Services and Software	12.14	14.19	17.64	18.66	13.65
批发和零售业	Wholesale and Retail Trades	131.90	170.04	205.71	250.46	282.74
住宿和餐饮业	Hotel and Catering Services	7.21	9.05	10.45	10.23	9.79
金融业	Financial Intermediation	39.12	55.61	77.11	90.97	129.09
房地产业	Real Estate	94.64	138.36	137.09	174.32	217.77
租赁和商务服务业	Leasing and Business Services	17.59	24.01	37.52	49.40	83.62
科学研究和技术服务业	Scientific Reasearch and Technical Services			9.68	10.90	16.87
居民服务和其他服务业	Services to Households and Other Services	10.49	20.08	38.24	52.64	57.85
教　育	Education	1.14	1.45	1.54	2.34	2.78
卫生和社会工作	Health and Social Work	1.61	1.71	1.53	2.64	3.28
文化、体育和娱乐业	Culture,Sports and Entertainment	2.36	2.80	2.90	3.52	3.38
公共管理、社会保障和社会组织	Public Management and Social Organization	6.39	9.41	31.13	40.49	58.79
其他行业	Others	41.13	31.65	33.26	40.79	49.95

注：1.资料来源于省地税局、省国税局，地税包含耕地占用税、契税。2.2010—2011年按国民经济行业分类(GB/T4754—2002)分，2012年起按国民经济行业分类(GB/T4754—2011)分。(以下相关表同)

Note:1.Data in this table is provided by Guizhou Provincial National Taxation Beaura and Local Taxation Beaura of Guizhou Province. Land tax includes 2.From 2010 to 2011,data in this table is classified by sector of the National Economy(GB/T4754-2002). And form 2012,data in this table is classified by sector of the National Economy (GB/T4754-2011).(The relative tables in this chapter are the same)

8-6 税收收入(按企业类型分)

Taxation Revenue (by Business Entities)

单位：亿元 (100 million yuan)

指　　标	Item	2010	2011	2012	2013	2014
总　计	**Total**	**831.97**	**1072.87**	**1308.63**	**1546.50**	**1787.08**
内资企业	Domestic Enterprises	745.52	966.07	1188.71	1405.02	1637.36
国有企业	State-owned Enterprises	117.19	126.59	154.24	182.57	196.92
集体企业	Collective-owned Enterprises	12.57	15.17	19.31	18.40	20.87
股份合作企业	Cooperative Enterprises	7.67	11.52	14.61	12.26	16.54
联营企业	Joint Ownership Enterprises	0.78	0.87	0.88	0.78	0.91
#国有控股	State-owned and State-controlled Enterprises	0.10	0.48	0.32	0.08	0.05
股份公司	Share-holding Corporations Limited	474.28	636.01	824.87	1006.37	1193.25
#国有控股	State-owned and State-controlled Enterprises	177.53	274.39	316.77	411.32	444.02
私营企业	Private Enterprises	87.90	100.32	111.52	106.01	95.60
其它企业	Other Enterprises	45.14	75.57	63.28	78.63	113.28
港澳台投资企业	Funded from Hong Kong, Macao and Taiwan	5.01	5.30	7.47	11.22	14.35
#国有控股	State-owned and State-controlled Enterprises	0.12	0.46	0.26	0.28	0.19
外商投资企业	Foreign Funded Enterprises	21.03	24.70	19.42	20.75	21.87
#国有控股	State-owned and State-controlled Enterprises	0.27	2.71	1.49	1.20	1.80
个体经营	Individual Enterprises	60.41	76.79	93.03	109.51	113.50
附：乡(镇)企业	Township (town) Enterprises	35.23	48.93	82.53	93.83	110.67

8-7 国税税收收入(按产业分)
National Tax Revenue (by Industry)

单位：亿元 (100 million yuan)

指 标	Item	2010	2011	2012	2013	2014
税收收入合计	**Total Tax Revenue**	**458.13**	**568.60**	**647.79**	**729.65**	**805.65**
第一产业	Primary Industry	1.16	1.03	1.35	2.01	2.45
第二产业	Secondary Industry	312.66	382.23	422.69	458.69	479.05
采矿业	Mining	70.37	82.10	85.08	70.83	66.08
制造业	Manufacturing	189.93	250.64	279.55	324.39	351.67
电力、燃气及水的生产和供应业	Production and supply of Electricity, Gas and Water	50.66	47.18	54.28	59.70	55.92
建筑业	Construction	1.69	2.31	3.78	3.76	5.39
第三产业	Tertiary Industry	144.31	185.33	223.74	268.95	324.14
交通运输、仓储及邮政业	Transport,Storage and Post	2.48	3.05	2.33	6.84	12.59
信息传输、计算机服务和软件业	Information Transmission,Computer Services and Software	6.15	7.09	9.33	8.96	6.02
批发和零售业	Wholesale and Retail Trades	89.03	111.23	132.19	164.35	188.52
住宿和餐饮业	Hotel and Catering Services	0.12	0.17	0.23	0.18	0.15
金融业	Financial Intermediation	11.38	19.84	27.57	27.37	41.49
房地产业	Real Estate	10.73	13.99	15.30	12.23	11.56
租赁和商务服务业	Leasing and Business Services	1.87	2.25	1.29	2.96	6.20
科学研究和技术服务业	Scientific Research and Technical Services			2.62	3.00	6.26
居民服务和其他服务业	Services to Households and Other Services	0.78	0.89	1.54	1.83	2.17
教 育	Education	0.09	0.13	0.14	0.19	0.13
卫生、社会保险和社会福利业	Health,Social Security and Social Welfare	0.10	0.15	0.15	0.14	0.25
文化、体育和娱乐业	Culture,Sports and Entertainment	0.18	0.24	0.25	0.49	0.99
公共管理和社会组织	Public Management and Social Organization	2.14	3.91	4.44	4.51	3.42
其他行业	Others	19.24	22.38	26.36	35.90	44.40

注：资料来源于省国税局（以下相关表同）。
Note: Data in the table are provided by Guizhou Provincial National Taxation Beaura (the same applies to the next table).

8-8 地方系统税收收入(按产业分)
Local Tax Revenue(by Industry)

单位：亿元 (100 million yuan)

指 标	Item	2010	2011	2012	2013	2014
税收收入合计	**Total Tax Revenue**	**373.83**	**504.27**	**660.84**	**816.85**	**981.43**
第一产业	Primary Industry	0.10	0.17	0.28	0.41	0.62
第二产业	Secondary Industry	136.22	192.03	261.37	317.72	356.06
采矿业	Mining	47.68	60.49	67.13	59.89	49.84
制造业	Manufacturing	36.16	43.20	51.00	55.96	54.95
电力、燃气及水的生产和供应业	Production and supply of Electricity, Gas and Water	9.99	12.24	16.44	15.00	15.94
建筑业	Construction	42.39	76.10	126.80	186.87	235.34
第三产业	Tertiary Industry	237.52	312.07	399.18	498.72	624.75
交通运输、仓储及邮政业	Transport,Storage and Post	13.62	15.99	16.80	13.47	6.76
信息传输、计算机服务和软件业	Information Transmission, Computer Services	5.99	7.10	8.31	9.70	7.63
批发和零售业	Wholesale and Retail Trades	42.87	58.81	73.53	86.11	94.22
住宿和餐饮业	Hotel and Catering Services	7.09	8.88	10.22	10.05	9.64
金融业	Financial Intermediation	27.73	35.77	49.54	63.60	87.60
房地产业	Real Estate	83.92	124.37	121.79	162.09	206.21
租赁和商务服务业	Leasing and Business Services	15.72	21.76	36.23	46.44	77.42
科学研究和技术服务业	Scientific Research and Technical Services			7.06	7.90	10.61
居民服务和其他服务业	Services to Households and Other Services	9.71	19.19	36.70	50.81	55.68
教 育	Education	1.05	1.32	1.40	2.15	2.65
卫生和社会工作	Health and Social Work	1.51	1.56	1.38	2.50	3.03
文化、体育和娱乐业	Culture,Sports and Entertainment	2.18	2.56	2.65	3.03	2.39
公共管理、社会保障和社会组织	Public Management Social Security and	4.25	5.50	26.69	35.98	55.37
其他行业	Others	21.89	9.27	6.90	4.89	5.55

注：资料来源于省地税局（以下相关表同）。
Note: Data in the table are provided by Local Taxation Beaura of Guizhou Province (the same applies to the next table).

8-9 国税税收收入(按企业类型分)
National Taxation Revenue (by Business Entities)

单位：亿元 (100 million yuan)

指 标	Item	2010	2011	2012	2013	2014
总 计	**Total**	**458.13**	**568.60**	**647.79**	**729.65**	**805.65**
内资企业	Domestic Enterprises	412.92	514.21	592.32	658.69	716.83
国有企业	State-owned Enterprises	59.33	62.20	72.89	86.14	95.99
集体企业	Collective-owned Enterprises	5.26	7.65	9.20	6.54	9.45
股份合作企业	Cooperative Enterprises	4.80	7.95	9.70	7.15	10.08
联营企业	Joint Ownership Enterprises	0.50	0.62	0.66	0.44	0.35
#国有控股	State-owned Holding Company	0.08	0.47	0.31	0.07	0.05
股份公司	Joint-stock Company	289.50	376.54	436.34	500.17	550.56
#国有控股	State-owned Holding Company	146.25	220.87	265.56	360.34	387.71
私营企业	Private Enterprises	50.92	55.19	59.54	52.99	46.46
其它企业	Other Enterprises	2.62	4.06	3.99	5.26	3.94
港澳台投资企业	Funded from Hong Kong, Macao and Taiwan	3.44	3.30	3.88	6.75	8.92
#国有控股	State-owned Holding Company	0.10	0.08	0.15	0.07	0.17
外商投资企业	Foreign Funded Enterprises	15.67	17.83	12.50	13.27	15.47
#国有控股	State-owned Holding Company	0.23	0.36	0.26	0.47	1.56
个体经营	Individual Enterprises	26.10	33.25	39.09	50.94	64.43
附：乡(镇)企业	Township (town) Enterprises	23.39	32.41	29.10	34.10	35.92

8-10 地方系统税收收入(按企业类型分)
Local Taxation Revenue (by Business Entities)

单位：亿元 (100 million yuan)

指 标	Item	2010	2011	2012	2013	2014
总 计	**Total**	**373.83**	**504.27**	**660.84**	**816.85**	**981.43**
内资企业	Domestic Enterprises	332.60	451.86	596.39	746.33	920.53
国有企业	State-owned Enterprises	57.86	64.39	81.35	96.43	100.93
集体企业	Collective-owned Enterprises	7.31	7.52	10.11	11.86	11.42
股份合作企业	Cooperative Enterprises	2.87	3.57	4.91	5.11	6.46
联营企业	Joint Ownership Enterprises	0.27	0.25	0.22	0.34	0.56
#国有控股	State-owned Holding Company	0.02	0.01	0.01	0.01	0.00
股份公司	Joint-stock Company	184.78	259.47	388.53	506.20	642.69
#国有控股	State-owned Holding Company	31.29	53.52	51.21	50.98	56.31
私营企业	Private Enterprises	36.98	45.13	51.98	53.02	49.14
其它企业	Other Enterprises	42.53	71.51	59.29	73.37	109.34
港澳台投资企业	Funded from Hong Kong, Macao and Taiwan	1.57	2.00	3.59	4.47	5.43
#国有控股	State-owned Holding Company	0.02	0.38	0.11	0.21	0.02
外商投资企业	Foreign Funded Enterprises	5.36	6.87	6.92	7.48	6.40
#国有控股	State-owned Holding Company	0.03	2.35	1.23	0.73	0.24
个体经营	Individual Enterprises	34.31	43.54	53.94	58.57	49.07
附：乡(镇)企业	Township (town) Enterprises	11.84	16.52	53.43	59.73	74.75

8-11 国家税收收入(分行业、分税种)(2014)

单位：亿元

指　　标	Item	合　计 Total
合　　计	**Total**	**805.65**
第一产业	Primary Industry	2.45
第二产业	Secondary Industry	479.05
采矿业	Mining	66.08
制造业	Manufacturing	351.67
电力、燃气及水的生产和供应业	Production and supply of Electricity,Gas and Water	55.92
建筑业	Construction	5.39
第三产业	Tertiary Industry	324.14
交通运输、仓储及邮政业	Transport,Storage and Post	12.59
信息传输、软件和信息技术服务业	Information Transmission,Computer Services and Software	6.02
批发和零售业	Wholesale and Retail Trades	188.52
住宿和餐饮业	Hotel and catering Services	0.15
金融业	Financial Intermediation	41.49
房地产业	Real Estate	11.56
租赁和商务服务业	Leasing and Business Services	6.20
科学研究和技术服务业	Scientific Research and Technical Services	6.26
居民服务、修理和其他服务业	Services to Households and Other Services	2.17
教　育	Education	0.13
卫生和社会工作	Health and Social Work	0.25
文化、体育和娱乐业	Culture,Sports and Entertainment	0.99
公共管理、社会保障和社会组织	Public Management Social Security and Social Organization	3.42
其他行业	Others	44.40

Taxation Revenue of the Central Government (By Industrial Sector and Taxation Category)

(100 million yuan)

国内 增值税 Domestic Value-added Tax	#一般纳税人 增值税 Value-added Tax from General Taxpayer	国内 消费税 Domestic Consumption Tax	企业 所得税 Corporate Income Tax	个人 所得税 Personal Income Tax	车辆 购置税 Vehicle Purchase Tax
388.76	**359.80**	**208.87**	**154.11**	**0.01**	**53.91**
0.17	0.12		0.04		2.24
243.81	236.51	191.36	42.96		0.93
64.17	63.21		1.78		0.13
128.59	127.00	191.36	31.20		0.52
50.57	45.94		5.25		0.11
0.48	0.35		4.73		0.18
144.77	123.18	17.51	111.12	0.01	50.72
9.76	5.06		0.78		2.05
4.87	4.64		1.12		0.02
115.35	106.89	17.51	51.90		3.76
0.02	0.01		0.13		0.01
0.25	0.20		41.14		0.10
0.09	0.06		11.33		0.13
4.64	1.78		1.35		0.21
4.14	2.79		2.06		0.06
1.37	0.71		0.52		0.28
0.02			0.05		0.06
0.01	0.01		0.19		0.05
0.81	0.75		0.16		0.01
3.08			0.14		0.20
0.37	0.27		0.24	0.01	43.79

8-12 地方系统税收收入(分行业、分税种)(2014)

单位：亿元

指标	Item	合计 Total	营业税 Business Tax	企业所得税 Enterprises Income Tax
合计	**Total**	**981.43**	**344.20**	**147.46**
第一产业	Primary Industry	0.62	0.21	0.04
第二产业	Secondary Industry	356.06	154.73	57.97
采矿业	Mining	49.84	1.49	12.75
制造业	Manufacturing	54.95	1.85	9.00
电力、燃气及水的生产和供应业	Production and supply of Electricity, Gas and Water	15.94	1.31	1.86
建筑业	Construction	235.34	150.08	34.36
第三产业	Tertiary Industry	624.75	189.26	89.46
交通运输、仓储及邮政业	Transport,Storage and Post	6.76	1.44	0.90
信息传输、软件和信息技术服务业	Information Transmission,Computer Services and Software	7.63	4.07	0.28
批发和零售业	Wholesale and Retail Trades	94.22	2.90	48.32
住宿和餐饮业	Hotel and Catering Services	9.64	6.08	0.36
金融业	Financial Intermediation	87.60	53.71	1.79
房地产业	Real Estate	206.21	72.20	21.13
租赁和商务服务业	Leasing and Business Services	77.42	21.58	7.12
科学研究和技术服务业	Scientific and Technical services	10.61	2.32	1.78
居民服务、修理和其他服务业	Resident Services, Repairs and other services	55.68	17.27	3.39
教育	Education	2.65	1.21	0.34
卫生和社会工作	Health and Social Work	3.03	0.06	0.11
文化、体育和娱乐业	Culture,Sports and Entertainment	2.39	0.89	0.26
公共管理、社会保障和社会组织	Public Management，Social Security and Social Organization	55.37	4.31	2.10
其他行业	Others	5.55	1.23	1.58

Taxation Revenue of the Local Government
(By Industrial Sector and Taxation Category)

(100 million yuan)

个人所得税 Personal Income Tax	城市维护建设税 Tax on City Maintenance and Construction	房产税 Tax on Real Estates	印花税 Stamp Tax	城镇土地使用税 Tax on the Use of Urban Land	土地增值税 Value-added Tax on Land	其他各税 Other Taxes
81.29	**57.30**	**23.43**	**11.64**	**18.44**	**64.64**	**233.03**
0.04	0.03	0.05	0.03	0.05	0.00	0.17
33.08	34.31	6.72	4.96	7.29	3.08	53.92
18.97	3.41	0.52	0.51	1.03	0.05	11.10
7.36	20.44	3.02	1.78	4.63	0.37	6.51
2.61	3.08	1.29	0.71	0.98	0.27	3.83
4.15	7.39	1.89	1.96	0.65	2.40	32.48
48.17	22.96	16.65	6.65	11.10	61.56	178.94
1.39	0.47	0.71	0.18	0.39	0.15	1.13
1.12	0.56	0.76	0.07	0.16	0.11	0.49
5.52	8.84	1.84	1.86	1.41	1.85	21.70
1.84	0.40	0.63	0.02	0.19	0.04	0.08
14.42	3.52	1.57	0.82	0.33	0.33	11.11
3.70	4.80	3.90	1.68	6.39	46.38	46.03
4.20	1.73	3.21	1.14	1.00	5.78	31.66
2.38	0.37	0.28	0.16	0.11	0.32	2.88
7.24	1.33	2.04	0.41	0.65	1.11	22.26
0.79	0.07	0.11	0.01	0.07		0.05
2.75	0.00	0.04	0.02	0.01		0.03
0.91	0.07	0.12	0.01	0.05	0.01	0.06
1.88	0.58	1.42	0.23	0.04	4.59	40.21
0.03	0.20	0.02	0.05	0.31	0.89	1.24

主要统计指标解释

一般公共预算收入 指政府为履行职能，按国家法律法规规定收取的纳入预算内管理的各项税收及非税收入总和。1994年我国实行分税制改革后，一般公共预算收入划分为中央固定收入、地方固定收入、中央与地方共享收入三部分。其中，地方一般公共预算收入（习惯上称地方财政收入）由地方固定收入和中央与地方共享收入地方分成部分组成，具体又可分为税收收入和非税收入两类。

一般公共预算支出 指地方政府为履行职能需要，通过预算内资金安排的用于维持政权运转及支持各项社会事业发展等方面的支出。主要包括：

(1)一般公共服务：指政府提供基本公共管理与服务的支出，包括人大事务、政协事务、政府办公厅(室)及相关机构事务、发展与改革事务、统计信息事务、财政事务、税收事务、审计事务、海关事务、人力资源事务、纪检监察事务、人口与计划生育事务、商贸事务、知识产权事务、工商行政管理事务、国土资源事务、海洋管理事务、测绘事务、地震事务、气象事务、民族事务、宗教事务、港澳台侨事务、档案事务、共产党事务、民主党派事务及工商联事务、群众团体事务、彩票事务等。

(2)国防：指政府用于国防方面的支出，包括用于现役部队、预备役部队、民兵、国防科研事业、专项工程、国防动员等方面的支出。

(3)公共安全：指政府维护社会公共安全方面的支出，包括武装警察、公安、国家安全、检察、法院、司法行政、监狱、劳教、国家保密、缉私警察等。

(4)教育：指政府教育事务支出，包括教育行政管理、学前教育、小学教育、初中教育、普通高中教育、普通高等教育、初等职业教育、中专教育、技校教育、职业高中教育、高等职业教育、广播电视教育、留学生教育、特殊教育、干部继续教育、教育机关服务等。

(5)科学技术：指用于科学技术方面的支出，包括科学技术管理事务、基础研究、应用研究、技术研究与开发、科技条件与服务、社会科学、科学技术普及、科技交流与合作等。

(6)文化教育与传媒：指政府在文化、文物、体育、广播影视、新闻出版等方面的支出。

(7)社会保障和就业：指政府在社会保障与就业方面的支出，包括社会保障和就业管理事务、民政管理事务、财政对社会保险基金的补助、补充全国社会保障基金、行政事业单位离退休、企业改革补助、就业补助、抚恤、退役安置、社会福利、残疾人事业、城市居民最低生活保障、其他城镇社会救济、农村社会救济、自然灾害生活救助、红十字事务等。

(8)医疗卫生与计划生育：指政府医疗卫生、计划生育方面的支出，包括医疗卫生管理事务支出、医疗服务支出、医疗保障支出、疾病预防控制支出、卫生监督支出、妇幼保健支出、农村卫生支出等。

(9)城乡社区：指政府城乡社区事务支出，包括城乡社区管理事务支出、城乡社区规划与管理支出、城乡社区公共设施支出、城乡社区住宅支出、城乡社区环境卫生支出、建设市场管理与监督支出等。

(10)农林水：指政府农林水事务支出，包括农业支出、林业支出、水利支出、扶贫支出、农业综合开发支出等。

(11)交通运输：指政府交通运输和邮政业方面的支出，包括公路运输支出、水路运输支出、铁路运输支出、民用航空运输支出、邮政业支出等。

Explanatory Notes on Main Statistical Indicators

General Public Finance Budget Revenue that the government is functioning, according to national laws and regulations charged into the budget management of the various tax and non-tax revenue totals. After the implementation of the tax reform in our country in 1994, General public revenue divided into the central fixed income, local fixed-income, central and local revenue sharing three parts. Among them, the local General public revenue (customarily known as local revenues) consists of Local fixed income and revenue sharing between central and local areas into parts, Specifically, it can be divided into tax revenues and non-tax revenue categories.

General Public Finance Budget Expenditure refers to local governments in order to fulfill functional needs, through budgetary funding arrangements for the operation and maintenance of the regime to support the development of social undertakings and other spending.It includes the following main items:

(1) Expenditure for general public services: It refers to the spending on the basic public management and services which provided by governments, including the expense on affairs of People's Congress, affairs of People's Political Consultative Conference, affairs of government general office and relative institutions, affairs of development and reform, affairs of statistics, affairs of finance, affairs of taxation, affairs of audit, affairs of customs, affairs of human resources and social security, affairs of discipline inspection and supervision, affairs of population and family planning, affairs of commerce and trade, affairs of intellectual property, affairs of administration for industry and commerce, affairs of land and resources, affairs of oceanic administration, affairs of surveying and mapping, affairs of earthquake, ethnic affairs, religious affairs, affairs of Hong Kong, Macao, Taiwan, and Overseas Chinese, affairs of archives administration, affairs of Chinese Communist Party, affairs of democratic parties and federation of industry and commerce, affairs of mass organization, and affairs of lottery, etc.

(2) Expenditure for national defence: It refers to the spending of government on national defence, including the expense on active force, reserve force, militia, scientific research on national defence, special projects, mobilization of national defence, etc.

(3) Expenditure for public security: It refers to the spending of government on maintaining social and public security, including the expense on armed police force, public security, state security, prosecution, courts, justice, prison, labour education and rehabilitation, protection of state secrecy, anti-smuggling police, etc.

(4) Expenditure for education: It refers to the spending of government on education, including the expense on the administration of education, pre-primary education, primary education, secondary education, high school education, regular higher education, primary vocational education, secondary vocational education, technical school education, vocational high school education and higher vocational education, radio and television education, student abroad education, special education, on the job training of cadres, education authorities services, etc.

(5) Expenditure for science and technology: It refers to the spending of government on science and technology (S&T), including the expense on the administration of S&T, basic research, applied research, research and development, conditions and services of S&T, popularization of social science, science and technology, exchanges and cooperation of S&T, etc.

(6) Expenditure for culture, sport and media: It refers to the spending of government on culture, cultural heritage, sports, radio, film, television, press and publication, etc.

(7) Expenditure for social safety net and employment effort: It refers to the spending of government on social safety net and employment, including the expense on administration of social safety net and employment, civil affairs, budgetary subsidy on the social insurance funds, subsidy on National Social Security Fund, retirees of administrative units and institutions, subsidy on enterprise reform, subsidy on employment effort, pension, placement of ex-serviceman, social welfare, the handicapped undertakings, the system of cost of living allowances for urban residents, other urban social relief, rural social relief, living relief of natural disasters, affairs of Red Cross Society, etc.

(8) Expenditure for medical and health care: It refers to the spending of government on medical and health care, including the expense on administration of medical and health care, medical services, health care, disease prevention and control, health inspection and supervision, women and children's health, rural health care, etc.

(9) Expenditure for urban and rural community affairs: It refers to the spending of government on urban and rural community affairs, including the expense on administration of urban and rural community, planning and management of urban and rural community, public facilities of urban and rural community, housing of urban and rural community, sanitation of urban and rural community, management and supervision on the construction market, etc.

(10) Expenditure for agriculture, forestry and water conservancy: It refers to the spending of government on agriculture, forestry and water conservancy, including the expense on agriculture, forestry, water conservancy, poverty alleviation, comprehensive agricultural development, etc.

(11) Expenditure for transportation: It refers to the spending of government on transportation and postal services, including the expense on road transportation, waterway transportation, railway transportation, civil aviation transportation, and postal services.

价格指数

9

Price Indices

9-1 居民消费价格分类指数

Consumer Price Indices by Category

(上年=100) (preceding year=100)

指 标	Item	2010	2011	2012	2013	2014
居民消费价格总指数	**General Consumer Price Index**	**102.9**	**105.1**	**102.7**	**102.5**	**102.4**
# 非食品价格指数	Non-Food Price Index	100.5	101.2	101.6	101.7	101.4
# 服务项目价格指数	Services Price Index	101.4	101.3	101.8	103.0	102.8
消费品价格指数	Consumer Goods Price Index	103.4	106.6	103.0	102.4	102.3
# **食品**	**Food**	**107.7**	**113.5**	**104.7**	**104.1**	**104.2**
粮食	Grain	120.5	116.8	104.5	103.3	102.6
淀粉及薯类	Starches and Tubers	110.7	108.9	107.2	107.5	106.0
干豆类及豆制品	Beans and Bean Products	109.7	107.9	100.6	102.9	103.0
油脂	Oil or Fat	100.4	116.5	104.4	100.2	94.1
肉禽及其制品	Meat, Poultry and Processed Products	104.9	124.5	101.3	103.8	101.3
食用畜肉及副产品	Livestock for Slaughtering and Sideline Products	102.5	129.9	100.1	103.7	98.7
禽	Poultry	114.7	113.4	100.1	102.9	110.7
肉禽加工制品	Products of Processed Meat and Poultry	101.9	109.5	112.3	105.8	104.7
蛋	Eggs	107.3	114.7	95.7	104.7	104.6
水产品	Aquatic Products	109.7	111.1	107.6	103.1	103.0
鱼	Fish	111.4	110.7	108.0	102.4	102.1
其他水产品	Other Aquatic Products	104.5	112.0	106.7	104.9	105.1
菜	Vegetables	116.6	108.7	109.0	101.6	104.8
鲜菜	Fresh Vegetables	114.3	108.3	110.8	101.3	104.5
调味品	Flavoring	105.3	107.3	102.7	103.3	102.1
糖	Carbohydrate	109.7	111.7	104.6	100.5	99.1
茶及饮料	Tea and Beverages	100.9	102.6	103.0	101.8	102.5
干鲜瓜果	Dried and Fresh Melons and Fruits	120.3	112.0	100.0	104.4	116.2
糕点饼干面包	Cake, Biscuit and Bread	102.3	110.5	105.6	102.0	101.3
奶及奶制品	Milk and Its Products	101.0	100.5	104.0	109.2	108.4

9-1 续表1 continued

(上年=100) (preceding year=100)

指 标	Item	2010	2011	2012	2013	2014
在外用膳食品	Dining Out	101.3	109.5	109.6	107.6	106.1
其他食品及食品加工服务	Other Foods and Manufacturing Services	100.8	103.5	106.6	101.5	103.8
烟酒及用品	**Tobacco, Liquor and Articles**	**102.0**	**102.4**	**102.8**	**101.5**	**99.8**
烟草	Tobacco	100.8	99.7	102.3	100.8	100.3
酒	Liquor	103.8	107.2	103.5	102.8	99.0
白酒	Distilled Spirit	106.5	110.0	104.5	102.9	97.9
啤酒	Beer	95.9	103.3	100.9	100.5	102
衣着	**Clothing**	**97.4**	**100.3**	**103.8**	**102.3**	**102.1**
服装	Garments	99.3	100.9	103.5	102.8	102.3
衣着材料	Clothing Material	103.1	113.2	107.1	101.1	100.0
鞋袜帽	Footgear and Hats	92.5	97.1	104.0	101.0	101.4
家庭设备用品及维修服务	**Household Facilities, Articles and Services**	**99.3**	**100.2**	**101.1**	**101.1**	**100.7**
耐用消费品	Durable Consumer Goods	98.6	98.7	99.1	100.9	101.1
家 具	Furniture	100.8	101.7	101.9	101.6	102.7
家庭设备	Household Facilities	97.6	97.3	97.7	100.5	100.3
室内装饰品	Interior Decorations	101.0	97.6	99.4	104.7	101.4
床上用品	Bed Articles	93.2	103.4	100.4	95.8	99.9
家庭日用杂品	Daily Use Household Articles	99.8	100.7	101.2	100.8	99.5
家庭服务及加工维修服务	Household Services and Maintenance and Renovation	109.7	103.2	111.5	107.4	104.0
医疗保健和个人用品	**Health Care and Personal Articles**	**101.3**	**102.6**	**102.5**	**101.5**	**101.6**
医疗保健	Health Care	100.9	103.5	102.3	101.0	101.3
医疗器具及用品	Medical Instrument and Articles	101.0	100.8	101.8	99.8	100.5
中药材及中成药	Traditional Chinese Medicine	103.8	115.1	108.2	103.0	102.4
西 药	Western Medicine	101.1	101.9	100.9	100.9	102.1
保健器具及用品	Health Care Appliances and Articles	99.5	99.6	99.7	100.3	100.1
医疗保健服务	Health Care Services	100.3	100.0	100.6	100.0	100.1

9-1 续表2 continued

(上年=100) (preceding year=100)

指 标	Item	2010	2011	2012	2013	2014
个人用品及服务	Personal Articles and Services	101.8	101.3	102.8	102.2	102.1
化妆美容用品	Cosmetics	101.7	100.4	100.2	100.0	100.1
卫生用品	Sanitation Articles	101.9	101.3	104.5	103.7	100.6
个人饰品	Personal Ornaments	100.1	103.7	100.1	97.6	97.7
个人服务	Personal Services	103.5	99.9	105.6	106.4	108.5
交通和通讯	**Transportation and Communication**	**100.8**	**100.1**	**99.6**	**99.6**	**100.2**
交 通	Transportation	102.6	102.9	101.4	101.3	101.1
交通工具	Transportation Facility	99.8	100.7	100.0	99.9	100.0
车用燃料及零配件	Fuels and Parts	111.3	109.7	103.3	101.1	99.6
车辆使用及维修	Fees for Vehicles Use and Maintenance	102.5	108.2	103.1	107.3	103.5
市区公共交通	Incity Traffic Fare	101.5	99.3	101.5	100.4	100.7
城市间交通	Intercity Traffic Fare	102.7	104.9	100.8	101.6	102.9
通 信	Communication	99.1	97.2	97.8	97.7	99.1
通信工具	Communication Facility	92.6	84.0	85.4	91.2	92.7
通信服务	Communication Service	100.4	100.6	100.5	98.9	100.2
娱乐教育文化用品及服务	**Recreation, Education and Culture Articles**	**100.4**	**99.9**	**101.2**	**101.8**	**102.4**
文娱用耐用消费品及服务	Durable Consumer Goods for Cultural and Recreational Use and Services	96.9	96.0	96.8	94.6	95.5
教 育	Education	101.0	101.4	102.7	103.0	104.4
文化娱乐用品	Culture and Recreational Articles	100.3	99.7	101.5	102.9	101.4
文化娱乐	Culture Articles	99.1	99.7	100.3	99.5	99.7
书报杂志	Newspapers and Magazines	101.1	100.3	102.2	104.9	100.7
文娱费	Expenditure on Culture and Recreation	100.2	99.5	101.8	103.9	102.2
旅游	Touring and Outing	106.2	100.1	101.5	104.9	104.2
居住	**Residence**	**102.4**	**102.8**	**101.4**	**103.0**	**101.8**
建房及装修材料	Building and Building Decoration Materials	100.4	102.5	100.9	101.5	100.5
租 房	Renting	102.5	99.5	103.2	105.8	104.3
自有住房	Private Housing	100.6	102.3	100.9	105.1	102.5
水、电、燃料	Water, Electricity and Fuels	105.0	103.9	101.9	100.9	101.2

9-2 商品零售价格分类指数

Retail Price Indices by Category

(上年=100) (preceding year=100)

指 标	Item	2010	2011	2012	2013	2014
商品零售价格总指数	**Retail Price Index**	**103.0**	**105.5**	**102.0**	**101.5**	**101.2**
食品类	Food	108.2	113.9	104.6	104.2	103.6
粮食	Grain	120.4	117.1	104.8	103.7	101.9
油脂	Oil or Fat	98.9	116.5	104.3	100.8	93.5
肉禽及其制品	Meat, Poultry and Processed Products	104.9	123.6	101.8	104.1	101.1
蛋	Eggs	107.2	115.7	97.9	106.1	104.2
水产品	Aquatic Products	108.2	112.3	107.3	103.5	102.5
鲜菜	Fresh Vegetables	114.4	109.5	110.6	101.1	104.4
干菜及菜制品	Dried Vegetables and Its Products	125.8	110.8	99.1	102.8	103.7
鲜果	Fresh Fruits	122.1	112.3	98.8	107.4	120.0
干(坚)果及瓜果制品	Dried Fruits and Its Products	120.8	113.4	101.3	100.8	99.8
在外用膳食品	Outward Dinner Food	101.3	109.3	109.9	107.3	106.1
饮料、烟酒	Beverages,Tobacco and Liquor	101.1	101.6	102.5	101.7	99.8
服装、鞋帽类	Garments,Shoes and Hats	98.3	100.4	103.5	102.9	102.3
纺织品类	Textiles	99.5	103.8	102.1	99.2	99.3
家用电器及音像器材	Household Appliances, Music and Video Equipment	97.9	96.3	97.2	97.3	98.3
文化办公用品	Cultural and Office Appliances	100.1	98.1	98.4	98.6	98.6
日用品	Articles for Daily Use	100.8	100.8	100.2	101.0	100.4
体育娱乐用品	Sports and Recreation Articles	99.2	100.3	101.4	99.6	100.4
交通、通信用品	Transportation and Communication Appliances	97.6	96.2	96.3	98.1	98.2
家具	Furniture	99.8	101.9	104.8	103.1	104.2
化妆品类	Cosmetics	99.7	100.6	101.9	102.2	100.1
金银珠宝类	Gold,Silver and Jewelry	108.9	111.7	101.5	95.1	91.3
中西药品及医疗保健用品类	Traditional Chinese and Western Medicines and Health Care Articles	102.6	106.2	104.2	102.1	101.6
书报杂志及电子出版物类	Books, Newspapers, Magazines and Electronic Publications	100.5	100.2	102.0	104.9	100.4
燃料类	Fuels	111.2	113.7	102.2	99.7	100.6
建筑材料及五金电料类	Building Materials and Hardware	102.5	102.7	99.0	99.3	99.4

9—3 工业生产者出厂价格分类指数

Ex-Factory Price Indices of Industrial Products by Category

(上年=100) (preceding year=100)

指 标	Item	2010	2011	2012	2013	2014
工业生产者出厂价格指数	**Producer Price Indices for Industrial Products**	**104.7**	**105.4**	**101.0**	**97.4**	**98.3**
按轻、重工业分	**Grouped by Light or Heavy Industries**					
轻工业	Light Industry	100.5	102.9	103.6	102.4	100.2
重工业	Heavy Industry	106.2	106.0	100.4	96.3	97.9
按用途分	**Grouped by Use**					
生产资料	Means of Production	105.5	106.2	100.3	96.1	97.8
采掘工业	Mining & Quarrying Industry	116.1	107.2	99.0	93.2	96.8
原材料工业	Raw Materials Industry	105.4	106.4	102.3	95.7	97.9
加工工业	Processing Industry	102.1	105.6	97.5	97.0	97.8
生活资料	Consumer Goods	100.9	102.8	103.5	102.4	100.3
食品类	Food	101.7	102.8	103.3	102.3	100.2
衣着类	Clothing	102.4	114.2	105.5	100.2	100.2
一般日用品	Articles for Daily Use	100.3	101.6	103.1	101.6	101.3
耐用消费品	Durable Consumer Goods	92.2	101.5	105.4	104.8	100.8
按工业大类行业分	**Grouped by Sector**					
#煤炭开采和洗选业	Mining and Washing of Coal	117.0	111.9	94.5	85.8	94.8
有色金属矿采选业	Mining and Processing of Non-Ferrous Metal Ores	105.6	104.5	98.1	96.2	91.5
非金属矿采选业	Mining and Processing of Nonmetal Ores	106.2	123.6	122.3	92.2	89.4
农副食品加工业	Processing of Food from Agricultural Products	102.5	111.9	110.5	107.0	101.3
食品制造业	Processing of Foodstuff	98.9	104.4	102.6	101.9	101.8
饮料制造业	Manufacture of Beverages	102.3	103.0	104.4	102.1	99.3
烟草制品业	Manufacture of Tobacco	100.6	99.7	101.7	100.9	100.2
纺织业	Manufacture of Textile	113.0	120.9	86.6	97.4	100.0
纺织服装、鞋、帽制造业	Manufacture of Textile Wearing Apparel, Footware and Caps	103.8	104.6	101.8	100.2	100.5
皮革、毛皮、羽毛(绒)及其制品业	Manufacture of Leather, Fur, Feather and Related Products	100.0	119.0	107.3	100.2	100.0

9-3 续表 Continued

(上年=100) (preceding year=100)

指 标	Item	2010	2011	2012	2013	2014
木材加工及木、竹、藤、棕、草制品业	Processing of Timber,Manufacture of Wood,Bamboo, Rattan,Palm and Straw Products	100.9	103.2	108.9	106.5	99.6
家具制造业	Manufacture of Furniture	103.1	119.8	100.6	100.1	100.3
造纸及纸制品业	Manufacture of Paper and Paper Products	104.4	103.0	95.6	102.5	97.0
印刷业和记录媒介的复制	Printing,Reproduction of Recording Media	99.3	100.0	98.6	99.8	102.4
文教体育用品制造业	Manufacture of Articles For Culture,Education and Sport Activities	100.0	109.3	109.3	102.4	107.3
石油加工、炼焦及核燃料加工业	Processing of Petroleum,Coking,Processing of Nuclear Fuel	110.6	112.4	94.3	85.0	97.5
化学原料及化学制品制造业	Manufacture of Raw Chemical Materials and Chemical Products	105.8	114.1	104.8	93.3	94.1
医药制造业	Manufacture of Medicines	103.7	101.9	101.0	102.1	100.3
橡胶制品业	Manufacture of Rubber	102.0	114.0	95.6	95.6	99.6
非金属矿物制品业	Manufacture of Non-metallic Mineral Products	93.1	102.2	96.7	102.8	99.4
黑色金属冶炼及压延加工业	Smelting and Pressing of Ferrous Metals	104.2	105.5	90.8	93.7	97.1
有色金属冶炼及压延加工业	Smelting and Pressing of Non-ferrous Metals	111.9	108.4	98.2	92.5	95.5
金属制品业	Manufacture of Metal Products	102.6	101.4	96.7	96.6	98.3
通用设备制造业	Manufacture of General Purpose Machinery	100.9	100.0	99.1	100.0	99.2
专用设备制造业	Manufacture of Special Purpose Machinery	99.9	105.0	102.2	104.3	101.0
交通运输设备制造业	Manufacture of Transport Equipment	97.8	100.0	90.6	95.6	91.9
电气机械及器材制造业	Manufacture of Electrical Machinery and Equipment	99.2	99.6	98.6	103.5	99.9
通信设备、计算机及其他电子设备制造业	Manufacture of Communication Equipment, Computers and Other Electronic Equipment	99.0	99.3	102.5	103.0	103.7
仪器仪表及文化、办公用机械制造业	Manufacture of Measuring Instruments and Machinery for Cultural Activity and Office Work	98.8	101.5	99.2	99.1	97.1
电力、热力的生产和供应业	Production and Supply of Electric Power and Heat Power	102.1	101.6	106.9	100.7	100.2
燃气生产和供应业	Production and Supply of Gas	120.3	102.4	104.8	115.5	104.7
水的生产和供应业	Production and Supply of Water	107.1	104.3	103.2	105.4	100.8

注：1.工业生产者出厂价格指数2010年为全部工业品出厂价格指数，统计口径不变。2.工业大类行业2010—2011年按国民经济行业分类(GB/T 4754—2002)分，2012年起按国民经济行业分类(GB/T 4754—2011)分。

Note:1.For the year 2010 and before,Ex-Factory Price Index of Industrial Producer referred to Total Ex-Factory Price Index of Industrial Products; statistical standards are unchanged. 2.From 2010 to 2011, industrial sectors are classified by Sector of the National Economy(GB/T4754-2002) and by Sector of the National Economy(GB/T4754-2011) in the year of 2012 .

9−4 工业生产者购进价格指数
Purchasing Price Index for Industrial Producer

(上年=100) (preceding year =100)

指　标	Item	2010	2011	2012	2013	2014
工业生产者购进价格指数	**Purchasing Price Indices for Industrial Producers**	**109.8**	**115.0**	**102.3**	**96.4**	**98.6**
燃料、动力类	Fuel and Power	110.1	121.6	107.2	96.3	100.3
黑色金属材料类	Ferrous Metals	104.0	109.9	93.2	93.8	98.0
#钢　材	Rolled-steel	103.3	108.0	96.2	93.8	95.7
有色金属材料和电线类	Nonferrous Metals	122.5	112.4	98.4	97.9	95.8
化工原料类	Raw Chemical Materials	110.2	116.4	94.6	85.2	92.9
木材及纸浆类	Timber and Paper Pulp	105.2	107.8	100.9	101.3	100.2
建筑材料及非金属矿类	Building Materials and Nonmetal Minerals Processing	96.7	117.8	116.1	102.2	98.1
其他工业原材料及半成品类	Other Industrial Raw Materials and Semi-products	108.8	106.4	103.9	104.9	101.2
农副产品类	Agricultural Products	115.1	109.2	106.1	104.9	101.7
纺织原料类	Textile Materials	105.0	118.1	100.0	104.2	105.1

注：工业生产者购进价格指数2010年为全部原材料、燃料、动力价格指数，统计口径不变。

Note:Purchasing Price Index of Industrial Producer referred to Total Indices of Purchasing Prices of Raw Materials,Fuels and Power in the year of 2010, and statistical standards are unchanged.

9−5 农业生产资料价格分类指数
Price Indices of Means of Agricultural Production by Category

(上年=100) (preceding year =100)

指　标	Item	2010	2011	2012	2013	2014
农业生产资料价格总指数	**General Price Index of Means of Agricultural Production**	**101.1**	**111.1**	**100.7**	**99.0**	**99.0**
小农具	Small Farm Tools	107.5	105.5	114.1	105.8	101.0
饲　料	Forage	109.4	104.1	97.8	100.7	100.9
产品畜	Commodity Animals	97.1	153.9	93.7	97.9	100.0
半机械化农具	Semi-mechanized Farm Tools	99.3	115.7	97.0	97.6	99.2
机械化农具	Mechanized Farm Machinery	98.9	106.0	99.5	99.3	99.3
化学肥料	Chemical Fertilizer	92.7	101.4	105.6	96.9	94.1
农药及农药器械	Pesticide & Its Appliances	99.1	100.6	106.4	101.3	102.3
化学农药	Chemical Pesticide	97.6	101.5	104.8	101.8	102.8
农药器械	Appliances for Pesticide	101.6	96.1	114.6	98.9	100.0
农机用油	Oil for Farm Machinery	107.5	103.8	100.8	99.1	98.2
其他农业生产资料	Others Means of Agricultural Production	99.9	107.8	97.9	101.5	104.8

9-6 固定资产投资和房地产销售价格指数

Price Indices of Investment in Fixed Assets and Real Estate

(上年=100) (preceding year =100)

指　　标	Item	2010	2011	2012	2013	2014
固定资产投资价格指数	**Price Indices of Investment in Fixed Assets**	**102.7**	**105.4**	**101.5**	**100.9**	**101.1**
建筑安装工程	Price Indices of Construction and Installation	103.6	107.5	102.0	101.5	101.3
人工费	Manpower	114.0	111.0	108.4	111.8	111.8
材料费	Materials	101.2	109.3	99.7	97.9	97.7
钢　材	Steel Products	102.2	114.6	96.2	93.3	93.6
木　材	Timber	108.0	110.0	101.3	104.1	101.0
水　泥	Cement	97.5	102.1	99.1	96.0	103.6
电　料	Electrical Materials	103.2	106.4	102.8	101.2	96.5
化工材料	Raw Chemical Materials	106.8	108.6	107.3	99.9	100.3
地方建筑材料	Local Building Materials	100.8	106.7	101.9	103.5	101.0
其他材料	Others	103.4	102.7	102.9	106.2	106.0
机械使用费	Costs for Using Machine	102.7	101.8	102.7	101.7	101.6
设备、工器具购置	Purchase of Equipment,Tools and Instruments	100.1	101.0	99.1	99.2	99.3
其他费用	Others	102.5	102.6	101.5	100.1	101.1
新建住宅价格指数(贵阳市)	**Price Indices of New Residential Housings(Guiyang)**	**108.2**	**104.4**	**101.2**	**104.5**	**102.6**
新建商品住宅价格指数(贵阳市)	Price Indices of New Commodity Residential Housings(Guiyang)	108.3	104.5	101.3	105.0	102.8

注：新建住宅价格指数2010年为房屋销售价格指数，新建商品住宅价格指数2010年为住宅销售价格指数，统计口径不一致。

Note:In the year of 2010,Price Indices of New Residential Housings referred to the Sales Price Indices of Real Estate;Price Indices of New Commodity Residential Housings referred to the Sales Price Indices of Residence Housings; and statistical standards are inconsistent.

主要统计指标解释

居民消费价格指数 是反映一定时期内城乡居民所购买的生活消费品价格和服务项目价格变动趋势和程度的相对数。

商品零售价格指数 是反映城乡商品零售价格变动趋势和程度的相对数。零售物价的变动直接反映城乡居民的生活支出和国家的财政收入，影响居民购买力和市场供需平衡，影响消费与积累的比例关系。

工业生产者价格指数 工业生产者价格包括工业企业产品第一次出售时的出厂价格和企业作为中间投入的原材料、燃料、动力购进价格(下简称工业生产者购进价格)。工业生产者价格调查的目的在于及时、准确、科学地反映各工业行业产品价格水平及其变动趋势和幅度，为国民经济核算、计算工业发展速度、宏观经济分析和调控、理顺价格体系等提供科学、准确的依据。

农业生产资料价格指数 是反映一定时期内农业生产资料价格变动趋势和程度的相对数。农业生产资料价格指数分为小农具、饲料、产品畜、役畜、半机械化农具、机械化农具、化学肥料、农药及农具械、农机用油、其他农业生产资料十大类。

固定资产投资价格指数 是反映固定资产投资额价格变动趋势和程度的相对数。固定资产投资额是由建筑安装工程投资完成额、设备、工器具购置投资完成额和其他费用投资完成额三部分组成的。编制固定资产投资价格指数应首先分别编制上述三部分投资的价格指数，然后采用加权算术平均法求出固定资产投资价格总指数。

Explanatory Notes on Main Statistical Indicators

Consumer Price Index reflects the trend and degree of changes in prices of consumer goods and services purchased by urban and rural residents during a given period.

Retail Price Index reflects the general change in retail prices of commodities. The change and adjustment in retail prices directly affect the living expenditure of urban and rural residents, government revenue, purchasing power of residents and the equilibrium of market supply and demand, and the ratio of consumption to accumulation.

Price Index of Industrial Producer enterprises and enterprises as the prices of intermediate inputs of raw materials, fuel and power purchase price (hereinafter referred to as industrial producer price). Industrial producer prices survey was designed to timely, accurate and scientifically reflect various industrial products industry trends and changes in the price level and the magnitude of national accounts to calculate the speed of industrial development, macroeconomic analysis and control, rationalize the price system to provide scientific and accurate basis.

Price Indices of Means of Agricultural Production reflect the trend and degree of changes in prices of means of agricultural production during a given period. Price indices of means of agricultural production are composed of 10 categories including small farm tools, feeds, domestic animals for meat, draught domestic animals, semi-mechanized farm machinery, mechanized farm machinery, chemical fertilizers, pesticides and spraying machinery, fuels for farm machinery and other means of agricultural production.

Price Index of Investment in Fixed Assets reflects the trend and degree of changes in prices of investment in fixed assets. The investment in fixed assets consists of three components, namely the investment in construction and installation, the investment in purchases of equipment and instrument, and the investment in other items. Price index of investment in fixed assets is calculated as the weighted arithmetic mean of the price indices of the three components of investment in fixed assets.

人民生活

10

People's Living Conditions

10-1 城乡人民生活水平

People's Livelihood in Urban and Rural Areas

指标	Item	2010	2011	2012	2013	2014
就业	**Employment**					
城镇居民家庭每户就业人口(人)	Average Number of Employed Persons per Urban Household(person)	1.43	1.43	1.45	1.61	1.56
城镇居民家庭每个就业者赡养人口(人)	Number of Dependents per Employee of Urban Household(person)	2.11	2.08	2.08	1.87	1.93
城镇平均每户就业面(%)	Proportion of Employment per Urban Household(%)	0.47	0.48	0.48	0.53	0.52
城镇登记失业人数(万人)	Registered Urban Unemployment Persons (10000 persons)	12.18	12.51	12.56	13.66	14.09
城镇登记失业率(%)	Registered Urban Unemployment Rate(%)	3.63	3.63	3.29	3.26	3.27
农村平均每户整、半劳动力(人)	Average Number of Full/Semi Laborer Force per Rural Household(person)	2.95	2.83	2.82	3.00	2.07
农村居民家庭每一劳动力赡养人口(人)	Number of Dependents per Laborer of Rural Household(person)	1.47	1.52	1.53	1.56	1.69
收入与支出	**Income and Expenditure**					
城镇常住居民人均可支配收入(元)	Annual Per Capita Disposable Income of Urban Households(yuan)	14142.7	16495	18700.5	20667	22548
城镇常住居民人均消费性支出(元)	Annual Per Capita Consumption Expenditure of Urban Householdss(yuan)	10058.3	11353	12585.7	13702.9	15255
在岗职工平均工资(元)	Average Wage of Staff and Workers in their Posts(yuan)	31458	37331	42733	49087	54685
农村常住居民人均可支配收入(元)	Annual Per Capita Net Income of Rural Households (yuan)	3472	4145	4753	5434	6671
农村居民人均生活消费支出(元)	Annual Per Capita Living Expenditure of Rural Households (yuan)	2852	3456	3902	4740	5970
生活质量	**Life Quality**					
居民家庭恩格尔系数(%)	**Household's Engle Coefficient(%)**					
城 镇	Urban	39.9	40.2	39.7	35.9	34.9
农 村	Rural	46.3	47.7	44.6	43.0	41.7
居住条件	**Residence Condition**					
城镇人均住宅建筑面积(平方米)	Per Capita Building Space in Urban Areas(sq.m)	27.42	27.83	27.86	34.84	36.58
农村居民人均住房面积(平方米)	Per Capita Living Space in Rural Areas(sq.m)	27.26	29.63	29.75	27.08	31.61
交通条件	**Traffic Condition**					
城市人均拥有道路面积(平方米)	Per Capita Area of Paved Roads in City(sq.m)	6.23	6.66	6.93	8.95	8.72
每百户城镇居民拥有家用汽车(辆)	Number of Family Vehicles Per 100 Urban Households(unit)	5.96	10.48	13.17	15.84	19.66
每百户农村居民拥有家用摩托车(辆)	Number of Motorcycles Per 100 Rural Households(unit)	30.76	35.98	39.02	41.37	48.38
通信条件	**Communication Condition**					
每百户拥有移动电话(部)	Mobile Telephone Per 100 Households(set)					
城 镇	Urban	183.54	204.75	214.73	211.72	228.15
农 村	Rural	102.10	156.96	173.26	190.06	218.13
城市公用设施普及占有率	City Public Utility Rate					
用水普及率(%)	Rate of Access to Tap Water(%)	86.5	86.9	87.6	88.5	90.2
燃气普及率(%)	Rate of Access to Gas(%)	54.5	55.0	55.2	58.7	60.3
人均公园绿地面积(平方米)	Per Capita Green Area(sq.m)	5.33	5.50	6.68	7.98	8.66

注：2013年全国城乡一体化住户调查改革，调查范围、调查样本、调查对象以及调查方式均进行重大改革。贵州城镇住户调查范围由17个县（市、区）扩大到44个，调查样本全部更换；农村住户调查范围由32个县（市、区）扩大到44个，调查样本全部更换。因此2013年起城乡住户有关数据请慎与往年比较（以下相关表同）。

Note: At 2013 in the National urban and rural household survey reform ,the survey range , survey samples , survey objects and investigation methods were carried out major reforms. The survey range of Guizhou urban household expanded from 17 counties(cities, districts) to 44, the survey samples all have been replacedl. So please carefully compare the relevant data of urban and rural residents for 2013 with data in previous relative tables in the chapter are the same) .

10-1 续表 continued

指 标	Item	2010	2011	2012	2013	2014
文化、教育和卫生	**Culture, Education and Health Care**					
文化	**Culture**					
广播节目综合人口覆盖率(%)	Radio Coverage Rate of the Population (%)	87.5	88.0	88.5	90.0	91.5
电视节目综合人口覆盖率(%)	TV Coverage Rate of the Population(%)	92.5	92.8	93.0	94.1	95.4
每百户彩色电视机拥有量(部/百户)	Number of Color TV per 100 Households(set)					
城镇	Urban	121.93	115.78	115.67	101.84	105.05
农村	Rural	91.07	93.93	95.94	96.53	98.88
每百户家用电脑拥有量(部/百户)	Number of Computers per 100 Households(set)					
城镇	Urban	56.79	63.89	71.22	55.72	63.56
农村	Rural	1.65	4.11	4.87	5.77	8.05
居民家庭文教娱乐支出比重(%)	Percentage of Household Expenditure on Education,Culture and Entertainment(%)					
城镇	Urban	12.5	11.7	11.1	14.2	13.6
农村	Rural	6.5	5.3	5.8	6.4	8.1
教育	**Education**					
学龄儿童入学率(%)	Enrollment Rate of School-age Children(%)	97.9	98.6	99.3	99.3	99.1
初中阶段毛入学率(%)	Enrollment Rate of Primary School Graduates Entering into Junior Secondary Schools(%)	97.6	94.2	97.4	101.1	102.5
高中阶段毛入学率(%)	Enrollment Rate of Juniorsecondary School Graduates Entering into Senior secondary Schools(%)	55.0	58.9	62.2	68.0	78.0
高等教育毛入学率(%)	Enrollment Rate of Senior secondary School Graduates Entering into Institution of Higher Education(%)	20.0	23.2	25.5	27.4	29.4
卫生	**Health Care**					
居民家庭医疗保健支出比重(%)	Percentage of Resident Expenditure on Health Care(%)					
城镇	Urban	5.4	5.1	5.2	4.6	6.1
农村	Rural	6.2	7.1	7.2	6.4	6.2
社会保障	**Social Security**					
城镇职工基本养老保险参保人数(万人)	Number of People Joining in Basic Pension Insurance(10 000 persons)	257.31	282.06	309.38	337.29	361.45
#参保职工	Number of Employees	190.29	210.71	231.67	248.91	268.30
城镇职工基本医疗保险参保人数(万人)	Number of Persons Joining in Urban Basic Medical Care System (10 000 persons)	293.52	314.06	329.27	344.72	354.76
失业保险参保人数(万人)	Number of Employees Joining in Unemployment Insurance (10 000 persons)	152.48	160.52	173.46	185.17	191.86
工伤保险参保人数(万人)	Number of Employees Joining in Injury Insurance (10 000 persons)	162.18	193.96	238.19	260.39	275.41
生育保险参保人数(万人)	Number of Persons Joining in Maternity Insurance(10 000 persons)	164.30	198.09	221.58	238.75	248.82
社会保险基金收入(亿元)	Revenue of Social Insurance Fund(100 million yuan)	201.56	256.94	310.85	351.06	386.81

注：城镇职工基本养老保险参保人数2010—2013年为基本养老保险参保人数，统计口径一致。

Note：The number of people who get Urban workers' basic pension refers to basic pension insurance number from 2010 to 2013, the statistics cabliers of both are the same.

10-2 城镇居民家庭生活基本情况
Basic Conditions of Urban Households Life

指　标	Item	2010	2011	2012	2013	2014
调查户数(户)	**Number of Households Surveyed(household)**	**1670**	**1720**	**1720**	**1129**	**1612**
平均每户常住家庭人口(人)	Average Household Size(person)	3.03	2.98	3.01	3.01	3.01
平均每户就业人员(人)	Number of Employed Persons Per Household (person)	1.43	1.43	1.45	1.61	1.56
平均每户就业面(%)	Proportion of Employment per Household(%)	0.47	0.48	0.48	0.53	0.52
平均每户国有经济单位职工人数(人)	Number of Staff and Workers in State-owned Units (person)	0.81	0.74	0.72	0.59	
平均每个就业者赡养人口(人)	Number of Dependents per Employee(person)	2.11	2.08	2.08	1.87	1.93
平均每人年可支配收入(元)	**Per Capita Annual Disposable Income (yuan)**	**14142.74**	**16495.01**	**18700.51**	**20667.07**	**22548.21**
平均每人年总收入(元)	**Per Capita Annual Income(yuan)**	**15138.80**	**17598.87**	**20042.88**	**21413.04**	
工资性收入	Income of Wages and Salaries	9627.99	10754.45	12309.17	13627.56	13147.52
工资及补贴收入	Income of Laborage and Allowance	9190.47	10359.48	11951.96	12901.49	
其他劳动收入	Income of other Labor	437.52	394.97	357.21	726.08	
经营者净收入	Net Business Income	1174.02	1614.67	1982.45	3244.92	3172.54
财产性收入	Income from Property	213.83	356.41	355.70	576.25	1746.58
转移性收入	Income from Transfer	4122.96	4873.34	5395.56	3964.30	4481.57
#养老金或离退休金	Annuities or Pension	3493.33	4229.54	4673.43	2798.38	4564.20
出售财物收入(元)	Income of Selling Property and Goods(yuan)	181.55	46.61	271.17	79.83	
平均每人消费性支出(元)	**Per Capita Annual Consumption Expenditure (yuan)**	**10058.29**	**11352.88**	**12585.70**	**13702.87**	**15254.64**
食　品	Food	4013.67	4565.85	4992.85	4915.02	5319.6
衣　着	Clothing	1102.41	1209.88	1399.00	1401.85	1245.89
居　住	Residence	890.75	1102.99	1013.53	1496.49	2432.50
家庭设备用品及服务	Household Facilities, Articles and Services	673.33	857.55	849.94	1083.77	1090.54
医疗保健	Health Care and Medical Services	546.84	578.33	654.53	633.72	927.39
交通和通信	Transport and Communication	1270.49	1395.28	1891.03	1870.08	1873.10
教育文化娱乐服务	Education, Culture and Recreation Services	1254.56	1331.43	1396.00	1950.28	2071.32
其他商品与服务	Miscellaneous Goods and Services	306.24	311.57	388.82	351.66	294.34
平均每人消费性支出构成(%)(人均消费性支出=100)	**Composition of Per Capita Annual Consumption Expenditure (%)**					
食　品	Food	39.9	40.2	39.7	35.9	34.9
衣　着	Clothing	11.0	10.7	11.1	10.2	8.2
居　住	Residence	8.9	9.7	8.0	10.9	15.9
家庭设备用品及服务	Household Facilities, Articles and Services	6.7	7.6	6.8	7.9	7.1
医疗保健	Health Care and Medical Services	5.4	5.1	5.2	4.6	6.1
交通和通信	Transport and Communication	12.6	12.3	15.0	13.6	12.3
教育文化娱乐服务	Education, Culture and Recreation Services	12.5	11.7	11.1	14.2	13.6
其他商品与服务	Miscellaneous Goods and Services	3.0	2.7	3.1	2.6	1.9

10-3 城镇居民家庭人均现金收支

Per Capita Annual Cash Income and Expenditure of Urban Households

单位：元 (yuan)

指 标	Item	2010	2011	2012	2013	2014
家庭总收入	**Total Households Income**	**15138.80**	**17598.87**	**20042.88**	**21413.04**	
#可支配收入	Disposable Income	14142.74	16495.01	18700.51	20667.07	21718.59
#工资性收入	Income of Wages and Salaries	9627.99	10754.45	12309.17	13627.56	13113.59
工资及补贴收入	Income of Laborage and Allowance	9190.47	10359.48	11951.96	12901.49	
其他劳动收入	Income of other Labor	437.52	394.97	357.21	726.08	
经营净收入	Net Business Income	1174.02	1614.67	1982.45	3244.92	3540.38
财产性收入	Income from Property	213.83	356.41	355.70	576.25	711.24
#利息收入	Interest Income	10.22	19.03	31.84	17.10	-46.26
股息与红利收入	Dividends and Bonus Income	4.29	12.63	11.76	120.20	162.97
转移性收入	Income from Transfer	4122.96	4873.34	5395.56	3964.30	4353.38
#养老金或离退休金	Annuities or Pension	3493.33	4229.54	4673.43	2798.38	4564.2
出售财物收入	Income of Selling Property and Goods	181.55	46.61	271.17	79.83	
家庭总支出	**Total Households Expenditure**	**13479.37**	**15558.27**	**17312.83**	**17138.08**	**19935.79**
消费支出	Consumption Expenditure	10058.29	11352.88	12585.70	13702.87	13311.96
财产性支出	Property Expenditure	52.40	88.39	87.07	49.01	96.09
转移性支出	Transfer Expenditure	1923.23	2364.36	2601.30	2423.39	828.34
#交纳的个人收入税	Individual Income Tax	20.67	15.95	14.70	12.36	33.05
各种非储蓄性保险支出	Various Nonsaving Insurance Expenditure	32.84	39.87	38.43	76.52	
其他转移性支出	Others	56.49	73.40	66.80	176.89	99.82
社会保障支出	Social Seurity Expenditure	859.17	996.60	1178.02	600.57	574.54
购房与建房支出	Expenditure of Purchasing or Building House	586.28	756.04	860.73	362.24	538.17

10-4 城镇居民家庭人均消费性支出

Per Capita Annual Consumption Expenditure of Urban Household

单位：元 (yuan)

指　标	Item	2010	2011	2012	2013	2014
消费性支出	**Consumption Expenditure**	**10058.29**	**11352.88**	**12585.70**	**13702.87**	**15254.64**
食　品	**Food**	**4013.67**	**4565.85**	**4992.85**	**4915.02**	**5319.60**
#粮　食	Grain	320.00	374.20	395.96	450.18	598.23
糖、烟、酒、饮料类	Sugar, Cigarette,Liquor and Beverage	494.98	508.79	592.09	710.69	783.30
在外饮食	Dining Out	818.58	918.02	1054.53	724.73	741.80
衣　着	**Clothing**	**1102.41**	**1209.88**	**1399.00**	**1401.85**	**1245.89**
居　住	**Residence**	**890.75**	**1102.99**	**1013.53**	**1496.49**	**2432.50**
#房　租	Rent	24.19	50.08	80.11	185.90	140.87
水　费	Water	98.60	94.38	101.47	132.89	124.81
电　费	Electricity	385.54	412.22	462.74	542.25	505.46
燃料费	Fuels	147.89	158.01	162.20	218.94	170.96
家庭设备用品及服务	**Household Facilities,Articles and Services**	**673.33**	**857.55**	**849.94**	**1083.77**	**1090.54**
#耐用消费品	Durable Consumer Goods	199.59	366.57	270.72	446.30	238.49
医疗保健	**Health Care and Medical Services**	**546.84**	**578.33**	**654.53**	**633.72**	**927.39**
交通和通信	**Transport and Communications**	**1270.49**	**1395.28**	**1891.03**	**1870.08**	**1873.10**
交　通	Transport	606.34	698.37	1146.18	1005.78	1028.95
通　信	Communications	664.15	696.91	744.85	864.30	844.15
教育文化娱乐服务	**Education,Culture and Recreation Services**	**1254.56**	**1331.43**	**1396.00**	**1950.28**	**2071.32**
#文化娱乐用品	Recreation Articles	269.35	323.35	315.85	313.64	335.89
书报杂志	Books,Newspaper and Magazines	31.26	29.84	26.53	29.53	31.51
文化娱乐服务	Recreation Services	491.18	520.72	580.28	639.24	731.11
其他商品和服务	**Miscellaneous Goods and Services**	**306.24**	**311.57**	**388.82**	**351.66**	**294.34**
恩格尔系数(%)	**Engel Coefficient(%)**	**39.9**	**40.2**	**39.7**	**35.9**	**34.90**

10-5 城镇居民家庭人均购买主要商品数量

Per Capita Annual Purchases of Major Commodities of Urban Househoulds

单位：公斤 (kg)

指 标	Item	2010	2011	2012	2013	2014
粮 食	Grain	70.69	78.88	68.13	82.82	69.68
食用植物油	Edible Vegetable Oil	8.70	9.91	8.40	11.81	9.54
猪 肉	Pork	25.66	27.89	24.93	28.37	24.38
牛、羊肉	Beef and Mutton	1.88	2.15	1.82	2.27	1.97
禽 类	Poultry	8.64	9.41	8.61	7.36	7.11
蛋 类	Eggs	5.70	6.68	5.70	5.21	5.02
水产品类(元)	Aquatic Products(yuan)	81.01	86.94	99.05	88.59	86.29
鲜 菜	Fresh Vegetables	93.57	106.12	92.88	92.95	76.70
糖类(元)	Sugar(yuan)	43.48	53.33	61.01	43.03	37.58
烟草类(元)	Cigarettes(yuan)	278.65	277.38	308.76	429.95	400.61
酒 类	Liquor	4.03	3.59	3.56	6.20	5.30
糕点类	Cake	3.08	3.34	2.90	3.23	3.19
干鲜瓜果类	Dried and Fresh Melons and Fruits	41.94	44.08	38.70	36.31	36.57
奶类及制品(元)	Milk and Its Products(yuan)	154.78	157.23	169.88	160.14	170.50

10-6 每百户城镇居民家庭耐用消费品拥有量

Number of Major Durable Consumer Goods Owned Per 100 Urban Households

单位：台 (set)

指 标	Item	2010	2011	2012	2013	2014
摩托车(辆)	Motorcycle(unit)	5.79	5.46	5.42	15.39	20.83
家用汽车(辆)	Automobile(unit)	5.96	10.48	13.17	15.84	19.66
洗衣机	Washing Machine	99.23	99.15	99.87	95.50	95.70
电冰箱	Refrigerator	94.56	97.21	97.63	89.98	90.69
彩色电视机	Color TV Set	121.93	115.78	115.67	101.84	105.05
家用电脑	Household Computer	56.79	63.89	71.22	55.72	63.56
组合音响(套)	Hi-Fi Stereo Component System(unit)	37.06	31.22	28.02	14.41	13.49
照相机(架)	Camera(unit)	28.03	29.01	29.87	21.78	21.87
微波炉	Microwave Oven	45.71	45.76	47.59	40.73	40.91
空调器	Air Conditioner	17.00	20.46	21.71	18.70	20.48
淋浴热水器	Water Heater for Shower	72.42	75.11	78.51	77.36	76.63
健身器材(套)	Healthy Equipment(unit)	4.20	3.30	4.06	2.22	3.84
移动电话(部)	Mobile Phone(unit)	183.54	204.75	214.73	211.72	228.15

10-7 按收入等级分城镇居民家庭收入、消费情况(2014)

Statistics of Income and Consumption of Urban Househoulds by Level of Income

指　标	Item	低收入户 (20%) Low Income Households	中低收入户 (20%) Lower Middle Income Households	中等收入户 (20%) Middle Income Households	中高收入户 (20%) Upper Middle Income Households	高收入户 (20%) High Income Households
平均每人年可支配收入(元)	**Per Capita Annual Disposable Income(yuan)**	**8895.42**	**15750.22**	**22377.71**	**29456.31**	**47117.24**
人均购买主要商品数量	**Per Capita Purchases of Major Commodities**					
粮食(千克)	Grain(kg)	64.28	64.69	72.23	75.78	75.28
食用植物油(千克)	Edible Vegetable Oil(kg)	7.40	8.60	11.01	11.13	10.55
猪肉(千克)	Pork(kg)	18.63	22.84	26.65	27.51	29.29
牛肉(千克)	Beef(kg)	0.88	1.28	1.87	2.44	2.95
鸡(千克)	Chicken(kg)	2.81	4.19	5.44	6.36	7.98
鸭(千克)	Duck(kg)	0.70	0.72	1.17	1.22	1.59
鲜蛋(千克)	Eggs(kg)	3.01	3.99	5.00	5.76	5.94
鱼(千克)	Fish(kg)	1.80	2.11	3.43	3.60	3.70
鲜菜(千克)	Fresh Vegetables(kg)	54.12	71.36	80.04	90.46	100.63
糖类(元)	Sugar(yuan)	28.16	26.52	42.73	44.64	54.34
烟草类(元)	Cigarettes(yuan)	219.71	280.29	437.86	510.89	696.15
白酒(千克)	Liquor(kg)	2.35	2.57	3.06	2.07	3.66
鲜果(千克)	Fresh Fruit(kg)	20.46	26.28	36.17	39.26	50.04
糕点(千克)	Cakes(kg)	1.28	1.79	2.33	3.59	3.65
鲜乳品(千克)	Fresh Milk Products(kg)	3.69	6.82	13.76	15.99	16.37
每百户耐用消费品拥有量	**Ownership of Major Durable Consumer Goods Per 100 Urban Households**					
摩托车(辆)	Motorcycle(unit)	31.61	26.13	20.30	14.93	11.22
家用汽车(辆)	Automobile(unit)	9.81	14.48	20.36	21.12	32.49
洗衣机(台)	Washing Machine(set)	96.24	92.43	85.56	96.85	97.39
电冰箱(台)	Refrigerator(set)	85.54	87.87	92.89	94.39	92.77
彩色电视机(台)	Color TV Set(set)	103.03	102.90	105.90	104.57	108.87
家用电脑(台)	Household Computer(set)	36.37	55.95	67.93	76.87	80.60
组合音响(套)	Hi-Fi Stereo Component System(unit)	104.40	108.60	16.32	17.04	12.77
照相机(架)	Camera(unit)	4.58	13.71	22.12	31.00	37.85
微波炉(台)	Microwave Oven(set)	15.80	32.63	42.38	54.16	59.42
空调器(台)	Air Conditioner(set)	9.09	11.30	20.23	22.41	39.32
淋浴热水器(台)	Water Heater for Shower(set)	55.74	67.86	82.80	86.95	89.75
健身器材(套)	Healthy Equipment(unit)	0.68	2.21	5.82	4.39	6.07
固定电话(部)	Telephone(unit)	67.47	48.36	50.89	52.77	55.75
移动电话(部)	Mobile Phone(unit)	235.33	233.33	245.06	230.38	196.82

10-8 农村居民家庭生活基本情况
Basic Conditions of Rural Households Life

指 标	Item	2010	2011	2012	2013	2014
调查户数(户)	**Households Surveyed(household)**	**2240**	**2240**	**2240**	**2014**	**2748**
平均每户常住人口(人)	Average Number of Persons Per Household (person)	4.34	4.32	4.31	4.68	3.49
平均每户整、半劳动力(人)	Average Number of Laborers Per Household (person)	2.95	2.83	2.82	3.00	2.07
平均每一劳动力赡养人口(人)	Average Number Persons Supported by a Laborer (person)	1.47	1.52	1.53	1.56	1.69
平均每百个劳动力中(人)	In Per 100 Laborers (person)					
文盲或半文盲	Illiterate or Semi-Illiterate	12.32	10.29	10.35	10.50	
小学程度	Elementary School	35.70	38.63	38.16	37.91	
初中程度	Junior High School	42.56	43.23	42.92	42.87	
高中程度	Senior High School	6.59	3.78	4.12	4.68	
中专程度	Technical Secondary School	1.91	1.69	1.93	2.04	
大专以上	Junior College	0.92	1.31	1.42	2.00	
劳动力平均受教育年限(年)	Average Fixed Number of Year of Receiving Education of the Laborers(year)	7.14	7.07	7.11	7.28	
平均每人年收入(元)	**Per Capita Annual Income (yuan)**					
总收入	Total Income	4560.52	5659.58	6443.90	7232.23	9351.90
工资性收入	Income from Wages and Salaries	1303.85	1713.52	1977.73	2572.61	2521.48
家庭经营收入	Income from Household Operations	2674.22	3367.61	3809.21	3922.00	5162.35
财产性收入	Income from Properties	117.19	59.50	71.54	78.37	95.63
转移性收入	Income from Transfers	465.26	518.96	585.42	659.25	1572.45
现金收入	Cash Income	3448.33	4439.54	5078.31	5982.67	7666.99
工资性收入	Income from Wages and Salaries	1303.65	1712.31	1976.43	2572.02	2519.76
家庭经营收入	Income from Household Operations	1571.86	2169.90	2460.43	2690.25	3549.75
财产性收入	Income from Properties	114.47	48.31	70.88	78.37	95.63
转移性收入	Income from Transfers	458.35	509.02	570.57	642.02	1471.85
平均每人年纯收入(元)	**Annual Average Net Income Per Capita(yuan)**	**3471.93**	**4145.35**	**4753.00**	**5434.00**	
工资性收入	Payment for Labour	1303.85	1713.52	1977.73	2572.61	
家庭经营纯收入	Income from Household Operations	1706.33	1980.21	2249.21	2355.85	
转移性收入	Income from Transfers	344.56	392.13	454.53	427.16	
财产性收入	Income from Properties	117.19	59.50	71.54	78.37	
平均每人年总支出(元)	**Annual Average Expenditure Per Capita(yuan)**	**4350.25**	**5722.46**	**6370.25**	**6752.89**	**10893.05**
#人均生活消费支出	Living Expenditure	2852.48	3455.76	3901.71	4740.18	5970.25
人均年末使用房屋面积(平方米)	Average Per Capita Living Space at the Year-end(sq.m)	27.26	29.63	29.75	27.08	31.61

10-9 农村居民家庭人均可支配收入
Per Capita Annual Net Income of Rural Households

单位：元 (yuan)

指标	Item	2010	2011	2012	2013	2014
农村常住居民人均可支配收入	**Annual Net Income**	**3471.93**	**4145.35**	**4753.00**	**5434.00**	**6671.22**
工资性收入	Income from Wage	1303.85	1713.52	1977.73	2572.61	2521.48
家庭经营收入	Income from Household Operation	1706.33	1980.21	2249.21	2355.85	2643.06
第一产业	Primary Industry	1396.65	1500.94	1686.76	1820.40	1977.53
农业收入	Farming	1081.82	1065.10	1275.43	1220.31	1192.96
林业收入	Forestry	42.99	63.41	78.38	62.03	113.97
牧业收入	Animal Husbandry	268.61	368.01	328.76	524.21	664.04
渔业收入	Fishery	3.23	4.41	4.19	13.85	6.56
第二产业	Secondary Industry	49.97	58.49	72.71	95.53	96.78
工业收入	Industry	9.30	12.91	21.97	37.51	
建筑业收入	Construction	40.66	45.57	50.74	58.02	47.81
第三产业	Tertiary Industry	259.72	420.78	489.74	439.92	568.74
交通运输邮电业收入	Transport, Post and Telecommunication Services	74.27	146.97	193.29	208.35	205.72
批发贸易餐饮业收入	Wholesale and Retail Trade & Catering Services	99.41	175.44	201.04	191.91	
社会服务业收入	Social Services	29.92	39.27	43.93	27.07	
其他家庭经营收入	Others	56.12	59.10	51.48	12.58	
转移性收入	Income from Transfer	344.56	392.13	454.53	427.16	1435.69
财产性收入	Income from Property	117.19	59.50	71.54	78.37	71.00

注：农村常住居民人均可支配收入2013年及以前为农民人均纯收入。

Note:Ruralpermanent residents's disposable income in 2013 and before was per capita net income of farms.

10-10 农村居民家庭人均年总支出
Per Capita Annual Gross Expenditures of Rural Households

单位：元 (yuan)

指　　标	Item	2010	2011	2012	2013	2014
全年总支出	**Gross Expenditure**	**4350.25**	**5722.46**	**6370.25**	**6752.89**	**10893.05**
#生活消费支出	Living Expenditure for Consumption	2852.48	3455.76	3901.71	4740.18	5970.25
食　品	Food	1319.43	1646.51	1740.58	2036.22	2488.50
衣　着	Clothing	137.49	186.22	226.81	254.25	341.63
居　住	Residence	621.80	639.32	758.37	980.78	1202.08
家庭设备、用品及服务	Household Facilities,Articles and Services	135.64	192.78	211.36	272.38	355.08
医疗保健	Medicines and Medical Services	178.07	246.28	282.51	302.30	372.98
交通和通信	Transport and Telecommunications	229.66	304.51	371.35	489.67	636.47
文教娱乐用品及服务	Culture,Education and Recreation Articles and Services	186.19	183.03	226.44	301.38	481.40
其他商品和服务	Miscellaneous Goods and Services	44.21	57.10	84.30	103.20	92.14
家庭经营费用支出	Expenditure for Household Operation	871.62	1218.87	1367.00	1353.40	2171.76
#种植业生产支出	Farming Production Costs	312.74	374.98	467.74	465.93	
牧业生产支出	Animal Husbandry Costs	484.31	628.23	644.05	625.49	787.16
购置生产用固定资产支出	Expenditure for Purchasing Productive Fixed Assets	102.89	209.95	183.17	170.29	
转移性支出	Transfer Expenditures	508.59	809.31	900.84	483.85	136.75
#寄给和带给在外人口	Posting or Taking to Outside City	30.67	74.84	99.89	91.54	
财产性支出	Property Expenditures	8.52	24.55	8.20	2.30	21.72
恩格尔系数(%)	**Engel Coefficient(%)**	**46.3**	**47.7**	**44.6**	**43.0**	**41.7**

10-11 农村居民家庭人均年现金收支
Per Capita Annual Cash Income and Expenditure of Rural Households

单位：元 (yuan)

指 标	Item	2010	2011	2012	2013	2014
现金收入合计	**Total Annual Cash Income**	**3448.33**	**4439.54**	**5078.31**	**5982.67**	**5717.71**
工资性收入	Income from Wage	1303.65	1712.31	1976.43	2572.02	2519.76
家庭经营现金收入	Income from Household Business Operation	1571.86	2169.90	2460.43	2690.25	1788.95
#出售产品收入	Income from Selling Product	1162.33	1440.86	1611.76	1810.94	
建筑业收入	Construction	52.15	65.33	76.45	88.44	61.55
交通运输邮电业收入	Transport, Post and Telecommunication Services	118.38	271.86	317.64	303.49	264.66
批发和零售贸易餐饮业收入	Wholesale and Retail Trade & Catering Services	120.40	251.27	310.52	325.12	
社会服务业收入	Social Service	31.66	45.10	49.65	39.29	
其他家庭经营现金收入	Others	45.35	35.11	32.99	28.23	
转移性现金收入	Transfer Cash Income	458.35	509.02	570.57	642.02	1335.10
#亲友赠送	Income from Friends' and Relatives' Presents	125.70	141.13	134.91	232.08	
抚恤金	Pension	3.63	3.11	3.30	8.18	4.35
财产性现金收入	Property Cash Income	114.47	48.31	70.88	78.37	73.90
#租金收入	Rental Income	26.45	18.26	22.67	37.28	
非收入所得合计	**Reward From Other Way**	**1046.65**	**1690.01**	**1663.71**	**1971.11**	**1350.87**
#银行、信用社贷款	Loans of Bank and Credit Union	130.30	271.12	226.41	185.76	
借入款	Borrowed Money	260.04	440.70	421.58	452.57	720.78
收回借出款	Drawing Back Loan	51.78	54.72	62.75	54.58	102.20
从银行、信用社取回存款	Drawing Money from Banks and Credit Union	165.05	200.05	241.46	412.48	832.12
收回投资款	Disinvestment		0.10	0.05	44.20	
现金支出合计	**Total Cash Expenditure**	**3339.45**	**4659.81**	**5390.31**	**5602.88**	**8773.58**
#生产费用支出	Expenditure for Operating Costs	666.48	1153.38	1316.52	1229.57	1790.80
生活消费支出	Living Expenditure for Consumption	2159.14	2670.71	3157.39	3888.31	4231.75
转移性支出	Transfer Expenditures	503.26	809.03	900.15	482.61	136.75
#寄给在外人口	Posting to Outside City	30.65	74.84	99.89	91.54	
非消费性现金支出	**Nonconsumptive Expenditure**	**599.03**	**668.28**	**613.96**	**1077.93**	
#归还银行、信用社存款	Deposits of Bank and Credit Union Recession	64.56	90.04	109.85	60.40	
借出款	Loan	18.14	25.86	17.88	15.78	13.54
归还借款	Loan Recession	99.02	150.47	159.16	158.60	192.86
存入银行、信用社	Deposit	286.23	187.3	129.65	244.57	59.68

10－12 农村居民家庭每人主要消费品消费量

Per Capita Annual Consumption of Major Consumer Goods in Rural Households

单位：公斤 (kg)

指　标	Item	2010	2011	2012	2013	2014
粮　食	Grain	164.63	162.62	149.10	151.57	163.55
#大　米	Rice	130.26	135.55	121.17	120.53	127.83
食　油	Edible Oil	3.01	4.34	4.80	5.98	8.05
肉禽及其制品	Meat,Poultry and Related Product	27.77	25.73	23.67	28.54	33.22
#猪　肉	Pork	25.21	23.04	20.98	24.58	32.11
家　禽	Poultry	1.98	2.10	2.05	2.43	3.30
蛋类及蛋制品	Eggs and Their Products	1.81	1.93	2.35	3.26	3.57
水产品	Aquatic Products	0.38	0.43	0.53	0.80	1.01
#鱼　类	Fish	0.33	0.39	0.48	0.72	0.92
蔬　菜	Vegetables	116.74	110.42	97.43	95.49	97.17
瓜　果	Melon and Fruits	8.93	10.33	12.39	10.88	17.31
食　糖	Sugar	0.78	0.68	0.70	0.74	0.94
卷　烟(盒)	Cigarette(pack)	22.44	25.34	25.83	24.26	30.31
酒	Liquor	6.83	7.52	7.75	8.82	9.96

10－13 每百户农村居民家庭年末耐用消费品拥有量

Number of Durable Consumer Goods Owned By Per 100 Rural Households at the Year-end

单位：台 (set)

指　标	Item	2010	2011	2012	2013	2014
彩色电视机	Color TV Set	91.1	93.9	95.9	96.5	98.9
电冰箱	Refrigerator	27.2	39.9	45.2	50.4	58.6
洗衣机	Washing Machine	55.2	62.5	69.8	69.6	75.2
热水器	Water Heater for Shower	6.2	9.7	12.0	13.8	19.6
摩托车(辆)	Motorcycle(unit)	30.8	36.0	39.0	41.4	48.4
电话机(部)	Telephone(unit)	37.5	17.9	15.4	13.9	13.2
移动电话(部)	Mobile Telephone(unit)	102.1	157.0	173.3	190.1	218.1

10−14 按收入五等份分农村居民家庭收入、消费情况（2014）
Income and Consumption of Rural Househoulds by Income Quintile

项　目	Item	低收入户 (20%) Low Income Households	中低收入户 (20%) Lower Middle Income Households	中等收入户 (20%) Middle Income Households	中高收入户 (20%) Upper Middle Income Households	高收入户 (20%) High Income Households
平均每人可支配收入(元)	**Per Capita Annual Income(yuan)**	**2428.28**	**4677.85**	**6357.06**	**8515.48**	**14216.70**
#现金可支配收入	Cash Income	1939.87	3820.63	5276.52	7302.88	12871.60
平均每人总支出(元)	**Per Capita Annual Expenditures(yuan)**	**9865.55**	**8182.78**	**9622.92**	**11833.10**	**16742.53**
#现金支出	Cash Expenditures	8264.63	6306.19	7518.38	9345.61	13891.79
平均每人主要消费品消费量（公斤）	**Per Capita Consumption of Majar Consumor Goods(kg)**					
粮　食	Grain	139.47	155.63	161.53	173.75	202.27
#大　米	Rice	105.55	119.94	129.27	136.18	161.50
食　油	Edible Oil	5.89	7.05	8.23	8.66	11.82
肉禽及其制品	Meat,Poultry and Related Product	24.04	29.98	33.49	37.63	46.39
#猪　肉	Pork	22.95	29.18	32.52	36.53	44.66
家　禽	Poultry	2.45	2.76	3.14	3.72	5.07
蛋类及蛋制品	Eggs and Their Products	2.87	3.24	3.53	3.99	4.70
水产品	Aquatic Products	0.84	0.85	0.80	1.15	1.60
#鱼　类	Fish	0.76	0.78	0.73	1.05	1.43
蔬　菜	Vegetables	79.22	89.11	97.35	107.53	123.81
瓜　果	Melon and Fruits	13.04	15.29	17.68	19.56	23.59
食　糖	Sugar	0.89	0.87	0.90	0.92	1.20
卷　烟(盒)	Cigarette(pack)	21.30	26.35	31.06	32.60	46.00
酒	Liquor	7.69	9.54	10.08	10.63	13.12
每百户耐用消费品拥有量	**Number of Durable Consumer Goods Owned By Per 100 Rural Households**					
彩色电视机(台)	Color TV Set(set)	97.79	98.10	101.26	97.01	100.24
电冰箱(台)	Refrigerator(set)	55.36	53.24	55.21	61.31	68.06
洗衣机(台)	Washing Machine(set)	73.76	71.92	74.99	75.93	79.31
热水器(台)	Water Heater(set)	11.77	14.87	18.22	24.49	28.68
摩托车(辆)	Motorcycles(set)	42.32	47.58	46.55	51.01	54.41
电话机(部)	Telephone(unit)	11.46	10.06	11.68	15.47	17.50
移动电话(部)	Mobile Telephone(unit)	212.83	211.25	214.38	226.49	225.66

10−15 农村居民家庭人均经营费用和生产性固定资产购置

Per Capita Expenditure for Household Operations and Expenditure for Purchasing Productive Fixed Assets of Rural Households

单位：元 (yuan)

指　标	Item	2010	2011	2012	2013	2014
家庭经营费用支出	**Expenditure for Household Operations**	**871.62**	**1218.87**	**1367.00**	**1353.40**	**2171.76**
#农业生产支出	Farming	312.74	374.98	467.74	465.93	582.11
林业生产支出	Forestry	2.65	8.64	12.35	16.60	10.19
牧业生产支出	Animal Husbandry	484.31	628.23	644.05	625.49	787.16
渔业生产支出	Fishery	2.51	1.03	2.33	2.51	4.99
工业生产支出	Industry	4.50	26.90	21.43	22.26	
建筑业支出	Construction	10.51	17.15	22.45	21.57	29.85
交通运输邮电业支出	Transport, Post and Telecommunication	26.82	86.41	85.12	57.69	95.61
批发和零售贸易、餐饮业支出	Wholesale and Retail Trade & Catering Services	18.40	63.42	96.43	106.60	
社会服务业支出	Social Services	1.07	4.78	4.91	9.88	
其他经营支出	Others	4.49	3.27	6.85	12.46	
购置生产用固定资产支出	**Expenditure for Purchasing Productive Fixed Assets**	**102.89**	**209.95**	**183.17**	**170.29**	**161.09**
#农林牧渔业机械	Machinery of Agricalture, Forestry, Animal Husbandry and Fishery	22.89	52.80	50.11	25.81	
工业机械	Industrial Machinery	5.74	5.91	0.35	2.15	
运输机械	Transportation Machinery	36.32	86.99	43.82	81.68	
役畜、产品畜	Draught Animals and Commodity Animals	16.46	38.80	47.04	39.06	76.70

主要统计指标解释

住户 指居住在一个住宅内，共同分享生活开支或收入的一群人。居住在同一房间内、不共同分享生活开支的人群，每个人都视为一个住户。住家保姆、住家家庭帮工视为单独的住户。

住户成员 指居住在一个住宅内，所有与本住户分享生活开支或收入的人员。

常住成员 指住户成员中，经常在家居住、或者调查期内居住时间超过一半的人员，以及本住户供养的学生。

季度调查的常住成员包括：

①过去三个月已经居住或未来三个月打算居住时间超过1.5个月的住户成员。

②过去三个月内每月至少在调查住宅居住一天以上，且没有在其他自有或独自租借的普通住宅中住过的人。或者说，在外与人合住或住在工棚、集体宿舍、工作地或其他临时性住所、又定期回家居住的人，也是本住户常住成员。

③由本住户供养的在校学生（包括大中专学生和研究生）。

就业面 指就业人口占家庭人口的百分比。

就业者负担人数 指家庭人口与就业人口之比。

整、半劳动力 整劳动力指男子18周岁到50周岁，女子18周岁到45周岁；半劳动力指男子16周岁到17周岁，51周岁到60周岁；女子16周岁到17周岁，46周岁到55周岁，同时具有劳动能力的人。虽然在劳动年龄之内，但已丧失劳动能力的人，不应算为劳动力；超过劳动年龄，但能经常参加劳动，计入半劳动力数内。常住人口中的职工，若这些职工为劳动力，就包括在本户的整半劳动力中。

可支配收入 指调查户在调查期内获得的、可用于最终消费支出和储蓄的总和，即调查户可以用来自由支配的收入。可支配收入既包括现金，也包括实物收入。按照收入的来源，可支配收入包含四项，分别为：工资性收入、经营净收入、财产净收入和转移净收入。计算公式为：

可支配收入=工资性收入+经营净收入+财产净收入+转移净收入

其中：经营净收入=经营收入−经营费用−生产性固定资产折旧−生产税

财产净收入=财产性收入−财产性支出

转移净收入=转移性收入−转移性支出

工资性收入 指就业人员通过各种途径得到的全部劳动报酬和各种福利，包括受雇于单位或个人、从事各种自由职业、兼职和零星劳动得到的全部劳动报酬和福利。

经营净收入 指住户或住户成员从事生产经营活动所获得的净收入，是全部经营收入中扣除经营费用、生产性固定资产折旧和生产税之后得到的净收入。计算公式具体为：

经营净收入=经营收入−经营费用−生产性固定资产折旧−生产税

财产净收入 指住户或住户成员将其所拥有的金融资产、住房等非金融资产和自然资源交由其他机构单位、住户或个人支配而获得的回报并扣除相关的费用之后得到的净收入。财产净收入包括利息净收入、红利收入、储蓄性保险净收益、转让承包土地经营权租金净收入、出租房屋净收入、出租其他资产净收入和自有住房折算净租金等。

财产净收入不包括转让资产所有权的溢价所得，这应该计入“非收入所得”。

转移净收入 计算公式为：转移净收入=转移性收入−转移性支出

转移性收入 指国家、单位、社会团体对住户的各种经常性转移支付和住户之间的经常性收入转移。包括政府、非行政事业单位、社会团体对居民转移的养老金或退休金、社会救济和补助、惠农补贴、政策性生活补贴、救灾款、经常性捐赠和赔偿以及报销医疗费等；住户之间的赡养收入、经常性捐赠和赔偿以及农村地区（村委会）在外（含国外）工作的本住户非常住成员寄回带回的收入等。

转移性收入不包括住户之间的实物馈赠。

城镇居民人均可支配收入（老口径） 指城镇家庭总收入扣除交纳的个人所得税和个人交纳的各项社会保障支出之后，按照城镇居民家庭人口平均的收入水平。其中家庭总收入是指该家庭中生活在一起的所有家庭人员从各种渠道得到的所有收入之和。更详细的解释可参照《城镇住户调查方案（2011 年统计年报和 2012 年定期报表）》。

农村居民人均纯收入（老口径） 指农村住户当年从各个来源得到的家庭总收入扣除有关费用性支出后，最终归农村居民所有的收入总和，按照农村住户人口平均的纯收入水平。更详细的解释可参照《农村住户调查方案（2011 年统计年报和 2012 年定期报表）》

消费支出 指住户用于满足家庭日常生活消费需要的全部支出，包括用于消费品的支出和用于服务性消费的支出。根据用途不同，消费支出可划分为食品烟酒、衣着、居住、生活用品及服务、交通通信、教育文化娱乐、医疗保健、其他用品及服务八大类。根据来源不同，消费支出可划分为现金消费支出、实物消费支出（含自产自用、来自单位、来自政府和其他社会组织）。

家庭收入分组方法 将所有调查户依户人均可支配收入由低到高排队，按 20%，20%，20%，20%，20%的比例依次分成：低收入户、中低收入户、中等收入户、中高收入户、高收入户等五组。

恩格尔系数 指食物支出金额在生活消费总支出金额中所占的比例。计算公式为：

$$恩格尔系数 = \frac{食品支出金额}{生活消费总支出金额} \times 100\%$$

Explanatory Notes on Main Statistical Indicators

Household refer to a group of people who live in a house, share a living expenses or income. Living in the same room, not to share the living expenses of the crowd, everyone is considered as a household. Nanny, home family workers are treated as a separate household。

Household Members refer to a member of the household who is living in a house, all of which share the expenses or income of the household.

Permanent Members refer to the members of the household who is often at home, or in the residence time of more than half of the residence time, and the students who support.

Quarterly Sruvey of Permanent Members include:

①The household members who have been living over the past three months or will live longer than 1.5 months in the next three months.

②The people who live In the investigation housing the past three months, at least over the past months, more than one day, and not live in ordinary homes, or on a lease. Or, in the outside and people share or live in sheds, dormitory, work or other temporary shelters and regular home living people, but also the households resident members.

③Students supported by the household.

Employment refers to the percentage of the population in the family.

The Number of Employed Persons refers to the ratio of the household population to the employment population.

Full/Semi Labour Force Full labour force refers to persons capable of work, aged 18-50 for males and 18-45 for females. Semi labour force refers to persons capable of work, aged 16-17 and 51-60 for males and 16-17 and 46-55 for females. Persons at their working ages but not capable of work are not to be included as labour force. Persons not at working ages but participating regularly in work are included in semi labour force. For staff and workers as resident population of the household, they are included as full or semi labour force of the household if they are in the labour force.

Disposable income refers to the income of the household survey period, which can be used for final consumption and savings, or the income of the household can be used for free. Disposable income includes both cash, but also in kind. According to the sources of income, disposable income includes four items, respectively, the wage income, net income, net income and net income. Calculation formula:

Disposable income = wage income + net income + property net income + transfer net income

Where: operating net income = operating income - operating expenses - production of fixed assets depreciation - production tax

Property net income = property income - property expenses

Transfer of net income = transfer income-transfer expenditure

Income from Wages refers to all the remuneration and benefits received by the employed persons through various means, including all the labor remuneration and benefits obtained from the employment of the unit or individual, in various kinds of freelance work, part - time, and sporadic labor.

Net Operating Income refers to the income of the household or household members engaged in the production and operation activities, is the net income of all operating expenses, production of fixed assets depreciation and production tax. Calculation formula is concrete:

Net operating income,=operating expenses-operating expenses-depreciation of productive fixed assets-production tax

Property Net Income refers to the income received by the household or household members of the financial assets, housing, and other non financial assets and natural resources, which are obtained by other institutional units, households or individuals, and net income after deducting expenses. Property net income includes interest income, dividend income, savings insurance net income, transfer contract land management right to rent, rental housing net income, rental income and other assets of the net rent and other assets.

Property net income does not include the premium income from the transfer of property rights, which should be included in the "non income".

Transfer of Net Income calculation formula is: the transfer of net income = transfer income - transfer expenditure

Transfer income refers to the transfer payments of the country, the unit, the social group to the tenants of a variety of recurrent and the transfer of the regular income between households. Including the government, the non administrative institutions, social groups of residents to move pension or retirement benefits, social benefits and subsidies, subsidies benefit farmers, policy subsidy, relief funds, regular donation and compensation and reimbursement of medical expenses; between tenants alimony income, often donations and compensation and rural areas (Village) (including foreign) of the households in non resident members return back to the income.

The transfer of income does not include the physical gifts between households.

The Per Capita Disposable Income of Urban Residents refers to the income tax and the average income level of the residents in urban families after the deduction of the income tax and the social security expenditure. The total household income is the sum of all the income of the family who lives in a variety of ways. More detailed explanation can be referred to the 《urban household survey (2011 statistical report and 2012 periodic report)》.

The Per Capita Net Income of Rural Residents (old caliber) refers to the total income of rural households in the year from various sources of household income after deducting the cost of the total income of rural residents, according to the average net income of rural households. A more detailed explanation can be referred to the 《Rural Household Survey Programme (2011 statistical report and the 2012 periodic report)》.

Consumer Spending refers to all the expenses that the household is used to meet the needs of the daily life of the family, including the expenses for the consumer goods and the expenses for the service. According to different purposes, the consumption expenditure can be divided into tobacco and food, clothing, housing, daily necessities and services, transportation and communication, education culture and entertainment, health care and other goods and services eight categories. According to different sources, consumer spending can be divided into cash consumption, real consumer spending (including self-produced their own, from the unit, from the government and other social organizations).

Household income grouping method According to the households, the average income per household was low to high, according to 20%, 20%, 20%, 20%, 20% of the proportion were divided into: low income households, middle and low income households, middle income households, middle and high income, high income households and other five groups.

Engel Coefficient refers to the percentage of expenditure on food in the total consumption expenditure, using the following formula:

$$\text{Engel Coefficient} = \frac{\text{expenditure on food}}{\text{total consumption expenditure}} \times 100\%$$

城市概况

11

General Survey of Cities

11-1 城市公用事业

City Public Utilities

指 标	Item	2010	2011	2012	2013	2014
城市建设	**City Areas and Floor Space of Buildings**					
城区面积(平方公里)	Urban Area (sq.km)	4103.09	4108.16	4543.68	4708.90	4918.41
建成区面积(平方公里)	Area of Built Districts (sq.km)	972.99	986.50	1121.68	1315.86	1371.15
城市建设用地面积(平方公里)	Area of Land Used for Urban Construction (sq.km)	1002.15	1005.73	1026.84	1141.93	1203.92
征用土地面积(平方公里)	Area of Land Put in Requisition for State Construction Projects (sq.km)	26.03	36.20	57.19	95.74	58.68
城市人口密度(人/平方公里)	Population Density of City Districts (persons/sq.km)	2481	2579	2410	2411	2368
城市供水、燃气	**Supply Water and Gas**					
年末供水综合生产能力(万立方米/日)	Production Capacity of Tap Water Supply at Year-end (10000 cu.m/day)	352.11	364.56	376.94	364.28	371.97
供水管道长度(公里)	Annual Length of Water Pipelines (km)	9376.00	11107.57	11629.67	12579.11	13608.14
建成区城市供水管道密度(公里/平方公里)	Water Pipelines Pensity of Built Districts of city(km/sq.km)	9.64	11.26	10.37	9.56	9.92
供水总量(万立方米)	Volume of Tap Water Supply (10000 cu.m)	63572	67766	71168	74730	79789
#生活用水	Water Consumption for Residential Use	33064	36091	38367	39631	42847
生产用水	Water Consumption for Productive Use	12109	11335	10728	10196	10379
用水人口(万人)	Number of Residents with Access to Tap Water (10000 persons)	880.83	920.40	959.30	1044.68	1050.33
人均日生活用水(升)	Per Capita Daily Consumption of Tap Water for Residential Use (liter)	116.88	127.82	128.92	131.39	134.53
用水普及率 (%)	Coverage Rate of Urban Population with Access to Tap Water (%)	86.5	86.9	87.6	88.5	90.2
人工煤气生产能力(万立方米)	Production Capacity of Gaswork Gas (10 000 cu.m)	191.80	187.00	187.00	102.00	102.00
管道长度(公里)	Length of Gas Pipelines (km)	3207.50	3264.27	3597.19	4065.69	4483.98
人工煤气	Gaswork	2829.70	2741.53	2902.89	2948.42	2954.25
液化石油气	Liquefied Petroleum Gas	182.72	182.72	184.95	189.95	129.39
天然气	Natural Gas	195.07	340.02	509.35	927.32	1400.34
全年供气总量	Annual Volume of Gas Supply					
人工煤气(万立方米)	Gaswork (10 000 cu.m)	26963	30515	34167	23788	16034
#家庭用量	Consumption of Gaswork Gas for Residential Use	11436	13118	14259	12177	8461
天然气(万立方米)	Natural Gas Supply (10 000 cu.m)	3546	5496	9879	16668	31311
#家庭用量	Consumption of Natural Gas for Residential Use	1160	674	1096	3118	12573
液化石油气 (吨)	Liquefied Petroleum Gas(ton)	94481	99396	101606	108144	113647
#家庭用量	Consumption of Liquefied Gas for Residential Use	86703	91742	93089	99340	106175
用气人口(万人)	Population with Access to Gas (10 000 persons)	554.35	582.54	603.88	666.26	701.73
人工煤气	Gaswork	166.76	207.69	176.05	126.60	127.50
液化石油气	Liquefied Petroleum Gas	375.94	350.98	372.81	402.53	419.23
天 然 气	Natural Gas	11.65	23.87	55.02	137.13	155.00
燃气普及率(%)	Coverage Rate of Urban Population with Access to Gas (%)	54.5	55.0	55.2	58.7	60.3
城市市政设施	**Municipal Infrastructure**					
年末实有道路长度(公里)	Length of Paved Roads at Year-end (km)	4081	4487	4875	5787	6325

11-1 续表 continued

指　　标	Item	2010	2011	2012	2013	2014
年末实有道路面积(万平方米)	Area of Paved Roads at Year-end(10 000sq.m)	6342	7054	7585	10166	11324
人均拥有道路面积(平方米)	Per Capita Area of Paved Roads(sq.m)	6.23	6.66	6.93	8.95	9.72
城市排水管道长度(公里)	Length of City Sewage Pipes(km)	5507	5977	6148	8146	8856
城市污水日处理能力(万立方米)	Daily Disposal Capacity of City Sewage (10 000 cu.m)	170.5	170.5	173.0	188.0	191.4
建城区城市排水管道密度(公里/平方公里)	Density of City Sewage Pipes(km/sq.km)	5.66	6.06	5.48	6.19	6.46
城市桥梁(座)	Number of City Bridges (unit)	735	776	783	901	931
城市道路照明灯(千盏)	Number of Street Lights (1 000 units)	302	391	428	540	590
城市公共交通	**Public Traffic**					
年末公共交通运营车辆数(辆)	Number of Public Vehicles under Operation at Year-end (Buses and Trolley Buses, etc.) (unit)	4984	5364	5429	6484	7355
运营线路网长度(公里)	Network Length (km)	6056	6212	6518	7161	9037
公共交通客运总量(万人次)	Passengers Transported by Public Vehicles (10 000person-times)	120219.6	130976	143499	153381	163336
出租汽车(辆)	Number of Taxi(unit)	15087	17196	20600	22946	24394
城市绿化和园林	**City Greening**					
城市园林绿地面积(公顷)	Area of Parks and Green Land (hectare)	45500	48024	51081	67029	71048
公园绿地面积	Park Green Areas	5422	5830	7311	9063	10090
人均公园绿地面积(平方米)	Per Capita Area of Parks and Green Land(sq.m)	5.33	5.50	6.68	7.98	8.66
公园个数(个)	Number of Parks and Zoos(unit)	130	146	147	161	160
公园面积(公顷)	Area of Parks (hectares)	4622	4941	5074	5743	6439
建成区绿化覆盖率(%)	Green Covered Area as % of Completed Area (%)	21.83	24.57	25.06	24.94	24.35
城市环境卫生	**Environmental Sanitation**					
清扫保洁面积(万平方米)	Area under Cleaning Program (10 000 sq.m)	5948	6982	7831	9028	9546
生活垃圾清运量(万吨)	Volume of Garbage Disposal (10 000 tons)	428.51	431.46	449.41	461.47	490.44
市容环卫专用车辆设备总数(台)	Number of Special Vehicles for Environmental Sanitation (unit)	1588	2320	2696	3134	3733
公共厕所(座)	Number of Public Lavatories (unit)	2147	2121	2110	2213	2311
#三类以上	Third Grade and Above	1463	1445	1461	1536	1689

注：资料来源于省住房城乡建设厅、省交通运输厅(以下相关表同)。

Note: Data is provided by provincial department of transport and housing construction of urban and rural department (The relative tables in the chapter are the same).

11-2 城市气象(2014)
Climate of Major Cities

城市名称	City	年平均气温(℃) Annual Average Temperature(℃)	年降水量(毫米) Annual Precipitation(mm)	年日照时数(小时) Annual Sunshine Hours(hour)	年平均相对湿度(%) Annual Average Relative Humidity(%)
贵阳市	Guiyang	14.7	1562.0	956.0	83
六盘水市	Liupanshui	13.1	1444.4	1204.3	81
遵义市	Zunyi	15.1	1069.8	1082.3	80
安顺市	Anshun	14.4	1334.6	1228.1	81
毕节市	Bijie	13.4	1013.8	970.5	81
铜仁市	Tongren	17.7	1609.8	900.7	80
兴义市	Xingyi	16.8	1958.5	1590.2	81
凯里市	Kaili	16.2	1205.4	1104.2	79
都匀市	Duyun	15.3	1763.5	729.5	84
清镇市	Qingzhen	15.0	1648.3	1195.4	80
赤水市	Chishui	18.0	1370.1	1089.6	84
仁怀市	Renhuai	15.9	1366.0	1041.6	79
福泉市	Fuquan	15.4	1263.4	853.2	81

注：1.资料来源于省气象局。2.地级市为所在城区的气象情况。(下表同)
Note:1.Data in the table are provided by the provincial bureau of meteorology. 2. (The same applies to the next table).

11-3 城市平均气温 (2014)
Monthly Average Temperature of Major Cities

单位：℃ (℃)

城市名称	City	1月 Jan.	2月 Feb.	3月 Mar.	4月 Apr.	5月 May	6月 June	7月 July	8月 Aug.	9月 Sept.	10月 Oct.	11月 Nov.	12月 Dec.
贵阳市	Guiyang	6.2	4.3	10.3	16.4	18.0	21.0	23.0	22.7	21.4	17.3	10.6	5.3
六盘水市	Liupanshui	4.5	5.1	9.9	15.5	17.0	18.9	20.4	19.8	19.0	14.9	9.1	3.3
遵义市	Zunyi	6.4	4.2	10.7	16.2	17.8	21.2	24.3	24.1	22.5	17.6	10.2	5.5
安顺市	Anshun	6.1	5.1	10.3	16.5	18.0	20.5	22.0	21.8	20.8	16.8	10.4	5.0
毕节市	Bijie	4.9	4.2	9.4	15.2	16.4	19.4	21.7	21.0	20.1	15.3	9.1	3.8
铜仁市	Tongren	8.6	6.1	13.0	17.8	21.1	24.7	27.5	26.6	24.7	20.3	13.3	8.6
兴义市	Xingyi	8.8	9.1	14.0	19.4	21.9	22.2	22.7	22.6	21.9	18.5	13.3	7.6
凯里市	Kaili	7.4	4.7	11.9	17.2	19.6	23.4	25.5	24.4	23.1	18.9	11.7	7.0
都匀市	Duyun	7.0	4.2	11.0	16.2	18.9	21.9	23.9	23.1	21.7	17.9	11.1	6.3
清镇市	Qingzhen	6.4	5.0	10.7	16.8	18.3	21.2	23.1	22.7	21.5	17.4	11.0	5.5
赤水市	Chishui	8.5	9.1	14.3	19.6	20.9	23.6	27.9	26.2	23.7	19.8	13.5	8.6
仁怀市	Renhuai	7.6	5.7	12.0	17.2	18.6	21.5	25.1	24.6	23.2	18.1	11.2	6.0
福泉市	Fuquan	6.7	4.1	11.2	16.6	18.8	22.2	24.4	23.6	22.2	17.9	11.3	6.3

11－4 城市建设(2014)
City Construction

城市名称	City	城区面积(平方公里) Urban Area (sq.km)	建成区面积(平方公里) Area of Built Districts (sq.km)	城市建设用地面积(平方公里) Area of Land Used for Urban Construction (sq.km)
贵 阳 市	Guiyang	1230.00	299.00	258.69
六盘水市	Liupanshui	129.00	42.50	41.13
遵 义 市	Zunyi	220.00	66.00	62.71
安 顺 市	Anshun	109.48	44.68	39.58
铜 仁 市	Tongren	53.30	34.68	31.60
兴 义 市	Xingyi	73.40	43.00	40.84
毕 节 市	Bijie	166.09	40.50	38.83
凯 里 市	Kaili	111.50	67.00	54.53
都 匀 市	Duyun	300.00	30.00	17.25
清 镇 市	Qingzhen	51.60	17.80	17.62
赤 水 市	Chishui	91.00	10.00	9.22
仁 怀 市	Renhuai	89.00	15.00	11.14
福 泉 市	Fuquan	19.20	13.60	12.51

11－5 城市设施水平(2014)
Level of Public Facilities in Cities

城市名称	City	城市用水普及率(%) Coverage Rate of Urban Population with Access to Tap Water (%)	城市燃气普及率(%) Coverage Rate of Urban Population with Access to Gas (%)	每万人拥有公共交通车辆(标台) Number of Public Transportation Vehicles Per 10 000 Population (unit)	人均城市道路面积(平方米) Per Capita Area of Paved Roads (sq.m)	人均公园绿地面积(平方米) Per Capita Park Green Areas (sq.m)
贵 阳 市	Guiyang	95.06	95.34	13.5	9.84	15.47
六盘水市	Liupanshui	90.88	91.18	8.1	12.34	16.66
遵 义 市	Zunyi	95.85	68.24	8.4	7.05	12.70
安 顺 市	Anshun	96.95	51.14	4.6	8.82	2.63
铜 仁 市	Tongren	90.27	30.60	5.9	7.84	5.42
兴 义 市	Xingyi	91.41	36.81	2.9	21.78	7.91
毕 节 市	Bijie	95.97	53.82	2.2	16.51	18.73
凯 里 市	Kaili	94.95	73.25	8.6	12.50	13.84
都 匀 市	Duyun	97.79	83.69	5.6	8.97	8.20
清 镇 市	Qingzhen	93.89	89.56	0.9	11.82	5.87
赤 水 市	Chishui	77.52	49.22	2.5	6.92	4.96
仁 怀 市	Renhuai	97.40	79.42	1.2	4.98	14.58
福 泉 市	Fuquan	96.26	53.48	0.7	9.19	14.44

11-6 城市供水（2014）
Tap Water Supply in Cities

城市名称	City	年末供水综合生产能力（万立方米/日）Production Capacity of Tap Water Supply (year-end) (10 000 cu.m/day)	年末供水管道长度（公里）Length of Water Supply Pipelines (year-end) (km)	全年供水总量（万立方米）Total Annual Volume of Water Supply (10 000 cu.m)	#生活用水 For Residential Use	#生产用水 For Productive Use	用水人口（万人）Number of Residents with Access to Tap Water (10 000 persons)	人均日生活用水量（升）Per Capita Daily Consumption of Tap Water for Residential Use(liter)
贵阳市	Guiyang	119.85	4217.76	29873.56	12928.41	4291.11	252.25	186.32
六盘水市	Liupanshui	10.00	950.00	2450.21	871.00	85.01	30.00	167.76
遵义市	Zunyi	23.40	305.00	5724.00	3833.00	578.00	75.00	152.62
安顺市	Anshun	9.30	242.80	2369.12	1403.23	489.63	50.30	88.75
铜仁市	Tongren	17.26	285.00	2303.86	1383.40	399.96	29.50	134.89
兴义市	Xingyi	12.50	392.00	2454.00	1560.00	360.00	29.80	152.52
毕节市	Bijie	12.00	588.00	2190.00	905.00	47.00	25.00	139.89
凯里市	Kaili	10.38	813.00	2471.00	1525.00	250.00	35.00	121.02
都匀市	Duyun	11.85	308.26	1933.54	877.22	372.90	23.02	157.31
清镇市	Qingzhen	5.50	202.50	1389.95	941.85	272.00	15.20	175.82
赤水市	Chishui	4.00	94.80	488.00	325.00	48.00	10.00	100.27
仁怀市	Renhuai	7.50	140.86	1184.30	792.00	141.00	13.49	178.72
福泉市	Fuquan	2.64	144.60	961.70	510.90	263.80	9.00	166.03

11－7 城市燃气(2014)
Supply of Gas in Cities

城市名称	City	人工煤气生产能力（万立方米/日） Production Capacity of Gaswork Gas (10 000 cu.m/day)	管道长度（公里） Length of GasPipelines(km)			全年供气总量 Volume of Gas Supply			用气人口（万人） Population with Accessto Gas (10 000 persons)		
			人工煤气 Coal Gas	液化石油气 Liquefied Petroleum Gas	天然气 Natural Gas	人工煤气（万立方米） Coal Gas (10 000 cu.m)	液化石油气（吨） Liquefied Petroleum Gas (ton)	天然气（万立方米） Natural Gas (10 000 cu.m)	人工煤气 Coal Gas	液化石油气 Liquefied Petroleum Gas	天然气 Natural Gas
贵阳市	Guiyang	95	2028		245	10292	40000	20080	89.0	72.0	92.0
六盘水市	Liupanshui	6	770			5092	488		29.0	1.1	
遵义市	Zunyi				192		11075	3663		43.0	10.4
安顺市	Anshun				109		4035	974		11.0	15.5
铜仁市	Tongren			91			2105			10.0	
兴义市	Xingyi				61		2846	146		11.0	1.0
毕节市	Bijie				116		2031	585		12.0	2.0
凯里市	Kaili				90		7553	1449		22.0	5.0
都匀市	Duyun			30	101		1818	197		18.0	1.7
清镇市	Qingzhen	1	156			650	1689		9.5	5.0	
赤水市	Chishui			4	24		252	1013		1.0	5.4
仁怀市	Renhuai				28		790	905		6.0	5.0
福泉市	Fuquan						1361			5.0	

11－8 城市市政设施（2014）

Municipal Infrastructure in Cities

城市名称	City	年末实有道路长度（公里）Length of Paved Roads (year-end) (km)	年末实有道路面积（万平方米）Area of Paved Roads (year-end) (10 000 sq.m)	城市桥梁（座）Number of City Bridges (unit)	城市排水管道长度（公里）Length of City Sewage Pipes (km)	城市污水日处理能力（万立方米）Daily Disposal Capacity of City Sewage (10 000 cu.m)	城市道路照明灯（千盏）Number of Street Lights (1 000 units)
贵 阳 市	Guiyang	1294.36	2611.07	311	3519.71	64.0	218.57
六盘水市	Liupanshui	177.00	407.30	25	75.50	6.5	25.48
遵 义 市	Zunyi	276.00	552.00	28	222.00	21.0	29.74
安 顺 市	Anshun	239.37	457.38	27	372.20	5.0	16.33
铜 仁 市	Tongren	233.00	256.05	26	156.75	5.3	7.30
兴 义 市	Xingyi	309.68	710.15	26	411.00	5.5	18.01
毕 节 市	Bijie	202.10	430.20	40	165.38	8.0	5.93
凯 里 市	Kaili	239.89	460.58	28	167.00	8.0	48.20
都 匀 市	Duyun	107.85	211.22	45	162.00	6.0	13.61
清 镇 市	Qingzhen	64.00	191.30	4	80.87	5.0	4.07
赤 水 市	Chishui	50.90	89.24	2	110.40	2.0	5.22
仁 怀 市	Renhuai	26.00	69.00	5	40.00	3.0	6.65
福 泉 市	Fuquan	74.80	85.96	6	93.80	1.5	2.24

11−9 城市绿地和园林(2014)

Parks and Green Areas in Cities

城市名称	City	建成区园林绿地面积(公顷) Area of Parks and Green Land(hectare)	公园绿地面积 ParkGreen Areas	公园(个) Number of Parks(unit)	公园面积(公顷) Area of Parks(hectare)	建成区绿化覆盖率(%) Green Covered Area as % of Completed Area (%)
贵阳市	Guiyang	12783	4104	13	2568	43.50
六盘水市	Liupanshui	513	550	7	620	23.25
遵义市	Zunyi	2320	994	6	534	39.42
安顺市	Anshun	927	136	2	90	23.09
铜仁市	Tongren	943	177	6	73	27.91
兴义市	Xingyi	686	258	5	58	17.77
毕节市	Bijie	1160	488	4	213	29.16
凯里市	Kaili	1187	510	7	684	25.69
都匀市	Duyun	581	193	6	129	19.50
清镇市	Qingzhen	670	95	1	7	40.22
赤水市	Chishui	258	64	2	15	27.20
仁怀市	Renhuai	323	202	1	1	26.80
福泉市	Fuquan	283	135	3	74	25.66

11−10 城市市容环境卫生(2014)

Urban Sanitation in Cities

城市名称	City	清扫保洁面积(万平方米) Area under Cleaning Program (10 000 sq.m)	生活垃圾清运量(万吨) Volume of Garbage Disposal (10 000 tons)	市容环卫专用车辆设备总数(台) Number of Special Vehicles for Environmental Sanitation (unit)	公共厕所(座) Number of Public Lavatories (unit)	#三类以上 Third Grade and Above	生活垃圾无害化处理率(%) Garbage harmless treatment rate (%)
贵阳市	Guiyang	2289	119.26	1061	540	540	96.2
六盘水市	Liupanshui	291	11.19	94	41	12	96.4
遵义市	Zunyi	552	42.20	286	312	312	92.6
安顺市	Anshun	290	15.15	330	46	46	81.1
铜仁市	Tongren	220	11.73	38	124	30	90.3
兴义市	Xingyi	158	9.60	39	99		97.9
毕节市	Bijie	355	17.23	130	51	50	93.7
凯里市	Kaili	463	11.78	60	38	38	91.9
都匀市	Duyun	190	12.19	83	38	38	96.0
清镇市	Qingzhen	122	4.86	63	19	19	95.9
赤水市	Chishui	70	3.80	26	15	15	88.0
仁怀市	Renhuai	69	7.88	107	44	42	97.7
福泉市	Fuquan	60	6.90	35	8		60.0

主要统计指标解释

供水综合生产能力 指按供水设施取水、净化、送水、出厂输水干管等环节设计能力计算的综合生产能力。包括在原设计能力的基础上，经挖、革、改增加的生产能力。计算时，以四个环节中最薄弱的环节为主确定能力。原则上按设计能力填报，对于经过更新改造后，实际生产能力与设计能力相差很大的，按实际能力填报。

供水管道长度 指从送水泵至用户水表之间所有管道的长度。不包括新安装尚未使用、水厂内以及用户建筑物内的管道。在同一条街道埋设两条或两条以上管道时，应按每条管道的长度计算。

供水总量 指报告期供水企业（单位）供出的全部水量。包括有效供水量和漏损水量。其中有效供水量指水厂将水供出厂外后，各类用户实际使用到的水量。包括售水量和免费供水量。

生活用水量 包括公共服务用水和居民家庭用水。公共服务用水指为城市社会公共生活服务的用水。包括行政事业单位、部队营区和公共设施服务、社会服务业、批发零售贸易业、旅馆饮食业以及其他公共服务业等单位的用水。居民家庭用水指城市范围内所有居民家庭的日常生活用水。包括城市居民、农民家庭、公共供水站用水。

用水普及率 指报告期末城区用水人口数与总人口的比率。计算公式：

$$用水普及率=\frac{城区用水人口（含暂住人口）}{城区人口+城区暂住人口}\times 100\%$$

人工煤气生产能力 指报告期末人工煤气生产厂制气、净化、输送等环节的综合生产能力，不包括备用设备能力。一般按设计能力计算，如果实际生产能力大于设计能力时，应按实际测定的生产能力计算。测定时应以制气、净化、输送三个环节中最薄弱的环节为主。

供气管道长度 指报告期末从气源厂压缩机的出口或门站出口至各类用户引入管之间的全部已经通气投入使用的管道长度。不包括煤气生产厂、输配站、液化气储存站、灌瓶站、储配站、气化站、混气站、供应站等厂(站)内的管道。按不同的材质、管径分别统计。

供气总量 指报告期燃气企业（单位）向用户供应的燃气数量。包括销售量和损失量。

燃气普及率 指报告期末使用燃气的人口与总人口的比率。计算公式为：

$$燃气普及率=\frac{城区用气人口（含暂住人口）}{城区人口+城区暂住人口}\times 100\%$$

桥梁 指为跨越天然或人工障碍物而修建的构筑物。包括跨河桥、立交桥、人行天桥以及人行地下通道等。

排水管道长度 指所有排水总管、干管、支管、检查井及连接井进出口等长度之和。计算时应按单管计算，即在同一条街道上如有两条或两条以上并排的排水管道时，应按每条排水管道的长度相加计算。

污水处理能力 指污水处理厂(或处理装置)每昼夜处理污水量的设计能力。

年末公共交通运营车辆数 指年末公交企业(单位)用于运营业务的全部车辆数。以企业(单位)固定资产台账中已投入运营的车辆数为准。

绿地面积 指报告期末用作园林和绿化的各种绿地面积。包括公园绿地、生产绿地、防护绿地、附属绿地和其他绿地的面积。其中公园绿地指城市中向公众开放的、以游憩为主要功能，有一定的游憩设施和服务设施，同时兼有健全生态、美化景观、防灾减灾等综合作用的绿化用地。它是城市建设用地、城市绿地系统和城市市政公用设施的重要组成部分。

公共绿地 指向公众开放的市级、区级、居住区级各类公园、街旁游园，包括其范围内的水域。其中居住区级公园应不小于1万平方米，街旁游园的宽度不小于8米，面积不小于400平方米。

生活垃圾清运量 指报告期收集和运送到各生活垃圾处理场（厂）和生活垃圾最终消纳点的生活垃圾的数量。统计时仅计算从生活垃圾源头和从生活垃圾转运站直接送到处理场和最终消纳点的清运量，对于二次中转的清运量不要重复计算。

气温 指空气的温度，我国一般以摄氏度(℃)为单位表示。气象观测的温度表是放在离地面约1.5米处通风良好的百叶箱里测量的，因此，通常说的气温指的是离地面1.5米处百叶箱中的温度。其统计计算方法为：月平均气温是将全月各日的平均气温相加，除以该月的天数而得。年平均气温是将12个月的月平均气温累加后除以12而得。

相对湿度 指空气中实际所含水蒸气密度和同温度下饱和水蒸气密度的百分比值。其统计方法与气温相同。

降水量 指从天空降落到地面的液态或固态(经融化后)水，未经蒸发、渗透、流失而在地面上积聚的深度。其统计计算方法为：月降水量是将全月各日的降水量累加而得。年降水量是将12个月的月降水量累加而得。

日照时数 指太阳实际照射地面的时间。其统计方法与降水量相同。

Explanatory Notes on Main Statistical Indicators

Production Capacity of Water Supply refers to the designed overall production capacity of water facilities, covering the four segments of water collection, purification, conveyance, and outflow through trunk pipelines. Increased capacity through transformation and innovation projects is included as well. The capacity is determined mainly on the weakest of the above-mentioned four segments. In principle, according to the design capacity reporting, for after renovation, the actual production capacity and design capabilities are vary greatly. It is according to the actual ability reported.

Length of Water Supply Pipelines refers to the total length of all the pipelines between the water pumps and the user water meters, excluding pipelines newly installed but not used yet, pipeline in the water factory, and pipeline in the user's buildings. Buried in the same street two or more pipes, each pipe length shall be calculated.

Total Volume of Water Supply refers to the total volume of water supplied by water-works (units) during the reference period, including both the effective water supply and loss during the water supply. The effective water supply refers to the water supply for the water supply factory, the actual use of various types of water users. Including the sale of water and free water supply.

Consumption of Water for Residential Use refers to water consumption of households for daily life and water consumption of public service facilities. The latter refers to water consumption for urban public services, including the consumption of government agencies and public institutions, military barracks, public facilities, wholesale and retail outlets, restaurants, hotels, and other units providing public services. Household water consumption refers to consumption of water for daily life of all households within the boundary of cities, including households of urban residents and farmers, and public water supply stations.

Coverage Rate of Urban Population with Access to Tap Water refers to the ratio of the urban population with access to tap water to the total urban population. The formula is:

$$\text{Coverage of urban population with access to tap water} = \frac{\text{Urban population with access to tap water}}{\text{Urban population}} \times 100\%$$

Production Capacity of Gaswork Gas refers to the overall production capacity of the urban gasworks in gas generation, purification and delivery at the end of the reference period, excluding capacity of the reserved facilities. In general, it is determined by the designed capacity, and when actual production capacity is larger than the designed capacity, the capacity is determined by the actual measurement on the weakest segment in the production, purification and delivery.

Length of Gas Pipelines refers to the total length of pipelines in use between the outlet of the compressor of gas-work or outlet of gas stations and the leading pipe of users, excluding pipelines within gasworks, delivery stations, LPG storage stations, refilling stations, gas-mixing stations and supply stations. It is according to different material, diameter, respectively statistics.

Volume of Gas Supply refers to the total volume of gas provided to users by gas-producing enterprises (units) in a year, including the volume sold and the volume lost.

Coverage Rate of Urban Population with Access to Gas refers to the ratio of the urban population with access to tap water to the total urban population. The formula is:

$$\text{Coverage rate of urban population with access to gas} = \frac{\text{Urban population with access to gas}}{\text{Urban population}} \times 100\%$$

Bridges refer to bridges built to cross over natural or man-made barriers, including bridges over rivers, overpasses for traffic and for pedestrians, underpasses for pedestrians, etc.

Length of Sewage Pipes refers to the total length of general drainage, trunks, branch and inspection wells, connection wells, inlets and outlets, etc. In the calculation, calculation shall be single-tube that is on the same street if two or more side by side drains, they should be added to the length of each drainage calculations.

Disposal Capacity of Sewage refers to the designed 24-hour capacity of sewage disposal by the sewage treatment works or facilities.

Number of Vehicles under Operation at Year-end refers to the total number of vehicles under operation by public transport enterprises (units) at the end of the year, based on the records of operational vehicles by the enterprises (units).

Green Area refers to the end of the reporting period used for landscaping and green area. Including the park green area, production green land, protective green land, attached green land, and other green space. Park green space refers to open to the public in the city, to the main function of recreation, with a certain recreational facilities and services, but also a comprehensive role of improving the ecological, landscaping, disaster prevention and mitigation, etc.. It is an important part of urban construction land, urban green space system and urban public facilities.

Public Green Area refers to green areas open to the public such as municipal, community and neighborhood parks and roadside parks, including waters within parks. Neighborhood parks should occupy an area larger than 10,000 square meters, and the width of roadside parks should occupy an area larger than 400 square meters, with a width of more that 8 meters.

Consumption Wastes Transported refers to volume of consumption wastes collected and transported to disposal factories or sites during the reference period. Consumption wastes are solid wastes regarded by laws and regulations as urban consumption wastes, including those from households, commercial activities, markets, cleaning of streets, public sites, offices, schools, factories, mining units and other sources.

Temperature refers to the air temperature, China uses Celsius as the unit. The thermometry used for water observation is put in a breezy shutter, which is 1.5 metres high from the ground. There fore the commonly used temperature refers to the temperature in the breezy shutter 1.5 metres away from the ground. The calculation method is as tollows.

Monthly average temperature is the summation of average daily temperature of one moth divided by the actual days of the particular month.

Annual average temperature is the summation of monthy average of a year divided by 12 months.

Relative Humidity refers to the ratio of actual water vapour pressure to the saturation water vapour pressure under the current temperature. The calculation method is the same as that of temperature.

Volume of Precipitation refers to the deepness of liquid state or solid state (thawed) water falling from the sky to the ground that has not been evaporated, infiltrated or run off. The calculation method is as follows monthly precipitation is the summation of daily precipitation of month. Annual precipitation is the summation of 12 months precipitation of a year.

Sunshine Hours refer to the actual hours of sun irradiating the earth. The calculation method is the same as that of the precipitation.

资源和环境

12

Resources and Environment

12-1 主要河流(省内部分)主要特征值(2014)
Major Feature of Some Part of The Main River

水 系	Water System	流域面积(平方公里) Drainage Area(sq.km)	河长(千米) Length of River (1000 m)	平均坡降(‰) Average Slope Falling(‰)
长江流域	**Changjiang River Drainage**			
#赤水河	Chishuihe	11341	442	1.52
乌 江	Wujiang	66798	993	1.02
清水江	Qingshuijiang	30252	1053	0.49
洪州河	Hongzhouhe	1129	285	0.87
㵲阳河	Wuyanghe	6505	446	0.99
锦 江	Jinjiang	4045	309	1.16
松桃河	Songtaohe	1427	191	1.55
松坎河	Songkanhe	2332	223	1.37
牛栏江	Niulanjing	2010	447	4.35
横江(洛泽河)	Hengjiang(Luozehe)	2944	340	4.18
珠江流域	**Zhujiang River Drainage**			
#南盘江	Nanpanjiang	7651		
北盘江	Beipanjiang	20953	456	2.61
红水河	Hongshuihe	15978		
都柳江	Duliujiang	15676	743	0.43
打狗河	Dagouhe	4206	392	1.40

注：资料来源于省水利厅。
Note:Data in the table are provided by the Provincial Hydrographic Regulatory Burea.

12-2 主要矿产资源(2014)
Major Mineral Resources

指　标	Item	资源储量 Reserves	居全国位次 Order in Whole Country
矿产资源	**Mineral Resources(Ensured Reserves)**		
煤炭(亿吨)	Coal(100 million tons)	573.54	5
锰矿(万吨)	Manganese(10000 tons)	36553.14	1
钒矿(万吨)	Vanadium(10000 tons)	475.06	3
铅矿(万吨)	Plumbum(10000 tons)	103.75	18
锌矿(万吨)	Zincum(10000 tons)	481.56	11
铝土矿(亿吨)	Bauxite Ore(100 million tons)	7.60	3
镁(炼镁白云岩)(万吨)	Magnesium(10000 tons)	11729.33	5
汞矿(万吨)	Hydrargyrum(10000 tons)	3.03	1
锑矿(万吨)	Antimony(10000 tons)	34.26	4
金矿(岩金)(吨)	Gold mine(ton)	286.57	8
稀土矿(万吨)	Rare Earth Mine(10000 tons)	86.01	6
冶金用砂岩(万吨)	Gritstone for Metallurgy(10000 tons)	8631.59	2
硫铁矿(亿吨)	Pyrites Ore(100 million tons)	8.55	2
重晶石(万吨)	Barite Ore(10000 tons)	9117.29	1
磷矿(亿吨)	Phosphorus Ore(100 million tons)	33.58	3
水泥用灰岩(亿吨)	Limestone for Cement(100 million tons)	20.40	22

注：资料来源于省国土资源厅。
Note:Data in this table are obtained from the Provisional Department of Land and Resoures.

12—3 森林资源

Forest Resources

指　标	Item	2010	2011	2012	2013	2014	2014年比2013年增长(%) Increase Rate in 2014 over 2013(%)
森林面积(万公顷)	**Forest Area(10000 Ha.)**	**713.80**	**732**	**828**	**845**	**863**	**2.2**
森林覆盖率(%)	Forest Coverage Rate (%)	40.52	41.53	47	48	49	1(百分点)
活立木总蓄积量(亿立方米)	Total Standing Fovest Stock (100 million stere)	3.33	3.89	3.97	4.09	4.31	5.4
完成造林面积(万公顷)	Area of Fulfilled Foyestation(10000 Ha.)	7.88	13.13	19.93	21.82	30.3	38.7
封山育林面积(万公顷)	Area of Seal Mountain Pass for Forestation(10000 Ha.)	13.21	14.48	8.10	8.37	8.73	4.3
实施退耕还林工程中：	**In Implement Cancel Infield for Forest Project**						
宜林荒山造林(万公顷)	Forestation for Feasible deserted Mountain(10000 Ha.)	1.33	1.20	1.00	1.20	0.47	-60.8
天然林保护工程中：	**In Savageness Forest Protect Project**						
封山育林(万公顷)	Seal Mountain Pass for Forestation (10000 Ha.)	4.66	0.60	0.67	0.67	0.67	持平
森林保护	**Forest Protection**						
森林火灾(起)	Forest Fire (unit)	2537	430	275	208	201	-3.4
森林火灾受害率(‰)	Rate of Fall Victim for Forest Fire (‰)	1.29	0.13	0.07	0.06	0.06	持平
森林病虫鼠害面积(万公顷)	Area of Fall Victim for Insect Pest(10000 Ha.)	26.85	27.18	20.60	23.56	22.84	-3.1
森林病虫鼠害防治面积(万公顷)	Prevention Area of Forest Insect Pest(10000 Ha.)	19.63	18.91	16.63	22.84	20	-12.4
森林病虫鼠害防治率(%)	Prevention Rate of Forest Insect Pest (%)	73.1	69.6	80.7	96.9	87.6	-9.3(百分点)

注：1.资料来源于省林业厅(以下相关表同)。2.森林面积、森林覆盖率2012年数据是以县为单位，以2006年底结束的全省第三次森林资源二类调查小班数据为基础，结合2011年度林地保护利用规划年度变更数据，以及2012年的森林资源增长和消耗的监测、抽样调查、核实而得出。

Note:1.The data in this table is obtained from Forest Department of Guizhou Province(The relative tables in the chapter are the same). 2.The data of forest area and forest coverage rate in 2012, which is based on the town as a unit,basing on data of the second category group investigation in Guizhou province's third inventory at the end of 2006,combining with the annal change data of 2011 Annual Forest Protection and utilization planning,and the data of forest growth and consumption in 2012,then finally obtained through the following steps:detection,sampling investigation, and verification.

12-4 自然保护区

Natural Reserves

指　标	Item	2010	2011	2012	2013	2014
自然保护区个数(个)	**Number of Nature Reserves (unit)**	**130**	**130**	**130**	**121**	**123**
#国家级自然保护区	Nature Reserves of National-level	9	9	9	9	9
省级自然保护区	Nature Reserves of Guizhou Province	4	4	4	7	7
地市级自然保护区	Nature Reserves of Region	21	21	21	21	21
县级自然保护区	Nature Reserves of County	96	96	96	84	86
自然保护区面积(万公顷)	Area of Nature Reserves (10000 hectares)	96.02	96.02	96.02	89.51	89.51
自然保护区面积占全省国土面积(%)	Percentage of Nature Reserves in Guizhou Province Land(%)	5.5	5.5	5.5	5.5	5.5
自然保护区中：	**In Nature Reserves**					
森林生态系统、野生动、植物类型(个)	Forest Biogeocenose,Wildness Animal and Plant(unit)	120	120	120	120	119
内陆湿地类型(个)	Wetlands inside Land(unit)	8	8	8	8	3
古生物遗迹类型(个)	Ancient Biology Relic(unit)	1	1	1	1	1
地质地貌类型(个)	Geological features(unit)	1	1	1	1	0

12-5 森林公园

Forest Parks

指　标	Item	2010	2011	2012	2013	2014	2014年比2013年增长(%) Increase Rate in 2014 over 2013(%)
森林公园(个)	Number of Forest Park (unit)	70	72	74	75	78	4.0
#国家级森林公园	Forest Park of National-level	21	21	22	22	25	13.6
省级森林公园	Forest Park of Guizhou Province-level	31	32	31	32	31	-3.1
森林公园面积(万公顷)	Area of Forest Park (10000 hectares)	25.4	26.1	26.2	26.2	27.2	3.9
森林公园面积约占全省国土面积(%)	Percentage of Forest Park Area to the Guizhou Total Land Areas(%)	1.5	1.5	1.5	1.5	1.6	0.1(百分点)

12-6 水资源和水质监测
Water Resource and Monitoring of Water Quality

指　标	Item	2010	2011	2012	2013	2014	2014年比2013年增长(%) Increase Rate in 2014 over 2013(%)
水资源总量(亿立方米)	**Total Water Resources (100 million cu.m)**	**956.54**	**626.02**	**974.02**	**759.78**	**1213.12**	**59.7**
#地表水	Surface Water Resources	956.54	626.02	974.02	759.78	1213.12	59.7
人均水资源量(立方米)	Per Capita Water Resources (cu.m)	2284	1805	2796	2169	3458	59.4
供水总量(亿立方米)	Water Supply(100 million cu.m)	101.45	99.19	100.82	92.61	95.31	2.9
#地表水	Surface Water Supply	93.75	98.89	98.05	90.62	82.34	-9.1
用水总量(亿立方米)	Water Use(100 million cu.m)	101.45	99.19	100.82	92.61	95.31	2.9
河流水质	**Water Quality of River**						
监测河流(条)	Monitored River (unit)	44	44	44	44	44	持平
监测河段断面(个)	Monitored Section of River (unit)	85	85	85	85	85	持平
满足规定水质类别的断面占总监测断面百分比(%)	the Sections Meeting the Standard of Water Quality I-III Genus As Percentage of total Monitored Sections(%)	71.8	72.9	83.5	82.3	81.2	-1.1 (百分点)
水质良好的出境断面(个)	Number of Favorable Water Quality Section(unit)	11	12	14	14	14	持平
湖泊水质	**Water Quality of Lake**						
监测湖库(个)	Monitored Lake (unit)	8	8	8	8	8	持平
监测点(个)	Monitored Point (unit)	25	25	25	25	25	持平
满足规定水质类别的监测点(个)	Ratio of the Points Meeting Water Quality I-III Genus(unit)	14	11	10	10	10	持平
占总监测点百分比(%)	As Percentage of total Monitored Points (%)	56.0	44.0	40.0	40.0	40.0	持平

注：资料来源于省水利厅、省环境保护厅。

Note:Data in the table are provided by the Provincial Department of Water Resources and Provincial Department of Environmental Protection.

12—7 环保系统机构、人员数

Number of Enviornmental Protection Agencies and Persons Engaged

指　标	Item	2010	2011	2012	2013	2014
机构总数(个)	**Number of Agencies(unit)**	**404**	**400**	**370**	**425**	**433**
#省	Province	13	14	14	14	14
地	Prefecture	48	53	57	66	70
县	County	306	296	292	345	349
年末人员总数(人)	**Number of Staff and Workers at the Year-end(person)**	**3220**	**3168**	**3633**	**3832**	**3945**
#省	Province	360	380	375	386	383
地	Prefecture	649	730	895	987	1011
县	County	2137	1984	2363	2459	2551
#科研人员	Scientific and Technical Personnel	101	93	93	93	107
监测人员	Monitoring Personal	720	838	857	1058	1163
监察人员	Supervising and Administrative Personnel	786	900	886	1156	1272

注：资料来源于省环境保护厅(以下相关表同)。
Note: The data in the table are provided by the provinvial Department of Environmental Protection(The relative tables in the chapter are the same).

12—8 环境保护资金投入

Investment in Environmental Protection

单位：亿元　　　　(100 million yuan)

指　标	Item	2010	2011	2012	2013	2014	2014年比2013年增长(%) Increase Rate in 2014over 2013(%)
环保资金投入	**Investment in Environmental Protection**	**89.52**	**106.70**	**97.35**	**133.70**	**175.25**	**31.1**
环保资金投入占地区生产总值比重(%)	Investment in Environmental Protection as Percent of GDP(%)	1.9	1.9	1.4	1.7	1.9	0.2(百分点)
环保资金投入中：	**In Investment of Environmental Protection**						
#老工业污染源治理	Old Industry Pollution Source Treatment	6.81	14.05	12.47	19.56	18.48	-5.5
建设项目“三同时”污染防治	"Three Simultaneities" Environmental Investment for New Project	16.47	13.74	5.37	2.85	18.39	545.2
城市环境基础设施建设	Investment in Urban Environmental Infrastructure	28.91	37.95	35.73	60.33	84.05	39.3
环境管理能力建设	Construction of Environment Management Capacity	1.81	1.21	1.83	3.19	3.87	21.3
工业污染治理设施运行费用	Operating Expense of Industry Pollution Treatment Facilities	35.52	39.75	41.95	47.77	50.46	5.6
征收排污费总额	**Pollutant Discharge Fees**	**4.47**	**4.58**	**4.73**	**5.41**	**4.30**	**-20.5**

注：“城市环境基础设施建设”数据2010年由省环境保护厅提供，2011年起由省住房城乡建设厅提供。
Note:The data of investment in urban environmental infrastructure was provided by Provincial Department of Environmental Protection 2010, but from 2011 they are provided by provincial Department of urban and Rural development.

12−9 废水治理

Waste Water Treatment

指 标	Item	2010	2011	2012	2013	2014	2014年比2013年增长(%) Increase Rate in 2014 over 2013（%）
废水排放总量（亿吨）	**Total Volume of Waste Water Discharged(100 million tons)**	**8.45**	**7.80**	**9.14**	**9.31**	**11.09**	**19.1**
#工业	Volume of Industrial Waste Water Discharged	2.55	2.07	2.34	2.29	3.27	42.7
生活	Volume of Residential Waste Water Discharged	5.89	5.73	6.80	7.01	7.81	11.5
废水中化学需氧排放量（万吨）	**COD Discharged from Industrial Waste Water(10000 tons)**	**34.83**	**34.22**	**33.30**	**32.81**	**32.67**	**-0.4**
#工业	Industrial Sector	6.07	6.55	6.47	6.32	6.73	6.4
生活	Residential Sector	22.05	21.49	19.97	19.81	19.52	-1.5
当年完成工业废水治理项目(个)	Item of Industry Waste Water Treatment Completed in This Year(unit)	45	82	122	34	31	-8.8
新增废水治理能力(万吨/日)	Newly Desinged Treatment and Utilization Capacity of Waste Water(10000 tons/day)	1.61	29.91	16.62	7.50	4.46	-40.5
城市污水处理率(%)	Treatment Rate of City Waste Water (%)	74.8	82.0	83.9	84.8	86.9	2.1（百分点）

注：2010年数据采用污染源普查动态更新数据(以下相关表同)。

Note:The data of 2010 were updated by the methods of survey of pollution sources dynamic(The relative tables in the chapter are the same).

12−10 空气质量及污染治理

Air Quality and Treatment of Industrial Waste Gas

指　标	Item	2010	2011	2012	2013	2014	2014年比2013年增长(%) Increase Rate in 2014 over 2013（%）
城市空气质量	**Atmosphere Quality of City**						
达到国家环境空气质量二级标准城市(个)	Number of Cities Reaching the National Grade II Standard of Atmosphere Quality of City (unit)	7	11	12	11	11	持平
占统计城市数(%)	Percentage in Total (%)	58.3	91.7	92.3	84.6	84.6	持平
城市空气污染物	**Contamination in City Atmosphere**						
二氧化硫年均浓度值(毫克/立方米)	Annud Average SO2 Concentration in Downtown(mg/cu.m)	0.048	0.044	0.038	0.039	0.026	-33.3
达到国家空气质量二级标准城市(个)	Number of Cities Reaching the National Grade II Standard of Atmosphere Quality of City (unit)	9	12	12	12	13	8.3
二氧化氮年均浓度值(毫克/立方米)	Annual Average NO2 Concentration in Downtown(mg/cu.m)	0.018	0.021	0.021	0.021	0.020	-4.8
达到国家空气质量一级标准城市(个)	Number of Cities Reaching the National Grade I Standard of Atmosphere Quality of City (unit)	12	12	13	13	13	持平
城市可吸入颗粒物年均浓度值(毫克/立方米)	Average Chroma of City Suspend Grain (mg/cu.m)	0.077	0.078	0.069	0.078	0.066	-15.4
达到国家空气质量二级标准城市(个)	Number of Cities Reaching the National Grade II Standard of Atmosphere Quality of City (unit)	10	11	13	12	11	-8.3
废气中污染物排放	**Contamination Discharged of Exhaust Gas**						
二氧化硫排放总量(万吨)	Volume of SO2 Emission(10000 tons)	116.17	110.42	104.11	98.64	92.58	-6.1
#工业	Industry	96.05	90.3	83.71	77.86	70.24	-9.8
生活及其它废气中二氧化硫排放量	Volume of SO2 from Living and Other Exhaust Gas Emission	20.13	20.12	20.40	20.78	22.34	7.5
烟(粉)尘排放总量(万吨)	Total Volume of soot(Dust) Emission (10000 tons)	29.08	28.97	29.45	26.45	37.79	42.9
#工业	Industry	24.88	24.34	25.65	22.53	34.30	52.3
生活及其它废气中烟(粉)尘排放量	Discharged Volume of soot(Dusts) from Living and Other Exhaust Gas Emission	3.32	3.69	2.82	3.92	3.48	-11.2
空气污染治理	**Air Pollution Treatment**						
工业废气中:	In Industrial Exhaust Gas						
二氧化硫去除率(%)	Rate of SO2 Removed (%)	59.9	66.3	69.0	70.3	77.2	6.9(百分点)
烟(粉)尘去除率(%)	Rate of Soot(Dust) Removed (%)	98.2	98.9	98.7	99.3	99.3	持平
当年完成废气治理项目(个)	Item of Exhaust Gas Treatment Fulfilled in This Year (unit)	34	29	45	51	50	-2.0
新增废气治理能力(万标立方米/小时)	New Exhaust Gas Treatment Capacity inThis Year (10000 stere/hour)	268.31	725.51	2777.86	7118.49	3348.46	-53.0
城市燃气普及率(%)	Popularization Rate of City Coal Gas (%)	54.5	55.0	55.2	58.7	60.3	1.6(百分点)

注："烟(粉)尘排放总量"为原"烟尘排放总量"，"烟(粉)尘去除率"为原"烟尘去除率"。

Note:"Total volume of soot(dust)emission"refers to the original"total volume of dust emission"."Rate of soot(dust) removed"refers to the original"Rate of soot removed".

12-11 固体废物生产及处理
Production and Treatment of Industrial Solid Wastes

指　标	Item	2010	2011	2012	2013	2014	2014年比2013年增长(%) Increase Rate in 2014 over 2013(%)
工业固体废物产生量(万吨)	**Volume of Industrial Solid Wastes Produced (10000 tons)**	**8187.68**	**7660.70**	**7835.25**	**8194.05**	**7394.22**	**-9.8**
工业固体废物倾倒丢弃量	Dumping Volume of Industrial Solid Waste Discarded	59.76	28.88	14.05	43.74	1.46	-96.7
工业固体废物治理	**Industrial Solid Wastes Treatment**						
当年完成工业固体废物治理项目(个)	Item of Industrial Solid Wastes Fulfilled in This Year (unit)	8	4	5	3	2	-33.3
工业固体废物综合利用量(万吨)	Volume of Industrial Solid Wastes Utilized(10000 tons)	4174.13	4089.09	4838.75	4135.41	4312.91	4.3
工业固体废物处置量(万吨)	Volume of Industrial Solid Wastes Treated (10000 tons)	2497.55	2102.95	2067.44	2275.60	1382.22	-39.3
工业固体废物综合利用率(%)	Ratio of Industrial Solid Wastes Utilized(%)	50.9	52.7	60.9	50.5	56.9	6.4 (百分点)
生活垃圾处理	**Consumption Wastes Treatment**						
生活垃圾清运总量(万吨)	Consumption Wastes Collected and Transported (10000 tons)	428.51	431.46	449.41	461.47	490.44	6.3
生活垃圾处理总量(万吨)	Consumption Wastes Treated (10000 tons)	294.92	296.15	324.07	351.56	386.59	10.0
#无害化处理量	Volume of Wastes Disposed	194.62	205.11	231.80	294.57	386.59	31.2
城市生活垃圾无害化处理率(%)	Treatment Rate of Consumption Wastes in Cities(%)	45.4	47.5	51.6	63.8	78.8	15.0 (百分点)

注："工业固体废物倾倒丢弃量"为原"工业固体废物排放量"。
Note:"Dumping volume of industrial solid waste discarded" refers to original "volume of industrial solid wastes discharged".

12－12 环境污染事故
Accident of Environment Pollution

指 标	Item	2010	2011	2012	2013	2014	2014年比2013年增 长(%) Increase Rate in 2014 over 2013(%)
环境污染事故(起)	**Number of Environmental Pollution Accidents(unit)**	**4**	**7**	**4**	**9**	**3**	**-66.7**
#重大事故	Fatal Accident		1	1			
较大事故	Major Accident		1				
一般事故	Commonly Accident	4	5	3	9	3	-66.7
#水污染事故	Water Pollution Accident	2	5	4	7	2	-71.4
空气污染事故	Air Pollution Accident	2	2		2	1	-50.0

12－13 自然灾害
Natural Disasters

指 标	Item	2010	2011	2012	2013	2014	2014年比2013年增长(%) Increase Rate in 2014 over 2013(%)
遭受自然灾害县个数(个)	Number of Counties Suffering from Natural Disasters(unit)	86	88	86	85	88	3.5
受灾人口(万人次)	The Population Affected by Natural Disasters (10000 person-times)	2633.40	2883.44	1227.66	2162.62	1385.28	-3.6
农作物受灾面积(万公顷)	Area of Crop Affected by Natural Disasters (10000 hectares)	195.64	253.75	55.27	157.81	62.82	-60.2
#绝收面积	The Gainless Area of Crop for Natural Disasters	55.72	51.51	6.74	36.28	9.74	-7.3
因自然灾害造成直接经济损失(亿元)	The Direct Economy Loss for Natural Disasters (100 million yuan)	179.77	250.67	66.21	140.06	196.76	28.8

注：资料来源于省民政厅。

Note: The data in the table are provided by the provinvial Department of Civil Affairs.

主要统计指标解释

流域 每条河流都有自己的干流和支流，干支流共同组成这条河流的水系。每条河流都有自己的集水区域，这个集水区域就称为该河流的流域。

矿产资源 矿产指由地质作用形成，富集于地壳中或出露于地表达到工农业利用要求的有用矿物。矿产是一种重要的自然资源，是社会发展的重要物质基础。

矿产保有储量 指探明的矿产储量（包括工业储量和远景储量），扣除已开采部分和地下损失量后的年末实有储量，是反映国家矿产资源现状的重要指标。

森林面积 指由乔木树种构成，郁闭度0.2以上(含0.2)的林地或冠幅宽度10米以上的林带的面积，即有林地面积。森林面积包括天然起源和人工起源的针叶林面积、阔叶林面积、针阔混交林面积和竹林面积，不包括灌木林地面积和疏林地面积。

森林覆盖率 指一个国家或地区森林面积占土地总面积的百分比。森林覆盖率是反映森林资源的丰富程度和生态平衡状况的重要指标。在计算森林覆盖率时，森林面积包括郁闭度0.2以上的乔木林地面积和竹林地面积，国家特别规定的灌木林地面积、农田林网以及四旁(村旁、路旁、水旁、宅旁)林木的覆盖面积。计算公式为：

$$森林覆盖率=\frac{森林面积}{土地总面积}\times 100\%$$

活立木总蓄积量 指一定范围内土地上全部树木蓄积的总量，包括森林蓄积、疏林蓄积、散生木蓄积和四旁树蓄积。

造林面积 指报告期内在荒山、荒地、沙丘、退耕地等一切可以造林的土地上，采用人工播种、飞机播种、植苗造林、分植造林等方法新植成片乔木林和灌木林，经过检查验收符合《造林技术规程》要求的单位面积株数，并按《中华人民共和国森林法实施条例》规定，成活率达85%以上(含85%，年降雨量在400毫米以下且无浇灌条件的地区造林成活率达70%以上)的总面积。四旁植树如一侧在四行以上，连片面积0.066公顷(一亩)以上，应统计在造林面积内。造林面积，通常按所有制(国有、国有集体合作、集体和个人)、造林方式(人工、飞机播种)、主要林种用途(用材林、经济林、防护林、薪炭林、特种用途林)分组进行统计。

水资源 水在自然界中以固体、液体和气态三种聚集状态存在，分布于海洋、陆地(包括土壤)以及大气之中，通过水循环形成水资源。水资源包括经人类控制并直接可供灌溉、发电、给水、航运、养殖等用途的地表水和地下水，以及江河、湖泊、井、泉、潮汐、港湾和养殖水域等。水资源是发展国民经济不可缺少的重要自然资源。

地表水和地下水 陆地上的水因空间分布不同，分为地表水和地下水。地表水指分别存在于河流、湖泊、沼泽、冰川和冰盖等水体中水分的总称，又称陆地水。地下水指储存在地面以下饱和岩土孔隙、裂隙及溶洞中的水。

水资源总量 一定区域内的水资源总量指当地降水形成的地表和地下产水量，即地表径流量与降水入渗补给量之和，不包括过境水量。

用水总量 指分配给用户的包括输水损失在内的毛用水量。

工业废水排放量 指经过企业厂区所有排放口排到企业外部的工业废水量。包括生产废水、外排的直接冷却水、超标排放的矿井地下水和与工业废水混排的厂区生活污水，不包括外排的间接冷却水(清污不分流的间接冷却水应计算在内)。

废水中化学需氧量（COD）排放量 指每年排放的废水中的COD的量。

工业SO_2排放量　指报告期内企业在燃料燃烧和生产工艺过程中排入大气的SO_2总量，计算公式为：

$$工业SO_2排放量=燃料燃烧过程中SO_2排放量+生产工艺过程中SO_2排放量$$

生活及其他SO_2排放量　以生活及其他煤炭消费量和其含硫量为基础，根据以下公式计算：

$$生活及其他SO_2排放量=生活及其他煤炭消费量\times 含硫量\times 0.8\times 2$$

工业烟尘排放量　指企业厂区内燃料燃烧过程中产生的烟气中夹带的颗粒物排放量。

工业粉尘排放量　指企业在生产工艺过程中排放的能在空气中悬浮一定时间的固体颗粒物排放量。如钢铁企业的耐火材料粉尘、焦化企业的筛焦系统粉尘、烧结机的粉尘、石灰窑的粉尘、建材企业的水泥粉尘等。不包括电厂排入大气的烟尘。

生活及其他烟尘排放量　指除工业生产活动以外的所有社会、经济活动及公共设施的经营活动中燃烧所排放的烟尘纯重量。以生活及其他煤炭消费量为基础进行测算。

工业固体废物产生量　指报告期内企业在生产过程中产生的固体状、半固体状和高浓度液体状废弃物的总量，包括危险废物、冶炼废渣、粉煤灰、炉渣、煤矸石、尾矿、放射性废物和其他废物等；不包括矿山开采的剥离废石和掘进废石(煤矸石和呈酸性或碱性的废石除外)。酸性或碱性废石指采掘的废石其流经水、雨淋水的PH值小于4或PH值大于10.5者。

工业固体废物综合利用量　指报告期内企业通过回收、加工、循环、交换等方式，从固体废物中提取或者使其转化为可以利用的资源、能源和其他原材料的固体废物量(包括当年利用往年的工业固体废物贮存量)，如用作农业肥料、生产建筑材料、筑路等。综合利用量由原产生固体废物的单位统计。

工业固体废物综合利用率　指工业固体废物综合利用量占工业固体废物产生量(包括综合利用往年贮存量)的百分率。计算公式为：

$$工业固体废物综合利用率=\frac{工业固体废物综合利用量}{工业固体废物产生量+综合利用往年贮存量}\times 100\%$$

工业固体废物处置量　指报告期内企业将固体废物焚烧或者最终置于符合环境保护规定要求的场所，并不再回取的工业固体废物量(包括当年处置往年的工业固体废物贮存量)。处置方式有填埋(其中危险废物应安全填埋)、焚烧、专业贮存场(库)封场处理、深层灌注、回填矿井及海洋处置(经海洋管理部门同意投海处置)等。

生活垃圾清运量　指报告期收集和运送到各生活垃圾处理场（厂）和生活垃圾最终消纳点的生活垃圾的数量。统计时仅计算从生活垃圾源头和从生活垃圾转运站直接送到处理场和最终消纳点的清运量，对于二次中转的清运量不要重复计算。

生活垃圾无害化处理率　指报告期内生活垃圾无害化处理量与生活垃圾产生量的比率。计算公式为：

$$生活垃圾无害化处理率=\frac{生活垃圾无害化处理量}{生活垃圾产生量}\times 100\%$$

在统计时，由于生活垃圾产生量不易取得，可用清运量代替。“垃圾清运量”在审核时要与总人口（包括暂住人口）对应，一般城市人均日产生垃圾为1kg左右。

环境污染事故　指由于违反环境保护法规的经济、社会活动与行为，以及意外因素的影响或不可抗拒的自然灾害等原因，致使环境受到污染，国家重点保护的野生动植物、自然保护区受到破坏，人体健康受到危害，社会经济和人民财产受到损失，造成不良社会影响的突发性事件。

Explanatory Notes on Main Statistical Indicators

Territory refers to territorial land, sea and air space under the administration of the People's Republic of China.

Mineral Resources refer to useful minerals that can be used for industrial or agricultural purposes enriched in lithosphere or on earth due to the geological process. Minerals are important natural resources, and important material base for social development.

Mineral reserves refer to proven mineral reserves (including industrial reserves and prospective reserves), after deducting the amount of mining and underground loss of the end of the year after the real reserves, it is an important indicator of the state of mineral resources.

Forest Area refers to the area of forest where trees and bamboo grow with canopy density above 0.2, including land of natural woods and planted woods, but excluding bush land and thin forest land. It reflects the total areas of afforestation.

Forest Coverage Rate refers to the ratio of area of afforested land to total land area. It is a very important indicator that reflects the status of abundance of forest resource and ecosystem balance. Forest area includes the area of trees and bamboo grow with canopy density above 0.2, the area of shrubby tree according to regulations of the government, the area of forest land inside farm land and the area of trees planted by the side of villages, farm houses and along roads and rivers. The formula for calculating forest coverage rate is as follows:

$$\text{Forestrycoverage rate}(\%) = \frac{\text{Area of Afforested Land}}{\text{Area of Total Land}} \times 100\%$$

Stock Volume of Forest refers to total stock volume of wood growing in forest area, which shows the total size and level of forest resources of a country or a region. It is also an important indicator illustrating the richness of forest resource and the status of forest ecological environment.

Total Area of Afforestation refers to the total area of land suitable for afforestation, including barren hills, idle land, sand dunes, rain for green land, on which acres of arbores or bushes are planted through manual planting, airplane planting, plant seedlings, etc. in accordance with the required density standards of the Technical Procedures of Afforestation, and with a survival rate of over 85% in line with the Implementing Rules of the Forest Law of the People's Republic of China (or a survival rate of 75% in areas with less that 400 mm of annual rainfall and without irrigation facilities). Included in the this category are trees planted alone the roadsides, riversides, or next to houses that occupy an area over 0.066 hectares, or where more than 4 lines of trees are planted. Total area of afforestation is further classified by ownership (state-owned, state-collective, collective or private), by approach of planting (manual, airplane), and by type of forests (timber, by-products, protection, fuel, special use, etc.).

Natural Resources refer to material resources that could be obtained from the nature by human being and used for production and living. Natural resources in general can be classified as renewable resources and non-renewable resources. Renewable resources refer to resources that could be renewed and recycled during a relatively short period of time, including land resource, water resource, climate resource, biology resource and marine resource. Non-renewable resources include resources that could not be renewed, such as minerals and geothermal resource.

Water Resource Water exists in the nature in solid, liquid and gaseous states, is distributed in the ocean, land (including earth) and air, and constitutes the water resource through the circulation of water. Water resource includes the surface water and underground water that is controlled by the human being for irrigation, power-generation, water supply, navigation and cultivation. It also includes rivers, lakes, wells, springs, tides, gulf and water area for cultivation. Water resource as an important natural resource is indispensable for the development of the national economy.

Surface Water and Underground Water Water on earth can be divided into surface water and underground water according to its distribution. Surface water refers to moisture exists in rivers, lakes, swamps, glaciers, icecaps and so on. It is also called land water. The underground water refers to water deposited underground in the cranny and the hole of saturated rock soil and in the water-eroded cave.

Total Water Resources refers to total volume of water resources measured as run-off for surface water from rainfall and recharge for groundwater in a given area, excluding transit water.

Water Use refers to gross water use distributed to users, including loss during transportation, broken down with use by agriculture, industry, living consumption and biological protection.

Waste Water Discharged by Industry refers to the volume of waste water discharged by industrial enterprises through all their outlets, including waste water from production process, directly cooled water, groundwater from mining wells which does not meet discharge standards and sewage from households mixed with waste water produced by industrial activities, but excluding indirectly cooled water discharged (It should be included if the discharge is not separated with waste water).

Volume of Chemical Oxygen Demand(COD) Generated by Urban Non-industrial Waster Water refers to chemical oxygen demand generated through the annual discharge of non-industrial waste water by urban households. It is estimated as:

SO_2 Emission through Industrial Activities refers to volume of sulphur dioxide emission from fuel burning and production process by enterprises during a given period of time. It is calculated as:

SO_2 emission through industrial activities = SO_2 emission from fuel burning + SO_2 emission from production process

SO_2 Emission through Non-industrial and Other Activities is calculated on the basis of consumption of coal by households and other activities and the sulphur content of coal with the following formula:

SO_2 emission through non-industrial and other activities = consumption of coal by households and other activities $\times$ sulphur content $\times 0.8 \times 2$

Industrial Soot Emission refers to volume of soot in smoke emitted in process of fuel burning in premises of enterprises.

Industrial Dust Emission refers to volume of dust emitted by production process of enterprises and suspended in the air for a given period of time, including dust from refractory material of iron and steel works, dust from coke-screening systems and sintering machines of coke plants, dust from lime kilns and dust from cement production in building material enterprises, but excluding soot and dust emitted from power plants.

Soot Emission by Consumption and Others refers to net volume of soot emitted by fuel burning from all social and economic activities and operation of public facilities other than industrial activities. It is calculated on the basis of coal consumption by households and others.

Industrial Solid Wastes Produced refers to total volume of solid, semi-solid and high concentration liquid residues produced by industrial enterprises from production process in a given period of time, including hazardous wastes, slag, coal ash, gangue, tailings, radioactive residues and other wastes, but excluding stones stripped or dug out in mining (gangue and acid or alkaline stones not included). A stone is acid or alkaline depending on the pH value of the water below 4 or above 10.5 when the stone is in, or soaked by, the water.

Industrial Solid Wastes Utilized refers to volume of solid wastes from which useful materials can be extracted or which can be converted into usable resources, energy or other materials by means of reclamation, processing, recycling and exchange (including utilizing in the year the stocks of industrial solid wastes of the previous year). Examples of such utilizations include fertilizers, building materials and road materials. The information shall be collected by the producing units of the wastes.

Rate of Utilization of Industrial Solid Wastes refers to the percentage of industrial solid wastes utilized over industrial solid wastes produced (including stocks of the previous years). It is calculated as:

$$\text{Rage of utilization of industrial solid wastes} = \frac{\text{volume of industrial solid wastes utilized}}{\text{industrial solid wastes produced} + \text{stock of previous years}} \times 100\%$$

Industrial Solid Wastes Disposed refers to quantity of industrial solid wastes which are burnt or placed ultimately in the sites meeting the requirements for environmental protection and not salvaged or recycled (including disposition in the year of those wastes of previous years). The disposition includes landfill (Safe landfills should be conducted for hazardous wastes), incineration, containment spaces, deep underground disposal, backfill in mining pits and disposal at sea.

Consumption Wastes Transported refers to volume of consumption wastes collected and transported to disposal factories or sites. Statistical calculations only when the source from garbage and garbage transfer station directly to the treatment plant and the final consumer satisfaction point clearance volume, for the secondary transit clearance volume can not be duplicated.

Ratio of Consumption Wastes Treated refers to consumption wastes treated over that produced. It is calculated as:

$$\text{Ratio of consumption wastes treated} = \frac{\text{consumption wastes treated}}{\text{consumption wastes produced}} \times 100\%$$

In practical statistics, as it is difficult to estimate, the volume of consumption wastes produced is replaced with that transported. During the audit, "Garbage clearance volume" and the total population to be (including temporary residents) corresponds, generally, urban waste generated per capita is about 1kg.

Environment Pollution and Destruction Accidents refer to sudden accidents, due to economic or social activities that are in contrast to environment protection laws or due to unforeseen factors or natural disasters, that lead to the environment pollution, the destruction of protected wild animals, plants or nature reserves, the damage to human health, the economic and property losses, and the negative impact on the society.

农 业 13

Agriculture

13-1 农村基本情况及农业生产条件
Basic Conditions of Rural Areas and Agricultural Production

指 标	Item	2010	2011	2012	2013	2014
农村基层组织	**Rural Grassroots Units**					
乡镇个数(个)	Number of Township and Town Governments(unit)	1446	1445	1439	1388	1262
村委会个数(个)	Number of Villagers' Committees(unit)	17672	17583	18099	16859	16747
农村社会基础设施	**Basic Facilities in Rural Areas**					
自来水受益村数(个)	Number of Villages with Access to Tap Water(unit)	13636	13922	14443	13997	14153
通汽车的村数(个)	Villages with Automobile(unit)	17388	17336	17717	16766	16507
通电话的村数(个)	Villages with Telephone Communication(unit)	16772	16823	17066	16191	15980
通有线广播的村数(个)	Villages with Wire Broadcast(unit)	6332	6690	7713	7336	7722
农业机械化	**Agricultural Mechanization**					
农用机械总动力(万千瓦)	Total Power of Agricultural Machinery(10000 kw)	1730.31	1851.40	2106.65	2240.80	2458.40
柴油机	Diesel Engine	1192.24	1308.11	1489.89	1601.13	1735.05
汽油机	Gas Engine	53.42	60.50	74.68	77.45	94.32
电动机	Electromotor	472.21	473.46	535.01	555.60	625.94
其他机械	Others	12.44	9.33	7.08	6.63	3.09
农村主要物资消耗	**Main Materials Consumption for Agricultural Use**					
农用化肥施用量(折纯法)(万吨)	Consumption of Chemical Fertilizer(pure) (10000 tons)	86.53	94.06	98.17	99.54	101.29
农药使用量(吨)	Consumption of Chemical Pesticides(ton)	12938	14469	14450.2	13744	13425
农用塑料薄膜使用量(吨)	Consumption of Farm Plastic Membrane(ton)	36174	40857	44062	48031	48949
农田水利建设	**Farmland and Water Conservancy**					
有效灌溉面积(千公顷)	Effective Irrigated Area(1000 hectares)	1195.33	1266.80	1317.59	1367.66	1429.49
旱涝保收面积(千公顷)	Area that Ensure Stable Yields Despite Droughtor Excessive Rain(1000 hectares)	646.02	659.31	666.41	672.47	679.29

注："农业机械化"资料来源于省农委，"农田水利建设"资料来源于省水利厅。

Note:The data of "agricultural mechanization" are provided by the Provincial Agricultural Commission; and the data of "farmland and water conservancy" are provided by the Provincial Department of Water Resources.

13-2 年末主要农业机械拥有量
Major Agricultural Machinery at the Year-end

指标	Item	2010	2011	2012	2013	2014	2014年比2013年增长(%) Increase Rate in 2014 over 2013(%)
大中型拖拉机(万台)	Number of Large and Medium-sized Tractors (10000 unit)	2.53	3.12	3.92	4.19	4.21	0.7
大中型拖拉机配套农具(万套)	Number of Large and Medium-sized Tractor Towing Farm Machinery (10000 unit)	1.36	1.38	1.43	1.53	1.62	5.4
小型拖拉机(万台)	Number of Small Tractors (10000 unit)	5.66	6.64	7.31	8.59	9.52	10.8
小型拖拉机配套农具(万套)	Small Tractor Towing Farm Machinery (10000 unit)	2.47	2.61	2.88	2.90	3.10	6.8
农用排灌电动机(万台)	Number of Drainage and Irrigation Electromotor Engines(10000 unit)	19.03	19.06	21.09	22.50	25.62	13.9
农用排灌柴油机(万台)	Number of Drainage and Irrigation Diesel Engines(10000 unit)	18.72	18.45	19.95	19.98	21.14	5.8
联合收割机(台)	Combine Harvesters(unit)	642	695	1057	1570	1812	15.4

注：资料来源于省农委。
Note:The data in this table are provided by the Provincial Agricultural Commission.

13-3 灌溉、除涝治水
Irrigation, Flood Prevention, Water and Soil Conservation

项目	Item	2010	2011	2012	2013	2014
水利投入(亿元)	Input of Water Conservancy(100 million yuan)	102.01	151.78	175.18	192.52	211.33
有效灌溉面积(千公顷)	Effective Irrigated Area(1000 hectares)	1195.33	1266.80	1317.59	1367.66	1429.49
节水灌溉面积(千公顷)	Water-saving Irrigated Area (1000 hectares)	391.74	396.00	403.28	304.37	313.28
除涝面积(千公顷)	Areas with Flood Prevention Measures(1000 hectares)	54.00	54.81	55.70	53.49	89.90
水土流失治理面积(千公顷)	Area of Soil Erosion under Control(1000 hectares)	2811.50	2956.00	3225.99	5816.53	6046.39
堤防长度(公里)	Total Length of Dikes(km)	1598.40	1634.60	2256.55	2453.58	3025.19
堤防保护面积(千公顷)	Area of Land Protected by Dikes (1000 hectares)	167.68	169.12	215.79	196.39	287.72

注：资料来源于省水利厅。
Note:Data in this table are provided by the Provincial Department of Water Resources.

13-4 农林牧渔业增加值

Value-Added of Farming,Forestry, Animal Husbandry, Fishery and Their Services

单位：亿元 (100 million yuan)

指 标	Item	2010	2011	2012	2013	2014
农林牧渔业增加值	**Added Value of FFAFS**	**625.04**	**726.21**	**891.91**	**1031.70**	**1316.08**
农 业	Farming	385.61	430.84	561.32	646.12	851.89
林 业	Forestry	28.07	31.99	37.03	47.71	68.15
畜牧业	Animal Husbandry	179.51	223.22	245.70	280.68	331.16
渔 业	Fishery	8.98	12.78	17.83	23.96	29.25
农、林、牧、渔服务业	FFAF Services	22.86	27.38	30.03	33.23	35.63
农林牧渔业增加值增长速度(%)	**Added Value of FFAFS growth rate(%)**	**4.7**	**1.2**	**8.6**	**5.8**	**6.5**
农 业	Farming	2.4	-0.3	10.6	5.7	8.1
林 业	Forestry	9.6	7.4	6.8	7.0	7.3
畜牧业	Animal Husbandry	8.0	1.0	5.0	4.9	1.8
渔 业	Fishery	11.2	23.7	21.2	20.0	19.7
农、林、牧、渔服务业	FFAF Services	8.9	10.4	3.2	4.8	3.3

13-5 农林牧渔业总产值

Gross Output Value of Farming,Forestry,Animal Husbandry, Fishery and Their Services

单位：亿元 (100 million yuan)

指 标	Item	2010	2011	2012	2013	2014	2014年比2013年增长(%) Increase Rate in 2014over 2013(%)
农林牧渔业总产值	**Gross Output Value of Farming,Forestry, AnimalHusbandry and Fishery**	**997.82**	**1165.46**	**1436.61**	**1663.02**	**2118.48**	**6.6**
农业产值	**Farming**	**587.31**	**655.30**	**864.86**	**997.13**	**1321.86**	**8.5**
谷物及其他作物的种植	Planting of Cereal and other Crops	340.56	340.36	389.45	447.34	438.67	5.2
蔬菜、园艺作物的种植	Planting of Vegetable and Gardening Crops	194.69	249.10	387.95	429.89	728.90	9.9
水果、坚果、饮料和香料作物的种植	Planting of Fruits, nuts, Beverages and Spice Crops	35.64	46.12	54.69	63.33	77.61	16.9
中药材的种植	Planting of Chinese Traditional Medicine	16.42	19.72	32.77	56.55	76.68	14.3
林业产值	**Forestry**	**41.01**	**46.66**	**54.19**	**69.87**	**99.62**	**7.5**
林木的培育和种植	Cultivating and planting of forest	5.49	5.90	6.90	13.55	26.42	10.7
木材和竹材的采运	Logging and Transporting of Timber & bamboo	11.47	12.51	14.46	17.15	16.39	-3.3
林产品的采集	Collecting of Forest Products	24.04	28.25	32.83	39.17	56.82	11.4
畜牧业产值	**Animal Husbandry**	**304.16**	**381.95**	**421.55**	**482.68**	**569.29**	**2.0**
牲畜的饲养	Animal Raising	56.13	70.05	85.31	102.50	141.98	4.4
猪的饲养	Hogs Raising	196.23	253.35	273.87	309.03	331.67	1.2
家禽的饲养	Poultry Raising	50.00	56.69	60.43	69.22	93.58	1.8
狩猎和捕捉动物	Hunting and Catching Animales	0.09	0.09	0.10	0.10	0.09	-7.4
其他畜牧业	Others	1.71	1.76	1.84	1.83	1.96	3.9
渔业产值	**Fishery**	**13.82**	**19.90**	**28.21**	**38.30**	**47.01**	**20.4**
农林牧渔服务业产值	**Gross Output Value of FFAF Services**	**51.52**	**61.65**	**67.80**	**75.04**	**80.70**	**3.6**

13-6 主要农作物播种面积
Sown Areas of Major Farm Crops

单位：千公顷 (1000 hectares)

指 标	Item	2010	2011	2012	2013	2014	2014年比2013年增长(%) Increase Rate in 2014 over 2013(%)
农作物总播种面积	**Total Sown Areas**	**4889.30**	**5021.22**	**5182.86**	**5390.11**	**5516.46**	**2.3**
#粮食作物	Grain Crops	3039.50	3055.56	3054.28	3118.42	3138.35	0.6
#稻 谷	Rice	695.81	681.53	682.95	684.45	681.96	-0.4
小 麦	Wheat	260.77	257.62	259.76	251.78	251.50	-0.1
玉 米	Corn	781.14	787.80	775.15	778.35	787.47	1.2
大 豆	Soja	128.95	132.78	133.82	128.17	130.62	1.9
薯 类	Tubers	894.83	912.94	919.41	937.90	944.50	0.7
#马铃薯	Potato	645.84	668.01	676.27	689.50	704.25	2.1
油 料	Oil-bearing Crops	529.14	536.14	547.50	560.76	582.14	3.8
#油菜籽	Rapeseeds	479.19	488.98	496.96	506.72	521.61	2.9
花 生	Peanuts	40.81	38.90	41.02	43.56	48.90	12.3
糖 料	Sugar Crops	13.74	12.02	21.83	27.93	27.85	-0.3
#甘 蔗	Sugarcane	13.70	11.98	21.71	27.92	27.84	-0.3
烟 叶	Tobacco	195.37	212.24	249.17	266.43	228.51	-14.2
#烤 烟	Flue-cured Tobacco	182.74	200.01	237.01	254.86	216.41	-15.1
药材类	Medicinal Materials	28.12	44.35	74.68	117.54	146.60	24.7
蔬 菜	Vegetable	647.92	708.52	774.32	847.72	924.25	9.0

13-7 主要农作物产品产量

Yields of Major Farm Crops

单位：万吨 (10000 tons)

指 标	Item	2010	2011	2012	2013	2014	2014年比2013年增长(%) Increase Rate in 2014over 2013(%)
粮食作物	**Grain Crops**	**1112.30**	**876.90**	**1079.50**	**1029.99**	**1138.50**	**10.5**
#稻 谷	Rice	445.65	303.93	402.43	361.30	403.24	11.6
小 麦	Wheat	24.83	50.38	52.39	51.51	61.50	19.4
玉 米	Corn	415.43	243.71	342.25	298.03	313.81	5.3
大 豆	Soja	15.99	7.11	7.84	8.04	11.78	46.5
薯 类	Tubers	174.13	239.31	235.83	263.36	289.91	10.1
#马铃薯	Potato	141.43	189.38	179.74	211.40	226.60	7.2
油料作物	**Oil-bearing Crops**	**60.34**	**78.85**	**87.38**	**91.53**	**98.05**	**7.1**
#油菜籽	Rapeseeds	51.62	71.81	78.18	81.78	86.69	6.0
花 生	Peanuts	7.68	6.07	7.86	8.25	9.71	17.7
甘 蔗	**Sugarcane**	**52.24**	**43.60**	**127.96**	**159.29**	**168.27**	**5.6**
烤 烟	**Flue-cured Tobacco**	**37.02**	**32.50**	**37.31**	**41.79**	**35.34**	**-15.4**
蔬 菜	**Vegetable**	**1202.04**	**1250.05**	**1375.63**	**1500.45**	**1625.62**	**8.3**

13-8 主要农作物单产

Yields of Major Farm Crops Per Mu

单位：公斤/亩 (kg/mu)

指 标	Item	2010	2011	2012	2013	2014	2014年比2013年增长(%) Increase Rate in 2014 over 2013(%)
粮食作物	**Grain Crops**	**244**	**191**	**236**	**220**	**242**	**9.8**
#稻 谷	Rice	427	297	393	352	394	12.0
小 麦	Wheat	63	130	134	136	163	19.5
玉 米	Corn	355	206	294	255	266	4.1
大 豆	Soja	83	36	39	42	60	43.8
薯 类	Tubers	130	175	171	187	205	9.3
#马铃薯	Potato	146	189	177	204	215	5.0
油料作物	**Oil-bearing Crops**	**76**	**98**	**106**	**109**	**112**	**3.2**
#油菜籽	Rapeseed	72	98	105	108	111	3.0
花 生	Peanuts	125	104	128	126	132	4.8
甘 蔗	**Sugarcane**	**2542**	**2427**	**3930**	**3804**	**4029**	**5.9**
烤 烟	**Flue-cured Tobacco**	**135**	**108**	**105**	**109**	**109**	**-0.4**

13−9 茶叶、水果面积及产量

Total Sown Areas and Yields of Tea,Fruit

指　标	Item	2010	2011	2012	2013	2014	2014年比2013年增长(%) Increase Rate in 2014 over2013(%)
面　积(千公顷)	**Area(1000 hectares)**						
茶园	Tea Field Area	167.19	196.37	251.52	313.24	369.26	17.9
桑园	Mulberry Field Area	4.63	4.47	3.92	3.01	3.81	26.5
柞坡	Breed Tussah Field Area	2.79	5.46	3.72	3.82	3.32	-13.0
果园	Orchards Filed Area	151.83	169.02	192.96	228.13	262.14	14.9
产　量(万吨)	**Yield(10000 tons)**						
茶　叶	Tea	5.23	5.84	7.44	8.94	10.71	19.8
水　果	Fruit	123.47	128.03	147.72	167.75	196.38	17.1
#园林水果	Garden Fruit	69.61	79.52	90.06	105.74	125.98	19.1
#苹　果	Apples	1.55	2.17	2.49	3.25	4.39	35.1
梨	Pears	18.21	19.54	21.72	24.09	27.31	13.4
柑　桔	Citrus	20.37	20.81	22.74	25.48	28.91	13.4
香　蕉	Bananas	0.61	0.59	0.61	0.56	0.58	3.6
杨　梅	Red Bayberry	2.90	3.19	3.19	3.49	5.06	45.0
猕猴桃	Chinese Gooseberrys	1.30	1.70	1.76	2.21	2.50	13.3
柿　子	Persimmons	1.36	1.25	1.46	1.46	1.50	2.8

13−10 造林及林产品产量

Areas of Forestation and Output of Forest Products

单位：吨 (ton)

指　标	Item	2010	2011	2012	2013	2014
当年造林面积(千公顷)	**Areas of Forestation in this year(1000 hectares)**	**78.8**	**131.3**	**199.3**	**218.2**	**302.7**
林产品产量	**Output of Forest Products**					
生　漆	Lacquer	1614	2001	1698	1827	6955
油桐籽	Tung-oil Seed	63815	75769	81638	70863	73095
油茶籽	Tea-oil Seed	20368	23166	26657	31220	69438
乌桕籽	Tallow-seed	2468	2487	2370	2305	2666
五倍籽	Nutgall	2216	1624	1922	2633	7207
棕　片	Palm-flake	4365	4530	4387	4321	5166
松　脂	Pine Resin	8215	12001	13014	13799	15992
竹笋片	Bamboo Shoot	20382	19897	20495	14456	17741
核　桃	Walnuts	15356	17364	23680	34315	57383
板　栗	Chestnut	19316	22653	26076	31621	53233

注：1."造林面积"数据来源于省林业厅。2.由于统计方法制度改变，2014年"林产品产量"数据来源于省林业厅。
Note:1."The areas of forestation" in the table are obtained from the Provincial Department of Forest.2 Due to the changing of statistics method, the of "out put of forestry products" in 2014 are provided by the Provincial Department of Forest.

13−11 畜牧业生产及水产品
Livestock Production and Aquatic Products

指　标	Item	2010	2011	2012	2013	2014	2014年比2013年增长(%) Increase Rate in 2014 over 2013(%)
当年出栏数	**Number of Slaughtered Fattened Hogs, Ox,Goats and Sheep**						
猪(万头)	Slaughtered Fattened Hogs(10000 heads)	1688.67	1689.66	1734.76	1832.28	1845.27	0.7
牛(万头)	Ox by Sold and Killed(10000 heads)	96.56	97.21	105.99	115.22	117.35	1.9
羊(万头)	Goats by Sold and Killed(10000 heads)	198.70	197.31	206.78	205.39	220.38	7.3
肉类总产量(万吨)	**Total Yield of Meat(10000 tons)**	**179.09**	**179.97**	**190.27**	**199.74**	**201.80**	**1.0**
#猪　肉	Pork	148.09	148.29	156.13	163.73	165.55	1.1
牛　肉	Beef	11.99	12.00	13.04	14.13	14.68	3.9
羊　肉	Mutton	3.40	3.37	3.53	3.51	3.75	7.0
禽　肉	Poultry	14.12	14.35	15.41	15.48	14.84	-4.1
其他畜产品产量	**Others**						
牛　奶(万吨)	Cow Milk(10000 tons)	4.59	4.85	5.10	5.45	5.71	4.7
禽　蛋(万吨)	Poultry Eggs(10000 tons)	12.51	13.65	14.65	15.44	16.20	4.9
蜂　蜜(吨)	Honey(ton)	1894	2029	2052	2468	2733	10.7
大牲畜年末存栏数(万头)	**Large Animals(year-end)(10000 heads)**	**627.64**	**550.82**	**541.03**	**536.90**	**572.05**	**6.5**
#牛	Cattle and Buffaloes	541.80	467.11	461.04	460.62	495.86	7.7
猪年末存栏数(万头)	**Hogs(year-end)(10000 heads)**	**1616.34**	**1521.60**	**1604.09**	**1604.10**	**1600.57**	**-0.2**
羊年末存栏数(万只)	**Sheep and Goats(year-end)(10000 heads)**	**261.10**	**256.49**	**290.09**	**299.59**	**337.40**	**12.6**
水产品(万吨)	**Aquatic Products(10000 tons)**	**8.79**	**10.88**	**13.47**	**16.70**	**20.99**	**25.7**

注：表中“水产品”数据来源于省农委。
Note:Data of "aquatic products" in the table are obtained from the Provincial Agricultural Commission.

主要统计指标解释

农业机械总动力 指主要用于农、林、牧、渔业的各种动力机械的动力总和。包括耕作机械、排灌机械、收获机械、农用运输机械、植物保护机械、牧业机械、林业机械、渔业机械和其他农业机械〔内燃机按引擎马力折成瓦(特)计算、电动机按功率折成瓦(特)计算〕。不包括专门用于乡、镇、村、组办工业、基本建设、非农业运输、科学试验和教学等非农业生产方面用的动力机械与作业机械。

农用化肥施用量 指本年内实际用于农业生产的化肥数量，包括氮肥、磷肥、钾肥和复合肥。化肥施用量要求按折纯量计算数量。折纯量是指把氮肥、磷肥、钾肥分别按含氮、含五氧化二磷、含氧化钾的百分之一百成份进行折算后的数量。复合肥按其所含主要成分折算。

有效灌溉面积 指具有一定的水源，地块比较平整，灌溉工程或设备已经配套，在一般年景下当年能够进行正常灌溉的耕地面积。

农林牧渔业总产值 指以货币表现的农、林、牧、渔业全部产品和对农林牧渔业生产活动进行的各种支持性服务活动的价值总量，它反映一定时期内农业生产总规模和总成果。农业总产值的计算方法通常是按农林牧渔业产品及其副产品的产量分别乘以各自单位产品价格求得；然后将四业产品产值及农林牧渔服务业产值相加即为农业总产值。

农作物播种面积 指实际播种或移植有农作物的面积。凡是实际种植有农作物的面积，不论种植在耕地上还是种植在非耕地上，均包括在农作物播种面积中。在播种季节基本结束后，因遭灾而重新改种和补种的农作物面积，也包括在内。

粮食产量 指全社会的产量。包括国有经济经营的、集体统一经营的和农民家庭经营的粮食产量，还包括工矿企业办的农场和其他生产单位的产量。粮食除包括稻谷、小麦、玉米、高粱、谷子及其他杂粮外，还包括薯类和豆类。其产量计算方法，豆类按去豆荚后的干豆计算；薯类(包括甘薯和马铃薯，不包括芋头和木薯)1963年以前按每4公斤鲜薯折1公斤粮食计算，从1964年开始改为按5公斤鲜薯折1公斤粮食计算。城市郊区作为蔬菜的薯类(如马铃薯等)按鲜品计算，并且不作粮食统计。其他粮食一律按脱粒后的原粮计算。

油料产量 指全部油料作物的生产量。包括花生、油菜籽、芝麻、向日葵籽、胡麻籽（亚麻籽）和其他油料。不包括大豆、木本油料和野生油料。花生以带壳干花生计算。

猪、牛、羊肉产量 指当年出栏并已屠宰、除去头蹄下水后带骨肉(即胴体重)的重量。

期初(末)畜禽存栏头(只)数 指报告期初(末)农村各种合作经济组织和国营农场、农民个人、机关、团体、学校、工矿企业、部队等单位以及城镇居民饲养的大牲畜、猪、羊、家禽等畜禽的存栏数。

水产品产量 指人工养殖的水产品和天然生长的水产品的捕捞量。包括海水的鱼类、虾蟹类、贝类和藻类以及内陆水域的鱼类、虾蟹类和贝类，不包括淡水生植物。

Explanatory Notes on Main Statistical Indicators

Total Power of Agricultural Machinery refers to total mechanical power of machinery used in agriculture, forestry, animal husbandry and fishery, including machinery for ploughing, irrigation and drainage, harvesting, transport, plant protection, animal husbandry, forestry and fishery and other agricultural machineries. (For the power of internal combustion engines, it is converted from its horsepower into watts while for electric motors the output power is converted into watts.) Machinery employed for non-agricultural purposes, such as the machines used in township-run and village-run industry, construction, non-agricultural transport, scientific experiments and teaching, are not included. Data are mainly from agricultural machinery agencies.

Consumption of Chemical Fertilizers in Agriculture refers to the quantity of chemical fertilizers applied in agriculture in the year, including nitrogenous fertilizer, phosphate fertilizer, potash fertilizer, and compound fertilizer. The consumption of chemical fertilizers is calculated in terms of volume of effective components by means of converting the gross weight of the respective fertilizers into weight containing effective component. Compound fertilizer is converted in regard to its major components.

Irrigated Area refers to area of land that are effectively irrigated, i.e. relatively level land, where there are water sources or complete sets of irrigation facilities to lift and move adequate water for irrigation purpose under normal conditions. Under normal situations, irrigated area is the sum of watered fields and irrigated fields where irrigation systems or equipment have been installed for regular irrigation purpose.

Gross Output Value of Agriculture, Forestry, Animal Husbandry and Fishery refers to the total value of products of agriculture, forestry, animal husbandry and fishery, and total value of services in support of agriculture, forestry, animal husbandry and fishery activities. It reflects the total scale and results of agricultural production during a given period. Gross output value of agriculture is obtained by multiplying the output of each product or by-product by its price, resulting in the output value of each single item. The sum of output values of all products of agriculture, forestry, animal husbandry and fishery and services in support to those industries is then equal to the gross output value of agriculture.

Sown Area of Crops refers to area of land sown or transplanted with crops regardless of being in cultivated area or non-cultivated area. Area of land re-sown due to natural disasters is also included.

Grain Output refers to the total output in the whole country including grains produced by State farms, collective units, rural households, as well as by farms affiliated to industrial and mining enterprises and other production units. Grain includes rice, wheat, corn, sorghum, millet and other miscellaneous grains as well as tubers and beans. Output of beans refers to dry beans without pods. The output of tubers (sweet potatoes and potatoes, not including taros and cassava) are converted into that of grain at the ratio 4:1, i.e. 4 kilograms of fresh tubers were equivalent to 1 kilogram of grain up to 1963. Since 1964 the ratio for conversion has been 5:1. Tubers supplied as vegetables (such as potatoes) in cities and suburbs are calculated as fresh vegetables and their output is not included in the output of grain. Output of all other grains refers to husked grain.

Output of Oil-bearing Crops refers to the total production of oil-bearing crops of various kinds, including peanuts (dry, in shell), rapeseeds, sesame, sunflower seeds, flax seeds, and other oil-bearing crops. Soybeans, oil-bearing woody plants, and wild oil-bearing crops are not included.

Output of Pork, Beef, and Mutton refers to the meat of slaughtered hogs, cattle, sheep and goats with head, feet, and offal taken away.

Number of Livestock or Poultry in Stock at Beginning (or End) of Period refers to the total number of large animals, pigs, sheep, fowls, etc. raised by rural cooperative organizations, State farms, rural individuals, government agencies, schools, industrial and mining enterprises, army, and urban residents at the beginning (or end) of the reference period.

Output of Aquatic Products refers to catches of both artificially cultured and naturally grown aquatic products, including fish, shrimps, crabs and shellfish in sea and inland water as well as seaweed. Freshwater plants are not included.

贵州2015
统计年鉴
GUIZHOU
STATISTICAL YEARBOOK

工业 Industry

14

14-1 规模以上工业企业单位数

Number of Industrial Enterprises above Designated Size

单位：个 (unit)

指 标	Item	2010	2011	2012	2013	2014
规模以上工业企业单位数	**Number of Industrial Enterprises above Designated Size**	**2963**	**2329**	**2752**	**3590**	**3895**
#国有控股企业	State-holding Industry Enterprises	516	431	470	502	509
按轻重工业分	**Grouped by Type of Light and Heavy Industry**					
轻工业	Light Industry	634	463	571	881	1075
重工业	Heavy Industry	2329	1866	2181	2709	2820
按企业规模分	**Grouped by Size of Enterprise**					
大型企业	Large Enterprises	30	71	80	98	101
中型企业	Medium-sized Enterprises	415	493	633	779	800
小型企业	Small Enterprises	2518	1631	1966	2503	2724
微型企业	Micro-enterprises		134	73	210	270
按登记注册类型分	**By Status of Registration**					
内资企业	Domestic Funded	2861	2253	2684	3518	3809
国有企业	State-owned Enterprises	309	253	267	225	156
集体企业	Collective-owned Enterprises	59	30	29	27	18
股份合作企业	Cooperative Enterprises	41	29	25	22	11
联营企业	Joint Ownership Enterprises	12	20	18	10	7
有限责任公司	Limited Liability Corporations	844	664	886	1381	1594
股份有限公司	Share-holding Corporations Limited	113	111	111	119	131
私营企业	Private Enterprises	1469	1129	1313	1700	1851
其他企业	Other Enterprises	14	17	35	34	41
港、澳、台商投资企业	Enterprises with Funds from Hong Kong,Macao and Taiwan	51	37	32	32	44
外商投资企业	Foreign Funded Enterprises	51	39	36	40	42

注：1.规模以上工业统计口径2010年为年主营业务收入500万元及以上的工业企业，2011年及以后为年主营业务收入2000万元及以上工业企业(以下相关表除特殊标注外，均同)。2.企业规模从2011年开始，按国家统计局新制定的《统计上大中小微企业划分办法》执行。

Note: 1.The statistics of industrial enterprises above designated size was the industrial enterprises with business income of 5 million yuan and above in 2010. And form 2011 it is the industrial with main business income of 20 million yuan. 2.From 2011,the standard of size is executed according to "Statistics issued by the division of the large, medium, small and micro-enterprises" which is the newly established by National Bureau of Statistics.

14-2 按行业分规模以上工业企业单位数

Number of Industrial Enterprises above Designated Size by Sector

单位：个 (unit)

指 标	Item	2010	2011
规模以上工业企业单位数	**Number of Industrial Enterprises above Designated Size**	**2963**	**2329**
采矿业	Mining	929	815
#煤炭开采和洗选业	Mining and Washing of Coal	827	743
黑色金属矿采选业	Mining and Processing of Ferrous Metal Ores	28	24
有色金属矿采选业	Mining and Processing of Non-Ferrous Metal Ores	30	15
非金属矿采选业	Mining and Processing of Non-metal Ores	44	32
制造业	Manufacturing	1814	1347
#农副食品加工业	Processing of Food from Agricultural Products	153	117
食品制造业	Manufacture of Foods	56	37
饮料制造业	Manufacture of Liquor, Beverages and Refined Tea	133	118
烟草制品业	Manufacture of Tobacco	3	6
纺织业	Manufacture of Textile	12	9
纺织服装、服饰业	Manufacture of Textile, Wearing Apparel and Accessories	7	3
皮革、毛皮、羽毛及其制品和制鞋业	Manufacture of Leather,Furs,Feather and Related Products, and Footware	2	2
木材加工和木、竹、藤、棕、草制品业	Processing of Timber, Manufacture of Wood, Bamboo, Rattan, Palm and Straw Products	69	41
家具制造业	Manufacture of Furniture	5	2
造纸及纸制品业	Manufacture of Paper and Paper Products	41	27
印刷业和记录媒介的复制	Printing and Reproduction of Recording Media	21	8
文教体育用品制造业	Manufacture of Articles for Culture, Education, Arts and Crafts, Sport and Entertainment Activities	3	2
石油加工、炼焦及核燃料加工业	Processing of Petroleum,Coking and Processing of Nuclear Fuel	27	26
化学原料及化学制品制造业	Manufacture of Raw Chemical Materials and Chemical Products	182	134
医药制造业	Manufacture of Medicines	96	76
橡胶制品业	Manufacture of Rubber	12	9
塑料制品业	Manufacture of Plastics	54	30
非金属矿物制品业	Manufacture of Non-metallic Mineral Products	345	248
黑色金属冶炼及压延加工业	Smelting and Pressing of Ferrous Metals	185	166
有色金属冶炼及压延加工业	Smelting and Pressing of Non-ferrous Metals	97	78
金属制品业	Manufacture of Metal Products	38	19
通用设备制造业	Manufacture of General Purpose Machinery	63	37
专用设备制造业	Manufacture of Special Purpose Machinery	39	29
交通运输设备制造业	Manufacture of Transport Equipment	67	46
电气机械及器材制造业	Manufacture of Electrical Machinery and Apparatus	58	42
通信设备、计算机及其他电子设备制造业	Manufacture of Communication Equipment, Computers and Other Electronic Equipment	21	16
仪器仪表及文化、办公用机械制造业	Manufacture of Measuring Instruments and Machinery	12	9
工艺品及其他制造业	Manufacture of Artwork and Other Manufacturing	11	7
废弃资源和废旧材料回收加工业	Utilization of Waste Resources	2	3
电力、燃气及水的生产和供应业	Production and Supply of Electric Power,Gas and Water	220	167
电力、热力生产和供应业	Production and Supply of Electric Power and Heat Power	177	148
燃气生产和供应业	Production and Supply of Gas	8	6
水的生产和供应业	Production and Supply of Water	35	13

注：1.表中数据按国民经济行业分类(GB/T4754—2002)划分。2.不再公布只有1个企业的行业、注册类型的数据。(以下相关表同)

Note: 1.Data in this table is classified by sector of the National Economy (GB/T4754-2002). 2.No published data with only one industry registered type. (the relative tables in the chapter are the same)

14-2 续表 Continued

单位：个 (unit)

指　　标	Item	2012	2013	2014
规模以上工业企业单位数	**Number of Industrial Enterprises above Designated Size**	**2752**	**3590**	**3895**
采矿业	Mining	937	1090	965
#煤炭开采和洗选业	Mining and Washing of Coal	843	916	782
黑色金属矿采选业	Mining and Processing of Ferrous Metal Ores	33	39	35
有色金属矿采选业	Mining and Processing of Non-Ferrous Metal Ores	17	29	29
非金属矿采选业	Mining and Processing of Non-metal Ores	44	106	119
制造业	Manufacturing	1640	2300	2714
#农副食品加工业	Processing of Food from Agricultural Products	139	199	233
食品制造业	Manufacture of Foods	49	76	88
酒、饮料和精制茶制造业	Manufacture of Liquor, Beverages and Refined Tea	146	248	292
烟草制品业	Manufacture of Tobacco	6	5	2
纺织业	Manufacture of Textile	10	15	16
纺织服装、服饰业	Manufacture of Textile, Wearing Apparel and Accessories	7	17	33
皮革、毛皮、羽毛及其制品和制鞋业	Manufacture of Leather,Furs,Feather and Related Products, and Footware	4	11	23
木材加工和木、竹、藤、棕、草制品业	Processing of Timber, Manufacture of Wood, Bamboo, Rattan, Palm and Straw Products	63	95	104
家具制造业	Manufacture of Furniture	7	16	24
造纸和纸制品业	Manufacture of Paper and Paper Products	29	39	45
印刷业和记录媒介复制业	Printing and Reproduction of Recording Media	11	16	19
文教、工美、体育和娱乐用品制造业	Manufacture of Articles for Culture, Education, Arts and Crafts, Sport and Entertainment Activities	5	15	18
石油加工、炼焦和核燃料加工业	Processing of Petroleum,Coking and Processing of Nuclear Fuel	31	33	23
化学原料和化学制品制造业	Manufacture of Raw Chemical Materials and Chemical Products	156	199	212
医药制造业	Manufacture of Medicines	79	93	107
橡胶和塑料制品业	Manufacture of Rubber and Plastics Products	44	70	98
非金属矿物制品业	Manufacture of Non-metallic Mineral Products	328	501	632
黑色金属冶炼和压延加工业	Smelting and Pressing of Ferrous Metals	193	193	172
有色金属冶炼和压延加工业	Smelting and Pressing of Non-ferrous Metals	66	87	85
金属制品业	Manufacture of Metal Products	38	72	109
通用设备制造业	Manufacture of General Purpose Machinery	35	49	60
专用设备制造业	Manufacture of Special Purpose Machinery	35	51	65
汽车制造业	Manufacture of Automotive	26	34	37
铁路、船舶、航空航天和其他运输设备制造业	Manufacture of Railroad, Marine, Aerospace and Other Transportation Equipment	31	37	42
电气机械和器材制造业	Manufacture of Electrical Machinery and Apparatus	55	71	97
计算机、通信和其他电子设备制造业	Manufacture of Communication Equipment, Computers and Other Electronic Equipment	22	28	43
仪器仪表制造业	Manufacture of Measuring Instruments and Machinery	9	9	10
其他制造业	Others	10	13	16
废弃资源综合利用业	Utilization of Waste Resources	5	7	8
电力、燃气及水的生产和供应业	Production and Supply of Electric Power,Gas and Water	175	200	216
电力、热力生产和供应业	Production and Supply of Electric Power and Heat Power	153	165	171
燃气生产和供应业	Production and Supply of Gas	8	16	20
水的生产和供应业	Production and Supply of Water	14	19	25

注：表中数据按国民经济行业分类（GB/T4754—2011）划分。（以下相关表同）
Note: Data in this table is classified by sector of the National Economy (GB/T4754-2011). (The relative tables in the chapter are the same)

14–3 规模以上工业增加值

Value added of Industry above Designated Size

单位：亿元 (100 million yuan)

指 标	Item	2010	2011	2012	2013	2014	2014年比2013年增长(%) Increase Rate in 2014 over 2013(%)
规模以上工业增加值	**Value added of Industry above Designated Size**	**1227.17**	**1638.71**	**2055.46**	**2531.92**	**3117.60**	**11.3**
#国有控股企业	State-holding Industry	749.55	917.55	1194.83	1319.74	1503.54	7.9
#私营企业	Private Enterprises	277.96	417.11	477.19	590.19	761.01	11.7
按轻重工业分	**Grouped by Type of Light and Heavy Industry**						
轻工业	Light Industry	413.99	545.78	773.04	969.29	1185.13	11.5
重工业	Heavy Industry	813.18	1092.93	1282.42	1562.63	1932.47	11.2
按企业规模分	**Grouped by Size of Enterprise**						
大型企业	Large Enterprises	465.95	580.70	904.47	1109.45	1206.87	5.8
中型企业	Medium-sized Enterprises	302.19	366.95	537.78	756.28	956.96	10.3
小型企业	Small Enterprises	459.03	651.60	600.11	658.12	937.85	20.3
微型企业	Micro-enterprises		39.46	13.10	8.07	15.91	33.6
按登记注册类型分	**By Status of Registration**						
国有企业	State-owned Enterprises	356.22	479.99	707.85	724.16	737.96	7.1
集体企业	Collective-owned Enterprises	6.81	2.75	9.91	8.72	3.89	-16.5
股份合作企业	Cooperative Enterprises	8.35	3.23	10.01	19.53	15.23	12.0
股份制企业	Share-holding Enterprises	612.56	813.19	889.82	1354.78	1917.08	14.1
外商及港澳台商投资企业	Enterprises with Funds from Foreign,Hong Kong, Macao and Taiwan	40.44	40.40	60.42	44.65	75.05	12.7
其他企业	Other Enterprises	202.80	299.16	377.45	380.08	368.40	6.7

注：工业增加值按收入法计算，增长速度按可比价计算(以下相关表同)。

Note:Value-added of industry above designated size is calculated by income approach and the increase rate is calculated at the comparable price(the relative tables in the chapter are the same).

14-4 按行业分规模以上工业增加值

Value added of Industry above Designated Size by Sector

单位：亿元 (100 million yuan)

指　标	Item	2010	2011
规模以上工业增加值	**Value added of Industry above Designated Size**	**1227.17**	**1638.71**
采矿业	Mining	297.43	446.32
#煤炭开采和洗选业	Mining and Washing of Coal	276.68	411.35
黑色金属矿采选业	Mining and Processing of Ferrous Metal Ores	5.58	5.71
有色金属矿采选业	Mining and Processing of Non-Ferrous Metal Ores	3.28	3.83
非金属矿采选业	Mining and Processing of Non-metal Ores	11.89	25.43
制造业	Manufacturing	721.35	952.38
#农副食品加工业	Processing of Food from Agricultural Products	11.50	20.01
食品制造业	Manufacture of Foods	15.41	13.99
饮料制造业	Manufacture of Beverages	162.79	238.88
烟草制品业	Manufacture of Tobacco	152.62	175.81
纺织业	Manufacture of Textile	1.12	2.11
纺织服装、服饰业	Manufacture of Textile, Wearing Apparel and Accessories	0.65	0.99
皮革、毛皮、羽毛及其制品和制鞋业	Manufacture of Leather,Furs,Feather and Related Products, and Footware	0.05	0.02
木材加工及木、竹、藤、棕、草制品业	Processing of Timber, Manufacture of Wood, Bamboo, Rattan, Palm and Straw Products	5.55	8.49
家具制造业	Manufacture of Furniture	1.30	1.45
造纸及纸制品业	Manufacture of Paper and Paper Products	3.81	4.64
印刷业和记录媒介的复制	Printing and Reproduction of Recording Media	6.60	6.62
文教体育用品制造业	Manufacture of Articles For Culture, Education and Sport Activity	0.32	0.4
石油加工、炼焦及核燃料加工业	Processing of Petroleum,Coking and Processing of Nuclear Fuel	13.46	11.89
化学原料及化学制品制造业	Manufacture of Raw Chemical Materials and Chemical Products	58.47	96.68
医药制造业	Manufacture of Medicines	40.50	52.02
橡胶制品业	Manufacture of Rubber	19.12	15.76
塑料制品业	Manufacture of Plastics	4.51	5.39
非金属矿物制品业	Manufacture of Non-metallic Mineral Products	47.86	61.41
黑色金属冶炼及压延加工业	Smelting and Pressing of Ferrous Metals	54.42	66.70
有色金属冶炼及压延加工业	Smelting and Pressing of Non-ferrous Metals	32.92	57.68
金属制品业	Manufacture of Metal Products	7.56	9.47
通用设备制造业	Manufacture of General Purpose Machinery	14.92	19.54
专用设备制造业	Manufacture of Special Purpose Machinery	5.77	7.88
交通运输设备制造业	Manufacture of Transport Equipment	31.50	32.82
电气机械及器材制造业	Manufacture of Electrical Machinery and Apparatus	8.66	8.05
通信设备、计算机及其他电子设备制造业	Manufacture of Communication Equipment, Computers and Other Electronic Equipment	8.94	10.50
仪器仪表及文化、办公用机械制造业	Manufacture of Measuring Instruments and Machinery for Cultural Activity and Office Work	1.91	3.05
工艺品及其他制造业	Manufacture of Artwork and Other Manufacturing	9.05	19.46
废弃资源和废旧材料回收加工业	Utilization of Waste Resources	0.07	0.68
电力、燃气及水的生产和供应业	Production and Supply of Electric Power,Gas and Water	208.40	240.01
#电力、热力生产和供应业	Production and Supply of Electric Power and Heat Power	203.60	234.89
燃气生产和供应业	Production and Supply of Gas	0.67	1.24
水的生产和供应业	Production and Supply of Water	4.13	3.88

14-4 续表 Continued

单位：亿元 (100 million yuan)

指 标	Item	2012	2013	2014	2014年比2013年增长(%) Increase Rate in 2014 over 2013(%)
规模以上工业增加值	**Value added of Industry above Designated Size**	**2055.46**	**2531.92**	**3117.60**	**11.3**
采矿业	Mining	523.79	641.94	789.17	9.8
#煤炭开采和洗选业	Mining and Washing of Coal	472.21	558.35	676.28	8.8
黑色金属矿采选业	Mining and Processing of Ferrous Metal Ores	9.54	16.25	20.17	14.3
有色金属矿采选业	Mining and Processing of Non-Ferrous Metal Ores	3.69	7.64	13.46	30.8
非金属矿采选业	Mining and Processing of Non-metal Ores	37.77	59.03	77.96	17.0
制造业	Manufacturing	1230.25	1564.04	1977.28	12.8
#农副食品加工业	Processing of Food from Agricultural Products	20.56	30.33	39.90	8.4
食品制造业	Manufacture of Foods	21.35	26.42	34.36	20.2
酒、饮料和精制茶制造业	Manufacture of Liquor, Beverages and Refined Tea	378.82	495.62	613.85	13.7
烟草制品业	Manufacture of Tobacco	246.89	274.74	302.19	8.8
纺织业	Manufacture of Textile	0.78	2.89	2.59	8.1
纺织服装、服饰业	Manufacture of Textile, Wearing Apparel and Accessories	1.82	3.19	6.80	86.3
皮革、毛皮、羽毛(绒)及其制品和制鞋业	Manufacture of Leather,Furs,Feather and Related Products, and Footware	1.84	4.16	7.69	29.7
木材加工及木、竹、藤、棕、草制品业	Processing of Timber, Manufacture of Wood, Bamboo, Rattan, Palm and Straw Products	15.49	24.93	33.12	12.3
家具制造业	Manufacture of Furniture	4.27	6.40	8.30	20.6
造纸及纸制品业	Manufacture of Paper and Paper Products	9.91	13.02	18.95	28.7
印刷和记录媒介复制业	Printing and Reproduction of Recording Media	4.60	6.21	9.71	16.3
文教、工美、体育和娱乐用品制造业	Manufacture of Articles for Culture, Education, Arts and Crafts, Sport and Entertainment Activities	0.64	1.00	2.70	96.4
石油加工、炼焦及核燃料加工业	Processing of Petroleum,Coking and Processing of Nuclear Fuel	20.68	20.52	17.62	-15.5
化学原料及化学制品制造业	Manufacture of Raw Chemical Materials and Chemical Products	109.43	124.84	141.46	10.0
医药制造业	Manufacture of Medicines	52.70	68.45	85.53	9.1
橡胶和塑料制品业	Manufacture of Rubber and Plastics Products	16.84	21.84	35.76	15.8
非金属矿物制品业	Manufacture of Non-metallic Mineral Products	66.34	106.79	190.56	23.6
黑色金属冶炼及压延加工业	Smelting and Pressing of Ferrous Metals	58.92	64.19	79.42	6.7
有色金属冶炼及压延加工业	Smelting and Pressing of Non-ferrous Metals	75.20	94.07	140.13	14.8
金属制品业	Manufacture of Metal Products	17.31	25.53	29.98	29.2
通用设备制造业	Manufacture of General Purpose Machinery	12.47	21.23	28.75	23.5
专用设备制造业	Manufacture of Special Purpose Machinery	9.57	12.92	21.76	39.3
汽车制造业	Manufacture of Automobiles	14.81	27.17	28.97	8.8
铁路、船舶、航空航天和其他运输设备制造业	Manufacture of Railroad, Marine, Aerospace and Other Transportation Equipment	23.92	27.90	34.87	17.9
电气机械及器材制造业	Manufacture of Electrical Machinery and Apparatus	10.75	13.99	21.90	33.7
计算机、通信和其他电子设备制造业	Manufacture of Communication Equipment, Computers and Other Electronic Equipment	14.52	20.93	20.73	20.7
仪器仪表制造业	Manufacture of Measuring Instruments and Machinery	3.75	3.60	2.80	-6.0
其他制造业	Other Manufacture	14.33	15.01	9.39	-56.1
废弃资源综合利用业	Utilization of waste Resources	0.57	1.48	2.95	64.0
电力、燃气及水的生产和供应业	Production and Supply of Electric Power,Gas and Water	301.42	325.94	351.15	6.6
#电力、热力生产和供应业	Production and Supply of Electric Power and Heat Power	295.39	318.03	340.17	6.6
燃气生产和供应业	Production and Supply of Gas	1.57	2.03	1.59	7.3
水的生产和供应业	Production and Supply of Water	4.46	5.87	9.39	28.1

14－5 规模以上工业总产值

Gross Output Value of Industry above Designated Size

单位：亿元 (100 million yuan)

指 标	Item	2010	2011	2012	2013	2014
规模以上工业总产值	**Gross Output Value of Industry above Designated Size**	**4206.37**	**5520.68**	**6544.02**	**8074.60**	**9507.33**
#国有控股企业	State-holding Enterprises	2429.41	2941.63	3284.31	3614.78	3966.86
按轻重工业分	**Grouped by Type of Light and Heavy Industry**					
轻工业	Light Industry	914.19	1192.92	1389.71	1864.15	2305.15
重工业	Heavy Industry	3292.18	4327.76	5154.31	6210.45	7202.18
按企业规模分	**Grouped by Size of Enterprise**					
大型企业	Large Enterprises	1523.30	2276.04	2769.32	2943.70	3071.41
中型企业	Medium-sized Enterprises	1349.06	1496.03	2013.99	2594.80	2927.48
小型企业	Small Enterprises	1334.01	1673.10	1729.46	2509.81	3342.34
微型企业	Micro-enterprises		75.51	31.25	26.29	166.10
按登记注册类型分	**By Status of Registration**					
内资企业	Domestic Funded	4048.82	5321.74	6375.58	7838.06	9177.68
国有企业	State-owned Enterprises	1212.22	1484.30	1812.38	1691.64	1365.87
集体企业	Collective-owned Enterprises	23.28	24.06	32.78	20.30	19.82
股份合作企业	Cooperative Enterprises	17.22	42.92	49.79	27.08	16.50
联营企业	Joint Ownership Enterprises	6.18	18.45	19.71	14.09	5.46
有限责任公司	Limited Liability Corporations	1501.31	1918.53	2389.65	3353.49	4537.25
股份有限公司	Share-holding Corporations Limited	440.28	603.50	470.07	618.21	684.87
私营企业	Private Enterprises	839.58	1214.36	1555.54	2092.04	2511.40
其他企业	Other Enterprises	8.74	15.62	45.66	21.21	36.51
港、澳、台商投资企业	Enterprises with Funds from Hong Kong, Macco and Taiwan	57.93	73.27	58.51	88.90	180.78
外商投资企业	Foreign Funded Enterprises	99.62	125.67	109.93	147.64	148.87

14-6 按行业分规模以上工业总产值

Gross Output Value of Industry above Designated Size by Sector

单位：亿元 (100 million yuan)

指 标	Item	2010	2011
规模以上工业总产值	**Gross Output Value of Industry above Designated Size**	**4206.37**	**5520.68**
采矿业	Mining	704.13	1102.35
#煤炭开采和洗选业	Mining and Washing of Coal	655.72	1015.81
黑色金属矿采选业	Mining and Processing of Ferrous Metal Ores	7.52	13.31
有色金属矿采选业	Mining and Processing of Non-Ferrous Metal Ores	12.00	14.38
非金属矿采选业	Mining and Processing of Non-metal Ores	28.89	58.43
制造业	Manufacturing	2554.94	3401.89
#农副食品加工业	Processing of Food from Agricultural Products	83.13	126.13
食品制造业	Manufacture of Foods	56.53	75.72
饮料制造业	Manufacture of Beverages	227.04	323.89
烟草制品业	Manufacture of Tobacco	208.65	253.47
纺织业	Manufacture of Textile	5.08	8.07
纺织服装、服饰业	Manufacture of Textile, Wearing Apparel and Accessories	3.63	3.53
皮革、毛皮、羽毛及其制品和制鞋业	Manufacture of Leather,Furs,Feather and Related Products, and Footware	1.17	1.89
木材加工及木、竹、藤、棕、草制品业	Timber Processing,Manufacture of Wood, Bamboo, Rattan,Palm and Straw Products	26.51	43.64
家具制造业	Manufacture of Furniture	1.63	7.12
造纸及纸制品业	Manufacture of Paper and Paper Products	24.36	38.02
印刷和记录媒介的复制	Printing and Reproduction of Recording Media	13.13	12.85
文教体育用品制造业	Manufacture of Articles For Culture, Education and Sport Activity	1.09	1.18
石油加工、炼焦和核燃料加工业	Processing of Petroleum,Coking and Processing of Nuclear Fue	67.18	75.98
化学原料及化学制品制造业	Manufacture of Raw Chemical Materials and Chemical Products	336.03	476.80
医药制造业	Manufacture of Medicines	180.61	227.31
橡胶制品业	Manufacture of Rubber	85.09	112.95
塑料制品业	Manufacture of Plastics	23.43	31.97
非金属矿物制品业	Manufacture of Non-metallic Mineral Products	182.22	273.54
黑色金属冶炼和压延加工业	Smelting and Pressing of Ferrous Metals	408.41	541.53
有色金属冶炼和压延加工业	Smelting and Pressing of Non-ferrous Metals	219.70	299.07
金属制品业	Manufacture of Metal Products	42.33	45.29
通用设备制造业	Manufacture of General Purpose Machinery	32.62	50.94
专用设备制造业	Manufacture of Special Purpose Machinery	36.00	37.61
交通运输设备制造业	Manufacture of Transport Equipment	144.21	163.30
电气机械和器材制造业	Manufacture of Electrical Machinery and Apparatus	75.45	92.13
通信、计算机及其他电子设备制造业	Manufacture of Communication Equipment, Computers and Other Electronic Equipment	43.00	47.64
仪器仪表及文化、办公用机械制造业	Manufacture of Measuring Instruments and Machinery for Cultural Activity and Office Work	9.24	10.25
工艺品及其他制造业	Manufacture of Artwork and Other Manufacturing	17.35	16.07
废弃资源和废旧材料回收加工业	Utilization of waste Resources	0.12	4.00
电力、燃气及水的生产和供应业	Production and Supply of Electric Power,Gas and Water	947.31	1016.44
#电力、热力生产和供应业	Production and Supply of Electric Power and Heat Power	913.38	980.17
燃气生产和供应业	Production and Supply of Gas	24.19	27.48
水的生产和供应业	Production and Supply of Water	9.74	8.79

14-6 续表 Continued

单位：亿元 (100 million yuan)

指　标	Item	2012	2013	2014
规模以上工业总产值	**Gross Output Value of Industry above Designated Size**	**6544.02**	**8074.60**	**9507.33**
采矿业	Mining	1352.90	1636.46	1885.27
#煤炭开采和洗选业	Mining and Washing of Coal	1244.16	1445.11	1607.47
黑色金属矿采选业	Mining and Processing of Ferrous Metal Ores	20.22	32.46	44.23
有色金属矿采选业	Mining and Processing of Non-Ferrous Metal Ores	16.52	31.47	57.21
非金属矿采选业	Mining and Processing of Non-metal Ores	72.00	127.42	176.36
制造业	Manufacturing	4017.15	5129.44	6265.79
#农副食品加工业	Processing of Food from Agricultural Products	146.22	220.62	270.76
食品制造业	Manufacture of Foods	69.48	95.51	125.93
酒、饮料和精制茶制造业	Manufacture of Liquor, Beverages and Refined Tea	438.60	597.52	715.96
烟草制品业	Manufacture of Tobacco	316.70	348.60	374.7
纺织业	Manufacture of Textile	5.04	11.13	13.46
纺织服装、服饰业	Manufacture of Textile, Wearing Apparel and Accessories	4.88	12.19	28.07
皮革、毛皮、羽毛及其制造业和制鞋业	Manufacture of Leather,Furs,Feather and Related Products, and Footware	15.66	25.27	39.12
木材加工和木、竹、藤、棕、草制品业	Processing of Timber, Manufacture of Wood, Bamboo, Rattan, Palm and Straw Products	71.01	112.62	137.48
家具制造业	Manufacture of Furniture	11.20	15.44	21.78
造纸和纸制品业	Manufacture of Paper and Paper Products	30.79	42.65	59.64
印刷和记录媒介复制业	Printing and Reproduction of Recording Media	12.15	18.82	26.72
文教、工美、体育和娱乐用品制造业	Manufacture of Articles for Culture, Education, Arts and Crafts, Sport and Entertainment Activities	2.84	7.38	14.58
石油加工、炼焦和核燃料加工业	Processing of Petroleum,Coking and Processing of Nuclear Fue	105.81	107.69	152.01
化学原料和化学制品制造业	Manufacture of Raw Chemical Materials and Chemical Product	555.67	645.66	684.96
医药制造业	Manufacture of Medicines	227.33	300.47	354.29
橡胶和塑料制品业	Manufacture of Rubber and Plastics Products	141.23	174.14	223.26
非金属矿物制品业	Manufacture of Non-metallic Mineral Products	362.09	610.93	888.12
黑色金属冶炼和压延加工业	Smelting and Pressing of Ferrous Metals	576.05	624.08	648.59
有色金属冶炼和压延加工业	Smelting and Pressing of Non-ferrous Metals	371.57	423.86	426.74
金属制品业	Manufacture of Metal Products	67.76	106.04	156.32
通用设备制造业	Manufacture of General Purpose Machinery	47.32	66.75	94.83
专用设备制造业	Manufacture of Special Purpose Machinery	39.20	71.08	102.21
汽车制造业	Manufacture of Automobiles	89.57	145.77	172.51
铁路、船舶、航空航天和其他运输设备制造业	Manufacture of Railwag, ship, Aerospace and Other Transport Equipments	126.67	111.67	163.43
电气机械和器材制造业	Manufacture of Electrical Machinery and Apparatus	86.95	130.50	179.03
计算机、通信和其他电子设备制造业	Manufacture of Computers, Communication and Other Electronic Equipment	63.89	61.13	130.41
仪器仪表制造业	Manufacture of Measuring Instruments and Machinery	9.91	10.34	11.38
其他制造业	Other Manufacture	17.77	23.57	38.73
废弃资源综合利用业	Utilization of Waste Resources	3.30	7.73	10.39
电力、燃气及水的生产和供应业	Production and Supply of Electric Power,Gas and Water	1173.97	1308.70	1356.27
#电力、热力生产和供应业	Production and Supply of Electric Power and Heat Power	1134.82	1263.73	1301.61
燃气生产和供应业	Production and Supply of Gas	29.41	31.69	37.79
水的生产和供应业	Production and Supply of Water	9.74	13.28	16.87

14-7 规模以上工业企业主要经济指标

Major Economic Indicators of Industrial Enterprises above Designated Size

指 标	Item	2010	2011	2012	2013	2014
固定资产净值年平均余额(亿元)	Average Balance of Net Value of Fixed Assets (100 million yuan)	2653.16	2693.51	2953.25	3574.57	4183.65
流动资产年平均余额(亿元)	Average Balance of Circulating Funds (100 million yuan)	2015.98	2654.50	2932.98	3643.86	4398.96
主营业务收入(亿元)	Revenue from Principal Business (100 million yuan)	3926.01	5022.11	5966.52	7357.43	8655.87
利税总额(亿元)	Total Profits and Taxes (100 million yuan)	671.39	901.37	1172.15	1268.68	1310.38
#利润总额	Total Profits	317.63	456.20	627.02	636.59	628.68
产值利税率(%)	Ratio of Pre-Tax Profit to Output Value(%)	15.96	16.33	17.91	15.71	13.78
资金利税率(%)	Ratio of Pre-Tax Profit to Assets(%)	12.62	16.85	19.91	17.58	15.27
销售利税率(%)	Ratio of Pre-Tax Profit to Sales(%)	17.10	17.95	19.65	17.24	15.14
资本保值增值率(%)	Increment Ratio of Capital(%)	125.32	118.66	121.72	117.66	115.87
总资产贡献率(%)	Ratio of Total Assets to Industrial Output Value(%)	12.84	14.56	15.97	19.11	13.00
资产负债率(%)	Asset-Liability Ratio(%)	64.85	64.67	64.90	58.20	63.68
流动资产周转次数(次/年)	Number of Times of Turnover of Circulating Fund(times/year)	1.75	1.95	1.89	1.72	1.86
成本费用利润率(%)	Ratio of After-tax Profits to Cost and Expenses(%)	9.04	9.98	11.89	14.53	8.03
产销率(%)	Proportion of Industrial Products Sold(%)	95.44	95.08	94.30	95.17	95.22

14-8 大中型工业企业主要经济指标

Major Economic Indicators of Large and Medium-sized Industrial Enterprises

指 标	Item	2010	2011	2012	2013	2014
固定资产净值年平均余额(亿元)	Average Balance of Net Value of Fixed Assets (100 million yuan)	2009.61	2206.42	2481.32	3024.00	3494.72
流动资产年平均余额(亿元)	Average Balance of Circulating Funds (100 million yuan)	1526.28	2065.99	2297.86	2814.22	3347.32
主营业务收入(亿元)	Revenue from Principal Business (100 million yuan)	2752.96	3542.89	4484.76	5135.87	5589.52
利税总额(亿元)	Total Profits and Taxes(100 million yuan)	516.99	739.50	981.36	1023.18	1024.28
#利润总额	Total Profits	240.89	371.65	520.55	490.38	467.07
资本保值增值率(%)	Increment Ratio of Capital(%)	122.88	120.38	119.19	117.82	116.97
总资产贡献率(%)	Ratio of Total Assets to Industrial Output Value(%)	12.72	14.93	16.33	14.39	13.02
资产负债率(%)	Asset-Liability Ratio(%)	65.46	65.14	65.40	66.20	64.90
流动资产周转次数(次/年)	Number of Times of Turnover of Circulating Fund (times/year)	1.63	1.78	1.81	1.70	1.59
成本费用利润率(%)	Ratio of After-tax Profits to Cost and Expenses(%)	9.88	11.74	13.29	10.65	9.38
产销率(%)	Proportion of Products Sold(%)	96.01	95.32	94.42	94.36	94.67

14-9 规模以上工业主要产品产量
Output of Major Industrial Products above Designated Size

单位：万吨 (10000 tons)

指 标	Item	2010	2011	2012	2013	2014
粗钢	Steel	360.48	434.01	531.27	531.44	551.81
成品钢材	Steel Products	391.04	462.77	560.22	573.28	552.39
铁合金	Iron Alloy	208.18	263.90	309.68	327.25	348.18
电解铝	Aluminium	88.79	90.36	104.35	112.28	65.21
氧化铝	Aluminum Oxide	134.84	211.03	270.04	360.32	407.93
铝材	Aluminium Material	1.49	13.16	11.70	27.15	58.17
磷矿石	Phosphorite Mineral	1579.21	2084.18	2281.95	2905.44	3397.42
生铁	Pig Iron	366.65	482.35	552.93	539.22	498.64
农用化肥	Chemical Fertilizer	384.92	360.37	503.82	524.26	533.52
轮胎外胎(万条)	Tires(10000 units)	558.59	536.77	622.78	602.15	546.46
水泥	Cement	3694.84	5250.89	6100.45	8352.95	9386.89
发电量(亿千瓦小时)	Electricity(100 million kwh)	1358.69	1359.01	1548.44	1620.08	1682.27
#水电	Hydropower	389.65	334.66	511.65	423.09	622.26
煤气生产量(亿立方米)	Gas Production (100 million cu.m)	67.81	84.15	98.63	92.17	83.95
卷烟(万箱)	Cigarettes(10000 cases)	239.24	245.23	249.35	254.29	258.36
饮料酒(万千升)	Alcohol Beverages(10000 kiloliters)	48.72	61.80	67.14	91.21	116.99
#白酒	White Spirit	16.04	25.49	26.83	30.49	38.05
食用植物油	Edible Vegetable Oil	10.22	12.23	23.09	32.69	35.79
中成药	Traditional Chinese Medicine	5.00	4.92	5.74	7.92	7.68
家用电冰箱(万台)	Household Refrigerators (10000 units)	196.35	169.54	159.04	155.33	168.22
彩色电视机(万部)	Color TV Sets(10000 units)	66.93	77.87	90.61	121.97	115.68

14-10 规模以上工业企业主要经济指标(2014)

Major Econornic Indicators of Industrial Entevprises above Designated Size

单位：亿元 (100 million yuan)

指 标	Item	工业总产值 Total Output Value of Industry	资产合计 Total Assets	主营业务收入 Revenue from Principal Business	利税总额 Total Profits and Taxes	#利润总额 Total Profits
总 计	**Total**	**9507.33**	**11747.39**	**8655.87**	**1310.38**	**628.68**
#国有控股企业	State-holding Enterprises	3966.86	7354.07	3831.49	761.39	317.31
#农村工业	Rural Industry	56.69	98.19	49.24	5.91	3.35
按登记注册类型分	**Grouped by Status of Registration**					
内资企业	Domestic-funded Enterprises	9177.68	11383.80	8348.43	1269.76	602.45
国有企业	State-owned Industry	1365.87	2001.30	1302.96	354.14	234.06
中央企业	Central Industry	659.05	906.53	650.80	18.08	-1.81
地方企业	Local Industry	706.83	1094.77	652.15	336.06	235.88
集体企业	Collective-owned Industry	19.82	7.84	18.04	0.76	0.31
股份合作企业	Cooperative Enterprises	16.50	21.73	11.58	2.64	1.46
联营企业	Joint Ownership Enterprises	5.46	7.89	5.24	1.00	0.79
有限责任公司	Limited Liability Corporations	4537.24	6284.31	4233.19	590.71	199.61
股份有限公司	Share-holding Enterprises	684.87	1182.91	560.44	63.09	26.21
私营企业	Private Enterprises	2511.40	1840.64	2188.22	254.29	138.73
其他企业	Others Enterprises	36.51	37.18	28.78	3.13	1.28
港、澳、台商投资企业	Enterprises with Funds from Hong kong, Macao and Taiwan	180.78	189.01	169.98	15.09	9.29
外商投资企业	Foreign Funded Enterprises	148.87	174.58	137.45	25.53	16.94
按轻重工业分	**Grouped by Light and Heavy Industry**					
轻工业	Light Industry	2305.15	2338.93	2064.98	781.11	397.58
重工业	Heavy Industry	7202.18	9408.46	6590.89	529.27	231.10
按企业规模分	**Grouped by Scale of Enterprise**					
大型企业	Large Enterprises	3071.41	5548.66	3024.14	724.25	311.08
型企业	Medium-sized Enterprises	2927.48	3753.51	2565.38	300.03	155.99
小型企业	Small Enterprises	3342.34	2257.43	2953.67	279.95	158.03
微型企业	Micro-enterprises	166.10	187.79	112.68	6.16	3.58

14-11 规模以上工业企业分行业主要经济指标(2014)

单位：亿元

指　　标	Item	企业单位数（个）Number of Enterprises (unit)
总　　计	**Total**	**3895**
采矿业	Mining	965
#煤炭开采和洗选业	Mining and Washing of Coal	782
黑色金属矿采选业	Mining and Processing of Ferrous Metal Ores	35
有色金属矿采选业	Mining and Processing of Non-Ferrous Metal Ores	29
非金属矿采选业	Mining and Processing of Non-metal Ores	119
制造业	Manufacturing	2714
农副食品加工业	Processing of Food from Agricultural Products	233
食品制造业	Manufacture of Foods	88
酒、饮料和精制茶制造业	Manufacture of Liquor, Beverages and Refined Tea	292
#白酒制造	Manufacture of Liquors	112
烟草制品业	Manufacture of Tobacco	2
纺织业	Manufacture of Textile	16
纺织服装、服饰业	Manufacture of Textile, Wearing Apparel and Accessories	33
皮革、毛皮、羽毛及其制品和制鞋业	Manufacture of Leather,Furs,Feather and Related Products, and Footware	23
木材加工和木、竹、藤、棕、草制品业	Processing of Timber, Manufacture of Wood, Bamboo, Rattan, Palm and Straw Products	104
家具制造业	Manufacture of Furniture	24
造纸和纸制品业	Manufacture of Paper and Paper Products	45
印刷和记录媒介复制业	Printing and Reproduction of Recording Media	19
文教、工美、体育和娱乐用品制造业	Manufacture of Articles for Culture, Education, Arts and Crafts, Sport and Entertainment Activities	18
石油加工、炼焦和核燃料加工业	Processing of Petroleum, Coking and Processing of Nuclear Fuel	23
化学原料和化学制品制造业	Manufacture of Raw Chemical Materials and Chemical Products	212
医药制造业	Manufacture of Medicines	107
橡胶和塑料制品业	Manufacture of Rubber and Plastics Products	98
非金属矿物制品业	Manufacture of Non-metallic Mineral Products	632
黑色金属冶炼和压延加工业	Smelting and Pressing of Ferrous Metals	172
有色金属冶炼和压延加工业	Smelting and Pressing of Non-ferrous Metals	85
金属制品业	Manufacture of Metal Products	109
通用设备制造业	Manufacture of General Purpose Machinery	60
专用设备制造业	Manufacture of Special Purpose Machinery	65
汽车制造业	Manufacture of Automobiles	37
铁路、船舶、航空航天和其他运输设备制造业	Manufacture of Railwag, ship, Aerospace and Other Transport Equipments	42
电气机械和器材制造业	Manufacture of Electrical Machinery and Apparatus	97
计算机、通信和其他电子设备制造业	Manufacture of Computers, Communication and Other Electronic Equipment	43
仪器仪表制造业	Manufacture of Measuring Instruments and Machinery	10
其他制造业	Other Manufacture	16
废弃资源综合利用业	Utilization of Waste Resources	8
电力、燃气及水的生产和供应业	Production and Supply of Electric Power,Gas and Water	216
电力、热力生产和供应业	Production and Supply of Electric Power and Heat Power	171
#电力生产	Production of Electric Power	86
电力供应	Distribution of Electric Power	85
燃气生产和供应业	Production and Supply of Gas	20
水的生产和供应业	Production and Supply of Water	25

Main Economic Indicators of Industrial Enterprises above Designated Size by Sector

(100 million yuan)

工业总产值 Total Output Value of Industry	资产合计 Total Assets	主营业务收入 Revenue from Principal Business	利税总额 Total Profits and Taxes	#利润总额 Total Profits
9507.33	**11747.39**	**8655.87**	**1310.38**	**628.68**
1885.27	2467.80	1562.76	203.19	82.80
1607.47	2301.91	1314.70	164.85	63.17
44.23	17.84	42.66	3.95	2.50
57.21	36.86	47.18	7.87	2.82
176.36	111.19	158.22	26.52	14.31
6265.79	6526.00	5764.87	1008.32	508.42
270.76	117.60	242.43	16.91	11.66
125.93	74.10	118.51	22.49	16.55
715.96	1183.55	628.88	368.79	261.58
556.38	1050.28	480.66	339.94	241.31
374.70	279.32	359.53	276.53	44.87
13.46	13.72	8.66	0.92	0.75
28.07	15.10	26.15	1.74	1.16
39.12	18.36	47.78	2.86	1.87
137.48	31.17	129.72	12.82	5.38
21.78	9.67	21.09	2.98	2.33
59.64	49.12	57.52	5.40	3.06
26.72	22.52	21.62	5.00	3.87
14.58	13.92	14.35	0.96	0.54
152.01	90.81	124.85	4.61	3.46
684.96	1300.65	808.41	37.45	18.08
354.29	330.66	297.57	55.16	34.68
223.26	166.74	160.56	11.64	6.95
888.12	819.75	800.76	88.03	53.75
648.59	410.03	600.91	9.83	-3.85
426.74	462.85	350.71	15.73	5.34
156.32	126.11	140.80	9.52	4.93
94.83	91.94	78.80	7.09	4.29
102.21	109.82	86.14	6.61	3.83
172.51	145.89	169.50	17.21	5.43
163.43	342.30	148.17	6.24	4.12
179.03	131.46	145.03	8.62	5.48
130.41	96.06	127.38	11.17	7.04
11.38	16.72	9.67	0.87	0.47
38.73	51.49	30.31	0.95	0.76
10.39	4.08	8.68	0.14	0.04
1356.27	2753.60	1328.25	98.85	37.47
1301.61	2579.82	1269.87	98.41	37.86
518.43	1850.36	474.03	72.97	39.01
783.18	729.46	795.84	25.44	-1.15
37.79	70.14	43.66	-1.92	-2.14
16.87	103.64	14.72	2.36	1.75

14-12 规模以上国有控股工业企业主要经济指标(2014)

单位：亿元

指 标	Item	企业单位数(个) Number of Enterprises (unit)
总 计	**Total**	**509**
按轻重工业分	**Grouped by Type of Light and Heavy Industry**	
轻工业	Light Industry	68
重工业	Heavy Industry	441
按企业规模分	**Grouped by Scale of Enterprise**	
大型企业	Large Enterprises	69
中型企业	Medium-sized Enterprises	238
小型企业	Small Enterprises	179
微型企业	Micro-enterprises	23
按工业行业分	**Grouped by Industrial Sector**	
采矿业	Mining	77
#煤炭开采和洗选业	Mining and Washing of Coal	65
黑色金属矿采选业	Mining and Processing of Ferrous Metal Ores	2
有色金属矿采选业	Mining and Processing of Nonferrous Metal Ores	2
非金属矿采选业	Mining and Processing of Nonmetal Ores	8
制造业	Manufacturing	263
#农副食品加工业	Processing of Food from Agricultural Products	12
酒、饮料和精制茶制造业	Manufacture of Wine,Soft drinks and Refined tea	10
烟草制品业	Manufacture of Tobacco	2
纺织服装、服饰业	Manufacture of Textile, Wearing Apparel and Accessories	3
木材加工和木、竹、藤、棕、草制品业	Timber Processing , Bamboo , Cane , Palm Fiber and Straw Products	5
印刷和记录媒介复制业	Printing,Reproduction of Recording Media	2
石油加工、炼焦和核燃料加工业	Processing of Petroleum,Coking and Processing of Nuclear Fuel	2
化学原料和化学制品制造业	Manufacture of Raw Chemical Materials and Chemical Products	44
橡胶和塑料制品业	Manufacture of Rubber and Plastics Products	4
非金属矿物制品业	Manufacture of Non-metallic Mineral Products	48
黑色金属冶炼和压延加工业	Smelting and Pressing of Ferrous Metals	10
有色金属冶炼和压延加工业	Smelting and Pressing of Non-ferrous Metals	13
金属制品业	Manufacture of Metal Products	14
通用设备制造业	Manufacture of General Purpose Machinery	16
专用设备制造业	Manufacture of Special Purpose Machinery	14
汽车制造业	Manufacture of Automobiles	7
铁路、船舶、航空航天和其他运输设备制造业	Manufacture of Railway, Ship, Aerospace and Other Transportation Equipment	24
电气机械和器材制造业	Manufacture of Electrical Equipment and Machinery	5
计算机、通信和其他电子设备制造业	Manufacture of Communication Equipment, Computers and Other Electronic Equipment	13
仪器仪表制造业	Manufacture of Measuring Instruments and Machinery for Cultural Activity and Office.Work	3
其他制造业	Other Manufacture	5
电力、燃气及水的生产和供应业	Production and Supply of Electric Power,Gas and Water	169
#电力、热力的生产和供应业	Production and Supply of Electric Power and Heat Power	141
燃气生产和供应业	Production and Supply of Gas	6
水的生产和供应业	Production and Supply of Water	22

Major Economic Indicators of State-controlled Industrial Enterprises above Designated Size

(100 million yuan)

工业总产值 Total Output Value of Industry	资产合计 Total Assets	主营业务收入 Revenue from Principal Business	利税总额 Total Profits and Taxes	#利润总额 Total Profits
3966.86	**7354.07**	**3831.49**	**761.39**	**317.31**
888.43	1299.48	835.04	591.74	273.68
3078.43	6054.58	2996.45	169.65	43.62
2565.39	4939.96	2566.39	661.39	272.98
1121.09	1919.35	1008.28	80.16	35.02
270.73	435.97	248.67	20.37	9.88
9.65	58.78	8.14	-0.54	-0.57
391.95	975.90	325.56	26.95	-2.12
364.09	955.76	307.63	23.10	-4.41
0.96	1.25	0.82	0.01	
6.37	2.57	6.07	0.78	0.06
20.53	16.32	11.04	3.06	2.23
2288.47	3812.89	2246.92	643.38	286.29
8.47	3.31	8.81	0.18	0.13
382.46	841.82	354.97	307.10	223.65
374.70	279.32	359.53	276.53	44.87
4.79	3.06	3.29	0.22	0.14
3.06	0.70	2.99	-0.03	-0.08
1.47	2.50	1.57	0.06	0.02
98.10	54.49	78.96	0.50	0.39
323.43	1067.31	469.68	5.41	-5.13
108.86	104.27	56.76	4.54	1.87
172.09	255.15	153.00	29.04	20.61
235.52	229.99	220.79	-6.46	-11.18
110.44	231.17	105.28	0.26	-4.75
48.05	72.39	48.25	2.58	0.96
36.53	50.43	29.79	2.89	1.51
19.88	54.28	12.53	0.45	-0.08
62.12	55.76	59.69	3.22	1.70
141.47	328.97	129.48	5.16	3.42
26.26	8.26	16.25	0.74	0.43
78.56	80.58	79.89	6.88	5.23
5.68	9.45	4.02	0.41	0.13
18.77	35.52	17.10	0.54	0.46
1286.43	2565.27	1259.00	91.08	33.16
1253.39	2433.52	1222.27	91.48	34.22
18.42	54.97	24.27	-2.46	-2.52
14.62	76.78	12.46	2.06	1.46

14-13 规模以上集体工业企业主要经济指标(2014)
Main Economic Indicators of All Collective-owned Industrial Enterprises above Designated Size

单位：亿元 (100 million yuan)

指 标	Item	企业单位数(个) Number of Enterprises (unit)	工业总产值 Total Output Value of Industry	资产合计 Total Assets	主营业务收入 Revenue from Principal Business	利税总额 Total Profits and Taxes	#利润总额 Total Profits
总 计	**Total**	**18**	**19.82**	**7.84**	**18.04**	**0.76**	**0.31**
#亏损企业	Loss Making Enterprise	10	12.21	4.10	10.82	-0.14	-0.31
按轻重工业分	**Grouped by Type of Light and Heavy Industry**						
轻工业	Light Industry	4	4.80	1.30	4.71	0.43	0.24
重工业	Heavy Industry	14	15.02	6.54	13.32	0.33	0.08
按企业规模分	**Grouped by Size of Enterprise**						
#中型企业	Medium-sized Enterprises	3	6.59	0.52	6.45	0.48	0.35
小型企业	Small Enterprises	14	9.92	6.81	8.39	0.26	-0.02
按工业行业分	**Grouped by Industrial Sector**						
#采矿业	Mining	4	5.68	0.87	5.19	0.25	0.33
#黑色金属矿采选业	Mining and Processing of Ferrous Metal Ores	4	5.68	0.87	5.19	0.25	0.33
制造业	Manufacturing	13	13.93	6.07	12.63	0.06	0.43
#非金属矿物制品业	Manufacture of Non-metallic Mineral Products	2	3.23	1.96	2.92	0.03	0.07
黑色金属冶炼和压延加工业	Smelting and Pressing of Ferrous Metals	3	1.15	1.26	1.15	-0.08	-0.03
有色金属冶炼和压延加工业	Smelting and Pressing of Non-ferrous Metals	2	4.42	1.04	3.53	-0.03	0.03
金属制品业	Manufacture of Metal Products	2	0.33	0.51	0.33	-0.09	-0.07

14-14 规模以上外商投资和港澳台商投资工业企业主要经济指标(2014)

Major Economic Indicators of all above Designated Size Industrial Enterprises Funded by Foreigners and Hong kong,Macao and Taiwan

单位：亿元 (100 million yuan)

指 标	Item	企业单位数(个) Number of Enterprises (unit)	工业总产值 Total Output Value of Industry	资产合计 Total Assets	主营业务收入 Revenue from Principal Business	利税总额 Total Profits and Taxes	#利润总额 Total Profits
总 计	**Total**	**86**	**329.65**	**363.59**	**307.43**	**40.62**	**26.22**
#亏损企业	Loss Making Enterprises	18	22.87	21.78	20.40	-1.29	-1.67
#港、澳、台商投资企业	Enterprises with Funds from Hong kong, Macao and Taiwan	44	180.78	189.01	169.98	15.09	9.29
合资经营企业(港或澳、台资)	Joint Venture Enterprises(with Funds from Hong Kong, Macao and Taiwan)	19	97.66	101.35	94.05	7.21	4.37
港澳台商独资经营企业	Enterprises with Sole Funds from Hong Kong,Macao and Taiwan	23	66.62	84.32	60.21	6.35	4.41
外商投资企业	Foreign Funded Enterprises	42	148.87	174.58	137.45	25.53	16.94
中外合作经营企业	Cooperation Enterprises	19	68.98	71.00	67.30	12.04	8.56
外资企业	Foreign Funded Enterprises	21	64.69	83.24	54.97	11.07	5.97
按轻重工业分	**Grouped by Type of Light and Heavy Industry**						
轻工业	Light Industry	35	117.92	104.20	106.74	24.05	15.81
重工业	Heavy Industry	51	211.73	259.39	200.70	16.57	10.41
按企业规模分	**Grouped by Size of Enterprise**						
大型企业	Large Enterprises	7	53.85	89.30	51.58	11.71	8.05
中型企业	Medium-sized Enterprises	21	112.68	154.87	106.46	18.59	12.25
小型企业	Small Enterprises	53	161.25	117.49	147.36	10.43	6.10
微型企业	Micro Enterprises	5	1.87	1.92	2.04	-0.10	-0.18
按工业行业分	**Grouped by Industrial Sector**						
采矿业	Mining	4	18.14	29.26	18.06	1.19	0.54
#黑色金属矿采选业	Mining and Processing of Ferrous Metal Ores	2	3.87	0.55	3.90	0.41	0.26
制造业	Manufacturing	78	289.10	234.31	268.43	36.97	24.61
#农副食品加工业	Processing of Food from Agricultural Products	7	13.57	4.56	12.52	0.16	0.02
酒、饮料和精制茶制造业	Manufacture of Liquor, Beverages and Refined Tea	8	37.71	28.95	41.16	12.86	9.13
造纸和纸制品业	Manufacture of Paper and Paper Products	2	0.62	0.68	0.56	0.06	0.03
印刷和记录媒介复制业	Printing,Reproduction of Recording Media	2	8.21	6.78	5.51	2.72	2.30
文教、工美、体育和娱乐用品制造业	Manufacture of Articles for Cluture, Education, Arts and Crafts, Sport and Entertainment Activities	2	1.97	3.01	1.58	-0.36	-0.37
石油加工、炼焦和核燃料加工业	Processing of Petro leum, Coking and Processing of Nuclear Fuel	2	49.63	5.45	49.27	0.04	-0.06
化学原料和化学制品制造业	Manufacture of Raw Chemical Materials and Chemical Products	5	7.88	19.11	7.53	1.47	1.05
医药制造业	Manufacture of Medicines	6	30.07	28.60	22.04	5.90	3.39
橡胶和塑料制品业	Manufacture of Rubber and Plastics	4	16.93	8.59	17.09	1.81	1.29
非金属矿物制品业	Manufacture of Non-metallic Mineral Products	20	42.98	69.30	37.00	5.90	3.62
黑色金属冶炼和压延加工业	Smelting and Pressing of Ferrous Metals	4	14.10	6.41	11.90	0.77	0.60
有色金属冶炼和压延加工业	Smelting and Pressing of Non-ferrous Metals	3	26.47	23.72	24.88	2.80	2.64
电气机械和器材制造业	Manufacture of Electrical Machinery and Apparatus	4	11.73	9.63	11.21	0.41	0.24
计算机、通信和其他电子设备制造业	Manufacture of Communication Equipment, Computers and Other Electronic Equipment	2	16.42	2.55	15.88	1.47	0.42
电力、燃气及水的生产和供应业	Production and Supply of Electric Power,Gas and Water	4	22.41	100.03	20.93	2.45	1.07
#电力、热力的生产和供应业	Production and Supply of Electric Power and Heat Power	2	16.20	47.57	16.17	1.43	0.21
水的生产和供应业	Production and Supply of Water	2	6.21	52.46	4.76	1.02	0.86

14-15 规模以上工业企业主要经济效益指标(2014)

Main Indicators on Economic Efficiency of all Industrial Enterprises above Designated Size

单位：% (%)

指标	Item	产值利税率 Ratio of Pre-Tax Profit to Output Value	资金利税率 Ratio of Pre-Tax Profit to Asset	销售利税率 Ratio of Pre-Tax Profit to Sales
总计	**Total**	**13.8**	**15.3**	**15.1**
内资企业	Domestic Enterprises	13.8	15.3	15.2
国有企业	State-owned	25.9	17.1	27.2
中央企业	Central	2.7	1.8	2.8
地方企业	Local	47.5	31.7	51.5
集体企业	Collective-owned	3.8	9.8	4.2
股份合作企业	Cooperation Enterprises	16.0	12.3	22.8
联营企业	Joint-owned Enterprises	18.3	7.0	19.1
有限责任公司	Limited Liability Corporations	13.0	14.9	14.0
股份有限公司	Share Holding Enterprises	9.2	7.8	11.3
私营企业	Private Enterprises	10.1	18.4	11.6
其他企业	Others	8.6	13.3	10.9
港、澳、台商投资企业	Enterprises with Funds from Hong kong,Macao and Taiwan	8.3	11.8	8.9
外商投资企业	Foreign Funded Enterprises	17.1	15.5	18.6
在总计中:	of the Total:			
#国有控股企业	State-controlled Enterprises	19.2	14.0	19.9
在总计中:	of the Total:			
#农村工业	Rural Industry	10.4	8.1	12.0
按轻重工业分	**Grouped by Type of Light and Heavy Industry**			
轻工业	Light Industry	33.9	44.3	37.8
重工业	Heavy Industry	7.3	7.8	8.0
按企业规模分	**Grouped by Size of Enterprise**			
大型企业	Large Enterprises	23.6	17.9	23.9
中型企业	Medium-sized Enterprises	10.2	10.7	11.7
小型企业	Small Enterprises	8.4	16.9	9.5
微型企业	Micro-enterprises	3.7	7.2	5.5
按工业行业分	**Grouped by Industrial Sector**			
采矿业	Mining	10.8	12.9	13.0
#煤炭开采和洗选业	Mining and Washing of Coal	10.3	11.1	12.5
黑色金属矿采选业	Mining and Processing of Ferrous Metal Ores	8.9	31.3	9.3
有色金属矿采选业	Mining and Processing of Non-Ferrous Metal Ores	13.8	43.4	16.7
非金属矿采选业	Mining and Processing of Non-metal Ores	15.0	43.7	16.8
制造业	Manufacturing	16.1	21.0	17.5
#农副食品加工业	Processing of Food from Agricultural Products	6.2	18.8	7.0
食品制造业	Manufacture of Foods	17.9	41.8	19.0
酒、饮料和精制茶制造业	Manufacture of Liquor, Beverages and Refined Tea	51.5	40.5	58.6
烟草制品业	Manufacture of Tobacco	73.8	115.3	76.9
纺织业	Manufacture of Textile	6.8	9.7	10.6
纺织服装、服饰业	Manufacture of Textile, Wearing Apparel and Accessories	6.2	19.6	6.7
皮革、毛皮、羽毛及其制品和制鞋业	Manufacture of Leather,Furs,Feather and Related Products, and Footware	7.3	24.2	6.0

14-15 续表 continued

单位：% (%)

指 标	Item	产值利税率 Ratio of Pre-Tax Profit to Output Value	资金利税率 Ratio of Pre-Tax Profit to Assets	销售利税率 Ratio of Pre-Tax Profit to Sales
木材加工和木、竹、藤、棕、草制品业	Processing of Timber, Manufacture of Wood, Bamboo, Rattan, Palm and Straw Products	9.3	49.4	9.9
家具制造业	Manufacture of Furniture	13.7	47.3	14.1
造纸和纸制品业	Manufacture of Paper and Paper Products	9.1	14.2	9.4
印刷和记录媒介复制业	Printing and Reproduction of Recording Media	18.7	27.9	23.1
文教、工美、体育和娱乐用品制造业	Manufacture of Articles for Culture, Education, Arts and Crafts,Sport and Entertainment Activities	6.6	10.3	6.7
石油加工、炼焦和核燃料加工业	Processing of Petroleum,Coking and Processing of Nuclear Fuel	3.0	6.6	3.7
化学原料和化学制品制造业	Manufacture of Raw Chemical Materials and Chemical Products	5.5	4.3	4.6
医药制造业	Maufacture of Medicines	15.6	25.3	18.5
橡胶和塑料制品业	Manufacture of Rubber and Plastics Produets	5.2	9.4	7.2
非金属矿物制品业	Manufacture of Non-metallic Mineral Products	9.9	14.6	11.0
黑色金属冶炼和压延加工业	Smelting and Pressing of Ferrous Metals	1.5	2.9	1.6
有色金属冶炼和压延加工业	Smelting and Pressing of Non-ferrous Metals	3.7	4.1	4.5
金属制品业	Manufacture of Metal Products	6.1	10.2	6.8
通用设备制造业	Manufacture of General Purpose Machinery	7.5	12.4	9.0
专用设备制造业	Manufacture of Special Purpose Machinery	6.5	7.3	7.7
汽车制造业	Manufacture of Automobiles	10.0	16.8	10.2
铁路、船舶、航空航天和其他运输设备制造业	Manufacture of Railway, Ship, Aerospace and other Transport Equipments	3.8	2.8	4.2
电气机械和器材制造业	Manufacture of Electrical Machinery and Apparatus	4.8	8.8	5.9
计算机、通信和其他电子设备制造业	Manufacture of Communication Equipment Computers and Other Electronic Equipment	8.6	21.3	8.8
仪器仪表制造业	Manufacture of Measuring Instruments and Machinery	7.6	6.4	9.0
其他制造业	Other Manufacture	2.5	2.6	3.1
废弃资源综合利用业	Utilization of Waste Resources	1.3	7.6	1.6
电力、燃气及水的生产和供应业	Production and Supply of Electric Power,Gas and Water	7.3	4.5	7.4
#电力、热力生产和供应业	Production and Supply of Electric Power and Heat Power	7.6	4.7	7.7
燃气生产和供应业	Production and Supply of Gas	-5.1	-5.0	-4.4
水的生产和供应业	Production and Supply of Water	14.0	4.2	16.0

14-16 规模以上国有控股工业企业主要经济效益指标(2014)

Major Indicators on Economic Efficiency of State-controlled Industrial Enterprises above Designated Size

单位：% (%)

指　标	Item	产值利税率 Ratio of Pre-Tax Profit to Output Value	资金利税率 Ratio of Pre-Tax Profit to Assets	销售利税率 Ratio of Pre-Tax Profit to Sales
总　计	**Total**	**19.2**	**14.0**	**19.9**
按轻重工业分	**Grouped by Type of Light and Heavy Industry**			
轻工业	Light Industry	66.6	57.1	70.9
重工业	Heavy Industry	5.5	3.9	5.7
按企业规模分	**Grouped by Size of Enterprise**			
大型企业	Large Enterprises	25.8	18.0	25.8
中型企业	Medium-sized Enterprises	7.2	6.7	8.0
小型企业	Small Enterprises	7.5	7.9	8.2
微型企业	Micro-enterprises	-5.6	-3.0	-6.6
按工业行业分	**Grouped by Industrial Sector**			
采矿业	Mining	6.9	5.0	8.3
#煤炭开采和洗选业	Mining and Washing of Coal	6.3	4.4	7.5
黑色金属矿采选业	Mining and Processing of Ferrous Metal Ores	1.0	2.1	1.2
有色金属矿采选业	Mining and Processing of Non-Ferrous Metal Ores	12.2	38.7	12.9
非金属矿采选业	Mining and Processing of Non-metal Ores	14.9	45.8	27.7
制造业	Manufacturing	28.1	22.9	28.6
#农副食品加工业	Processing of Food from Agricultural Products	2.1	4.6	2.0
酒、饮料和精制茶制造业	Manufacture of Liquor, Beverages and Refined Tea	80.3	46.4	86.5
烟草制品业	Manufacture of Tobacco	73.8	115.3	76.9
纺织服装、服饰业	Manufacture of Textile, Wearing Apparel and Accessories	4.6	8.0	6.7
木材加工和木、竹、藤、棕、草制品业	Processing of Timber,Manufacture of Wood, Bamboo,Rattan,Palm and Straw Products	-1.0	-4.3	-1.0
印刷和记录媒介复制业	Printing and Reproduction of Recording Media	4.1	2.8	3.8
石油加工、炼焦和核燃料加工业	Processing of Petroleum,Coking and Processing of Nuclear Fuel	0.5	1.3	0.6
化学原料和化学制品制造业	Manufacture of Raw Chemical Materials and Chemical Products	1.7	0.8	1.2
橡胶和塑料制品业	Manufacture of Rubber and Plastics Produets	4.2	5.8	8.0

14-16 续表 continued

单位：% (%)

指 标	Item	产值利税率 Ratio of Pre-Tax Profit to OutputValue	资金利税率 Ratio of Pre-Tax Profit to Assets	销售利税率 Ratio of Pre-Tax Profit to Sales
非金属矿物制品业	Manufacture of Rubber	16.9	15.8	19.0
黑色金属冶炼和压延加工业	Smelting and Pressing of Ferrous Metals	-2.7	-3.3	-2.9
有色金属冶炼和压延加工业	Smelting and Pressing of Non-ferrous Metals	0.2	0.1	0.2
金属制品业	Manufacture of Metal Products	5.4	4.4	5.3
通用设备制造业	Manufacture of General Purpose Machinery	7.9	9.9	9.7
专用设备制造业	Manufacture of Special Purpose Machinery	2.3	1.2	3.6
汽车制造业	Manufacture of Automobiles	5.2	7.3	5.4
铁路、船舶、航空航天和其他运输设备制造业	Manufacture of Railway, Ship, Aerospace and Other Transport Equipments	3.6	2.4	4.0
电气机械和器材制造业	Manufacture of Electrical Machinery and Apparatus	2.8	9.0	4.6
计算机、通信和其他电子设备制造业	Manufacture of Communication Equipment,Computers and Other Electronic Equipment	8.8	15.5	8.6
仪器仪表制造业	Manufacture of Measuring Instruments and Machinery	7.2	5.2	10.2
其他制造业	Other Manufacture	2.9	2.1	3.2
电力、燃气及水的生产和供应业	Production and Supply of Electric Power,Gas and Water	7.1	4.4	7.2
电力、热力的生产和供应业	Production and Supply of Electric Power and Heat Power	7.3	4.6	7.5
燃气生产和供应业	Production and Supply of Gas	-13.4	-8.0	-10.1
水的生产和供应业	Production and Supply of Water	14.1	3.9	16.5

14-17 规模以上集体工业企业主要经济效益指标(2014)

Main Indicators on Economic Benefit of Collective-owned Industrial Enterprises above Designated Size

单位：% (%)

指 标	Item	产值利税率 Ratio of Pre-Tax Profit to Output Value	资金利税率 Ratio of Pre-Tax Profit to Assets	销售利税率 Ratio of Pre-Tax Profit to Sales
总 计	**Total**	**3.8**	**9.8**	**4.2**
#亏损企业	Loss Making Enterprises	-1.1	-4.9	-1.3
按轻重工业分	**Grouped by Type of Light and Heavy Industry**			
轻工业	Light Industry	9.0	52.0	9.1
重工业	Heavy Industry	2.2	4.8	2.5
按企业规模分	**Grouped by Size of Enterprise**			
中型企业	Medium-sized Enterprises	7.3	48.0	7.4
小型企业	Small Enterprises	2.2	4.3	2.5
按工业行业分	**Grouped by Industrial Sector**			
采矿业	Mining	5.8	19.7	6.4
#黑色金属矿采选业	Mining and Processing of Ferrous Metal Ores	5.8	30.6	6.4
制造业	Manufacturing	3.1	8.0	3.4
#非金属矿物制品业	Manufacture of Non-metallic Mineral Products	2.2	3.7	2.4
黑色金属冶炼和压延加工业	Smelting and Pressing of Ferrous Metals	-2.6	-2.3	-2.6
有色金属冶炼和压延加工业	Smelting and Pressing of Non-ferrous Metals	0.7	5.9	0.8
金属制品业	Manufacture of Metal Products	-21.2	-12.9	-21.2

14-18 大中型工业企业主要经济指标占全省规模以上工业比重(2014)

Percentages of Main Indicators of Large and Medium Industrial Enterprises as the whole Industrial Enterprises above Designated Size

单位：亿元 (100 million yuan)

指 标	Item	规模以上工业 Industrial Enterprises above Designated Size	#大中型工业企业 Large and Medium industrial Enterprises		#国有大中型 State-owned Large and Medium Industrial Enterprises	
			绝对数 Absolute Figure	占规模以上工业比重(%) Percentage Taken to Industrial Enterprises above Designated Size(%)	绝对数 Absolute Figure	占规模以上工业比重(%) Percentage Taken to Industrial Enterprises above Designated Size(%)
企业单位数(个)	Number of Industrial Enterprises(unit)	3895	901	23.1	107	2.7
#亏损企业个数(个)	Number of Loss Making Industrial Enterprises(unit)	739	200	27.1	22	3.0
工业总产值	Gross Output Value of Industry	9507.33	5998.89	63.1	1305.06	13.7
工业增加值	Value-added of Industry	3117.60	2163.83	69.4	696.72	22.3
资产总计	Total Assets	11747.39	9302.17	79.2	1915.02	16.3
流动资产年平均余额	Average Balance of Circulating Funds	4398.96	3347.32	76.1	879.00	20.0
固定资产净值年平均余额	Annual Average Balance Net Value of Fixed Assets	4183.65	3494.72	83.5	1099.10	26.3
负债总计	Total Liabilities	7480.21	6037.22	80.7	924.64	12.4
主营业务收入	Revenue from Principal Business	8655.87	5589.52	64.6	1244.06	14.4
主营业务成本	Cost of Sales	6732.87	4181.90	62.1	867.55	12.9
主营业务税金及附加	Sales Tax and Extra Charges	314.44	270.11	85.9	35.86	11.4
亏损企业亏损额	Total Deficit of Loss Making Industrial Enterprises	136.32	108.42	79.5	9.12	6.7
利税总额	Total Profits and Taxes	1310.38	1024.28	78.2	348.43	26.6
资金利税率(%)	Ratio of Pre-Tax Profit and Assets(%)	15.30	14.97	97.8	17.61	115.1

14-19 规模以上大中型工业企业分行业主要经济指标(2014)

单位：亿元

指　　标	Item	企业单位数(个) Number of Enterprises (unit)
总　　计	**Total**	**901**
采矿业	Mining	341
#煤炭开采和洗选业	Mining and Washing of Coal	320
黑色金属矿采选业	Mining and Processing of Ferrous Metal Ores	8
有色金属矿采选业	Mining and Processing of Non-Ferrous Metal Ores	2
非金属矿采选业	Mining and Processing of Non-metal Ores	11
制造业	Manufacturing	456
#农副食品加工业	Processing of Food from Agricultural Products	16
食品制造业	Manufacture of Foods	6
酒、饮料和精制茶制造业	Manufacture of Liquor, Beverages and Refined Tea	42
烟草制品业	Manufacture of Tobacco	1
纺织业	Manufacture of Textile	4
纺织服装、服饰业	Manufacture of Textile, Wearing Apparel and Accessories	3
皮革、毛皮、羽毛及其制品和制鞋业	Manufacture of Leather, Fur, Feathers and other Products and Footwear	10
木材加工和木、竹、藤、棕、草制品业	Processing of Timber, Manufacture of Wood, Bamboo,Rattan, Palm and Straw Products	21
家具制造业	Manufacture of Fumiture	2
造纸和纸制品业	Manufacture of Paper and Paper Products	5
印刷和记录媒介复制业	Printing, and Reproduction of Recording Media	2
文教、工美、体育和娱乐用品制造业	Manufacture of Articles for Culture, Education, Arts and Crafts, Sport and Entertainment Activities	3
石油加工、炼焦和核燃料加工业	Processing of Petroleum, Coking and Processing of Nuclear Fuel	6
化学原料和化学制品制造业	Manufacture of Raw Chemical Materials and Chemical Products	46
医药制造业	Manufacture of Medicines	28
橡胶和塑料制品业	Manufacture of Plastics	9
非金属矿物制品业	Manufacture of Non-metallic Mineral Products	76
黑色金属冶炼和压延加工业	Smelting and Pressing of Ferrous Metals	37
有色金属冶炼和压延加工业	Smelting and Pressing of Non-ferrous Metals	22
金属制品业	Manufacture of Metal Products	12
通用设备制造业	Manufacture of General Purpose Machinery	14
专用设备制造业	Manufacture of Special Purpose Machinery	9
汽车制造业	Manufacture of Automobiles	16
铁路、船舶、航空航天和其他运输设备制造业	Manufacture of Railway, Ship, Aerospace and Other Transport Equipments	24
电气机械和器材制造业	Manufacture of Electrical Machinery and Apparatus	13
计算机、通信和其他电子设备制造业	Manufacture of Communication Equipment, Computers and Other Electronic Equipment	16
仪器仪表制造业	Manufacture of Measuring Instruments and Machinery	5
其他制造业	Other Manufacture	7
电力、燃气及水的生产和供应业	Production and Supply of Electric Power,Gas and Water	104
电力、热力的生产和供应业	Production and Supply of Electric Power and Heat Power	93
燃气生产和供应业	Production and Supply of Gas	3
水的生产和供应业	Production and Supply of Water	8

Main Indicators on Economic of Large and Medium Industrial Enterprises by Sector

(100 million yuan)

工业总产值 Total Output Value of Industry	资产合计 Total Assets	主营业务收入 Revenue from Principal Business	利税总额 Total Profits and Taxes	#利润总额 Total Profits
5998.89	**9302.17**	**5589.52**	**1024.28**	**467.07**
1008.49	1863.21	868.85	119.60	42.45
923.30	1791.04	791.82	105.13	33.65
15.32	7.52	15.27	1.33	0.64
3.22	3.16	3.24	0.21	0.09
66.65	61.49	58.52	12.93	8.07
3741.63	5050.78	3508.67	819.59	395.86
37.62	24.79	35.44	1.80	0.65
43.73	37.13	38.03	11.63	9.07
510.46	1028.93	461.11	341.27	245.65
368.02	234.04	352.45	274.41	43.84
6.40	5.92	2.66	0.11	0.05
11.66	5.71	10.20	0.17	0.13
31.84	15.10	40.76	2.32	1.50
57.05	12.69	54.36	5.60	2.46
5.06	3.51	4.50	0.88	0.64
16.19	33.59	14.73	2.41	1.05
4.52	7.84	4.72	1.41	1.05
2.33	3.47	1.92	-0.33	-0.35
79.09	75.07	57.57	2.68	1.89
488.92	1171.81	633.07	18.71	5.76
246.24	245.94	213.86	44.75	28.43
135.65	123.14	82.40	6.84	3.51
334.10	451.16	285.84	48.11	32.33
445.68	317.25	412.68	7.41	-3.63
323.83	414.93	259.51	9.10	2.20
40.76	72.93	41.98	2.42	0.81
40.71	55.38	32.35	3.46	1.77
25.56	53.04	21.24	0.86	0.14
146.61	124.93	145.67	16.07	4.61
141.47	328.97	129.48	5.16	3.42
75.15	59.53	57.68	3.73	2.43
82.80	83.64	85.26	7.24	5.48
8.64	11.99	7.03	0.76	0.49
29.58	46.39	21.90	0.58	0.46
1248.78	2388.17	1212.00	85.09	28.76
1222.28	2282.34	1181.51	86.32	30.43
17.78	47.19	23.16	-2.47	-2.52
8.72	58.64	7.33	1.24	0.85

14−20 规模以上工业销售产值(2014)
Output Value of Industrial Sales above Designated Size

单位：亿元 (100 million yuan)

指 标	Item	销售产值 Sales Value	#出口交货值 Delivery Value of Industry
总 计	**Total**	**9052.59**	**122.94**
#国有控股企业	State-controlled Enterprises	3752.25	104.65
按登记注册类型分	**By status of Registration**		
内资企业	Domestic Enterprises	8731.48	117.45
国有企业	State-owned Enterprises	1298.53	21.15
中央企业	Central	651.06	1.53
地方企业	Local	647.47	19.61
集体企业	Collective-owned Enterprises	17.56	
股份合作企业	Cooperation Enterprises	11.35	
联营企业	Joint-owned Enterprises	5.46	
有限责任公司	Limited Liability Corporations	4334.97	70.71
股份有限公司	Share holding Cerporations Limited	599.56	21.76
私营企业	Private Enterprises	2428.69	3.83
其他企业	Others	35.37	
港、澳、台商投资企业	Enterprises with Funds from Hong kong,Macao and Taiwan	183.92	2.13
外商投资企业	Foreign Funded Enterprises	137.18	3.36
按轻重工业分	**Grouped by Type of Light and Heavy Industry**		
轻工业	Light Industry	2124.07	29.16
重工业	Heavy Industry	6928.52	93.78
按企业规模分	**Grouped by Scale of Enterprise**		
大型企业	Large Enterprises	2870.44	98.41
中型企业	Medium-sized Enterprises	2808.93	12.39
小型企业	Small Enterprises	3210.87	8.34
微型企业	Micro-enterprises	162.35	3.80

14-21 规模以上工业主要产品产量、销售量和产销率(2014)

Output, Sales Volume, Ratio of Produots Solcl of Major Industrial Products above Designated Size

指 标	Item	产 量 Output	销售量 Sales Volume	产销率(%) Ratio of Products Sold(%)	2014年比2013年增长(%) Increase Rate in 2014 over 2013(%)	
					产 量 Output	销售量 Sales Volume
磷矿石(折含P_2O_5 30%)(万吨)	Phosphorite Mineral(10000 tons)	3397.42	2504.83	73.7	12.5	23.3
配混合饲料(万吨)	Forage(10000 tons)	115.82	113.64	98.1	22.0	28.1
成品糖(万吨)	Refined(10000 tons)	5.55	5.39	97.0	49.1	-14.1
乳制品(吨)	Dairy Products(ton)	78659.00	77502.00	98.5	16.8	16.0
罐头(吨)	Canned Food(ton)	24773.29	24262.39	97.9	19.6	23.7
饮料酒(万千升)	Alcohol Beverages(10000 kiloliter)	116.99	106.16	90.7	32.5	38.5
#白酒	White Spirit	38.05	31.47	82.7	11.0	22.0
啤酒	Beer	78.63	74.69	95.0	46.1	46.9
软饮料(万吨)	Soft Drink(10000 tons)	342.52	322.22	94.1	32.7	21.4
卷烟(万箱)	Cigarettes(10000 cases)	258.36	248.95	96.4	1.6	-0.5
纱(万吨)	Yarn(10000 tons)	3.97	3.12	78.6	113.4	71.0
丝(吨)	Silk(ton)	291.00	302.00	103.8	24.6	30.4
服装(万件)	Garment(10000 pieces)	4288.72	4124.26	96.2	82.2	97.7
人造板(万立方米)	Artificial Board(10000cu.m)	304.57	307.06	100.8	12.2	16.2
机制纸(万吨)	Machine-made Paper(10000 tons)	28.00	22.01	78.6	12.5	27.3
硫酸(折100%)(万吨)	Sulfuric Acid(10000 tons)	689.41	66.71	9.7	5.7	80.5
氢氧化钠(烧碱折100%)(万吨)	Caustic Soda(10000 tons)	6.32	6.24	98.7	-8.8	1.1
碳化钙(电石折300升/千克)(万吨)	Calcium Carbide(10000 tons)	7.38	7.61	103.1	-67.9	-66.6
合成氨(万吨)	Synthetic Ammonia(10000 tons)	229.75	123.72	53.9	9.7	35.0
农用化学肥料总计(折纯)(万吨)	Chemical Fertilizers(10000 tons)	533.52	512.23	96.0	4.8	6.4
#氮肥(折含N100%)	Nitrogen Fertilizers	230.80	213.31	92.4	-0.3	-2.9
#尿素	Carbamide	93.89	89.92	95.8	-12.4	-16.7
磷肥(折合P_2O_5 100%)	Phosphate Fertilizers	299.11	297.93	99.6	8.8	14.6

14-21 续表 continued

指 标	Item	产 量 Output	销售量 Sales Volume	产销率(%) Proportion of Products Sold(%)	2014年比2013年增长(%) Increase Rate in 2014 over 2013 (%)	
					产 量 Output	销售量 Sales Volume
纯苯(吨)	Pure Benzene(ton)	7372	7382	100.1	-52.9	-52.9
合成洗涤剂(万吨)	Synthetic Detergents(10000 tons)	9.81	9.66	98.5	11.1	12.0
轮胎外胎(万条)	Tires(10000 tires)	546.46	534.03	97.7	-9.3	-9.7
塑料制品(万吨)	Plastic Products(10000 tons)	61.66	57.47	93.2	6.8	16.8
#农用薄膜(吨)	Rural Use Membrane(ton)	8310.00	8281.00	99.7	12.2	12.1
水泥(万吨)	Cement(10000 tons)	9386.89	9102.32	97.0	15.5	14.5
生铁(万吨)	Pig Iron(10000 tons)	498.64	59.24	11.9	-5.4	-28.8
粗钢(万吨)	Crude Steel(10000 tons)	551.81	37.28	6.8	-2.0	6.4
成品钢材(万吨)	Steel Products(10000 tons)	552.39	552.32	100.0	-1.9	-1.7
#盘条(线材)(万吨)	Wire Rod(10000 tons)	179.25	178.20	99.4	-1.3	-1.4
无缝钢管(吨)	Seamless Steel Pipe(ton)	9480.21	9112.88	96.1	-24.5	-28.9
铁合金(万吨)	Iron Alloy(10000 tons)	348.18	337.24	96.9	4.7	4.3
十种有色金属(万吨)	Ten kinds of Nonferrous Metals(10000 tons)	71.89	66.85	93.0	-39.9	-42.5
#铅(吨)	Lead(ton)	19662.00	20377.00	103.6	20.5	26.0
锌(万吨)	Zinc(10000 tons)	2.06	1.81	87.8	-29.7	-34.1
电解铝(万吨)	Aluminum(10000 tons)	65.21	60.30	92.5	-41.9	-44.7
氧化铝(万吨)	Aluminum oxide(10000 tons)	407.93	406.73	99.7	13.4	30.8
铝材(万吨)	Aluminium Material(10000 tons)	58.17	57.46	98.8	99.0	102.3
金属切削机床(台)	Metal-cutting Machine Tools(set)	2071	1764	85.2	20.8	-10.5
小型拖拉机(辆)	Mini-tractors(set)	5190	5190	100.0	-57.9	-56.4
交流电动机(万千瓦)	Alternating Current Motor(10000 kw)	30.31	29.73	98.1	-28.4	-14.3
家用电冰箱(万台)	Household Refrigerators(10000 sets)	168.22	167.08	99.3	8.3	7.0
集成电路(万块)	Integrated Circuits(10000 units)	1991.79	705.83	35.4	9.9	9.9
彩色电视机(万台)	Color TV Sets(10000 sets)	115.68	115.68	100.0	-5.2	-5.6

14-22 高技术产业基本情况

Basic Statistics on High-tech Industry

指 标	Item	2010	2011	2012	2013	2014
规模以上高技术企业数(个)	Number of Enterprises (unit)	155	157	187	147	170
从业人员年平均人数(万人)	Annual Average Number of Employees (10 000 persons)	6.77	6.82	7.43		7.81
工业总产值(亿元)	Gross Output Value(100 million yuan)	320.96	392.87	423.57	518.96	638.31
主营业务收入(亿元)	Revenue from Principal Business (100 million yuan)	260.26	316.59	345.80	412.53	531.80
利税总额(亿元)	Pre-Tax Profits(100 million yuan)	33.21	35.18	45.17	50.90	69.41
利润总额(亿元)	Profits (100 million yuan)	21.38	22.38	28.07	30.47	43.92

注：高技术产业统计口径2010—2012年为年主营业务收入500万元及以上工业企业，2013年起为年主营业务收入2000万元及以上工业企业。
Note: From 2010 to 2012, High tech industry's statistics caliber was the industrial enterprise with the main business income of 5 million yuan and above. The standard of main business income changed to 20 millions yuan from 2013.

主要统计指标解释

工业 指从事自然资源的开采，对采掘品和农产品进行加工和再加工的物质生产部门。具体包括：(1)对自然资源的开采，如采矿、晒盐等(但不包括禽兽捕猎和水产捕捞)；(2)对农副产品的加工、再加工，如粮油加工、食品加工、缫丝、纺织、制革等；(3)对采掘品的加工、再加工，如炼铁、炼钢、化工生产、石油加工、机器制造、木材加工等，以及电力、自来水、煤气的生产和供应等；(4)对工业品的修理、翻新，如机器设备的修理、交通运输工具（如汽车）的修理等。

工业统计调查单位为独立核算法人工业企业。

独立核算法人工业企业指从事工业生产经营活动的单位。独立核算法人工业企业应同时具备以下条件：①依法成立，有自己的名称、组织机构和场所，能够承担民事责任；② 独立拥有和使用资产、承担负债、有权与其他单位签订合同；③独立核算盈亏，并能够编制资产负债表。

国有及国有控股企业 指国有企业加上国有控股企业。国有企业（即原全民所有制工业或国营工业）指企业全部资产归国家所有、并按《中华人民共和国企业法人登记管理条例》规定登记注册的非公司制的经济组织。包括国有企业、国有独资公司和国有联营企业。1957年以前的公私合营和私营工业、后均改造为国营工业，1992年改为国有工业，这部分工业的资料不单独分列时，均包括在国有企业内。国有控股企业是对混合所有制经济的企业进行的“国有控股”分类。它是指这些企业的全部资产中国有资产（股份）相对其他所有者中的任何一个所有者占资（股）最多的企业。该分组反映了国有经济控股情况。

本篇涉及的其他企业登记注册类型的解释详见综合篇。

资产总计 指企业过去的交易或者事项形成的、由企业拥有或者控制的、预期会给企业带来经济利益的资源。资产一般按流动性分为流动资产和非流动资产。其中流动资产可分为货币资金、交易性金融资产、应收票据、应性账款、预付款项、其他应收款、存货等；非流动资产可分为长期股权投资、固定资产、无形资产及其他非流动资产等。根据会计“资产负债表”中“资产总计”项目的期末余额数填报。

流动资产合计 资产满足以下条件之一应归为流动资产：(1）预计在一个正常营业周期中变现、出售或耗用，主要包括存货、应收账款等；(2）主要为交易目的而持有；（3）预计在资产负债表日起一年内（含一年）变现；(4）自资产负债日起一年内，交换其他资产或清偿负债的能力不受限制的现金或现金等价物。包括货币资金、应收票据、应收账款、存货等项目。根据会计“资产负债表”中“流动资产合计”项目的期末余额数填报。

负债合计 指企业过去的交易或者事项形成的，预期会导致经济利监流出企业的现时义务。负债一般按偿还期长短分为流动负债和非流动负情。根据会计“资产负债表”中“负债合计”项目的期末余额数填报。

主营业务收入 指企业确认的销售商品、提供劳务等主营业务的收入。根据会计“主营业务收入”科目的期末贷方余额填报。

主营业务成本 指企业经营主要业务所发生的成本总额。根据会计“主营业务成本”科目的期末借方余额填报。

主营业务税金及附加 指企业经营主要业务应负担的营业税、消费税、城市维护建设税教育费附加等。根据会计“主营业务税金及附加”科目的期末借方余额填报。

利润总额 指企业在一定会计期间的经营成果，是生产经营过程中各种收入扣除各种耗费后的盈余，反映企业在报告期内实现的盈亏总额。根据会计“利润表”中“利润总额”项目的本期金额数填报。

应交增值税 指企业按税法规定，从事货物销售或提供加工、修理修配劳务等增加货物价值的活动本期应交纳的税金。计算公式为：

应交增值税=销项税额−（进项税额−进项税额转出）−出口抵减内销产品应纳税额−减免税款+出口退税

进项税额指企业在报告期内购入货物或接受应税劳务而支付的、准予从销项税额中抵扣的增值税额。

销项税额指企业在报告期内销售货物或提供应税劳务应收取的增值税额。

总资产贡献率 反映企业全部资产的获利能力，是企业经营业绩和管理水平的集中体现，是评价和考核企业盈利能力的核心指标。计算公式为：

$$\text{总资产贡献率}=\frac{\text{利润总额}+\text{税金总额}+\text{利息支出}}{\text{平均资金总额}}\times 100\%$$

公式中：税金总额为主营业务税金及附加与应交增值税之和；平均资产总额为期初期末资产之和的算术平均值。

资产负债率 该指标既反映企业经营风险的大小，也反映企业利用债权人提供的资金从事经营活动的能力。计算公式为：

$$\text{资产负债率}=\frac{\text{负债总额}}{\text{资产总额}}\times 100\%$$

资产与负债均为报告期期末数。

流动资产周转次数 指一定时期内流动资产完成的周转次数、反映投入工业企业流动资金的周转速度。计算公式为：

$$\text{流动资产周转次数}=\frac{\text{产品销售收入}}{\text{全部流动资产平均余额}}$$

公式中：全部流动资产平均余额为期初和期末的流动资产之和的算术平均值。

成本费用利润率 反映企业投入的生产成本及费用的经济效益，同时也反映企业降低成本所取得的经济效益。计算公式为：

$$\text{成本费用利润率}=\frac{\text{利润总额}}{\text{成本费用总额}}\times 100\%$$

公式中：成本费用总额为主营业务成本、销售费用、管理费用、财务费用之和。

Explanatory Notes on Main Statistical Indicators

Industry refers to the material production sector which is engaged in the extraction of natural resources and processing and reprocessing of minerals and agricultural products, including (1) extraction of natural resources, such as mining, salt production (but not including hunting and fishing); (2) processing and reprocessing of farm and sideline produces, such as rice husking, flour milling, wine making, oil pressing, silk reeling, spinning and weaving, and leather making; (3) manufacture of industrial products, such as steel making, iron smelting, chemicals manufacturing, petroleum processing, machine building, timber processing; water and gas production and electricity generation and supply; (4)repairing of industrial products such as the repairing of machinery and means of transport (including cars).

In industrial statistics surveys, the units of enquiry are corporate industrial enterprises with independent accounting systems.

Corporate industrial enterprises with independent accounting systems refer to enterprises engaging in industrial production activities, which meet the following requirements: (1) They are established legally, having their own names, organizations, Iocation and able to take civil liability; (2) They possess and use their assets independently, assume liabilities and are entitled to sign contracts with other units; (3) They are financially independent and compile their own balance sheets.

State-owned and State-holding Enterprises refer to state-owned enterprises plus State-holding enterprises. State-owned enterprises (originally known as State-run enterprises with ownership by the whole society) are non-corproate economic entities registered in accordance with the Regulation of the People's Republic of China on the Management of Registration of Legal Enterprises, where all assets are owned by the State. Included in this category are State-owned enterprises, State-funded corporations and State-owned joint-operation enterprises. Joint State-private industries and private industries, which existed before 1957, were transformed into state-run industries since 1957, and into State-owned industries after 1992. Statistics on those enterprises are included in the State-owned industries instead of being grouped them separately. State-holding enterprises are a sub-classification of enterprises with mixed ownership, referring to enterprises where the percentage of State assets (or shares by the State) is larger than any other single share holder of the same enterprise. This sub-classification illustrates the control of the State over a particular industry.

For explanation of enterprises of other types of registration covered in this chapter, please refer to General Survey.

Total Assets refer to all resources that are owned or controlled by enterprises through previous trades or transactions with expectation of making economic profits. Classified by the degree of liquidity, total assets include current assets, and non-current assets. Current assets can be classified into monetary assets, trading financial assets, notes receivable, accounts receivable, advanced payments, other prepaid money and inventories. Non-current assets can be divided into long-term equity investment, fixed assets, intangible assets and other non-current assets. Date on this indicator can be obtained by the year-end figures of total assets in the Assets and Liability Table of accounting records of enterprises.

Total Current Assets refers to the assets that meet one of the following requirements: (1) expected to be cashed, sold or used in a normal operation cycle, mainly including inventory and accounts receivable; (2) be owned for trading prupose mainly; (3) expected to be cashed in one year (including one year) from the day of the Assets and Liability Table; (4) unlimited cash or cash equivalents that can be exchanged with other assets or being capable of settling debts during one year since the day of Assets and

Liability Table. Included are monetary assets, notes receivable, accounts receivable and inventories. Data on this indicator can be obtained by the year-end figures of total current assets in the Assets and Liability Table of the accounting records of enterprises.

Total Liabilities refer to payable liabilities of enterprises that accumulated from previous trades or transactions with expectation of economic profits leaking out. In terms of payment, it can be divided into liquid liabilities and long-term liabilities. Data on this item is obtained from the year-end figures on total liabilities from the Assets and Liability Table of the accounting record of the enterprises.

Revenue from Principal Business refers to the income confirmed of an enterprise from the principal business of selling products and providing labor services. Data on this indicator can be obtained from the year-end credit balance of "revenue from principal business" in the accounting record of enterprise.

Cost of Principal Business refers to the total cost occurred from the principal business of the enterprise. Date can be obtained from the year-end debit balance of "cost of principal business" in the accounting record of enterprise.

Tax and Extra Charges from Principal Business refers to the sales tax, consumption tax, urban maintenance and construction tax and education expenses shouldered by the enterprise from its principal business. Date are obtained from the year-end debit balance of "tax and extra charges from principal business" in the accounting record of enterprise.

Total Profits refers to the operation results in a certain accounting period, and it is the balance of various incomes minus various spendings in the course of operation reflecting the total profits and losses of enterprises in reference period. Date are obtained from the amount of "total profits" in the "profit table" of the accounting record of enterprise.

Value-added Tax Payable refers to the payable tax of enterprises which engaged in selling of goods or providing services that bring added value to the goods, such as processing, repairing, fitting and other activities should be paid according to Tax Law. The formula is as follows:

Value-added Tax Payable = tax on sales – (tax on purchase – transferred tax on purchase) – exports deduct tax payable on domestic sales – tax relief + the export tax rebate.

Tax on Purchase refers to the value-added tax payable by enterprises that purchase goods or receiving taxable services during the reference period and this part of the tax is allowed to be deducted from the tax on sales.

Tax on Sales refers to the value-added tax chargeable by enterprises that sell goods or provide taxable services during the reference period.

Ratio of Profits, Taxes and Interests to Average Assets reflects the profit-making capability of all assets of the enterprise and is a key indicator manifesting the performance and management and evaluating the profit-making potential of the enterprise. It is calculated as follows:

$$\text{Ration of Profits, Taxes and Interests to Average Assets}(\%) = \frac{\text{total profits+total taxes+interest payment}}{\text{average assets}} \times 100\%$$

In the above formula, total taxes is the sum of tax of and extra charges on the principal business and value-added tax payable; and average assets is the arithmetic mean of the sum of beginning assets and ending assets.

Ratio of Debts to Assets reflects both the operation risk and the capability of the enterprise in making use of the capital from the creditors. It is calculated as follows:

$$\text{Ratio of Debts to Assets}(\%) = \frac{\text{total debts}}{\text{total assets}} \times 100\%$$

Both assets and debts are figures at the end of the reference period.

Turnover of Current Assets refers to the number of times of turnover of current assets in a given period of time, which reflects the speed of the turnover of current assets of industrial enterprises, and is calculated as follows:

$$\text{Turnover of Working Capital} = \frac{\text{sales revenue of products}}{\text{average balance of total working capital}}$$

In the above formula, average balance of total current assets refers to the arithmetic mean of the sum of current assets at the beginning and at the end of the reference period.

Ratio of Profits to Total Industrial Costs refers to the ratio of profits realized in a given period to the total costs in the same period, which reflects the economic efficiency of input cost and is calculated as follows:

$$\text{Ratio of Profits to Total Industrial Cost}(\%) = \frac{\text{total profits}}{\text{total costs}} \times 100\%$$

Total costs in the above formula are the sum of cost of principal business, marketing cost, management cost and financial cost.

15 建筑业
Construction

15-1 建筑业主要指标

Main Economic Indicators on Construction Enterprises

指　　标	Item	2010	2011	2012	2013	2014
建筑业企业个数(个)	**Number of Enterprises (unit)**	**605**	**581**	**628**	**678**	**841**
年末从业人员(万人)	Number of Emplyed Persons at the Year-end (10000 persons)	33.83	33.14	35.57	41.22	45.64
自有固定资产原价(亿元)	Fixed Assets Owned(original value)(100 million yuan)	87.43	92.00	101.17		114.17
自有固定资产净价(亿元)	Fixed Assets Owned(net value)(100 million yuan)	57.16	57.33	61.62		65.96
自有机械设备台数(万台)	Number of Machinery and Equipment Owned(10000 sets)	7.97	7.26	6.74		
自有机械设备净值(亿元)	Net Value of Machinery and Equipment Owned (100 million yuan)	27.85	33.08	24.45		
自有机械设备总功率(万千瓦)	Total Power of Machinery and Equipment Owned (10000 kw)	142.88	153.03	143.00		
建筑业总产值(亿元)	**Gross Output Value of Construction (100 million yuan)**	**622.96**	**824.72**	**1039.95**	**1365.00**	**1640.24**
建筑业增加值(亿元)	**Value Added of Construction(100 million yuan)**	**283.19**	**365.13**	**460.48**	**577.18**	**717.69**
#本年固定资产折旧	Depreciation of Fixed Assets	5.44	5.56	6.75		9.57
应付职工薪酬	Wages Payable	75.25	90.07	121.89		166.30
工程结算税金及附加	Taxes and Extra Charges on Project Settle Accounts	22.67	29.86	34.65		53.52
管理费用中的税金	Taxes in Management Expenses	0.8	0.83	1.34		1.21
营业利润	Operating Profits	9.78	14.31	12.51		35.55
房屋建筑施工面积(万平方米)	**Floor Space of Buildings under Construction (10000 sq.m)**	**5756**	**6779**	**8254**	**12174**	**13890**
房屋建筑竣工面积(万平方米)	**Floor Space of Buildings Completed(10000 sq.m)**	**1350**	**1530**	**1863**	**2450**	**2801**
利润总额(亿元)	Total Profits(100 million yuan)	10.48	14.4	16.30		35.07
税金总额(亿元)	Total Taxes(100 million yuan)	26.24	34.08	40.69		63.16
劳动生产率(元/人)	**Overall Labor Productivity(yuan/person)**					
按总产值计算	In Terms of Gross Output Value	196170	222471	319469	368122	367684
按增加值计算	In Terms of Value-added	89177	98494	141459	155658	160881
技术装备率(元/人)	Value of Machines Per Laborer(yuan/person)	8232	9982	8148		
动力装备率(千瓦/人)	Power of Machines Per Laborer(kw/person)	4.22	4.52	4.76		
房屋建筑面积竣工率(%)	Ratio of Floor Space of Buildings Completed(%)	23.5	22.6	22.6	20.13	20.17
产值利润率(%)	Ratio of Profit to Gross Output Value(%)	1.7	1.7	1.6		2.1
产值利税率(%)	Ratio of Pre-tax Profit to Gross Output Value(%)	5.9	5.9	5.5		5.9

注：应付职工薪酬2010-2011年为应付工资数据。

Note: From 2010 to 2011, data of accrued payroll refers to the wages payable.

15-2 建筑业主要生产指标(2014)

指　标	Item	企业个数(个) Number of Construction Enterprises (unit)	年末从业人员(万人) Number of Persons Engaged (10000 persons)	签订合同额(亿元) Value of Signed Contract (100 million yuan)	#本年新签合同额 New Value of Signed Contract in this year
总　计	**Total**	**841**	**45.64**	**4196.67**	**2188.63**
#国有及国有控股	State-owned and state-controlled Construction Enterprises	144	30.41	3538.42	1786.10
#施工总承包企业	General Contractors	641	43.74	4096.56	2116.48
专业承包企业	Special Contractors	200	1.90	100.11	72.15
按登记注册类型分组	**By Registration Status**				
#内资企业	Domestic Funded	841	45.64	4196.67	2188.63
#国有企业	State-owned	56	7.08	809.78	439.96
集体企业	Collective-owned	86	2.54	81.88	62.55
股份有限公司	Company Limited with Share Holding	33	1.72	561.18	241.38
私营企业	Private Enterprises	283	4.22	230.65	151.09
按国民经济行业分组	**By Sector**				
房屋和土木工程建筑业	Building and Civil Engineering Construction	650	42.72	3750.77	1874.48
房屋工程建筑	Building Engineering Construction	518	30.18	2489.02	1372.43
土木工程建筑	Civil Engineering Construction	132	12.54	1261.75	502.05
建筑安装业	Construction Installation	82	2.10	361.10	253.19
建筑装饰业	Construction Decoration	69	0.43	47.80	31.98
其他建筑业	Others	40	0.39	37.00	28.98

Main Production Indicators on Construction Enterprises

建筑业总产值(亿元) Total Output Value of Construction (100 million yuan)	#在省外完成的产值 Value of Construction Which Fulfilled outside of Guizhou Province	#建筑工程 Output Value of Constr-uction	#安装工程 Output Value of Instal-lation	房屋建筑施工面积(万平方米) Floor Space of Buildings under Constru-ction (10000 sq.m)	#本年新开工面积 Started This Year	#实行投标承包面积 Verified Eligible Area of the First Time
1640.24	**265.86**	**1437.49**	**108.19**	**13889.68**	**3257.91**	**9709.93**
1264.19	262.14	1116.38	76.34	10828.43	2332.42	8082.92
1570.09	262.75	1397.75	88.38	13863.03	3254.70	9706.47
70.15	3.11	39.74	19.81	26.65	3.21	3.46
1640.24	265.86	1437.49	108.19	13889.68	3257.91	9709.93
258.06	54.85	211.65	25.43	3096.52	198.07	537.44
57.55		50.78	2.14	452.94	154.83	258.10
193.12	45.62	185.57	1.98	2518.86	527.85	2299.68
128.91	2.51	114.11	9.16	1296.77	352.96	729.03
1445.50	219.36	1323.07	51.51	13429.81	3172.76	9300.96
1004.20	168.91	913.96	26.16	13209.65	3129.06	9128.52
441.30	50.45	409.11	25.35	220.16	43.70	172.44
141.10	45.62	71.82	54.47	440.53	85.15	408.97
21.84	0.88	17.15	1.53			
31.80		25.45	0.68	19.34		

15−3 建筑业企业房屋建筑(2014)

指　标	Item	竣工面积 (万平方米) Floor Space of Buildings Completed (10000sq.m)	#厂房、仓库 Workshop Storehouse	#住 宅 Residential Buildings	#教育用房 Educational Buildings
总　计	**Total**	**2800.77**	**138.75**	**1821.43**	**277.80**
#国有及国有控股	Construction Enterprises of State-owned and state-controlled	1531.49	96.32	1104.03	121.70
#施工总承包企业	General Contractors	2794.40	137.96	1820.92	277.63
专业承包企业	Special Contractors	6.37	0.79	0.51	0.17
按登记注册类型分组	**By Registration Status**				
#内资企业	Domestic Funded	2800.77	138.75	1821.43	277.80
#国有企业	State-owned	365.25	15.45	273.09	9.16
集体企业	Collective-owned	232.31	8.29	127.61	24.71
股份有限公司	Company Limited with Share Holding	243.47	9.95	175.94	33.36
私营企业	Private Enterprises	463.77	10.22	279.24	54.05
按国民经济行业分组	**By Sector**				
#房屋和土木工程建筑业	Building and Civil Engineering Construction	2701.53	129.59	1746.96	275.70
房屋工程建筑	Building Engineering Construction	2634.17	121.34	1697.92	275.42
土木工程建筑	Civil Engineering Construction	67.36	8.25	49.04	0.28
建筑安装业	Construction and Installation	94.67	9.16	74.04	2.10

House Buildings by Construction Enterprises

		总造价					
#卫生医疗用房 Medical Buildings	#科研用房 Scientific Research Buildings	(元/平方米) Total cost of Buildings Completed (yuan/sq.m)	#厂房、仓库 Workshop Storehouse	#住宅 Residential Buildings	#教育用房 Educational Buildings	#卫生医疗用房 Medical Buildings	#科研用房 Scientific Research Buildings
47.39	**10.31**	**1401**	**1594**	**1337**	**1445**	**1385**	**1295**
26.43	3.40	1542	1698	1388	1727	1485	1378
47.23	10.31	1402	1594	1338	1445	1386	1295
0.16		875	1598	804	944	1319	
47.39	10.31	1401	1594	1337	1445	1385	1295
7.31	2.64	1055	1981	939	952	736	1429
4.54	1.63	1268	1139	1248	1306	1227	1109
	1.04	1925	1123	1860	1673		1300
7.10	2.68	1302	2204	1363	1230	1278	1182
44.09	10.31	1411	1634	1348	1449	1356	1295
44.09	10.31	1396	1588	1336	1449	1356	1295
		1960	2301	1762	1445		
3.30		1164	1029	1096	871	1784	

主要统计指标解释

建筑业总产值(即自行完成施工产值) 是以货币形式表现的建筑业企业在一定时期内生产的建筑业产品和提供服务的总和。建筑业总产值包括：

(1)建筑工程产值：指列入建筑工程预算内的各种工程价值。

(2)安装工程产值：指设备安装工程价值，不包括被安装设备本身价值。

(3)其他产值：建筑业总产值中除建筑工程、安装工程以外的产值。包括房屋构筑物修理产值、非标准设备制造产值、总包企业向分包企业收取的管理费以及不能明确划分的施工活动所完成的产值。

a.房屋构筑物修理产值：指房屋和构筑物修理所完成的产值，但不包括被修理房屋、构筑物本身价值和生产设备的修理价值。

b.非标准设备制造产值：指加工制造没有定型的非标准生产设备的加工费和原材料价值(如化工厂、炼油厂用的各种罐、槽，矿井生产统一使用的各种漏斗、三角槽、阀门等)以及附属加工厂为本企业承建工程制作的非标准设备的价值。

建筑业增加值 指建筑业企业在报告期内以货币表现的建筑业生产经营活动的最终成果。建筑业现价增加值按生产法和分配法（收入法）两种方法计算，以收入法的计算结果为准，即从收入的角度出发，根据生产要素在生产过程中应得的收入份额计算。

自有机械设备台数 指归本企业所有，属于本企业固定资产的生产性机械设备年末总台数。包括施工机械、生产设备、运输设备以及其他设备。

自有机械设备总功率 指本企业自有施工机械、生产设备、运输设备以及其他设备等列为在册固定资产的生产性机械设备年末总功率，按设定能力或查定能力计算。包括机械本身的动力和为该机械服务的单独动力设备，如电动机等。计量单位用千瓦，动力换算可按1马力＝0.735千瓦折合成千瓦数。电焊机、变压器、锅炉不计算动力。

房屋建筑施工面积 指在报告期内施工的全部房屋建筑面积，包括本期新开工的房屋面积、上期施工跨入本期继续施工的房屋面积、上期停缓建在本期恢复施工的房屋面积、本期竣工的房屋面积及本期施工后又停缓建的房屋面积。

房屋建筑竣工面积 指在报告期内房屋建筑按照设计要求全部完工，达到了住人和使用条件，经验收鉴定合格，正式移交使用单位的房屋建筑面积。

Explanatory Notes on Main Statistical Indicators

Gross Output Value of Construction refers to total of construction products and services, expressed in money terms, produced or rendered by construction and installation enterprises during a given period of time. It includes:

(1) Output value of construction projects: the value of projects covered by the project budgets;

(2) Output value of installation projects: the value of the installation of equipment, (excluding the value of the equipment to be installed);

(3) Other output values: the output value of construction industry apart from that of construction projects and installation projects. It includes: output value of repair of buildings and structures; output value of non-standard equipment manufacturing; overhead expenses received by contracted enterprises from the sub-contracted enterprises and the completed output value of construction activities for which there is no clear definition.

a. Output value of repair of buildings and structures: the value created through the repairs of buildings or structures. It does not include the value of buildings or structures being repaired and the value of the repair of production equipment;

b. Output value of manufactured non-standard equipment: the value of non-standard production equipment, including raw materials and manufacturing cost, made for the construction project (i.e., chemical plant; kettles or tanks used by refineries; various fillers, triangle tanks, valves used by mines). It also includes the output value of equipment manufactured by subsidiary workshops.

Value-added of Construction refers to the final result of the activities of production and operation of enterprises of the construction industry in monetary terms during the reference period. Value-added of construction is calculated by both production approach and income approach, with the figures from the income approach as the final figures., Under the income approach,, calculation starts from the perspective of income and is based on the share of income derived from the production process by the relevant factors of production.

The Number of Machinery and Equipment refer to the total number of all enterprises, the production of machinery and equipment belonging to the fixed assets of the enterprises at the end of the year. Including construction machinery, production equipment, transportation equipment and other equipment.

Total Power of Its Own Mechanical Equipment refers to the enterprise own construction machinery, production equipment, transportation equipment and other equipment for the fixed assets register production machinery and equipment at the end of the total power, according to the set or fixed capacity calculation. The power of the machine itself and the individual power equipment for the service, such as the motor, etc.. The calculation unit of power, power conversion can be reduced to 1 HP = 0.735 kw. Electric welding machine, transformer, boiler is not calculated power.

Floor Space of Buildings Under Construction refers to floor space of buildings under construction during the reference period, including newly started buildings, buildings started earlier and continued during the reference period, and buildings suspended earlier but restarted during the reference period, buildings completed during the reference period, and buildings under construction and then suspended during the reference period.

Floor Space of Buildings Completed refers to the floor space of buildings that are completed in the reference period in accordance with the requirements of the design, up to the standard for putting them into use, and have been checked and accepted by concerned departments as qualified ones.

16 运输和邮电

Transport, Postal and Telecommunication Services

16-1 境内运输线路长度

Length of Domestic Transport Routes

单位：公里 (km)

指标	Item	2010	2011	2012	2013	2014	2014年比2013年增长(%) Increase Rate in 2014 over 2013(%)
铁路营业里程	**Length of Railways in Operation**	**2002**	**2070**	**2058**	**2093**	**2373**	**13.4**
#复线里程	Double-tracking Length	643	643	667	667	938	
公路线路里程	**Total Length of Highways**	**151644**	**157820**	**164542**	**172564**	**179079**	**3.8**
按行政等级分	**Classified by Administrative Level**						
国道	State Road	3924	4132	4436	4560	4654	2.1
#国家高速公路	Expressway	1259	1467	1772	1890	1985	5.1
省道	Provincial Road	7463	7769	8071	8582	9199	7.2
县道	County Road	17311	17350	17572	17572	17574	持平
乡道	Township Road	18465	18447	18455	18463	18489	0.1
村道	Village Road	103785	109384	115267	122629	128399	4.7
专用公路	Accommodation Highway	697	737	741	759	764	0.7
按技术等级分	**Classified by Technical Grade**						
等级公路	Standard Highway	72557	79643	86577	95419	107573	12.7
高速公路	Expressway	1507	2022	2630	3284	4007	22.0
#四车道	Four-lane	1507	1979	2587	3204	3926	22.6
一级	First Class	153	164	179	256	393	53.9
二级	Second Class	3578	3831	4060	4128	4497	8.9
三级	Third Class	8222	8367	8453	8466	8714	2.9
四级	Fourth Class	59096	65258	71255	79285	89962	13.5
等外公路	Substandard Highway	79087	78177	77965	77145	71506	-7.3
按路面类型分	**Classified by Pavement**						
有铺装路面(高级)	Paved Road (advanced)	10474	14859	21610	31799	45085	41.8
沥青混凝土	Asphalt Concrete	3663	4512	5781	6862	9364	36.5
水泥混凝土	Cement Concrete	6810	10347	15830	24937	35721	43.2
简易铺装路面	Simple Paved Road	26589	29167	31988	34357	35147	2.3
未铺装路面	Not-paved Road	114581	113794	110944	106408	98848	-7.1
晴雨通车里程	Can be open to traffic in rainy or sunny days	151644	157820	164542	172564	179079	3.8
可绿化里程	Can be green	141768	147643	153072	160440	166501	3.8
养护里程	Maintained Road	151644	157820	164542	172564	178213	3.3
内河航道里程	**Length of Navigable Inland Waterways**	**3563**	**3563**	**3563**	**3563**	**3664**	**2.8**

注：1.资料来源于省交通运输厅、成都铁路分局(以下相关表同)。2.公路线路里程包括村道里程。3.2014年铁路复线里程数据为成都铁路局管辖范围内的数据。

Note:1.Data in the table are obtained from the Provincial Department of Transports and Chengdu Railway Branch(The relative tables in the chapter are the same). 2.Since 2008, the total length of highways has included the length of village road. 3.The data of Double-tracking vailway length in 2014 belongs to the domin ation area of railway Burean in Chengdu.

16-2 民用航空运输
Civil Aviation Transportation

指　标	Item	2010	2011	2012	2013	2014	2014年比2013年增长(%) Increase Rate in 2014 over 2013(%)
机场个数(个)	**Numbei of Civil Airports(unit)**	**6**	**6**	**6**	**9**	**10**	**11.1**
通航城市(个)	Cities Reachable (unit)	59	62	59	68	81	19.1
#国际及地区城市	International and Regional Cities	6	6	5	7	12	71.4
运输航班(架次)	Flight Movements (unit)	64835	72009	81928	107450	140219	30.5
进出港旅客(万人次)	**Passengers Get in and Get out of the Airports(10000 person-times)**	**637.59**	**747.02**	**890.99**	**1125.46**	**1420.68**	**26.2**
#进港旅客	Passengers Get in the Airports	302.82	353.01	421.25	532.77	663.25	24.5
民航货邮吞吐量(万吨)	**Volume of Freight Handled in Civil Aviation(10000 tons)**	**6.17**	**6.93**	**7.97**	**7.76**	**8.31**	**7.1**

注：1.资料来源于贵州省机场集团有限公司。2.通航城市数量仅为贵阳龙洞堡机场通航城市。

Note:1.Data in the table are provided by Airports Group Corporation Ltd. of Guizhou Province.2.The number of navigable city only for navigable city of guiyang airport.

16-3 民用汽车拥有量
Possession of Civil Vehicles

单位：万辆　　(10000 units)

指　标	Item	2010	2011	2012	2013	2014	2014年比2013年增长(%) Increase Rate in 2014 over 2013(%)
民用汽车合计	**Total**	**121.30**	**140.12**	**166.72**	**202.76**	**246.36**	**21.5**
#载客汽车	Passenger Vehicles	82.19	101.14	126.47	158.03	195.17	23.5
载货汽车	Trucks	32.73	34.23	36.72	41.50	47.77	15.1
#私人汽车	Private Vehicles	92.77	109.54	134.19	167.87	208.95	24.5

注：资料来源于省交警总队车辆管理所。

Note:Data in the table are obtained from the vehicle management office of the provincial traffic police corps.

16-4 快递业务量

Express delivery services

指　　标	Item	2010	20111	2012	2013	2014
快递（万件）	**Express Services(10000 pcs)**	**1120.92**	**1533.90**	**1800.98**	**2931.23**	**4669.09**
#国内同城快递	Local Express Service	124.71	172.66	202.57	398.35	950.20
#国内异地快递	National Express Service	990.63	1356.34	1593.08	2519.23	3702.48
#国际及港澳台	Hong Kong, Macao, Taiwan and International Express Service	5.58	4.90	5.33	13.64	16.40
快递业务收入（亿元）	**Revenue from Express Service(10000 yuan)**	**2.95**	**3.66**	**4.04**	**6.03**	**9.82**

注：资料来源于省邮政管理局。

Note: data in this table is provided by provincial postal administration.

16-5 旅客运量及周转量

Passenger Traffic and Passenger-Kilometers

指　　标	Item	2010	2011	2012	2013	2014
旅客运量(万人)	**Total Passenger Traffic(10000 persons)**	**97793**	**120554**	**142809**	**83435**	**86572**
铁　路	Railways	3437	3939	3902	4322	4409
公　路	Highways	92426	114429	136454	77358	80231
水　运	Waterways	1930	2186	2453	1755	1932
旅客周转量(亿人公里)	**Passenger-Kilometers(100 million passenger-km)**	**514.41**	**631.74**	**718.22**	**593.62**	**635.50**
铁　路	Railways	189.38	204.58	199.20	211.21	217.39
公　路	Highways	320.46	422.01	513.07	377.87	412.92
水　运	Waterways	4.57	5.15	5.95	4.54	5.19

注：1.公路、水路运输量采用全国公路水路运输量专项调查数据。 2.由于交通运输部对公路、水运运输量统计方案进行调整，2013年相关数据统计口径发生变化，相同指标数据与往年不可比。(下表同)

Note:1.National highway and waterway transportation volume survey data is used to highway and waterway transportation volume. 2.Because of the traffic department of transportation adjust the highway projects, the same indicators of waterway transport statistics in 2013 are not comparable with the correlation data in 2012 . (table below is the same)

16-6 货物运输量及周转量

Freight Traffic and Ton-Kilometers

指　　标	Item	2010	2011	2012	2013	2014
货物运输量(万吨)	**Total Freight Traffic (10000 tons)**	**40310**	**44890**	**52765**	**72700**	**85673**
铁　路	Railways	7991	7219	6665	6458	6319
公　路	Highways	31409	36684	45000	65100	78017
水　运	Waterways	910	987	1100	1142	1337
货物周转量(亿吨公里)	**Total Freight Ton-Kilometers (100 million ton-km)**	**1012.20**	**1060.69**	**1177.78**	**1292.11**	**1442.24**
铁　路	Railways	706.45	696.36	693.68	655.85	634.35
公　路	Highways	293.00	350.10	467.60	610.64	776.95
水　运	Waterways	12.75	14.23	16.50	25.62	30.94

16-7 电信主要指标

Major Indicators of Telecommunications

指　　标	Item	2010	2011	2012	2013	2014	2014年比2013年增长（%） Increase Rate in 2014 over 2013(%)
电信业务收入(亿元)	Business Revenue of Telecommunications (100 million yuan)	147.38	164.56	187.47	217.55	222.02	2.1
电信业务总量(亿元)	Business of Volume Telecommunications (100 million yuan)	566.40	204.35	244.11	278.15	353.98	16.4
交换机总容量(万门)	Capacity of Telephone Exchanges (10000 line)	3673.01	4838.00	5026.53	5870.04	5671.60	-3.4
移动电话交换机容量(万户)	Capacity of Mobile Telephone Exchanges (10000 subscribers)	2724.50	4433.00	4106.76	4954.00	4928.00	-0.5
长途光缆线路长度(万公里)	Length of LongDistance OpticalCable Lines(10000km)	3.02	3.45	3.32	3.50	46.13	3.7
年末固定电话用户数(万户)	Number of Telephone Subscribers at Year-end (10000 subscribers)	432.61	403.96	380.00	362.99	339.10	-6.6
#农村电话用户数	Number of Rural Telephone Subscribers	184.37	149.07	115.55	93.39	77.75	-16.7
城市电话用户	Number of Local(urban)Telephone Subscribers	248.24	254.90	264.45	269.60	261.36	-3.8
#公　用	Number of Public Telephone Subscribers	39.29	34.63	33.43	31.86	30.74	-3.5
移动电话用户(万户)	Number of Mobile Telephone Subscribers (10000 subscribers)	1964.40	2175.22	2515.00	2871.75	3059.85	6.5
移动短信业务量(亿条)	Short Message Services (100 million messages)	120.84	129.26	124.49	140.06	123.36	-11.9
互联网宽带接入端口(万个)	Broad Band Subscribers Port of Internet (10 000 ports)	231.69	437.87	435.79	575.95	668.40	14.8
电话普及率(包括移动电话)(部/百人)	Popularization Rate of Telephone (Include Mobile Telephone) (sets/100 persons)	68.90	74.35	83.27	93.25	97.98	4.7
#移动电话普及率	Popularization Rate of Mobile Telephone	56.46	62.71	72.34	82.78	88.21	5.4
已通电话的行政村比重(%)	Percentage of Administrative Village with Phone Sets(%)	100	100	100	100	100	持平
国内长途电话(万分钟)	Number of Long Distance Telephone Calls Inside Country(10000 minutes)	138922	111354	88786	77143	66294	-14.8
国际及港澳长途电话(万分钟)	Number of Long Distance Telephone Calls outside Country or to Macao、Hong Kong(10000 minutes)	121.83	111.00	79.22	65.95	50.31	-23.7

注：1.资料来源于省通信管理局。2.电信业务总量增长速度按可比价计算。3.电信业务总量2011年起采用2010年不变价计算。

Note:1.Data in the table are obtained from the provincial communications authority bureau. 2.The increase rate of business volume of telecommunication services is calculated at comparable prices. 3. Business volume calculates in 2010 constant prices from 2011.

16-8 邮政、电信主要指标

Major Indicators of Post

指 标	Item	2010	2011	2012	2013	2014	2014年比2013年增长(%) Increase Rate in 2014 over 2013(%)
邮电局所总数(处)	**Number of Post and Telecommunication Offices(unit)**	**19372**	**21496**	**19482**	**20582**	**21380**	**3.9**
邮政	Post	1795	1425	1307	1326	1737	31.0
电信	Telecommunication	17577	20071	18175	19256	19643	2.0
邮路网路总长度(公里)	Number of Postal Routes(km)	96174	99155	136429	154810	407046	
#汽车邮路	Number of Highway Postal Routes	55901	58062	76734	38400	43177	12.4
铁路邮路	Number of Railways Postal Routes	6413	6413	5880	5880	2536	-56.9
邮政业务总量(亿元)	Business Volume of Post (100 million yuan)	15.50	14.97	17.93	22.64	27.75	22.6
函件(万件)	Number of Letters(10000 pcs)	5939	5041	6036	5192	3809.37	-26.6
报刊、杂志累计订销数(万份)	Issue of Newspapers and Magazines(10000 copies)	32084	35056	38027	40469	40002.68	-1.2
国内快递(万件)	Pieces of Express Mail Services inside Nation (10000 pcs)	1115	1529	1796	1071	4652.68	
国际快递(万件)	Pieces of Express Mail Services outside Nation (10000 pcs)	5.60	4.90	5.33	2.63	16.4	
邮政储蓄期末余额(亿元)	Post Deposits at the Year-end(100 million yuan)	269.34	347.38	457.89	556.61	623.63	12.0
集邮业务(万枚)	Stamps for Collection(10000 pcs)	1226	1907	1918	2720.4	2616.1	-3.8
长话业务电路(2M)	Long Distance Cable Lines(2M)	127660	118618	178267	665440	1024266	53.9

注：1.资料来源于省邮政管理局、省邮政储蓄银行。2.邮电局所总数含电信部门特约代理点。3.2014年国家邮政局对相关指标口径、名称调整，邮路网路总长度2010—2013年为邮路总长度，国内快递和国际快递2010—2013年分别为“国内特快专递”和“国际特快专递”，更名指标数据与往年数据不可比。4.邮政业务总量增长速度按可比价计算。5.长话业务电路统计口径2011年及以前为固定长话电路业务(2M)、移动长话电路业务(2M)指标；2012年起包含固定长话电路业务(2M)、移动长话电路业务(2M)、数据及互联网电路业务等，与以往年份数据不可比。6.国内、国际特快专递含快递企业数据。

Note:1. These information comes from the province postal service, the postal savings bank. 2. The total number of the post office containing special agents in telecom department. 3.In 2014 years CSPB caliber, name adjustment of relevant indicators, the total length “postal” index change to post road network, the total length of "domestic express delivery" and "international express mail" indicators were converted into domestic express and international express delivery, relative data and normal data cannot be renamed. 4. Growth rate of postal business volume was calculated at comparable price. 5.Before 2011 ,long-distance services circuit statistics caliber were for fixed long-distance business (2M), mobile long-distance circuit business (2M) indicator; 2012 contains fixed long-distance business (2M), mobile long-distance circuit business (2M), data and Internet business circuit, etc., which cann't compare with former years. 6. Domestic and international express mail include data ofdelivery enterprise.

主要统计指标解释

铁路营业里程 又称营业长度，指投入客货运输营业或临时营业的线路长度。

公路线路里程 指报告期末公路的实际长度。包括城间、城乡间、乡（村）间能行驶汽车的公共道路，公路通过城镇街道的里程，公路桥梁长度、隧道长度、渡口宽度。不包括城市街道里程，断头路里程，农（林）业生产用道路里程，工（矿）企业等内部道路里程。按已竣工验收或交付使用的实际里程计算；两条或多条公路共同经由同一路段的重复里程，只计算一次。

内河航道里程 指在一定时期内，能通航运输船舶及排筏的天然河流、湖泊水库、运河及通航渠道的长度。包括全年季节性通航累计三个月以上的航道，不包括仅供零散流放竹、木排的河道。两省以河为界的航道里程，双方均按一半计算，以免重复。该指标可以反映内河水运网的规模、水平和发展情况。

货(客)运量 指在一定时期内，各种运输工具实际运送的货物(旅客)数量。货运按吨计算，客运按人计算。货物不论运输距离长短、货物类别，均按实际重量统计。旅客不论行程远近或票价多少，均按一人一次客运量统计；半价票、小孩票按一人统计。

货物(旅客)周转量 指在一定时期内，由各种运输工具运送的货物(旅客)数量与其相应运输距离的乘积之总和。计算货物周转量通常按发出站与到达站之间的最短距离，也就是计费距离计算。计算公式为：

货物(旅客)周转量＝Σ货物(旅客)运输量×运输距离

移动电话用户 指通过移动电话交换机进入移动电话网、占用移动电话号码的电话用户。用户数量以报告期末在移动电话营业部门实际办理登记手续进入移动电话网的户数进行计算，一部移动电话统计为一户。

固定电话用户 指在电信运营企业营业网点办理开户登记手续并已接入固定电话网上的全部电话用户。包括普通电话用户、公用电话用户、窄带综合业务数字网(N—ISDN)用户、智能网专用接入终端用户等。按行政区划分为城市电话用户和农村电话用户。1997年以前，市内电话用户是指接入县城及县以上城市的电话网上的电话用户；农村电话用户是指接入县邮电局农话台及县以下农村电话交换点，以县城为中心(除市话用户外)联通县、乡(镇)、行政村、村民小组的用户。从1997年起，电话用户数分组以用户所在区域划分，调整为城市电话用户和乡村电话用户，与过去的按市内电话和农村电话划分方法不同。电话用户总数、电话机总部数统计范围不变。

城市电话用户 指直辖市、省辖市、地级市、县级市的市区、市郊区及县城(包括县人民政府所在地的县城关区或行政建制相当于县人民政府所在地的镇)范围内接入局用交换机的电话用户数，包括分布在农村地区的独立工矿区、林区、驻军等接入局用交换机的电话用户数。

农村电话用户 指县城关区以下的集镇和农村接入局用交换机的电话用户数。

Explanatory Notes on Main Statistical Indicators

Length of Railways in Operation also is known as operating length and refers to the investment business or temporary operating passenger and freight transport line length.

Length of Highways refers to the actual length of road during the reporting period. Statistical range: The length of highways includes that the car can travel on public roads in intercity, urban and rural areas, township (village). Road through the town streets mileage, length of roads and bridges, tunnel length, crossing width. It does not include the length of streets in big and medium-sized cities and highways built for the production purpose at factories, mines, forest areas and agricultural areas. Statistical principles: It is on the basis of final acceptance or delivery of the actual mileage calculation. If two or more highways go the same section of the way, the length of the section is only calculated for once and no duplication is allowed.

Length of Navigable Inland Waterways is an indicator reflecting the size and development of inland water network. It refers to the length of the natural rivers, lakes, reservoirs, canals, and ditches open to navigation during a given period, which enables transportation by ships and rafts. It includes the channels open to navigation for over an accumulated period of 3 months in a year, yet this does not include the river courses which are only used to float odd logs and bamboo rafts. For fear of repeating calculation, the length of waterways of boundary rivers between two provinces is reckon in a half for each province. This indicator can reflect the scale, level and development situation of the inland waterway network.

Freight (Passenger) Traffic refers to the volume of freight (passenger) transported with various means. Freight transport is calculated in tons and passenger traffic is calculated in the number of persons. Despite the type of freight and travelling distance, the freight transport is calculated in the actual weight of the goods: and despite the travelling distance and ticket price, the passenger traffic is calculated by the principle that one person can be counted only once in one travel. The passenger who travel with a half price ticket or a child ticket is also calculated as one person.

Freight Ton-kilometers (Passenger-kilometers) refer to the sum of the products of the volume of transported cargo (passengers) multiplying by the transport distance, usually using ton-kilometer and passenger-kilometer as units for measurement. Normally, the shortest distance between the departure station and the destination station (i.e., the payable distance) is the basis to calculate the freight ton-kilometers. The formula is as follows:

$$\text{Freight Ton-kilometers (Passenger-kilometers)} = \sum \{\text{Freight (Passenger) Traffic} \times \text{Distance of Transportation}\}$$

Mobile Telephone Subscribers are connected with the mobile telephone communication network through the mobile telephone switchboards and occupy mobile phone numbers. In the reporting period the number of users in the mobile phone operating divisions actual registration number of households into the mobile phone network to calculate a statistic as a mobile phone.

Local Telephone Subscribers refers to all subscribers who have gone through registration procedures in the operation points of enterprises engaged in telecommunications and are hence connected to the local telecommunications service provider through fixed line network. Included are general subscribers, public telephones subscribers, N-ISDN subscribers and intelligent network terminal subscribers. They are also classified in terms of administrative districts as urban telephone subscribers and rural telephone subscribers according to location. Before 1997, the "local phone users" refers to access cities above county and county telephone line telephone subscribers; "Rural

Telephone User" refers to access the post office, if farmers Taiwan county and below county rural telephone exchange points, to the county as the center (except local subscriber outside) Unicom county and township (town), administrative villages, village groups of users. From 1997 onwards, the number of telephone users adjust to the user group area classified as "urban telephone subscribers" and "rural telephone subscribers," with the past by local and rural telephone divided in different ways. But the number of telephone users and telephone statistical range are unchanged.

Urban Telephone Subscribers refers to number of telephone subscribers, located at municipalities, cities under the jurisdiction of province, cities at prefecture level, downtown and suburb of city at county level town and county towns (including country towns where county government located, and towns of county level according to the administrative organizational system), that are connected to the public line telephone network, including rural mineral area, forest area, military area.

Rural Telephone Subscribers refers to telephone subscribers, located at the towns below the level of county town and villages, that are connected to the public line telephone network.

批发和零售业

17

Wholesale and Retail Trades

17-1 社会消费品零售总额
Total Retail Sales of Consumer Goods

单位：亿元 (100 million yuan)

指标	Item	2010	2011	2012	2013	2014
社会消费品零售总额	**Total Retail Sales of Consumer Goods**	**1531.64**	**1899.92**	**2266.27**	**2601.20**	**2936.85**
按地域分	**By Area**					
城镇	Urban	1253.74	1561.07	1863.59	2148.26	2425.25
乡村	Rural	277.90	338.85	402.68	452.94	511.60
按行业分	**By Sector**					
批发和零售业	Wholesale and Retail Trade	1373.41	1710.15	2049.70	2370.95	2679.29
住宿和餐饮业	Hotel and Catering Services	158.23	189.77	216.57	230.25	257.56

17-2 限额以上批发业和零售业
Basic Conditions of Enterprises above Designated Size of Wholesale and Retail Trades

指标	Item	2010	2011	2012	2013	2014
批发业	**Wholesale Trade**					
法人企业(个)	Number of Corporation Enterprises(unit)	306	332	487	640	780
年末从业人数(人)	Engaged persons Year-end(person)	41066	45691	51372	51442	57986
商品购进额(亿元)	Total Purchases Value(100 million yuan)	776.73	1124.58	1419.29	1878.97	2042.79
商品销售额(亿元)	Total Sales Value(100 million yuan)	1095.34	1309.90	1907.99	2391.89	2750.52
期末商品库存额(亿元)	Stock(year-end)(100 million yuan)	93.47	127.38	175.80	223.23	230.47
零售业	**Retail Trade**					
法人企业(个)	Number of Corporations Enterprises(unit)	494	555	793	1178	1463
年末从业人数(人)	Engaged Persons at Year-end(person)	38154	44045	54865	67485	78431
商品购进额(亿元)	Total Purchases value(100 million yuan)	423.39	588.27	764.09	970.87	1139.38
商品销售额(亿元)	Total Sales value(100 million yuan)	487.38	690.58	898.82	1143.96	1399.19
期末商品库存额(亿元)	Total stock at Year-end(100 million yuan)	42.11	59.71	76.89	89.11	151.30
年末零售营业面积(万平方米)	Retail Operating Area at year-end(10000 sq.m)	212.03	230.85	203.48	294.38	357.01

17-3 限额以上批发业企业(2014)

单位：万元

指 标	Item	法人企业(个) Number of Corporation Enterprises (Unit)
合 计	**Total**	**780**
按登记注册类型分	**by Status of Registration Status**	
内资企业	**Domestic Funded Enterprises**	**777**
国有企业	State-owned Enterprises	52
集体企业	Collective-owned Enterprises	22
股份合作企业	Cooperative Enterprises	1
联营企业	Joint Ownership Enterprises	
有限责任公司	Limited Liability Corporations	346
国有独资公司	State Sole Funded Corporations	39
其他有限责任公司	Other Limited Liability Corporations	307
股份有限公司	Share-holding Corporations Ltd.	27
私营企业	Private Enterprises	328
私营独资企业	Private-funded Enterprises	3
私营有限责任公司	Private Limited Liability Corporations	311
私营股份有限公司	Private Share-holding Co.Ltd	14
其他企业	Other Enterprises	1
港、澳、台商投资企业	**Enterprises with Funds From HongKong, Macao and Taiwan**	
外商投资企业	**Foreign Funded Enterprises**	**3**
中外合资经营企业	Joint-venture Enterprises	3
按国民经济行业分	**by Sector**	
#农、林、牧产品批发	**Wholesale of Agricultural,Forestry and Livestock Products**	**11**
谷物、豆及薯类批发	Wholesale of Grain, Beans and Potatoes	3
种子批发	Wholesale of Seeds	2
饲料批发	Wholesale of Feed	3
牲畜批发	Wholesale of Livestock	2
其他农畜产品批发	Others	1
食品、饮料及烟草制品批发	**Wholesale of Food,Beverages and Tobaccos**	**129**
#米、面制品及食用油批发	Wholesale of Rice,Flour and Edible Oil	25
糕点、糖果及糖批发	Wholesale of Pastries, Candy and Sugar	1
果品、蔬菜批发	Wholesale of Fruit and Vegetables	6
肉、禽、蛋及水产品批发	Wholesale of Meat, Poultry, Eggs and Aquatic Products	13
盐及调味品批发	Wholesale of Salt and Condiment	15
营养和保健品批发		1
酒、饮料及茶叶批发	Wholesale of Wine,Beverages and Tea	58
烟草制品批发	Wholesale of Tobaccos	10
纺织、服装及家庭用品批发	**Wholesale of Textiles,Wearing Apparel and Household Artides**	**36**

注：表中行业分类按国民经济行业分类(GB/T4754—2011分)(以下相关表同)。

Basic Conditions of Enterprises above Designated Size of Wholesale Trade

(10000 yuan)

从业人数 (人) Engaged Persons (person)	购进 总额 Total Value	销售 总额 Total value	批发 Wholesale Trade	零售 Retail Trade	年末 库存额 Stock (year-end)
57986	**20427859.8**	**27505212.0**	**25103764.6**	**2401447.4**	**2304690.7**
57728	**20322648.9**	**27392360.6**	**24991894.9**	**2400465.7**	**2303302.2**
23190	5370011.6	7227222.2	7194240.7	32981.5	1113810.7
975	117539.3	120510.9	105471.5	15039.4	21566.6
10	2050.3	2303.1	2303.1		514.1
20813	10575471.9	15105366.8	13220224.0	1885142.8	746439.6
3977	4115228.6	7820583.3	6582368.0	1238215.3	327176.4
16836	6460243.3	7284783.5	6637856.0	646927.5	419263.2
1943	1497723.0	1894751.6	1547266.1	347485.5	105433.7
10787	2757060.8	3039314.0	2919933.2	119380.8	315527.5
20	16186.1	17045.8	14836.7	2209.1	285.5
10342	2633664.7	2905614.1	2789727.1	115887.0	309438.9
425	107210.0	116654.1	115369.4	1284.7	5803.1
10	2792.0	2892.0	2456.3	435.7	10.0
258	**105210.9**	**112851.4**	**111869.7**	**981.7**	**1388.5**
258	105210.9	112851.4	111869.7	981.7	1388.5
361	**39590.7**	**41999.0**	**40348.0**	**1651.0**	**8840.5**
160	7556.9	10525.7	10426.2	99.5	2772.4
106	9456.8	8400.2	8400.2		4722.2
28	15834.0	15818.6	15818.6		1062.6
47	2929.4	3684.4	3667.8	16.6	39.8
20	3813.6	3570.1	2035.2	1534.9	243.5
29502	**6086700.6**	**10952541.1**	**10191238.1**	**761303.0**	**1305921.3**
1600	198897.6	203610.9	186638.4	16972.5	101207.0
39	618.9	4348.4	3987.8	360.6	654.2
443	103816.8	105047.2	68747.9	36299.3	1540.1
598	48854.6	52469.5	50177.4	2292.1	3770.2
1012	159229.1	191864.1	183098.6	8765.5	15277.8
173	25250.6	25808.3	25808.3		4386.5
5626	1427715.6	4473164.5	3779123.2	694041.3	154029.0
20011	4122317.4	5896228.2	5893656.5	2571.7	1025056.5
2197	**390700**	**397949**	**379497**	**18452**	**77548**

Note: industries in this table are classifiated by sector of national economy industry(GB/T4754-2011)(the relative tables in this chapter are the same)

17-3 续表

单位：万元

指 标	Item	法人企业(个) Number of Corporation Enterprises (Unit)
服装批发	Wholesale of Garments	7
鞋帽批发	Wholesale of Shoes and Hats	3
化妆品及卫生用品批发	Wholesale of Cosmetics and Hygiene Products	3
厨房、卫生间用具及日用杂货批发	Wholesale of Kitchen and Lavatory Appliance and Daily Consumer Groceries	4
家用电器批发	Wholesale of Household Electrical Appliances	18
其他家庭用品批发	Wholesale of Other Daily Consumer Goods	1
文化、体育用品及器材批发	**Wholesale of Culture,Sports Appliances and Equipments**	**13**
#文具用品批发	Wholesale of Stationery	4
图书批发	Wholesale of Books	6
首饰、工艺品及收藏品批发	Wholesale of Jewelry,Arts and Crafts and Collections	1
其他文化用品批发	Wholesale of Other Cultural Articles	2
医药及医疗器材批发	**Wholesale of Medicines and Medical Appliances**	**79**
西药批发	Wholesale of Western Medicines	58
中药批发	Wholesale of Traditional Chinese Medicines	18
医疗用品及器材批发	Wholesale of Medical Articles and Appliances	3
矿产品、建材及化工产品批发	**Wholesale of Mineral Products,Building Materials and Chemical Products**	**402**
#煤炭及制品批发	Wholesale of Coal and Related Products	142
石油及制品批发	Wholesale of Petroleum and Related Products	19
非金属矿及制品批发	Wholesale of Non-metallic Minerals and Related Products	10
金属及金属矿批发	Wholesale of Metal Materials	70
建材批发	Wholesale of Building Materials	53
化肥批发	Wholesale of Chemical Fertilizer	61
其他化工产品批发	Wholesale of Other Chemical Materials	47
机械设备、五金交电及电子产品批发	**Wholesale of Machinery,Hardware and Electronic Products**	**99**
农业机械批发	Wholesale of Agricultural Machinery	4
汽车批发	Wholesale of Motor Vehicles	23
汽车零配件批发	Wholesale of Auto Parts	8
摩托车及零配件批发	Wholesale of Motorcycle Parts & Accessories	6
五金产品批发	Wholesale of Hardware Products	8
电气设备批发	Wholesale of Electrical Equipment	1
计算机、软件及辅助设备批发	Wholesale of Computer,Software and Assistance Appliances	7
通讯及广播电视设备批发	Wholesale of Communication , Radio and Television Equipments	4
其他机械设备及电子产品批发	Wholesale of Other Machinery Equipments and Electric Products	38
贸易经纪与代理	**Trade Broker and Agency**	
其他批发	**Others Wholesale not Classified Elsewhere**	**11**
再生物资回收与批发	Wholesale and Reclaim of Regeneration Materials	3
其他未列明的批发	Other Wholesale Unlisted	8

continued

(10000 yuan)

从业人数 (人) Engaged Persons (person)	购进总额 Total Value	销售总额 Total value	批发 Wholesale Trade	零售 Retail Trade	年末库存额 Stock (year-end)
324	47413	50228	49278	950	11092
246	21080.3	23384.5	22836.4	548.1	2030
160	9497.0	11286.4	11286.4		3514
242	17391.5	18545.4	17445.2	1100.2	3438
1190	290823.1	289718.4	275073.3	14645.1	57130
35	4495.1	4785.8	3577.5	1208.3	345
512	**202721.1**	**207374.5**	**204918.0**	**2456.5**	**20722**
103	25290.8	28268.0	27900.0	368.0	7296
349	165441.8	166505.1	166008.0	497.1	11723
3	2143.6	2646.1	2190.6	455.5	140
57	9844.9	9955.3	8819.4	1135.9	1563
5698	**1076947.7**	**1315063.1**	**1230900.2**	**84162.9**	**135583**
4484	841469.8	1049363.6	985811.4	63552.2	92549
1158	226885.3	252720.4	232109.7	20610.7	42137
56	8592.6	12979.1	12979.1		897
15064	**11439874.7**	**13273050.9**	**11794120.5**	**1478930.4**	**620290**
5538	2425790.5	2762725.9	2693971.9	68754.0	50355
3241	1209306.2	2491529.2	1145113.3	1346415.9	49722
168	131699.3	140679.4	140679.4		2898
1712	2389392.5	2456462.8	2437912.1	18550.7	138870
749	836445.8	879007.6	859060.1	19947.5	86374
1885	2927249.5	2902865.4	2881386.1	21479.3	196538
1771	1519990.9	1639780.6	1635997.6	3783.0	95533
4186	**1121173.9**	**1238612.8**	**1184350.2**	**54262.6**	**133603**
68	14415.0	16923.2	12229.4	4693.8	3126
632	154004.6	159312.2	147862.2	11450.0	15500
324	320273.9	345388.4	344244.5	1143.9	7362
157	101030.1	104225.1	103698.3	526.8	9979
190	61310.3	65507.6	65169.4	338.2	8030
8	4074.1	4258.1	4200.0	58.1	90
217	38722.1	40532.5	34287.8	6244.7	3218
267	87777.1	95885.0	91596.0	4289.0	22263
2323	339566.7	406580.7	381062.6	25518.1	64036
466	**70150.7**	**78622.1**	**78393.1**	**229.0**	**2182**
174	23010.3	27648.0	27419.0	229.0	727
292	47140.4	50974.1	50974.1		1456

17-4 限额以上批发业企业主要财务指标(2014)

Main Financial Indicators of Enterprises above Designated Size of Wholesale Trade

单位：万元 (10000 yuan)

指标	Item	主营业务收入 Revenue from Principal Business	主营业务成本 Cost of Principal Business	主营业务税金及附加 Taxes and Other Charges on Principal Business	销售费用 Selling Expenses	营业利润 Operating Profits
总计	**Total**	**23716768**	**19718829**	**332750**	**848604**	**2115062**
按登记注册类型分	**by Statys of Registration**					
内资企业	**Domestic Funded Enterprises**	**23620313**	**19626878**	**332610**	**843091**	**2110528**
国有企业	State-owned Enterprises	6236932	4673782	244792	320948	671635
集体企业	Collective-owned Enterprises	131159	114413	584	3895	6278
股份合作企业	Copperative Enterprise	1969	1806	10	79	7
联营企业	Joint Ownership Enterprises					
有限责任公司	Limited Liability Corporations	12733682	10662695	66142	366158	1356865
国有独资公司	State Sole Fundal Corporations	6199348	4567449	49259	166059	1330135
其他有限责任公司	Other Limited Liability Corporations	6534333	6095246	16883	200099	26730
股份有限公司	Share-holding Co.Ltd	1794945	1664718	13392	39042	61846
私营企业	Private Enterprises	2718735	2506684	7688	112903	13870
私营独资企业	Private-funded Enterprises	16646	15096	302	369	341
私营有限责任公司	Private Limited Liability Corporations	2600972	2396473	7275	109913	13096
私营股份有限公司	Private Share-holding Co.Ltd	101117	95116	111	2622	433
其他企业	Other Enterprises	2892	2780	2	67	28
港、澳、台商投资企业	**Enterprises with Funds From HongKong, Macao and Taiwan**					
外商投资企业	**Foreign Funded Enterprises**	**96455**	**91950**	**140**	**5513**	**4533**
中外合资经营企业	Joint-venture Enterprises	96455	91950	140	5513	4533
按国民经济行业分	**by Sector**					
农、林、牧产品批发	**Wholesale Agricultural, Forestry Livestock Products**	**39779**	**37229**	**58**	**493**	**72**
#谷物、豆及薯类批发	Wholesale of Grain, Beans and Potatoes	10138	9749	39	120	-21
种子批发	Wholesale of Seeds	8400	6987		272	395
饲料批发	Wholesale of Feed	13933	13558	15		-281
牲畜批发	Wholesale of Livestock	3598	3237	4	101	-19
其他农畜产品批发	Others	3710	3699			-3
食品、饮料及烟草制品批发	**Wholesale of Food,Beverages and Tobaccos**	**8541864**	**5300276**	**282225**	**488058**	**2055221**
#米、面制品及食用油批发	Wholesale of Rice,Flour and Edible Oil	197896	173339	241	10262	-1125
糕点、糖果及糖批发	Wholesale of Pastries, Candy and Sugar	3876	3605	5		207
果品、蔬菜批发	Wholesale of Fruit and Vegetables	100394	96048	1095	724	1660
肉、禽、蛋及水产品批发	Wholesale of Meat, Poultry, Eggs and Aquatic Products	48147	41335	1380	3298	989
盐及调味品批发	Wholesale of Salt and Condiment	176327	140438	1038	11218	5890
营养和保健品批发		22167	21030	56		283
酒、饮料及茶叶批发	Wholesale of Wine，Beverages and Tea	2893424	1072516	62121	253649	1417926
烟草制品批发	Wholesale of Tobaccos	5099634	3751966	216288	208907	629392
纺织、服装及家庭用品批发	**Wholesale of Textiles,Wearing Apparel and Household Artides**	**344077**	**315921**	**710**	**17323**	**2103**

17-4 续表 continued

单位：万元 (10000 yuan)

指 标	Item	主营业务收入 Revenue from Principal Business	主营业务成本 Cost of Principal Business	主营业务税金及附加 Taxes and Other Charges on Principal Business	销售费用 Selling Expenses	营业利润 Operating Profits
服装批发	Wholesale of Garments	42921	39617	74	1724	62
鞋帽批发	Wholesale of Shoes and Hats	19987	17578	60	1010	135
化妆品及卫生用品批发	Wholesale of Cosmetics and Hygiene Products	10047	8788	16	131	123
厨房、卫生间用具及日用杂货批发	Wholesale of Kitchen and Lavatory Appliance and Daily Consumer Groceries	17477	16092	68	848	-568
家用电器批发	Wholesale of Household Electrical Appliances	249555	230004	485	13430	2337
其他家庭用品批发	Wholesale of Other Daily Consumer Goods	4090	3842	7	179	14
文化、体育用品及器材批发	**Wholesale of Culture,Sports Appliances and Equipments**	**166546**	**135524**	**605**	**3803**	**23859**
#文具用品批发	Wholesale of Stationery	24161	22904	66	634	196
体育用品及器材批发	Wholesale of Sporting Goods					
图书批发	Wholesale of Books	131265	102231	178	2935	23729
首饰、工艺品及收藏品批发	Wholesale of Jewelry,Arts and Crafts and Collectibles	2646	2292	344		5
其他文化用品批发	Wholesale of Other Cultural Articles	8474	8096	17	234	-71
医药及医疗器材批发	**Wholesale of Medicines and Medical Appliances**	**1136631**	**1029875**	**2772**	**48461**	**17074**
西药批发	Wholesale of Western Medicine	906820	829421	1999	29963	14964
中药批发	Wholesale of Chinese Traditional Medicines	218718	190759	723	18100	1623
医疗用品及器材批发	Wholesale of Medical Articles and Appliances	11093	9695	49	397	486
矿产品、建材及化工产品批发	**Wholesale of Mineral Products,Building Materials and Chemical Products**	**12343420**	**11844132**	**43991**	**242563**	**15269**
#煤炭及制品批发	Wholesale of Coal and Related Products	2611773	2454948	10875	92138	-42411
石油及制品批发	Wholesale of Petroleum and products	2111525	2050637	2651	42893	-1843
非金属矿及制品批发	Wholesale of Non-metallic Minerals and Products	122838	118457	1380	753	1752
金属及金属矿批发	Wholesale of Metal Materials	2224288	2151415	3525	24343	25963
建材批发	Wholesale of Building Materials	777295	739620	1467	9288	5351
化肥批发	Wholesale of Chemical Fertilizer	2923119	2842077	13228	33885	9748
其他化工产品批发	Wholesale of Other Chemical Materials	1572583	1486978	10865	39263	16709
机械设备、五金交电及电子产品批发	**Wholesale of Machinery,Hardware and Electronic Products**	**1073926**	**994408**	**2025**	**44897**	**-1703**
农业机械批发	Wholesale of Agricultural Machinery	15649	13663	29	893	116
汽车批发	Wholesale of Motor Vehicles	142316	135706	320	3015	-1541
汽车零配件批发	Wholesale of Auto Parts	292936	279250	187	10443	179
摩托车及零配件批发	Wholesale of Motorcycle Parts & Accessories	88458	84106	120	2319	1179
五金产品批发	Wholesale of Hardware Products	56301	51506	99	1679	1143
电气设备批发	Wholesale of Electrical Equipment	4249	4074	9	15	5
计算机、软件及辅助设备批发	Wholesale of Computer,Software and Assistance Appliances	34643	32806	67	436	250
通讯及广播电视设备批发	Wholesale of Communications and Broadcasting Equipment	82559	77831	247	413	-2457
其他机械设备及电子产品批发	Others	356816	315468	945	25684	-577
贸易经纪与代理	**Trade Broker and Agency**					
其他批发	**Others Wholesale not Classified Elsewhere**	**70526**	**61463**	**364**	**3006**	**3166**
再生物资回收与批发	Wholesale and Reclaim of Regeneration Materials	23445	20337	121	409	1228
其他未列明批发	Other Wholesale Unlisted	47081	41125	243	2597	1938

17–5 限额以上零售业企业(2014)

单位：万元

指 标	Item	法人企业(个) Number of Corporations Enterprises (Unit)
合 计	**Total**	**1463**
按登记注册类型分	**by Status of Registration**	
内资企业	**Domestic Funded Enterprises**	**1439**
国有企业	State-owned Enterprises	43
集体企业	Collective-owned Enterprises	8
股份合作企业	Cooperation Enterprises	3
联营企业	Joint Ownership Enterprises	1
#集体联营企业	Collective Joint Ownership Enterprises	1
有限责任公司	Limited Liability Corporations	612
国有独资公司	State Sole Funded Corporations	22
其他有限责任公司	Other Limited Liability Corporations	590
股份有限公司	Share-holding Corporations Ltd.	30
私营企业	Private Enterprises	735
私营独资企业	Private-funded Enterprise	75
私营合伙企业	Private Partnership Enterprises	8
私营有限责任公司	Private Limited Liability Corporations	626
私营股份有限公司	Private Share-holding Co.Ltd	26
其他	Other Enterprises	7
港、澳、台商投资企业	**Enterprises with Funds From Hongkong, Macao and Taiwan**	**13**
#合资经营企业(港或澳、台资)	Joint-venture Enterprises	8
港、澳、台商独资经营企业	Enterpises with Sole Fund	5
外商投资企业	**Foreign Funded Enterprises**	**11**
#中外合资经营企业	Joint-venture Enterprises	2
外资企业	Enterprises with Sole Fund	9
外商投资股份有限公司	Share-holding Corporations Ltd. With Foreign Investment	
按国民经济行业分	**by Sector**	
综合零售	**Integrated Retail**	**230**
百货零售	Retail of General Merchandise	101
超级市场零售	Retail of Supermarkets	118
其他综合零售	Other Integrated Retail	11
食品、饮料及烟草制品专门零售	**Retail of Food,Beverages and Tobaccos**	**168**
粮油零售	Retail of Grain and Oil	37
糕点、面包零售	Retail of Pastries and Bread	2
果品、蔬菜零售	Retail of Fruits and Vegetables	6
肉、禽、蛋及水产品零售	Retail of Meat, Poultry, Eggs and Aquatic Products	5
营养和保健品零售	Retail of Nutrition and health products	1
酒、饮料及茶叶零售	Retail of Wine,Beverages and Tea	91
烟草制品零售	Retail of Tobaccos	1
其他食品零售	Other Food Retail	25
纺织品、服装及日用品专门零售	**Sperial Retail of Textiles,Wearing Apparel and Household Artides**	**31**
#纺织品及针织品零售	Retail of Textiles and Knitwear	1
服装零售	Retail of Garments	21
鞋帽零售	Retail of Shoes and Hats	3

Basic Conditions of Enterprises above Designated Size in Retail Trade

(10000 yuan)

从业人数 (人) Engaged Persons (person)	购进总额 Total Vslus	销售总额 Total Vslus	批发 Wholesale Trade	零售 Retail Trade	年末库存额 Stock (year-end)
78431	**11393825**	**13991866**	**1686029**	**12305837**	**1513032**
72892	**10806913**	**13306157**	**1657638**	**11648519**	**1467158**
1293	196119	194402	25528	168873	17542
79	33401	33540	8054	25486	3852
250	35980	44002		44002	1361
16	27427	29415		29415	765
16	27427	29415		29415	765
35772	5020090	5425189	525338	4899851	587687
837	57160	91605	8497	83108	22390
34935	4962930	5333585	516842	4816743	565297
6568	2422382	4238135	721625	3516510	92768
28489	3066923	3334767	376643	2958125	762545
1271	75581	80930	2761	78169	8982
180	10350	10695		10695	1421
26419	2921825	3183261	363361	2819901	744736
619	59167	59880	10521	49360	7406
425	4591	6707	450	6257	638
2486	**291464**	**372043**	**28391**	**343652**	**20125**
1151	247487	316142	16087	300055	16218
1335	43977	55902	12304	43597	3907
3053	**295447**	**313666**		**313666**	**25750**
1145	160042	148497		148497	12392
1908	135406	165169		165169	13358
26577	**1496229**	**1705527**	**15864**	**1689664**	**158942**
8431	685378	851736	7838	843899	46685
15521	730364	768095	1231	766864	103063
2625	80487	85695	6795	78901	9195
3905	**381082**	**458428**	**132327**	**326101**	**59541**
1084	48843	54202	5907	48295	18165
20	493	1227		1227	92
432	20657	25454	19201	6253	552
91	109955	110236	48888	61348	151
14	554	531		531	103
1775	158549	216719	51573	165146	34777
92	18490	23236		23236	2076
397	23540	26823	6758	20065	3625
2065	**121260**	**157576**	**12773**	**144803**	**24323**
12	759	807		807	56
1862	103536	138440	11823	126617	21916
63	2879	3156		3156	46

17-5 续表

单位：万元

指 标	Item	法人企业(个) Number of Corporations Enterprises (Unit)
化妆品及卫生用品零售	Retail of Cosmetics and Hygiene Products	1
钟表、眼镜零售	Retail of Horologe and Spectacles	3
厨房用具及日用杂品零售	Retail of Kitchen utensils and household goods	1
其他日用品零售	Retail of Other Daily Consumer Use	1
文化、体育用品及器材专门零售	**Retail of Culture,Sporting Apliances and Equipments**	**55**
文具用品零售	Retail of Stationery	3
体育用品及器材零售	Retail of Sports Goods	2
图书零售、报刊零售	Retail of Books, newspapers and periodicals	35
音像制品及电子出版物零售	Retail of Audio and Visual Products and Electronic Publications	1
珠宝首饰零售	Retail of Jewelry	7
工艺美术品及收藏品零售	Retail of Arts and Crafts and Collections	2
乐器零售	Retail of Musical Instruments	1
照相器材零售	Retail of Photographic Equipment	3
其他文化用品零售	Retail of Other Cultural Articles	1
医药及医疗器材专门零售	**Retail of Medicines and Medical Appliances**	**88**
药品零售	Retail of Medicines	71
医疗用品及器材零售	Retail of Medicines and Medical Appliances	17
汽车、摩托车、燃料及零配件专门零售	**Retail of Motor Vehicles, Motorcycles, Fuel and Parts**	**626**
汽车零售	Retail of Motor Vehicles	523
汽车零配件零售	Retail of Auto Parts and Accessories	9
摩托车及零配件零售	Retail of Motorcycles,Parts and Accessories	29
机动车燃料零售	Retail of Fuel of Motor Vehicles	65
家用电器及电子产品专门零售	**Special Retail of Household Electric Appliances and Electronic Products**	**194**
家用试听设备零售	Retail of Listen household equipment	33
日用家电设备零售	Retail of Household appliances	93
计算机、软件及辅助设备零售	Retail of Computer,Software and Assistant Appliances	48
通讯设备零售	Retail of Communication Equipments	19
其他电子产品零售	Retail of Other Electronic Products	1
五金、家具及室内装修材料专门零售	**Special Retail of Hardware, Furniture and Interior Decoration Materials**	**36**
#五金零售	Retail of Hardware	9
家具零售	Retail of Furniture	20
木质装饰材料零售	Retail of Wooden decorative materials	1
陶瓷、石材装饰材料零售	Retail of Ceramics, Stone Decoration Materials	1
其他室内装修材料零售	Retail of Other Interior Decoration Materials	5
货摊、无店铺及其他零售	**Stalls,Non-shop and Other Retails**	**35**
#互联网零售	Retail of Internet	2
邮购及电视、电话零售	Retail of Mail order, TV and telephone	1
旧货零售	Retail of Second-hand Goods	1
生活用燃料零售	Retail of life Fuel	15
其他未列明的零售	Other Retails Unlisted	16

continued

(10000 yuan)

从业人数 (人) Engaged Persons (person)	购进 总额 Total Vslus	销售 总额 Total Vslus	批发 Wholesale Trade	零售 Retail Trade	年末 库存额 Stock (year-end)
18	3490	3519		3519	816
63	4281	4393	830	3564	1017
39	4776	5853		5853	341
8	1539	1409	121	1288	131
1828	**161875**	**174890**	**20931**	**153959**	**24883**
31	4411	4575	624	3951	392
57	2166	2634	258	2375	1151
1327	128734	134692	14394	120298	12145
84	8325	7760		7760	1732
206	9823	14445		14445	6935
14	919	1413	137	1277	444
6	635	699		699	59
51	3693	4233	1088	3145	1740
52	3170	4439	4430	9	287
7966	**732138**	**778030**	**259871**	**518158**	**83888**
7609	638355	661916	229476	432441	74901
357	93783	116113	30396	85717	8987
28138	**7649804**	**9721450**	**1062823**	**8658627**	**1073522**
20605	4681687	4928116	235476	4692639	970601
111	43265	49271	11620	37651	4609
401	32412	34749	1367	33381	5624
7021	2892441	4709315	814360	3894955	92689
5706	**582444**	**659943**	**103991**	**555952**	**64640**
804	66674	70858	5183	65675	12393
3186	370461	421710	33057	388653	34106
774	64442	76020	18880	57140	6330
722	75135	81917	46872	35046	11467
220	5733	9437		9437	343
563	**47630**	**54883**	**3487**	**51396**	**11707**
79	11927	14491	995	13496	2087
381	15341	15347	904	14443	7671
24	2417	3027		3027	822
25	14021	18221	689	17532	599
54	3924	3798	899	2898	528
1683	**221363**	**281140**	**73962**	**207177**	**11587**
18	22400	32762	28745	4017	709
570	113067	147726	13027	134699	1678
3	721	729		729	12
685	59109	70365	18113	52251	4118
407	26066	29558	14077	15481	5070

17-6 限额以上零售业企业主要财务指标(2014)

Main Financial Indicators of Enterprises above Designated Size of Retail Trade

单位：万元 (10000 yuan)

指标	Item	主营业务收入 Revenue from Principal Business	主营业务成本 Cost of Principal Business	主营业务税金及附加 Taxes and Other Charges on Principal Business	销售费用 Selling Expenses	营业利润 Operating Profits
总计	**Total**	**11699778**	**10453245**	**45404**	**564769**	**404054**
按登记注册类型分	**by Status of Registration**					
内资企业	**Domestic Funded Enterprises**	**11115832**	**9970727**	**41795**	**501441**	**359930**
国有企业	State-owned Enterprises	191962	170472	417	9526	3115
集体企业	Collective-owned Enterprises	32117	29794	66	745	3483
股份合作企业	Cooperation Enterprises	38846	35951	71	1214	406
联营企业	Joint Ownership Enterprises	29415	23559	32	1236	2747
#集体联营企业	Collective Joint Ownership Enterprises	29415	23559	32	1236	2747
有限责任公司	Limited Liability Corporations	4667713	4179308	25326	260799	81644
国有独资公司	State Sole Funded Corporations	83312	62109	2313	7491	4634
其他有限责任公司	Other Limited Liability Corporations	4584401	4117199	23013	253308	77010
股份有限公司	Share-holding Corporations Ltd.	3161418	2827791	3509	93502	228211
私营企业	Private Enterprises	2987698	2698443	12324	133962	39699
私营独资企业	Private-funded Enterprises	76613	66954	702	3251	2998
私营合伙企业	Private Partnership Enterprises	9923	8452	88	559	257
私营有限责任公司	Private Limited Liability Corporations	2836649	2564713	11151	127817	34910
私营股份有限公司	Private Share Holding Co.Ltd	64513	58324	384	2336	1534
其他	Other Enterprises	6664	5411	50	458	626
港、澳、台商投资企业	**Enterprises with Funds From HongKong, Macao and Taiwan**	**318428**	**267928**	**1879**	**33678**	**21607**
合资经营企业(港或澳、台资)	Joint-venture Enterprises	268458	228078	1596	21185	22104
合作经营企业(港或澳、台资)	Cooperative Enterprises					
港、澳、台商独资经营企业	Enterpises with Sole Fund	49970	39850	283	12494	-498
其他港、澳、台商投资企业	Others					
外商投资企业	**Foreign Funded Enterprises**	**265519**	**214590**	**1729**	**29650**	**22517**
中外合资经营企业	Joint-venture Enterprises	126921	102100	1006	11069	13341
外资企业	Enterprises with Sole Fund	138598	112491	724	18581	9176
按国民经济行业分	**by Sector**					
综合零售	**Integrated Retail**	**1458382**	**1220031**	**12062**	**167348**	**64466**
百货零售	Retail of General Merchandise	700708	586968	8073	75226	42251
超级市场零售	Retail of Supermarkets	677323	564668	3749	86572	19317
其他综合零售	Other Integrated Retail	80351	68395	241	5550	2898
食品、饮料及烟草制品专门零售	**Retail of Food,Beverages and Tobaccos**	**409595**	**349765**	**5339**	**29222**	**6170**
粮油零售	Retail of Grain and Oil	52103	48755	175	2974	-3754
糕点、面包零售	Retail of Pastries and Bread	1159	895	53	22	123
果品、蔬菜零售	Retail of Fruits and Vegetables	22800	20280	53	1220	943
肉、禽、蛋奶及水产品零售	Retail of Meat, Poultry, Eggs and Aquatic Products	94688	89831	63	2310	67
营养和保健品零售	Retail of nutrition and health care products	515	438	15	20	13
酒、饮料及茶叶零售	Retail of Wine,Beverages and Tea	193394	154084	4383	19645	4975
烟草制品零售	Retail of Tobaccos	19860	15200	84	1138	2942
其他食品零售	Other Food Retail	25075	20284	515	1893	862
纺织品、服装及日用品专门零售	**Special Retail of Textiles,Wearing Apparel and Household Articles**	**130234**	**103880**	**1031**	**16541**	**5449**
纺织品及针织品零售	Retail of Textiles and Knitwear	689	601	2	51	9
服装零售	Retail of Garments	113810	90157	859	15182	4967
鞋帽零售	Retail of Shoes and Hats	2709	2335	33	215	84

17-6 续表 continued

单位：万元 (10000 yuan)

指 标	Item	主营业务收入 Revenue from Principal Business	主营业务成本 Cost of Principal Business	主营业务税金及附加 Taxes and Other Charges on Principal Business	销售费用 Selling Expenses	营业利润 Operating Profits
化妆品及卫生用品零售	Retail of Cosmetic and Hygiene Products	3007	2718	2	200	9
钟表、眼镜零售	Retail of Horologe and Spectacles	3813	3389	10	344	18
厨房用具及日用杂品零售	Retail of Kitchen utensils and household goods	5002	4036	27	549	182
其他日用品零售	Retail of Other Daily Consumer Use	1204	645	98		181
文化、体育用品及器材专门零售	**Retail of Culture,Sports Apliances and Equipments**	**162024**	**131221**	**1099**	**10439**	**7942**
文具用品零售	Retail of Stationery	3852	3192	351	85	157
体育用品及器材零售	Retail of Sporting Goods	2251	1909	27	158	56
图书、报刊零售	Retail of Books, newspapers and periodicals	125814	101638	166	8358	6640
音像制品及电子出版物零售	Retail of Audio and Visual Products and Electronic Publications	7526	5810	5	562	396
珠宝首饰零售	Retail of Jewelry	13364	10854	530	868	284
工艺美术品及收藏品零售	Retail of Arts and Crafts and Collections	1291	847	8	24	332
乐器零售	Retail of Musical Instruments	598	543	0	31	20
照相器材零售	Retail of Photographic Equipment	3535	3131	5	135	0
其他文化用品零售	Retail of Other Cultural Articles	3794	3297	9	218	57
医药及医疗器材专门零售	**Retail of Medicines and Medical Appliances**	**679872**	**594292**	**2548**	**36001**	**13359**
药品零售	Retail of Medicines	581135	509229	2034	33038	8434
医疗用品及器材零售	Retail of Medical Articles and Appliances	98736	85062	514	2963	4925
汽车、摩托车、燃料及零配件专门零售	**Retail of Motor Vehicles, Motorcycles, Fuel and Parts**	**7955668**	**7290673**	**16581**	**220309**	**278440**
汽车零售	Retail of Motor Vehicles	4388609	4076504	11431	118091	46613
汽车零配件零售	Retail of Auto Parts and Accessories	42515	39899	134	966	797
摩托车及零配件零售	Retail of Motorcycles,Parts and Accessories	32774	27267	1374	930	2325
机动车燃料零售	Retail of Fuel of Motor Vehicles	3491770	3147003	3643	100323	228706
家用电器及电子产品专门零售	**Special Retail of Household Electric Appliances and Electronic Products**	**584838**	**512819**	**3993**	**43200**	**5192**
家用试听设备零售	Retail of Listen household equipment	64514	56088	279	3630	1625
日用家电设备零售	Retail of Household appliances	374386	326600	2699	32078	1831
计算机、软件及辅助设备零售	Retail of Computer,Software and Assistant Appliances	67631	60532	587	2250	1249
通讯设备零售	Retail of Communication Equipments	69805	63151	360	5224	-795
其他电子产品零售	Retail of Other Electronic Products	8502	6447	68	18	1283
五金、家具及室内装修材料专门零售	**Special Retail of Hardware, Furniture and Interior Decoration Materials**	**48250**	**40922**	**740**	**1444**	**2776**
#五金零售	Retail of Hardware	12732	11590	64	93	261
家具零售	Retail of Furniture	13924	10724	481	802	1011
木质装饰材料零售	Retail of Wood Decorative Materials	2587	2035	10	314	104
陶瓷、石材装饰材料零售	Retail of ceramic and stone ecoration materials	15573	14021	75	91	1148
其他室内装修材料零售	Retail of Other Interior Decoration	3434	2553	110	143	253
货摊、无店铺及其他零售	**Stalls,Non-shop and Other Retails**	**270916**	**209642**	**2010**	**40263**	**20260**
#互联网零售	Retail of Flow Stalls	28004	19005	216	174	8569
邮购及电视、电话零售	Retail of Mail order,TV and Telephone	150501	113067	1277	36118	6809
旧货零售	Retail of Second-hand Goods	605	462	24	66	4
生活用燃料零售	Retail of life Fuel	63839	54326	273	2943	3785
其他未列明零售	Other Retails Unlisted	27967	22783	220	962	1092

17-7 商品交易市场
Commodity Exchange Markets

单位：个 (unit)

指 标	Item	2010	2011	2012	2013	2014
商品交易市场	**Number of Commodity trading markets**	**2216**	**2211**	**1658**	**1521**	**1494**
消费品市场数	**Number of Consumable Markets**	**2175**	**2170**	**1614**	**1443**	**1449**
消费品综合市场	Consumable Goods Integrative Market	1190	1176	705	586	616
农副产品市场	Agricultural Subproduct Market	890	894	811	742	717
农副产品综合市场	Agricultural Subproduct Integrative Market	844	846	786		
农副产品专业市场	Agricultural Subproduct Special Market	46	48	25		
工业消费品市场	Industrial Consumable Goods Market	59	58	58	42	43
工业消费品综合市场	Industrial Consumable Goods Integrative Market	51	50	32		
工业消费品专业市场	Industrial Consumer Goods Special Market	8	8	26		
其他消费品市场	Other Consumable Goods Market	36	42	40	73	73
生产资料市场数	**Number of Production Markets**	**41**	**41**	**44**	**78**	**45**
生产资料综合市场	Production Integrative Comprehensive Markets	4	4	3	12	4
工业生产资料市场	Industrial Production Markets	27	27	31	28	32
机动车交易市场	Motor vehicle Markets	9	11	12		
钢材交易市场	Steel Markets	6	5	7		
煤炭交易市场	Coal and Charcoal Markets	2	2	1		
木材交易市场	Wood Markets	6	5	6		
其他工业生产资料市场	Other Means of Industrial Production Market	4	4	5		
农业生产资料市场	Agricultural Production Markets	5	5	7	8	7
农业生产资料综合市场	Agricultural Production Comprehensive Markets	3	3	4		
农业生产资料专业市场	Agricultural Production Special Markets	2	2	3		
其他生产资料市场	Others	5	5	3	30	2

注：资料来源于省工商局。

Note:Data in the table are provided by the provincial administration for industry and commerce.

主要统计指标解释

社会消费品零售总额 指企业（单位、个体户）通过交易直接售给个人、社会集团非生产、非经营用的实物商品金额，以及提供餐饮服务所取得的收入金额。个人包括城乡居民和入境人员，社会集团包括机关、社会团体、部队、学校、企事业单位、居委会或村委会等。

社会消费品零售总额包括：（1）售给城乡居民作为生活用的商品和修建房屋用的建筑材料；（2）售给社会集团的各种办公用品和公用消费品；（3）售给机关、团体、学校、部队、企业、事业单位的职工食堂和旅店(招待所)附设专门供本店旅客食用，不对外营业的食堂的各种食品、燃料；企业、单位和国营农场直接售给本单位职工和职工食堂的自己生产的产品；（4）售给部队干部、战士生活用的粮食、副食品、衣着品、日用品、燃料；（5）售给来华的外国人、华侨、港澳台同胞的消费品；（6）居民自费购买的中、西药品、中药材及医疗用品；（7）报社、出版社直接售给居民和社会集团的报纸、图书、杂志，集邮公司出售的新、旧纪念邮票、特种邮票、首日封、集邮册、集邮工具等；（8）旧货寄售商店自购、自销部分的商品；（9）煤气公司、液化石油气站售给居民和社会集团的煤气灶具和罐装液化石油气；（10）农民售给非农业居民和社会集团的商品。不包括售给国民经济各部门企业、事业单位(包括国有经济的农场)生产经营用的各种原材料、燃料、设备、工具等和售给批发和零售贸易业、住宿和餐饮业作为转卖用的商品，旧货寄售商店受托寄售卖出的商品，服务业的营业收入，邮局出售邮票的收入，自来水、电力、煤气生产(供应)单位的产品供应收入，也不包括农民之间的商品销售。

商品购进额 指从本企业以外的单位和个人购进（包括从国外直接进口）作为转卖或加工后转卖的商品金额（含增值税）。商品购进包括：（1）从工农业生产者、批发和零售业企业、住宿和餐饮业企业、出版社或报社的出版发行部门和其他服务业企业购进的商品；（2）从机关团体、事业单位购进的商品；（3）从海关、市场管理部门购进的缉私和没收的商品；（4）从居民收购的废旧商品等，不包括：（1）企业为本单位自身经营用，不是作为转卖而购进的商品，如材料物资、包装物、低值易耗品、办公用品等；（2）未通过买卖行为而收入的商品，如接受其他部门移交的商品、借入的商品、收入代其他单位保管的商品、其他单位赠送的样品、加工回收的成品等；（3）经本单位介绍，由买卖双方直接结算，本单位只收取手续费的业务；（4）销售退回和买方拒付货款的商品；（5）商品溢余。

商品销售额 指对本单位以外的单位和个人出售的商品金额（包括售给本单位消费用的商品，含增值税）。商品销售包括：（1）售给城乡居民和社会集团消费用的商品；（2）售给农业、工业、建筑业、服务业等国民经济各行业用于生产、经营用的商品，包括售予批发和零售业作为转卖或加工后转卖的商品；（3）对国（境）外直接出口的商品。不包括：（1）未通过买卖行为付出的商品，如随机构变动移交给其他企业单位的商品、借出的商品、归还受其他单位委托代保管的商品、付出的加工原料和赠送给其他单位的样品等；（2）经本单位介绍，由买卖双方直接结算，本单位只收取手续费的业务；（3）购货退回的商品；（4）商品损耗和损失；（5）出售本单位自用的废旧物资。

商品库存额 对于批发和零售业法人单位和个体经营户，是指报告期末取得所有权的全部商品金额（含增值税）；对于批发和零售业产业活动单位，是指报告期末实际在库且归属法人具有所有权的全部商品金额（含增值税）。它反映批发和零售业企业(单位)的商品库存情况和对市场商品供应的保证程度。商品库存包括：(1)存放在批发和零售业经营单位(如门市部、批发站、经营处)仓库、货场、货柜和货架中的商品；(2)挑选、整理、包装中的商品；(3)已记入购进而尚未运到本单位的商品，即发货单或银行承兑凭证已到而货未到的商品；(4)寄放他处的商品，如因购货方拒绝承付而暂时存放在购货方的商品和已办完加工成品收回手续而未提回的商品；(5)委托其他单位代销(未作销售或调出)尚未售出的商品；(6)代其他单位购进尚未交付的商品。库存商品不包括所有权不属于本单位的商品、委托外单位加工生产尚未收回成品的商品、外贸企业代理其他单位从国外进口尚未付给订货单位的商品、代国家物资储备部门保管的商品等。

Explanatory Notes on Main Statistical Indicators

Total Retail Sales of Consumer Goods refers to enterprises (units and self-employed) by trading sold directly to individuals, social groups, non production and non business use of the physical amount of goods, and provide catering services achieved the amount of revenue. Individuals, including urban and rural residents and immigration personnel, social groups, including organs, social groups, troops, schools, enterprises and institutions, neighborhood committees, etc.

The retail sales of consumer goods include: (1) commodities sold to urban and rural residents for their daily use and building materials sold to them for the construction or repair of houses; (2) office appliances and supplies sold to institutions; (3) food and fuels sold to canteens of institutions, enterprises ,schools ,military units and to canteens of hotels and hostels that only serve their guests ,and commodities produced by enterprises ,institutions or state farms and sold directly to their employees or their canteens; (4) grain and non-staple food, clothing ,daily articles and fuels sold to military personnel; (5)consumer goods sold to foreigners, overseas Chinese, and Chinese compatriots from Taiwan, Hong Kong and Macao during their stay in the mainland of China; (6) Chinese and western medicines, herbs and medical facilities purchased by residents; (7) newspapers, books and magazines directly sold to residents and social groups by publishers, new and old commemorative stamps, special stamps, first-day covers, stamp albums and other stamp-collection articles sold by stamp companies; (8) consumer goods purchased and then sold by second-hand shops; (9) stoves and other heating facilities and liquefied gas sold by gas companies to households and institutions; and (10) commodities sold by farmers to non-agricultural residents and social groups. Excluded under this heading are: raw materials, fuels, equipment, tools sold to enterprises, institutions and state farms for production purpose; commodities sold to trade establishments for re-selling; commissioned sales at second-hand shops; operational income of urban public utilities; stamps sold at post offices; income of water, power, gas production and supply establishments from the supply of their products; and sales of commodities among farmers.

Purchases of Commodities refer to the total value of purchases of commodities by enterprises (establishments) from other establishments or individuals (including direct import from abroad) for the purpose of re-selling, either with or without further processing of the commodities purchased. The commodities include: (1) commodities purchased from agricultural and industrial producer, wholesaler, retailer, publishing hourse and other service business; (2) commodities purchased from institutions and government departments; (3) confiscated goods purchased from the custums authorities or market management agencies; (4) second-hand goods and wastes purchased from residents; The commodities exclude 1 commodities purchased by enterprises (establishments) for use in their own business operation, commodities obtained without buying or selling procedures such as materials, consumable goods of low value, office appliances,etc. 2 received goods without trading, such as goods handed over from others, borrowed goods, preserved goods for others, donated goods from others, processed and retrieved goods, etc. 3. goods of direct settlement between buyer and seller with handling fees introduced by others, 4. goods returned or refused to pay by the buyer, 5. excessive goods.

Sales of Commodities refer to value of commodities sold by the establishments to other establishments and individuals (including goods sold for self consumption, including the value-added tax). The commodities include: (1) commodities sold to urban and rural residents and social groups for their consumption; (2) commodities sold to establishments in all industries for their production and operation, including agriculture, industry, construction, transportation, post and telecommunications, catering services, and public utility including commodities sold to wholesale and retail establishments for re-selling, with or without further processing; and (3) commodities for direct export to abroad. Excluded are (1) extended commodities without trading, such as goods handed over to other enterprises and institutions becase of the change of organizations, lent goods, returned goods preserved for others, extended processing materials and samples donated to others, (2) goods of direct settlement between buyer and seller with handling fees introduced by others, 3. goods returned after purchase, (4) damaged and spoiled goods, (5) waste and used goods of self use.

Stock of Commodities refers to total commodities possessed by wholesaler and retailer of various types of registration status at the end of the reference period, reflecting the commodity stock level of various wholesaler and retailer and the potential for market supply. It includes: (1) commodities located in storage, garages, counters, and shelves of operating places (such as sale stores, wholesale centres, and operating offices); (2) commodities in the process of being selected, sorted, and packed; (3) commodities not arrived but recorded as purchase in the account, i.e. commodities not arrived but payment receipts for the commodities from the sellers or the banks arrived; (4) commodities deposited in other places rather than places mentioned above, for instance: commodities in the hold of purchasers temporarily due to the refusal of payment and commodities not taken back after going through the formalities; (5) commodities entrusted to other units to sell but not sold yet; (6) commodities purchased for other units but not delivered yet. Commodities not included as stock are those not owned by the enterprises (units), commodities on commission for processing but not yet delivered, imported commodities of agency of foreign trade enterprise but not yet delivered to ordering units and finally those put in stock on behalf of the state material reserves units.

18 住宿、餐饮业和旅游业

Hotel, Catering Services and Tourism

18-1 限额以上住宿业和餐饮业

Basic Conditions of Enterprises above Designated Size in Hotels and Catering Services

指　　标	Item	2010	2011	2012	2013	2014
住宿业	**Hotels**					
法人企业(个)	Number of Corporations Enterprises(unit)	234	260	318	395	464
年末从业人数(人)	Engaged Hersons at year-end(person)	23289	26236	31793	32580	34125
营业额(亿元)	Business Revenue (100 million yuan)	20.53	27.07	35.88	41.99	46.70
#客房收入	From Hotel Rooms	11.71	15.58	20.31	25.25	28.57
餐费收入	From Meals	7.35	9.30	12.25	13.12	14.01
客房数(万间)	Number of Rooms(10000 rooms)	2.79	3.05	3.76	4.39	6.02
床位数(万张)	Number of Beds(10000 beds)	5.07	5.20	6.32	7.31	9.51
年末餐饮营业面积(万平方米)	Business Area of Catering Services at year-end(10000 sq.m)	23.03	49.19	64.65	56.81	66.68
餐饮业	**Catering Services**					
法人企业(个)	Number of corporation Unit (unit)	134	153	183	304	385
年末从业人数(人)	Employed Persons(person)	12088	15234	17593	19645	17355
营业额(亿元)	Business Revenue (100 million yuan)	11.65	15.88	19.02	21.12	22.70
#餐费收入	From Meals	10.45	13.63	16.42	17.99	19.10
年末餐饮营业面积(万平方米)	Business Area of Catering Services at Year-end(10000 sq.m)	23.51	36.24	40.44	53.90	58.73

18-2 限额以上住宿业企业(2014)

单位：万元

指 标	Item	法人企业(个) Number of Corporations Enterprises (unit)	从业人员平均人数(人) Engaged Persons at Year-end (person)	营业额 Business Revenue	#客房收入 from Hotel Rooms	#餐费收入 from Meals
合计	**Total**	**464**	**33149**	**467047**	**285698**	**140101**
按登记注册类型分	**by Status of Registration**					
内资企业	**Domestic Funded Enterprises**	**457**	**32099**	**449581**	**275396**	**133830**
国有企业	State-owned Enterprises	35	2819	40340	22641	13671
集体企业	Collective-owned Enterprises	12	319	8910	6387	2044
股份合作企业	Cooperative Enterprises					
联营企业	Joint Ownership Enterprises					
有限责任公司	Limited Liability Corporations	172	16177	244285	138206	81387
国有独资公司	State Sole Funded Corporations	6	1210	24545	9545	11269
其他有限责任公司	Other Limited Liability Corporations	166	14967	219740	128662	70118
股份有限公司	Share-holding Corporations Ltd.	5	278	2484	1912	350
私营企业	Private Enterprises	226	12089	147328	102328	34161
私营独资企业	Private-funded Enterprises	46	1950	31020	21561	7098
私营合伙企业	Private Psrtrership Enterprises	14	613	7698	4762	2375
私营有限责任公司	Private Limited Liability Corporations	154	8782	100672	71509	22972
私营股份有限公司	Private Share Holding Co.Ltd	12	744	7938	4497	1716
其他企业	Other Enterprises	7	417	6235	3922	2217
港、澳、台商投资企业	**Enterprises with Funds From Honkong, Macao and Taiwan**	**6**	**840**	**14312**	**8878**	**4826**
#合资经营企业	Joint-venture Enterprises	2	612	10244	6583	3167
独资经营企业	Enterpises with Sole Fund	3	194	3324	1867	1409
投资股份有限公司	Share-holding Corporations Ltd. with Investment	1	34	744	428	251
外商投资企业	**Enterprises with Foreign Investment**	**1**	**210**	**3154**	**1424**	**1445**
中外合资经营企业	Joint-venture Enterprises	1	210	3154	1424	1445
按国民经济行业分	**by Sector**					
旅游饭店	Tourist Hotel	316	26569	382167	228312	120129
一般旅馆	Fonda	134	5824	77571	52909	17627
其他住宿业	Others	14	756	7309	4477	2346

Basic Conditions of Enterprises above Designated Size in Hotel Services

(10000 yuan)

主营业务收入 Revenue from Principal Business	主营业务成本 Cost of Principal Business	主营业务税金及附加 Taxes and Other Charges on Principal Business	利润总额 Total profit	资产总计 Total Assets	#流动资产合计 Total Current Assets	#固定资产合计 Total Fixed Assets	负债合计 Total Liabilities	所有者权益 Total Owners' Equity
462012	**204673**	**25608**	**-35207**	**1440502**	**511044**	**648158**	**1024834**	**415668**
444723	**198281**	**24494**	**-34681**	**1412130**	**507669**	**626455**	**1013705**	**398426**
39078	17355	2214	-2883	63503	19194	37839	32866	30637
9470	5425	592	1913	17528	1606	15674	3139	14388
240278	104052	13126	-31493	834764	297923	373178	669325	165439
23641	5567	1338	2597	43177	28204	13014	27427	15751
216636	98484	11789	-34090	791586	269719	360164	641898	149688
2430	674	421	-93	7803	2920	4677	4255	3548
147344	67881	7839	-1446	479612	184765	187495	297429	182183
32667	18376	1657	3581	70165	10536	53422	18717	51448
7424	3721	439	338	9537	2136	5359	3269	6269
99763	42213	5365	-5637	380342	161324	122667	262191	118151
7491	3571	378	272	19568	10769	6047	13253	6315
6123	2894	303	-680	8921	1262	7593	6690	2231
14135	**5933**	**827**	**-216**	**17242**	**2371**	**13978**	**8581**	**8661**
10244	4126	601	-524	12213	1126	10989	7661	4552
3146	1322	181	182	3416	1207	1425	751	2666
744	485	45	126	1613	37	1564	170	1443
3154	**460**	**287**	**-310**	**11129**	**1004**	**7725**	**2548**	**8581**
3154	460	287	-310	11129	1004	7725	2548	8581
378889	167546	20942	-31363	1227894	436884	556127	907228	320666
75915	34181	4289	-2481	196940	68490	82726	106496	90444
7208	2946	377	-1363	15669	5670	9305	11111	4558

18-3 限额以上餐饮业企业(2014)

单位：万元

指　标	Item	法人企业(个) Number of corporation Enterprises (unit)	从业人员平均人数(人) On average of staff (engaged persons)	营业额 Business Revenue	#餐费收入 From Meals
合计	**Total**	**385**	**17160**	**227014**	**191001**
按登记注册类型分	**by Status of Registration**				
内资企业	**Domestic Funded Enterprises**	**384**	**16932**	**223094**	**187203**
国有企业	State-owned Enterprises	9	679	7635	3882
集体企业	Collective-owned Enterprises	1	31	214	178
股份合作企业	Cooperative Enterprises	1	23	268	268
联营企业	Joint Ownership Enterprises				
有限责任公司	Limited Liability Corporations	105	6088	81655	70029
国有独资公司	State Sole Funded Corporations	1	90	1048	1048
其他有限责任公司	Other Limited Liability Corporations	104	5998	80607	68981
股份有限公司	Share-holding Corporations Ltd.	3	283	5538	3244
私营企业	Private Enterprises	257	9519	123728	106376
私营独资企业	Private-funded Enterprises	87	1696	26686	23458
私营合伙企业	Private Psrtrership Enterprises	12	735	9435	8678
私营有限责任公司	Private Limited Liability Corporations	152	6640	84431	72516
私营股份有限公司	Private Share Holding Co.Ltd	6	448	3177	1723
其他	Other Enterprises	8	309	4055	3226
外商投资企业	**Enterprises with Foreign Investment**	**1**	**228**	**3921**	**3798**
#外商投资股份有限公司	Share-holding Corporations Ltd. with Foreign Investment	1	228	3921	3798
按国民经济行业分	**by Sector**				
正餐服务	Restaurant	376	16824	223509	187537
快餐服务	Fast Food	3	160	1951	1951
饮料及冷饮服务	Beverages and Cold Drinks	3	97	700	690
#咖啡馆服务	Coffee Library Services	2	64	435	425
酒吧服务	Bar Serviles	1	33	265	265
其他餐饮业	Others	3	79	856	823
#餐饮配送服务	Food Delivery Service	2	46	553	520
其他未列明餐饮业	Other food and beverage industry not Listed	1	33	303	303

Basic Conditions of Enterprises above Designated Size in Catering Services

(10000 yuan)

主营业务收入 Revenue from Principal Business	主营业务成本 Cost of Principal Business	主营业务税金及附加 Taxes and Other Charges on Principal Business	利润总额 Total profit	资产总计 Total Assets	#流动资产合计 Current Assets	#固定资产合计 Total Fixed Assets	负债合计 Total Liabilities	所有者权益 Total Owners' Equities
220639	**123630**	**11172**	**3656**	**359388**	**164911**	**128746**	**238902**	**120529**
216719	**122377**	**10948**	**2991**	**355330**	**161431**	**128651**	**236350**	**119023**
7399	2840	462	-111	6525	2507	2030	4946	1579
214	89	12	-65	480	36	398	911	-431
268	138	15	15	364	20	162	169	195
77235	46179	3592	913	123738	57837	40632	81205	42576
1048	622	52	282	15189	7102	48	5217	9973
76187	45557	3540	631	108549	50736	40584	75989	32603
5538	1778	314	1000	6136	5672	439	5628	508
122042	68957	6336	1225	216230	94787	83769	142772	73458
26325	18500	1348	2019	22905	9174	12478	8861	14044
9083	4052	374	1088	13548	3826	6493	4046	9502
83495	45030	4389	-1686	139710	59561	50774	93937	45773
3139	1376	226	-197	40068	22226	14025	35928	4139
4023	2396	217	15	1858	571	1223	719	1139
3921	**1253**	**224**	**665**	**4058**	**3480**	**95**	**2552**	**1506**
3921	1253	224	665	4058	3480	95	2552	1506
217134	121503	11010	3544	355367	162244	127491	237758	117652
1951	1112	115	-22	1074	800	263	266	808
700	426	32	66	1332	517	735	399	933
435	233	13	38	904	423	401	181	723
265	192	19	29	428	94	334	218	210
856	589	15	68	1615	1349	257	479	1136
553	464	1	10	1528	1270	255	459	1069
303	125	14	58	87	79	3	20	67

18-4 旅游业
Tourism

指　　标	Item	2010	2011	2012	2013	2014
旅行社总数(个)	**Total Number of Travel Agencies(unit)**	**260**	**270**	**302**	**321**	**338**
出境游组团旅行社	International Travel Agencies	11	11	13	16	19
国内及入境旅游旅行社	Domestic Travel Agencies	249	259	289	305	319
旅行社职工人数(人)	**Number of Staff and Workers of Travel Agencies(person)**	**3132**	**3240**	**3624**	**3852**	**4684**
出境游组团旅行社	International Travel Agencies	225	226	260	316	452
国内及入境旅游旅行社	Domestic Travel Agencies	2907	3014	3364	3536	4232
旅游总人数(万人次)	**Total Number of Tourists(10000 person-times)**	**12913.02**	**17019.36**	**21401.18**	**26761.28**	**32134.94**
入境旅游人数	Number of Overseas Visitor Arrivals	50.01	58.51	70.50	77.70	85.50
外国人	Foreigners	18.61	23.62	30.42	31.97	35.94
港澳同胞	Chinese Compatriots From Hong Kong and Macao	13.64	16.91	20.85	22.93	24.55
台湾同胞	Chinese Compatriots From Taiwan Province	17.76	17.98	19.23	22.80	25.01
国内旅游人数	Total Number of Domestic Tourists	12863.01	16960.85	21330.68	26683.58	32049.44
旅游总收入(亿元)	**Tourism Earnings(100 million yuan)**	**1061.23**	**1429.48**	**1860.16**	**2370.65**	**2895.98**
国际旅游外汇收入(万美元)	Foreign Exchange Earnings from International Tourism (USD 10000)	12957.88	13507.18	16893.60	20143.41	21671.23
国内旅游收入(亿元)	Earnings from Domestic Tourism (100 million yuan)	1052.64	1420.70	1849.49	2358.18	2882.66
三大旅行社接待入境旅游人数(万人次)	**Number of International Tourists Received by Three Major Travel Service (10000 person-times)**	**1.76**	**1.51**	**1.27**	**7.08**	**8.23**
中国国际旅行社	China International Travel Service	0.23	0.39	0.77	0.73	0.53
贵州海外旅游总公司	Guizhou Overseas Tourism Corporation	1.47	0.69	0.14	2.55	4.68
中国青年旅行社	China Youth Travel Service	0.06	0.43	0.36	3.80	3.02

注：资料来源于省旅游局(以下相关表同)。

Note:Data in the table are obtained from the provincial tourism administration(The relative tables are the same).

18-5 来黔境外旅游人数及人均消费支出
Number of Overseas Tourists Visiting Guizhou and Average Per Capita Spending

指 标	Item	2010	2011	2012	2013	2014	2014年比2013年增长(%) Increase Rate in 2014 over 2013(%)
来黔境外旅游人数（万人次）	**Number of Foreign Tourists Visiting Guizhou(10000 person-times)**	**50.01**	**58.51**	**70.50**	**77.70**	**85.50**	**10.0**
外国人	Foreigner	18.61	23.62	30.42	31.98	35.94	12.4
港澳同胞	Chinese Compatriots From Hong Kong and Macao	13.64	16.91	20.85	22.92	24.55	7.1
台湾同胞	Compatriots from Taiwan	17.76	17.98	19.23	22.80	25.01	9.7
平均每人逗留天数(天/人)	Average Days Tourists Stay in Guizhou Per Capita (day/person)	1.43	1.39	1.43	1.41	1.44	2.1
平均每人每天消费支出(美元/人、天)	Average Per Capita Daily Spending (USD/person-day)	171.76	168.68	167.13	181.05	180.65	-0.2

18-6 接待外国旅游人数(按地区分)
Number of Overseas Tourists Visiting Guizhou(by Country/Territory)

单位：人次 (person-time)

指 标	Item	2010	2011	2012	2013	2014	2014年比2013年增长(%) Increase Rate in 2014 over 2013(%)
接待外国旅游人数	**Number of Overseas Tourists Visiting Guizhou**	**186054**	**236244**	**304168**	**319743**	**359356**	**12.4**
亚 洲	Asia	85383	104624	122958	131790	138688	5.2
非 洲	Africa	1110	1536	2165	2250	4580	103.6
欧 洲	Europe	44799	57619	81799	85065	103327	21.5
拉丁美洲	Latin America	35239	45379	61853	64987	67391	3.7
大洋洲	Oceania	16861	23518	30354	30406	31482	3.5
其 他	Others	2662	3568	5039	5245	13888	164.8

18-7 旅游外汇收入

Foreign Exchange Earnings from Tourism

单位：万美元 (USD 10000)

指　标	Item	2010	2011	2012	2013	2014	2014年比2013年增长(%) Increase Rate in 2014 over 2013(%)
旅游外汇收入	**Tourism foreign exchange earnings**	**12957.88**	**13507.18**	**16893.60**	**20143.41**	**21671.20**	**7.6**
长途交通	Long Distance Transportation	5001.74	5200.26	5084.97	5881.90	5981.26	1.7
游　览	Sightseeing	596.06	540.29	658.85	1087.70	931.86	-14.3
住　宿	Accommodation	1399.45	1701.9	1756.93	2598.50	2383.84	-8.3
餐　饮	Food and Beverage	997.76	729.39	1114.98	1631.60	1625.34	-0.4
商品销售	Shopping	2410.17	3241.72	4983.61	5398.40	5894.57	9.2
娱　乐	Entertainment	583.10	634.84	929.15	725.20	1516.99	109.2
邮电通讯	Postal and Communication Services	362.83	324.17	439.23	543.90	476.77	-12.3
市内交通	Local Transportation	220.28	108.06	388.55	745.30	671.81	-9.9
其他服务	Other Services	1386.49	1026.55	1537.33	1530.90	2188.79	43.0

18-8 旅馆业接待经营

Operation of Hotels

指　标	Item	2010	2011	2012	2013	2014	2014年比2013年增长(%) Increase Rate in 2014 over 2013(%)
接待能力	**Capacity**						
年末客房数(间)	Guest Rooms (Year-end) (unit)	25191	26120	29358	32058	31320	-2.3
年末客房床位数(张)	Guest Beds (Year-end) (bed)	45683	46204	51687	55738	53922	-3.3
客房开房率(%)	Room Occupancy Rate(%)	63.6	64.2	64.3	59.9	57.7	-3.7
#星级宾馆	Star-rated Hotels	65.1	64.6	64.1	60.6	57.7	-4.7
实际住宿人次数(万人次)	Actual Number of Guests (10000 person-times)	625.63	740.49	775.15	823.39	767.31	-6.8
#海外来黔	Overseas Visitors	50.01	58.51	70.50	77.70	85.50	10.0
实际住宿人天数(万人天)	Actual Number of Guests and Days of Stay (10000 person-days)	866.84	997.23	1092.97	1198.42	1135.62	-5.2
#海外来黔	Overseas Visitors	71.39	81.22	101.18	109.60	123.46	12.6
经营和财务	**Management and Financial**						
营业收入(万元)	Operational Revenue(10000 yuan)	195639	228252	245265	261241	239211	-8.4

18-9 星级饭店

Star-rated Hotels

单位：个　　(unit)

指　标	Item	2010	2011	2012	2013	2014
星级饭店个数	**The number of Star-rated Hotels**	**344**	**340**	**368**	**377**	**358**
按经济类型分	**Grouped by Ownership**					
国有经济	State-owned	103	90	80	77	63
集体经济	Collective-owned	241	250	287	299	294
外商投资经济	Foreign Funded			1	1	1
按规模分	**Grouped by Capacity**					
客房总数300间以上	With Above than 300 Rooms	3	3	5	7	7
客房总数200−299间	With 200-299 Rooms	14	16	16	20	17
客房总数100−199间	With 100-199 Rooms	54	63	76	84	81
客房总数99间以下	With Less than 100 Rooms	273	258	271	266	253

18-10 风景名胜区
National Parks

名　称	Name	级　别	地　址
红枫湖风景名胜区	Hongfeng Lake National Park	国家级	贵州省贵阳市清镇市
黄果树风景名胜区	Huangguoshu Waterfalls National Park	国家级	贵州省安顺市镇宁、关岭县
龙宫风景名胜区	The Dragon Palace National Park	国家级	贵州省安顺市西秀区
织金洞风景名胜区	Zhijin Cave National Park	国家级	贵州省毕节市织金县
九洞天风景名胜区	Jiudongtian National Park	国家级	贵州省毕节市大方、纳雍县
马岭河峡谷风景名胜区	Malinghe Canyon National Park	国家级	贵州省黔西南州兴义市
㵲阳河风景名胜区	Wuyang River National Park	国家级	贵州省黔东南州镇远、施秉、黄平县
黎平侗乡风景名胜区	Liping Dong-Village National Park	国家级	贵州省黔东南州黎平县
荔波樟江风景名胜区	Libo Zhangjiang National Park	国家级	贵州省黔南州荔波县
都匀斗篷山——剑江风景名胜区	Duyun Doupeng Mountain----Jianjiang National Park	国家级	贵州省黔南州都匀市
赤水风景名胜区	Chishui National Park	国家级	贵州省遵义市赤水市
九龙洞风景名胜区	Jiulong Cave National Park	国家级	贵州省铜仁市
紫云格凸河风景名胜区	Ziyun Getu River National Park	国家级	贵州省安顺市紫云县
平塘风景名胜区	Pingtang National Park	国家级	贵州省黔南州平塘县
瓮安江界河风景名胜区	Wengan Jiangjie River National Park	国家级	贵州省黔南州瓮安县
榕江苗山侗水风景名胜区	Rongjiang Mountain and Water Landscapes with Miao and Dong Cultures National Park	国家级	贵州省黔东南州榕江县
石阡温泉群风景名胜区	Shiqian Hot Well Flock National Park	国家级	贵州省铜仁市石阡县
沿河乌江山峡风景名胜区	Yanhe Wujiang River Sanxia National Park	国家级	贵州省铜仁市沿河县
百花湖风景名胜区	Baihua Lake National Park	省级	贵州省贵阳市乌当区
花溪风景名胜区	Huaxi National Park	省级	贵州省贵阳市花溪区
息烽风景名胜区	Xifeng National Park	省级	贵州省贵阳市息烽县
修文阳明风景名胜区	Xiuwen Yangming National Park	省级	贵州省贵阳市修文县
贵阳香纸沟风景名胜区	Guiyang Xiangzhigou National Park	省级	贵州省贵阳市乌当区
开阳风景名胜区	Kaiyang National Park	省级	贵州省贵阳市开阳县
贵阳相思河风景名胜区	Guiyang Xiangsi River National Park	省级	贵州省贵阳市乌当区
清镇暗流河风景名胜区	Qingzhen Undercurrent River National Park	省级	贵州省贵阳市清镇市
普定梭筛风景名胜区	Puding Suoshai National Park	省级	贵州省安顺市普定县
关岭花江大峡谷风景名胜区	Guanling Huajiang Canyon National Park	省级	贵州省安顺市关岭县
平坝天台山——斯拉河风景名胜区	Pingba Tiantai Mountain ----Sila River National Park	省级	贵州省安顺市平坝区
百里杜鹃风景名胜区	One-Hundred-Li Azalea Belt National Park	省级	贵州省毕节市大方、黔西县
贵州屋脊赫章韭菜坪风景名胜区	Guizhou Fastigium Hezhang Jiucaiping National Park	省级	贵州省毕节市赫章县
鲁布革风景名胜区	Lubuge National Park	省级	贵州省黔西南州兴义市
泥凼石林风景名胜区	Nidang shilin National Park	省级	贵州省黔西南州兴义市
安龙招堤风景名胜区	Anlong Zhaodi National Park	省级	贵州省黔西南州安龙县
贞丰三岔河风景名胜区	Zhenfeng Sancha River National Park	省级	贵州省黔西南州贞丰县

18−10 续表 continued

名 称	Name	级 别	地 址
晴隆三望坪风景名胜区	Qinglong Sanwangping National Park	省级	贵州省黔西南州晴隆县
兴仁放马坪风景名胜区	Xingren Fangmaping National Park	省级	贵州省黔西南州兴仁县
岑巩龙鳌河风景名胜区	Cengong Longao River National Park	省级	贵州省黔东南州岑巩县
剑河风景名胜区	Jianhe National Park	省级	贵州省黔东南州剑河县
镇远高过河风景名胜区	Zhenyuan Gaoguo River National Park	省级	贵州省黔东南州镇远县
雷山风景名胜区	Leishan National Park	省级	贵州省黔东南州雷山县
锦屏三板溪——隆里古城风景名胜区	Jinping Sanbanxi----Longli National Park	省级	贵州省黔东南州锦屏县
丹寨龙泉山——岔河风景名胜区	Danzhai Longquanshan----Chahe National Park	省级	贵州省黔东南州丹寨县
从江风景名胜区	Congjiang National Park	省级	贵州省黔东南州从江县
龙里猴子沟风景名胜区	Longli Monkey Fossa National Park	省级	贵州省黔南州龙里县
福泉洒金谷风景名胜区	Fuquan Sajingu National Park	省级	贵州省黔南州福泉市
惠水涟江——燕子洞风景名胜区	Huishui Lianjiang--Yanzi Cave National Park	省级	贵州省黔南州惠水县
长顺杜鹃湖——白云山风景名胜区	Changshun Dujuan Lake--Baiyun Mountain National Park	省级	贵州省黔南州长顺县
三都都柳江风景名胜区	Sandu Duliu River National Park	省级	贵州省黔南州三都县
贵定洛北河风景名胜区	Guiding Luobei River National Park	省级	贵州省黔南州贵定县
独山深河桥风景名胜区	Dushan Shenhe Bridge National Park	省级	贵州省黔南州独山县
遵义娄山风景名胜区	Zunyi Loushan Mountain National Park	省级	贵州省遵义市桐梓县
绥阳宽阔水风景名胜区	Suiyang Kuankuoshui National Park	省级	贵州省遵义市绥阳县
仁怀茅台风景名胜区	Renhuai Moutai National Park	省级	贵州省遵义市仁怀市
习水风景名胜区	Xishui National Park	省级	贵州省遵义市习水县
余庆大乌江风景名胜区	Yuqing Wujiang River National Park	省级	贵州省遵义市余庆县
湄潭湄江风景名胜区	Meitan National Park	省级	贵州省遵义市湄潭县
梵净山——太平河风景名胜区	Fanjing Mountain----Taiping River National Park	省级	贵州省铜仁市江口县
印江木黄风景名胜区	Yinjiang Muhuang National Park	省级	贵州省铜仁市印江县
思南乌江白鹭洲风景名胜区	Sinan Wujiang River Bailuzhou National Park	省级	贵州省铜仁市思南县
松桃豹子岭——寨英风景名胜区	Songtao Baozi Mountain----Zhaiying National Park	省级	贵州省铜仁市松桃县
万山夜郎谷风景名胜区	Wanshan Yelang Canyon National Park	省级	贵州省铜仁市万山区
玉屏北洞萧笛之乡风景名胜区	Yuping Beidong Xiaodi-Village National Park	省级	贵州省铜仁市玉屏县
六枝牂牁江风景名胜区	Liuzhi Zangke River National Park	省级	贵州省六盘水市六枝特区
盘县古银杏风景名胜区	Panxian Ancientry Gingko National Park	省级	贵州省六盘水市盘县特区
盘县大洞竹海风景名胜区	PanXian Dadong Banboo Sea National Park	省级	贵州省六盘水市盘县特区
盘县坡上草原风景名胜区	PanXian Grassland on Mountain National Park	省级	贵州省六盘水市盘县特区
南开风景名胜区	Nankai National Park	省级	贵州省六盘水市水城特区
务川洪渡河风景名胜区	Wuchuan hongduhe National Park	省级	贵州省遵义市务川县
罗甸大小井风景名胜区	Luodian daxiaojin National Park	省级	贵州省黔南州罗甸县
德江乌江傩文化风景名胜区	Dejiang Wjiang Riverside National Park	省级	贵州省铜仁市德江县

18-11 全国重点文物保护单位
Historical and Cultrual Relics under Key Protection

名　称	Name	地址
平坝天台山伍龙寺	Pingba Tiantai Wulong Temple	贵州省安顺市平坝区
云山屯古建筑群(含本寨)	The Ancientry Construction of Yunshantun(Including the Village)	贵州省安顺市西秀区
安顺文庙	Anshun Temple	贵州省安顺市西秀区
穿洞遗址	The Ruins of Chuandong	贵州省安顺市普定县
宁谷遗址	The Ruins of Ninggu	贵州省安顺市西秀区
黔西观音洞遗址	The Site of Kwan-yin Cave Qianxi	贵州省毕节市黔西县
赫章可乐遗址	The Ruins of Kele in Hezhang	贵州省毕节市赫章县
织金古建筑群	The Ancientry Construction Zhijin	贵州省毕节市织金县
川滇黔省革命委员会旧址	Finish the committee old address of Chuan Dian Qian province revolution	贵州省毕节市大方县
奢香墓	The Mausoleum of Lady She Xiang	贵州省毕节市大方县
大屯土司庄园	Datun Headman's Castle	贵州省毕节市毕节市
马头寨古建筑群	The Ancientry Construction of Matouzhai	贵州省贵阳市开阳县
阳明洞和阳明祠	Yangming Cave and Yangming Ancestral Temple	贵州省贵阳市修文县、云岩区
文昌阁和甲秀楼	Wenchang Pavilion and Jiaxiu Floor	贵州省贵阳市贵阳市
息烽集中营旧址(含玄天洞)	The Site of Concentration Camp Xifeng(including Tien-dong)	贵州省贵阳市息烽县
大洞遗址	The Site of Dadong Cave	贵州省六盘水市盘县
郎德上寨古建筑群	The Ancientry Construction Langdeshangzhai	贵州省黔东南州雷山县
地坪风雨桥	Diping Pavilion Bridge	贵州省黔东南州黎平县
飞云崖古建筑群	The Ancientry Construction of Feishanya	贵州省黔东南州黄平县
旧州古建筑群	The Ancientry Construction of Jiuzhou	贵州省黔东南州黄平县
黎平会议会址	The Site of Liping Conference	贵州省黔东南州黎平县
和平村旧址	The former site of Peace village	贵州省黔东南州镇远县
青龙洞	Qinglong Cave	贵州省黔东南州镇远县
增冲鼓楼	Zengchong Drum-tower	贵州省黔东南州从江县
福泉城墙	Ming Dynasty Wall in Fuquan	贵州省黔南州福泉市
葛镜桥	Gejing Bridge	贵州省黔南州福泉市
交乐墓群	Jiaole Tombs	贵州省黔西南州兴仁县
“二十四道拐”抗战公路	"twenty-four Shui" road war	贵州省黔西南州晴隆县
石阡万寿宫	Shiqian Wanshou Palace	贵州省铜仁市石阡县
万山汞矿遗址	The Site of Wanshan Hydrargyrum	贵州省铜仁市万山区
东山古建筑群	The Ancient Building Complex of Dongshan	贵州省铜仁市铜仁市
寨英古建筑群	The Ancient Building Complex of Zhaiying	贵州省铜仁市松桃县
思唐古建筑群	The Ancientry Construction Sitang	贵州省铜仁市思南县
黔东特区革命委员会旧址	The site of Qiandong SAR revolution committee	贵州省铜仁市沿河县、德江县、印江县
遵义会议会址	The Site of Zunyi Conference	贵州省遵义市红花岗区
遵义海龙屯	Zunyi Hailongtun	贵州省遵义市汇川区
杨粲墓	Yangcan Tomb	贵州省遵义市汇川区
红军四渡赤水战役旧址	The former site of Battle of the Red Army Siduchishui	贵州省遵义市习水县、仁怀市、汇川区
湄潭浙江大学旧址	The former site of Zhejiang University in Meitan	贵州省遵义市湄潭县

注：资料来源于省文化厅，表中文物单位为第一至六批全国重点文物保护单位。

Note:Data in this table come from the Provinvial Department of Culture.The units in this table are the sixth batch of national key cultural relics protection units form the firse batch to the sixth batch.

18−11 续表 continued

名　称	Name	地址
龙广观音洞遗址	The Ruins of Guanglong Cave	贵州省黔西南州安龙县
普安铜鼓山遗址	The Ruins of Puan Timbal Hill	贵州省黔西南州普安县
茶马古道	Tea-Horse Road	四川、云南、贵州
务川大坪墓群	Wuchuan Daping Tombs	贵州省遵义市务川县
兴义万屯墓群	Xingyi Wan Tuen Tombs	贵州省黔西南州兴义市
平坝棺材洞	Pingba coffin hole	贵州省安顺市平坝区
惠水仙人桥洞葬	Huishui Fairy bridge Burial cave	贵州省黔南州惠水县
黔南水族墓群	Qiannan Aquarium Tombs	贵州省黔南州三都县、荔波县
小冲墓群	Small punch Tombs	贵州省六盘水市盘县
明十八先生墓	Eighteen persons' Tomb of Ming Dynasty	贵州省黔西南州安龙县
鲍家屯水利工程	Baojiatun Hydraulic	贵州省安顺市西秀区
镇远城墙	Zhenyuan walls	贵州省黔东南州镇远县
安顺武庙	Anshun Wumiao	贵州省安顺市西秀区
隆里古建筑群	The Ancient Building Complex of Longli	贵州省黔东南州锦屏县
石阡府文庙	Shiqian Temple	贵州省铜仁市石阡县
榕江大利村古建筑群	The Ancient Building Complex in the village Rongjiang Dali	贵州省黔东南州榕江县
楼上村古建筑群	The Ancient Building Complex in the village Loushang	贵州省铜仁市石阡县
岩门长官司城	Yanmen Long lawsuit City	贵州省黔东南州黄平县
锦屏飞山庙	Jinping Feishan Temple	贵州省黔东南州锦屏县
高阡鼓楼	Gaoqian Drum-tower	贵州省黔东南州从江县
宰俄鼓楼	Zaie Drum-tower	贵州省黔东南州从江县
金勾风雨桥	Jingou Pavilion Boasting	贵州省黔东南州从江县
鲁屯牌坊群	Lu Tun archway	贵州省黔西南州兴义市
复兴江西会馆	Jiangxi Hall in the town of Fuxing	贵州省遵义市赤水市
三门塘古建筑群	The Ancient buildings Complex in the Village of Sanmentang	贵州省黔东南州天柱县
敖氏和罗氏墓群石刻	Ao and Roche' Tombs of Carved stone	贵州省毕节市金沙县
尚稽陈玉璧祠	Chenyu Temple in the town of Shangji	贵州省遵义市遵义县
兴义刘氏庄园	The Liu manor in Xingyi	贵州省黔西南州兴义市
茅台酒酿酒工业遗产群	Maotai wine industry heritage group	贵州省遵义市仁怀市
王若飞故居	Wang Ruofei's former residence	贵州省安顺市西秀区
述洞独柱鼓楼	Duzhu Drum-tower in the Village of Shudong	贵州省黔东南州黎平县
重安江水碾群	Chongan River Shuinian group	贵州省黔东南州黄平县

注：表中文物单位为第七批全国重点文物保护单位。

Note:The units in this table are the seventh batch of national key cultural relics protection units.

18-12 星级饭店

Star-rated Hotels

名 称	Name	星级 Level	评定日期 Date of Assess	客房数 Rooms	床位数 Beds	地 址 Address	电 话 Telephone
贵州天怡豪生大酒店	Guizhou Howard Johnson Plaza Hotel	5	2005.03	310	439	贵阳市枣山路29号	0851-86518888
喜来登贵航大酒店	Sheraton Guiyang Hotel	5	2010.08	346	629	贵阳市中华南路49号	0851-85888888
黔西南州金州翠湖宾馆	Jinzhoucuihu Hotel in Qianxinanzhou	5	2010.12	203	294	兴义市瑞金南路60号	0859-3619999
贵阳世纪金源大饭店	Empark Grand Hotel - Guiyang	5	2012.03	520	755	贵阳市金阳新区金阳南路6号	0851-83928888
富康国际酒店	Fortune International Hotel	5	2013.12	420	614	兴义市瑞金路19号	0859-3666666
保利富豪温泉酒店	Regal Poly Guiyang Hotel	5	2013.12	209	332	贵阳市乌当区顺海中路88号	0851-86328888
贵州饭店	Guizhou Park Hotel	4	1998.07	382	660	贵阳市北京路66号	0851-86823888
贵州鲜花酒店	Guizhou Flower Hotel	4	2001.12	260	403	贵阳市中华南路1号	0851-85867888
贵州柏顿酒店	Trade-Point Hotel Guizhou	4	2001.05	254	343	贵阳市延安东路18号	0851-85827888
贵州丽豪大饭店	Gui Zhou Regal Hotel	4	2005.07	220	355	贵阳市瑞金北路115号	0851-86521888
贵龙饭店	Gui Long Hotel - Guiyang	4	2001.06	168	316	贵阳市神奇路52号	0851-85593888
能辉酒店	Neng Hui Hotel	4	2003.12	125	205	贵阳市瑞金南路38号	0851-85898888
贵州武岳酒店	Guizhou Wuyue Hotel	4	2007.09	192	306	贵阳市南厂路1号	0851-88651777
贵州雅迪尔国际大酒店	Gui Zhou Yonder International Hotel	4	2010.04	218	342	贵阳市中华南路7号	0851-85578888
贵州峰润喀斯特酒店	Guizhou Casite Hotel	4	2011.01	197	309	南明区神奇路1号	0851-88196888
金芦笙小镇精品特色酒店	Jinlusheng town boutique Featured Hotels	4	2011.04	138	245	宝山南路88号	0851-85623999
贵州民族大酒店	Guizhou Ethnic Hotel	4	2011.08	121	209	南明区箭道街23号	0851-85571888
贵阳蓝天宾馆	Guiyang Blue Sky Hotel	4	2011.08	112	191	南明区解放路158号	0851-85795988
西苑锦润酒店	Xiyuan Jinrun Hotel	4	2011.08	134	214	小河区锦江路5号	0851-85975555
西湖花园大酒店	West Lake Garden Hotel	4	2011.08	252	451	宝山北路133号	0851-85292802
都市怡景酒店	City Scene Hotel	4	2011.10	117	202	贵阳市都司路122号	0851-85848888
贵州铝厂宾馆	Guizhou Aluminum Hotel	4	2011.11	78	134	贵阳市白云区刚玉街57号	0851-84896111
贵阳夏日康桥酒店	Guiyang Summer Cambridge Hotel	4	2011.11	89	141	贵阳市白云区白云南路299号	0851-84439655
贵阳诺富特酒店	Guiyang Novotel Hotel	4	2012.08	242	314	贵阳市中华南路8号	0851-85881888
贵阳林城万宜酒店	Guiyang Linchengwanyi Hotel	4	2012.12	388	639	贵阳市遵义路326号	0851-86878888
遵义大世界酒店	Zuyi Grand World Hotel	4	2008.12	167	238	遵义市汇川区珠海路一号	0851-28666666
遵义东方酒店	Zunyi Oriental Hotel	4	2008.12	203	326	遵义市中华南路2号	0851-28867777
赤水中悦大酒店	Zhong Yue Hotel	4	2008.12	140	253	赤水市南正街22号	0851-22823888
遵义森林大酒店	Zunyi Woods Hotel	4	2011.12	121	212	遵义市汇川区深圳路新客运大楼	0851-28988888
遵义金城大酒店	Zunyi Jincheng Hotel	4	2012.01	131	215	遵义市香港路中段	0851-28621666
国酒门温泉酒店	GJM Hotspring Hotel	4	2012.12	67	132	仁怀市盐津河风景区国酒门旁	0851-22316666
金黔嘉华大酒店	Jinqianjiahua Hotel	4	2012.12	169	281	桐梓县娄山关镇河滨大道南段888号	0851-26666666
遵义市丽都酒店	Zunyi Lidu Hotel	4	2012.12	111	168	遵义市香港路638号	0851-28959999
安顺凯旋大酒店	Triumphal Hotel - Anshun	4	2006.12	246	403	安顺市开发区南马广场	0851-33461999
泰翔柏丽酒店	Taixiang Boutique Hotel	4	2012.08	116	183	安顺市开发区西航路	0851-38186666
关岭坝陵酒店	Guanling Baling Hotel	4	2012.08	232	432	关岭县关索镇大龙滩高速公路出口	0851-37116888
荔波县三力酒店	San Li Hotel in Libo county	4	2007.09	462	828	荔波县玉屏镇思铭大道	0854-3615888
贵侯苑商务大酒店	Guihouyuan Business Hotel	4	2009.03	85	138	都匀市开发区龙山大道	0854-7121111
伯爵花园酒店	Earl Garden Hotel	4	2009.01	149	204	都匀市开发区斗篷山路	0854-8199999
三都福丰假日酒店	Sandu Fufeng Holiday Hotel	4	2011.12	165	236	三都县三合镇龙嘴角移民新村	0854-3029999
福泉大酒店	Fuquan Hotel	4	2012.08	148	257	福泉市金山办事处洒金北路174号	0854-2212888
凯里嘉瑞禾腾龙酒店	Jiaruihe Tenglong Hotel - Kaili	4	2004.05	166	311	凯里市宁波东路	0855-8066666
凯里金冠酒店	Kaili Jin Guan Hotel	4	2006.11	168	316	凯里市支庄路18号	0855-8068888
金凯美悦酒店	Gold Camery Hotel	4	2008.09	109	187	凯里市北京西路	0855-8276688
天柱大酒店	Tianzhu Hotel	4	2012.08	80	144	天柱县凤城镇北部新区1号	0855-7821888
铜仁宝鑫大酒店	Baoxin Hotel - Tongren	4	2006.07	151	280	铜仁市东太大道88号	0856-5937888
松桃松闽大酒店	Songtao Song Min Hotel	4	2012.01	142	220	贵州省松桃县麻阳街24号	0856-6966666
铜仁温州大酒店	Tongren Wenzhou Hotel	4	2012.10	115	177	铜仁市大庆北路85号	0856-6968888
铜仁江华国际大酒店	Tongren Jin Hua International Hotel	4	2012.10	158	238	铜仁市火车站转盘	0856-5266091
毕节腾龙凯悦酒店	Tenglong Kaiyue Hotel - Bijie	4	2006.12	254	343	毕节市桂花路2号	0857-8291111
毕节大酒店	Bijie Hotel	4	2008.09	151	269	毕节市砂石路	0857-8689999
宏洲国际大酒店	Hongzhou International Hotel	4	2011.10	203	298	织金县城关镇金北路151号	0857-7758888
毕节大众国际酒店	Bijie Dazhong International Hotel	4	2012.05	179	321	毕节市翠屏路12号	0857-8933333
六盘水时代假日酒店	Liupanshui Times Holiday Hotel	4	2009.08	265	381	六盘水钟山区钟山中路66号	0858-8108888

18-12 续表1 continued

名　　称	Name	星级 Level	评定日期 Date of Assess	客房数 Rooms	床位数 Beds	地　址 Address	电　话 Telephone
六盘水凤凰祥林大酒店	Liupanshui Fenghuang Xianglin Hotel	4	2010.12	130	224	六盘水市凤凰新区青峰路18号	0858-8296789
六盘水红果大酒店	Liupanshui Hongguo Hotel	4	2011.12	189	353	盘县红果经济开发区凤鸣路	0858-3631888
牂牁江假日酒店	Zangkejiang Holiday Hotel	4	2012.12	114	178	六枝特区人民路22号	0858-8101666
铜仁南长城国际大酒店	Tongren South Great Wall International Hotel	4	2013.04	202	292	铜仁市南长城路金滩商业休闲港	0856-5939999
松桃国际大酒店	Songtao International Hotel	4	2013.06	228	345	松桃县东城新区七星大道	0856-8333333
贵州华联大酒店	Guizhou Hualian Large Hotel	4	1999.09	143	218	贵阳市中华中路137号	0851-5810999
长顺浩瀚大酒店	Changshun vast Large Hotel	4	2013.06	111	191	长顺县城南新区城南大道一号	0854-6828888
沿河乌江酒店	Yanhe Wujiang Hotel	4	2013.11	121	206	沿河县环城路	0856-6977777
杜鹃花大酒店	Rhododendron Large Hotel	4	2013.12	141	282	黔西县文化路口	0857-4836666
贵州黎明澳斯特酒店	Guizhou Dawn Macao Crest Hotel	4	2013.12	165	267	金沙县黎明路1号	0857-7212888
黔西县水西大酒店	Qianxi County Water West Large Hotel	4	2013.12	80	141	黔西县文峰办事处公园路	0857-4833333
贵山大酒店	Guishan Large Hotel	4	2014.01	235	351	贵阳市云岩区省府路39号	0851-85254166
黔灵大酒店	Qianling Hotel	3	2000.04	152	273	贵阳市北京路225号	0851-88271521
贵阳神奇星岛酒店	Guiyang Shenqixingdao Hotel	3	2002.09	101	180	贵阳市贵开路1号	0851-86751888
贵州立云酒店	Guizhou Liyun Hotel	3	2002.12	254	468	贵阳市浣沙路5号	0851-88126666
紫林宾馆	Zilin Hotel	3	2004.02	195	365	贵阳市延安中路110号	0851-85283000
久远饭店	Jiuyuan Hotel	3	2004.08	169	300	贵阳市瑞金南路36号	0851-85849999
贵阳市金品大酒店	Guiyang Jinpin Hotel	3	2004.12	112	196	贵阳朝阳洞路建材巷1号	0851-88216666
贵阳南翔酒店	Guiyang Nanxiang Hotel	3	2004.12	63	108	贵阳市延安西路185号	0851-86522888
贵州宏业宾馆	Guizhou Hongye Hotel	3	2005.02	75	143	贵阳市解放路87号	0851-85566755
花溪溪山酒店	Huaxi Xishan Hotel	3	2006.01	49	96	贵阳市花溪区迎宾路	0851-83630166
贵阳鸿鼎大酒店	Guiyang Hongding Large Hotel	3	2006.11	110	200	贵阳市沙冲路198号	0851-83839988
新联大厦	New Union Building	3	1997.12	120	200	贵阳市外环东路227号	0851-86765555
红阳宾馆	Hongyang Hotel	3	2005.01	73	140	贵阳花溪区150号信箱	0851-83853306
金泉酒店	Jinquan Hotel	3	2007.01	91	172	贵阳花溪区花谷路6号	0851-83851484
贵阳机场宾馆	Guiyang Airport Hotel	3	2007.11	168	315	贵阳市	0851-85498585
黔景宾馆	Qianjing Hotel	3	2007.12	117	246	贵阳市	0851-83990188
京瑞宾馆	Jingrui Hotel	3	2005.06	134	300	贵阳市北京路194号	0851-86891602
贵阳瑞金酒店	Ruijin Hotel	3	2008.06	168	312	贵阳市瑞金南路62号	0851-85209999
贵州铁路通达饭店	Guizhou Railway Tongda Hotel	3	2008.11	234	468	贵阳市遵义路86号	0851-88213888
贵阳益宏酒店有限公司	Guiyang Yihong Hotels Ltd.	3	2009.12	99	157	贵阳市油榨街2号	0851-83818888
云岩浣溪假日大酒店	Yunyan Huanxi Holiday Hotel	3	2010.05	138	230	贵阳市浣沙路104号	0851-88598888
花溪玉龙宾馆	Huaxi Yulong Hotel	3	2011.03	35	70	花溪区大吉路1号	0851-83863865
聚鑫酒店	Juxin Hotel	3	2011.04	114	189	贵阳市环城北路228号	0851-86851999
贵武花园大酒店	Guiwu Garden Hotel	3	2011.09	91	151	贵阳市金阳新区云潭南路	0851-85625678
水云天酒店	Water sky hotel	3	2011.09	60	126	贵阳市南明区翠微巷60号	0851-85515666
南江度假酒店	Nanjiang Holiday Hotel	3	2011.07	146	257	开阳南江大峡谷景区内	0851-87524089
红枫湖旅游度假村	Hongfeng Lake Tourist Resort	3	2011.07	126	207	清镇市望城坡	0851-88575042
清镇皇朝大酒店	Qingzhen Dynasty Hotel	3	2011.07	90	144	清镇市云岭东路	0851-82581888
贵州林都酒店	Guizhou Lindu Hotel	3	2011.12	105	189	云岩区延安西路2号	0851-85360367
贵阳腾晖酒店	Guiyang Tenghui Hotel	3	2012.05	76	131	贵阳市修文县翠屏路	0851-82327777
遵义港澳大酒店	Zunyi Gang'ao Hotel	3	2005.11	100	179	遵义市澳门路8号	0851-28716655
遵义宾馆	Zunyi Hotel	3	2000.01	259	465	遵义市石龙路3号	0851-28224902
遵义京腾丽湾酒店	Zunyi Jingtengliwan Hotel	3	2006.11	139	250	遵义市北京路	0851-28649898
茅园宾馆	Maoyuan Hotel	3	2004.01	56	110	遵义仁怀市茅台镇	0851-22386290
习水绿洲酒店	Xishui Lvzhou Hotel	3	2006.11	84	230	遵义习水县经济开发区	0851-22732100
广电酒店	Guangdian Hotel	3	2007.09	107	192	遵义市中华北路广电大厦	0851-28700888
仁怀市名酒宾馆	Renhuai Mingjiu Hotel	3	2007.09	71	119	仁怀市国酒大道	0851-23226999
嘉联宾馆	Jialian Hotel	3	2008.12	64	119	赤水市人民南路运管大厦	0851-22820222
鹏程大酒店	Pengcheng Hotel	3	2010.01	51	92	余庆县城内	0851-24625868
赤天化宾馆	Chitianhua hotel	3	2010.01	95	168	赤水市	0851-22887081
湄潭大酒店	Meitan Hotel	3	2010.12	82	136	湄潭县兴湄北路35号	0851-24366595
金竹大酒店	Jinzhu Hotel	3	2011.12	89	167	赤水市文化办财神涂	0851-22853555
佳乐家酒店	Jialejia Hotel	3	2012.11	106	171	遵义市大连路	0851-24626888

18-12 续表2 continued

名 称	Name	星级 Level	评定日期 Date of Assess	客房数 Rooms	床位数 Beds	地 址 Address	电 话 Telephone
余庆广电酒店	Yuqing Guangdian Hotel	3	2011.11	56	91	余庆县香港路	0851-23195555
安顺西秀山宾馆	Anshun Xixiushan Hotel	3	2002.04	92	153	安顺市南华路48号	0851-33223900
神奇福运大酒店	Shenqifuyun Hotel	3	2002.09	90	160	安顺市外环西南路3号	0851-33290000
黔中大厦	Qianzhong Building	3	2005.07	66	113	安顺市南华路68好	0851-33292019
白马湖山庄	Baima Lake Villa	3	2005.07	33	59	安顺市镇宁县白马哨	0851-36791111
安顺若飞宾馆	Anshun Ruofei Hotel	3	2001.04	41	73	安顺市南华路48号	0851-33225325
龙宫酒店	Dragon Palace Hotel	3	2006.01	41	79	安顺市龙宫风景名胜区	0851-33661388
关岭黔岭宾馆	Guanling Qianling Hotel	3	2006.11	50	92	关岭县外环路128号	0851-37228888
安顺纽曼宾馆	Anshun Newman Hotel	3	2008.03	36	70	安顺市	0851-33467777
龙宫水电宾馆	Longgong Shuidian Hotel	3	2009.11	31	60	安顺市龙宫风景名胜区	0851-33661166
廊桥华油酒店	Langqiao Huayou Hotel	3	2010.07	82	152	安顺市塔山西路15号	
平坝白云大酒店	Pingba Baiyun Hotel	3	2010.07	47	52	平坝区城关镇高新区	
安顺凤凰山大酒店	Anshun Fenghuangshan Hotel	3	2011.12	121	240	安顺市塔山东路58号	0851-33225998
君临大酒店	Junlin Hotel	3	2012.05	123	202	安顺市新大十字塔山西路1号	0851-33350777
紫鑫酒店	Zixin Hotel	3	2012.06	102	184	西秀区黄果树大街消防支队内	0851-33332777
新华宾馆	Xinhua Hotel	3	2012.06	108	189	开发区西航路138号	0851-33459888
鑫焰酒店	Xinyan Hotel	3	2012.06	52	87	平坝区南客运站大楼	0851-34616789
汇景酒店	Huijing Hotel	3	2012.06	51	93	普定县龙潭加油站对面	0851-38718888
都匀港龙大酒店	Duyun Ganglong Hotel	3	2002.08	132	214	都匀市河滨路134号	0854-8222895
金利源大酒店	Jinliyuan Hotel	3	2010.01	89	182		0854-3619188
五月花景山酒店	Wuyuehua Jingshan Hotel	3	2005.01	89	121	都匀市剑江中路112号	0854-8756999
西苑假日酒店	Xiyuan Holiday Hotel	3	2007.09	54	99	都匀市开发区	0854-8758888
锦绣园	Jinxiuyuan Park	3	2005.09	48	101	龙里县城郊	0854-5669508
顺庆大酒店	Shunqing Hotel	3	2005.03	112	182	荔波樟江北街	0854-3610388
荔波吉妮丽吉大酒店	Libo Jeanne Liji Hotel	3	2006.11	79	155	荔波县教师新村	0854-3619666
神泉大酒店	Shenquan Hotel	3	2005.03	46	96	罗甸县政府路	0854-7620758
都匀市桥城宾馆	Duyun Qiaocheng Hotel	3	2007.09	92	166	都匀市文明路50号	0854-8222189
独山县南方大酒店	Dushan Southern Hotel	3	2007.09	61	91	独山县四通路十八号	0854-3238525
荔波县金谷宾馆	Libo Jingu Hotel	3	2007.09	80	178	荔波县樟江北路	0854-3613888
纪龙大酒店	Jilong Hotel	3	2005.09	44	80	龙里县	0854-5620333
贵定县环岛大酒店	Guiding Huandao Hotel	3	2009.01	30	36	贵定县城关镇八一村	0854-5221000
瓮安县金福大酒店	Weng'an Jinfu Hotel	3	2009.03	62	100	瓮安县文峰中路	0854-2635100
荔波县大鹏商务酒店	Libo Dapeng Business Hotel	3	2008.03	95	184	荔波县漳江中路12号	0854-3615499
独山县翠泉宾馆	Dushan Cuiquan hotel	3	2009.04	63	114	独山县	0854-3239018
三江宏晟度假酒店	Sanjiang Hongsheng Holiday Hotel	3	2010.08	30	40	福泉市金山办事处双桥村金鸡山	0854-2210999
怡景苑宾馆	Yijingyuan hotel	3	2010.08	54	107	荔波县漳江北街42号	0854-3618300
夜郎大酒店	Yelang Hotel	3	2010.12	70	126	惠水县和平镇建设路	0854-6234567
桂花园度假酒店	Guihuayuan Holiday Hotel	3	2011.09	54	103	都匀市大河村村卫生院对面	0854-8190559
九九大酒店	Jiujiu Hotel	3	2011.12	51	94	贵州省长顺县和平西路	0854-6898888
瓮安灵江大酒店	Weng'an Lingjiang Hotel	3	2012.06	30	47	瓮安县新区武装部	0854-2776666
凯里凯莱酒店	Kaili Gloria Plaza Hotel	3	2006.12	96	182	凯里市韶山南路21号	0855-8277888
凯里鸿祺宾馆	Kaili Hongqi Hotel	3	2006.08	84	140	凯里市韶山南路3号	0855-8275555
黎平大酒店	Liping Hotel	3	2006.11	80	148	黎平德风镇富民北路	0855-6210666
贵州清酒醉翁宾馆	Guizhou Qingjiuzuiweng Hotel	3	2004.05	46	92	镇远县	0855-5823238
施秉县三丰迎宾馆	Shibing Sanfeng Guest House	3	2004.05	89	190	施秉县平宁桥	0855-4227188
凯铁大酒店	Kaitie Hotel	3	2008.09	63	121	凯里市清江路	0855-3811999
凯里大酒店	Kaili Hotel	3	2008.09	156	275	凯里市韶山北路	0855-8277778
忠德园假日酒店	Zhongdeyuan Holiday Hotel	3	2008.09	70	160	凯里市环城东路	0855-8538888
港赛大酒店	Gangsai Hotel	3	2008.09	63	114	黎平县城内	0855-6230888
久恰里吉温泉度假酒店	Jiugeliji Spa Resort	3	2008.09	60	115	剑河县温泉风景区内	0855-5158288
清源酒店	Qingyuan Hotel	3	2008.12	30	56	下司镇皮划艇激流回旋训练基地	0855-2685666
营盘坡民族宾馆	Yingpanpo National Hotel	3	2009.07	92	163	凯里市	0855-3837779
凯里市天华宾馆	Kaili Tianhua Hotel	3	2009.07	82	153	凯里市	0855-8276411
镇远县铁溪度假酒店	Zhenyuan Tiexi Resort	3	2009.07	33	57	镇远县	0855-5721888

18-12 续表3 continued

名 称	Name	星级 Level	评定日期 Date of Assess	客房数 Rooms	床位数 Beds	地 址 Address	电 话 Telephone
剑河县馨泉山庄	Jianhe Xinquan Villa	3	2009.11	38	74	剑河县	0855-5158168
凯里宾馆	Kaili Hotel	3	2010.04	57	130	凯里市	0855-8066100
从江县奥悦酒店	Congjiang Aoyue Hotel	3	2009.11	33	66	从江县	0855-6411808
金正酒店	Jinzheng Hotel	3	2010.06	67	107	凯里市经济开发区	0855-8558988
麻江县怡景湾酒店	Majiang Yijing Hotel	3	2010.08	34	48	麻江县下司镇	0855-2684777
华侨大酒店	Huaqiao Hotel	3	2010.11	70	110	三穗城关	0855-3855555
柏悦酒店	Boyue Hotel	3	2010.11	56	101	凯里市	0855-8270000
万豪酒店	Wanhao Hotel	3	2010.11	72	128	凯里市	0855-8603999
镇远府城宾馆	Zhenyuan Fucheng Hotel	3	2011.11	69	130	镇远县兴隆街	0855-5711888
台江金红阳生态酒店	Taijiang Jinhongyang Eco-hotel	3	2011.11	63	120	台江国家级南宫森林公园景区18号	
杉木河酒店	Shanmuhe Hotel	3	2011.03	57	115	施秉县舞阳河路	0855-4221177
西江黔森大酒店	Xijiang Qian Sen Hotel	3	2011.03	72	140	西江千户苗寨黔森路1号	0855-3347909
源丰商务酒店	Yuanfeng Business Hotel	3	2005.07	62	99	铜仁市锦江南路1号	0856-5222222
思南远航大酒店	Sinan Yuanhang Hotel	3	2009.06	62	110	思南县城北街29号	0856-7220777
江口县索菲特大酒店	Jiangkou Sofite Hotel	3	2009.12	57	112	江口县三星西路17号	0856-6622288
德江县金平大酒店	Dejiang Jinping Hotel	3	2009.12	44	83	德江县清龙镇	0856-8527555
铜仁市金顶酒店	Tongren Jinding Hotel	3	2009.12	41	73	铜仁市清水大道80号	0856-5211168
铜仁市梵天索菲特酒店	Tongren Brahma Sofitel Hotel	3	2010.12	57	97	铜仁锦江大道8号	0856-5218888
沿河沙洲大酒店	Yanhe Shazhou Hotel	3	2010.11	55	87	铜仁市沿河县沙坨电站	0856-6998666
玉屏宾馆	Yuping Hotel	3	2010.12	66	114	玉屏县平溪镇人民路333号	0856-3227888
沿河金红大酒店	Yanhe Jinhong Hotel	3	2010.12	57	130	铜仁市沿河县城南路	0856-8228055
龙都大酒店	Longdu Hotel	3	2011.06	139	216	铜仁市清水大道128号	0856-4133333
松桃世纪华园大酒店	Songtao Shijiyuan Hotel	3	2012.04	50	87	松桃县大十字	0856-2681555
铜仁盛世佳华酒店	Tongren Shengshijiahua Hotel	3	2012.06	64	125	铜仁市清水路火车站旁	0856-6903888
铜仁世纪大酒店	Tongren Century Hotel	3	2012.06	149	272	铜仁市清水南路公园道1号	0856-5629999
铜仁亨达酒店	Tongren Hengda Hotel	3	2012.06	55	92	铜仁市火车站旁	0856-5230999
金沙县黄金大酒店	Jinsha Huangjin Hotel	3	2008.07	95	179	金沙县长安街138号	0857-7258888
洪南大酒店	Hongnan Hotel	3	2008.09	81	117	毕节市迎宾大道	0857-8292888
赫章夜郎大酒店	Hezhang Yelang Hotel	3	2008.12	145	255	赫章县城南路	0857-3238998
煌都帝豪酒店	Huangdudihao Hotel	3	2008.09	78	120	黔西县城内	0857-4888888
黔西化屋度假酒店	Qianxi Huawu Holiday Hotel	3	2011.08	36	66	黔西县新仁乡化屋村	0857-4634166
纳雍华熙酒店	Nayong Huaxi Hotel	3	2010.01	114	173	纳雍县城南大道	0857-3685777
金海大酒店	Jinhai Hotel	3	2011.09	67	120	毕节市洪南路	0857-8615555
草海大酒店	Caohai Hotel	3	2011.09	108	188	威宁威双大道	0857-7115388
红楼酒店	Honglou Hotel	3	2004.06	48	90	大方县奢香大道南段	0857-5233712
金龙酒店	Jinlong Hotel	3	2012.07	79	142	织金县金北路	0857-7755777
金鑫酒店	Jinxin Hotel	3	2012.07	78	138	大方县奢香大道北段	0857-2198888
奢香大酒店	Shexiang Hotel	3	2012.11	79	136	七星关区清毕路长弘花苑内	0857-8631888
六盘水金三角大酒店	Liupanshui Jinsanjiao Hotel	3	2006.12	44	79	六盘水市明湖路3号	0858-8233888
雨田酒店	Yutian Hotel	3	2005.07	75	126	六盘水钟山西路48号	0858-8261888
黔锦假日酒店	Qianjin Holiday Hotel	3	2012.03	137	208	盘县红果经济开发区	0858-3668995
兴凯花园酒店	Xingkai Garden Hotel	3	2010.03	76	122	盘县红果镇杜鹃西路1号	0858-3635059
城城大厦	Chengcheng Building	3	2005.07	68	128	兴义市神奇路159号	0859-3112222
龙宇大酒店	Longyu Hotel	3	2007.11	56	112	兴义市神奇西路26号	0859-3126888
盘江宾馆	Panjiang Hotel	3	2005.07	123	231	兴义市盘江西路4号	0859-3223456
兴义神禧大酒店	Xingyi Shenxi Hotel	3	2008.05	80	158	兴义市坪东路	0859-3818188
贞丰县贞丰宾馆	Zhenfeng Hotel	3	2009.09	120	214	贞丰县金丰大道29号	0859-6777777
贞丰县怡景酒店	Zhenfeng Yijing Hotel	3	2009.09	36	60	贞丰县	0859-6613777
兴义市三生酒店	Xingyi Sansheng Hotel	3	2009.09	111	200	兴义市瑞金北路中段	0859-3244888
安龙泰安宾馆	Anlong Tai'an Hotel	3	2012.02	75	132	贵州省安龙县西区开发大道	0859-5555222
海钰酒店	Haiyu Hotel	3	2012.02	152	266	兴义市瑞金北路10号	0859-8711111
印江腾龙酒店	Yinjiang Dragon Hotel	3	2013.01	55	100	印江县城西环开发区	0857-6228888
镇远县名城宾馆	Zhenyuan County City Hotel	3	2013.04	63	119	镇远县步行街	0855-5720888
中瑞天禧酒店	Zhongrui Tianxi Hotel	3	2013.04	112	196	凯里市迎宾大道环城南路（行政中心南侧）	0855-3830000

18-12 续表4 continued

名　称	Name	星级 Level	评定日期 Date of Assess	客房数 Rooms	床位数 Beds	地　址 Address	电　话 Telephone
盘县大浪淘沙假日酒店	Panxian Da Lang Tao Sha Holiday Hotel	3	2013.04	74	137	盘县	
盘县大酒店	Panxian Large Hotel	3	2013.04	165	276	盘县	
镇远大酒店	Zhenyuan Large Hotel	3	2013.06	90	162	镇远县和平街	0855-3878888
博雅宾馆	Boya Hotel	3	2008.12	40	76	绥阳县北大街	0852-6223855
南星酒店	South Star Hotel	3	2013.11	63	107	开发区星光路中段	0852-2280000
紫云宾馆	Ziyun Hotel	3	2013.11	112	200	紫云县商业街	0853-5238888
印江豪情大酒店	Yinjiang Passion Large Hotel	3	2013.12	30	54	印江县木黄镇	0856-6360080
印江金穗酒店	Yinjiang Golden Spike Hotel	3	2013.12	36	66	印江县县府路	0856-6318888
万山宾馆	Wanshan Hotel	3	2013.12	50	79	万山区体育馆旁	0856-3520868
思南电力宾馆	Sinan Power Hotel	3	2013.12	30	58	思南县思唐镇安化社区275号	0856-7229948
黔西景鸿酒店	Qianxi Jinghong Hotel	3	2013.12	48	88	黔西县文峰办大水塘	13765851366
莱凯桐都大酒店	Les Cayes Tong Large Hotel	3	2013.11	110	182	正安县桐乡北路	0852-3176666
构皮滩大酒店	Goupitan Large Hotel	3	2013.11	89	160	余庆县构皮滩镇	0852-4737777
岑巩县双龙大酒店	Cengong County double Dragon Large Hotel	3	2014.04	89	175	岑巩县舞水南路8号	0855-3891555
枫叶山庄	Fengye Villa	2	2000.01	66	129	贵阳市红枫发电总厂内	0851-82554168
天洋楼大酒店	Tianyanglou Hotel	2	2004.09	42	100	贵阳市民权路5号	0851-85832088
贵州民族宾馆	Guizhou National Hotel	2	2004.12	86	170	贵阳市市北路68号	0851-88633666
开阳金都宾馆	Kaiyang Jindu Hotel	2	2004.01	41	87	贵阳市开阳县环城北路	0851-85832088
仁达饭店	Renda Hotel	2	2004.09	112	300	贵阳市中华北路319号	0851-86825301
开阳尚怡宾馆	Kaiyang Shangyi Hotel	2	2009.04	22	41	开阳县	0851-87251666
开阳江南宾馆	Kaiyang Jiangnan Hotel	2	2010.05	35	65	开阳县城关镇环城北路	0851-87224688
万乐商务酒店	Wanle Business Hotel	2	2011.11	65	87	贵阳市白云区同心路1号	0851-86617999
一家快捷酒店	Yijia Inn	2	2011.11	43	48	贵阳市白云区白云南路402号	0851-84485308
君安宾馆	Jun'an Hotel	2	2011.10	92	148	贵阳黔灵西路62号	0851-86816999
七天连锁酒店花溪行政中心店	Seven Days Hotel Chain Huaxi Administrative Center Store	2	2011.12	93	99	贵阳市花溪区清溪路493号	0851-88516677
平达快捷酒店	Pinda Inn	2	2011.11	38	47	开阳县城关镇环城北路68号	0851-87228369
南江农庄	Nanjiang Farm	2	2011.12	21	30	开阳县南江乡杉木冲	13595005415
开阳舜熙酒店	Kaiyang Xishun Hotel	2	2011.12	21	32	开阳县城关镇吉祥路	0851-87315399
贵阳金关大酒店	Guiyang Jinguan Hotel	2	2011.12	70	120	贵阳市云岩区金关村	0851-84766665
瑞海酒店	Ruihai Hotel	2	2001.12	74	108	遵义市外环路沙坝	0851-28866333
名族酒店	Mingzu Hotel	2	2004.06	46	86	遵义市红花岗武装部	0851-28433888
蓝天宾馆	Blue Sky Hotel	2	2005.12	138	248	遵义市北京路99号	0851-28622916
通达酒店	Tongda Hotel	2	2001.06	148	276	遵义市北京路134号	0851-28822925
正华大酒店	Zhenghua Hotel	2	2002.05	46	105	桐梓县娄山关镇	0851-26657869
利永宾馆	Liyong Hotel	2	2004.05	83	136	仁怀市国酒中路	0851-22250882
聚贤楼宾馆	Juxianlou Hotel	2	2005.12	33	50	绥阳县博雅苑陈列馆内	0851-26233848
娄山关生态乐园酒店	Loushanguan Eco Paradise Hotel	2	2009.01	27	49	桐梓县娄山关镇娄山村	0851-26825333
彩阳酒店	Caiyang Hotel	2	2008.12	35	49	桐梓县城	0851-23208788
香山宾馆	Xiangshan Hotel	2	2008.12	67	129	遵义市红花岗区大兴路狮子桥头	0851-28234444
赤水大酒店	Chishui Hotel	2	2008.12	36	74	赤水市西内环路106号	0851-22821334
云门囤宾馆	Yunmentun Hotel	2	2009.01	38	71	遵义县三渡镇花桥村	0851-26581555
枫香温泉	Fengxiang Spa	2	2009.01	38	82	遵义县枫香镇	0851-27572608
凤岗宾馆	Fenggang hotel	2	2009.01	57	105	凤岗县县府路	0851-25224567
恒源酒店	Hengyuan Hotel	2	2009.01	37	66	凤岗县政通路	0851-25222768
腾达酒店	Tenda Hotel	2	2005.06	27	54	安顺市	0851-37228886
长城宾馆	Great Wall Hotel	2	2009.07	29	48	安顺平坝区武装部	0851-34227333
福源酒店	Fuyuan Hotel	2	2012.06	36	72	开发区北航路广电大楼旁	0851-33320666
西苑酒店	Xiyuan Hotel	2	2006.04	50	106	都匀市剑江中路	0854-8682132
都匀丽都酒店	Duyun Lidu Hotel	2	2005.09	63	97	都匀州地税局培训中心	0854-8318869
樟江大厦	Zhangjiang Building	2	2003.04	34	76	荔波县城内	0854-3618888
荔波宾馆	Libo Hotel	2	2003.04	36	67	荔波县政府大院内	0854-3612169
鲁黔宾馆	Luqian Hotel	2	2003.04	20	40	荔波县樟江中路	0854-3617098
锦源宾馆	Jinyuan Hotel	2	2004.01	17	39	荔波县广场东路	0854-3618818
水上人间	Water world	2	2003.12	21	47	荔波县内	0854-8939979

18-12 续表5 continued

名 称	Name	星级 Level	评定日期 Date of Assess	客房数 Rooms	床位数 Beds	地 址 Address	电 话 Telephone
松源宾馆	Songyuan Hotel	2	2003.12	20	37	荔波县内	0854-8967651
东方宾馆	Dongfang Hotel	2	2003.04	20	38	荔波县内	0854-3618968
青旅大酒店	CYTS Hotel	2	2006.05	30	70	荔波县广场东路	0854-3613158
蓝天宾馆	Blue Sky Hotel	2	2003.04	30	60	荔波县城	0854-3619831
荔伊宾馆	Liyi Hotel	2	2006.05	27	52	荔波县城樟江北街	0854-8808668
荔波前锦宾馆	Libo Qianjin Hotel	2	2006.09	39	94	荔波	13595418295
怡心宾馆	Yixin Hotel	2	2005.09	15	24	三都三启镇县府路	0854-3927818
望月宾馆	Wangyue Hotel	2	2006.04	48	87	罗甸县委	0854-7611554
腾龙宾馆	Tenglong Hotel	2	2006.09	27	45	平塘县	0854-7222888
银河大酒店	Yinhe Hotel	2	2008.12	23	41	平塘县	0854-7230988
金胜宾馆	Jinsheng Hotel	2	2008.12	25	44	平塘县	0854-7223688
富源宾馆	Fuyuan Hotel	2	2008.12	18	40	荔波县	0854-3619298
金容宾馆	Jinrong Hotel	2	2008.12	25	51	荔波县	0854-3613818
祥和宾馆	Xianghe Hotel	2	2008.12	30	64	荔波县	0854-3616177
金林宾馆	Jinlin Hotel	2	2008.12	30	59	荔波县	0854-3619780
东篱宾馆	Dongli Hotel	2	2008.12	30	60	荔波县	0854-3619758
名豪大酒店	Minghao Hotel	2	2008.12	40	69	瓮安县	0854-2625555
东利酒店	Dongli Hotel	2	2008.12	24	34	瓮安县	0854-2621889
水电宾馆	Shuidian Hotel	2	2008.12	20	29	瓮安县	0854-2624584
杜鹃苑宾馆	Dujuanyuan Hotel	2	2008.12	48	87	长顺县	0854-6936222
凤凰宾馆	Fenghuang Hotel	2	2008.12	40	90	三都县	0854-3927898
三林时尚酒店	Sanlinshishang Hotel	2	2008.12	52	88	都匀市	0854-8239828
惠水县百联商务酒店	Huishui Bailian Business Hotel	2	2009.12	32	58	惠水县涟江中路中段	0854-6283989
荔波县溪桥宾馆	Libo Xiqiao Hotel	2	2009.12	53	103	荔波县樟江东路17号	0854-3618666
荔波县齐鲁宾馆	Libo Qilu Hotel	2	2009.12	25	50	荔波县玉屏镇文明路24号	0854-3617118
贵储酒店	Guichu Hotel	2	2010.06	30	50	贵定县	0854-5236666
贵定飞龙大酒店	Guiding Feilong Hotel	2	2010.06	28	54	贵定县	0854-5233298
三都地中海宾馆	Sandu Dizhonghai Hotel	2	2010.07	22	35	三都县城中心	0854-3028777
三都润丰宾馆	Sandu Runfeng Hotel	2	2010.07	23	27	三都县三合镇团结路	0854-3929123
祥华酒店	Xianghua Hotel	2	2010.08	26	56	龙里县龙山镇青龙路	0854-5636088
馨豪酒店	Xinhao Hotel	2	2010.08	37	68	龙里县龙山镇兴龙路	0854-5635789
育才宾馆	Yucai Hotel	2	2010.11	36	67	荔波县建设西路41号	0854-3619852
虹泰宾馆	Hongtai Hotel	2	2010.09	20	38	平塘县平湖镇环城路	0854-7225888
聚丰园宾馆	Jufengyuan Hotel	2	2010.09	20	30	平塘县新区大道	0854-7230568
银都宾馆	Yindu Hotel	2	2010.11	48	63	贵定县红旗大道1号	0854-5231878
惠馨时尚酒店	Huixin Fashion Hotel	2	2011.12	23	29	贵州省惠水县和平镇涟江北路	0854-6225333
乐喜商务酒店	Lexi Business Hotel	2	2012.09	40	60	都匀市开发区沙坝供销社综合楼	0854-8518688
凯里市西湖大酒店	Kaili Westlake Hotel	2	2002.12	44	83	凯里市北京西路74号	0855-3826888
国穗大酒店	Guosui Hotel	2	2003.01	28	52	凯里市国税务局大院内	0855-8276888
岑巩县凯华大酒店	Cengong Kaihua Hotel	2	2007.01	65	128	岑巩县	0855-3895988
从江宾馆	Congjiang hotel	2	2008.12	34	67	从江县	0855-6418669
仁和大酒店	Renhe Hotel	2	2008.12	29	43	从江县	0855-6412900
雷山县圣城嘉源酒店	Leishan Shengchengjiayuan Hotel	2	2008.12	27	51	雷山县	0855-3336718
麻江县下司第一楼	Majiang Xiasi Diyilou	2	2008.12	32	65	麻江县	0855-2684000
金鼎龙大酒店	Jindinglong Hotel	2	2009.04	22	41	雷山县城关镇	0855-5158168
剑河温泉剑泉山庄	Jianhe Spa and Jianquan Villa	2	2008.05	33	61	剑河县	0855-5158088
马家岩大酒店	Majiayan Hotel	2	2010.05	36	70	黄平县	0855-2431199
凯里香山大酒店	Kaili Xiangshan Hotel	2	2010.07	40	68	凯里市北京西路39号	0855-8601099
施秉县王府酒店	Shibing Wangfu Hotel	2	2012.06	33	62	施秉县城关镇中沙大道	0855-4326999
石阡宾馆	Shiqian hotel	2	2005.06	61	115	石阡县汤山镇	0856-7652777
沿河天龙大酒店	Yanhe Tianlong Hotel	2	2005.09	96	350	沿河县城南路23号	0856-8228054
思南县明星宾馆	Sinan Mingxing Hotel	2	2009.12	26	54	思南县民政局内	0856-7225085
玉屏贵阳大酒店	Yuping Guiyang Hotel	2	2010.08	30	60	玉屏火车站附近	0856-3228886
天生桥假日酒店	Tianshengqiao Holiday Hotel	2	2011.12	16	29	铜仁市碧江区川东镇云盘村32号	13668562598

18-12 续表6 continued

名称	Name	星级 Level	评定日期 Date of Assess	客房数 Rooms	床位数 Beds	地址 Address	电话 Telephone
滨江假日酒店	Binjiang Holiday Hotel	2	2012.09	56	110	松桃县滨江花园D区6号	0856-2835899
黔闽商务酒店	Qianmin Business Hotel	2	2012.11	31	58	松桃县滨江花园A区2号	0856-2323888
洪山宾馆	Hongshan Hotel	2	2004.08	208	388	毕节市洪山路1号	0857-8251829
金辉酒店	Jinhui Hotel	2	2006.07	60	102	金沙县城内	0857-7251999
毕节迎宾馆	Bijie Guest House	2	2009.07	49	90	毕节市环东路1号	0857-8312222
织金平远酒店	Zhijin Pingyuan Hotel	2	2009.07	43	83	织金县沿河路	0857-7636999
威宁明珠酒店	Weining Mingzhu Hotel	2	2009.07	27	51	威宁县开发区	0857-6233088
赫章维尔乐宾馆	Hezhang wei'erle Hotel	2	2009.07	20	33	赫章县南环路	0857-3239898
纳雍良源大酒店	Nayong Liangyuan Hotel	2	2009.12	40	100	纳雍县农贸街1号（法院旁）	0857-3536116
金沙富豪大酒店	Jinsha Fuhao Hotel	2	2010.01	17	27	新武装部旁	0857-7235555
名望宾馆	Mingwang Hotel	2	2010.08	15	23	赫章县城关镇环城路	0857-3221513
金沙安底温泉度假中心	Jinsha Andi Hot Spring Holiday Center	2	2011.12	24	64	金沙县安底镇温泉村	0857-7388333
黔西龙华大酒店	Qianxi Longhua Large Hotel	2	2009.06	36	61	黔西县城关镇水西大道燕山街口	0857-4240333
黔西星旗酒店	Qianxi Star Hotel	2	2009.09	77	132	黔西县城关镇莲城大道星旗大厦	0857-4243777
六枝工矿迎宾馆	Liuzhi Gongkuang Guest House	2	2002.05	57	114	六枝特区团结路13号	0858-5713548
凯豪大酒店	Kaihao Hotel	2	2007.01	40	72	六枝特区交通西路	0858-5319999
六枝宾馆	Liuzhi Hotel	2	2005.01	65	160	六枝平寨镇友谊路	0858-5322660
丰鑫假日酒店	Fengxin Holiday Hotel	2	2012.05	75	120	六枝特区团结路5号	0858-5898888
安龙县麗月鸿钰酒店	Anlong Liyuehongyu Hotel	2	2010.01	36	63	安龙县	0859-5216111
南昆宾馆	Nankun Hotel	2	2004.11	44	69	兴义市顶效开发区	0859-2282188
盘江紫薇园宾馆	Panjiang Ziweiyuan Hotel	2	2006.09	42	87	安龙县	0859-5211888
黔西南州隆泰酒店	Qianxinanzhou Longtai Hotel	2	2007.07	27	53	兴义市	
西苑锦润酒店	Xiyuan Jinrun Hotel	2	2013.04	135	226	都匀市	0854-5679999
瓮安县天琦旅馆	Weng'an county Tianqi Hotel	2	2013.04	21	27	瓮安县文峰南路	
瓮安县阳关宾馆	Weng'an county Yangguan Hotel	2	2013.04	24	47	瓮安县雍阳镇气象局旁	
德江金宏大酒店	Dejiang Jinhong Large Hotel	2	2013.05	56	93	贵州省德江县青龙镇香树路131号	0856-4160888
白云区七天连锁酒店	Baiyun District Seven Days Hotel Chain	2	2013.05	101	108	贵阳市白云区刚玉街8号	0851-84899066
白云区白云假日酒店	Baiyun District Baiyun Holiday Hotel	2	2013.05	40	76	贵阳市白云区同心西路147号	0851-88171188
美豪商务酒店	Meihao Business Hotel	2	2013.06	33	54	六盘水市盘县红果杜鹃西路69号	18685813990
黔海酒店	Qianhai Hotel	2	2013.06	48	71	龙山镇三林路	0854-5673555
龙架山宾馆	Long Hill Hotel	2	2013.06	103	210	龙山镇三林路	0854-5620338
松桃净裕酒店	Songtao Jingyu Hotel	2	2013.11	20	30	松桃县普觉镇	0856-2689188
大方和泰快捷酒店	Dafang Hetai Fast Hotel	2	2013.11	92	161	大方县奢香大道北段	0857-5688789
鸿雁宾馆	Hongyan Hotel	1	2004.06	39	97	黔西县东路	0857-4225666
亲情宾馆	Qingqin Hotel	1	2006.09	19	34	平塘县	13985085075
玖玖宾馆	Jiujiu Hotel	1	2006.09	15	27	平塘县	13385185973
紫金大酒店	Zijin Hotel	1	2006.09	15	40	平塘县	13885455082
思南县电力宾馆	Sinan Dianli Hotel	1	2003.07	25	53	思南县中山街55号	0856-7229948
从江观音阁山庄	Congjiang Guanyinge Villa	1	2007.03	30	52	从江县	0855-6418488
黄平谦和大酒店	Huangping Qianhe Hotel	1	2006.12	27	54	黄平县	0855-2436366
黄平丰丰宾馆	Huangping Feng Feng Hotel	1	2006.12	43	86	黄平县	0855-2438298
岑巩兴岑大酒店	Cengong Xingcen Hotel	1	2007.09	15	25	岑巩县	0855-3575333
岑巩万向宾馆	Cengong Wanxiang Hotel	1	2007.09	17	30	岑巩县	0855-3573086
瑞权宾馆	Ruiquan Hotel	1	2010.06	70	110	黔西南州	0859-3815588
青松宾馆	Qingsong Hotel	1	2010.12	78	143	罗甸县	0854-7620518
天竹名人酒店	Tianzhumingren Hotel	1	2011.10	32	108	贵阳市乌当区航天大道1号	0851-86402020
港湾快捷酒店	Gangwan Inn	1	2011.08	42	65	贵阳市白云区建设路4号	0851-84611112
赛非尔商务宾馆	Saifeier Business Hotel	1	2011.11	38	45	贵阳市白云区金塘北街四合院	0851-84480899
博纳快捷酒店	Bona Inn	1	2011.11	43	62	贵阳市白云区大山洞尖山路	0851-85619999
麒麟酒店	Kylin Hotel	1	2012.12	29	43	罗甸县信邦大道二级路口	0854-87837888
白云区金义酒店	Baiyun District Jin Yi Hotel	1	2013.02	41	50	贵阳市白云区铝建路344号	0851-84619577
佳佳宾馆	Jia Jia Hotel	1	2013.02	50	80	贵州省凤冈县龙泉镇龙凤大道218号	13314401996
腾龙商务酒店	Dragon Business Hotel	1	2013.02	35	62	贵州省凤冈县	0851-25119199

主要统计指标解释

住宿业 指有偿为顾客提供临时住宿的服务活动。不包括提供长期住宿场所的活动，如出租房屋、公寓等，列入房地产开发经营。

餐饮业 指在一定场所，对食物进行现场烹饪、调制，并出售给顾客主要供现场消费的服务活动。

营业额 指住宿和餐饮业法人企业（单位）在经营活动中因提供服务或销售商品等取得的收入。包括客房收入、餐费收入、商品销售额和其他收入。其中，客房收入指住宿和餐饮业法人企业（单位）在经营活动中因提供住宿服务取得的收入。餐费收入指住宿和餐饮业法人企业（单位）因为顾客提供就餐服务取得的收入，包括经烹饪、调制加工后出售的各种食品，如主食、炒菜、凉拌菜等的收入。

入境游客人数 指报告期内来中国(大陆)观光、度假、探亲访友、就医疗养、购物、参加会议或从事经济、文化、体育、宗教活动的外国人、港澳台同胞等游客(即入境旅游人数)。统计时，入境游客按每入境1次统计1人次。

入境游客包括入境过夜游客和入境一日游游客。

国内游客人数 指报告期内在中国(大陆)观光游览、度假、探亲访友、就医疗养、购物、参加会议或从事经济、文化、体育、宗教活动的中国(大陆)居民，其出游的目的不是通过所从事的活动谋取报酬。统计时，国内游客按每出游1次统计1人次。

国内游客包括国内过夜游客和国内一日游游客。

国际旅游(外汇)收入 入境游客在中国(大陆)境内旅行、游览过程中用于交通、参观游览、住宿、餐饮、购物、娱乐等全部花费。

出境游组团旅行社 指从事招徕、组织、接待中国内地居民出国旅游，赴香港特别行政区、澳门特别行政区和台湾地区旅游，以及招徕、组织、接待在中国内地的外国人、在内地的香港特别行政区、澳门特别行政区居民和在大陆的台湾地区居民出境旅游的业务的旅行社。

国内及入境旅游旅行社 指从事招徕、组织和接待中国内地居民在境内旅游的业务和从事招徕、组织、接待外国旅游者来我国旅游，香港特别行政区、澳门特别行政区旅游者来内地旅游，台湾地区居民来大陆旅游，以及招徕、组织、接待在中国内地的外国人，在内地的香港特别行政区、澳门特别行政区居民和在大陆的台湾地区居民在境内旅游的业务的旅行社。

国内旅游收入 国内游客在旅游过程中(由游客或游客的代表为游客)支付的一切旅游支出就是国家(省、区、市)的国内旅游收入。旅游支出应包括过夜游客和一日游游客在整个游程中行、游、住、食、购、娱，以及为亲友、家人购买纪念品、礼品等方面的旅游支出，不包括为商业目的购物、购买房、地、车、船等资本性或交易性的投资、馈赠亲友的现金及给公共机构的捐赠。

星级饭店 指设备、设施、服务符合《旅游饭店星级的划分与评定》（GB/T14308−2003），通过相关旅游管理部门评定，并取得星级饭店称号的饭店（含预备星级饭店）。

Explanatory Notes on Main Statistical Indicators

Hotel Services refer to the activities of enterprises providing paid services of lodging to the customer, excluding the activities of providing long period of services of lodging, such as leased house and apartments, which are shown in development and operation of real estate.

Catering Services refer to the activities of enterprises prvideing on-the-spot services of selling food cooked and prepared to the customer in certain sites

Business Revenue refers to revenue received from providing services or selling commodities by enterprises and establishments engaged in hotels and catering services, including income from hotels, from catering services, from selling of commodities and from other services. Income from hotels refers to income of enterprises and establishments engaged in hotels and catering services by providing lodging services. Income from catering services refers to income of enterprises and establishments engaged in hotels and catering services by providing catering services, including selling of cooked or prepared foods, such as staple food, cooked dishes, or cold dishes.

Visitor arrivals refer to the number of foreigners, Chinese compatriots from Hong Kong, Macao and Taiwan Chinese who come to China for sight-seeing, vacation, visiting relatives, medical treatment, shopping, attending conference, or to engage in economic, cultural, sports and religious activities(That tourist arrivals). In compiling statistics, each time of entering China is counted as one person-time.

Inbound tourists are including inbound overnight tourists and inbound tour tourists.

Number of domestic tourists refers to the number of Chinese (mainland) residents who travel within China (mainland) for sight-seeing, vacation, visiting relatives, medical treatment, shopping, attending conference, or to engage in economic, cultural, sports and religious activities. In compiling statistics, each time of travelling is counted as one person-time.

Domestic tourists are including domestic overnight visitors and domestic day trip visitors.

Foreign Exchange Earnings from International Tourism refer to the total expenditure of foreigners, overseas Chinese, Chinese compatriots from Hong Kong, Macao and Taiwan during their stay in the mainland of China on transportation of sighting, accommodation, food, shopping and entertainment.

Outbound travel agencies is engaged in the solicitation, organization, hospitality Chinese mainland residents to travel abroad, to visit Hong Kong SAR, Macao SAR and Taiwan tourism and attract, organize the reception of foreigners in the Chinese mainland, the mainland Hong Kong SAR, Macao SAR residents and residents of Taiwan on the mainland outbound travel business travel.

Domestic and inbound tourism travel is engaged in soliciting travel, organization and hospitality Chinese mainland residents to travel in the territory and engaged in soliciting business, organization, reception of foreign tourists to China's tourism, Hong Kong SAR, Macao SAR mainland tourists to travel to the mainland for Taiwan residents tourism and attract, organization, reception of foreigners in China Mainland, the Mainland Hong Kong SAR, Macao SAR residents and residents of Taiwan on the mainland tourism business in the territory of the travel agency.

Income from Domestic tourism revenue domestic tourists in the tourism process (by the representatives of visitors or tourists for tourists) payment of all tourism expenditure is the national (provincial, autonomous regions and municipalities) of domestic tourism tourism revenue. Travel expenses shall include overnight visitors and day visitors in the entire run Bank of China, travel, housing, food, shopping and entertainment, as well as friends, family, buy souvenirs, gifts and other aspects of tourism expenditure, not including for commercial purposes, shopping, purchase house, ground, cars, boats and other capital investment or trading, cash and gift donations to public institutions.

Star-rated Hotels refer to hotels rated with stars as assessed by the relevant tourism authorities according to GB/T14308-2003 standard with reference to their infrastructure, facilities and service levels.

贵州2015
统计年鉴
GUIZHOU
STATISTICAL YEARBOOK

19 金融业

Financial Intermediation

19−1 金融机构人民币存贷款余额

Total Deposits and Total Loans of Financial Institutions

单位：亿元 (100 million yuan)

指　标	Item	2010	2011	2012	2013	2014	2014年比2013年增长(%) Increase Rate in 2014 over 2013(%)
资金来源合计	**Sources of Funds**	**7029.92**	**8300.17**	**9891.66**	**12234.52**	**14036.29**	**14.7**
各项存款	Total Deposits	7363.92	8742.79	10540.06	13265.01	15263.26	15.1
#财政存款	Fiscal Deposits	361.52	447.67	412.56	424.78	534.84	25.9
个人存款	Personal Deposits	3244.99	3934.48	4806.09	5919.05	6620.56	11.9
资金运用合计	**Uses of Funds**	**7029.92**	**8300.17**	**9891.66**	**12234.52**	**14036.29**	**14.7**
各项贷款	Total Loans	5747.53	6841.92	8274.78	10104.30	12368.30	22.4
#短期贷款	Short-term Loans	1015.30	1293.00	1744.63	2244.51	2803.96	24.9
中长期贷款	Medium-term & Long-term Loans	4582.34	5439.64	6405.81	7759.30	9403.72	21.2

注：1.资料来源于中国人民银行贵阳中心支行。2.个人储蓄存款2010年为城乡居民储蓄存款。
Note:1.Data in the table are obtained from Guiyang Central Branch of PBC.2.Deposits in 2010 refer to deposits of urban and rural residents.

19−2 保险

Insurance

单位：个 (unit)

指　标	Item	2010	2011	2012	2013	2014	2014年比2013年增长(%) Increase Rate in 2014 over 2013(%)
机构数	**Total**	**883**	**930**	**949**	**991**	**1052**	**6.2**
省级分公司	Provincial Branches	20	22	23	23	25	8.7
地市级分公司	Branches at Prefecture Level	110	117	123	137	146	6.6
县级支公司	Branches at County Level	328	384	416	447	496	11.0
办事处或营业部	Business Offices and Departments	38	38	38	38	36	-5.3
营销服务部	Marketing Deparements	387	369	349	346	349	0.9
职工人数	**Total**	**10472**	**11283**	**11390**	**11860**	**12827**	**8.2**
省级分公司	Provincial Branches	2552	2666	2732	2761	2792	1.1
地市级分公司	Branches at Prefecture Level	4650	5444	5335	5542	5868	5.9
县级支公司	Branches at County Level	2546	2597	2504	2741	3340	21.9
办事处或营业部	Business Offices and Departments	60	33	218	291	354	21.6
营销服务部	Marketing Departments	664	543	601	525	473	-9.9

注：资料来源于中国保险监督管理委员会贵州监管局(以下相关表同)。
Note:Data in the table are obtained from the provincial insurance regulatory bureau(the relative tables in the chapter are the same).

19-3 财产保险

Property Insurance

单位：万元 (10000 yuan)

指　　标	Item	2010	2011	2012	2013	2014	2014年比2013年增长(%) Increase Rate in 2014 over 2013(%)
保费收入	**Premium**	**489187**	**617886**	**738037**	**934898**	**1173603**	**25.5**
企业财产保险	Enterprise Property Insurance	28222	38138	35794	40438	40015	-1.0
机动车辆保险	Motor Vehicle Insurance	392399	480928	593675	755887	930033	23.0
货物运输保险	Freight Transport Insurance	7289	7290	6713	6625	6657	0.5
责任保险	Liability Insurance	20552	29781	34106	37825	44302	17.1
信用保证保险	Export Credit and Guarantee Insurance	1346	7624	12478	14946	24239	62.2
农业保险	Agriculture Insurance	920	2119	6876	16194	43949	171.4
其他保险	Other Insurance	38459	52006	48396	62983	84409	34.0
储金	**Deposits**	**4362**	**5822**	**7225**	**41765**	**7369**	**-82.4**
赔案件数(万件)	**Cases of Claims(10000 cases)**	**42**	**50**	**66**	**86**	**125**	**45.5**
赔款支出	**Claim and Payment**	**192351**	**262491**	**395728**	**468568**	**588310**	**25.6**
企业财产保险	Enterprise Property Insurance	6159	10467	28811	11836	17981	51.9
机动车辆保险	Motor Vehicle Insurance	163175	225500	324388	397667	490885	23.4
货物运输保险	Freight Transport Insurance	408	517	412	443	837	89.0
责任保险	Liability Insurance	8013	10904	17514	17984	23992	33.4
信用保证保险	Export Credit and Guarantee Insurance	68	193	558	1049	2148	104.8
农业保险	Agriculture Insurance	1686	1311	2316	7108	11033	55.2
其他保险	Other Insurance	12842	13598	21728	32481	41435	27.6
未决赔款	**Outstanding Claim**	**117217**	**189131**	**196770**	**250852**	**321479**	**28.2**

注：本表包括人保财险、太保产险、平安产险、天安保险、安邦保险、阳光产险、大地产险、国寿产险、都邦产险、太平保险、华安产险、鼎和产险、华泰产险、安诚产险、锦泰产险15家财产保险分公司数据(下表同)。

Note:.Data in the table include figures of the Guizhou Branches of PICC,Pacific Property Insurance Company, Ping'an Property Insurance Company, Tianan Insurance Company,Anbang Insurance Company,Yangguang Property Insurance Company, Dadi Property Insurance Company, China Li Property & Casualty Insurance Company, DuBang Insurance,Dinghe Insurance Company，Huatai Insuurance company and An-cheng Insurance Company (the same applies to the next table) .

19-4 财产保险主要指标(2014)

Major Indicators on Property Insurance

指 标	Item	合 计 Total	企业财产保险 Enterprise Property Insurance	家庭财产保险 Family Property Insurance	机动车辆保险 Motor Vehide Insurance	工 程 保 险 Engin-eering Insurance	责 任 保 险 Liability Insu-rance	保 证 保 险 Guarantee Insu-rance	信 用 保 险 Export Credit Insurance
承保件数(万件)	Amount Insured (10000 cases)	1061	2	5	495	0	10	1	0
保险金额或责任限额(亿元)	Insurance Value or Liability Limit (100 million yuan)	48410	3663	716	14387	921	16559	22	3
签单保费(万元)	Premium of Sign Bill (10000 yuan)	1172847	40476	7934	930159	25538	44234	24116	133
赔付件数(万件)	Amount Claim and Payment (10000 cases)	125	0	0	101	0	1	0	
已决赔款(万元)	Settled claim (10000 yuan)	565745	16627	3931	472568	7556	23087	2461	
未决赔款(万元)	Outstanding clain (10000 yuan)	321479	34951	762	225148	16379	19517	58	

19-4 续表 continued

指 标	Item	船 舶 保 险 Ship Insurance	货物运输保险 Freight Transport	特殊风险保险 Special Risk Insurance	农 业 保 险 Agric-ultural Insurance	健康险 Health Insu-rance	意外伤害保险 Accident Injury Insurance	其他险 Others Insu-rance
承保件数(万件)	Amount Insured(10000 cases)	0.05	6.34		0.51	9.19	272.76	258.47
保险金额或责任限额(亿元)	Insurance Value or Liability Limit (100 million yuan)	2.11	1016.92	10.17	706.90	1958.63	8443.77	0.31
签单保费(万元)	Premium of Sign Bill(10000 yuan)	179.90	6649.54	77.54	43756.30	12920.42	36411.58	261.39
赔付件数(万件)	Amount Claim and Payment (10000 cases)		0.02		2.29	2.07	0.75	16.94
已决赔款(万元)	Settled claim(10000 yuan)	49.15	814.75	46.26	10283.28	8588.43	19540.23	192.35
未决赔款(万元)	Outstanding clain(10000 yuan)	683.80	453.67	1.45	7882.12	3618.45	12021.39	4.16

注：赔付件数指已决赔付件数。

Note:Amount Claim and Payment refers to indemnity Expenditure.

19－5 人寿保险

Life Insurance

单位：万元 (10000 yuan)

指　　标	Item	2010	2011	2012	2013	2014	2014年比2013年增长(%) Increase Rate in 2014 over 2013(%)
保费收入	**Premium**	**735914**	**700228**	**764119**	**881254**	**957021**	**8.6**
#新单保费	Premium of New Guarantee Slip	423733	368371	310106	342673	355082	3.6
#个人业务	Personal Business	702187	670327	733130	814520	876164	7.6
人寿保险	Life Insurance	662714	624908	676263	741759	781899	5.4
意外伤害险	Accident Injury Insurance	11983	13608	16385	21633	29090	34.5
健康险	Health Insurance	27490	31811	40482	51127	65174	27.5
团体业务	Group Business	33727	29901	30988	66734	80857	21.2
人寿保险	Life Insurance	14277	7051	7285	7262	7001	-3.6
意外伤害险	Accident Injury Insurance	11396	15121	14618	19346	20373	5.3
健康险	Health Insurance	8054	7730	9085	40126	53484	33.3
有效保单件数(万件)	**Cases of Virtual Guarantee Slip(10000 cases)**	**416**	**459**	**491**	**545**	**608**	**11.6**
赔款及给付支出	**Claim and Payment**	**113982**	**132696**	**157626**	**255813**	**308371**	**20.5**
个人业务	Personal Business	74656	93250	110036	193168	206479	6.9
赔款支出	Benefit Paid	7753	9495	7967	9625	10661	10.8
年金给付	Payment for Annuity	11862	14179	22935	38340	32937	-14.1
满期给付	Payment for Expiration	43237	54158	60679	125087	137244	9.7
死伤医疗给付	Payment for Death and Injured person	11804	15418	18454	22336	25636	14.8
团体业务	Group Business	39326	39446	47591	45891	101892	122.0
赔款支出	Benefit Paid	13253	10766	13123	20269	52988	161.4
年金给付	Payment for Annuity	3283	2465	3130	3340	4795	43.6
满期给付	Payment for Expiration	21412	25039	30248	35585	42676	19.9
死伤医疗给付	Payment for Death and Injured Person	1378	1177	1090	1232	1432	16.3

注：本表数据包含国寿、太保寿险、平安寿险、新华人寿、泰康人寿、平安养老、太平人寿、人保寿险、生命人寿、泰康养老10家人寿保险分公司数据(下表同)。

Note: Data in the table include figures of the Guizhou Branches of China Life Insurance Company,Pacific Life Insurance Company, Ping'an Life Insurance Company, Xinhua Life Insurance Company, Taikang Life Insurance Company , Ping'an pension Insurance and Life Insurance Company (the same applies to the next table) .

19—6 人寿保险主要指标(2014)
Major Indicators on Life Insurance

单位：万元 (10000 yuan)

指标项目	Item	合 计 Total	寿险业务 Life Insurance Business	普通寿险 Normal Life Insurance	个人业务 Personal	团体业务 Group	分红寿险 Share out Bonus	个人业务 Personal	团体业务 Group
保费收入	Premium	957021.07	788900.09	277189.17	270860.21	6328.96	500698.34	500026.67	671.67
期末有效保险金额(亿元)	Virtual Insurance Value at the year-end(100 million yuan)	25314.49	2875.38	2133.03	2002.11	130.92	489.27	486.80	2.48
期末有效承保人次(万人)	Virtual Insurance Person-time at the year-end (10000 persons)	5670.16	854.17	682.50	664.37	18.14	134.22	125.48	8.74
期末有效承保保单件数(万件)	Cases of Virtual Guarantee Slip at the year-end (10000 cases)	607.77	361.48	205.68	199.74	5.95	121.12	119.58	1.55
赔款和给付支出	Expenditure for Claim and Payment	308371	237603	76297	27554	48743	158957	158952	6
#赔款支出	Settled Claim	63650							
死伤医疗给付	Payment for Death,Injury or Medical Treatmnet	27068	20066	12176	10898	1278	6238	6238	
满期给付	Mature Payment	179920	179804	50053	7377	42676	129055	129055	
年金给付	Payment for Annuity	37733	37733	14068	9279	4790	23665	23659	6
退保金	Insurance withdrawed	219995.24	218666.36	21002.24	20670.65	331.59	197658.57	197653.31	5.26
在售产品数量（个）	Amount of Products under Selling(unit)	2003	768	319	266	53	357	341	16

19—6 续表 continued

单位：万元 (10000 yuan)

指标项目	Item	投资连结产品 Life Insurance Product in inve-stment	万能寿险 Omnip-otence Life Insu-rance	健康险业务 Health Insu-rance	个人业务 Personal	团体业务 Group	意外伤害保险业务 Unforeseen Injury Insurance
保费收入	Premium	222.47	10790.12	118658.10	65173.94	53484.16	49462.88
期末有效保险金额(亿元)	Virtual Insurance Value at the year-end (100 million yuan)	4.68	248.40	16103.08	1260.22	14842.86	6336.04
期末有效承保人次(万人)	Virtual Insurance Person-time at the year-end(10000 persons)	0.63	36.81	2981.03	905.42	2075.61	1834.96
期末有效承保保单件数(万件)	Cases of Virtual Guarantee Slip at the year-end(10000 cases)	0.57	34.10	90.86	82.60	8.26	155.43
赔款和给付支出	Expenditure for Claim and Payment	24	2324	58379	13897	44482	12389
#赔款支出	Settled Claim			51261	6932	44328	12389
死伤医疗给付	Payment for Death,Injury or Medical Treatmnet	12	1641	7002	6848	154	
满期给付	Mature Payment	12	684	116	116		
年金给付	Payment for Annuity						
退保金	Insurance withdrawed	0.12	5.43	1328.88	1328.07	0.81	
在售产品数量（个）	Amount of Products under Selling (unit)	20	72	822	536	286	826

19−7 贵州上市公司股票发行情况(A股)(2014)

Summary List of Stocks Publicly Issued by Guizhou Enterprises(A Shares)

单位：亿股 (100 million shares)

上市公司名称	Listed Companies	上市时间 Listed Time	板块类别 Setor of Listed Companies	总股本(亿股) Total Capital Stock	流通股 Gover-nment Share	募集资金总额(亿元) Total Amount Issued (100 million yuan)
中天城投	Century Zhong Tian Investment Jiont Stock Co.,Ltd.	1994.02.02	主板	17.17	12.83	31.52
黔轮胎	Gui Zhou Tyre Co., Ltd.	1996.03.08	主板	7.75	4.89	40.20
中航重机	Guizhou Liyuan Hydraulic Components Co., Ltd.	1996.11.06	主板	7.78	7.78	54.44
振华科技	China Zhenhua(Group) Science & Technology Co., Ltd.	1997.07.03	主板	4.69	3.58	25.51
天成控股	Controlled Company Co., Ltd.	1997.11.27	主板	5.09	5.09	10.98
高鸿股份	Gohigh Data Networks Technology Co., Ltd.	1998.06.09	主板	5.91	4.85	26.82
南方汇通	South Huiton Co., Ltd.	1999.06.06	主板	4.22	4.22	6.19
渝能源	Chongqing Energy Co., Ltd.	1999.09.23	主板	3.78	3.78	1.80
赤天化	Guizhou Chitianhua Corp.	2000.02.21	主板	9.50	9.50	21.54
红星发展	Guizhou Redstat Developing Co., Ltd.	2001.03.20	主板	2.91	2.91	3.80
盘江股份	Guizhou Panjiang Refined Coal Co., Ltd.	2001.05.31	主板	16.55	16.55	76.87
贵州茅台	Kweichow Moutai Co., Ltd.	2001.08.27	主板	11.42	11.42	22.44
贵航股份	Guizhou Guihang Automotive Components Co., Ltd.	2001.12.27	主板	2.89	2.89	12.97
益佰制药	Guizhou Yibai Phamacy Co., Ltd.	2004.03.23	主板	3.96	3.58	13.97
贵绳股份	Guizhou Guisheng Co., Ltd.	2004.05.14	主板	2.45	2.45	9.78
航天电器	Guizhou Spaceflight Dianqi Co., Ltd.	2004.07.26	中小板	3.30	3.30	6.12
久联发展	Guizhou Jiulian Development Co., Ltd.	2004.09.08	中小板	3.27	3.27	14.92
黔源电力	Guizhou Qianyuan Electric Power Co., Ltd.	2005.03.03	中小板	3.05	3.05	13.78
信邦制药	Guizhou Xinbang Pharmaceutical Co., Ltd.	2010.04.16	中小板	5.00	2.28	19.70
贵州百灵	Guizhou Bailing Group Pharmaceutical Co., Ltd.	2010.06.03	中小板	4.70	2.06	14.80
朗玛信息	Longmastrr Inforation & Technology Co., Ltd.	2012.02.16	创业版	1.13	0.27	6.33

注：1.资料来源于中国证监会贵州监管局。2.ST国创于2011年3月9日迁入贵州，2013年更名为渝能源。3.募集资金总额包括首发、增发、配股、可转债等募集的资金。

Note:1.Data in the table are provided by the Guizhou Securities Regulatory Bureau of the CSRC. 2.ST GUIZHOU GUOCHUANG ENERGY HOLDING(GROUP)CO.,LTD. Removed to Guizhou on March9,2011Renamed as CHONGQING ENERGY CO., LTD in 2013. 3.Total Raised Capita including money raised by the first, issuing, convert-ible bonds of listed companies.The total amount of funds raised of Guizhou Panjiang Refined coalco.,LTD.indude infusion of funds.

主要统计指标解释

存款 指企业、机关、团体或居民根据资金必须收回的原则，把货币资金存入银行或其他信用机构保管并取得一定利息的一种信用活动形式。根据存款对象的不同可划分为企业存款、财政存款、机关团体存款、基本建设存款、城镇储蓄存款、农村存款等科目。它是银行信贷资金的主要来源。

贷款 指银行或其他信用机构根据资金必须归还的原则，按一定利率，为企业、个人等提供资金的一种信用活动形式。我国银行贷款分为流动资金贷款、固定资产贷款、城乡个体工商户贷款以及农业贷款等科目。

保费 指投保人为取得保险保障，按保险合同约定向保险人支付的费用。

赔款 指保险人对保险事故造成的损失，根据合同约定向被保险人或受益人给予的经济补偿。

给付 人身保险合同中，保险人向被保险人或受益人给付保险金的行为。

Explanatory Notes on Main Statistical Indicators

Deposit is a form of credit by which enterprises, institutions, organizations or households can put money into banks and other credit institutions for safekeeping and interest earning under the principle of free withdrawal. According to different depositors, deposits are divided into enterprise deposits, treasury deposits, deposits of government agencies and organizations, capital construction deposits, urban savings deposits, rural deposits and other deposits. Deposits are major sources of the credit funds of banks.

Loan is a form of credit by which banks and other credit institutions provide funds at certain interest rate to enterprises and individuals in the light of the principle of unconditional repayment. Loans from Chinese banks include circulating capital loans, fixed assets loans, loans to urban and rural individuals engaged in industrial and commercial business and agricultural loans.

Premium refers to the fee that in order to obtain insurance coverage and in accordance with the insurance contract, the insured paid to the insurer.

Settled Claim is the economic compensation that for the insurance losses caused by the accident and according to the contract, the insurer paid to the insured or the beneficiary.

Payment is the Insurance payments behavior that in the life insurance contract, the insurer paid for the insured or the beneficiary.

20 教育和科技

Education, Science and Technology

20-1 各级各类学校数

Number of Schools by Level and Type

单位：所 (unit)

指　标	Item	2010	2011	2012	2013	2014
研究生培养机构	Institutions Providing Postgraduate Programs	8	8	9	9	8
普通高等学校	Regular Institutions of Higher Education	47	48	49	52	55
#成人高等学校	Institutions of Higher Education for Adult	4	4	4	4	4
中等职业教育	Vocational Secondary Education	249	227	229	218	209
调整后中等职业教育	Adjusted Vocational Secondary Schools	35	32	34		1
普通中等专业教育	Regular Specialized Secondary Schools	63	54	54	58	63
职业高中	Vocational Senior Secondary Schools	130	126	125	146	133
成人中等专业学校	Adult Specialized Secondary Schools	21	15	16	14	12
普通中学	Regular Secondary Schools	2592	2641	2661	2664	2604
高　中	Senior Secondary Schools	444	447	446	448	438
初　中	Junior Secondary Schools	1639	1635	1621	1609	1593
九年一贯制学校	From Grade 1 to 9	531	559	594	607	573
小　学	Primary Schools	12422	12008	11529	10632	9275
幼儿园	Kindergartens	2196	2677	3159	4016	4767
特殊教育	Special Education	53	52	56	60	65
工读学校	Schools for Juvenile Delinquents	4	4	5	6	7
成人中学	Adult Secondary Schools	33	13	51	23	28
成人技术培训学校	Adult Technical Training Schools	7711	8202	7863	6994	7098
成人小学	Adult Primary Schools	5405	5059	4935	4169	3560

注：资料来源于省教育厅(以下相关表同)。

Note:Data in the table are provided by the Provincial Department of Education(The relative tables in the chapter are the same).

20－2 各级各类学校专任教师数
Number of Full-time Teachers by Level and Type of School

单位：人 (person)

指 标	Item	2010	2011	2012	2013	2014
专任教师	**Number of Full-time Teachers**					
培养研究生的单位	Institutions Providing Postgraduate Programs	2760	2971	3133	3409	3316
普通高等学校	Regular Institutions of Higher Education	20351	21855	22803	25351	28144
#成人高等学校	Institutions of Higher Education for Adult	296	314	361	368	371
中等职业教育	Vocational Secondary Education	11291	11635	12585	14326	16342
调整后中等职业教育	Adjusted Vocational Secondary Schools	1211	1339	1712		55
普通中等专业教育	Regular Specialized Secondary Schools	3857	3677	3841	4816	5861
职业高中	Vocational Senior Secondary Schools	4883	5354	5784	8209	9181
成人中等专业学校	Adult Specialized Secondary Schools	1190	1233	1216	1265	1209
其它机构	Other Institutions	150	32	32	36	36
普通中学	Regular Secondary Schools	143128	147396	156325	162309	171988
高 中	Senior Secondary Schools	33072	36223	41572	46964	52365
初 中	Junior Secondary Schools	110056	111173	114753	115345	119623
小 学	Primary Schools	197913	197094	197983	192953	192850
幼儿园	Kindergartens	14623	18120	23846	34188	43081
特殊教育	Special Education	796	901	996	1093	1241
工读学校	Schools for Juvenile Delinquents	76	65	82	88	120
成人中学	Adult Secondary Schools	169	33	35	21	60
成人技术培训学校	Adult Technical Training Schools	3983	5515	5339	5920	6203
成人小学	Adult Primary Schools	4463	3403	3155	2789	2249

20-3 各级各类学校招生数

Number of New Students Enrollment by Level and Type of School

单位：人 (person)

指　标	Item	2010	2011	2012	2013	2014
研究生	Postgraduates	4246	4417	4769	4937	5097
普通高等教育	Regular Institutions of Higher Education	101548	107841	127963	131245	145849
成人高等教育	Adult Higher Education	26580	26054	32661	38368	43256
#成人高等学校	Institutions of Higher Education for Adult	2345	3041	4004	5290	5050
中等职业教育	Vocational Secondary Education	155527	148242	150784	247135	235809
调整后中等职业教育	Adjusted Vocational Secondary Schools	13675	16283	20395		1100
普通中等专业教育	Regular Specialized Secondary Schools	62260	61181	58945	91983	89722
职业高中	Vocational Senior Secondary Schools	62199	66736	68119	111222	100713
成人中等专业教育	Adult Specialized Secondary Education	17393	4042	3325	43930	44274
#成人中等专业学校	Adult Specialized Secondary Schools	14584	1788	986	517	1145
普通中学	Regular Secondary Schools	1008606	1022950	1050119	1046445	1016349
高　中	Senior Secondary Schools	240208	277290	318188	330212	349047
初　中	Junior Secondary Schools	768398	745660	731931	716233	667302
小　学	Primary Schools	656919	626379	591024	510554	554793
幼儿园	Kindergartens	627154	632789	668389	694176	763491
特殊教育	Special Education	2755	2858	2904	2684	2769
工读学校	Schools for Juvenile Delinquents	432	660	609	538	253

注：2013年实施教育“9+3”计划，加大成人中等专业教育力度（以下相关表同）。

Note: In 2013，the implementation of education " 9 +3" program has increased adult secondary professional education efforts. (The relative tables in the chapter are the same)

20-4 各级各类学校在校生数

Number of Students Enrollment by Level and Type of School

单位：人 (person)

指 标	Item	2010	2011	2012	2013	2014
在校生数	**Total Enrollment**					
研究生	Postgraduate	11406	12436	13344	14057	14667
普通高等教育	Regular Institutions of Higher Education	323293	344100	383815	419040	460401
成人高等教育	Adult Higher Education	86630	79615	85575	101698	116719
#成人高等学校	Institutions of Higher Education for Adult	5827	6064	6488	11457	12789
中等职业教育	Vocational Secondary Education	375740	379908	383367	475512	544462
调整后中等职业教育	Adjusted Vocational Secondary Schools	32084	39497	47532		1650
普通中等专业教育	Regular Specialized Secondary Schools	169033	170659	165583	204053	220320
职业高中	Vocational Senior Secondary Schools	145853	151786	158059	220885	246681
成人中等专业教育	Adult Specialized Secondary Education	28770	17966	12193	50574	75811
#成人中等专业学校	Adult Specialized Secondary Schools	24855	14057	8008	2290	2010
普通中学	Regular Secondary Schools	2767503	2827096	2873822	2960110	3010982
高 中	Senior Secondary Schools	620221	689042	772972	857077	942656
初 中	Junior Secondary Schools	2147282	2138054	2100850	2103033	2068326
小 学	Primary Schools	4334971	4087382	3800803	3555333	3463056
幼儿园	Kindergartens	769144	877824	982511	1077687	1198864
特殊教育	Special Education	16231	14474	13657	12721	13535
工读学校	Schools for Juvenile Delinquents	233	400	549	623	501
成人中学	Adult Secondary Schools	16869	1203	7500	768	1163
成人技术培训学校	Adult Technical Training Schools	2058138	2180591	2014520	1755865	1693020
成人小学	Adult Primary Schools	239936	128006	135401	110207	128434

20－5 各级各类学校毕业生数

Number of Graduates by Level and Type of School

单位：人 (person)

指　标	Item	2010	2011	2012	2013	2014
毕业生数	**Graduates**					
研究生	Postgraduate	2910	3335	3820	4093	4396
普通高等教育	Regular Institutions of Higher Education	74777	83016	85285	92395	99562
成人高等教育	Adult Higher Education	24365	29953	23343	22657	24335
#成人高等学校	Institutions of Higher Education for Adult	2015	2166	1742	2217	3314
中等职业教育	Vocational Secondary Education	100997	90966	100340	100281	108500
调整后中等职业教育	Adjusted Vocational Secondary Schools	7101	6933	10647		
普通中等专业教育	Regular Specialized Secondary Schools	50118	46622	47080	50400	51645
职业高中	Vocational Senior Secondary Schools	39099	35230	39931	44881	45393
成人中等专业教育	Adult Specialized Secondary Education	4679	2181	2682	5000	11462
#成人中等专业学校	Adult Specialized Secondary Schools	4643	1913	1560	749	563
普通中学	Regular Secondary Schools	811669	830799	859136	868894	912527
高　中	Senior Secondary Schools	171704	180203	195861	210409	238495
初　中	Junior Secondary Schools	639965	650596	663275	658485	674032
小　学	Primary Schools	798173	773003	760174	723478	664842
幼儿园	Kindergartens	328152	365936	477201	491678	499442
特殊教育	Special Education	1350	1244	1389	1378	1470
工读学校	Schools for Juvenile Delinquents	393	652	268	588	178
成人中学	Adult Secondary Schools	7701	3243	10005	3313	3517
成人技术培训学校	Adult Technical Training Schools	2065482	2195836	1984866	1740821	1631110
成人小学	Adult Primary Schools	214867	129893	125809	99934	124921

20-6 教师职称

Technical Rank of Teachers

单位：人 (person)

指 标	Item	2010	2011	2012	2013	2014
高等学校教师数	**Regular Institutions of Higher Education**	**20647**	**22169**	**23164**	**25719**	**28515**
正高级	Senior	1801	2038	2166	2515	2684
副高级	Sub-senior	5913	6544	7129	8103	8773
中 级	Middle	8403	8863	8726	9000	9297
初 级	Junior	3288	3383	3387	3663	4408
无职称	No Rank	1242	1341	1756	2438	3353
中等职业学校教师数	**Vocational Secondary Schools**	**11291**	**11635**	**12585**	**14326**	**16342**
正高级	Senior	60	68	89	22	36
副高级	Sub-senior	2065	2101	2302	2405	2632
中 级	Middle	4583	4605	4708	4775	5100
初 级	Junior	3457	3492	3698	4099	4941
无职称	No Rank	1126	1369	1788	3025	3633
普通中学教师数	**Regular Secondary Schools**	**143128**	**147396**	**156325**	**162309**	**171988**
中学高级	Senior-rank of Secondary Teacher	14826	16522	18031	19840	24535
中学一级	First-rank of Secondary Teacher	43485	46402	49150	52650	56566
中学二级	Second-rank of Secondary Teacher	64423	63548	63585	62142	61182
中学三级	Third-rank of Secondary Teacher	8570	6640	5030	4084	3772
未评职称	No Rank of Secondary Teacher	11824	14284	20529	23593	25933
小学教师数	**Regular Primary Schools**	**197913**	**197094**	**197983**	**192953**	**192850**
中学高级	Senior-rank of Secondary Teacher	205	763	326	555	516
小学高级	Senior-rank of Primary Teacher	77589	82258	81489	83842	94840
小学一级	First-rank of Primary Teacher	80881	76802	75320	69341	60301
小学二级	Second-rank of Primary Teacher	21409	18572	15801	14883	14448
小学三级	Third-rank of Primary Teacher	1141	971	840	1219	564
未评职称	No rank of Primary Teacher	16688	17728	24207	23113	22181

20-7 各级各类学校女学生和女教师数

Female Students and Teachers by Level and Type of School

单位：人 (person)

指　标	Item	2010	2011	2012	2013	2014
在校女生数	**Number of Female Students Entrollment**					
普通高等教育	Regular Institutions of Higher Education	163824	178663	201277	223391	251116
成人高等教育	Adult Higher Education	39923	40274	43189	56646	66826
中等职业教育	Vocational Secondary Education	184525	193289	199383	252847	284816
普通中学	Regular Secondary Schools	1316239	1356343	1387546	1430914	1453719
#高　中	Senior Secondary Schools	290983	330129	377426	425058	472304
初　中	Junior Secondary Schools	1025256	1026214	1010120	1005856	981415
小　学	Primary Schools	2038362	1913008	1775234	1654132	1609910
女教师数	**Number of Female Teachers**					
普通高等学校	Regular Institutions of Higher Education	9712	10690	11131	12591	14049
成人高等学校	Institutions of Higher Education for Adult	157	167	191	196	201
中等职业学校	Secondary Vocational Schools	4746	5053	5534	6360	7597
普通中学	Regular Secondary Schools	52088	55196	60701	64728	71113
#高　中	Senior Secondary Schools	12618	14186	16829	19864	22871
初　中	Junior Secondary Schools	39470	41010	43872	44864	48242
小　学	Primary Schools	90208	91253	94049	92794	95082

20-8 各级各类学校师生比

Student-Teacher Ratio by Level and Type of School

单位：学生/教师 (Student/Teacher)

指 标	Item	2010	2011	2012	2013	2014
普通高等学校	Regular Institutions Of Higher Education	15.89	15.74	16.83	16.53	16.36
普通高中	Regular Senior Secondary School	18.75	19.02	18.59	18.25	18.00
初中	Regular Junior Secondary School	19.51	19.23	18.31	18.23	17.29
小 学	Primary School	21.90	20.74	19.20	18.43	17.96

20-9 各级各类学校学生入学率

Enrollment Rate by Level and Type of School

单位：% (%)

指 标	Item	2010	2011	2012	2013	2014
小学学龄儿童入学率	Enrollment Rate of Primary Schools	97.9	98.6	99.3	99.3	99.1
小学毕业生升学率	Percentage of Graduates of Primary Schools Entering into Junior Secondary Schools	96.3	96.5	96.3	99.0	100.0
初中阶段毛入学率	Rate of Primary School Graduates Entering into Junior Secondary Schools	97.6	94.2	97.4	101.1	102.5
高中阶段毛入学率	Rate of Junior Secondary School Graduates Entering into Senior Secondary Schools	55.0	58.9	62.2	68.0	78.0
高等教育毛入学率	Rate of Senior Secondary School Graduates Entering into Institution of Higher Learning	20.0	23.2	25.5	27.4	29.4

20−10 普通高等学校(2014)
Regular Institutions of Higher Education

单位：人 (person)

类别	Sort	学校数(所) Number of Schools (unit)	毕业生数 Graduates with Degrees or Diplomas	招生数 New Enrollment	在校学生人数 Enro-llment	教职员工 Teachers, Staff & Workers	#专任教师 Full-time Teachers	#正、副教授 Senior and Sub-senior Professors
普通高等院校	**Regular Institutions of Higher Education**	**55**	**99562**	**145849**	**460401**	**38899**	**28144**	**11351**
综合大学	Comprehensive Universities	18	33051	47731	150287	12490	8913	3377
理工院校	Science & Engineering	8	11841	21684	51517	3964	2941	634
医药院校	Medicine & Pharmacy	10	14234	22300	72095	6691	4912	2374
师范院校	Teacher Training	12	24840	30916	111648	9892	7225	3224
财经院校	Finance & Economics	4	8266	15566	48409	3541	2571	915
政法院校	Politics and Law	1	2168	1774	4646	443	300	132
民族院校	Ethnic Minortities	2	5162	5878	21799	1878	1282	695
高等职业技术学院	**Vocational and Technical Colleges**	**22**	**31173**	**57283**	**139012**	**10248**	**7843**	**1895**

20−11 普通高等学校分科专任教师数(2014)
Number of Full-time Teachers in Institutions of Higher Education by Field of Study

单位：人 (person)

类别	Sort	专任教师数 Full-time Teachers	正高级 Senior	副高级 Subsenior	中级 Middle	初级 Junior	无职称 No Rank
总计	**Total**	**28144**	**2670**	**8681**	**9183**	**4264**	**3346**
哲学	Philosophy	957	93	348	276	130	110
经济学	Economics	1592	143	440	588	216	205
法学	Law	1630	146	570	568	203	143
教育学	Education	2644	220	825	815	388	396
文学	Literature	3815	297	1265	1318	513	422
历史学	History	563	69	202	193	51	48
理学	Science	3538	365	1217	1029	499	428
工学	Engineering	5061	368	1396	1738	908	651
农学	Agriculture	823	136	308	250	49	80
医学	Medicine	4269	631	1337	1216	676	409
管理学	Management	1675	127	402	579	342	225
艺术学	Art	1577	75	371	613	289	229

20−12 研究生数

Number of Postgraduates

单位：人 (person)

指 标	Item	2010	2011	2012	2013	2014
招研究生数	Number of New Postgraduates Enrollment	4246	4417	4769	4937	5097
#女 性	Female	2206	2248	2362	2648	2816
在校研究生数	Number of Postgraduates Enrollment	11406	12436	13344	14057	14667
#女 性	Female	5622	6211	6673	7390	7852
毕业研究生数	Number of Postgraduates Graduate	2910	3335	3820	4093	4396
#女 性	Female	1269	1570	1837	2085	2282

20−13 技工学校

Technical Schools

单位：人 (person)

指 标	Item	2013	2014	2014年比2013年增 长(%) Increase Rate in 2014over 2013(%)
学校数（所）	Number of Schools (unit)	34	34	持平
招生数	Number of Enrollment	21912	34648	58.1
在校学生数	Number of Students	40985	61458	50.0
毕业生数	Number of Graduates	6721	7810	16.2
教职工数	Teachers and Staff	3867	5620	45.3
专任教师数	Full-time Teachers	3455	5591	61.8
文化技术理论课教师	Classroom Teachers	2040	2979	46.0
生产实习课指导教师	Practical Training Teachers	758	1149	51.6
理论实习一体化教师	Classroom cum Practical Training Teachers	657	1463	122.7

注：资料来源于省人力资源社会保障厅。

Note: Date in the table are obtained from Provincial Department of Human Resources and Social Security.

20-14 中等职业学校(机构)数（2014）
Number of Secondary Vocational Schools

单位：个 (unit)

指　标	Item	总 计 Total	地方部门 Local Departments	教育部门 Departments of Education	非教育部门 Departments of Non-Education	民 办 Private
中等职业学校	**Secondary Vocational Schools**	**209**	**154**	**112**	**42**	**55**
调整后中等职业学校	Adjusted Secondary Vocational Schools	1	1	1		
普通中等专业学校	Regular Specialized Secondary Schools	63	59	29	30	4
成人中等专业学校	Adult Specialized Secondary Schools	12	11	3	8	1
职业高中学校	Vocational Junior Secondary Schools	133	83	79	4	50

20-15 中等职业学校(2014)
Secondary Vocational Schools

单位：人 (person)

指　标	Item	学校数(所) Schools (unit)	毕业生数 Graduates	招生数 New Enrollment	在校学生数 Total Enrolment	教职员工 Teachers, Staff & Workers	#专任教师 Full-time Teachers
中等职业学校	**Secondary Vocational Schools**	**209**	**108500**	**235809**	**544462**	**20257**	**16342**
调整后中等职业学校	Adjusted Vocational Secondary Schools	1		1100	1650	61	55
普通中等专业学校	Regular Specialized Secondary Schools	63	51645	89722	220320	7770	5861
成人中等专业学校	Adult Specialized Secondary Educaiton	12	11462	44274	75811	1614	1209
职业高中	Vocational Senior Secondary Schools	133	45393	100713	246681	10754	9181
#其他机构(教学点)	Others Institutions					58	36

20−16 中等职业学校（机构)学生分科类情况（2014）
Students in Secondary Vocational Schools by Field of Study

单位：人 (person)

指标	Item	招生数 New Enrollment	#应届毕业生 Current Year Graduates	#初中毕业生 Junior Secondary School Graduates	在校学生数 Total Enrollment	毕业生数 Graduates	#获得职业资格证书 With Certificate On Professional Competence
总　计	**Total**	**235809**	**205163**	**193440**	**544462**	**108500**	**93567**
农林牧渔类	Agriculture,Forestry,Animal Husbandry and Fishery	21438	15034	10632	45874	11154	9134
资源环境类	Resources and Environment	2445	2341	2296	10294	1678	1582
能源与新能源类	Energy and New Energy	1162	1151	869	2676	487	430
土木水利类	Civil and Hydraulic Engineering	13084	12159	11789	31924	7005	6485
加工制造类	Manufacturing	21785	19492	18605	51275	11078	10013
石油化工类	Petroleum and Chemical	978	406	406	2041	556	528
轻纺食品类	Light Inclustry,Textile and Food	4168	3393	3218	9756	1387	995
交通运输类	Transport	29189	25652	25239	56356	7785	6874
信息技术类	Information Technologies	38565	33055	32681	87475	18188	16159
医药卫生类	Medicine and Health	29310	27379	25748	70543	13008	9715
休闲保健类	Leisure and Health-care	2081	1800	1795	3784	247	247
财经商贸类	Finance and Trade	9279	7714	7632	24388	5763	4828
旅游服务类	Tourism and services	17017	13566	12447	39151	6362	5161
文化艺术类	Culture and Art	6716	5697	5476	13154	2552	2206
体育与健身	Sports and Fitness	476	473	473	1115	402	370
教育类	Education	29576	29053	28361	79279	18373	16455
司法服务类	Justice Services	870	822	811	1736	573	546
公共管理与服务类	Public Management and Services	4712	3861	2874	7649	679	628
其　他	Other	2958	2115	2088	5992	1223	1211

20—17 民族教育
Minority Nationality Education

指　标	Item	2010	2011	2012	2013	2014
学校数(所)	**Number of Schools(unit)**					
普通高校	Regular Institutions of Higher Education	2	2	2	2	2
普通中学	Regular Secondary Schools	121	194	205	211	206
小　学	Primary Schools	161	637	614	605	588
专任教师数(人)	**Full-time Teachers(person)**					
普通高校	Regular Institutions of Higher Education	4407	5189	5872	5777	7105
成人高校	Adult Institutions of Higher Education	42	40	49	64	98
普通中学	Regular Secondary Schools	58519	60519	64441	66469	69363
#高　中	Senior Secondary Schools	13044	14041	16552	18816	20463
中等职业学校	Secondary Vocational Schools	2778	3501	3351	3719	4030
小　学	Primary Schools	82892	80267	84680	81916	77444
在校生数(人)	**Number of Total Enrollment(person)**					
普通高等教育	Regular Institutions of Higher Education	110549	117205	141345	144480	169124
成人高等教育	Adult Institutions of Higher Education	17428	22601	27640	35373	36488
普通中学	Regular Secondary Schools	1092467	1127199	1148755	1195659	1233687
#高　中	Senior Secondary Schools	243987	275147	313056	349855	384598
中等职业学校	Secondary Vocational Schools	125407	135113	138442	179593	194642
小　学	Primary Schools	1775808	1697558	1596713	1519620	1491503
毕业生数(人)	**Number of Graduates(person)**					
普通中学	Regular Secondary Schools	315968	325984	343094	346312	365203
#高　中	Senior Secondary Schools	66977	70296	77553	84314	97856
小　学	Primary Schools	316272	304096	303243	292089	277398

20－18 民办教育
Private Education

指　　标	Item	2010	2011	2012	2013	2014
学校数(所)	**Number of Schools(unit)**					
普通高等学校	Regular Institutions of Higher Education	9	10	11	11	11
中等职业教育学校	Secondary Vocational Schools	70	62	64	64	55
普通中学	Regular Secondary Schools	319	346	372	404	411
#高　中	Senior Secondary Schools	89	94	92	93	94
小　学	Primary Schools	259	269	273	260	261
在校学生数(人)	**Number of Total Enrollment(person)**					
普通高等学校	Regular Institutions of Higher Education	54552	58030	64527	73850	82312
中等职业教育学校	Secondary Vocational Schools	49919	41267	40114	39057	41558
普通中学	Regular Secondary Schools	155165	169007	183239	199010	217087
#高　中	Senior Secondary Schools	44672	55248	58441	63377	75836
小　学	Primary Schools	162362	173050	173542	160602	158272
教职员工数(人)	**Teachers, Staff and Workers(person)**					
普通高等学校	Regular Institutions of Higher Education	3251	3818	4111	4655	5430
中等职业教育学校	Secondary Vocational Schools	2610	2226	2175	2163	1984
普通中学	Regular Secondary Schools	9719	13771	15814	18330	20490
小　学	Primary Schools	7456	4770	5094	4454	4807
专任教师数(人)	**Full-time Teachers(person)**					
普通高等学校	Regular Institutions of Higher Education	2653	2993	3037	3520	3998
中等职业教育学校	Secondary Vocational Schools	1448	1264	1302	1331	1341
普通中学	Regular Secondary Schools	6811	10138	11766	13575	15206
小　学	Primary Schools	6146	3928	4181	3631	3828

20-19 成人教育

Adult Education

指　标	Item	2010	2011	2012	2013	2014
学校数(所)	**Number of Schools(unit)**					
成人高等教育学校	Adult Institutions of Higher Education	4	4	4	4	4
成人中等专业教育学校	Adult Specialized Secondary Schools	21	15	16	14	12
成人中学	Adult Secondary Schools	33	13	51	23	28
成人技术培训学校	Adult Technical Training Schools	7711	8202	7863	6994	7098
成人小学	Adult Primary Schools	5405	5059	4935	4169	3560
在校生数(万人)	**Number of Students Enrollment(10000 persons)**					
成人高等教育	Adult Institutions of Higher Education	8.66	7.96	8.56	10.17	11.67
成人中等专业教育	Adult Specialized Secondary Schools	2.88	1.80	1.22	5.06	7.58
成人中学	Adult Secondary Schools	1.69	0.12	0.75	0.08	0.12
成人技术培训学校	Adult Technical Training Schools	205.81	218.06	201.45	175.59	169.3
成人小学	Adult Primary Schools	23.99	12.80	13.54	11.02	12.84
毕业生数(万人)	**Number of Graduates(10000 persons)**					
成人高等教育	Adult Institutions of Higher Education	2.44	3.00	2.33	2.27	2.43
成人中等专业教育	Adult Specialized Secondary Schools	0.47	0.22	0.27	0.50	1.15
成人中学	Adult Secondary Schools	0.77	0.32	1.00	0.33	0.35
成人技术培训学校	Adult Technical Training Schools	206.55	219.58	198.49	174.08	163.11
成人小学	Adult Primary Schools	21.49	12.99	12.58	9.99	12.49

20−20 科技活动

Scientific and Technological Activities

指　标	Item	2013	2014	2014年比2013年增长(%) Increase Rate in 2014 over 2013(%)
科技活动人员(人)	**Persons Engaged in Scientific and Technological Activities (person)**	**69101**	**71771**	**3.9**
科研机构	**Scientific Research Institutions**			
科研机构数(个)	Number of Institutions(unit)	357	449	25.8
科研用仪器设备原价(万元)	Original Cost of Instrument and Equipment for Scientific Research(10000yuan)	446569	432228	-3.2
#进　口	Import	121437	122116	0.6
研究与实验发展(R&D)	**Research and Development**			
研究与试验发展(R&D)人员(人)	R&D Personnel(person)	36113	38158	5.7
#博士毕业	Doctor	2067	2472	19.6
硕士毕业	Master	5934	7049	18.8
研究与试验发展(R&D)经费支出(万元)	Expenditure on R&D(10000yuan)	471850	554795	17.6
科技产出	**S&T Output**			
专利申请数(件)	Number of Patents Application(unit)	4598	5449	18.5
#发明专利	Inventions	2018	2699	33.7
专利授权数(件)	Number of Patents Granted(unit)	516	652	26.4
#发明专利	Inventions	151	182	20.5
有效发明专利数(件)	Number of Patents In Force(unit)	2672	4080	52.7
专利所有权转让及许可数(件)	Number of Patents Ownership Assigned and Granted (unit)	30	53	76.7
专利所有权转让及许可收入(万元)	Revenue from Patents Ownership Assigned and Granted(10000yuan)	217	9512	4283.4
植物新品种权授予数(项)	Number of New Plant Breed Rights Granted(unit)	17	15	-11.8
形成国家或行业标准数(项)	Number of Standards Adopted by State or Industry(unit)	188	172	-8.5
发表科技论文(篇)	Scientific Papers Issued(piece)	18629	19360	3.9
出版科技著作(种)	Publication on Science an Technology(kind)	490	588	20.0

20-21 研究与试验发展(R&D)活动
Scientific Research and Development

指　标	Item	2013	2014	2014年比2013年增长(%) Increase Rate in 2014 over 2013(%)
有研究与试验发展(R&D)活动单位(个)	**Number of Institutions Having R&D Activities(unit)**	**359**	**416**	**15.9**
R&D人员	**Bisic Statistics on R&D Personnel**			
R&D人员(人)	R&D Personnel(person)	36113	38158	5.7
#女性	Female	11588	11727	1.2
#研究人员	Research Personnel	20109	21979	9.3
#全时人员	Full-time Personnel	18582	20115	8.2
非全时人员	Part-time Personnel	17531	18043	2.9
#博士毕业	Doctor	2067	2472	19.6
硕士毕业	Master	5934	7049	18.8
本科毕业	Bachelor	11969	12433	3.9
其他学历	Others	16143	16204	0.4
R&D人员折合全时当量(人年)	Full-time Equivalent of R&D Personnel(person-year)	23888	23962	0.3
#研究人员	Research Personnel	12067	12656	4.9
#基础研究	Basic Research	3080	3418	11.0
应用研究	Applied Research	3070	3263	6.3
试验发展	Experimental Development	17736	17281	-2.6
R&D经费	**Expenditure on R&D**			
R&D经费内部支出(万元)	Intramural Expenditure on R&D (10000yuan)	471850	554795	17.6
#基础研究	Basic Research	53888	59759	10.9
应用研究	Applied Research	49680	63878	28.6
试验发展	Experimental Development	368282	431158	17.1
#日常性支出	Daily Expenditure	399301	471326	18.0
#人员劳务费	Personnel Service Fees	109830	141056	28.4
资产性支出	Expenditure on Assets	72548	83468	15.1
#仪器和设备	Insrument and Equipment	51185	63321	23.7
#政府资金	Government Appropriation Funds	123526	132720	7.4
企业资金	Self-raised Funds by Enterprises	315922	388509	23.0
境外资金	Overseas Funds	323	503	55.7
其他资金	Other Funds	32079	33063	3.1
经费投入强度(%)	**Intensity of Funds Input(%)**	**0.59**	**0.60**	**0.01(百分点)**
R&D项目(课题)	**Projects of R&D**			
R&D项目(课题)数(项)	Projects of R&D(unit)	14284	16203	13.4
R&D项目(课题)参加人员折合全时当量(人年)	Participants(person-year)	21000	21787	3.7
#研究人员	Research Personnel	10691	11366	6.3
R&D项目(课题)经费内部支出(万元)	Intramural Expenditure (10000yuan)	399251	457529	14.6

20-22 规模以上工业企业科技活动
Scientific and Technological Activities above Designated Size

指 标	Item	2011	2012	2013	2014
科技活动人员(人)	**Persons Engaged in Scientific and Technological Activities (person)**	**30593**	**33009**	**36826**	**38210**
科研机构	**Scientific Research Institutions**				
科研机构数(个)	Number of Institutions(unit)	163	148	165	224
科研用仪器设备原价(万元)	Original Cost of Instrument and Equipment for Scientific Research(10000yuan)	363719	341337	345935	302154
#进 口	Import	68306	73325	83242	70781
研究与实验发展(R&D)	**Research and Development**				
研究与试验发展(R&D)人员(人)	R&D Personnel(person)	12309	16509	21071	20771
#研究人员	Research Personnel	4882	6391	7579	8197
#全时人员	Full-time Personnel	7135	9764	12095	13071
#博士毕业	Doctor	102	99	64	123
硕士毕业	Master	523	756	471	1030
研究与试验发展(R&D)人员折合全时当量(人年	Full-time Equivalent of R&D Personnel(Person-year)	9564	12135	16049	15659
#研究人员	Research Personnel	3945	4850	6327	6305
#基础研究	Basic Research		9	16	37
应用研究	Applied Research	114	188	346	289
试验发展	Experimental Development	9450	11939	15687	15332
研究与试验发展(R&D)经费支出(万元)	Expenditure on R&D(10000yuan)	275217	315079	342541	410132
#基础研究	Basic Research		177	101	486
应用研究	Applied Research	3159	4379	4952	11371
试验发展	Experimental Development	272058	310523	337488	398276
#日常性支出	Daily Expenditure	257837	288505	309056	362687
#人员劳务费	Personnel Service Fees	47662	62238	71593	98072
资产性支出	Expenditure on Assets	17380	26574	33485	47446
#仪器和设备	Insrument and Equipment	16798	22298	30952	41739
#政府资金	Government Appropriation Funds	25322	31114	47086	38657
企业资金	Self-raised Funds by Enterprises	239918	266602	286509	364976
境外资金	Overseas Funds	74	83	125	294
其他资金	Other Funds	9903	17280	8820	6206
科技产出	**Statistics on S&T Outputs**				
专利申请数(件)	Number of Patents Application(unit)	2034	2794	3446	4051
#发明专利	Inventions	813	1347	1516	1918
有效发明专利数(件)	Number of Valid Patents for Invention(unit)	990	1370	1985	3146
专利所有权转让及许可数(件)	Number of Patents Ownership Assigned and Granted (unit)	31	18	26	42
专利所有权转让及许可收入(万元)	Revenue from Patents Ownership Assigned and Granted(10000yuan)	500	145		9363
形成国家或行业标准数(项)	Number of Standards Adopted by State or Industry (unit)	263	169	165	158
发表科技论文(篇)	Scientific Papers Issued(piece)	1015	1170	1014	1165

注:规模以上工业企业指年主营业务收入2000万元及以上工业企业。

Note:The industrial enterprises which are above designated size refer to the industrial enterprises with the sales revenue above 20 million

20-23 规模以上工业企业新产品开发及生产情况(2014)

New product Development and production above Designated Size

指标	Item	新产品开发项目数(项) The number of new pruduct development (unit)	新产品开发经费支出(万元) Spending for the New Product Development (10000 yuan)	新产品销售收入(万元) Sales Revenue of New Product (10000 yuan)	#出口 Expots
合　计	**Total**	**1802**	**383864**	**4083736**	**560790**
#大中型工业企业	Large and Medium-sized Industrial Enterprises	1289	292629	3573373	558643
按登记注册类型分	**by Status of Registration**				
内资企业	Domestic Funded Enterprises	1760	375289	3914283	560764
#国有企业	State-owned Enterprises	156	45954	917319	124117
有限责任公司	Limited Liability Corporations	824	239424	2303971	397634
股份有限公司	Share-holding Corporations Ltd.	539	74891	460040	37513
港、澳、台商投资企业	Enterprises with Funds From Honkong, Macao and Taiwan	27	4861	68104	
外商投资企业	Foreign Funded Enterprises	15	3714	101349	26
按行业分	**By Industrial Sector**				
#煤炭开采和洗选业	Mining and Washing of Coal	38	832	30	
食品制造业	Manufacture of Foods	9	881	12539	
酒、饮料和精制茶制造业	Manufacture of Liquor, Beverages and Refined Tea	96	26481	842987	125617
烟草制品业	Manufacture of Tobacco	2	0	116994	
石油加工、炼焦及核燃料加工业	Processing of Petroleum, Coking, Processing of Muclear Fuel			26483	
化学原料及化学制品制造业	Manufacture of Chemical Raw Material and Chemical Products	84	49564	970922	364240
医药制造业	Manufacture of Medicines	237	30690	488850	
非金属矿物制品业	Manufacture of Nonmetallic Mineral Products	12	1861	44067	
黑色金属冶炼和压延加工业	Manufacture and Processing of Ferrous Metals	15	2922	35127	437
有色金属冶炼和压延加工业	Manufacture and Processing of Mu-ferrous Metals	13	1599	28094	22
金属制品业	Manufacture of Metal Product	41	9778	92760	2679
通用设备制造业	Manufacture of General Purpose Machinery	79	7405	91301	265
专用设备制造业	Manufacture of Special Purpose Machinery	51	9176	77778	185
汽车制造业	Manufacture of Automotive	134	19820	131918	4082
计算机、通信和其他电子	Manufacture of Communication Equipment, Computer and other Electronic Equipment	368	36779	141444	3485
电力、热力生产和供应业	Production and Supply of Electric Power and Heat Power.	40	1931	202	

20-24 政府属独立研究与开发机构科技活动

Scientific and Technological Activities of Government-affiliated Independent Research Institutions

指 标	Item	2010	2011	2012	2013	2014	2014年比2013年增长(%) Increase Rate in 2014 over 2013(%)
科技机构数(个)	**Number of S&T Institutions(unit)**	**107**	**105**	**106**	**105**	**106**	**1.0**
县级以上自然类研究与开发机构	The Scientific Research and Development Institution above the county level.	62	60	63	62	63	1.6
县级以上社会、人文科学研究机构	The Research Institutions of Social and Human Studies above the county level.	4	4	4	4	4	持平
县级以上部门属科技情报与文献机构	Department of S&T Informations and Literature Institutions at County and Higher Levels	6	6	6	6	6	持平
县级政府部门属研究与开发机构	Scientific Research and Development Institutions at County Level	11	10	9	8	8	持平
县级以上研究与开发转制机构	Conversed Scientific Research and Development Institution at County and Higher Levels	24	25	24	25	25	持平
科技活动人员数(人)	**Personnel Engaged in S&T Activities(person)**	**4594**	**5019**	**4627**	**4948**	**5499**	**11.1**
县级以上自然类研究与开发机构	The Scientific Research and Development Institution above the county level.	2847	3218	3032	3106	3300	6.2
县级以上社会、人文科学研究机构	The Research Institutions of Social and Human Studies above the county level.	226	223	224	226	213	-5.8
县级以上部门属科技情报与文献机构	Department of S&T Informations and Literature Institutions at County and Higher Levels	120	128	130	150	142	-5.3
县级政府部门属研究与开发机构	Scientific Research and Development Institutions at County Level	101	102	103	104	89	-14.4
县级以上研究与开发转制机构	Conversed Scientific Research and Development Institution at County and Higher Levels	1300	1348	1138	1362	1755	28.9
大学本科及以上学历人数(人)	**University,College and Above(person)**	**3103**	**3612**	**3432**	**3792**	**4266**	**12.5**
县级以上自然类研究与开发机构	The Scientific Research and Development Institution above the county level.	1848	2273	2182	2330	2581	10.8
县级以上社会、人文科学研究机构	The Research Institutions of Social and Human Studies above the county level.	205	200	200	201	190	-5.5
县级以上部门属科技情报与文献机构	Department of S&T Informations and Literature Institutions at County and Higher Levels	74	84	97	112	114	1.8
县级政府部门属研究与开发机构	Scientific Research and Development Institutions at County Level	26	28	29	31	29	-6.5
县级以上研究与开发转制机构	Conversed Scientific Research and Development Institution at County and Higher Levels	950	1027	924	1118	1352	20.9

注：资料来源于省科技厅(以下相关表同)。

Note: Data in the table are obtained from the Department of Science and Technology(The relative tables in the chapter are the same)

20-24 续表 continued

指 标	Item	2010	2011	2012	2013	2014	2014年比2013年增长(%) Increase Ratein 2014 over 2013(%)
经费收入总额(万元)	**Funding for S&T Activities(10000 yuan)**	**140870**	**175937**	**210700**	**258654**	**285659**	**10.4**
县级以上自然类研究与开发机构	The Scientific Research and Development Institution above the county level.	84360	96246	112779	104276	123615	18.5
县级以上社会、人文科学研究机构	The Research Institutions of Social and Human Studies above the county level.	3266	3469	4574	5956	5904	-0.9
县级以上部门属科技情报与文献机构	Department of S&T Informations and Literature Institutions at County and Higher Levels	1851	1972	2845	2576	2941	14.2
县级政府部门属研究与开发机构	Scientific Research and Development Institutions at County Level	1140	1259	1335	1170	1130	-3.4
县级以上研究与开发转制机构	Conversed Scientific Research and Development Institution at County and Higher Levels	50253	72992	77151	144676	152069	5.1
经费支出总额(万元)	**Expenditures on S&T Activities (10000 yuan)**	**139117**	**171663**	**182102**	**254670**	**265331**	**4.2**
县级以上自然类研究与开发机构	The Scientific Research and Development Institution above the county level.	73690	87132	105898	109580	116474	6.3
县级以上社会、人文科学研究机构	The Research Institutions of Social and Human Studies above the county level.	2724	3262	4584	4951	4225	-14.7
县级以上部门属科技情报与文献机构	Department of S&T Informations and Literature Institutions at County and Higher Levels	1957	2003	2780	2634	2679	1.7
县级政府部门属研究与开发机构	Scientific Research and Development Institutions at County Level	1350	1394	1417	1152	1050	-8.9
县级以上研究与开发转制机构	Conversed Scientific Research and Development Institution at County and Higher Levels	59396	77872	67423	136353	140903	3.3
研究与试验发展经费支出(R&D经费支出)(万元)	**Expenditure on R&D(10000 yuan)**	**24771**	**30422**	**36899**	**55735**	**59558**	**6.9**
县级以上自然类研究与开发机构	The Scientific Research and Development Institution above the county level.	19682	20024	25426	42667	46414	8.8
县级以上社会、人文科学研究机构	The Research Institutions of Social and Human Studies above the county level.	839	1001	1690	1510	2014	33.4
县级以上部门属科技情报与文献机构	Department of S&T Informations and Literature Institutions at County and Higher Levels	257				375	
县级政府部门属研究与开发机构	Scientific Research and Development Institutions at County Level	30		29			
县级以上研究与开发转制机构	Conversed Scientific Research and Development Institution at County and Higher Levels	3963	9398	9754	11558	10755	-6.9

20-25 省部级以上成果登记(完成人员)

Staffs Personnel of Provincial or Ministerial Level and above

单位：人次 (person-time)

指 标	Item	2010	2011	2012	2013	2014
合 计	**Total**	**1306**	**979**	**1479**	**1712**	**2009**
按学历分	**by Type of Diploma**					
博士	Doctor	143	133	215	242	314
硕士	Master	279	255	365	419	555
大本	Undergraduate Student	720	515	751	954	1001
大专	Junior College Student	139	68	114	75	115
中专	Senoir Middle School	20	8	27	13	17
其他	Below Senoir Middle School	5		7	9	7
按年龄结构分	**by Type of Age**					
35岁以下(含35岁)	thirty-five and below	388	328	380	500	570
36-45岁	thirty-six to forty-five	500	353	568	625	762
46-55岁	forty-six to fifty-five	341	238	393	466	541
56-65岁	fifty-six to sixty-five	55	45	106	94	123
65岁以上	above sixty-five	22	15	32	27	13
按技术职称分	**by Type of Title**					
院士	Academicians			1	2	
正高	Senior Title	277	198	345	398	444
副高	Sub-senior Title	380	302	468	531	751
中级	Middle Title	486	345	464	551	594
初级	Primary Title	134	91	120	149	137
其他	No Rank	29	43	81	81	83

20-26 省部级以上成果登记（数量及投资额）

Number of Achievements and Investment of Projects at Provincial or Ministerial Level and above（number & investment）

指　　标	Item	2010	2011	2012	2013	2014
成果登记(项)	**Achievement Registration(item)**	**125**	**90**	**132**	**141**	**147**
发明专利授权数(件)	Invention of Patent Authorigations Granted (piece)	67	240	120	150	174
制订标准数(个)	Number of Standards for Formulation (unit)	12	8	21	8	7
按成果类别分(项)	by Typt of Achievement Sort (item)					
#基础研究	Basic Research	16	19	28	26	22
应用研究	Applied Research	109	71	104	115	124
按成果应用属性分(项)	by Typt of Achievement Application Property (item)					
#原始性创新	Original Invention	63	22	11	8	9
国外引进消化 吸收创新	Absorb and Digest Invention of Foreign Indraught	15	11	18	26	12
国内技术二次开发	Twice Development of Inner Technology	31	38	75	81	103
项目投资额(万元)	**Project Investment (10000 yuan)**	**95331**	**212819**	**109689**	**58093**	**295362**
国家资金	Government Funds	12317	6127	11886	4376	2122
部门资金	Department Funds	18234	947	10798	3905	36693
地方资金	Local Funds	31433	6223	37697	5324	6297
基金投入	Fund Input	158	135	1176	228	124
自有资金	Self-raised Funds	23420	195620	35323	43807	249584
银行贷款	Loans from Bank		200	200	200	500
国外资金	Foreign Funds.		12	6		
其他资金	Other Funds	9769	3555	12603	253	42
净利润(万元)	**After-Tax Profit (10000 yuan)**	**78889**	**354367**	**120310**	**125554**	**296395**
实交税金(万元)	**Tax (10000 yuan)**	**17699**	**104371**	**41289**	**83925**	**134026**

20–27 事业、企业单位各类专业技术人员

Specialized Technical Personnel in Enterprises and institutions

单位：万人 (10000 persons)

指　标	Item	2010	2011	2012	2013	2014	2014年比2013年增长(%) Increase Rate in 2014 over 2013(%)
总　计	**Total**	**56.43**	**57.72**	**59.15**	**61.91**	**64.22**	**3.7**
#女　性	Female	23.19	24.16	25.55	27.79	29.63	6.6
按专业分	**By Specialized Subject**						
#工程技术人员	Engineering Technical Personnel	5.86	5.73	5.74	6.07	6.26	3.1
农业技术人员	Agricultural Technical Personnel	2.41	2.49	2.47	2.38	2.35	-1.3
卫生技术人员	Medical Technical Persomnel	7.27	7.84	8.12	9.10	9.58	5.3
科学研究人员	Scientific Research Personnel	0.15	0.16	0.20	0.19	0.25	31.6
教学人员	Teaching Personnel	36.12	37.09	38.20	39.24	40.16	2.3
按专业技术职务分	**By Professional Titles**						
#高　级	Senior	3.24	3.76	4.08	4.69	5.48	16.8
中　级	Medium	17.38	18.59	18.86	20.35	22.94	12.7
初　级	Junior	33.61	32.54	32.90	31.71	29.92	-5.6
按学历分	**By Education Background**						
大学本科以上	University,College and above	18.86	21.32	24.00	27.90	31.79	13.9
大学专科	Specialized Institutions of Higher Education	26.16	26.35	26.35	26.11	25.46	-2.5
中专以下	Senior Middle School and the Level below	11.41	10.05	8.80	7.91	6.97	-11.9

注：1.资料来源于省人力资源社会保障厅。 2.本表数据按岗位统计，不含非公经济单位和中央驻黔单位数据。3.事业单位部分专业技术人员划到管理人员统计。

Note: 1.Data in the table are obtained from the Provincal Department of Human Resources and Social Security.2.Data in this table are counted by post, and don't include non-public economic units and the central unit of data in Guizhou.3.Since 2010, due to adjustment of statistical cabliers part of the professional and technical personnel of institutions have designated to manage personnel and statistics.

20−28 专利申请受理及授权
Patent Application Accepted and Granted

单位：件 (item)

指　标	Item	2010	2011	2012	2013	2014	2014年比2013年增长(%) Increase Rate in 2014over 2013(%)
受理专利总计	**Total Patent Applications Accepted**	**4414**	**8351**	**11296**	**17405**	**22471**	**29.1**
按种类分	**Grouped by Sort**						
发　明	Inventions	1322	2358	3103	3988	8203	105.7
实用新型	Utility Models	2441	3170	4111	6456	7335	13.6
外观设计	Designs	651	2823	4082	6961	6933	-0.4
按对象分	**Grouped by Applicant**						
非职务发明创造	Non-service Creations and Inventions	1631	2072	2192	3089	7896	155.6
职务发明创造	Service Creations and Inventions	2783	6279	9104	14316	14575	1.8
大专院校	Universities and Colleges	172	312	366	1056	1176	11.4
科研单位	Research Institutions	633	357	530	626	542	-13.4
工矿企业	Industrial and Mineral Enterprises	1937	5507	7949	12100	12413	2.6
机关团体	Government Agencies and Organizations	41	103	259	534	444	-16.9
授权专利总计	**Total Patent Authorigations Granted**	**3034**	**3386**	**6054**	**7915**	**10107**	**27.7**
按种类分	**Grouped by Sort**						
发　明	Inventions	434	596	635	776	1047	34.9
实用新型	Utility Models	1904	1885	3149	3916	5207	33.0
外观设计	Designs	696	905	2270	3223	3853	19.5
按对象分	**Grouped by Applicant**						
非职务发明创造	Non-service Creations and Inventions	961	992	1283	1731	1369	-20.9
职务发明创造	Service Creations and Inventions	2073	2394	4771	6184	8738	41.3
大专院校	Universities and Colleges	116	141	182	345	460	33.3
科研单位	Research Institutions	366	378	269	333	377	13.2
工矿企业	Industrial and Mineral Enterprises	1569	1841	4214	5426	7795	43.7
机关团体	Government Agencies and Organizations	22	34	106	80	106	32.5

注：资料来源于省科技厅。

Note: Data in the table are obtained from the Provincial Intellectual Property Right Bureau.

20－29 科协系统科学技术普及情况

Popularization of science and Technology

指　　标		Item	2013	2014	2014年比2013年增长（%）
科学技术普及活动		**Science and Teohnology Popularization Activityes**			
举办科普宣讲活动	（次）	Popular Science Propaganda Activities(unit)	3020	5028	66.5
宣讲活动受众人数	（万人次）	Audience of Preaching Activity (10000 Person-time)	311	372	19.6
参加活动科技人员	（万人次）	Personnel Participated in the Activities of aud Technical (10000 Person-time)	8	10	26.0
科普基础设施建设		**Imfrastrueture Corstruction in Popularizatime of Science**			
科技馆	（个）	Number of Science and Technology Museum	3	3	持平
全年参观人数	（万人次）	Number of Participcmts (10000 Person-time)	28	19	-31.2
#少儿参观人数		Number of Child and Youth's participation	19	12	-36.8
科普画廊建筑面积（宣传栏、橱窗）	（平方米）	Gallery construction Area in popularization of science(square meter)	42801	52258	22.1
科普画廊展示面积	（平方米）	Gallery Exhibition Area in popularization of science(square meter)	64920	87836	35.3

主要统计指标解释

普通高等学校 指通过国家普通高等教育招生考试，招收高中毕业生为主要培养对象，实施高等学历教育的全日制大学、独立设置的学院，独立学院和高等专科学校、高等职业学校及其他普通高教机构。

成人高等学校 指通过国家成人高等教育招生考试，招收具有高中毕业或同等学历的人员为主要培养对象，利用函授、业余、脱产等多种形式，对其实施高等学历教育的学校。包括：职工高等学校、农民高等学校、管理干部学院、教育学院、独立函授学院、广播电视大学、其他成人高教机构。

小学学龄儿童入学率 指调查范围内已入小学学习的学龄儿童占校内外学龄儿童总数(包括弱智儿童，不包括盲聋哑儿童)的比重。计算公式为：

小学学龄儿童入学率=已入学的小学学龄儿童数/校内外小学学龄儿童总数×100%

科技活动 指在自然科学、农业科学、医药科学、工程与技术科学、人文与社会科学领域(简称科学技术领域)中，与科技知识的产生、发展、传播和应用密切相关的有组织的活动。可分为研究与试验发展(R&D)、研究与试验发展成果应用及相关的科技服务三类活动。

科技活动人员 指直接从事科技活动、以及专门从事科技活动管理和为科技活动提供直接服务，累计的实际工作时间占全年制度工作时间10%及以上的人员。(1)直接从事科技活动的人员包括：在独立核算的科学研究与技术开发机构、高等学校、各类企业及其他事业单位内设的研究室、实验室、技术开发中心及中试车间(基地)等机构中从事科技活动的研究人员、工程技术人员、技术工人及其它人员；虽不在上述机构工作，但编入科技活动项目(课题)组的人员；科技信息与文献机构中的专业技术人员；从事论文设计的研究生等。(2)专门从事科技活动管理和为科技活动提供直接服务的人员，包括：独立核算的科学研究与技术开发机构、科技信息与文献机构、高等学校、各类企业及其他事业单位主管科技工作的负责人，专门从事科技活动的计划、行政、人事、财务、物资供应、设备维护、图书资料管理等工作的各类人员，但不包括保卫、医疗保健人员、司机、食堂人员、茶炉工、水暖工、清洁工等为科技活动提供间接服务的人员。该指标用来反映投入科技活动人力的规模。

研究与试验发展(R&D) 指在科学技术领域，为增加知识总量、以及运用这些知识去创造新的应用进行的系统的创造性的活动，包括基础研究、应用研究、试验发展三类活动。国际上通常采用R&D活动的规模和强度指标反映一国的科技实力和核心竞争力。

基础研究 指为了获得关于现象和可观察事实的基本原理的新知识(揭示客观事物的本质、运动规律，获得新发现、新学说)而进行的实验性或理论性研究，它不以任何专门或特定的应用或使用为目的。其成果以科学论文和科学著作为主要形式。用来反映知识的原始创新能力。

应用研究 指为获得新知识而进行的创造性研究，主要针对某一特定的目的或目标。应用研究是为了确定基础研究成果可能的用途，或是为达到预定的目标探索应采取的新方法(原理性)或新途径。其成果形式以科学论文、专著、原理性模型或发明专利为主。用来反映对基础研究成果应用途径的探索。

试验发展 指利用从基础研究、应用研究和实际经验所获得的现有知识，为产生新的产品、材料和装置，建立新的工艺、系统和服务，以及对已产生和建立的上述各项作实质性的改进而进行的系统性工作。其成果形式主要是专利、专有技术、具有新产品基本特征的产品原型或具有新装置基本特征的原始样机等。在社会科学领域，试验发展是指把通过基础研究、应用研究获得的知识转变成可以实施的计划(包括为进行检验和评估实施示范项目)的过程。人文科学领域没有对应的试验发展活动。主要反映将科研成果转化为技术和产品的能力，是科技推动经济社会发展的物化成果。

研究与试验发展人员 指参与研究与试验发展项目研究、管理和辅助工作的人员，包括项目组(课题)人员，企业科技行政管理人员和直接为项目(课题)活动提供服务的辅助人员。不包括全年从事研究与试验发展活动工作量不到0.1年的人员。反映投入从事拥有自主知识产权的研究开发活动的人力规模。

研究与试验发展人员全时当量 指全时人员折合成全时工作量与所有非全时人员折合成全时工作量的总计。一个全时人员的折合全时工作量计为1，非全时人员按实际投入工作量进行累加。例如：有两个全时人员和三个非全时人员(工作量分别为20%、30%和70%)，则全时当量为1+1+0.2+0.3+0.7=3.2人年。为国际上比较科技人力投入而制定的可比指标。

专业技术人员 指从事专业技术工作和专业技术管理工作的人员，即企事业单位中已经聘任专业技术职务从事专业技术工作和专业技术管理工作的人员，以及未聘任专业技术职务，现在专业技术岗位上工作的人员。包括工程技术人员，农业技术人员，科学研究人员，卫生技术人员，教学人员，经济人员，会计人员，统计人员，翻译人员，图书资料、档案、文博人员，新闻出版人员，律师、公证人员，广播电视播音人员，工艺美术人员，体育人员，艺术人员及企业政治思想工作人员，共十七个专业技术职务类别。用来反映科技人力资源情况。

科技活动经费内部支出 指报告年内用于科技活动的实际支出，包括劳务费、科研业务费、科研管理费，非基建投资购建的固定资产、科研基建支出以及其他用于科技活动的支出。不包括生产性活动支出、归还贷款支出及转拨外单位支出。反映科技投入实际完成情况。

专利 一般是专利权的简称，指专利权人对发明创造享有的专利权。即国家依法在一定时期内授予发明创造或者其权利继受者独占使用其发明创造的权利。

专利同时也指具体专利技术，即受国家认可并在公开的基础上进行法律保护的技术或者方案。

专利还可指具体的物质文件，即国家颁发的确认申请人对其发明创造享有的专利证书或记载发明创造内容的专利文献。

发明 对产品、方法或其改进所提出的新的技术方案。

Explanatory Notes on Main Statistical Indicators

Regular Institutions of Higher Education refer to recruiting graduates from senior secondary schools as the main target by National Matriculation TEST. They include full-time universities, colleges, institutions of higher professional education, institutions of higher vocational education, institutions of higher vocational education and others.

Institutions of Higher Education for Adults refer to educational establishments, enrolling staff and workers with senior secondary school or equivalent education, and providing higher education courses in many forms of correspondence, spare time, or full time for adults. Professionals thus trained receive a qualification equivalent to graduates studying regular courses at regular universities, colleges and professional colleges. Institutions of higher learning for adults include schools of higher education for staff and workers, schools of higher education for peasants, colleges for management cadres, pedagogical colleges, independent correspondence colleges, Radio and TV universities and other educational establishments.

Enrollment Ratio of Primary Schools refers to the proportion of school age children enrolled at schools to the total number of school age children both in and outside schools (including retarded children, but excluding blind, deaf and mute children). The formula is:

$$\text{Net Enrolment Ratio of Primary Schools}=\frac{\text{Total Primary School-age Children at Schools}}{\text{Total Primary School-age Children Whether or Not Attending School}}\times 100\%$$

Scientific and Technological Activities(S&T Activities) refer to organized activities which are closely related with the creation, development, dissemination and application of the scientific and technical knowledge in the fields of natural sciences, agricultural science, medical science, engineering and technological science, humanities and social sciences (referred to as scientific and technological fields). S&T activities can be classified in to 3 categories: research and development (R&D) activities, application of R&D results, and related S&T services.

Personnel Engaged in S&T Activities refer to personnel directly engaged in S&T activities, in the management of S&T activities, and in providing direct service to S&T activities, who spend over 10% of the total working hours in a year in S&T activities. (1) Personnel directly engaged in S&T activities include researchers, engineers, technicians and other related personnel engaged in S&T activities in independent-accounting R&D institutions, institutions of higher learning, and in research institutes, laboratories, technology development centers and central experiment workshops under enterprises and institutions. Also included are people working in S&T research project teams, professional and technical personnel working in S&T information archiving institutes, and graduate students working on the design of their thesis. (2) Personnel engaged in the management of S&T activities and in providing direct service to S&T activities include senior management people responsible for S&T activities in independent-accounting R&D institutions, S&T information archiving institutes, institutions of higher learning, and in enterprises and institutions where S&T activities are undertaken. Also included are people responsible for the planning, administration, personnel management, financial management, logistics supply, equipment maintenance, information and library management that are related with S&T activities. People providing indirect services are excluded, such as security, medical service, drivers, plumbers, cleaners and those providing catering and related service. This indicator reflects the size of personnel engaged in S&T activities.

Research and Development (R&D) refers to systematic and creative activities in the field of science and technology aiming at increasing the knowledge and using the knowledge for new application. R&D includes 3 categories of activities: basic research, applied research and experimentation for development. The scale and intensity of R&D are widely used internationally to reflect the strength of S&T and the core competitiveness of a country in the world.

Basic Research refers to empirical or theoretical research aiming at obtaining new knowledge on the fundamental principles regarding phenomena or observable facts to reveal the intrinsic nature and underlying laws and to acquire new discoveries or new theories. Basic research takes no specific or designated application as the aim of the research. Results of basic research are mainly released or disseminated in the form of scientific papers or monographs. This indicator reflects the innovation capacity for original knowledge.

Applied Research refers to creative research aiming at obtaining new knowledge on a specific objective or target. Purpose of the applied research is to identify the possible uses of results from basic research, or to explore new (fundamental) methods or new approaches. Results of applied research are expressed in the form of scientific papers, monographs, fundamental models or invention patents. This indicator reflects the exploration of ways to apply the results of basic research.

Experiments and Development refer to systematic activities aiming at using the knowledge from basic and applied researches or from practical experience to develop new products, materials and equipment, to establish new production process, systems and services, or to make substantial improvement on the existing products, process or services. Results of experiment and development activities are embodied in patents, exclusive technology, and monotype of new products or equipment. In social sciences, experiment and development activities refer to the process of converting the knowledge from basic or applied researches into feasible programmes (including conduct of demonstration projects for assessment and evaluation). There are no experiment and development activities in the science of humanities. This indicator reflects the capability of transferring the results of S&T into technique and products, and measures the realization of S&T in spearheading the economic and social development.

R & D Personnel refer to persons engaged in research, management and supporting activities of R & D, including persons in the project teams, persons engaged in the management of S&T activities of enterprises and supporting staff providing direct service to the research projects, and not including annual research and experimental development activities in less than 0.1 years of staff workload. This indicator reflects the size of personnel engaged in R&D activities with independent intellectual property.

Full-time Equivalent of R&D Personnel refers to the sum of the full-time persons and the full-time equivalent of part-time persons converted by workload. A full-time staff equivalent to full-time work is counted as a part-time personnel according to actual efforts to accumulate. For instance, if there are 2 full-time persons and 3 part-time workers (20%, 30% and 70% of working hours respectively on R&D activities), the full-time equivalent are 2+0.2+0.3+0.7=3.2 person-years. This is an internationally comparable indicator of S&T manpower input.

Professional and Technical Personnel refer to persons engaged in professional and technical work or in the management of professional and technical activities, i.e., people with professional or technical positions who are engaged in professional and technical work or in the management of professional and technical activities, and people without professional or technical positions but are working on professional or technical posts. They include professionals and technicians working in 17 categories of technical occupations including engineering, agriculture, scientific researches, medical service, teaching, economic research and application, accounting, statistics, translation, libraries, archives, cultural and museum service, journalism and publication, lawyers, notarization service, radio and television broadcasting, handicraft and fine arts, sports, performing art, and political workers in enterprises. This indicator reflects the condition of human resources in S&T.

Self-raised Funds by Enterprises refers to self-raised funds by enterprises from their own expenditure or from other enterprises and funds received by universities or research institutions from enterprises for scientific research or technical development projects. Excluded in this category are funds from government agencies, financial institutions or from foreign institutions.

Patent is an abbreviation for the patent right and refers to the exclusive right of ownership by the inventors or designers for the creation or inventions, given from the patent offices after due process of assessment and approval in accordance with the Patent Law.

Patent also refers to a specific patented technology that recognized by the State and public legal protection on the basis of technical or program.

Patent document also refers to a specific substance, which confirm that the applicant issued by the state enjoyed their inventions patented inventions certificate or record the content of patent documents.

Inventions refer to new technical proposals to the products or methods or their modifications.

21 文化、体育和卫生

Culture, Sports and Public Health

21－1 文化事业机构和人员

Number of Institution and Personel in Culture Industry

指　标	Item	2010	2011	2012	2013	2014	2014年比2013年增长(%) Increase Rate in 2014over 2013(%)
机构总计(个)	**Total Number of Institutions(unit)**	**2041**	**2075**	**2213**	**2241**	**2235**	**-0.3**
艺术事业	Art Institutions	65	56	90	113	113	持平
文物事业	Cultural Relics	145	130	151	152	150	-1.3
图书馆事业	Libraries	93	94	93	94	95	1.1
群众文化事业	Mass Culture	1524	1579	1661	1687	1686	-0.1
文艺科研	Cultural and Art Research Institutions	4	4	2	2	2	持平
其他文化事业	Other Culture Units	210	212	216	193	189	-2.1
人员总计(人)	**Total Number of Persons Engaged(person)**	**12949**	**14945**	**16380**	**17996**	**17902**	**-0.5**
艺术事业	Arts	2421	2259	2531	3955	3744	-5.3
文物事业	Cultural Relics	1665	1691	2166	1693	1551	-8.4
图书馆事业	Libraries	937	950	976	1014	1015	0.1
群众文化事业	Mass Culture	4790	5223	5320	5986	6006	0.3
文艺科研	Cultural and Art Research Institutions	31	33	21	21	20	-4.8
其他文化事业	Others	3105	4789	5366	5327	5566	4.5

注：1.资料来源于省文化厅(以下相关表同)。2.机构和人员数不含文化市场新分的机构和人员数。3.2013年对1个机构两块牌子从业人员进行重新划分，因此文物业从业人员有所减少。

Note: 1.Data in the table are provided by the Provinvial Department of Culture(The relative tables in the chapter are the same). 2. Number of Instituiions and Personnel in the table exclude newly increased Institutions and Personnel. 3. In 2013,one institution with two brands practitioners were divided again, so the property practitioners has decreased.

21-2 文化事业单位数

Basic Statistics on Culture Establishment

单位：个 (unit)

指　标	Item	2010	2011	2012	2013	2014
艺术表演场所	Arts Centers	7	11	10	6	6
公共图书馆	Public Libraries	93	94	93	94	95
博物馆、纪念馆	Museums and Memorials	59	53	66	75	74
群众艺术馆、文化馆	Mass Art Centers and Cultural Centers	95	97	97	98	98
档案馆	Archives	107	107	107	107	107

注:1.2013年博物馆、纪念馆统计范围增加民间博物馆机构。2.2013年非文化部门艺术表演场所减少4个。

Note:1.The statistical range of museums and memorials has included folk museum agencies in 2013. 2.Non-cultural department arts centers reduced in 2013.

21-3 文化娱乐业(2014)

Culture and Entertainment Industry

指　标	Item	机构数(个) Institutions (unit)	从业人员(人) Number of Employed Persons(person)	营业收入(万元) Operating Revenue (10000 yuan)	营业利润(万元) Primary Business Profit (10000 yuan)
总　计	**Total**	**5021**	**33424**	**301172**	**104961**
非国有艺术表演团体	Non-state Performing Arts Groups	64	1976	4735	-325
娱乐场所	Places of Entertainment	2557	20347	182661	61284
互联网上网服务营业场所（网吧）	Internet access service establishments (internet cafes)	2400	11101	113777	44002

21-4 艺术表演场所(2014)

Art Preformances Places

指　标	Item	机构数(个) Number of Instit-utions (unit)	从业人员(人) Number of Staff and Workers (person)	座席数(个) Seats (unit)	演(映)出场次(场) Number of Perfo-rmances (show)	#艺术演出场次 Art Perfo-rmance	观众人次(万人次) Number of Spectators (10000 person-times)
总　计	**Toatl**	**6**	**76**				
#省　级	Province Level	4	60				
地 级	Prefectural Level	2	16				
县 级	County Level						
#文化系统	Cultural Organizations and Institutions	6	76				

注：2014年文化系统6个艺术表演场所均处于改制转型中，全年无演出。

Note: There were 6 of 6 performing arts venues in cultural system in the restructuring and transformtion, with no performances throughout the year.

21－5 文化部门艺术表演团体(2014)
Art Troupes of Culture Sector

指　　标	Item	剧团数(个) Number of Troupes (unit)	从业人员(人) Number of Employed Persons (person)	国内演出(场) Number of Domestic Performances (show)	#在农村演出 Shows in Rural Areas	国内观众人数(万人次) Number of Domestic Spectators (10000 person-times)
总　　计	**Total**	**40**	**1537**	**2700**	**1220**	**300.35**
按隶属关系分	**Grouped by Ownership**					
#国有剧团	State-owned Troupes	32	1258	2080	1020	201.95
按剧种分	**Grouped by Art Troupes**	**40**	**1537**	**2700**	**1220**	**300.35**
话剧、儿童剧、滑稽剧团	Drama, Children's Play and Comedy Troupes	1	65	100	30	1.25
歌舞、音乐类	Song and Dance Troupe,Music Troupes	33	972	1970	970	237.50
京剧、昆曲类	Local Beijing Opera Troupes,Kunqu Troupes	1	50	120		5.50
地方戏曲类	Local Opera Troupes	2	215	240	40	14.10
杂技、魔术、马戏类	Acrobatics , Magic, Circus Troupes	1	82	130	70	12.00
曲艺类	Art class	1	86	120	110	23.00
综合性艺术表演团体	General Art Performing Troupes	1	67	20		7.00

21－6 群众文化馆(站)(2014)
Mass Culture Centers(Stations)

指　　标	Item	合计 Total	文化馆 Culture Centers	文化站 Culture Stations
馆(站)个数(个)	**Number of Centers(unit)**	**1686**	**98**	**1588**
组织各类讲座次数(次)	Organizing Lectures(time)	348	348	
组织文艺活动次数(次)	Organizing Art Performances(time)	16786	4543	12243
举办业余文艺训练班(班次)	Conducting Amateur Art Training Courses(class)	9113	2546	6567
#结业人数(万人次)	Number of Persons Completed(10000 person-times)	64.86	21.43	43.43
举办展览次数(次)	Number of Exhibitions(unit)	3154	477	2677

21-7 广播、电视
Radio and Television Industry

指 标	Item	2010	2011	2012	2013	2014
广播电视台(座)	Broadcasting and Television Stations(unit)	79	79	84	85	84
广播节目综合人口覆盖率(%)	Radio Coverage Rate of the Population(%)	87.5	88.0	88.5	90.0	91.5
#农村	Rural	85.6	86.1	86.6	88.6	
广播节目自办套数(套)	Number of Radio Programs with Ownership(set)	27	31	39	38	40
#公共广播	Public Radio	27	31	39	38	40
广播节目制作时间(万小时)	Length of Radio Programs Produced(10 000 hours)	6.23	10.58	12.94	12.06	12.50
公共广播节目播出时间(万小时)	Length of Public Radio Programs Broadcasted (10 000 hours)	15.78	18.92	20.87	22.55	22.74
电视节目综合人口覆盖率(%)	TV Coverage Rate of Population(%)	92.5	92.8	93.0	94.1	95.4
#农村	Rural	91.4	91.7	91.9	93.4	
有线广播电视用户数(万户)	Users of Cable Radio and TV (10 000 households)	335.23	396.57	396.61	394.28	386.18
#农村	Rural	91.26	210.53	218.20	44.70	
数字电视用户数(万户)	Number of Users of Digital TV(10 000 households)	234.51	349.67	357.69	394.28	386.18
有线广播电视入户率(%)	Popularization Rate of Cable Radio and TV(%)	29.9	34.3	32.9	32.1	30.8
#农村	Rural	9.9	22.0	22.2	4.5	
电视节目自办套数(套)	Number of TV Programs with Ownership(set)	101	101	101	102	102
#公共电视	Public TV	101	101	101	102	102
电视节目制作时间(万小时)	Length of TV Programs Produced(10 000 hours)	4.35	3.10	4.61	4.15	4.27
公共电视节目播出时间(万小时)	Length of Public TV Programs Broadcasted (10 000 hours)	24.69	22.71	24.00	23.50	24.07
电视剧播出数(万部)	Number of TV Plays Broadcasted(10 000 sets)	0.30	0.26	0.26	0.25	0.21
#进口电视剧播出数(部)	Imported TV Plays(set)	140	127	115	107	50
电视剧播出数(万集)	Number of TV Plays Broadcasted(10 000 parts)	7.24	6.45	6.29	5.75	4.67
#进口电视剧播出数	Imported TV Plays	0.38	0.26	0.23	0.24	0.12

注：1.资料来源于省新闻出版广电局(以下相关表同)。2.2014年国家新闻出版广电总局取消农村统计指标.

Note: 1.Data in the table is provided by Guizhou provinvial press and publication bureau. (The relative tables in the chapter are the same). 2.State Press and Publication Administration of Radio canceled rural statistical indicators in 2014.

21−8 广播、电视节目播出时间(2014)
Broadcasting Hours of Radio and Television Programs

单位：小时 (hour)

指　标	Item	全　年 公共节目播出时间 Broadcasting Hours	#新闻资讯类节目 News	#专题服务类节目 Special Subject	#综合益智类节目 General Entertainment
广播电台	**All Radio Broadcasting Stations**	**393546**	**83123**	**75327**	**84496**
省　级	Province Level	227433	43630	46219	50464
地　级	Prefectural Level	105759	21053	22973	27801
县　级	County Level	60354	18440	6135	6231
电视台	**All Television Stations**	**425176**	**121675**	**40801**	**16200**
省　级	Province Level	240732	70080	25098	12476
地　级	Prefectural Level	122171	6348	11519	1708
县　级	County Level	62273	45247	4184	2016

21−9 图书出版
Books Published

指　标	Item	2010	2011	2012	2013	2014
出版图书(种)	**Number of Publications(kind)**	**823**	**856**	**966**	**894**	**845**
#新出版	New Publications	642	545	575	667	721
总印数(万册)	Printed Copies(10000 copies)	8069	8492	7304	6278	10099
总印张数(万印张)	Printed Sheets(10000 sheets)	55778	57278	48304	44066	64882

21-10 杂志出版
Magazines Published

指 标	Item	2010	2011	2012	2013	2014
出版杂志(种)	**Number of Publications(kind)**	**88**	**88**	**88**	**88**	**90**
每期平均印数(万册)	Average Printed Copies Per Issue(10000 copies)	85	78	86	84	84
总印数(万册)	Printed Copies(10000 copies)	1300	1413	1485	1575	1523
总印张数(万印张)	Printed Sheets(10000 sheets)	7117	7257	7062	7792	7890

21-11 报纸出版
Newspaper Published

指 标	Item	2010	2011	2012	2013	2014
出版报纸(种)	**Number of Publications(kind)**	**44**	**44**	**44**	**43**	**42**
每期平均印数(万份)	Average Printed Copies Per Issue(10000 copies)	162	175	170	156	147
总印数(万份)	Printed Copies(10000 copies)	37004	44931	41704	38954	36409
总印张数(万印张)	Printed Sheets(10000 sheets)	145831	200712	178188	162120	156095

21-12 报纸分类出版数量(2014)
Number of Newspaper Published by Category

指 标	Item	出版报纸(种) Number of Public-ations (kind)	每期平均印数(万份) Average Publication Per Issue (10000 copies)	总印数(万份) Total Printed (10000 copies)	总印张数(万印张) Total Printed Sheets (10000 sheets)
总 计	**Total**	**6**	**51**	**16622**	**94419**
#贵州日报	Guizhou Daily	1	16.09	5871.46	15635.79
贵州都市报	Guizhou Urban Newspaper	1	16.01	5733.12	40131.84
贵阳晚报	Guiyang Evening Newspaper	1	13.15	4708.34	36779.01
文 摘	Tabloid	1	1.30	65.00	585.00
每周广播电视报	Broadcasting and Television Weekly Newspaper	2	4.70	244.40	1287.00

21-13 体育运动员
Athletes

单位：人 (person)

指 标	Item	2010	2011	2012	2013	2014
优秀运动员	**Excellent Athletes**	**145**	**189**	**173**	**173**	**153**
#女运动员	Female	50	67	66	74	55
专职教练员	**Full-time Coaches**	**215**	**219**	**167**	**219**	**212**
#女专职教练员	Female	56	61	46	67	58
等级运动员发展人数	**Number of Certified Athletes**	**450**	**488**	**511**	**301**	**279**
等级裁判员发展人数	**Number of Certified Referees**	**153**	**5130**	**939**	**2059**	**2315**

注：资料来源于省体育局(以下相关表同)。
Note: The data in the table are provided by the provinvial Sport Administration(The relative tables in the chapter are the same).

21-14 体育运动获奖
Medals Won by Guizhou Athletes in Domestic and International Competitions

单位：项 (unit)

指 标	Item	2010	2011	2012	2013	2014
国内外大赛第一名	Number of the First-Order	16	12	9	7	23
国内外大赛第二名	Number of the Second-Order	19	21	2	13	11
国内外大赛第三名	Number of the Third-Order	12	28	5	17	15

21－15 公共体育场地

Number of Public Stadiums and Gymnasiums

单位：个 (unit)

指 标	Item	2013	2014
总 计	**Total**	**1653**	**3740**
#体育场馆	Stadiums	3	11
全民健身活动中心	The National fitness activities center	18	6
乡镇体育健身场所	Villages and Towns sports fitness sites	111	295
村级农民体育健身场所	Villages farmer sports fitness sites	911	2948

注：2014年起体育系统报表制度改变，只统计体育系统的场地数.2013年数据为第六次全国体育场地普查初步汇总数据。
Note:The reporting system of sport system has changed since 2014, which is only account spots number.data of 2013 was preliminary summary data of the sixth national stadium census.

21－16 群众体育活动

Activities of Mass Sports

指 标	Item	2013	2014
社会体育指导员发展情况（人）	Development of Social sports Instructors	22930	24109
国家级	National level	206	206
一级	First-level	5749	6592
二级	Second-level	4657	4993
三级	Three-level	12318	12318
青少年体育俱乐部(个)	Athletic Club for Youngsters(unit)	103	108
全民健身工程(条)	Body-building Activities of The Whole Nation(unit)	340	310

21-17 卫生事业
Health Care

指 标	Item	2010	2011	2012	2013	2014
卫生机构(个)	**Number of Health Institutions(unit)**	**5637**	**5683**	**27379**	**29182**	**28995**
#医院、卫生院	Hospitals and Township Hospitals	2005	2071	2210	2429	2612
床位数(万张)	**Number of Beds(10000 beds)**	**10.53**	**11.75**	**13.65**	**16.33**	**18.17**
#医院、卫生院床位	Number of Hospital and Township Hospitals Beds	9.75	10.80	12.97	15.58	17.84
卫生人员合计(万人)	**Number of Employed Personnel in Health Care Institutions (10000 persons)**	**12.13**	**13.29**	**19.21**	**22.23**	**23.73**
#卫生技术人员	Medical Technical Personnels	10.25	11.22	12.98	15.66	16.98
#执业(助理)医师	Licensed(Assistant) Doctors	4.22	4.40	4.92	5.59	5.78
#注册护士	Registered Nurse	3.60	4.16	4.87	5.94	6.71
医疗机构病床使用率(%)	**Utilization Rate in Medical Institutions(%)**	**79.7**	**79.6**	**83.2**	**81.3**	**77.1**
人均卫生费(元)	**Expenditure for Health of each Person(yuan)**	**947**	**1221**	**1378**	**1580**	**1578**
平均每千人拥有:	**Per 1000 Person:**					
床位数(张)	Beds(set)	3.00	2.77	3.21	3.81	4.20
#医院、卫生院床位	Number of Hospital Beds	2.78	2.55	3.05	3.64	4.12
卫生人员(人)	Number of Employed Personnel in Health Care Institutions(person)	3.46	3.14	4.52	5.19	5.49
#卫生技术人员	Medical Technical Personnels	2.92	2.65	3.06	3.65	3.93
#执业(助理)医师	Licensed(Assistant) Doctors	1.20	1.04	1.12	1.30	1.34
医院服务情况	**Hospital Services**					
诊疗人次(万人次)	Visits (10000 person-times)	2536.82	2910.53	3464.00	4063.16	4474.63
入院人数(万人)	Inpatients (10000 persons)	211.91	243.34	325.04	406.70	443.42
出院人数(万人)	Patients Discharged from Hospital (10000 persons)	208.93	240.59	320.49	401.46	438.95
每百门诊急诊入院人数(人)	Inpatients per 100 Outpatient and Emergency Visits (person)	8.50	8.70	9.75	10.43	10.29
病床使用率(%)	Utilization Rate of Beds (%)	86.4	87.1	89.11	85.81	82.71
出院者平均住院日(天)	Average Stay Days in Hospital(day)	9.70	9.20	8.90	8.50	8.50

注：1.资料来源于省卫生计生委,表中2011年及以前数据不含村卫生室,2012年起含村卫生室(以下相关表同)。2.医院服务情况指医院类别的医疗服务情况。3.每千人口指标2010年以常住人口数为基数计算，2011年起以户籍人口数为基数计算。人均卫生费2010—2011年为测算数，2012—2013年为推算数。

Note:1.Data in the table is provided by the Committee of Population and Family Planning of Guizhou Provincial. In the year of 2011 and before data in this table exclude health clinics of village, but including health clinics of village from 2012(the same applies to the next table). 2.The Hospital Services include all medical institutions refer to hospitals' services.3.Indicators of per thousand population are calculated based on resident population, while based on Household registration population in 2011. Per capita health costs in 2011 were measured, while data in 2012 and 2013 was calculated .

21-18 卫生机构、床位、人员数(2014)

Number of Health Institutions,Beds and Personnels

指　标	Item	机构数(个) Institutions (unit)	床位数(张) Hospital Beds (Bed)	人员数(人) Number of Personels (person)	#卫生技术人员数 Medical Technical Personels
合　计	**Total Number of Institutions**	**28995**	**181728**	**237317**	**169799**
医　院	Hospitals	1067	135332	129727	108335
#市	City	446	64936	72131	59698
县	County	621	70396	57596	48637
#综合医院	Genaral Hospital	821	102355	100475	84412
县医院	Hospitals at County Level	70	29153	26640	23435
中医医院	Hospital Specialized in TCM	83	17490	16187	13798
中西医结合医院	Combine Hospitals of Chinese and Western Medicine	16	1437	1043	882
民族医院	Nationality Medicine Hospital	9	521	543	432
专科医院	Other Specialized Hospitals	135	13306	11382	8735
护理院	Nursing Hospital	3	223	97	76
疗养院(所)	Sanitariums	1	98	42	41
社区卫生服务中心(站)	Total Health Service Centers for Community	596	2797	6348	5355
社区卫生服务中心	Health Service Centers for Community	157	2797	3195	2642
社区卫生服务站	Health Service Stations for Community	439		3153	2713
卫生院	Health Centers	1445	38670	33241	29492
#农村乡镇卫生院	Health Centers of Villages and Towns in Country	1427	38178	32845	29183
中心卫生院	Health Centers Focus Villages and Towns	561	21752	17007	15079
乡卫生院	Health Centers of Commonly Villages and Towns	866	16426	15838	14104
门诊部、诊所、医务室	Outpatient Department Clinic and Infirmary	3446		8782	8485
#私人办诊所	Private Clinique	2811		6570	6461
专科防治所(站)	Specialized Disease Prevention and Treatment Centers	9	455	384	287
疾控中心(卫生防疫站)	CDC(Epidemic Prevention Station)	101		4944	3953
#县疾控中心	CDC at County Level	71		2690	2237
卫生监督机构	Sanitation Supervise Centers	94		1659	1386
#县卫生监督机构	Sanitation Supervise Centers at County Level	66		949	788
妇幼保健院(所、站)	MCH Center	100	4376	5355	4596
#县妇幼保健院(所、站)	MCH Centers at County level	61	2385	2501	2156
医学科学研究机构	Research Institution of Medicine Science	2		22	21
村卫生室	Health Clinics of Village	20945		37962	1668
其他卫生机构	Other Health Project Institution	1189		8851	6180
按主办单位分	**Total Number of Institutions**				
政府办	Government Office	5392	126815	143116	119218
卫计部门办	Health Department	4381	123908	135016	113281
社会办	Industrial and Other Department	12432	18864	43879	17906
个人办	Private	11171	36049	50272	32675
按经济类型分	**Total Number of Institutions**				
公立	The Public	13263	137675	170101	130375
国有	State-owned	6071	136816	155315	129114
集体	Collective	7192	859	14786	1261
民营	Private	15732	44053	67216	39424
联营	Joint venture	191	795	800	471
私营	Private	14250	36166	56224	31968
其他	other	1291	7092	10192	6985

21-19 卫生防疫防治和妇幼卫生事业

Sanitation and Epidemic Prevention,Maternity and Child Care

指　标	Item	2010	2011	2012	2013	2014
专科疾病防治院（所、站）机构数(个)	**Prevention and Treatment Centers or Stations (unit)**	**8**	**9**	**7**	**10**	**9**
人员总数(人)	Number of Personnels(person)	186	243	202	261	384
#卫生技术人员数	Medical Technical Personnels	144	191	162	212	287
床位数(张)	Hospital Beds(bed)	199	280	440	486	455
疾病预防控制中心机构数(个)	**Institutions of Sanitation and Antiepidemic Agencies(unit)**	**103**	**103**	**101**	**101**	**101**
人员总数(人)	Number of Personnels(person)	4561	4542	4737	4952	4944
#卫生技术人员数(人)	Medical Technical Personnels(person)	3689	3629	3627	3958	3953
妇幼保健机构数(个)	**Institutions of Maternity and Child Care(unit)**	**89**	**94**	**96**	**98**	**100**
人员总数(人)	Number of Personnels(person)	3692	3888	4216	4889	5355
#卫生技术人员数(人)	Medical Technical Personnels(person)	3151	3341	3601	4201	4596
床位数(张)	**Hospital Beds(bed)**	**3049**	**4398**	**3785**	**4141**	**4376**

21－20 县及县以上医院、卫生院(2014)

Hospitals and Health Centers at County Level and above

指 标	Item	机构合计(个) Institutions (unit)	诊疗人次数(万人次) Number of Visits and Inpatients (10000 person-times)	#门 诊(万人次) Number of Visits in Clinics (10000 person-times)	入院人数(万人) Inpatients (10000 person)	出院人数(万人) Outpatients (10000 person)
县及县以上医院合计	**Hospitals at County Level and above**	**1067**	**4474.63**	**3853.24**	**443.42**	**438.95**
#综合医院	Comprehensive Hospitals	821	3573.74	3068.90	356.07	352.88
中医医院	Hospital of Chinese Medicine	83	595.18	511.63	56.96	56.31
妇幼保健院(所、站)	**Maternity and Child Care Hospital(Centers orStations)**	**100**	**299.57**	**234.65**	**20.67**	**19.93**
#妇幼保健院	Maternity and Child Care Hospital	55	247.38	184.84	17.19	16.42
卫生院合计	**Township Hospitals**	**1445**	**2371.18**	**2212.84**	**165.42**	**164.59**
#农村乡镇卫生院	Rural Township Hospitals	1427	2354.07	2197.96	163.25	162.42
中心卫生院	Central Township Hospitals	561	1251.20	1165.42	94.53	94.08
乡卫生院	Ecumenic Township Hospitals	866	1102.86	1032.54	68.73	68.34

21－20 续表 continued

指 标	Item	平均开放病床数(张) Average Sickbeds Setup (bed)	病床周转次数(次/年) Turnover of Beds (time/year)	病床工作日(日/床) Number of Days Per Bed in Use (day/Bed)	病床使用率(%) Utilization Rate of Beds(%)	出院者平均住院日(天/人) Average Stay Days in Hospital (day/Person)	每百门(急)诊入院人数(人) Hospital Admissions Per 100 Out-Patient Times and Emergency Patient-Times (person)
县及县以上医院合计	**Hospitals at and above County Level**	**128490**	**34.2**	**301.9**	**82.71**	**8.5**	**10.29**
#综合医院	Comprehensive Hospitals	97084	36.3	303.0	83.00	8.1	10.39
#中医医院	Hospital of Chinese Medicine	16790	33.5	316.1	86.61	9.1	9.87
妇幼保健院(所、站)	**Maternity and Child Care Hospital(Centers orstations)**	**4113**	**48.5**	**256.4**	**70.25**	**5.1**	**7.53**
#妇幼保健院	Maternity and Child Care Hospital	3084	53.2	289.9	79.41	5.3	7.67
卫生院合计	**Township Hospitals**	**36827**	**44.7**	**217.6**	**59.63**	**4.6**	**7.31**
#农村乡镇卫生院	Rural Township Hospitals	36400	44.6	217.5	59.59	4.6	7.26
中心卫生院	Central Township Hospitals	20784	45.3	226.8	62.14	4.7	7.91
乡卫生院	Ecumenic Township Hospitals	15616	43.8	205.2	56.21	4.4	6.54

21-21 县、乡、村三级医疗、预防、保健

Health Organization at County,Town and Village Level

指　标	Item	2010	2011	2012	2013	2014	2014年比2013年增长(%) Increase Rate in 2014 over 2013(%)
县医院个数(个)	**Number of Hospitals at County Level(unit)**	**70**	**70**	**70**	**70**	**70**	**持平**
平均每院病床数(张)	Average Number of Beds Per Hospital(bed)	230.01	242.36	278.74	333.17	416.47	25.0
平均每院人员数(人)	Average Personnels Per Hospital(person)	193.10	233.37	258.26	322.06	380.57	18.2
#平均每院卫生技术人员数	Average Medical Technical Personnels Per Hospital	167.53	203.16	224.81	282.39	334.79	18.6
县妇幼保健院(所、站)机构数(个)	**Maternity and Child Care Centers at County Level (unit)**	**58**	**57**	**58**	**57**	**61**	**7.0**
平均每院(所、站)床位数(张)	Average Number of Beds Per Station (bed)	26.91	28.54	33.43	38.84	39.10	0.7
平均每院(所、站)人员数 (人)	Average Personnels Per Station (person)	28.98	30.49	33.38	36.61	41.00	12.0
#每院(所、站)卫生技术人员数	Medical Technical Personnels Per Stati on	25.47	26.91	33.38	31.89	35.34	10.8
县疾病预防控制中心机构数(个)	**Institutions of Epidemic Prevention Station at County Level(unit)**	**69**	**69**	**71**	**75**	**71**	**-5.3**
平均每所站人员数(人)	Personnels Per Station(person)	35.01	35.14	37.48	37.84	37.89	0.1
#平均每站卫生技术人员数	Average Medical Technical Personnels Per Station	29.83	29.45	31.34	31.75	31.51	-0.8
农村乡镇卫生院机构数(个)	**Institutions of Rural Township Hospitals(unit)**	**1437**	**1436**	**1438**	**1430**	**1427**	**-0.2**
农村乡镇卫生院床位数 (张)	Number of Beds of Rural Township Hospitals(bed)	28123	29541	33148	36812	38178	3.7
平均每院床位数(张)	Average Number of Beds Per Hospital(bed)	19.57	20.57	23.05	25.74	26.75	3.9
平均每千农业人口乡镇卫生院床位数(张)	Average Number of Beds of Rural Township Hospitals Per 1000 Rural Personnels(bed)	0.80	0.83	0.93	1.03	1.06	2.8
农村乡镇卫生院人员数(人)	Personnels of Rural Township Hospitals (person)	20893	23047	26113	29725	32845	10.5
平均每院人员数(人)	Average Personnels Per Hospital(person)	14.54	16.05	18.16	20.79	23.02	10.7
平均每千农业人口乡镇卫生院人员数(人)	Average Medical Technical Personnels of Rural Township Hospitals Per 1000 Rural Personnels(person)	0.59	0.65	0.73	0.83	0.91	9.5
村卫生室个数(个)	**Number of Villages with Medical Treatment Sations(unit)**	**19783**	**20260**	**21445**	**21220**	**20945**	**-1.3**
村卫生室覆盖率(%)	Coverage Rate of Township Hospitals(%)	90.1	93.8	100.0	100.0	100.0	持平
开展合作医疗的村数(个)	Number of Villages of Carrying out Rural Cooperative Medical Treatment(unit)	17672	17583	18099	16869	18878	11.9
开展合作医疗的村覆盖率(%)	Coverage Rate of Villages of Carrying out Rural Cooperative Medical Treatment(%)	100.0	100.0	100.0	100.0	100.0	持平
平均每村设置医疗点数(个)	Average Number of Medical Treatment Stations Per Village(unit)	1.12	1.15	1.18	1.26	1.24	-1.2
乡村医生和卫生员数(人)	Doctors and Health Workers(person)	31517	34587	37760	36328	36294	-0.1
#乡村医生所占比例(%)	Proportion of Rural Doctors(%)	78.0	76.7	73.4	75.5	75.0	-0.5(百分点)
平均每村乡村医生和卫生员数(人)	Average Number of Doctors and Health Workers Per Village(person)	1.78	1.97	2.09	2.15	1.73	-19.5
平均每千农业人口乡村医生和卫生员数(人)	Average Number of Doctors and Health Workers Per 1000 Rural Personnels (person)	0.90	0.97	1.06	1.01	1.00	-1.0

注：1.县医院指卫生部门办的县综合医院，且不含县级市和区。2."村卫生室覆盖率"=设置村卫生室的村数/行政村总数。

Note: 1.Hospitals at county level running by the health department refers to general hospital,and exclude county-level city and district. 2."the coverage rate of township hospitals"=number of villages with medical treatment sations/the number of administrative villages.

21－22 28种传染病报告发病及死亡人数(2014)

List of 28 Infectious Diseases Reported and Number of Death

单位：人 (person)

顺 位 No.	发病 Diseases 疾病名称 Diseases	发病人数 Persons	死亡 Death 疾病名称 Diseases	死亡人数 Persons
1	肺结核 Pulmonary Tuberculosis	43320	艾滋病 AIDS	382
2	病毒性肝炎 Viral Hepatitis	25486	肺结核 Pulmonary Tuberculosis	153
3	梅毒 Syphilis	9505	狂犬病 Hydrophobia	68
4	细菌性和阿米巴性痢疾 Dysentery	3493	乙脑 Encephalitis B	
5	淋病 Gonorrhea	1288	新生儿破伤风 Newborn Tetanus	6
6	伤寒副伤寒 Typhoid and Paratyphoid Fever	694	病毒性肝炎 Viral Hepatitis	8
7	艾滋病 AIDS	1038	梅毒 Syphilis	3
8	猩红热 Scarlet Fever	512	细菌性和阿米巴性痢疾 Dysentery	
9	流行性乙型脑炎 Encephalitis B	63	钩端螺旋体病 Leptospirosis	2
10	狂犬病 Hydrophobia	69	流行性脑脊髓膜炎 Epidemic Encephalitis	
11	流行性出血热 Hemorrhage Fever	87	流行性出血热 Hemorrhage Fever	1
12	百日咳 Pertussis	31	人感染高致病性禽流感 Highly Pathogenic Bird Flu	
13	麻疹 Measles	151	淋病 Gonorrhea	
14	钩端螺旋体病 Leptospirosis	8	伤寒副伤寒 Typhoid and Paratyphoid Fever	
15	新生儿破伤风 Newborn Tetanus	31	疟疾 Malaria	
16	疟疾 Malaria	3493	麻疹 Measles	1
17	流行性感冒(包含甲型H1N1流感) A(H1N1)Flu	2236	流行性感冒(包含甲型H1N1流感) A(H1N1)Flu	1
18	布鲁氏菌病 Brucellosis	56	炭疽 Anthrax	3
19	流行性脑脊髓膜炎 Epidemic Encephalitis	5	鼠疫 The Plague	
20	炭疽 Anthrax	14	血吸虫病 Schistosomiasis	
21	人感染高致病性禽流感 Highly Pathogenic Bird Flu		百日咳 Pertussis	
22	血吸虫病 Schistosomiasis		布鲁氏菌病 Brucellosis	
23	霍乱 Cholera		猩红热 Scarlet Fever	
24	鼠疫 The Plague		登革热 Dengue Fever	
25	登革热 Dengue Fever	2	霍乱 Cholera	
26	传染性非典型肺炎 SARS		传染性非典型肺炎 SARS	
27	脊髓灰质炎 Poliomyelitis		脊髓灰质炎 Poliomyelitis	
28	白喉 Diphtheria		白喉 Diphtheria	

21-23 28种传染病报告发病率、死亡率及病死率(2014)

List of Incidence,Death and Mortality Rates of 28 Infectious Disease Reported

顺位 No.	发病 Disease Incidence 疾病名称 Diseases	发病率 (1/10万) Incidence (1/100 000)	死亡 Death 疾病名称 Diseases	死亡率 (1/10万) Death Rate (1/100 000)	病死 Mortality Rate 疾病名称 Diseases	病死率 (%) Mortality Rate(%)
1	肺结核 Pulmonary Tuberculosis	123.6930	狂犬病 Hydrophobia	0.1942	人禽流感 Highly Pathogenic Bird Flu	
2	病毒性肝炎 Viral Hepatitis	72.7710	艾滋病 AIDS	1.0907	狂犬病 Hydrophobia	98.5507
3	梅毒 Syphilis	27.1399	肺结核 Pulmonary Tuberculosis	0.4369	艾滋病 AIDS	36.8015
4	细菌性和阿米巴性痢疾 Dysentery	9.9737	流行性乙型脑炎 Encephalitis B		新生儿破伤风 Newborn Tetanus	19.3548
5	淋病 Gonorrhea	3.6777	病毒性肝炎 Viral Hepatitis		流脑 Epidemic Encephalitis	
6	伤寒+副伤寒 Typhoid and Paratyphoid Fever	1.9816	新生儿破伤风 Newborn Tetanus	0.0171	钩端螺旋体病 Leptospirosis	25.0000
7	艾滋病 AIDS	2.9638	梅毒 Syphilis	0.0086	流行性乙型脑炎 Encephalitis B	
8	猩红热 Scarlet Fever	1.4619	细菌性和阿米巴性痢疾 Dysentery		流行性出血热 Hemorrhage Fever	1.1494
9	流行性乙型脑炎 Encephalitis B	0.1799	流脑 Epidemic Encephalitis		肺结核 Pulmonary Tuberculosis	0.3532
10	狂犬病 Hydrophobia	0.1970	流行性出血热 Hemorrhage Fever	0.0029	淋病 Gonorrhea	
11	流行性出血热 Hemorrhage Fever	0.2484	人禽流感 Highly Pathogenic Bird Flu		梅毒 Syphilis	0.0316
12	百日咳 Pertussis	0.0885	淋病 Gonorrhea		细菌性和阿米巴性痢疾 Dysentery	
13	麻疹 Measles	0.4312	伤寒+副伤寒 Typhoid and Paratyphoid Fever		病毒性肝炎 Viral Hepatitis	
14	钩端螺旋体病 Leptospirosis	0.0228	疟疾 Malaria		炭疽 Anthrax	21.4286
15	新生儿破伤风 Newborn Tetanus	0.0885	流行性感冒(包含甲型H1N1流感) A(H1N1)Flu	0.0029	流行性感冒(包含甲型H1N1流感) A(H1N1)Flu	0.0447
16	疟疾 Malaria	0.0799	炭疽 Anthrax	0.0086	鼠疫 The Plague	
17	流行性感冒(包含甲型H1N1流感) A(H1N1)Flu	6.3845	麻疹 Measles	0.0029	麻疹 Measles	0.6623
18	布鲁氏菌病 Brucellosis	0.1599	血吸虫病 Schistosomiasis		疟疾 Malaria	
19	流脑 Epidemic Encephalitis	0.0143	鼠疫 The Plague		百日咳 Pertussis	
20	炭疽 Anthrax	0.0400	百日咳 Pertussis		血吸虫病 Schistosomiasis	
21	人禽流感 Highly Pathogenic Bird Flu		淋病 Gonorrhea		伤寒+副伤寒 Typhoid and Paratyphoid Fever	
22	登革热 Dengue Fever	0.0057	布鲁氏菌病 Brucellosis		布鲁氏菌病 Brucellosis	
23	血吸虫病 Schistosomiasis		猩红热 Scarlet Fever		猩红热 Scarlet Fever	
24	鼠疫 The Plague		登革热 Dengue Fever		登革热 Dengue Fever	
25	霍乱 Cholera		霍乱 Cholera		霍乱 Cholera	
26	传染性非典型肺炎 SARS		传染性非典型肺炎 SARS		传染性非典型肺炎 SARS	
27	脊灰 Poliomyelitis		脊灰 Poliomyelitis		脊灰 Poliomyelitis	
28	白喉 Diphtheria		白喉 Diphtheria		白喉 Diphtheria	

21-24 5岁以下儿童和孕产妇死亡率

Mortality Rate of the Maternal and Children Aged under 5

指 标	Item	2010	2011	2012	2013	2014
新生儿死亡率(‰)	**Newborn Mortality Rate(‰)**	**7.1**	**5.1**	**5.9**	**4.6**	**5.1**
城 市	Urban	6.3	4.7	4.9	3.7	2.9
农 村	Rural	7.3	5.1	6.8	5.1	6.2
婴儿死亡率(‰)	**Infant Mortality Rate(‰)**	**11.9**	**8.6**	**11.4**	**9.2**	**7.9**
城 市	Urban	10.9	8.4	6.8	6.3	4.7
农 村	Rural	12.2	8.9	13.8	10.7	9.5
5岁以下儿童死亡率(‰)	**Mortality Rate of Children under 5(‰)**	**15.0**	**11.2**	**15.1**	**13.0**	**11.7**
城 市	Urban	14.0	10.8	8.1	8.9	7.0
农 村	Rural	15.3	11.3	18.7	15.1	14.2
孕产妇死亡率(1/10万)	**Maternal Mortality Rate(1/100 000)**	**35.4**	**24.5**	**32.0**	**22.4**	**29.4**
城 市	Urban	35.7	30.2	32.0	26.3	30.8
农 村	Rural	35.3	22.5	34.2	21.4	29.1

注：2010—2011年数据源自妇幼卫生年报表，2012年起数据源自妇幼卫生监测数据。

Note:Data is obtained from the Annual Report of Maternal and Child Health in 2010 and 2011.The remaining data of 2012 originated from maternal and child health surveillance data.

21-25 新型农村合作医疗

Conditions of New Cooperative Medical System

指 标	Item	2010	2011	2012	2013	2014
开展新农合县（市、区、特区)数(个)	Number of Counties Implementing of NCMS (unit)	88	88	88	88	88
参加新农合人数(万人)	Number of Enrollees(10000 persons)	3029.17	3074.80	3112.21	3213.95	3247.40
参合率(%)	Enrollment Rate(%)	96.3	97.1	98.0	98.7	98.9
当年筹资总额(亿元)	Total Fund Raised at Current Year (100 million yuan)	44.35	68.73	90.25	107.34	127.82
人均筹资(元)	Per Capita Premiums(yuan)	140	230	290	330	390
当年基金支出(亿元)	Payout at Current Year(10000 million yuan)	37.12	52.25	85.75	116.40	123.28
补偿受益人次(万人次)	Number of Beneficiaries from Reimbursement (10000 person-times)	3949.88	4408.91	4890.82	5520.51	5755.28

主要统计指标解释

文化事业机构 指由文化部门主办或实行行业管理的文化及相关产业机构以及由文化部门主办的非文化及相关产业机构等。

艺术表演团体 指由文化部门主办或实行行业管理（经文化行政部门审批并领取营业性演出许可证），专门从事表演艺术等活动的各类专业艺术表演团体，含民间职业剧团（不包括群众业余文艺表演团队）。

艺术表演观众人数(人次) 指在国内和国外的艺术表演的观众人数。包括售票、包场等有演出收入的场次人数和政府采购的公益性演出场次人数及参加汇演、调演等无演出收入的公开演出场次人数，包括流动舞台车演出场次人数，不包括彩排和内部观摩等无演出收入的场次人数。

广播节目综合人口覆盖率 指根据国家广电总局制定的《广播电视人口覆盖率统计技术标准和方法》进行统计调查的，在对象区内采用无线、有线、卫星等技术手段能够收听到包括中央、省、地市、县广播节目其中任意一套的人口数占全国总人口数的百分比。

电视节目综合人口覆盖率 指根据国家广电总局制定的《广播电视人口覆盖率统计技术标准和方法》进行统计调查的，在对象区内采用无线、有线、卫星等技术手段能够收看到包括中央、省、地市、县级电视节目中任意一套的人口数占全国总人口数的百分比。

等级运动员发展人数 指经考核正式批准授予等级运动员称号的人数。运动员等级分为国际级运动健将、运动健将、一级运动员、二级运动员。

等级裁判员发展人数 指经考核正式批准授予等级裁判员称号的人数。裁判员等级分为国际级裁判员、国家级裁判员、一级裁判员、二级裁判员。

体育场 指有400米跑道(中心含足球场)，有固定道牙，跑道6条以上，并有固定看台的室外田径场地。体育场按看台容纳观众人数分为：甲级25000人以上，乙级15000−25000人，丙级5000−15000人，丁级5000人以下。

体育馆 指有固定看台，可供篮球、排球、羽毛球、乒乓球、体操等项目训练比赛活动用的室内运动场地。体育馆按看台容纳观众人数分为：甲级6000人以上，乙级4000−6000人，丙级2000−4000人，丁级2000人以下。

医院 包括综合医院、中医医院、中西医结合医院、民族医院、各类专科医院和护理院。包括医学院校附属医院，不包括专科疾病防治院、妇幼保健院和疗养院。

社区卫生服务中心(站) 指为本社区居民提供预防、医疗、保健、康复、健康教育、计划生育技术服务等的基层卫生机构。包括社区卫生服务中心和社区卫生服务站。

卫生技术人员 包括执业医师、执业助理医师、注册护士、药师(士)、检验及影像技师(士)、卫生监督员和见习医(药、护、技)师(士)等卫生专业人员(不包括药剂员、检验员、护理员等)，不包括从事管理工作的卫生技术人员(如院长、副院长、党委书记等)。其中见习医师(士)指毕业于高中等院校医学专业但尚未取得医师执业证书的医师和医士。

执业医师 指具有《医师执业证》及其“级别”为“执业医师”且实际从事临床工作的人员，不包括取得执业证书但从事管理工作的人员（如院长、书记等）。执业医师类别分为临床、中医、口腔和公共卫生。

执业助理医师 指具有《医师执业证》及其“级别”为“执业助理医师”且实际从事临床工作的人员，不包括取得执业证书但从事管理工作的人员。执业助理医师类别分为临床、中医、口腔和公共卫生。

孕产妇死亡率 $$孕产妇死亡率=\frac{该年该地区孕产妇死亡人数\times 100000}{某年某地区活产率\times 100000}$$

5岁以下儿童死亡率 $$5岁以下儿童死亡率=\frac{该年该地区5岁以下儿童死亡人数}{某年某地区活产率}\times 1000‰$$

婴儿死亡率 指某地区一年内出生未满28天（0—27天）的婴儿死亡人数与该地区当年全部活产数的比率。

$$婴儿死亡率=\frac{该年该地区婴儿死亡人数}{某年某地区活产数}\times 10000‰$$

参加新农合人数 指根据本地新农合的实施方案，到本年度新农合筹资截止时，已缴纳参加新农合资金的人口数。

Explanatory Notes on Main Statistical Indicators

Cultural Institutions defined by the cultural industry management department sponsored or cultural institutions and related industries as well as non-organized by the cultural sector and related industries and cultural institutions.

Art Troupe defined by the cultural industry management department sponsored or carried (by the cultural administrative departments for approval and obtain business performance license), specializing in the performing arts and other activities of the various professional performing arts groups, including the professional troupes (Excluding the masses of amateur theatrical performance team).

Number of Spectators at Art Performance refers to the domestic and foreign performing arts attendance. Including ticketing, private use, which are the number of performances and screenings of revenue for government procurement and participation in the number of public performances show and other non-public performances show the number of performances, including the number of mobile stage vehicle, not including rehearsals and internal observation and other the number of non-performing income screenings.

Radio Coverage of Population refers to the percentage of population, which can listen to one of central, provincial, city, prefecture, and county radio programs by wireless, cable, satellite and other technical means, in the surveying area, to national total population, according to Statistical Standard and Method on Television and Radio Coverage of Population established by the State Administration of Broadcasting, Film and Television.

Television Coverage of Population refers to the percentage of population, which can watch one of central, provincial, city, prefecture, and county television programs by wireless, cable, satellite and other technical means, in the surveying area, to national total population, according to Statistical Standard and Method on Television and Radio Coverage of Population established by the State Administration of Broadcasting, Film and Television.

Number of Athletes in Grades refers to the number of athletes who have been given titles through examination. The titles of athletes include international masters of sports, masters of sports, first-grade and second-grade.

Number of Referees in Grades refers to the number of referees who have been given titles after examination. They are classified as international referees, national referees and referees of the first and second grades.

Stadiums refer to stadiums for track and field events with six lane 400-meter tracks around soccer fields, permanent track marks and permanent bleachers. Stadiums are classified according to seating capacity. They include: Class A stadiums seating 25000 people each. Class B stadiums seating 15000 to 25000 people each. Class C stadiums seating 5000 to 15000 people each, and Class D stadiums seating fewer than 5000 people.

Gymnasiums refer to indoor sports grounds with permanent seats in which basketball, volleyball. badminton, table tennis and gymnastics competitions can be held. Gymnasiums are classified according to seating capacity. They include Class A gymnasiums seating over 6000 people. Class B gymnasiums seating 4000 to 6000 people. Class C gymnasiums seating 2000 to 4000 people, and Class D gymnasiums seating fewer than 2000 people.

Hospitals include: polyclinics, traditional Chinese medical hospitals, hospitals integrated with traditional Chinese therapeutics and western therapeutics, ethical hospitals, various specialties hospitals and nursing hospitals, including medical colleges affiliated hospitals, but excluding specialized prevention and treatment hospital and health centers and nursing homes.

Community Health Service Centers (stations) refer to the primary units that provide the health care for community residents, such as disease prevention and control, medical treatment, health care, rehabilitation, health education, family planning technical services, including community health service centers and community health service stations.

Medical Technical Personnel refers to practicing physicians, practicing physician assistant, registered nurses, pharmacists (who), inspection and imaging technician (who), health supervisors and trainee doctors (medicine, nursing, technology) division (disabilities) and other health professionals (not including pharmacy staff , inspectors, care workers, etc.), not including those engaged in the management of health and technical personnel (such as president, vice president, party secretary, etc.). The trainee doctors (who) refers graduated from high school and other institutions but has not yet obtained physician medical specialty physicians and healers practicing certificate.

Licensed Doctors refer to the medical workers who have obtained the licenses of qualified doctors and are employed in medical treatment, disease prevention or healthcare institutions, excluding the licensed doctors engaged in management job. The classification of licensed doctors is clinician, Chinese medicine, dentist and public health.

Licensed Assistant Doctors refer to the medical workers who have obtained the licenses of qualified assistant doctors and are employed in medical treatment, disease prevention or healthcare institutions, excluding the licensed assistant doctors engaged in management job. The classification of licensed assistant doctors is clinician, Chinese medicine, dentist and public health.

Maternal Mortality Rate

$$\text{Maternal Mortality Rate} = \frac{\text{number of maternal deaths} \times 100000}{\text{live births} \times 100000}.$$

Mortality Rate of Children under 5

$$\text{Mortality Rate of Children under 5} = \frac{\text{death number of children under 5}}{\text{live birth}} \times 1000‰.$$

Newborn Mortality Rate refers to the ratio of neonatal deaths of new birth under the age of 28 days (0-27 days) in a year of the region to the total number of live births of this region.

$$\text{Newborn Mortality Rate} = \frac{\text{death number of newborn}}{\text{live birth}} \times 1000‰.$$

Number of Persons Participated in the New Rural Cooperative Medical System refers to the number of persons who have given payment to the new cooperative medical system by the deadline of fundraising during the year according to the implementation plan of the new system.

22 社会服务及其他

Social Services and Others

22-1 律师、公证、调解工作
Lawyers,Notarization and Mediation

指 标	Item	2010	2011	2012	2013	2014
律师工作	**Lawyers**					
法律律师事务所(个)	Number of Law Offices(unit)	244	267	286	328	357
专职律师(人)	Full-time Lawyers(person)	1809	2030	2359	2778	3509
辅助工作人员(人)	Assistant(person)	952	879	468	551	1404
聘请常年法律顾问(个)	Number of Permanent Legal Advisors(person)	7392	8973	4708	4738	4398
全年办理(件)	Number of Cases in Whole Year(case)	81398	84788	78097	138712	129181
刑事案件诉讼代理	Agent of Criminal Cases	6532	5698	5882	8282	7874
民事诉讼代理	Agent of Civil Cases	13437	14156	16969	18860	20630
行政诉讼代理	Agent of Administrative Action	572	431	627	856	507
经济案件诉讼代理	Agent of Economic Cases	5300	5783	6049	8695	9006
非诉讼法律事务	Agent of Non-litigious Legal Affairs	1367	1860	1569	1579	1120
解答法律询问	Agent of Legal Advisory Services	52623	55172	53228	85915	84839
代写法律事务文书	Agent of Legal Document Written on Behalf of Clients	6076	6620	8650	11885	7700
调解成功	Successful Mediation	791	851	3792	2640	1453
公证工作	**Notarization**					
公证处(个)	Number of Notary Offices(unit)	97	97	97	97	97
公证员(人)	Notaries(person)	226	256	230	235	258
公证辅助人员(人)	Assistant Notaries(person)	92	63	77	143	226
办理公证文书(件)	Number of Notarized Documents(case)	79398	75353	77937	96634	96627
#经济合同公证	Notarized Documents on Economic Affairs	17630	15335	20924	27882	29114
#涉外公证	Foreign-related Notarization	10189	10023	11046	15051	15837
国内公证	Domestic Notarization	67451	63482	45967	68752	80790
公证费收入(万元)	Income of Notarization(10000 yuan)	935	1280	1263	2664	3148
人民调解工作	**Number of People's Mediation**					
人民调解委员会(个)	Number of People's Mediation Committees(unit)	22275	22976	22498	22543	20082
人民调解人员(人)	Number of Mediators(person)	109270	115699	115315	115804	104983
调解民间纠纷(件)	Number of Civil Disputes Mediated(case)	134667	198778	184749	187966	180113
调解成功率(%)	The Rate of Success of Mediation(%)	97.1	96.7	95.7	96.9	97.9
基层法律服务工作	**Law Service at Basic Level**					
法律服务所(个)	Offices for Law Service(unit)	484	451	477	436	473
法律工作者(人)	Law Staffs(person)	2138	1431	1774	1913	2137
代理案件(件)	Cases Deputed(case)	9914	12654	12691	13594	14296
避免经济损失(万元)	Number of Avoided Economical Loss(10000 yuan)	12472	24869	21853	24586	86565
刑释解教人员安置帮教工作	**Settling and Assisting and Teaching Work for People That Has Been Released After Serving a Sentence**					
设立工作机构(个)	Institutions Established(unit)	99	99	102	94	98
工作人员(人)	Staffs(person)	279	194	197	189	210
安置人数(人)	Number of Persons Settled Down(person)	16973	24209	14764	25137	31227
帮教人数(人)	Number of Persons Assisted and Teached(person)	15794	27642	33598	31853	37578

注：资料来源于省司法厅(下表同)。

Note:Data in the table are obtained from provinvial department of justice(the same applies to the next table).

22-2 国内公证文书分类

Domestic Notarial Documents by Type

单位：件 (piece)

指　　标	Item	2014
总　　计	**Total**	
经济合同(协议)合计	**Total Economic contracts (agreements)**	**29114**
#买卖合同(购销、房屋买卖)	Contract of sale (purchase and sales, house sale)	2534
企业经营合同(联营合同、企业租赁、资产经营责任制)	Business Contracts (joint venture contract, corporate leasing, asset management responsibility)	164
借款合同(贷款)	Loan Agreement (Loan)	9167
劳务(劳动)合同	Labor (labor) Contract	5
建筑工程合同(建筑工程承包)	Construction Contracts (Construction Contract)	1
承包合同(农林牧副渔承包、工商服务承包、乡镇企业承包)	Contract (agriculture, forestry, animal husbandry and fisherycontracting, business services contracting, township enterprises contracting)	32
租赁合同(财产租赁、房屋租赁)	Lease Contract (property lease, rental)	693
扶养协议(遗赠扶养协议、赡养协议)	Support Agreement(Legacy support agreement, maintenance agreement)	43
出国留学协议(留学协议)	Study abroad agreement(Study protocol)	140
其他(其他民事协议、计划生育)	Other (Other Civil Agreements,Planned Parenthood)	2707
民事法律关系公证合计	**Total civil legal relations Notary**	**755**
#收养关系(收养、解除收养)	Adoptive Relationship (adoption, termination of adoptive)	25
继承(继承权)	Inherit(Inheritance)	12480
财产权(产权、宅基地使用权)	Property rights (property， land use rights)	20
亲属关系	Kinship	806
组织资格(法人(代表)资格)	Organization Qualifications(Legal (Representative) Qualification)	无
单方法律行为	**Unilateral legal acts(By the end of 2012 after the Justice Department modified statistical reports,the notarial matters were classified)**	**32150**
#委托(委托书、法人委托书)	Delegate (power of attorney, power of attorney)	15027
声明(声明书)	Statement	11854
赠与(赠与书)	handsel(Gift book)	2619
遗嘱	testament	1174
现场监督类	**Site supervision class**	**1728**
#招标投标	Bidding	105

22-3 消费者协会受理投诉

Cases Accepted and Heard by Consumer Association

单位：件 (piece)

指　标	Item	2010	2011	2012	2013	2014
总　计	**Total**	**5981**	**4986**	**3931**	**5479**	**3051**
#家用电器类	Household Appliances	1517	1228	876	1248	678
#视听产品	Televison	253	218	58	64	45
电冰箱	Refrigerators	110	77	10	8	3
洗衣机	Washing Machines	93	86	20	1	2
空调器	Air-Conditioner	58	77	24		1
摩托车	Motorcycles	47	53	6	3	2
医疗器械	Assistant Things of Medical Treatment	7	13	3	7	6
服装鞋帽	Garment,Shoes and Caps	712	550	588	730	462
家　具	Furniture	75	58	38	102	40
食　品	Foods	325	368	361	522	275
房屋及装修建材	Houses and Fitment Material	469	364	283	441	282
#房　屋	Houses	151	87	47	80	94
装饰材料	Fitment Material	191	170	141	197	77
电信服务	Telecome	589	641	283	147	100
邮政业服务	Mail	46	35	42	66	38
农用生产资料类	Agricultural Production Materials	168	93	115	126	75
其他类	Others	492	407	265	473	197

注：资料来源于省消费者协会。

Note: Data in the table are obtained from provinvial consumers association.

22-4 检察院主要业务

Cases of Procuratorate

指　标	Item	2010	2011	2012	2013	2014
职务犯罪(件)	**Crime by Taking Advantage of Duty(case)**					
受案	Cases Accepted	1223	1003	1019	951	1437
立案	Cases Registered	983	929	977	922	1037
结案	Cases Settled	978	908	1013	907	972
批准、决定批捕	**Total of Arrests**					
案件数（万件）	Cases (10000 cases)	1.94	1.88	2.16	2.19	2.25
人数（万人）	Persons (10000 persons)	3.07	2.89	3.22	3.11	3.13
决定起诉	**Total of Public Prosecutions**					
案件数（万件）	Cases (10000 cases)	2.28	2.24	2.63	2.75	2.91
人数（万人）	Persons (10000 persons)	3.59	3.42	3.93	4.00	4.15

注：资料来源于省人民检察院。

Note:Data in the table are obtained from the provincial people's procuratorate.

22-5 人民法院刑事一审案件收案

First Trail Criminal Cases Accepted by Courts

单位：件　　(case)

指　标	Item	2010	2011	2012	2013	2014	2014年比2013年增长(%) Increase Rate in 2014over 2013(%)
总　计	**Total**	**23294**	**22570**	**26448**	**27819**	**30094**	**8.2**
危害国家安全罪	Offences Against State Security	2	2	3	5	3	-40.0
危害公共安全罪	Offences Against Public Security	2368	2334	3115	3417	3784	10.7
破坏社会主义市场经济秩序罪	Offences Against Socialist Economic Order	399	360	433	519	650	25.2
侵犯公民人身权利民主权利罪	Offences Against Citizens' Personal and Democratic Rights	5327	4944	5382	5196	5581	7.4
侵犯财产罪	Offences Against Properties	9854	9320	10730	9891	9501	-3.9
妨害社会管理秩序罪	Offences Against Social Management of Order	4250	4688	5622	7939	9557	20.4
危害国防利益罪	Offences Against National Defense			2	1	2	100.0
贪污贿赂罪	Offences on Corruption and Bribery	938	801	1016	738	876	18.7
渎职罪	Offences on Dereliction of Duty	143	116	137	113	139	23.0
其他	Other	13	5	8		1	

注：资料来源于省高级人民法院(以下相关表同)。

Note:Date in the table are obtained from provincial higher people's court(The relative tables in the chapter are the same).

22-6 人民法院刑事一审案件结案

First Trail Criminal Cases Settled by Courts

单位：件 (case)

指 标	Item	2010	2011	2012	2013	2014	2014年比2013年增长(%) Increase Rate in 2014over 2013(%)
总 计	**Total**	**23143**	**22412**	**26260**	**27534**	**28597**	**3.9**
危害国家安全罪	Offences Against State Security	2	1	3	5	3	-40.0
危害公共安全罪	Offences Against Public Security	2362	2326	3096	3405	3673	7.9
破坏社会主义市场经济秩序罪	Offences Against Socialist Economic Order	393	352	418	492	564	14.6
侵犯公民人身权利民主权利罪	Offences Against Citizens' Personal and Democratic Rights	5275	4898	5344	5113	5185	1.4
侵犯财产罪	Offences Against Properties	9839	9295	10694	9844	9179	-6.8
妨害社会管理秩序罪	Offences Against Social Management of Order	4232	4655	5577	7885	9186	16.5
危害国防利益罪	Offences Against National Defense			2	1	2	100.0
贪污贿赂罪	Offences on Corruption and Bribery	894	776	983	684	695	1.6
渎职罪	Offences on Abuse and Dereliction of Duty	133	104	135	105	109	3.8
其他	Other	13	5	8		1	

22-7 人民法院刑事案件中青少年犯罪

Juvenile Delinquency Among Criminal Cases

单位：人 (person)

指 标	Item	2010	2011	2012	2013	2014	2014年比2013年增长(%) Increase Rate in 2014 over 2013 (%)
刑事罪犯总数	**Number of Criminals**	**28735**	**28171**	**30239**	**35272**	**31483**	**-10.74**
#青少年罪犯	Juvenile Criminals	10106	9266	9503	10645	10024	-5.83
#不满18岁	Less Than 18	3516	3014	2993	3282	2940	-10.42
18-25岁	Aged 18-25	6590	6252	6510	7363	7084	-3.79
青少年罪犯占刑事罪犯(%)	Proportion of Juvenile Criminals to Total Criminals(%)	35.2	32.9	31.4	30.2	31.8	1.6(百分点)

22-8 生产安全
Production Safety

指 标	Item	2010	2011	2012	2013	2014
各类事故死亡人数合计(人)	**Number of Deaths for Production Security Accidents(person)**	**1936**	**1655**	**1301**	**1156**	**1040**
工矿商贸企业	Enterprises of Industry,Mining,Commerce and Trade	659	523	296	206	140
煤 矿	Coal Mine	388	256	117	105	59
金属与非金属矿	Metallic and Non-metallic Mine	47	69	34	8	9
建筑业	Construction	105	81	74	62	44
其 他	Others	119	117	71	31	28
火 灾	Fire Accidents	64	54	31	66	59
道路交通	Roadway Traffic Accidents	1136	1020	931	847	795
铁路交通	Railway Traffic Accidents	75	49	38	34	46
其 他	Others	2	9	5	3	
亿元地区生产总值生产安全事故死亡人数(人/亿元)	Number of Deaths of Production Security Accidents Per of GDP (person/100 million yuan)	0.42	0.29	0.19	0.14	0.11
工矿商贸企业从业人员10万人死亡率(人/10万人)	Number of Deaths Per 100000 Persons of Employed Personels of Enterprises of Industry,Mining, Commerceand Trade (person/100000 persons)	6.45	5.08	2.88	1.77	1.32
煤矿百万吨死亡人数(人/百万吨)	Number of Deaths Per Unit of Yields of Coal Mine (person/per million tons)	2.43	1.64	0.65	0.50	0.32
道路交通万车死亡人数(人/万车)	Number of Deaths of Roadway Traffic Accidents Per Unit of Vehicles(person/10000 sets)	4.01	3.32	2.62	2.10	1.76

注：资料来源于省安全监管局，其中火灾死亡人数来源于省公安厅。

Note: Data in the table are obtained from provincial production safety supervision management administration, among them, fire death toll is from the Provincial Public Security Department.

22-9 火灾

Fire Accidents

指 标	Item	2013	2014
实际发生数(起)	**Number of Fire Accidents(case)**	**2915**	**4221**
按火灾原因分	**Grouped by Cause**		
生产作业	Operation	110	150
电 气	Electric	1277	1784
吸 烟	Smoking	64	104
生活用火不慎	Not Careful with Cooking Fire	518	802
玩 火	Playing with Fire	111	182
自 燃	Natural Fire	57	91
不 明	Uncertain	125	77
其 他	Others	653	1031
死亡人数(人)	Number of Deaths(person)	66	59
受伤人数(人)	Number of Injuries(person)	41	27
直接财产损失(万元)	Direct Economic Losses(10000 yuan)	11203	17667
平均每起事故损失(万元)	Average Loss of Fire (10000 yuan)	3.84	4.19

注：资料来源于省公安厅(下表同)。2013年数据有修改。

Note: Data in the table are obtained from provincial department of public security(the same applies to the next table).

22-10 交通事故(2014)

Traffic Accidents

指 标	Item	发生数(起) Number of Traffic Accidents(case)	死亡人数 (人) Number of Deaths (person)	受伤人数(人) Number of Injuries (person)	损失折款(万元) Losses Converted into Cash(10000 yuan)
总 计	**Total**	**1145**	**795**	**1412**	**1282.45**
#重大事故	Extraordinarily Serious Accidents				
较大事故	Serious Accidents	37	145	80	116.82
机动车	Motor Vehicles	1082	749	1386	1256.13
#汽 车	Automobiles	720	515	917	1118.80
摩托车	Motorcycles	337	207	437	118.16
拖拉机	Tractors	10	10	7	1.92
非机动车	Non-motor-driven Vehicles	14	7	13	2.38
#自行车	Bicycles	2	1	3	0.10
行人乘车人	Pedestrians and Passengers	49	39	13	23.94

注：重大事故为一次死亡10—29人，较大事故为一次死亡3—9人。

Note: A major accident refers to 10-29 people died at a time , and a larger accident refers to 3-9 people died at a time.

22-11 社会保险
Social Insurance

指　标	Item	2010	2011	2012	2013	2014
社会保险基金	**Social Security Fund**					
社会保险基金收入(亿元)	Reveneu(100 million yuan)	201.56	256.94	310.85	351.06	386.81
社会保险基金支出(亿元)	Expenses(100 million yuan)	151.41	181.74	229.08	279.25	319.42
社会保险基金累计结余(亿元)	Balance at year-end(100 million yuan)	267.93	343.13	366.79	502.47	569.86
城乡居民基本养老保险	**The New Rural Social Pension Insurance**					
城乡居民基本养老保险参保人数(万人)	The number of insured (10 000 persons)	223.72	849.74	1226.78	1439.34	1586.64
城乡居民基本养老保险基金收入(亿元)	Reveneu(100 million yuan)	6.94	24.84	36.51	43.84	47.78
城乡居民基本养老保险基金支出(亿元)	Expenses(100 million yuan)	3.53	14.35	27.63	28.90	32.00
城镇职工基本养老保险	**Basic Pension Insurance of urban Staff**					
城镇职工基本养老保险参保人数(万人)	Number of Persons Joining Basic Pension Insurance(10 000 persons)	257.31	282.06	309.38	337.29	361.45
#参保职工	Number of Employees	190.29	210.71	231.67	248.91	268.30
城镇职工基本养老保险基金收入(亿元)	Reveneu(100 million yuan)	144.85	179.25	216.94	240.21	259.83
城镇职工基本养老保险基金支出(亿元)	Expenses(100 million yuan)	107.74	127.57	153.07	178.45	207.80
离退休人员社区管理服务率(%)	Rate of Community Management and Services for Retirees(%)	57.0	61.1	70.2	73.2	75.0
基本医疗保险	**Urban Employees Basic Medical Care Insurance**					
基本医疗保险参保人数(万人)	Number of Persons Joining Basic Medical Care Insurance(10 000 persons)	602.48	629.00	648.30	672.09	687.14
城镇职工	Urban Worker	293.52	314.06	329.27	344.72	354.76
#农民工	Migrant Worker	14.01	14.76	13.79	17.83	16.79
#城镇居民	Urban Residents	308.96	314.94	319.03	327.37	332.38
基本医疗保险基金收入(亿元)	Reveneu(100 million yuan)	45.23	61.26	72.93	84.33	96.274
城镇职工	Urban Worker	41.64	54.31	65.75	76.32	88.416
城镇居民	Urban Residents	3.59	6.95	7.18	8.01	7.858
基本医疗保险支出(亿元)	Expenses(100 million yuan)	35.89	46.22	65.41	80.12	94.04
城镇职工	Urban Worker	33.08	42.44	60.50	74.14	86.74
城镇居民	Urban Residents	2.82	3.78	4.91	5.98	7.30
失业保险	**Unemployment Insurance**					
失业保险参保人数(万人)	Number of Persons Joining Unemployment Insurance(10 000 persons)	152.48	160.52	173.46	185.17	191.86
领取失业金人数(万人)	Beneficiaries of Unemployment Insurance Fund(10 000 persons)	1.21	1.08	1.02	1.33	1.54
失业保险基金收入(亿元)	Reveneu(100 million yuan)	7.58	11.64	14.91	17.97	20.29
失业保险基金支出(亿元)	Expenses(100 million yuan)	5.29	2.34	6.49	13.09	9.77
# 失业金（亿元）	Jobless Claims	0.71	0.82	0.78	1.01	1.45
职业培训补贴支出(亿元)	Expenses of Professional Training (100 million yuan)	0.14	0.14	0.38	0.24	0.18
工伤保险	**Work Injury Insurance**					
工伤保险参保人数(万人)	Number of Persons Joining Injury Insurance (10 000 persons)	162.18	193.96	238.19	260.39	275.41
#农民工（亿元）	Migrant Worker	59.65	69.78	81.13	87.46	90.25
工伤保险基金收入(亿元)	Reveneu(100 million yuan)	6.26	9.12	11.02	13.07	14.13
工伤保险支出(亿元)	Expenses(100 million yuan)	4.84	6.55	7.97	11.45	11.99
生育保险	**Maternity Insurance**					
生育保险参保人数(万人)	Number of PersonsJoining in Basic Maternity Insurance(10 000 persons)	164.30	198.09	221.58	238.75	248.82
生育保险基金收入(亿元)	Reveneu(100 million yuan)	1.23	1.47	2.22	3.50	4.14
生育保险支出(亿元)	Expenses(100 million yuan)	0.47	0.61	1.05	2.11	3.12

注：1.资料来源于省人力资源社会保障厅。2.2014年起，城乡居民基本养老保险为新型农村社会养老保险。城镇职工基本养老保险参保人数为基本养老保险参保人数。

Note: 1.Date in the table are obtained from Provincial Department of Human Resources and Social Security. 2.Since 2014, basce pension insurance for urban and rural residents refers to the new rural saial pension insurance. Urban employecs basic pension insurance dhanged to The original number of basic pension insurance .

22-12 社会福利机构
Social Welfare Institutions and Enterprises

单位：个 (unit)

项 目	Item	2010	2011	2012	2013	2014	2014年比2013年增长(%) Increase Rate in 2014over 2013(%)
总 计	**Total**	**1454**	**1722**	**7020**	**14986**	**21077**	**40.6**
提供住宿的社会服务活动机构	Social Welfare Institutions with Acammoclations	974	1185	1240	1286	947	-26.4
社会福利企业	Social Welfare Enterprises	84	81	59	48	41	-14.6
优抚事业单位	Administration Agencies for Martyrs	59	62	63	81	80	-1.2
救助类单位	Collecting and Repatriation Units	61	64	71	72	75	4.2
殡仪服务单位	Funeral and Interment services Institutions	116	119	128	139	148	6.5
彩票发行单位	Lottery Issuing Units	13	15	15	12	13	8. 3
社区服务单位	Community Service Facilities	147	196	5444	13348	19773	48.1

注：1.资料来源于省民政厅。2.提供住宿的社会服务活动机构2010—2013年为收养性福利单位，2014年起调整为提供住宿的社会服务活动机构，包括：为老年人与残疾人提供收留抚养服务的机构、为智障与精神病人提供收留抚养服务的机构、为儿童提供收留抚养和救助服务的机构、其他提供住宿的服务机构。其中，农村养老机构2014年大幅减少，系因民政部调整口径，将原农村养老服务机构中未办理法人登记的农村敬老院全部调整至社区服务设施中的社区养老服务机构中。（以下相关表同）

Note:1.The data in the table are provided by the provincial department of civol affairs. 2.In 2010-2013,institutions where provide social services accommodation were regarded as adapting welfare unit, while those institution were adjusted to provide social service activities,including institution where provide where provid accomoodations for elderly , disabilities,mental patients or children with services, and institutions provide other services.Among them,rural pension agency dropped significantly in 2014. it might because the Ministry of Civil Affairs was adjus cabliers, which tansfer unregistered rural nursing home to communities pension institutions.(The relative tables in the chapter are the same)

22-13 社会福利机构工作人员
Staff Employed by Social welfare Institutions and Enterprises

单位：人 (person)

项 目	Item	2010	2011	2012	2013	2014	2014年比2013年增长(%) Increase Rate in 2014over 2013(%)
总 计	**Total**	**13433**	**14679**	**35677**	**75184**	**102058**	**35.7**
提供住宿的社会服务活动机构	Social Welfare Institutions with Accommodations	3522	4274	4658	5488	5955	8.5
社会福利企业	Social Welfare Enterprises	5512	5216	3343	2424	2145	-1.2
优抚安置事业单位	Administration Agencies for Martyrs	293	466	314	351	338	-3.7
救助类单位	Collecting and Repatriation Units	339	347	371	429	431	0.5
殡仪服务单位	Funeral and Interment services Institutions	2669	2925	2985	3192	3483	9.1
彩票发行单位	Lottery Issuing Units	147	160	181	188	236	25.5
社区服务单位	Community Service Facilities	951	1291	23825	63112	89470	41.8

22−14 社会服务及设施和民政事业发展主要指标

Main Indicators of Social Services & Facilities and Civil Administration Career Development

指　标	Item	2010	2011	2012	2013	2014	2014年比2013年增长(%) Increase Rate in 2014 over 2013(%)
城市社区服务设施数(个)	**Number of Urban Community Service Facilities(unit)**	**5920**	**6593**	**11587**	**4721**	**3110**	**-34.1**
#城市社区服务单位数	Number of Community Service Institutions	147	196	5444	2268	2586	14.0
城镇便民利民服务网点(个)	Number of Urban Service Points for Civilian(unit)	25715	26587	27699	14577	15515	6.4
乡镇敬老院覆盖率(%)	Coverage Rate of Villages and Town Elderly Welfare Homes(%)	56.5	68.3	72.3	78.4	81.4	3.8
收养性福利单位床位数(张)	Number of Beds of Welfare Home (unit)	28358	44025	52996	67129	86111	28.3
收养性福利单位床位利用率(%)	Using Rate of Bed(%)	60.2	61.8	53.4	53.0	49.8	-6.0
享受城市低保人数(万人)	Number of Persons Receiving Lowest Cost of living in Urban Area (10000 persons)	53.98	54.34	53.00	51.00	47.00	-7.8
城市低保生活保障支出(万元)	Expenditure of Lowest Cost of living in Urban Area(10000 yuan)	101685	143028	155819	174125	167700	-3.7

注：1.城市社区服务设施数，2010−2012年为城镇社区服务机构数。2.民政部对2014年报中其他社区服务设施统计口径进行调整，不再统计除残疾人康复站外的非民政部门指导管理的其他社区服务设施，故城市社区服务设施数较上年下降。

Note: 1.The number of city community service facilities from 2010 to 2012 is the urban community service organizations. 2.Ministry of Civil Affairs has adjust the cabliers of other community service facilities, and will never counts other communities service facilities except facilities managed by disabled rehabilitation station, so the number of city community service facilities decrease compare with last year.

22−15 社会福利救济主要支出

Major Expenditures of Welfare Relief Funds

单位：万元　　　　(10000 yuan)

指　标	Item	2010	2011	2012	2013	2014	2014年比2013年增长(%) Increase Rate in 2014 over 2013(%)
总　计	**Total**	**522166**	**830472**	**891463**	**972636**	**970604**	**-0.2**
优抚对象补助金额	Funds for Family Members of Martyrs and Disabled Veterans	81660	95162	110456	130472	123959	-5.0
#国家支出	Government Funds	81660	95162	110456	130472	123959	-5.0
传统救济对象的国家救济金额	Funds for Family Members of Traditional Relief	14628	29995	33180	35930	45596	26.9
最低生活保障支出	Expenditure for Persons Receiving Lowest Cost-of-living	419143	692908	731412	786453	777983	-1.0
城　市	For Urban Areas	101685	143028	155819	174125	167700	-3.7
农　村	For Rural Areas	317458	549880	575593	612328	610283	-0.3
收养性社会福利单位支出	Funds for Adopting Social Welfare Institution	6735	12407	16415	19781	23065	16.6
#国家支出	Government Funds	6735	12407	16415	19781	23065	16.6

注：1.优抚对象包括：死亡抚恤，伤残抚恤，在乡复员、退伍军人生活补助，义务兵优待金，其他优抚支出。 2.传统救济对象包括：五保供养，城市“三无”救助，流浪乞讨人员救助，临时救助，传统救济。

Note:1.Entitled groups including:death pension, disability pension, in the township demobilized, veterans living allowance, compulsory special allowances, special care and other expenses. 2.Traditional Relieves groups including:five guarantees, the city "three noes" rescue, vagrants and beggars,temporary relief, traditional Relief.

22-16 享受补助、救济人员

Persons Receiving Subsidies and Relief Funds

单位：万人 (10000 persons)

指　　标	Item	2010	2011	2012	2013	2014	2014年比2013年增长(%) Increase Rate in 2014 over 2013(%)
城乡居民最低生活保障人数	**Number of Urban and Rural Residents Receiving Minimum Living Allowance**	**588.72**	**585.23**	**566**	**528**	**463**	**-12.3**
城　市	Urban Area	53.98	54.34	53	51	47	-7.8
农　村	Rural Area	534.74	530.89	513	477	416	-12.8
传统救济人数	Number of Persons Receiving Traditional Relief Funds	1.70	1.71	1.74	1.83	2.15	17.5
提供住宿的社会服务活动机构“三无”对象人数	Number of Persons Adopted by Adopting Social Welfare Institutions	1.35	2.25	2.34	3.05	2.90	-4.9

注：提供住宿的社会服务活动机构“三无”对象人数里包含社区养老机构中农村养老人数。

Note:"three noes"objects of social service institutions provide accommodations including the number of rural old-age pension in community organizations.

22-17 享受国家定期抚恤、补助、救济人员数

Persons Receiving Regular Subsidy and Commiseration of Country

单位：人 (person)

指　　标	Item	2010	2011	2012	2013	2014	2014年比2013年增长(%) Increase Rate in 2014over 2013(%)
合　　计	**Total**	**191988**	**223071**	**263107**	**261395**	**232737**	**-11.0**
伤残抚恤人数	Number of Persons Receiving Disability Commiseration	15844	15809	16057	15999	14801	-7.5
“三属”抚恤人数	Number of Persons Comfort and Compensated Bereaved Family	5121	4931	4810	4759	3652	-23.3
烈士家属	Family Numbers of Martyr	3019	2911	2781	2734	1967	-28.1
牺牲、病故军人家属	Family Numbers of Immolate & Die of Illness Armyman	2102	2020	2029	2025	1685	-16.8
定期补助人数	Number of Persons Receiving Regular Subsidies	171023	202331	242240	240637	214284	-11.0
#复退军人定补人数	Number of Ex-servicemen	83506	80397	76315	69774	45738	-34.4
参战、参试定补人数	Number of Persons Receiving Regular Subsidies for War and Test	87034	88530	90147	90285	86861	-3.8

注：参战、参试定补人数指参加对越自卫反击战及核试验等人员。

Note:Persons receiving regular subsidies for sar and sest refer to these persons taking part in acting in self-defence war and nuclear test.

22-18 残疾人事业基本情况
Basic Information of Person with Disablility

单位：人 (person)

指　　标	Item	2013	2014
康复	**Rehabilitation**		
视力残疾康复	Rehabilitation of Persons with Visual Disability		
贫困白内障患者免费手术(例)	Free Surgeries for Poor Cataract Patients(case)	9220	9292
低视力者配用助视器	Persons with Low-vision Fitted with Vision-aids	3807	2745
盲人定向行走训练	Blind Persons Receiving Orientation Skill Training	2275	2300
聋儿康复	**Rehabilitation of Children with Hearing Disability**		
年收训聋儿	Deaf Children Newly Trained in the year	381	383
培训家长	Parents Trained	759	690
精神病防治康复	**Prevention and Rehabilitation of Mental Illness (PRMI)**		
开展精神病防治康复工作市县数(个)	Counties Carried on the Works of Prevention and Treatment of Psychiatric Diseases(unit)	86	86
接受治疗的精神病患者	Treatment Provided for Patients with Sever Psychiatric Diseases	13675	14262
孤独症儿童训练	Children with Autism Trained	309	308
肢体残疾康复	**Rehabilitation of Persons with Physical Disability**		
肢体残疾人社区康复训练	Rehabilitation Training Institution for Persons with Mobility Impairment	1415	1419
脑瘫儿童机构康复训练	Rehabilitation Training Institutions for Children with Cerebral Palsy	398	374
贫困肢体残疾儿童矫治手术	Rehabilitation of Children with Physical Disability in Poverty	218	252
智力残疾康复	**Rehabilitation of Persons with Intellectual Disability**		
智残儿童社区康复训练	Children with Intellectual Disability Receiving Rehabilitation Training at Community	369	369
智残儿童机构康复训练	Children with Intellectual Disability Receiving Rehabilitation Training at Institutions	370	562
辅助器具供应服务数(件)	**Assistive Devices Provided(piece)**	**18476**	**18464**
贫困残疾人假肢装配例数(例)	**Artificial limb Assembled (case)**	**734**	**528**
大　腿	for Ham	284	206
小　腿	for Shank	359	260
特殊假肢	Special Artificial limb	91	62
社区康复协调员培训	**Workers Trained for Disabled porsn at Community**	**1926**	**1488**

22-18 续表 Continued

单位：人 (person)

指　标	Item	2013	2014
教育	**Education**		
未入学适龄残疾儿童少年	School-age Disabled Children Unable to Enter School	4427	4635
职业教育与培训	Vocational Education and Training		
机构数(个)	Facilities (unit)	40	40
教育与培训人数(人次)	Number or Educated and Trained (person-time)	4423	5142
就业	**Employment**		
城镇残疾人就业状况	Employment of Urban Handicapped		
当年安排就业	Persons Employed in the Year	5928	6774
#按比列就业	Employed by Quote Scheme	1379	1572
公益性岗位安置	Employed at Public Institution	176	143
集中就业	Employed in Collective Form	1149	1384
个体及其他形式就业	Self-employed or Employed in Other Forms	3224	3675
农村残疾人就业状况	Employment of Rural Handicapped		
就　业	Employed	791526	747962
残疾人就业服务机构(个)	Employment Service Institutions for Handicapped (unit)		
省	Provinces	1	1
市、州	Prefectures	9	9
县、市、区	County、Cities	63	63
盲人按摩	**Massage by Persons with Visual Disability**		
保健按摩人员培训	Massage Therapists Training	467	496
医疗按摩人员培训	Keep-fit Massage Training	27	48
扶贫	**Poverty Alleviation**		
本年度脱贫人数	Disabled Persons Overcoming Poverty	68873	59499
农村贫困残疾	Rural Disabled persons in Poverty	867102	852285
当地低收入残疾	Disabled Persons at the Local Low-income Level	587793	486040
残联组织建设	**Organization of the Disabled Persons' Federation**		
残疾人工作者	Workers Working for the Disabled	3294	3237

注：资料来源于省残联。
Note :Data in the table are provided by Disabled Federation of Gui zhou Province.

22－19 婚姻

Marriages and Divorces

指 标	Item	2010	2011	2012	2013	2014
准予登记结婚(对)	**Registered Marriages(couple)**	**375051**	**373423**	**417840**	**429812**	**437203**
#初婚(人)	First Marriages(person)	692590	679348	780707	835350	852237
再婚(人)	Remarriages(person)	57512	67498	54973	24274	22169
#女性	Female	27696	34236	29838	12462	11267
涉外婚姻(对)	**Registered Marriages with Foreigner and the Citizen of Hong Kong,Macao,Taiwan(couple)**	**369**	**500**	**440**	**438**	**409**
#国内公民(人)	Domestic Citizen(person)	369	500	439	438	409
#女性	Female	330	457	367	359	333
离婚人数(人)	**Divorces(person)**	**127938**	**144420**	**162460**	**171478**	**191428**
#民政部门批准	Permitted by Civil Administration Department	89384	104032	118810	124674	141696

注：资料来源于省民政厅。
Note: Data in the table are provided by provincial Civil Affairs Department

22－20 殡葬服务情况

Funeral and Interment Services

指 标	Item	2010	2011	2012	2013	2014
殡葬类单位数（个）	Number of Funeral and Interment Enterprises	116	119	128	139	148
从业人员（人）	Employed Persons(Porson)	2669	2925	2985	3192	3483
火化炉数（台）	Number of Cremators(unit)	129	86	101	117	124
火化数（万具）	Cremated Remains(10000 units)	5.49	6.11	6.44	6.82	7.21
#安葬数（万具）	Number of the Buried(10000 units)	1.59	1.79	1.28	1.67	1.85
火化率（%）	Cremation Rate(%)	22.54	25.16	26.41	27.82	29.94

注：安葬数为当年安葬数。
Note: Number of the buried refers to the number in current year.

主要统计指标解释

公证员 指按照《公证法》规定，在公证机构从事公证业务的执业公证员、公证助理员、行政人员、其他人员。

办理公证文书 指公证处在一定时期内办结的公证文书件数。公证文书按司法部规定或批准的格式制作，包括国内公证和涉外公证两部分。国内公证分为经济合同公证和民事法律关系公证两大类。

人民调解人员 指人民调解委员会委员和人民调解委员会聘任的，负责对《人民调解法》规定人民调解委员会可以受理的民间纠纷进行调解的人员。

调解民间纠纷 是指人民调解委员会通过说服、疏导等方法，促成当事人在平等协商基础上自愿达成调解协议，解决民间纠纷的活动。

批准、决定逮捕 指人民检察院对公安机关、国家安全机关、监狱管理机关提出逮捕的犯罪嫌疑人进行审查，根据事实，依法做出逮捕决定。该指标主要反映人民检察院对提请逮捕犯罪嫌疑人进行审查后依法做出批准逮捕决定的情况。

青少年罪犯 指人民法院在报告期内判决发生法律效力的有罪判决中14周岁以上不满25周岁的罪犯。其中14周岁以上不满18周岁的罪犯为未成年罪犯。

城市居民最低生活保障人数 指在报告期末家庭平均收入在当地规定的最低生活保障线以下的家庭人员及国家规定有民政部门救济的特殊人员和60年代精减退职老职工救济人员等。

农村居民最低生活保障人数 指报告期末在建立农村最低生活保障制度的地区，得到当地政府或集体给予最低生活保障的农业人口家庭人数。

城市社区服务设施数 是指社区服务站、社区服务中心、其他社区服务设施的总和。是面向老年人及家庭的商品递送、医疗保健、家庭保洁、日间照料、陪伴服务等为社区居家老服务的设施和突出综合服务功能，将党员活动室、就业保障网络、社区卫生服务站、文化活动室、图书馆、“爱心超市”社区捐款接收站点、警务站（室）、老年活动室、未成年人文化活动场所等具有综合服务功能的设施。原则上，每个社区服务站设施的最低标准时能满足社区居委会办公所需，并配置多功能社区活动场所，建筑面积不低于200平方米。在此基础上可根据社区居民的实际需求，重点强化若干类服务功能。

基本养老保险参保人数 指报告期末按照国家法律、法规和有关政策规定参加基本养老保险并在社保经办机构已建立缴费记录档案的人数，包括中断缴费但未终止养老保险关系的职工人数，报告期末参加基本养老保险的离休、退休和退职人员，不包括只登记未建立缴费记录档案的人数。

基本医疗保险参保人数 指报告期末按国家有关规定参加基本医疗保险的人数。包括参加保险的职工人数和退休人员人数。

失业保险参保人数 指报告期末按照国家法律、法规和有关政策规定参加了失业保险的城镇企业事业单位的职工及地方政府规定参加失业保险的其他人员的人数。

工伤保险参保人数 指报告期末依据国家有关规定参加工伤保险的职工人数和有雇工的个体工商户的雇工数。

生育保险参保人数 指报告期末依据有关规定参加生育保险的职工人数。

Explanatory Notes on Main Statistical Indicators

Notary Personnel refers to judicial workers of the state notary offices handling notarization work according to law. They include notaries, assistant notaries, and other people working for notary offices.

Notarized Documents refer to the documents settled by notary offices in a year. The notary documents are drawn up in accordance with the regulations of the Ministry of Justice, including domestic documents and foreign-related documents. Domestic documents are divided into two major categories, documents on economic contracts and documents on civil legal relations.

Mediators refer to workers on peoples mediation committees responsible for mediating in civil disputes and cases of slight infraction of the law. They include members of the mediation committees and mediators of mediation groups.

Mediation of civil disputes refers to the people's mediation committee through persuasion, persuasion and other methods, to facilitate the parties to reach a voluntary agreement on the basis of equality, the settlement of civil disputes.

Approval for Arrest refers to the decision made by people's procuratorate office, in accordance with the law and relevant facts, to approve the arrest of the suspect(s) as proposed by the public security departments, state security departments or prisons authority. This indicator reflects approved arrests made by people's procuratorate offices that are proposed by related departments.

Juvenile Criminals refers to the offenders within the age range of 14 to 25 convicted guilty by the court during the reporting period while those between 14 and 18 are defined as minor offenders.

Number of Urban Residents Entitled to Minimum Living Allowances refers to the number of those whose average family income is below a minimum local standard by the end of the reporting period and special staff who were relieved by states provide State regulations and the District Department and 1960s streamline relief workers older workers retire, etc.

Number of Rural Residents Entitled to Minimum Living Allowances refers to the number of those receiving the minimum living allowances from the local government or community in the rural areas where this allowances system is in place as of the end of the reporting period.

Number of Service Facilities in Urban Communities refers to community service centers, community service centers, other community service facilities combined. Is for the elderly and home delivery of goods, health care, household cleaning, day care, companionship services, home care services for community facilities and outstanding comprehensive service functions, will party room, employment security networks, community health service stations, cultural activities room, library, "love supermarket" community donations receiving stations, police stations (room), old activity room, minors and other cultural activities with comprehensive service functions of the facility. In principle, each community service station facilities to meet the minimum standards required for community neighborhood committee office, and configure the multi-purpose community activities, building area of not less than 200 square meters. On this basis, according to the actual needs of community residents, focusing on enhancing certain types of services.

Number of Basic Pension Insurance refer to the people participating in the basic pension insurance programme according to national laws, regulations and related policies at the end of the reference period, who have already had payment records in social security management agencies, including those who have interrupt payment without terminating the insurance programme. Those who have registered in the programme but with no payment records are not included.

Number of Medical Insurance refers to the number of people participating in the basic medical care insurance programme according to related regulations as at the end of reference period, including number of staff and workers and retirees participating in this insurance programme.

Number of Unemployment Insurance refers to the number of staff and workers in urban enterprises or institutions who have participated in the unemployment insurance programme according to relevant policies and regulations, and other people who have participated according to local government regulations, as at the end of reference period.

Number of Work Injury Insurance refers to the number of staff and workers who have participated in the work injury insurance programme according to relevant national regulations and hirelings who were hired by individual industrial and commercial households.

Number of Maternity Insurance refers to the number of staff and workers who have participated in the maternity insurance programme according to relevant regulation at the end of the reporting period.

民营经济

23

Private Economy

23-1 民营经济基本情况(2014)
Basic Conditions of Private Economy

指 标	Item	单位数 Number of Enterprises			资 产 Assets			从业人员 Emplyed Persons		
		单位数(个) Number of Enterprises (units)	增长(%) Increase Rate (%)	占全省企业单位数的比重(%) The proportion of the provincial total (%)	资产(金)数额(亿元) Amount of Assets (100 million)	增长(%) Increase Rate (%)	占全省企业单位资产(金)比重(%) The proportion of the provincial total (%)	人数(万人) Persons (10000 persons)	增长(%) Increase Rate (%)	占全省企业单位从业人员比重(%) The proportion of the provincial total (%)
一、民营企业	**Private Enterprise**	**134490**	**75.5**	**95.5**	**23871.78**	**105.9**	**35.6**	**245.50**	**41.7**	**68.4**
按登记注册类型分	By Status of Registration									
私营企业	Private Enterprises	81223	69.6	57.6	6908.32	86.1	10.3	123.66	33.1	34.4
集体企业	Collective-owned Enterprises	1889	-14.7	1.3	997.89	83.8	1.5	6.74	-13.9	1.9
股份合作企业	Cooperative Enterprises	1049	21.0	0.7	3100.80	588.7	4.6	3.43	25.8	1.0
集体联营企业	Collective Joint Ownership Enterprises	235	190.1	0.2	13.30	382.3	0.0	0.37	80.9	0.1
其他联营企业	Other Joint Ownership Enterprises	151	77.6	0.1	8.67	114.9	0.0	0.27	-6.4	0.1
其他有限责任公司	Other Limited Liability Corporations	33866	71.4	24.0	9853.08	127.7	14.7	79.93	42.3	22.3
股份有限公司	Share-holding Corporations Limited	1995	22.4	1.4	2250.28	-8.5	3.4	8.83	24.0	2.5
其他内资企业	Other domestic Funded enterprises	14082	244.3	10.0	739.44	696.8	1.1	22.27	273.3	6.2
按行业分	**By Industry**									
第一产业	Primary Industry	25187	164.6	17.9	423.86	313.0	0.6	27.66	227.2	7.7
第二产业	Secondary Industry	37053	52.4	26.3	7218.21	38.3	10.8	118.48	16.8	33.0
第三产业	Tertiary Industry	72250	68.9	51.3	16229.71	158.8	24.2	99.35	57.0	27.7
工 业	Industry	32721	51.9	23.2	6280.88	27.3	9.4	99.38	13.5	27.7
建筑业	Construction	4332	56.4	3.1	937.34	228.9	1.4	19.10	37.4	5.3
交通运输、仓储和邮政业	Transportat, Storage and Post	2653	73.2	1.9	192.74	250.6	0.3	6.67	45.0	1.9
批发和零售业	Wholesale and Retail Trades	33399	66.5	23.7	2644.11	142.7	3.9	31.90	50.8	8.9
住宿和餐饮业	Hotels and Catering services	4507	102.4	3.2	235.39	59.1	0.4	9.17	22.4	2.6
金融业	Finance Intemediation	1376	61.5	1.0	5551.66	335.0	8.3	4.06	56.8	1.1
房地产业	Real Estate	6469	24.4	4.6	5254.45	59.9	7.8	13.65	34.9	3.8
其他服务业	Other service industries	23846	84.7	16.9	2351.35	464.2	3.5	33.91	95.5	9.4
二、个体经营户	**privately owned business**	**1280048**	**20.7**	**100.0**	**657.60**	**38.5**	**100.0**	**220.81**	**19.3**	**100.0**

注:1."个体经营户"资料来源于省工商局。 2.表中计算增长速度的基期数据为第三次经济普查数据。

Note:Data of "privately owned business "is from Provincial Industrial and Commercial Bureau. 2 Base data that used to calculate the rate of growth is from the third time economic census.

23−2 民营经济增加值

Value-added of Private Economy

单位：亿元 (100 million yuan)

指　标	Item	2010	2011	2012	2013	2014
民营经济增加值	**Value—added of Private Economy**	**1610.76**	**2103.98**	**2759.40**	**3493.52**	**4275.38**
第一产业	Primary Industry	165.63	197.77	378.24	508.27	655.34
第二产业	Secondary Industry	674.31	856.50	1128.85	1500.89	2010.34
工　业	Industry	579.44	728.81	1042.88	1376.85	1858.84
建筑业	Construction	94.87	127.69	85.97	124.04	151.50
第三产业	Tertiary Industry	770.82	1049.71	1252.31	1484.36	1609.70
#交通运输、仓储和邮政业	Transport,Storage and Post	234.88	320.63	388.18	437.20	469.37
批发和零售业	Wholesale and Retail Trades	178.61	234.14	248.36	257.85	278.44
住宿和餐饮业	Hotels and Catering Services	148.74	193.28	240.62	273.34	299.06
房地产业	Real Estate	124.70	146.60	56.13	82.19	91.06

注：2012年起民营经济增加值核算口径调整(以下相关表同)。
Note: The accounting caliber of the added value of private economy was adjusted in 2012(the related tables in the chapter are the same) .

23−3 民营经济分产业增加值占该产业增加值比重

Value-added of Private Economy Unit as Percentage to GDP

单位：% (%)

指　标	Item	2010	2011	2012	2013	2014
民营经济增加值占比	**Gross Domestic Product**	**35.0**	**36.9**	**40.3**	**43.2**	**46.1**
第一产业	Primary Industry	26.5	27.2	42.4	50.9	51.2
第二产业	Secondary Industry	37.5	39.0	42.1	45.8	52.1
工　业	Industry	38.2	39.8	47.0	51.3	59.2
建筑业	Construction	33.5	35.0	18.7	21.0	21.1
第三产业	Tertiary Industry	35.4	37.7	38.2	38.9	39.0
#交通运输、仓储和邮政业	Transport,Storage and Post	48.9	54.3	56.5	56.6	56.6
批发和零售业	Wholesale and Retail Trades	48.6	52.2	48.3	44.3	44.6
住宿和餐饮业	Hotels and Catering Services	82.3	86.1	90.3	92.7	92.7
房地产业	Real Estate	89.3	91.5	31.8	40.5	41.3

23-4 民营经济固定资产投资(2014)

Private Economic Investment in Fixed Assets

单位：亿元 (100 million yuan)

指 标	Item	2014	比上年增长(%) Increase Rate (%)
民营经济固定资产投资	**Private Fixed Asset Investment**	**4145.83**	**19.9**
按登记注册类型分	By Status of Registration		
私 营	Private Enterprises	1840.45	32.9
集 体	Collective Ownership Enterprises	21.97	-2.8
股份合作	Cooperative Company	23.35	12.5
集体联营	Collective Joint Ownership Enterprises	1.25	-73.5
其他联营	Other Joint Ownership Enterprises	3.20	121.1
其他有限责任公司	Other Limited Liability Corporations	1851.43	15.3
股份有限公司	Share-holding corporations Limited	198.26	7.9
其他内资	Other domestic Funded enterprises	172.51	-6.4
个体经营	Self-employed	33.41	-33.8
按行业分	By Industry		
第一产业	Primary Industry	152.79	35.1
第二产业	Secondary Industry	1495.80	19.9
工 业	Industry	1493.64	20.2
建筑业	Construction	2.15	-57.8
第三产业	Tertiary Industry	2497.25	19.0
交通运输、仓储和邮政业	Transport,Storage and Post	39.87	-1.4
批发和零售业	Wholesale & Retail Trades	84.75	63.7
住宿和餐饮业	Hotels & Catering Trade	62.00	18.1
金融业	Finance Intermediation	4.26	45.7
房地产业	Real Estate	2004.23	15.2
其他服务业	Other service industries	302.14	43.4

注：本表统计口径为计划总投资500万元及以上固定资产项目投资和房地产开发项目投资。

Note: This table's statistical caliber is the fixed assets investment projects in plan of total investment at 5 million yuan and above and real estate investment projects.

23-5 规模以上民营经济工业企业主要经济指标(2014)

Main Economic Indicators of Industrial Enterprises above Designated Size of Private Economy

单位：亿元 (100 million yuan)

指　标	Item	企业数(个) Number of Enterprises (unit)	工业总产值(当年价) Gross Industial OutputValue (current price)	固定资产原价 Original Value of Fixed Assets	主营业务收入 Revenue from Principal Business	利润总额 Total Profits
总　计	**Total**	**3302**	**5263.03**	**1363.80**	**4568.16**	**285.91**
#亏损企业	Loss Making Enterprises	581	831.23	290.47	599.34	-47.53
按轻重工业分	**Grouped by Type of Light and Heavy Industry**					
轻工业	Light Industry	973	1304.01	259.28	1127.41	108.81
重工业	Heavy Industry	2329	3959.02	1104.52	3440.74	177.10
按企业规模分	**Grouped by Size of Enterprise**					
大型企业	Large Enterprises	21	365.34	121.98	337.52	27.81
中型企业	Medium-sized Enterprises	376	1288.74	504.28	1073.98	78.80
小型企业	Small Enterprises	2905	3608.95	737.54	3156.65	179.30
按登记注册类型分	**Grouped by Registration Categories**					
#集体企业	Collective-owned Enterprises	18	19.81	2.19	18.03	0.32
股份合作企业	Share-holding Cooperative Enterprises	11	16.50	3.15	11.58	1.46
联营企业	Joint Owned Enterprises	5	4.87	1.35	4.79	0.77
有限责任公司	Limited Liability Corporations	1289	2429.56	656.60	2095.85	128.13
股份有限公司	Share-holding Corporations Limited	87	244.38	84.13	220.91	15.22
私营企业	Private Enterprises	1851	2511.40	608.32	2188.22	138.73
其他企业	Others Enterprises	41	36.51	8.06	28.78	1.28

注：本表统计口径为年主营业务收入2000万元及以上工业企业。

Note: Above scale industrial private economic statistics refer to the revenue from principal business of 20 million yuan and above of industrial enterprises.

23-5 续表

单位：亿元

指　　标	Item	企业数（个）Number of Enterprises (unit)
按工业行业分	**Grouped by Industrial Sector**	**3302**
煤炭开采和洗选业	Mining and Washing of Coal	717
黑色金属矿采选业	Mining and Processing of Ferrous Metal Ores	31
有色金属矿采选业	Mining and Processing of Non-Ferrous Metal Ores	26
非金属矿采选业	Mining and Dressing of Non-metal Ores	110
开采辅助活动	Support Activities for Mining	
其他采矿业	Mining of other ores	
农副食品加工业	Processing of Food from Agricultural Products	213
食品制造业	Manufacture of Foods	86
酒、饮料和精制茶制造业	Manufacture of Liquor, Beverages and Refined Tea	275
纺织业	Manufacture of Textile	15
纺织服装、服饰业	Manufacture of Textile, Wearing Apparel and Accessories	29
皮革、毛皮、羽毛及其制品和制鞋业	Manufacture of Leather,Furs,Feather and Related Products, and Footware	21
木材加工和木、竹、藤、棕、草制品业	Processing of Timber, Manufacture of Wood,Bamboo, Rattan, Palm and Straw Products	99
家具制造业	Manufacture of Furniture	23
造纸和纸制品业	Manufacture of Paper and Paper Products	42
印刷和记录媒介复制业	Printing and Reproduction of Recording Media	15
文教、工美、体育和娱乐用品制造业	Manufacture of Articles For Culture, Education, Arts and Crafts and Sport and Entertainment Activities	15
石油加工、炼焦和核燃料加工业	Processing of Petroleum, Coking and Processing of Nuclear Fuel	20
化学原料和化学制品制造业	Manufacture of Raw Chemical Materials and Chemical Products	163
医药制造业	Manufacture of Medicines	100
橡胶和塑料制品业	Manufacture of Rubber and Plastics Products	90
非金属矿物制品业	Manufacture of Non-metallic Mineral Products	564
黑色金属冶炼和压延加工业	Smelting and Pressing of Ferrous Metals	158
有色金属冶炼和压延加工业	Smelting and Pressing of Non-ferrous metal	69
金属制品业	Manufacture of Metal Products	95
通用设备制造业	Manufacture of General Purpose Machinery	44
专用设备制造业	Manufacture of Special Purpose Machinery	50
汽车制造业	Manufacture of Automobiles	29
铁路、船舶、航空航天和其他运输设备制造业	Manufacture of Railway, ship, Aerospace and other Transport Equipments	17
电气机械和器材制造业	Manufacture of Electrical Machinery and Apparatus	88
计算机、通信和其他电子设备制造业	Manufacture of Communication, Computers and Other Electronic Equipment	28
仪器仪表制造业	Manufacture of Measuning Instruments and Machinery	6
其他制造业	Other Manufacture	11
废弃资源综合利用业	Utilization of waste Resources	8
电力、热力生产和供应业	Production and supply of Electric Power and Heat Power	28
燃气生产和供应业	Production and supply of Gas	14
水的生产和供应业	Production and supply of Water	2

注：工业行业按国民经济行业分类(GB/T4754—2011)进行分类。

Continued

(100 million yuan)

工业总产值 (当年价) Gross Industial OutputValue (current price)	固定资产原价 Original Value of Fixed Assets	主营业务收入 Revenue from Principal Business	利润总额 Total Profits
5263.03	**1363.80**	**4568.16**	**285.91**
1243.38	369.47	1007.07	67.58
39.41	4.15	37.94	2.24
48.61	5.50	38.98	2.61
143.79	24.60	135.14	11.96
248.21	38.49	220.73	11.49
119.00	19.61	112.68	16.42
296.69	81.50	233.96	28.90
12.44	2.58	8.33	0.75
22.52	3.36	22.12	1.01
26.33	3.14	24.85	0.81
134.42	12.04	126.73	5.46
18.28	3.03	18.14	1.74
55.10	9.66	54.27	2.88
17.04	8.37	14.55	1.55
12.17	2.44	12.34	0.88
51.28	13.86	43.62	3.16
353.64	87.97	331.20	22.15
323.70	59.24	275.05	31.19
97.47	14.21	86.71	3.80
673.05	218.76	610.76	29.52
398.97	55.32	368.22	6.73
289.82	112.63	220.55	7.46
108.27	15.44	92.55	3.97
58.30	7.79	49.01	2.79
75.51	14.15	67.34	3.77
109.85	31.61	109.14	3.70
20.99	8.53	17.76	0.64
141.04	16.47	117.57	4.80
35.44	5.86	31.60	1.40
5.34	0.77	5.29	0.35
19.96	4.55	13.21	0.29
10.39	0.86	8.68	0.04
32.02	101.97	31.43	3.43
19.37	5.86	19.38	0.37
0.86		0.86	0.08

Note:Data in this table is classified by sector of the National Economy (GB/T4754-2011).

23-6 限额以上民营经济批发零售企业主要经济指标(2014)

Main Economic Indicators of Wholesale and Retail Trade Enterprises above Designated Size of Private Economy

单位：万元 (10000 yuan)

指 标	Item	企业个数(个) Number of Enterprises (unit)	固定资产原价 Original Value of Fixed Assets	主营业务收入 Prime Operating Revenue	主营业务税金及附加 Tax and associate charge	利润总额 Total Profits
批发业	**Wholesale Trade**	**624**	**293165**	**6931992**	**24815**	**40419**
按登记注册类型分组	**By status of Registration**					
内资企业	State-owned Enterprises	624	293165	6931992	24815	40419
#集体企业	Collective-owned Enterprises	22	17325	131159	584	1128
股份合作企业	Cooperative Enterprises	1	246	1969	10	7
有限责任公司	Limited Liability Corporations	254	153206	3831058	13422	10956
其他有限责任公司	Other Limited Liability Corporations	254	153206	3831058	13422	10956
股份有限公司	Share-holding Companies Ltd.	18	49192	246180	3110	11407
私营企业	Private Enterprises	328	72512	2718735	7688	16894
私营独资企业	Private-funded Enterprises	3	57	16646	302	225
私营合伙企业	Private Partnership Enterprise					
私营有限责任公司	Private Limited Liability Corporations	311	69861	2600972	7275	16192
私营股份有限公司	Private Share-holding Corporations Ltd.	14	2594	101117	111	477
其他企业	Other Enterprises	1	684	2892	2	28
按批发行业分组	**by Wholesale Trade Sector**					
农畜产品批发业	Wholesale of Agriculture and Livestock Products	10	2655	35446	58	964
食品、饮料及烟草制品批发	Wholesale of Food, Beverage and Tobacco	88	21315	642308	5172	29581
纺织、服装及日用品批发	Wholesale of Textiles, Wearing Apparel and Household Articles	35	3720	334390	691	2778
文化、体育用品及器材批发	Wholesale of Culture, Sports Appliances and Equipments	5	752	18975	37	131
医药及医疗器材批发	Wholesale of Medicines and Medical Appliances	65	34467	1004781	2459	16562
矿产品、建材及化工产品批发	Wholesale of Mineral Products, Building Materials and Chemical Products	323	206892	4117541	14591	-9708.3
机械设备、五金交电及电子产品批发	Wholesale of Mechanical, Hardware and Electronic products	91	19174	760114	1674	-500
其他批发	Other Wholesale	7	4189	18438	134	611

23-6 续表

continued

单位：万元 (10000 yuan)

指标	Item	企业个数(个) Number of Enterprises (unit)	固定资产原价 Original Value of Fixed Assets	主营业务收入 Prime Operating Revenue	主营业务税金及附加 Tax and associate charge	利润总额 Total Profits
零售业	**Retail Trade**	**1327**	**495356**	**7275023**	**34012**	**96136**
按登记注册类型分组	**By status of Registration**					
内资企业	State-owned Enterprises	1327	495356	7275023	34012	96136
#集体企业	Collective-owned Enterprises	8	4271	32117	66	3511
股份合作企业	Share-holding Cooperative Enterprises	3	2860	38846	71	561
联营企业	Joint Ownership Enterprises	1	3849	29415	32	
有限责任公司	Limited Liability Corporations	556	241376	3900127	20838	55920
国有独资公司	State-owned Companies					
其他有限责任公司	Other Limited Liability Corporations	556	241376	3900127	20838	55920
股份有限公司	Share-holding Companies Ltd.	17	42406	280157	631	596
私营企业	Private Enterprises	735	198542	2987698	12324	34770
私营独资企业	Private-funded Enterprises	75	9469	76613	702	1980
私营合伙企业	Private Partnership Enterprise	8	927	9923	88	257
私营有限责任公司	Private Limited Liability Corporations	626	183690	2836649	11151	31035
私营股份有限公司	Private Share-holding Corporations Ltd.	26	4455	64513	384	1499
其他企业	Other Enterprises	7	2051	6664	50	779
按零售行业小类分组	**By Retail Trade Sector**					
综合零售	Integrated Retail	209	93467	1064229	8515	30653
食品、饮料及烟草制品专门零售	Special Retail of Food, Beverage and Tobaccos	134	33984	286092	3040	8982
纺织、服装及日用品专门零售	Special Retail of Textiles, Garments and Daily	27	8028	84370	669	1316
文化、体育用品及器材专门零售	Special Retail of Culture, Sports Appliances and Equipments	24	2219	63836	813	1665
医药及医疗器材专门零售	Special Retail of Medicines and Medical Appliances	81	15721	441992	1827	7504
汽车、摩托车、燃料及零配件专门零售	Special Retail of Motor Vehicles, Motorcycles, Fuels and Parts	599	291077	4515773	12943	28751
家用电器及电子产品专门零售	Special Retail of Household Electric Appliances and Electronic Products	192	21829	571500	3919	4238
五金、家具及室内装修材料专门零售	Special Retail of Hardware, Furniture and Interior Decoration Materials	35	4496	47645	735	1635
货摊、无店铺及其他零售	Stalls, Non-shop and Other Retails	26	24536	199587	1552	11394

23−7　限额以上民营经济住宿餐饮企业主要经济指标(2014)

单位：万元

指　　标	Item	企业个数(个) Number of Enterprises(unit)
住宿业	**Quartering Services**	**399**
按登记注册类型分组	**By Status of Registration**	
内资企业	State-owned Enterprises	399
#集体企业	Collective-owned Enterprises	12
股份合作企业	Share-holding Cooperative Enterprises	
有限责任公司	Limited Liability Corporations	149
其他有限责任公司	Other Limited Liability Corporations	149
股份有限公司	Share-holding Companies Ltd.	5
私营企业	Private Enterprises	226
私营独资企业	Private-funded Enterprises	46
私营合伙企业	Private Partnership Enterprise	14
私营有限责任公司	Private Limited Liability Corporations	154
私营股份有限公司	Private Share-holding Companies Ltd.	12
其他企业	Other Enterprises	7
按住宿行业分组	By Accommodation Industry Sector	
旅游饭店	Tourist Hotel	270
一般旅馆	Fonda	117
其他住宿服务	Other Hotel Services	12
餐饮业	**Catering Services**	371
按登记注册类型分组	**by Status of Registration**	
内资企业	State-owned Enterprises	371
#集体企业	Collective-owned Enterprises	1
股份合作企业	Share-holding Cooperative Enterprises	1
有限责任公司	Limited Liability Corporations	101
其他有限责任公司	Other Limited Liability Corporations	101
股份有限公司	Share-holding Corporations Ltd.	3
私营企业	Private Enterprises	257
私营独资企业	Private-funded Enterprises	87
私营合伙企业	Private Partnership Enterprise	12
私营有限责任公司	Private Limited Liabilities Companies	152
私营股份有限公司	Private Share-holding Companies Ltd.	6
其他企业	Others	8
按餐饮行业分组	**By Catering industry Sector**	
正餐服务	Restaurant	362
快餐服务	Fast Food	3
饮料及冷饮服务	Beverages and Cold Drinks	3
其他餐饮服务业	Others	3

Main Economic Indicators of Accommodation and Catering Enterprises above Designated Size of Private Economy

(10000 yuan)

固定资产原价 Original Value of Fixed Assets	主营业务收入 Prime Operating Revenue	主营业务税金及附加 Taxes and Other charges on Principal Business	利润总额 Total Profits
552704	**340996**	**18813**	**-24285**
552704	340996	18813	-24285
16579	9470	592	1913
290274	175629	9658	-23979
290274	175629	9658	-23979
5528	2430	421	-93
230549	147344	7839	-1446
61167	32667	1657	3581
7708	7424	439	338
153952	99763	5365	-5637
7722	7491	378	272
9773	6123	303	-680
460503	274243	15092	-21173
82822	63068	3541	-2551
9379	3685	180	-561
150743	197587	10100	3575
150743	197587	10100	3575
656	214	12	-65
269	268	15	15
43214	65502	3205	1386
43214	65502	3205	1386
631	5538	314	1000
104382	122042	6336	1225
13811	26325	1348	2019
7985	9083	374	1088
67943	83495	4389	-1686
14643	3139	226	-197
1591	4023	217	15
149083	194081	9938	3463
569	1951	115	-22
818	700	32	66
273	856	15	68

23-8 资质以上民营经济建筑企业主要经济指标(2014)

Main Economic Indicators of Construction Enterprises above Qualification of Private Economy

指 标	Item	有工作量企业数(个) Number of Workload Enterprises(unit)	建筑业总产值(亿元) Gross Output Value of Construction (100 million yuan)	平均人数(人) Annual Average Number of Employed Persons (person)
总 计	**Total**	**578**	**376.05**	**163436**
按登记注册类型分组	**By status of Registration**			
内资企业	State-owned Enterprises	578	376.05	163436
#联营企业	Joint Ownership Enterprises	1	0.04	23
其他联营企业	Others Joint Ownership Enterprises	1	0.04	23
有限责任公司	Limited Liability Corporations	255	166.38	77389
其他有限责任公司	Other Limited Liability Corporations	255	166.38	77389
股份有限公司	Share-holding Companies Limited	24	23.18	10789
私营企业	Private Enterprises	222	128.91	49658
私营独资企业	Private-funded Enterprises	1	0.93	221
私营合伙企业	Private Partnership Enterprise			
私营有限责任公司	Private Limited Liability Companies	206	108.38	42592
私营股份有限公司	Private Share-holding Corporations Ltd.	15	19.60	6845
按建筑业行业中类分组	**Grouped by Classification of Construction Industry**			
房屋和土木工程建筑业	Housing Construction and Civil Engineering Industry	432	344.77	149416
建筑安装业	Construction Installation Industry	67	15.05	7251
建筑装饰业	Building Descoration Industry	50	7.62	3865
其他建筑业	Other Construction Industries	29	8.61	2904
按企业资质等级分组	**By Qualification level**			
施工总承包	General Construction Contract	422	344.52	148100
一级	First Grade	10	37.34	12714
二级	Second Grade	122	148.76	65714
三级及以下	Third Grade and Below	290	158.42	69672
专业承包	Professional Contract	156	31.53	15336
一级	First Grade	6	2.66	1466
二级	Second Grade	60	17.87	7638
三级及以下	Third Grade and Below	90	11.00	6232

24 民族自治地方

Minority Nationality Autonomous Areas

24-1 民族自治地方选行政区划
Administrative Division of Minority Nationality Autonomous Areas

单位：个 (unit)

民族自治州(县)名称	Autonomous State(County)	地级 Prefectural Level	县级 County Level	#县级市 City at County Level	成立时间 Time of Comeinto Existence	土地面积(平方公里) Total Land Area(sq.km)
黔西南布依族苗族自治州	Qianxinan(Bouyei & Miao)Autonomous State	1	8	1	1982年05月01日	16804
黔东南苗族侗族自治州	Qiandongnan(Miao & Dong)Autonomous State	1	16	1	1956年07月23日	30337
黔南布依族苗族自治州	Qiannan(Bouyei & Miao)Autonomous State	1	12	2	1956年08月08日	26197
道真仡佬族苗族自治县	Daozhen(Gelao & Miao)Autonomous County		1		1987年11月29日	2156
务川仡佬族苗族自治县	Wuchuan(Gelao & Miao)Autonomous County		1		1987年11月26日	2773
镇宁布依族苗族自治县	Zhenning(Bouyei & Miao)Autonomous County		1		1963年09月11日	1703
关岭布依族苗族自治县	Guanling(Bouyei & Miao)Autonomous County		1		1981年12月31日	1468
紫云苗族布依族自治县	Ziyun(Miao & Bouyei)Autonomous County		1		1966年02月11日	2284
威宁彝族回族苗族自治县	Weining(Yi,Hui & Miao)Autonomous County		1		1954年11月11日	6296
玉屏侗族自治县	Yuping(Dong)Autonomous County		1		1984年11月07日	516
印江土家族苗族自治县	Yinjiang(Tujia & Miao)Autonomous County		1		1987年11月20日	1961
沿河土家族自治县	Yanhe(Tujia)Autonomous County		1		1987年11月23日	2469
松桃苗族自治县	Songtao(Miao)Autonomous County		1		1956年12月31日	2861
三都水族自治县	Sandu(Shui)Autonomous County		1		1957年01月02日	2384

注：资料来源于省民政厅。
Note: Data in the table are provided by the provinvial department of civil affairs.

24-2 少数民族分布
Geographic Distribution of Minority Nationalities

民族	Nationality	分布的主要地区	Main Geographic Distribution
苗族	Miao	黔东南州、黔南州、黔西南州、松桃县、紫云县、务川县、水城县	Qiandongnan,Qiannan,Qianxinan,Songtao, Ziyun Wuchuan,Shuicheng
布依族	Bouyei	黔南州、黔西南州、镇宁县、紫云县	Qiannan,Qianxinan,Zhenning,Ziyun
侗族	Dong	黔东南州、玉屏县、碧江区、石阡县	Qiandongnan,Yuping,Bijiang,Shiqian
土家族	Tujia	铜仁市	Tongren
彝族	Yi	毕节市、六盘水市	Bijie,Liupanshui
仡佬族	Gelao	遵义市、关岭县、石阡县	Zunyi,Guanling,Shiqian
水族	Shui	三都县	Sandu
回族	Hui	威宁县、兴仁县、平坝区、兴义市	Weining,Xingren,Pingba,Xingyi
白族	Bai	毕节市、盘县	Bijie,panxian
瑶族	Yao	黔东南州、荔波县	Qiandongnan,Libo
壮族	Zhuang	从江县、独山县、荔波县、都匀市	Congjiang,Dushan,Libo,Duyun
畲族	She	凯里市、麻江县、都匀市、福泉市	Kaili,Majiang,Duyun,Fuquan
毛南族	Maonan	平塘县、独山县、惠水县	Pingtang,Dushan,Huishui
蒙古族	Mongoloid	毕节市、石阡县、思南县	Bijie,Shiqian,Sinan
仫佬族	Mulam	凯里市、麻江县、黄平县	Kaili,Majiang,Huangping
满族	Man	黔西县、大方县、金沙县、云岩区	Qianxi,Dafang,Jinsha,Yunyan
羌族	Qiang	石阡县、江口县	Shiqian,Jiangkou

24-3 民族自治地方经济社会主要指标

Major Social and Economic Indicators of Minority Nationality Autonomous Areas

指　　标	Item	2013	2014	2014年比2013年增长(%) Increase Rate in 2014 over 2013(%)
人口	**Population**			
年末常住人口(万人)	Number of Resident Population at Year-end(10000 persons)	1356.74	1355.78	-0.1
#少数民族人口	Minority Population	873.06	872.44	-0.1
地区生产总值	**Gross Domestic Product**			
地区生产总值(亿元)	Gross Domestic Product(100 million yuan)	2343.01	2855.13	14.9
固定资产投资	**Investment in Fixed Assets**			
固定资产投资(亿元)	Total Investment in Fixed Assets(100 million yuan)	2136.87	2705.33	26.6
财政、金融	**Government Finance and Banking**			
公共财政预算收入(亿元)	Public Government Revenue(100 million yuan)	278.43	313.82	12.7
公共财政预算支出(亿元)	Public Government Expenditure(100 million yuan)	940.82	1053.88	12.0
金融机构人民币各项存款余额(亿元)	Total Savins Deposit Balance at Year-end (100 million yuan)	2832.45	3160.29	11.6
#储蓄余额(亿元)	Urban and Rural Resident Savings Deposit Balance (100 million yuan)	1690.41	1908.34	12.9
金融机构人民币各项贷款余额(亿元)	Total Loan Balance at Year-end(100 million yuan)	1795.05	2198.22	22.5
农业	**Agriculture**			
农林牧渔业总产值(亿元)	Gross Output Value of Farming, Forestry, Animal Husbandry and Fishery(100 million yuan)	740.83	919.70	24.1
粮食产量(万吨)	Grain Output(10000 tons)	476.80	516.85	8.4
油菜籽产量(万吨)	Output of Rapeseeds(10000 tons)	27.27	22.94	-15.9
大牲畜年底存栏数(万头)	Large Domestic Animals(year-end)(10000 heads)		296.89	
猪年底存栏数(万头)	Hogs(year-end)(10000 heads)	691.17	681.07	-1.5
羊年底存栏数(万只)	Sheep and Goats(year-end)(10000 heads)	187.04	194.04	3.7
工业（规模以上）	**Industry**			
企业数（个）	Number of enterprises(unit)	1336	1635	22.4
工业增加值（亿元）	Value added of industry(100 million yuan)	567.75	736.64	14.6
运输邮电	**Transportation, Post and Telecommunication**			
公路里程(公里)	Length of Highways(km)	83746	89496	6.9
邮路总长度(公里)	Length of Postal Routes(km)	21662	40143	85.3
商业	**Trade**			
社会消费品零售总额(亿元)	Total Retail Sales of Consumer Goods(100 million yuan)	607.50	746.03	22.8
人均水平	**Per Capita Standard of Living**			
人均地区生产总值(元)	Per Capita Gross Domestic Product(yuan)	17297	21059	21.7
人均一般公共预算收入(元)	Per Capita Local Financial Revenue(yuan)	2055	2315	12.6
城乡居民人均储蓄(元)	Per Capita Urban and Rural Resident Savings(yuan)	12480	14076	12.8

注:1.规模以上工业统计口径为年主营业务收入2000万元及以上工业企业（以下相关表同）。2.人均水平数据按常住半年人口计算。
Note: 1. Above scale industrial statistics refer to the main business income of 20 million yuan and above industrial enterprise(the same applies to the next table). 2.Data of per capita standard of living are calculated according to resident population staying at home for 6 months.

24-4 民族自治地方经济社会主要指标(2014)

Major Economic Indicators of Minority Nationality Autonomous Areas

指　标	Item	民族自治地方 Minority Nationality Autonomous Areas	民族自治州 Minority Nationality Autonomous State	民族自治县 Minority Nationality Autonomous County
人口	**Population**			
年末常住半年人口(万人)	Number of Population at The Year-end (10000 persons)	1355.78	952.17	430.35
#少数民族人口	Minority Population	872.44	645.19	261.74
人口密度(人/平方公里)	Population Density(person/sq.km)	137.79	129.83	156.75
地区生产总值(亿元)	**Gross Domestic Product(100 million yuan)**	**2855.13**	**2174.42**	**724.45**
第一产业	Primary Industry	568.16	389.22	191.99
第二产业	Secondary Industry	940.52	749.63	197.53
第三产业	Tertiary Industry	1346.45	1035.57	334.93
农业	**Agriculture**			
乡村从业人口(万人)	Rural Employment(10000 persons)	952.51	648.66	324.64
农用机械总动力(万千瓦)	Total power of Agricultural machinery(10000 kw)	825.44	590.08	256.96
化肥使用量(折纯量)(万吨)	Consumption of Chemical Fertilizers(10000 tons)	47.74	24.47	23.67
有效灌溉面积(千公顷)	Irrigated Areas(1000 hectares)	428.86	269.96	164.96
农作物播种面积(千公顷)	Total Sown Areas (1000 hectares)	2325.78	1610.32	763.11
#粮　食	Grain	1284.51	878.01	434.02
油菜籽	Rapeseeds	232.80	164.92	68.70
粮食总产量(万吨)	Total Grain Yield(10000 tons)	516.85	346.59	180.04
油菜籽产量(万吨)	Output of Rapeseeds(10000 tons)	22.94	12.42	11.74
烤烟产量(万吨)	Output of Flue -cured Tobacco (10000 tons)	62.87	55.36	7.51
茶叶产量(万吨)	Output of Tea (10000 tons)	4.44	2.92	1.58
当年造林面积(千公顷)	Afforested Areas in 2014(1000 hectares)	141.96	109.20	34.68
牲畜当年存栏数	Animals in Hand			
大牲畜(万头)	Large Animals(10000 heads)	296.89	201.28	104.86
猪(万头)	Hogs(10000 heads)	681.07	446.41	248.98
羊(万只)	Sheep and Goats(10000 heads)	194.04	110.33	84.18
牲畜当年出栏数	Number of Slaughtered Animals			
大牲畜(万头)	Large Animals(10000 heads)	75.49	44.11	32.99
猪(万头)	Hogs(10000 heads)	808.67	545.28	266.11
羊(万只)	Sheep and Goats(10000 heads)	131.41	65.69	66.23
肉类总产量(万吨)	Output of Meat(10000 tons)	70.45	40.51	31.68
水产品产量(万吨)	Total Aquatic Products(10000 tons)	10.91	7.82	3.31
农林牧渔业总产值(亿元)	Gross Output Value of Farming,Forestry,Animal Husbandry and Fishery(100 million yuan)	919.70	627.10	308.34
#农　业	Farming	563.68	376.25	196.58

24-4 续表 continued

指 标	Item	民族自治地方 Minority Nationality Autonomous Areas	民族自治州 Minority Nationality Autonomous State	民族自治县 Minority Nationality Autonomous County
林 业	Forestry	55.17	47.22	9.17
牧 业	Animal Husbandry	255.89	170.29	90.19
渔 业	Fishery	29.44	22.78	7.18
工业(规模以上)	**Industry(above designated size)**			
企业单位数(个)	Number of Enterprises(unit)	1635	1216	430
工业销售产值(亿元)	Sales Output Value of Industry(100 million yuan)	2444.51	2009.52	441.05
工业增加值(亿元)	Value-added of Industry(100 million yuan)	736.64	633.07	106.36
利润总额(亿元)	Total Profits(100 million yuan)	44.60	14.36	30.27
固定资产投资	**Investment in Fixed Assets**			
固定资产投资完成额(亿元)	All Investment in Fixed Assets in the Whole Province (100 million yuan)	2705.33	1897.17	857.85
商业	**Trade**			
社会消费品零售总额(亿元)	Total Retail Sales of Consumer Goods (100 million yuan)	746.03	597.10	159.66
财政、金融	**Government Finance and Banking**			
一般公共预算收入(亿元)	Public Govemment Revenue (100 million yuan)	313.82	271.60	44.98
一般公共预算支出(亿元)	Public Govemment Expenditure(100 million yuan)	1053.88	807.57	266.31
金融机构人民币各项存款余额(亿元)	Deposits Balance(100 million yuan)	3160.29	2552.56	649.45
#储蓄余额	Urban and Rural Resident Savings Deposit Balance	1908.34	1495.62	440.66
金融机构人民币各项贷款余额(亿元)	Loans Balance(100 million yuan)	2198.22	1758.14	470.12
交通运输	**Traffic**			
公路里程(公里)	Length of Highways(km)	89496	62814	39732
邮电、通讯	**Post and Telecommunications**			
邮政所总数(处)	Number of Post Offices(unit)	532	397	155
邮路总长度(公里)	Length of Postal Routes(km)	40143	32947	7485
农村投递线路总长度(公里)	Rural Delivery Routes(km)	41876	20204	21932
固定电话年末用户(万户)	Number of Fixed Telephone Subscribers at the Year-end (10000 units)	93.83	69.16	25.68

24-5 民族自治地方一般公共预算收入(2014)
General Public Financial Budget Revenue of Minority Nationality Autonomous Areas

单位：万元 (10000 yuan)

指　标	Item	民族自治地方 Miniority Nationality Autonomous Area	民族自治州 Nationality Minority Autonomous State	民族自治县 Minority Nationality Autonomous County
一般公共预算收入	**General Public Financial Budget Revenue**	**3138228**	**2716018**	**449813**
税收收入	**Tax Revenue**	**2273930**	**1959659**	**322426**
#增值税	Value-added Tax	174912	152549	23233
营业税	Business Tax	620089	526390	99368
企业所得税	Corporate Income Tax	145947	129010	17912
个人所得税	Individual Income Tax	56035	48335	7977
资源税	Resource Tax	43556	39011	5102
城市维护建设税	City Maintenance and Construction Tax	103567	90657	13492
耕地占用税	Farm Land Occupation Tax	516730	465663	56729
契　税	Deed Tax	128502	113103	16058
非税收入	**Non -tax Revenue**	**864298**	**756359**	**117387**
#专项收入	Specid program Receipts	90113	78705	11883
行政事业性收费收入	Change of Administrative and Institntional Units	194108	161843	34264
罚没收入	Penalty Receipts	84932	71581	14434
国有资本经营收入	Operation Income of State-owned Assets	7999	3035	4964
国有资源(资产)有偿使用收入	Income from use of Stated-owned Resources(Assets)	407146	366942	45925

注：资料来源于省财政厅(下表同)。
Note:Data in the table are obtained from Guizhou Provincial Finance Department(the same applies to the next table).

24-6 民族自治地方一般公共预算支出(2014)
General Public Financial Budget Expenditure of Minority Nationality Autonomous Areas

单位：万元 (10000 yuan)

指　标	Item	民族自治地方 Miniority Nationality Autonomous Area	民族自治州 Minority Nationality Autonomous State	民族自治县 Minority Nationality Autonomous County
一般公共预算支出	**General Public Financial Budget Expenditure**	**10583832**	**8075730**	**2663118**
一般公共服务	Expenditure for General Public Service	1590955	1317432	319826
国　防	Expenditure for National Defense	14229	11805	2474
公共安全	Expenditure for Public Security	473230	378715	101457
教　育	Expenditure for Education	2268927	1683342	632222
科学技术	Expenditure for Science and Technology	81743	70827	12924
文化体育与传媒	Expenditure for Culture,Sports and Media	151264	127635	26043
社会保障和就业	Expenditure for Social Safety Net and Employment Effort	957791	726564	244371
医疗卫生	Expenditure for Medical and Health Care	1126842	829753	318825
节能环保	Expenditure for Environmental Protection	288276	215680	74513
城乡社区事务	Expenditure for Urban and Rural Community Affairs	261019	206775	55655
农林水事务	Expenditure for Agriculture,Forest and Water conservancy	1759191	1339296	448325
交通运输	Expenditure for Transportation	134532	103667	32345
其他支出	Expenditure for Other Expenditures	93963	72536	21719

经济强县

Economically Strong Counties

25

25-1 经济强县主要指标(一)(2014)

Major Indicators of Economically Strong County (1)

单位：亿元 (100 million yuan)

县(市、区) 名称	County (City,Section)	地区生产总值 Gross Domestic Product	第一产业 Primary Industry	第二产业 Secondary Industry	第三产业 Tertiary Industry	2014年比2013年增长(%) Increase Rate in 2014 over 2013(%)	人均地区生产总值(元) Per Capita Gross Domestic Product(yuan)	2014年比2013年增长(%) Increase Rate in 2014 over 2013(%)
云岩区	Yunyan	615.91	0.52	186.30	429.09	13.8	62117	13.3
南明区	Nanming	528.51	3.33	117.37	407.81	15.5	60970	14.1
花溪区	Huaxi	362.52	14.88	196.84	150.80	14.8	57351	13.7
乌当区	Wudang	123.73	11.55	59.66	52.52	16.4	52992	14.6
白云区	Baiyun	150.75	4.67	78.72	67.36	17.3	55285	15.9
观山湖区	Guanshanhu	131.87	2.46	47.56	81.85	15.4	56871	10.0
清镇市	Qingzhen	219.39	19.01	100.19	100.19	14.3	46990	13.0
修文县	Xiuwen	119.78	16.00	54.85	48.93	17.5	45981	15.9
息烽县	Xifeng	128.47	12.56	68.06	47.85	16.4	58515	15.1
开阳县	Kaiyang	160.89	23.03	89.71	48.15	16.3	44260	15.5
红花岗区	Honghuagang	299.39	13.57	92.91	192.91	16.0	44282	15.5
汇川区	Huichuan	216.60	8.79	108.51	99.30	15.8	47819	15.3
仁怀市	Renhuai	442.87	19.49	306.20	117.18	13.4	80471	13.1
赤水市	Chishui	71.45	11.85	32.86	26.74	16.6	29693	16.2
遵义县	Zunyi	273.97	49.17	134.99	89.81	16.8	29217	16.4
桐梓县	Tongzi	108.54	22.71	44.32	41.51	16.5	20756	16.0
钟山区	Zhongshan	343.66	4.50	181.18	157.98	15.9	57344	18.0
盘　县	Panxian	426.30	32.93	281.37	112.00	16.1	40896	15.7
西秀区	Xixiu	201.39	21.09	75.62	104.68	16.2	26233	15.6
平坝区	Pingba	87.64	10.51	49.80	27.33	17.1	29331	16.5
都匀市	Duyun	153.92	14.23	54.60	85.09	15.4	33822	13.9
福泉市	Fuquan	112.04	12.44	51.24	48.36	16.5	38342	14.0
凯里市	Kaili	186.71	11.46	62.00	113.25	17.4	34997	16.7
兴义市	Xingyi	282.83	30.71	106.67	145.45	16.0	35861	15.8
七星关区	Qixingguan	258.90	47.87	97.37	113.66	15.4	22814	15.2
金沙县	Jinsha	187.53	23.94	105.01	58.58	16.0	33725	15.9
碧江区	Bijiang	110.81	9.10	42.94	58.77	17.1	36055	15.8
水城县	Shuicheng	181.11	20.52	101.95	58.64	15.8	24496	13.0
兴仁县	Xingren	91.93	14.53	34.88	42.52	15.7	21951	15.8
龙里县	Longli	64.33	8.46	40.32	15.55	17.1	40180	24.3
玉屏县	Yuping	55.44	5.87	31.21	18.36	15.8	46352	15.0

25-2 经济强县主要指标(二)(2014)

Major Indicators of Economically Strong County (2)

单位：亿元 (100 million yuan)

县(市、区)名称	County (City,Section)	一般公共预算收入 General Public Government Budget Revenue	一般公共预算支出 General Public Govenment Budget Expenditure	金融机构人民币各项存款余额 Total Deposits of Financial Institutions	金融机构人民币各项贷款余额 Total Loans of Financial Institutions	社会消费品零售总额 Total Retail Sales of Consumer Goods	固定资产投资 Investment in Fixed Assets	城镇常住居民人均可支配收入(元) Per Capita Annual Disposable Income of Urban Households (yuan)	农村常住居民人均可支配收入(元) Per Capita Net Income of Rural Residents (yuan)
云岩区	Yunyan	32.64	37.80			275.83	343.52	25840	12839
南明区	Nanming	39.83	43.41			302.74	433.70	25796	12722
花溪区	Huaxi	29.47	52.00			187.63	385.98	24374	11327
乌当区	Wudang	15.30	23.91			30.33	154.90	24435	11924
白云区	Baiyun	21.87	28.54			38.40	357.36	24508	12833
观山湖区	Guanshanhu	37.34	38.35			90.52	356.46	24446	12103
清镇市	Qingzhen	11.90	28.26	142.75	98.12	35.92	258.62	23627	10439
修文县	Xiuwen	7.03	20.09	57.61	41.74	20.16	209.56	23601	9807
息烽县	Xifeng	6.88	20.74	69.85	63.95	17.33	228.26	22420	9787
开阳县	Kaiyang	10.22	23.30	93.02	84.13	31.94	268.04	23745	10227
红花岗区	Honghuagang	21.85	35.03			172.91	335.64	24965	10210
汇川区	Huichuan	13.32	20.36			92.42	157.46	24965	10228
仁怀市	Renhuai	25.81	40.27	451.42	182.55	72.60	257.58	24283	8548
赤水市	Chishui	4.90	19.30	89.30	69.81	20.85	118.18	21722	8350
遵义县	Zunyi	16.55	40.65	238.26	172.98	59.22	347.18	24089	9788
桐梓县	Tongzi	6.56	26.37	99.96	55.31	22.42	155.12	20588	8155
钟山区	Zhongshan	16.85	25.76			145.11	323.99	22759	9044
盘县	Panxian	46.14	79.54	218.74	168.87	68.77	517.97	20137	6933
西秀区	Xixiu	20.07	43.85			54.96	333.09	22410	8129
平坝县	Pingba	8.04	24.94	104.28	84.09	20.67	141.86	20593	6863
都匀市	Duyun	14.23	29.56	283.06	169.76	55.66	239.38	23518	8410
福泉市	Fuquan	11.52	23.18	76.04	76.89	18.66	118.34	22091	7495
凯里市	Kaili	36.13	47.61	339.39	239.70	87.41	353.81	22401	7879
兴义市	Xingyi	30.58	52.92	391.27	300.78	119.28	317.70	23122	8190
七星关区	Qixingguan	19.61	48.03	329.12	237.74	95.67	306.26	22727	6382
金沙县	Jinsha	15.91	34.97	88.13	78.31	27.90	301.12	23001	7146
碧江区	Bijiang	11.09	23.91	246.78	187.51	40.28	166.71	21957	8458
水城县	Shuicheng	19.51	44.35			15.16	300.56	19603	6400
兴仁县	Xingren	13.25	32.22	62.74	66.51	15.47	122.35	20816	6345
龙里县	Longli	6.71	17.65	57.57	44.26	12.62	108.59	21860	7513
玉屏县	Yuping	3.58	12.87	32.87	42.35	8.04	58.56	20937	7921

注：固定资产投资统计口径为计划总投资50万元及以上固定资产投资项目和房地产开发投资项目。

Note: The caliber of fixed asset investment refers to those projects planned to invest 500 thousand yuan at least in fixed assets investment projects and real estate development investment projects.

26 扶贫与开发

Anti-poverty and Development

26-1 扶贫开发重点县主要指标占全省比重(2014)

Major Indicators of Basilic County of Anti-poverty and Development and Its Percentage to Provincial Total

单位：亿元 (100 million yuan)

指 标	Item	全省合计 Provincial Total	扶贫开发重点县合计 Poverty Counties Total	扶贫开发重点县占全省比重(%) As Percentage to Provincial Total(%)
国土面积(万平方公里)	Area of Territory(10000 sq.km)	17.61	11.63	66.0
年末常住人口(万人)	Permanent Resident Population at the Year-end (10000 persons)	3508.00	1782.70	50.8
地区生产总值	Gross Domestic Product	9266.39	3532.29	38.1
一般公共预算收入	General Public Financial Budget Revenue	1366.67	281.82	20.6
一般公共预算支出	General Public Financial Budget Expenditure	3542.80	1183.31	33.4
农林牧渔业总产值	Gross Output Value of Agricalture, Forestry, Animal Husban dry and Fishery	2118.48	1185.04	55.9
粮食产量(万吨)	Output of Grain(10000 tons)	1138.50	708.72	62.3
规模以上工业增加值	Value-added of Industry above Designated Size	3117.60	951.63	30.5
社会消费品零售总额	Total Retail Sales of Consumer Goods	2936.85	839.97	28.6
个人储蓄存款	Personal Savings Deposits	6620.56	1939	29.3

26-2 贫困人口及发生率(2014)

Number of Poverty Population and It's Arisen Rate

市(州) 县(市、区、特区) 名　称	County (City,Section, Special Region)	农村贫困人口 (万人) Poverty Population (10 000 persons)	农村贫困 发生率(%) Arisen Rate of Poverty (%)
全省合计	**Provincial Total**	**623.00**	**18.00**
扶贫开发重点县小计	**Basilic Counties of Antipoverty and Development**	**486.14**	**27.30**
贵阳市	**Guiyang**	**3.40**	**1.37**
南明区	Nanming		
云岩区	Yunyan		
花溪区	Huaxi	0.25	0.98
乌当区	Wudang	0.28	2.12
白云区	Baiyun		
观山湖区	Guanshanhu	0.20	1.43
开阳县	Kaiyang	0.70	2.17
息烽县	Xifeng	0.56	2.95
修文县	Xiuwen	0.51	1.83
清镇市	Qingzhen	0.90	2.25
六盘水市	**Liupanshui**	**50.99**	**19.55**
钟山区	Zhongshan	1.49	8.85
△六枝特区	Liuzhi	10.04	16.98
△水城县	Shuicheng	19.48	24.81
△盘　县	Panxian	19.98	18.79
遵义市	**Zunyi**	**72.98**	**10.80**
红花岗区	Honghuagang	1.25	6.13
汇川区	huichuan	1.51	6.98
遵义县	Zunyi	9.44	7.88
桐梓县	Tongzi	5.53	7.98
绥阳县	Suiyang	3.93	7.63
△正安县	Zhengan	9.83	16.38
△道真县	Daozhen	5.02	16.36
△务川县	Wuchuan	7.89	18.74
凤冈县	Fenggang	3.61	9.06
湄潭县	Meitan	3.66	8.38
余庆县	Yuqing	2.07	7.84
△习水县	Xishui	11.95	17.78
赤水市	Chishui	2.38	10.05
仁怀市	Renhuai	4.91	8.25
安顺市	**Anshun**	**43.83**	**17.72**
西秀区	Xixiu	5.11	8.16
平坝区	Pingba	3.92	12.63
△普定县	Puding	9.18	20.77
△镇宁县	Zhenning	7.91	21.76
△关岭县	Guanling	8.63	24.16
△紫云县	Ziyun	9.08	24.27
毕节市	**Bijie**	**138.99**	**19.75**
七星关区	Qixingguan	17.71	15.86
△大方县	Dafang	20.04	23.51
黔西县	Qianxi	11.97	13.60
金沙县	Jinsha	6.40	14.51
△织金县	Zhijin	23.81	27.32
△纳雍县	Nayong	19.05	22.39
△威宁县	Weining	23.91	18.63
△赫章县	Hezhang	16.10	21.77

26-2 续表 continued

市(州) 县(市、区、特区) 名 称	County (City,Section, Special Region)	农村贫困人口(万人) Poverty Population (10 000 persons)	农村贫困发生率(%) Arisen Rate of Poverty (%)	市(州) 县(市、区、特区) 名 称	County (City,Section, Special Region)	农村贫困人口(万人) Poverty Population (10 000 persons)	农村贫困发生率(%) Arisen Rate of Poverty (%)
铜仁市	**Tongren**	**77.54**	**20.61**	镇远县	Zhenyuan	4.25	24.31
碧江区	Bijiang	2.31	14.08	△岑巩县	Cengong	4.93	25.39
万山区	Wanshan	2.41	17.58	△天柱县	Tianzhu	9.92	27.65
△江口县	Jiangkou	4.01	18.78	△锦屏县	Jinping	6.14	28.54
玉屏县	Yuping	2.24	17.27	△剑河县	Jianhe	6.92	28.29
△石阡县	Shiqian	8.47	21.20	△台江县	Taijiang	4.39	28.78
△思南县	Sinan	13.25	21.32	△黎平县	Liping	11.27	24.48
△印江县	Yinjiang	7.93	19.13	△榕江县	Rongjiang	10.54	33.73
△德江县	Dejiang	9.90	25.79	△从江县	Congjiang	9.05	29.01
△沿河县	Yanhe	14.17	22.95	△雷山县	Leishan	3.60	26.48
△松桃县	Songtao	12.85	18.89	△麻江县	Majiang	4.81	32.76
黔西南州	**Qianxinan**	**58.29**	**18.48**	△丹寨县	Danzhai	4.61	29.24
兴义市	Xingyi	5.84	8.56	**黔南州**	**Qiannan**	**73.60**	**20.70**
△兴仁县	Xingren	7.10	16.12	都匀市	Duyun	4.31	13.28
△普安县	Puan	5.11	15.17	福泉市	Fuquan	4.27	18.61
△晴隆县	Qinglong	10.11	32.77	△荔波县	Libo	4.23	25.56
△贞丰县	Zhenfeng	8.36	20.65	贵定县	Guiding	4.33	16.64
△望谟县	Wangmo	8.72	27.82	瓮安县	Wengan	5.07	11.59
△册亨县	Ceheng	6.81	29.17	△独山县	Dushan	7.45	22.73
△安龙县	Anlong	6.24	14.40	△平塘县	Pingtang	8.17	25.98
黔东南州	**Qiandongnan**	**103.38**	**26.58**	△罗甸县	Luodian	9.66	30.27
凯里市	Kaili	4.56	12.33	△长顺县	Changshun	6.51	26.56
△黄平县	Huangping	9.79	27.90	龙里县	Longli	2.88	14.95
△施秉县	Shibing	2.82	26.81	惠水县	Huishui	6.10	14.89
△三穗县	Sansui	5.78	29.09	△三都县	Sandu	10.62	32.30

注：△为新阶段扶贫开发工作重点县。

Note: These counties with '△' refer to basilic counties of antipoverty and development.

26-3 扶贫开发重点县主要指标(2014)

单位：亿元

扶贫开发重点县名称	County	年末常住人口(万人) Population (year-end) (10000 persons)	地区生产总值 Gross Domestic Product	一般公共预算收入 General Public Financial Budget Revenue	一般公共预算支出 General Public Financial Budget Expenditure	农林牧渔业总产值 Gross Output Value of Agriculture, Forestry, Animal Husbandry and Fishery
扶贫开发重点县合计	**Total**	**1782.70**	**3532.29**	**281.82**	**1183.31**	**1185.04**
六盘水市	**Liupanshui**					
六枝特区	Liuzhi	49.78	127.52	12.22	32.19	28.70
水城县	Shuicheng	74.01	181.11	19.51	44.35	33.10
盘　县	Panxian	104.33	426.30	46.14	79.54	53.11
遵义市	**Zunyi**					
正安县	Zhengan	38.39	59.81	4.01	23.39	34.34
※道真县	Daozhen	24.47	39.75	3.17	18.06	23.65
※务川县	Wuchuan	31.95	42.99	3.58	20.40	25.84
习水县	Xishui	51.80	112.55	7.80	32.77	37.49
安顺市	**Anshun**					
普定县	Puding	38.02	71.20	6.04	21.27	19.40
※镇宁县	Zhenning	28.49	64.14	5.67	20.79	16.75
※关岭县	Guanling	30.28	60.90	3.62	18.25	19.73
※紫云县	Ziyun	27.19	45.02	3.77	20.15	22.47
毕节市	**Bijie**					
大方县	Dafang	77.94	158.74	13.47	39.09	45.32
织金县	Zhijin	78.55	136.35	11.16	39.23	41.44
纳雍县	Nayong	67.31	148.69	6.43	30.70	34.29
※威宁县	Weining	126.82	152.03	7.94	51.92	75.70
赫章县	Hezhang	65.36	91.07	2.97	31.05	45.48
铜仁市	**Tongren**					
江口县	Jiangkou	17.36	33.42	1.55	13.15	16.42
石阡县	Shiqian	30.47	47.67	2.89	24.32	29.15
思南县	Sinan	49.95	88.20	4.24	32.89	36.82
※印江县	Yinjiang	28.46	58.91	2.65	22.81	28.46
德江县	Dejiang	37.05	73.30	4.24	27.99	31.78
※沿河县	Yanhe	45.03	72.60	3.67	29.67	33.11
※松桃县	Songtao	48.93	88.93	4.58	31.38	36.82

注：固定资产投资统计口径为计划总投资50万元及以上固定资产投资项目和房地产开发投资项目。

Major Indicators on Basilic County of Anti-poverty and Development

(100 million yuan)

粮食产量(万吨) Output of Grain (10000 tons)	人均粮食(公斤) Per Capita Output of Grain (kg)	农村常住居民人均可支配收入(元) Per Capita Annual Net Income of Rural Households(yuan)	规模以上工业增加值 Value-added of Industry above Designated Size	个人储蓄存款 Savings Deposit	固定资产投资 Investment in Fixed Assets	社会消费品零售总额 Total Retail Sales of Consumer Goods
708.72	**331**		**951.63**	**1939.03**	**4588.75**	**700.60**
21.18	358	6404	23.10	61.37	193.61	32.33
22.63	288	6400	113.43		300.56	15.16
35.49	334	6933	229.23	133.26	517.97	68.77
22.48	375	6786	6.13	60.19	70.75	17.20
14.40	469	6785	3.48	51.85	51.26	10.96
17.28	410	6757	3.27	46.06	58.18	11.05
25.41	378	7082	56.61	68.64	178.98	21.49
						139.37
10.48	237	6116	23.46	29.72	84.58	15.67
10.06	277	5969	4.72	28.86	62.73	16.70
9.63	269	5986	3.78	31.33	45.75	18.47
9.76	261	5868	2.12	23.24	40.73	12.91
26.20	307	6260	33.85	73.12	174.12	26.07
33.18	381	6184	24.28	70.90	247.56	25.90
25.80	303	5873	43.33	50.71	211.32	21.30
47.80	372	6196	19.41	54.65	181.06	25.85
24.96	337	5857	11.27	45.53	109.56	18.97
6.72	315	6162	4.34	27.65	65.15	7.42
12.99	325	6148	5.37	38.09	44.84	8.52
22.09	355	5996	16.50	67.37	135.83	20.04
13.62	329	6037	8.04	42.39	78.85	10.73
17.83	464	5907	10.03	39.61	74.07	14.03
19.92	323	5960	9.04	50.33	116.18	15.04
23.71	349	5915	21.41	60.38	114.87	19.19

Note: The Statistic soope of investment in fixed asset refers to those projects which planned to invest 500 thousand yuan at least in investment in fixed assets and real estate development investment projects.

26-3 续表

单位：亿元

扶贫开发重点县名称	County	年末常住人口(万人) Population (year-end) (10000 persons)	地区生产总值 Gross Domestic Product	一般公共预算收入 General Public Financial Budget Revenue	一般公共预算支出 General Public Financial Budget Expenditure	农林牧渔业总产值 Gross Output Value of Agriculture, Forestry, Animal Husbandry and Fishery
黔西南州	**Qianxinan**					
兴仁县	Xingren	41.78	91.93	13.25	32.22	27.32
普安县	Puan	25.60	50.45	7.15	20.96	14.75
晴隆县	Qinglong	24.80	44.45	4.29	16.98	14.39
贞丰县	Zhenfeng	30.54	76.54	9.51	26.77	22.89
望谟县	Wangmo	24.46	36.16	2.45	23.09	21.10
册亨县	Ceheng	19.14	28.96	2.20	14.83	13.16
安龙县	Anlong	35.94	73.05	5.96	22.26	28.02
黔东南州	**Qiandongnan**					
黄平县	Huangping	26.25	37.43	2.93	17.14	18.73
施秉县	Shibing	13.06	27.33	1.92	10.34	9.62
三穗县	Sansui	15.50	30.81	2.78	13.35	9.42
岑巩县	Cengong	16.04	31.96	3.16	14.17	10.40
天柱县	Tianzhu	26.04	59.10	4.88	19.15	17.33
锦屏县	Jinping	15.35	30.34	1.46	13.03	8.78
剑河县	Jianhe	18.06	31.18	2.96	13.74	11.94
台江县	Taijiang	11.10	22.20	1.73	10.51	7.85
黎平县	Liping	38.86	57.25	3.77	23.98	20.10
榕江县	Rongjiang	28.59	41.40	5.00	20.12	17.79
从江县	Congjiang	29.02	41.07	3.54	20.19	17.70
雷山县	Leishan	11.68	20.98	2.03	12.74	7.97
麻江县	Majiang	12.20	22.32	1.65	12.01	8.43
丹寨县	Danzhai	12.23	21.34	1.12	19.37	7.85
黔南州	**Qiannan**					
荔波县	Libo	12.71	41.49	2.71	14.62	11.45
独山县	Dushan	26.93	55.01	3.33	16.69	19.86
平塘县	Pingtang	23.88	42.41	2.91	17.69	18.58
罗甸县	Luodian	25.65	50.82	2.09	17.94	18.39
长顺县	Changshun	18.62	41.37	2.95	14.04	16.11
※三都县	Sandu	26.74	43.74	2.76	20.00	15.74

continued

(100 million yuan)

粮食产量（万吨）Output of Grain (10000 tons)	人均粮食（公斤）Per Capita Output of Grain (kg)	农村常住居民人均可支配收入（元）Per Capita Annual Net Income of Rural Households(yuan)	规模以上工业增加值 Value-added of Industry above Designated Size	个人储蓄存款 Savings Deposit	固定资产投资 Investment in Fixed Assets	社会消费品零售总额 Total Retail Sales of Consumer Goods
17.06	387	6345	25.63	36.80	122.35	15.47
8.35	248	5729	21.26	25.20	59.13	6.93
8.63	280	5463	13.85	23.08	63.83	5.71
11.71	289	6134	41.74	37.93	80.52	8.03
7.56	241	5206	3.23	18.19	40.09	3.93
5.22	224	5361	3.17	18.13	30.71	2.23
19.04	439	6086	19.73	44.04	71.99	10.27
10.55	301	5816	3.82	35.04	42.51	9.90
5.65	537	6497	2.23	31.07	30.12	6.73
5.32	268	6168	6.07	24.02	42.15	11.11
6.31	325	6144	11.85	25.23	40.76	9.17
11.43	319	6349	16.83	49.93	75.89	15.54
5.76	268	5705	11.36	30.36	28.29	8.26
6.17	252	5825	3.48	27.09	35.07	8.59
4.18	274	5580	5.53	16.63	36.11	5.02
12.64	274	5945	9.01	52.29	69.95	16.89
8.16	261	5766	7.83	35.61	50.73	11.42
10.81	346	6126	4.33	24.38	58.97	11.33
4.55	335	6064	1.41	18.00	23.24	5.52
4.66	317	5870	3.14	22.25	39.03	6.13
4.62	293	5862	7.87	19.44	49.91	4.91
4.74	286	6916	11.27	25.96	55.05	8.85
11.15	340	7029	16.24	45.21	59.62	14.64
10.90	347	6666	2.19	25.99	53.29	10.69
10.40	326	7160	7.95	25.91	65.23	10.34
9.75	398	6768	11.65	18.07	56.01	8.48
9.78	297	6758	2.79	27.95	49.68	10.74

市(州)、县(市、区、特区)资料

27

Main Statistics of City (State,Prefecture) and County (City,District,Special Region)

27-1 各市(州)地区生产总值及增速(2014)

Gross Domestic Product and Its Composition by Region

市（州）名称	City (State, Prefecture)	地区生产总值 Gross Domestic Product	第一产业 Primary Industry	第二产业 Secondary Industry	#工业 Industry	第三产业 Tertiary Industry	人均地区生产总值(元) Per Capita Gross Domestic Product (yuan)
绝对数(亿元)	**Absolute Figure (100 million yuan)**						
贵阳市	Guiyang	2497.27	108.02	976.59	678.00	1412.66	55019
六盘水市	Liupanshui	1042.73	75.75	567.08	500.14	399.90	36228
遵义市	Zunyi	1874.36	267.47	860.69	716.75	746.20	30484
安顺市	Anshun	520.06	78.56	189.67	149.98	251.83	22569
毕节市	Bijie	1266.70	252.78	522.77	425.88	491.15	19369
铜仁市	Tongren	647.73	149.68	193.35	140.82	304.70	20826
黔西南州	Qianxinan	670.96	113.42	240.55	198.73	316.99	23821
黔东南州	Qiandongnan	701.71	124.55	214.19	148.17	362.97	20161
黔南州	Qiannan	801.75	151.25	294.89	222.95	355.61	24791
比上年增长(%)	**Composition(%)**						
贵阳市	Guiyang	13.9	6.6	13.9	12.1	14.3	
六盘水市	Liupanshui	14.1	7.0	13.4	12.3	16.4	
遵义市	Zunyi	14.4	6.6	15.3	12.8	15.4	
安顺市	Anshun	14.8	6.8	16.0	14.2	16.0	
毕节市	Bijie	14.0	7.0	15.4	13.7	15.0	
铜仁市	Tongren	14.3	6.5	16.0	14.3	17.2	
黔西南州	Qianxinan	14.6	6.6	16.0	14.2	15.6	
黔东南州	Qiandongnan	14.4	6.8	14.7	14.2	16.8	
黔南州	Qiannan	14.5	6.6	16.9	14.5	14.7	

注：表中绝对数按当年价格计算，增长速度按可比价格计算。

Note:Data of absolute figures in the table are calculated at current prices,and increase rates are calculated at comparable prices.

27-2 各市(州)年末常住人口

Permanent Population at the year-end by Region

单位：万人 (10000 persons)

市(州)名称	City (State,Prefecture)	2010	2011	2012	2013	2014
贵阳市	Guiyang	432.93	439	445.17	452.19	455.60
六盘水市	Liupanshui	285.43	285	285.90	287.45	288.20
遵义市	Zunyi	613.29	610	611.70	614.25	615.49
安顺市	Anshun	230.04	228	228.34	230.05	230.81
毕节市	Bijie	654.57	652	652.41	653.82	654.12
铜仁市	Tongren	309.63	308	309.44	310.40	311.65
黔西南州	Qianxinan	281.02	280	281.20	282.22	281.12
黔东南州	Qiandongnan	348.52	346	347.27	348.34	347.75
黔南州	Qiannan	323.51	321	322.64	323.50	323.30

27—3 各市(州)户籍人口
Household Registered Population by Region

市(州)名称	City (State,Prefecture)	总户数(万户) Total Number of Household (10000 households)		平均每户人数(人) Population of Per Household(person)		年末人口数(万人) Total Population at The Year-end(10000 persons)	
		2013	2014	2013	2014	2013	2014
贵阳市	Guiyang	117.30	119.11	3.23	3.21	379.09	382.91
六盘水市	Liupanshui	100.47	102.73	3.24	3.20	325.41	328.34
遵义市	Zunyi	233.71	236.63	3.33	3.33	778.46	787.03
安顺市	Anshun	85.05	86.77	3.36	3.34	285.62	289.98
毕节市	Bijie	235.89	240.39	3.69	3.66	870.57	880.79
铜仁市	Tongren	125.02	129.56	3.43	3.34	429.21	432.28
黔西南州	Qianxinan	101.02	100.36	3.46	3.51	349.22	351.87
黔东南州	Qiandongnan	132.06	133.36	3.51	3.50	463.44	466.20
黔南州	Qiannan	123.66	125.62	3.28	3.23	405.12	406.08

注：资料来源于省公安厅(下表同)。
Note:Data in the table are obtained from Guizhou Provincial Department of Public Security.(the same table below)

27—3 续表 Continued

单位：万人 (10000 persons)

市(州)名称	City (state,Prefecture)	按农业与非农业分 By Agricultural and Non-Agricultural				按性别分 Grouped by sex			
		农业 Agricultural		非农业 Non-Agricultural		男 Male		女 Female	
		2013	2014	2013	2014	2013	2014	2013	2014
贵阳市	Guiyang	191.66	193.77	187.43	189.14	192.78	194.44	186.31	188.47
六盘水市	Liupanshui	251.86	254.32	73.56	74.02	171.79	173.34	153.62	155
遵义市	Zunyi	647.18	655.00	131.28	132.03	404.33	409.25	374.13	377.78
安顺市	Anshun	243.85	247.71	41.77	42.27	148.18	150.42	137.44	139.56
毕节市	Bijie	805.83	815.21	64.74	65.58	456.16	462.24	414.41	418.55
铜仁市	Tongren	375.34	376.31	53.87	55.97	226.16	228.41	203.04	203.86
黔西南州	Qianxinan	313.45	315.98	35.77	35.89	180.23	182.07	168.99	169.81
黔东南州	Qiandongnan	406.36	408.73	57.08	57.47	246.30	248.01	217.15	218.19
黔南州	Qiannan	348.64	349.23	56.48	56.85	211.28	212.37	193.84	193.71

27−4 各市(州)非私营单位在岗职工年平均人数、年平均工资(2014)

Number of Staff and Workers and Their Annual Average Wages in Non-private units by Region

市(州) 名 称	City (State, Prefecture)	合 计 Total	国有经济 State -owned units	城镇集体经济 Urban Collective-owned Units	其他经济类型 Units of Other Types of Ownership	2014年比2013年增长(%) Increase Rate in 2014 over 2013(%)
在岗职工年平均人数(万人)	**Number of Staff and Workers(10000 persons)**	**275.81**	**151.61**	**5.29**	**118.91**	**2.3**
贵 阳 市	Guiyang	91.60	36.21	1.22	54.17	3.2
六盘水市	Liupanshui	22.45	7.75	0.24	14.46	-3.8
遵 义 市	Zunyi	39.64	23.93	0.74	14.97	7.3
安 顺 市	Anshun	15.87	8.91	0.70	6.26	1.0
毕 节 市	Bijie	30.54	21.12	0.49	8.93	6.5
铜 仁 市	Tongren	16.55	12.66	0.47	3.42	6.0
黔西南州	Qianxinan	15.02	9.77	0.44	4.82	6.1
黔东南州	Qiandongnan	23.15	17.48	0.42	5.25	8.5
黔 南 州	Qiannan	20.98	13.77	0.57	6.64	8.2
年平均工资(元)	**Annual Average Wages (yuan)**	**54685**	**56918**	**59458**	**51627**	**11.4**
贵 阳 市	Guiyang	59334	65838	44612	55317	16.8
六盘水市	Liupanshui	52130	53630	109351	50389	12.4
遵 义 市	Zunyi	57152	57205	60629	56896	13.2
安 顺 市	Anshun	49204	54226	47876	42203	7.1
毕 节 市	Bijie	48781	50718	66816	43214	6.6
铜 仁 市	Tongren	54161	56891	53728	44104	13.4
黔西南州	Qianxinan	53060	55731	58502	47148	6.6
黔东南州	Qiandongnan	49342	50251	84876	43468	8.1
黔 南 州	Qiannan	52682	55398	63697	46101	11.5

27-5 各市(州)投资、消费(2014)

Investment in Fixed Assets by Region

单位：亿元 (100 million yuan)

市(州)名称	City (State, Prefecture)	固定资产投资 Investment in Fixed Assets	社会消费品零售总额 Total retail sales of social consumer goods
贵阳市	Guiyang	2336.06	951.12
六盘水市	Liupanshui	895.36	261.40
遵义市	Zunyi	1365.27	570.40
安顺市	Anshun	427.32	139.37
毕节市	Bijie	1128.77	269.38
铜仁市	Tongren	597.66	148.09
黔西南州	Qianxinan	521.11	171.85
黔东南州	Qiandongnan	680.45	229.19
黔南州	Qiannan	695.60	196.06

注：固定资产投资统计口径为计划总投资500万元及以上固定资产项目投资和房地产开发项目投资，不含跨区域项目投资。

Note:Data in the table refer to those projects planned to invest 5 million yuan at least in investment in fixed assets and real estate development. but it doesn't include investment in cross-regional projects.

27-6 各市(州)能源利用效率(2014)

Energy Using Effutency by Region

市(州)名称	City (State, Prefecture)	单位地区生产总值能耗(吨标准煤/万元) Energy Consumption Per Unit of GDP(ton of SEC/10000 yuan)	单位地区生产总值能耗比上年增长(%) Growth Rate of Energy Consumption Per Unit of GDP over Preceding Year(%)	单位地区生产总值电耗(千瓦小时/万元) Electricity Consumption Per Unit of GDP (KWh/10000 yuan)	单位地区生产总值电耗比上年增长(%) Growth Rate of Electricity Consumption Per Unit of GDP over Preceding Year(%)
贵阳市	Guiyang	1.2247	-5.08	1159	-12.6
六盘水市	Liupanshui	2.3539	-9.20	1500	-8.2
遵义市	Zunyi	1.1761	-5.65	1043	-18.5
安顺市	Anshun	1.8088	-9.50	1704	-17.2
毕节市	Bijie	1.6451	-4.51	1175	0.9
铜仁市	Tongren	1.4497	-5.20	1627	-3.1
黔西南州	Qianxinan	1.5251	-4.64	1695	4.7
黔东南州	Qiandongnan	1.6846	-6.87	1806	-7.0
黔南州	Qiannan	1.6036	-3.20	1619	6.6

27-7 各市(州)一般公共预算收入(2014)

General Public Financial Budget Revenue by Region

市(州)名称	City (State, Prefecture)	一般公共预算收入(亿元) General Public Financial Budget Revenue (100 million yuan)	税收收入 Tax revenue	#增值税 Value Added Tax	#营业税 Business Revenue	#企业所得税 Corporate Income Tax	#个人所得税 Individual Income Tax	非税收入 Non-tax revenue	#专项收入 Special Program Roceipts	2014年比2013年增长(%) Increase Rate in 2014 over 2013(%)
贵阳市	Guiyang	331.60	271.85	32.56	101.42	26.26	8.92	59.74	16.83	19.6
六盘水市	Liupanshui	128.74	89.09	8.96	15.71	4.42	2.37	39.65	4.21	4.2
遵义市	Zunyi	159.65	125.50	19.33	37.56	8.01	4.39	34.15	6.36	16.7
安顺市	Anshun	58.48	44.64	3.30	15.03	3.19	1.02	13.84	1.51	24.7
毕节市	Bijie	116.15	71.72	9.31	18.92	4.87	3.52	44.43	9.32	-7.5
铜仁市	Tongren	50.13	37.75	3.36	13.76	2.38	0.96	12.38	1.65	12.0
黔西南州	Qianxinan	94.50	70.69	5.37	16.70	3.92	2.36	23.80	2.37	16.1
黔东南州	Qiandongnan	92.63	62.27	3.91	16.56	4.50	1.24	30.36	1.59	7.7
黔南州	Qiannan	84.47	63.00	5.98	19.38	4.48	1.23	21.47	3.90	15.4

注：资料来源于省财政厅(下表同)。
Note:Data in the table were obtained from Guizhou Provincial Financial Department(the same applies to the next table).

27-8 各市(州)一般公共预算支出(2014)

General Public Financial Budget Expenditure by Region

市(州)名称	City (State, Prefecture)	一般公共预算支出(亿元) General Public Financial Budget Expenditure (100 million yuan)	#一般公共服务 Expenditure for General Public Service	#教育 Expenditure for Education	#科学技术 Expenditure for Science and Technology	#文化体育与传媒 Expenditure for Culture, Sports and Media	#社会保障和就业 Expenditure for Safety Net and Emdoyment Effort	#医疗卫生 Expenditure for Medical and Health Care	#节能环保 Expenditure for Enviro-nmental Protection	#农林水事务 Expenditure for Agriculture, Forestry and Water Conservancy	2014年比2013年增长(%) Increase Rate in 2014 over 2013(%)
贵阳市	Guiyang	448.63	78.49	80.47	12.38	8.25	31.94	33.30	16.36	34.82	14.0
六盘水市	Liupanshui	224.79	33.13	44.50	1.35	3.13	19.73	21.37	6.71	34.58	2.6
遵义市	Zunyi	396.32	51.97	87.12	3.55	5.96	34.13	49.73	12.28	57.43	8.1
安顺市	Anshun	172.82	23.56	32.97	1.22	2.65	20.49	17.80	5.55	26.49	14.0
毕节市	Bijie	361.34	35.46	90.36	1.59	3.91	32.80	47.61	7.62	46.65	4.1
铜仁市	Tongren	256.48	24.48	57.54	1.76	3.41	27.17	28.11	6.94	43.51	8.7
黔西南州	Qianxinan	236.91	32.95	51.68	2.06	2.83	19.41	21.33	7.39	41.93	12.9
黔东南州	Qiandongnan	308.72	55.24	62.05	2.28	5.53	28.99	33.98	6.16	47.74	10.7
黔南州	Qiannan	261.94	43.55	54.61	2.75	4.41	24.26	27.66	8.02	44.26	13.8

27—9 各市(州)金融机构人民币存贷款余额(2014)

Saving Deposits and Loans Balance of Financial Institutions by Region

单位：亿元 (100 million yuan)

市(州)名称	City (State, Prefecture)	金融机构人民币各项存款余额 Total Deposits	#个人储蓄存款 Personal Savings Deposits	金融机构人民币各项贷款余额 Total Loans
贵 阳 市	Guiyang	6992.20	2010.58	6560.51
六盘水市	Liupanshui	817.09	416.88	701.20
遵 义 市	Zunyi	2567.60	1308.23	1527.74
安 顺 市	Anshun	660.28	344.08	518.95
毕 节 市	Bijie	916.79	568.72	689.48
铜 仁 市	Tongren	754.14	475.76	601.65
黔西南州	Qianxinan	759.35	365.65	539.97
黔东南州	Qiandongnan	925.79	604.00	613.65
黔 南 州	Qiannan	867.43	525.98	604.52

注：资料来源于中国人民银行贵阳中心支行。
Note:Data in the table are obtained from the People's bank of China Guiyang Branch.

27—10 各市(州)城镇常住居民家庭人均年收支(2014)

Per capita Income and Expenditure of Urban Households by Region

单位：元 (yuan)

市(州)名称	City (State, Prefecture)	城镇常住居民家庭人均可支配收入 Per Capita Annual Disposable Income of Urban Households	位次 Order	城镇常住居民家庭人均消费性支出 Per Capita Annual Consumption Expenditnre of Urban Households	位次 Order
贵 阳 市	Guiyang	24961	1	17492	1
六盘水市	Liupanshui	21168	6	13542	5
遵 义 市	Zunyi	22728	2	14891	2
安 顺 市	Anshun	21042	7	13803	4
毕 节 市	Bijie	21231	5	13199	7
铜 仁 市	Tongren	20224	9	13171	8
黔西南州	Qianxinan	21300	4	13470	6
黔东南州	Qiandongnan	20990	8	12606	9
黔 南 州	Qiannan	21698	3	13855	3

27-11 各市(州)农村常住居民家庭人均年收支(2014)

Per Capita Net Income and Living Expenditure of Rural Households by Region

单位：元 (yuan)

市(州)名称	City (State, Prefecture)	农村常住居民人均可支配收入 Per Capita Net Income of Rural Households	位次 Order	农村常住居民人均期内现金可支配收入 Annual Per Capita Cash Income of Rural Households	位次 Order	农村常住居民人均生活消费支出 Annual Per Capita Living Expenditures of Rural Households	位次 Order
贵 阳 市	Guiyang	10826	1	10371	1	8724	1
六盘水市	Liupanshui	6791	4	6288	3	6042	5
遵 义 市	Zunyi	8365	2	7389	2	7334	2
安 顺 市	Anshun	6671	5	6162	5	6160	4
毕 节 市	Bijie	6223	8	5004	8	5638	6
铜 仁 市	Tongren	6233	7	5353	7	5376	9
黔西南州	Qianxinan	6345	6	5440	6	5532	7
黔东南州	Qiandongnan	6139	9	4943	9	5476	8
黔 南 州	Qiannan	7265	3	6287	4	6459	3

27-12 各市(州)所在城市分类价格指数

Urban Residents Consumer Price Indices of Major Cities by Region

(上年=100) (preceding year=100)

城市名称	City	居民消费价格指数 Residents Consumer Price Index		商品零售价格指数 Retail Price Index of Commodities	
		2013	2014	2013	2014
贵 阳 市	Guiyang	103.2	102.7	101.9	101.2
六盘水市	Liupanshui	103.3	101.3	103.0	101.3
遵 义 市	Zunyi	102.7	102.0	101.0	101.6
安 顺 市	Anshun	102.1	102.3	101.5	101.7
毕 节 市	Bijie	101.4	103.2	100.0	102.0
铜 仁 市	Tongren	102.4	102.0	101.7	101.1
兴 义 市	Xingyi	101.9	101.9	100.2	100.5
凯 里 市	Kaili	102.6	101.3	101.8	100.0
都 匀 市	Duyun	102.7	102.3	101.4	100.9

27-13 各市(州)乡村从业人员数(2014)

Rural Employment by Region

单位：万人 (10000 persons)

市(州)名称	City (State, Prefecture)	合计 Total	农业 Agric-ulture	工业 Indu-stry	建筑业 Constru-ction	交通运输仓储和邮政业 Trans-port, Storage and Post	信息传输、计算机服务和软件业 Information Transmission, Computer Services and Software	批发与零售业 Whole-sale and Retail Trade	住宿和餐饮业 Hotel and Catering Services	其他行业 Other Services
贵阳市	Guiyang	115.77	47.39	11.09	11.67	4.47	1.57	6.92	4.77	27.88
六盘水市	Liupanshui	142.95	74.69	11.93	8.01	3.81	0.31	4.43	2.04	37.74
遵义市	Zunyi	419.75	169.90	37.20	33.20	10.57	2.40	22.71	9.99	133.79
安顺市	Anshun	152.07	78.82	8.98	9.68	3.53	0.69	4.20	2.91	43.26
毕节市	Bijie	463.29	227.01	32.19	23.17	9.10	1.91	15.49	8.45	145.96
铜仁市	Tongren	224.77	108.00	13.52	13.91	3.90	0.77	6.12	3.34	75.23
黔西南州	Qianxinan	186.35	106.13	12.44	11.02	5.51	0.72	6.72	3.15	40.65
黔东南州	Qiandongnan	239.80	125.45	12.33	11.74	4.03	0.57	5.92	3.57	76.20
黔南州	Qiannan	222.51	109.97	12.22	11.47	4.32	0.49	7.30	3.99	72.76

27-14 各市(州)农业机械总动力及拥有量(2014)

Total Power and Possession of Agricultural Machinery by Region

市(州)名称	City (State, Prefecture)	农业机械总动力(万千瓦) Total Power of Agricultural Machinery (10000 kw)	大中型拖拉机(台) Number of Large and Medium-sized Agricultural (set)	小型拖拉机(台) Number of Small Tractors (set)	农用水泵(台) Agricultural Water Pump (unit)
贵阳市	Guiyang	181.69	2693	3523	29773
六盘水市	Liupanshui	185.00	1734	6267	22312
遵义市	Zunyi	408.55	7631	8070	112361
安顺市	Anshun	185.73	3805	3587	56465
毕节市	Bijie	365.62	5717	45060	35266
铜仁市	Tongren	293.25	3999	9788	74578
黔西南州	Qianxinan	252.37	3093	5177	50844
黔东南州	Qiandongnan	290.10	4001	5386	56555
黔南州	Qiannan	296.10	9476	8311	83717

注：资料来源于省农委。
Note:Data in this table are obtained from the Agricultural Committee of Guizhou Province.

27−15 各市(州)农林牧渔业总产值(2014)

Gross Output Value of Farming,Forestry, Animal Husbandary, Fishery and Their Services by Region

单位：亿元 (100 million yuan)

市(州)名称	City (State, Prefecture)	合计 Total	农业 Farming	林业 Forestry	牧业 Animal Husbandary	渔业 Fishery	农林牧渔服务业 Services of FFAF	2014年比2013年增长(%) Increase Rate in 2014 over 2013 (%)
贵阳市	Guiyang	170.68	120.00	1.04	46.35	2.22	1.07	6.8
六盘水市	Liupanshui	122.17	73.65	6.88	37.05	0.38	4.21	7.0
遵义市	Zunyi	456.56	292.25	21.62	128.29	9.31	5.09	6.9
安顺市	Anshun	131.55	81.52	3.28	41.53	4.43	0.79	6.9
毕节市	Bijie	389.29	268.66	4.91	108.70	1.32	5.68	7.0
铜仁市	Tongren	249.48	156.32	7.34	69.23	9.60	6.99	6.7
黔西南州	Qianxinan	192.61	121.02	8.62	52.76	7.95	2.27	7.0
黔东南州	Qiandongnan	210.11	111.04	29.34	56.24	9.22	4.27	7.1
黔南州	Qiannan	224.37	144.19	9.27	61.29	5.60	4.03	6.8

27−16 各市(州)农用化肥施用量(2014)

Consumption of Chemical Fertilizers for Agricultural Use by Region

单位：吨 (ton)

市(州)名称	City (State, Prefecture)	合计 Total	氮肥 Nitrogenous Fertilizer	磷肥 Phosphate Fertilizer	钾肥 Potash Fertilizer	复合肥 Compound Fertilizer	2014年比2013年增长(%) Increase Rate in 2014over2013(%)
贵阳市	Guiyang	62733	28384	5652.16	8952.5	19744.53	-2.3
六盘水市	Liupanshui	70570	45066	7136.5	5180	13187.5	2.2
遵义市	Zunyi	223664	118669	27095.4	23225	54674.6	1.6
安顺市	Anshun	65987	29178	11602.8	5393.64	19812.24	7.9
毕节市	Bijie	215773	111406	19367.52	20142.5	64857.66	0.4
铜仁市	Tongren	104884	50717	13590	9021	31556	4.5
黔西南州	Qianxinan	80638	47663	11519.68	9067.9	12387.4	-0.9
黔东南州	Qiandongnan	78943	28506	10790	5474	34173	-0.4
黔南州	Qiannan	109756	60284	11948	9801	27723	4.7

注：本表按折纯法计算。

Note:Consumption of chemical fertilizers is required in calculation to convert the gross weight into weight containing 100% effective component.

27－17 各市(州)主要农作物播种面积(2014)

Sown Areas of Major Farm Crops by Region

单位：千公顷 (1000 hectares)

市(州)名称	City (State, Prefecture)	总计 Total	粮食作物 Sown Areas of Grain Arops	#夏粮 Summer Grain Crops	按品种分 #稻谷 Rice	#小麦 Wheat	#玉米 Corn	#大豆 Soja	油菜籽 Rapeseeds	烤烟 Flue-cured Tobacco
贵阳市	Guiyang	286.62	112.74	26.91	33.37	3.95	40.74	6.75	38.97	8.95
六盘水市	Liupanshui	256.02	183.00	78.82	15.74	26.37	70.19	6.59	8.11	7.36
遵义市	Zunyi	1302.15	782.52	244.53	159.90	29.16	153.80	39.13	132.71	57.83
安顺市	Anshun	284.75	149.07	31.50	54.69	10.01	46.85	4.50	55.50	8.01
毕节市	Bijie	1170.66	681.00	284.88	41.77	67.02	173.62	35.66	62.75	58.39
铜仁市	Tongren	609.97	355.96	102.60	94.06	21.23	70.87	16.26	69.06	20.50
黔西南州	Qianxinan	441.54	250.05	70.39	51.31	52.18	85.74	5.70	28.62	25.34
黔东南州	Qiandongnan	596.17	308.05	81.46	127.59	4.21	46.40	10.16	55.11	14.07
黔南州	Qiannan	568.58	315.96	89.79	108.91	33.80	83.75	11.67	70.77	15.95

27－18 各市(州)主要农产品产量(2014)

Output of Major Farm Crops by Region

单位：万吨 (10000 tons)

市(州)名称	City (State, Prefecture)	粮食 Grain	#夏粮 Summer Grain Crops	2014年比2013年增长(%) Increase Rate in 2014 over 2013	油菜籽 Rapeseeds	烤烟 Fluecured Tobacco	茶叶 Tea	水果 Fruits
贵阳市	Guiyang	45.92	8.80	6.1	6.51	1.73	0.35	16.85
六盘水市	Liupanshui	81.41	19.83	0.6	0.99	1.53	0.06	4.81
遵义市	Zunyi	291.55	66.09	12.2	25.61	10.17	4.58	33.35
安顺市	Anshun	68.26	7.80	8.1	8.02	1.46	0.29	14.29
毕节市	Bijie	250.12	66.52	9.7	13.31	7.57	0.21	15.83
铜仁市	Tongren	134.46	33.85	14.6	11.20	3.24	2.31	21.18
黔西南州	Qianxinan	102.10	14.86	11.2	3.75	4.58	0.59	11.18
黔东南州	Qiandongnan	118.77	18.58	7.9	7.18	2.39	0.99	37.78
黔南州	Qiannan	125.72	20.82	6.4	10.13	2.66	1.34	41.11

27−19 各市(州)牲畜出、存栏量(2014)

Amount of Livestocks in Hand and Slaughtered by Region

单位：头、只 (head)

市(州)名称	City (State, Prefecture)	出栏 Amount of Slaughtered Livestocks			存栏 Amount of Livestock in Hand		
		猪 Hogs	牛 Cattle and Buffalo	羊 Sheep and Goats	猪 Hogs	牛 Cattle and Buffalo	羊 Sheep and Goats
贵阳市	Guiyang	1301543	57273	24704	956557	248441	42356
六盘水市	Liupanshui	1122187	76469	140676	1141553	337163	230072
遵义市	Zunyi	4711375	207897	614079	3504338	916675	806594
安顺市	Anshun	1202181	120804	60941	1205756	491386	83260
毕节市	Bijie	3505233	210705	373526	3254144	857159	655841
铜仁市	Tongren	2282767	140516	685736	2145268	571976	772549
黔西南州	Qianxinan	1502170	133707	277608	1375024	574330	530657
黔东南州	Qiandongnan	1810818	142118	188851	1399050	683515	312646
黔南州	Qiannan	2141500	147780	190211	1690004	650569	260309

27−20 各市(州)主要畜产品、水产品产量(2014)

Output of Major Livestock Products and Aquatic Products by Region

市(州)名称	City (State, Prefecture)	肉类总产量(万吨) Total Output of Meat (10000 tons)	2014年比2013年增长(%) Increase Rate in 2014 over 2013	禽蛋(万吨) Poulty Eggs (10000 tons)	水产品(吨) Aquatic Products(ton)
贵阳市	Guiyang	15.41	1.6	2.43	9800
六盘水市	Liupanshui	12.10	1.7	0.63	1014
遵义市	Zunyi	48.99	1.8	4.07	48381
安顺市	Anshun	14.78	2.1	1.53	14960
毕节市	Bijie	38.06	8.0	2.82	9984
铜仁市	Tongren	24.87	2.1	2.15	30747
黔西南州	Qianxinan	16.77	1.6	2.07	47400
黔东南州	Qiandongnan	19.48	3.6	1.10	26490
黔南州	Qiannan	21.02	2.2	0.35	21164

注：“水产品”数据来源于省农委。

Note: "Output of aquatic products" in this table are obtained from the Agricultural Commission of Guizhou province.

27-21 各市(州)规模以上工业增加值(2014)

Total Gross Industrial Value-added above Designated Size by Region

单位：亿元 (100 million yuan)

市(州)名称	City (State, Profecture)	工业增加值 Industrial Value-added	轻工业 Light Industry	重工业 Heavy Industry
贵 阳 市	Guiyang	636.06	315.84	320.22
六盘水市	Liupanshui	456.36	5.40	450.96
遵 义 市	Zunyi	818.86	605.60	213.26
安 顺 市	Anshun	129.29	27.85	101.44
毕 节 市	Bijie	304.31	72.96	231.35
铜 仁 市	Tongren	139.99	46.09	93.90
黔西南州	Qianxinan	224.65	18.41	206.24
黔东南州	Qiandongnan	155.47	32.58	122.89
黔 南 州	Qiannan	252.95	74.57	178.38

注：统计口径为年主营业务收入2000万元及以上的工业企业(下表同)。

Note: The Statistical caliber of the table refers to the industries which main business revenue achieve 20 millions yuan and above. (The same applies to the next table).

27-22 各市(州)规模以上工业企业主要工业产品产量(2014)

Ouput of Major Industrial Products above Designated Size by Region

市(州)名称	City (State, Profecture)	发电量(亿千瓦小时) Electricity (100 million kwh)	化 肥(万吨) Chemical Fertilizer(10000 tons)	水 泥(万吨) Cement (10000 tons)
贵 阳 市	Guiyang	114.29	324.12	1292.11
六盘水市	Liupanshui	347.30		920.05
遵 义 市	Zunyi	262.81	42.71	1740.88
安 顺 市	Anshun	66.85	16.63	737.70
毕 节 市	Bijie	338.79	22.68	824.72
铜 仁 市	Tongren	111.63	2.52	540.21
黔西南州	Qianxinan	266.58	32.55	908.23
黔东南州	Qiandongnan	88.40		643.35
黔 南 州	Qiannan	85.61	92.30	1779.64

27-23 各市(州)公路里程(2014)

Length of Highways by Region

单位：公里 (km)

市(州)名称	City (State, Profecture)	公路里程 Total Length of Highways	#等级公路 Expressway and class Ⅰ to Ⅳ Highway	#高速公路 Expressway	#有铺装路面(高级) Paved Road (advanced)	#沥青混凝土 Asphalt concrete
贵阳市	Guiyang	9709.72	8861.59	303.84	5653.93	808.13
六盘水市	Liupanshui	12899.62	10351.06	246.07	3394.44	1092.62
遵义市	Zunyi	27041.81	14705.48	682.95	6186.42	1799.81
安顺市	Anshun	13710.52	5337.09	286.00	2880.67	644.01
毕节市	Bijie	29443.47	18232.85	414.14	4708.68	977.84
铜仁市	Tongren	23819.57	12983.78	422.61	6918.45	795.12
黔西南州	Qianxinan	16847.24	11821.24	335.15	3894.86	736.39
黔东南州	Qiandongnan	28832.23	13871.92	700.19	6843.43	1356.19
黔南州	Qiannan	16775.01	11408.13	615.87	4603.80	1153.47

注：资料来源于省交通运输厅。

Note:Data in the table are obtained from Guizhou Provincial Department of Transportation.

27-24 各市(州)邮政、电信主要指标(2014)

Major Indicators of Telecommunications and Post by Region

市(州)名称	City (State, Profecture)	年末固定电话用户数(万户) Number of Telephone Subscribers at Year-end (10000 subscribers)	移动电话用户(万户) Number of Mobile Telephone Subscribers (10000 subscribers)	互联网宽带接入用户(万户) Number of Subscribers of Internet Service (10000 subscribers)	交换机总容量(万门) Capacity of Telephone Exchanges (10000 line)	报刊、杂志累计订销数(万份) Issue of Newspapers and Magazines (10000 copies)	邮政储蓄期末余额(亿元) Post Deposits at the Year-end(100 million yuan)
贵阳市	Guiyang	102.90	810.14	105.44	962.53	11968.66	65.82
六盘水市	Liupanshui	21.58	250.32	22.91	304.17	2990.88	35.98
遵义市	Zunyi	71.85	551.69	61.01	773.01	6698.47	161.60
安顺市	Anshun	19.73	172.35	20.62	298.72	2426.98	25.46
毕节市	Bijie	28.82	351.98	27.47	625.86	1996.40	63.79
铜仁市	Tongren	19.13	211.30	21.02	383.62	3338.67	74.65
黔西南州	Qianxinan	17.28	205.93	25.60	382.17	2526.88	40.08
黔东南州	Qiandongnan	31.22	269.29	35.11	458.62	4479.87	77.83
黔南州	Qiannan	26.62	236.84	28.59	428.58	3575.87	78.42

注：1.资料来源于省通信管理局、省邮政管理局、省邮政储蓄银行。2.交换机总容量指标市州汇总数不等于全省数据。

Note:1.Date in the table are obtained from the Provincal Communications Authority Bureau, the Provincial Postal Service and Postal Savings bank of China Guizhou Branch. 2.The sum total of Capacity of Telephone Erchanges by region is not equal to the total of province.

27-25 各市(州)教育事业主要指标(2014)

Major Indicators of Education by Region

市(州)名称	City (State, Prefecture)	高等教育 Higher Education		普通中学 Secondary Schools		小学 Primary Schools	
		学校数(所) Number of schools (unit)	在校学生(人) Students Enrollment (person)	学校数(所) Number of schools (unit)	在校学生(人) Students Enrollment (person)	学校数(所) Number of schools (unit)	在校学生(人) Students Enrollment (person)
贵阳市	Guiyang	31	381838	311	258105	571	320000
六盘水市	Liupanshui	2	10289	225	254276	673	255335
遵义市	Zunyi	6	66988	448	531452	1369	530582
安顺市	Anshun	4	17295	152	170589	714	233135
毕节市	Bijie	3	19543	466	680952	2170	842014
铜仁市	Tongren	3	23763	252	318748	1074	344112
黔西南州	Qianxinan	2	11105	266	249709	851	322908
黔东南州	Qiandongnan	3	32244	255	299114	916	337591
黔南州	Qiannan	5	28722	229	248037	937	277379

注：1.资料来源于省教育厅。2.高等教育学校数包括：中科院地化所、普通高等学校、成人高等学校，高等教育在校学生包括：研究生、普通高等教育、成人高等教育。

Note:1.Data in the table are obtained from Guizhou Provincial Department of Education.2.Institutions of higher education include Localization of Chinese Academy of Sciences,regular schools of higher education,and adult institutions of higher education.Students enrollment include those students enrolling in postgradu-ates education,ragular institutions of higher education and adult institution of higher education.

27-26 各市(州)卫生人员数(2014)

Number of Employed Persons in Health Care Institutions by Region

单位：人 (person)

市(州)名称	City (State, Prefecture)	总计 Total	卫生技术人员 Medical Technical Personnel	#执业(助理)医师 Licensed (Assistant) Doctors	执业医师 Licensed Doctor	#注册护士 Registered Nurse	#药师(士) Pharmacist	#技师(士) Laboratory Technician	乡村医生和卫生员 Village Doctors and Assistants	其他技术人员 Other Technical Personnel	管理人员 Admini-strative Personnel	工勤技能人员 Logistics Technical Workers
贵阳市	Guiyang	43364	34776	13043	12008	15501	1526	1788	3314	1786	2196	2875
六盘水市	Liupanshui	18105	12368	4267	3374	4823	502	705	1207	668	922	1151
遵义市	Zunyi	43666	31411	10461	8274	12613	1355	1789	3144	2043	1792	2417
安顺市	Anshun	12440	8354	2785	2214	3415	322	476	798	419	725	536
毕节市	Bijie	37022	24319	7307	4949	9644	874	1269	2143	1601	1497	1350
铜仁市	Tongren	22374	14990	4275	3444	5630	572	958	1530	686	925	986
黔西南州	Qianxinan	15538	11005	3891	3005	4007	468	576	1044	500	714	682
黔东南州	Qiandongnan	25370	18209	6123	4215	6639	678	1104	1782	760	1006	833
黔南州	Qiannan	19438	14367	5650	4137	4859	609	889	1498	406	1028	720

注：资料来源于省卫生计生委。(以下相关表同)

Note:Data in the table are obtained from Guizhou Provincial Department of Health and Fanily Planning(the same applies to relative tables below).

27-27 各市(州)每千人口拥有卫生技术人员数(2014)

Medical Technical Personnel in Health Care Institutions Per 1000 Persons by Region

单位：人 (person)

市(州)名称	City (State, Prefecture)	卫生技术人员 Medical Technical Personnel		执业(助理)医师 Lecensed(Assistant) Doctors		注册护士 Registered Nurses	
		合计 Total	每千人口拥有 Per 1000 Person	合计 Total	每千人口拥有 Per 1000 Person	合计 Total	每千人口拥有 Per 1000 Person
贵阳市	Guiyang	34776	9.08	13043	3.41	15501	4.05
六盘水市	Liupanshui	12368	3.77	4267	1.30	4823	1.47
遵义市	Zunyi	31411	3.99	10461	1.33	12613	1.60
安顺市	Anshun	8354	2.88	2785	0.96	3415	1.18
毕节市	Bijie	24319	2.76	7307	0.83	9644	1.09
铜仁市	Tongren	14990	3.47	4275	0.99	5630	1.30
黔西南州	Qianxinan	11005	3.13	3891	1.11	4007	1.14
黔东南州	Qiandongnan	18209	3.91	6123	1.31	6639	1.42
黔南州	Qiannan	14367	3.54	5650	1.39	4859	1.20

注：每千人口数根据2014年各市（州）户籍人口数计算。

Note:Number per thousand population are based on household population of 2014.

27-28 各市(州) 社区卫生服务中心(站)医疗服务情况(2014)

Medical Services of Community Health Service Centers(Stations) by Region

市(州)名称	City (State, Prefecture)	社区卫生服务中心 Community Health Service Centers						社区卫生服务站 Community Health Service Stations	
		诊疗人次(万人次) Visits (10 000 person-times)	入院人数(人) Inpatients (person)	病床使用率(%) Utilization Rate (%)	出院者平均住院日(日) Average Stay Days in Hospital (day)	医师日均担负诊疗人次(人次) Daily Visits Each Doctor (person-time)	医师日均担负住院床日(日) Daily Inpatients Each Doctor (day)	诊疗人次(万人次) Visits (10 000 person-times)	医师日均担负诊疗人次(人次) Daily Visits Each Doctor (person-time)
贵阳市	Guiyang	74.38	7593	36.18	8.80	7.90	0.70	46.29	9.00
六盘水市	Liupanshui	6.93	4480	49.36	1.50	16.30	3.50	43.33	8.50
遵义市	Zunyi	35.65	24974	71.47	4.60	9.80	2.30	82.97	10.10
安顺市	Anshun	6.16	8002	74.98	6.40	7.20	4.30	19.01	6.40
毕节市	Bijie	20.28	16198	60.73	4.90	6.50	2.30	6.41	8.80
铜仁市	Tongren	14.49	5945	41.29	4.70	12.60	1.70	20.46	13.00
黔西南州	Qianxinan							32.12	11.50
黔东南州	Qiandongnan	7.54	5008	71.82	4.10	4.00	0.80	0.12	2.50
黔南州	Qiannan	18.44	8754	58.49	4.00	7.20	1.00	9.91	12.80

注:黔西南州无社区卫生服务中心。

Note:Nan zhou where is eastern to Guizhou has no hygiene service center.

27−29 各市(州)医疗卫生机构服务情况(2014)

Services in Hospitals by Region

市(州)名称	City (State, Prefecture)	诊疗人次(万人次) Visits (10 000 person-times)	#医院 Hospital	#农村乡镇卫生院 Rural Township Hospitals	入院人数(万人) Inpatients (10000 persons)	#医院 Hospital	#农村乡镇卫生院 Rural Township Hospitals	出院人数(万人) Patients Discharged from Hosptials (10000 persons)	#医院 Hospital	#农村乡镇卫生院 Rural Township Hospitals
贵阳市	Guiyang	2569.43	1177.67	212.52	76.54	67.16	3.62	74.98	66.37	3.56
六盘水市	Liupanshui	704.44	234.44	166.93	39.64	26.55	10.58	39.61	26.55	10.55
遵义市	Zunyi	2719.52	877.59	463.91	144.14	91.88	47.86	142.99	91.05	47.59
安顺市	Anshun	668.80	220.08	82.75	41.56	25.32	12.88	41.03	24.85	12.84
毕节市	Bijie	1790.28	502.57	339.41	95.29	67.37	23.12	94.40	66.50	23.15
铜仁市	Tongren	1126.42	348.82	278.04	64.02	45.45	16.36	63.51	45.15	16.18
黔西南州	Qianxinan	1005.67	304.14	192.92	48.60	30.28	14.61	48.02	29.83	14.50
黔东南州	Qiandongnan	1267.15	410.48	285.70	70.47	47.38	20.76	69.98	47.05	20.63
黔南州	Qiannan	1158.52	398.82	331.89	58.74	42.02	13.47	58.29	41.62	13.42

27−29 续表 continued

市(州)名称	City (State, Prefecture)	每百门诊急诊入院人数(人) Inpatientsper 100 Outpatient and Emergency Visits (person)	#医院 Hospital	#农村乡镇卫生院 Rural Township Hospitals	病床使用率(%) Utilization Rate of Beds (%)	#医院 Hospital	#农村乡镇卫生院 Rural Township Hospitals	出院者平均住院日(天) Average Stay Days in Hospital (day)	#医院 Hospital	#农村乡镇卫生院 Rural Township Hospitals
贵阳市	Guiyang	4.84	5.83	1.72	85.50	89.72	44.32	10.60	11.00	5.50
六盘水市	Liupanshui	8.63	11.85	6.59	75.80	79.06	64.15	8.50	9.70	6.30
遵义市	Zunyi	10.09	10.77	10.86	86.33	90.29	77.11	6.90	8.20	4.50
安顺市	Anshun	12.68	11.87	18.03	79.56	84.05	63.56	6.20	8.20	2.70
毕节市	Bijie	11.35	14.35	7.14	62.42	67.48	47.69	6.90	7.60	5.30
铜仁市	Tongren	9.70	13.87	6.17	71.71	77.44	57.30	6.70	7.40	5.00
黔西南州	Qianxinan	9.27	10.26	8.00	78.61	88.43	55.62	5.70	7.10	3.40
黔东南州	Qiandongnan	10.15	12.16	7.63	75.61	82.88	59.02	7.00	8.10	4.60
黔南州	Qiannan	7.74	10.94	4.21	79.86	87.45	67.61	7.10	8.10	5.30

27−30 各市(州)火灾(2014)

Fires by Region

市(州)名称	City (State, Prefecture)	火灾(起) Fire Accidents (case)	死亡(人) Deaths (person)	受伤(人) Injuries (person)	直接财产损失(万元) Averoge Number of Fires(10000 yuan)
贵阳市	Guiyang	1729	12	4	7343
六盘水市	Liupanshui	174			79
遵义市	Zunyi	310	6	3	2033
安顺市	Qiandongnan	157	1	7	552
毕节市	Bijie	414	6	1	1212
铜仁市	Tongren	211	6	2	823
黔西南州	Qianxinan	477	6	3	481
黔东南州	Qiannan	491	16	5	4373
黔南州	Anshun	258	6	2	771

注：资料来源于省公安厅。
Note:Data in the table are obtained from Guizhou Provincial Department of Public Security.

27−31 各县(市、区、特区)地区生产总值(2014)

Gross Domestic Product by County(City,District,Special region)

单位：亿元 (100 million yuan)

县(市、区、特区)名称	County (City, District, Special region)	地区生产总值 Gross Domestic Product	第一产业 Primary Industry	第二产业 Secondary Industry	#工业 Industry	第三产业 Tertiary Industry	2014年比2013年增长(%) Increase Rate in 2014over 2013(%)
南明区	Nanming	528.51	3.33	117.37	45.81	407.81	15.5
云岩区	Yunyan	615.91	0.52	186.30	138.21	429.09	13.8
花溪区	Huaxi	362.52	14.88	196.84	156.24	150.80	14.8
乌当区	Wudang	123.73	11.55	59.66	46.56	52.52	16.4
白云区	Baiyun	150.75	4.67	78.72	68.93	67.36	17.3
观山湖区	Guanshanhu	131.87	2.46	47.56	17.53	81.85	15.4
开阳县	Kaiyang	160.89	23.03	89.71	66.16	48.15	16.3
息烽县	Xifeng	128.47	12.56	68.06	61.34	47.85	16.4
修文县	Xiuwen	119.78	16.00	54.85	42.16	48.93	17.5
清镇市	Qingzhen	219.39	19.01	100.19	48.91	100.19	14.3
钟山区	Zhongshan	343.66	4.50	181.18	163.33	157.98	15.9
六枝特区	Liuzhi	127.52	17.79	51.09	43.53	58.64	15.9
水城县	Shuicheng	181.11	20.52	101.95	87.52	58.64	15.8
盘　县	Panxian	426.30	32.93	281.37	243.04	112.00	16.1
红花岗区	Honghuagang	299.39	13.57	92.91	70.79	192.91	16.0
汇川区	Huicuan	216.60	8.79	108.51	96.94	99.30	15.8
遵义县	Zunyi	273.97	49.17	134.99	105.68	89.81	16.8
桐梓县	Tongzi	108.54	22.71	44.32	29.37	41.51	16.5
绥阳县	Suiyang	73.77	24.31	21.05	13.57	28.41	17.0
正安县	Zhengan	59.81	19.11	13.89	6.47	26.81	17.4
※道真县	Daozhen	39.75	13.76	7.49	4.06	18.50	17.8
※务川县	Wuchuan	42.99	15.13	8.57	3.83	19.29	16.5
凤冈县	Fenggang	49.92	17.03	11.97	6.57	20.92	16.7
湄潭县	Meitan	66.15	18.05	18.72	13.55	29.38	16.7
余庆县	Yuqing	54.92	13.86	17.73	10.28	23.33	17.6
习水县	Xishui	112.55	20.64	51.79	36.48	40.12	16.9
赤水市	Chishui	71.45	11.85	32.86	26.49	26.74	16.6
仁怀市	Renhuai	442.87	19.49	306.20	296.73	117.18	13.4
西秀区	Xixiu	201.39	21.09	75.62	66.95	104.68	16.2
平坝区	Pingba	87.64	10.51	49.80	39.09	27.33	17.1
普定县	Puding	71.20	11.05	31.16	26.74	28.99	15.0
※镇宁县	Zhenning	64.14	10.06	19.44	10.34	34.64	15.4
※关岭县	Guanling	60.90	12.49	16.21	5.88	32.20	15.2
※紫云县	Ziyun	45.02	13.36	8.86	4.10	22.80	14.7
七星关区	Qixingguan	258.90	47.87	97.37	79.65	113.66	15.4
大方县	Dafang	158.74	29.58	67.38	54.55	61.78	15.4
黔西县	Qianxi	158.64	26.99	68.02	52.45	63.63	15.8
金沙县	Jinsha	187.53	23.94	105.01	88.48	58.58	16.0
织金县	Zhijin	136.35	27.06	54.22	38.73	55.07	15.8
纳雍县	Nayong	148.69	21.98	79.25	70.59	47.46	15.9
※威宁县	Weining	152.03	47.46	43.12	33.26	61.45	15.0
赫章县	Hezhang	91.07	27.89	21.31	17.31	41.87	13.9
碧江区	Bijiang	110.81	9.10	42.94	30.78	58.77	17.1
万山区	Wanshan	31.11	6.54	13.91	10.78	10.66	16.6

注：1.※为少数民族自治县(以下相关表同)。2.表中绝对数按当年价格计算，增长速度按可比价格计算。

Note:1.Counties with ※ refer to autonomous counties(The relative tables in this chapter are the same).2.Absolute Figures in the table are calculated at prices,and increase rates are calculated at comparable prices.

27-31 续表 continued

单位：亿元 (100 million yuan)

县(市、区、特区)名 称	County (City, District, Special region)	地区生产总值 Gross Domestic Product	第一产业 Primary Industry	第二产业 Secondary Industry	#工 业 Industry	第三产业 Tertiary Industry	2014年比2013年增长(%) Increase Rate in 2014 over 2013(%)
江口县	Jiangkou	33.42	8.37	9.84	4.97	15.21	14.2
※玉屏县	Yuping	55.44	5.87	31.21	28.07	18.36	15.8
石阡县	Shiqian	47.67	14.97	7.21	4.16	25.49	15.0
思南县	Sinan	88.20	23.03	21.16	13.81	44.01	15.5
※印江县	Yinjiang	58.91	18.82	12.81	9.18	27.28	16.1
德江县	Dejiang	73.30	20.98	14.91	9.37	37.41	15.5
※沿河县	Yanhe	72.60	19.83	13.53	7.61	39.24	15.5
※松桃县	Songtao	88.93	22.16	29.65	24.61	37.12	15.5
兴义市	Xingyi	282.83	30.71	106.67	93.23	145.45	16.0
兴仁县	Xingren	91.93	14.53	34.88	27.30	42.52	15.7
普安县	Puan	50.45	8.67	23.27	19.16	18.51	15.9
晴隆县	Qinglong	44.45	8.56	16.35	12.50	19.54	16.1
贞丰县	Zhenfeng	76.54	13.07	39.32	34.03	24.15	15.8
望谟县	Wangmo	36.16	12.44	4.79	2.70	18.93	14.1
册亨县	Ceheng	28.96	9.28	3.64	2.66	16.04	14.1
安龙县	Anlong	73.05	16.17	24.88	21.04	32.00	15.7
凯里市	Kaili	186.71	11.46	62.00	41.89	113.25	17.4
黄平县	Huangping	37.43	10.03	4.73	2.41	22.67	15.7
施秉县	Shibing	27.33	5.86	7.24	5.73	14.23	14.3
三穗县	Sansui	30.81	5.50	9.09	5.49	16.22	17.3
镇远县	Zhenyuan	54.27	9.88	24.87	20.75	19.52	16.3
岑巩县	Cengong	31.96	6.26	10.58	9.48	15.12	15.7
天柱县	Tianzhu	59.10	10.92	23.06	18.66	25.12	16.3
锦屏县	Jinping	30.34	4.70	10.69	9.59	14.95	16.3
剑河县	Jianhe	31.18	7.34	5.74	3.75	18.10	14.1
台江县	Taijiang	22.20	4.44	5.02	3.37	12.74	15.5
黎平县	Liping	57.25	11.73	16.61	8.14	28.91	15.2
榕江县	Rongjiang	41.40	11.65	11.65	5.48	18.10	15.0
从江县	Congjiang	41.07	10.78	12.35	4.38	17.94	15.3
雷山县	Leishan	20.98	4.68	4.71	2.71	11.59	14.8
麻江县	Majiang	22.32	4.63	6.44	5.53	11.25	10.5
丹寨县	Danzhai	21.34	4.67	6.20	3.75	10.47	15.1
都匀市	Duyun	153.92	14.23	54.60	32.32	85.09	15.4
福泉市	Fuquan	112.04	12.44	51.24	37.74	48.36	16.5
荔波县	Libo	41.49	8.43	12.15	9.75	20.91	15.5
贵定县	Guiding	62.42	9.45	27.78	20.14	25.19	16.1
瓮安县	Wengan	86.85	17.47	32.77	29.04	36.61	15.9
独山县	Dushan	55.01	13.76	17.81	15.98	23.44	16.5
平塘县	Pingtang	42.41	13.78	8.11	5.05	20.52	16.1
罗甸县	Luodian	50.82	12.48	17.77	13.77	20.57	15.6
长顺县	Changshun	41.37	10.45	10.45	8.88	20.47	15.3
龙里县	Longli	64.33	8.46	40.32	32.33	15.55	17.1
惠水县	Huishui	63.47	17.25	21.60	17.73	24.62	15.3
※三都县	Sandu	43.74	13.05	6.64	2.84	24.05	14.2

27-32 各县(市、区、特区)人均地区生产总值(2014)

Per Capita Gross Domestic Product by County(City，District，Special region)

单位：元 (yuan)

县(市、区、特区)名称	County (City, District, Special region)	人均地区生产总值 Per Capita Gross Domestic Product(yuan)	位次 Order
南明区	Nanming	60970	3
云岩区	Yunyan	62117	2
花溪区	Huaxi	57351	5
乌当区	Wudang	52992	9
白云区	Baiyun	55285	8
观山湖区	Guanshanhu	56871	7
开阳县	Kaiyang	44260	15
息烽县	Xifeng	58515	4
修文县	Xiuwen	45981	13
清镇市	Qingzhen	46990	11
钟山区	Zhongshan	57344	6
六枝特区	Liuzhi	25648	32
水城县	Shuicheng	24496	34
盘　县	Panxian	40896	16
红花岗区	Honghuagang	44282	14
汇川区	Huichuan	47819	10
遵义县	Zunyi	29217	27
桐梓县	Tongzi	20756	46
绥阳县	Suiyang	19385	59
正安县	Zhengan	15592	79
※道真县	Daozhen	16275	75
※务川县	Wuchuan	13473	87
凤冈县	Fenggang	16101	77
湄潭县	Meitan	17558	69
余庆县	Yuqing	23278	35
习水县	Xishui	21734	44
赤水市	Chishui	29693	25
仁怀市	Renhuai	80471	1
西秀区	Xixiu	26233	30
平坝区	Pingba	29331	26
普定县	Puding	18760	61
※镇宁县	Zhenning	22544	39
※关岭县	Guanling	20134	51
※紫云县	Ziyun	16589	73
七星关区	Qixingguan	22814	37
大方县	Dafang	20372	49
黔西县	Qianxi	22990	36
金沙县	Jinsha	33725	23
织金县	Zhijin	17361	71
纳雍县	Nayong	22095	42
※威宁县	Weining	11992	88
赫章县	Hezhang	13937	86
碧江区	Bijiang	36055	19
万山区	Wanshan	27158	28
江口县	Jiangkou	19289	60
※玉屏县	Yuping	46352	12
石阡县	Shiqian	15657	78
思南县	Sinan	17667	68
※印江县	Yinjiang	20722	47
德江县	Dejiang	19852	54
※沿河县	Yanhe	16125	76
※松桃县	Songtao	18223	63
兴义市	Xingyi	35861	20
兴仁县	Xingren	21951	43
普安县	Puan	19705	58
晴隆县	Qinglong	17919	66
贞丰县	Zhenfeng	25059	33
望谟县	Wangmo	14544	82
册亨县	Ceheng	15128	80
安龙县	Anlong	20314	50
凯里市	Kaili	34997	21
黄平县	Huangping	14245	84
施秉县	Shibing	20910	45
三穗县	Sansui	19833	55
镇远县	Zhenyuan	26629	29
岑巩县	Cengong	19863	53
天柱县	Tianzhu	22678	38
锦屏县	Jinping	19746	57
剑河县	Jianhe	17250	72
台江县	Taijiang	19982	52
黎平县	Liping	14719	81
榕江县	Rongjiang	14460	83
从江县	Congjiang	14128	85
雷山县	Leishan	17947	65
麻江县	Majiang	18280	62
丹寨县	Danzhai	17435	70
都匀市	Duyun	33822	22
福泉市	Fuquan	38342	18
荔波县	Libo	32619	24
贵定县	Guiding	26095	31
瓮安县	Wengan	22362	40
独山县	Dushan	20422	48
平塘县	Pingtang	17760	67
罗甸县	Luodian	19817	56
长顺县	Changshun	22211	41
龙里县	Longli	40180	17
惠水县	Huishui	17949	64
※三都县	Sandu	16361	74

27-33 各县(市、区、特区)年末常住人口

Permanent Population at Year-end by County(City,District,Special region)

单位：万人 (10000 persons)

县(市、区、特区)名 称	County (City，District，Special region)	2010	2011	2012	2013	2014
南明区	Nanming	83.07	84.47	85.06	86.30	87.07
云岩区	Yunyan	95.83	97.60	98.39	99.09	99.21
花溪区	Huaxi	36.05	36.39	36.72	63.08	63.34
乌当区	Wudang	37.75	39.22	41.68	23.23	23.47
白云区	Baiyun	26.49	26.87	27.13	27.18	27.35
观山湖区	Guanshanhu	24.85	25.60	25.89	22.72	23.66
开阳县	Kaiyang	35.85	35.74	35.92	36.29	36.42
息烽县	Xifeng	21.31	21.33	21.53	21.90	22.01
修文县	Xiuwen	24.93	25.17	25.48	25.91	26.19
清镇市	Qingzhen	46.80	46.96	47.39	46.49	46.88
钟山区	Zhongshan	61.76	61.88	62.28	59.78	60.08
六枝特区	Liuzhi	49.56	49.36	49.46	49.66	49.78
水城县	Shuicheng	70.52	70.29	70.43	73.86	74.01
盘 县	Panxian	103.59	103.47	103.73	104.15	104.33
红花岗区	Honghuagang	65.74	66.83	67.17	67.48	67.74
汇川区	Huichuan	43.90	44.78	45.01	45.23	45.36
遵义县	Zunyi	94.52	93.24	93.23	93.64	93.90
桐梓县	Tongzi	52.23	51.68	51.94	52.20	52.38
绥阳县	Suiyang	38.04	37.87	38.06	38.15	37.96
正安县	Zhengan	38.97	38.14	38.14	38.33	38.39
※道真县	Daozhen	24.42	24.13	24.26	24.38	24.47
※务川县	Wuchuan	32.19	31.70	31.70	31.87	31.95
凤冈县	Fenggang	31.32	30.67	30.83	30.98	31.03
湄潭县	Meitan	37.77	37.27	37.46	37.64	37.71
余庆县	Yuqing	23.49	23.34	23.45	23.57	23.62
习水县	Xishui	52.32	51.77	51.77	51.77	51.80
赤水市	Chishui	23.72	23.82	23.92	24.04	24.09
仁怀市	Renhuai	54.66	54.77	54.76	54.98	55.09
西秀区	Xixiu	76.63	75.95	76.07	76.64	76.90
平坝区	Pingba	29.85	29.58	29.62	29.83	29.93
普定县	Puding	37.88	37.54	37.59	37.89	38.02
※镇宁县	Zhenning	28.41	28.15	28.20	28.40	28.49
※关岭县	Guanling	30.20	29.95	29.99	30.21	30.28
※紫云县	Ziyun	27.07	26.82	26.87	27.08	27.19
七星关区	Qixingguan	113.86	113.00	113.20	113.47	113.50
大方县	Dafang	77.74	78.00	77.73	77.90	77.94
黔西县	Qianxi	69.68	69.00	68.84	68.99	69.02
金沙县	Jinsha	56.15	56.00	55.47	55.59	55.62
织金县	Zhijin	78.48	78.00	78.36	78.53	78.55
纳雍县	Nayong	67.09	67.00	67.14	67.28	67.31
※威宁县	Weining	126.56	126.00	126.48	126.73	126.82
赫章县	Hezhang	65.01	65.00	65.19	65.33	65.36
碧江区	Bijiang	36.23	29.52	30.24	30.54	30.93
万山区	Wanshan	4.79	11.25	11.33	11.43	11.48

注：由于行政区划调整，2013年起花溪区、乌当区、观山湖区、清镇市、凯里市、麻江县数据为现行行政区划统计数。

Note:Due to admisoration division adjustent, from 2013, data refers to statistics of the current administration division.

27-33 续表 continued

单位：万人 (10000 persons)

县(市、区、特区)名 称	County (City, District, Special region)	2010	2011	2012	2013	2014
江口县	Jiangkou	17.30	17.21	17.29	17.29	17.36
※玉屏县	Yuping	11.86	11.75	11.83	11.93	11.99
石阡县	Shiqian	30.45	30.27	30.35	30.42	30.47
思南县	Sinan	49.99	49.72	49.79	49.90	49.95
※印江县	Yinjiang	28.44	28.29	28.35	28.40	28.46
德江县	Dejiang	36.84	36.62	36.71	36.80	37.05
※沿河县	Yanhe	45.01	44.88	44.96	45.02	45.03
※松桃县	Songtao	48.72	48.49	48.59	48.67	48.93
兴义市	Xingyi	78.53	78.20	78.50	78.88	78.86
兴仁县	Xingren	41.85	41.70	41.90	41.98	41.78
普安县	Puan	25.47	25.40	25.50	25.61	25.60
晴隆县	Qinglong	24.70	24.60	24.70	24.81	24.80
贞丰县	Zhenfeng	30.42	30.30	30.40	30.55	30.54
望谟县	Wangmo	25.20	25.10	25.20	25.26	24.46
册亨县	Ceheng	19.07	19.00	19.10	19.15	19.14
安龙县	Anlong	35.79	35.70	35.90	35.98	35.94
凯里市	Kaili	47.92	48.22	48.57	53.29	53.41
黄平县	Huangping	26.34	26.14	26.21	26.30	26.25
施秉县	Shibing	13.06	13.02	13.03	13.08	13.06
三穗县	Sansui	15.60	15.50	15.53	15.57	15.50
镇远县	Zhenyuan	20.40	20.28	20.32	20.40	20.36
岑巩县	Cengong	16.22	16.04	16.10	16.14	16.04
天柱县	Tianzhu	26.42	25.80	26.00	26.08	26.04
锦屏县	Jinping	15.51	15.26	15.34	15.38	15.35
剑河县	Jianhe	18.08	18.02	18.04	18.09	18.06
台江县	Taijiang	11.24	11.02	11.09	11.12	11.10
黎平县	Liping	39.16	38.70	38.85	38.93	38.86
榕江县	Rongjiang	28.68	28.60	28.63	28.67	28.59
从江县	Congjiang	29.13	29.07	29.09	29.12	29.02
雷山县	Leishan	11.73	11.63	11.67	11.70	11.68
麻江县	Majiang	16.78	16.52	16.60	12.22	12.20
丹寨县	Danzhai	12.26	12.17	12.20	12.25	12.23
都匀市	Duyun	44.43	44.04	44.29	45.54	45.48
福泉市	Fuquan	28.44	28.17	27.93	29.24	29.20
荔波县	Libo	14.50	14.39	14.50	12.73	12.71
贵定县	Guiding	23.13	22.95	23.10	23.92	23.92
瓮安县	Wengan	38.10	37.74	38.43	38.86	38.82
独山县	Dushan	26.53	26.34	25.93	26.95	26.93
平塘县	Pingtang	22.86	22.71	23.02	23.88	23.88
罗甸县	Luodian	25.68	25.55	25.00	25.64	25.65
长顺县	Changshun	19.12	18.98	18.64	18.64	18.62
龙里县	Longli	18.09	17.95	17.96	16.03	15.99
惠水县	Huishui	34.27	34.04	34.99	35.37	35.35
※三都县	Sandu	28.36	28.14	28.85	26.73	26.74

27-34 各县(市、区、特区)户籍人口(2014)

Household Registered Population by County (City，District，Special region)

单位：万人 (10000 persons)

县(市、区、特区)名称	County (City，District，Special region)	年末总人口 Permanent Population at the year-end	县(市、区、特区)名称	County (City，District，Special region)	年末总人口 Permanent Population at the year-end
南明区	Nanming	56.56	万山区	Wanshan	15.69
云岩区	Yunyan	62.82	江口县	Jiangkou	24.36
花溪区	Huaxi	49.29	※玉屏县	Yuping	15.44
乌当区	Wudang	20.13	石阡县	Shiqian	41.59
白云区	Baiyun	19.71	思南县	Sinan	67.69
观山湖区	Guanshanhu	22.20	※印江县	Yinjiang	44.49
开阳县	Kaiyang	44.40	德江县	Dejiang	54.08
息烽县	Xifeng	26.31	※沿河县	Yanhe	66.84
修文县	Xiuwen	30.84	※松桃县	Songtao	71.05
清镇市	Qingzhen	50.65			
			兴义市	Xingyi	84.26
钟山区	Zhongshan	47.59	兴仁县	Xingren	54.47
六枝特区	Liuzhi	71.44	普安县	Puan	33.99
水城县	Shuicheng	89.25	晴隆县	Qinglong	34.16
盘　县	Panxian	120.06	贞丰县	Zhenfeng	42.28
			望谟县	Wangmo	31.69
红花岗区	Honghuagang	52.90	册亨县	Ceheng	23.86
汇川区	Huichuan	36.78	安龙县	Anlong	47.15
遵义县	Zunyi	123.53			
桐梓县	Tongzi	74.21	凯里市	Kaili	50.58
绥阳县	Suiyang	55.55	黄平县	Huangping	38.20
正安县	Zhengan	64.71	施秉县	Shibing	17.18
※道真县	Daozhen	34.56	三穗县	Sansui	22.44
※务川县	Wuchuan	46.17	镇远县	Zhenyuan	27.32
凤冈县	Fenggang	43.78	岑巩县	Cengong	22.91
湄潭县	Meitan	49.56	天柱县	Tianzhu	40.86
余庆县	Yuqing	30.39	锦屏县	Jinping	22.95
习水县	Xishui	74.57	剑河县	Jianhe	26.17
赤水市	Chishui	31.01	台江县	Taijiang	16.36
仁怀市	Renhuai	69.31	黎平县	Liping	53.83
			榕江县	Rongjiang	36.40
西秀区	Xixiu	89.22	从江县	Congjiang	35.24
平坝区	Pingba	36.44	雷山县	Leishan	15.45
普定县	Puding	48.38	麻江县	Majiang	22.84
※镇宁县	Zhenning	38.94	丹寨县	Danzhai	17.47
※关岭县	Guanling	38.51			
※紫云县	Ziyun	38.49	都匀市	Duyun	48.26
			福泉市	Fuquan	32.72
七星关区	Qixingguan	157.29	荔波县	Libo	17.53
大方县	Dafang	113.98	贵定县	Guiding	29.23
黔西县	Qianxi	96.86	瓮安县	Wengan	46.96
金沙县	Jinsha	67.41	独山县	Dushan	34.97
织金县	Zhijin	113.76	平塘县	Pingtang	32.38
纳雍县	Nayong	101.81	罗甸县	Luodian	34.60
※威宁县	Weining	147.62	长顺县	Changshun	25.66
赫章县	Hezhang	82.05	龙里县	Longli	22.64
			惠水县	Huishui	44.91
碧江区	Bijiang	31.03	※三都县	Sandu	36.22

注：资料来源于省公安厅。
Note: Data in the table above are obtained from the Public Security Department of Guizhou Province.

27-35 各县(市、区、特区)固定资产投资

Investment in Fixed Assets by County(City,District,Special region)

单位：万元 (10000 yuan)

县(市、区、特区)名称	County (City,District, Special region)	2013	2014	2014年比2013年增长(%) Increase Ratein 2014 over 2013(%)
南明区	Nanming	3761574	4337026	15.3
云岩区	Yunyan	2869976	3435173	19.7
花溪区	Huaxi	3173122	3859756	21.6
乌当区	Wudang	1314721	1548985	17.8
白云区	Baiyun	2984541	3573608	19.7
观山湖区	Guanshanhu	3074241	3564560	15.9
开阳县	Kaiyang	2203196	2680386	21.7
息烽县	Xifeng	1731600	2282607	31.8
修文县	Xiuwen	1719768	2095575	21.9
清镇市	Qingzhen	2145873	2586171	20.5
钟山区	Zhongshan	2562435	3239893	26.4
六枝特区	Liuzhi	1525674	1936080	26.9
水城县	Shuicheng	2383072	3005603	26.1
盘　县	Panxian	4077028	5179742	27.0
红花岗区	Honghuagang	2589403	3356411	29.6
汇川区	Huicuan	1191782	1574569	32.1
遵义县	Zunyi	2669970	3471798	30.0
桐梓县	Tongzi	1286573	1551157	20.6
绥阳县	Suiyang	754939	979421	29.7
正安县	Zhengan	556803	707501	27.1
※道真县	Daozhen	402228	512568	27.4
※务川县	Wuchuan	443489	581846	31.2
凤冈县	Fenggang	383370	500731	30.6
湄潭县	Meitan	803332	1040694	29.5
余庆县	Yuqing	539482	698898	29.5
习水县	Xishui	1403007	1789752	27.6
赤水市	Chishui	910186	1181809	29.8
仁怀市	Renhuai	1726010	2575812	49.2
西秀区	Xixiu	1853094	3330859	79.7
平坝区	Pingba	658957	1418582	115.3
普定县	Puding	573228	845817	47.6
※镇宁县	Zhenning	438352	627338	43.1
※关岭县	Guanling	305519	457537	49.8
※紫云县	Ziyun	271973	407261	49.7
七星关区	Qixingguan	2415326	3062606	26.8
大方县	Dafang	1395386	1741211	24.8
黔西县	Qianxi	1698953	1854304	9.1
金沙县	Jinsha	2373936	3011213	26.8
织金县	Zhijin	1883512	2475623	31.4
纳雍县	Nayong	1692315	2113202	24.9
※威宁县	Weining	1562973	1810634	15.8
赫章县	Hezhang	881396	1095632	24.3
碧江区	Bijiang	1322411	1667102	26.1
万山区	Wanshan	400624	508548	26.9

注：统计口径为计划总投资50万元及以上固定资产项目投资和房地产开发项目投资，不包括跨县(市、区)域项目投资及220KV及以上输电线路投资。

Note: Data in the table refers to those projects that planned to invest 500,000 yuan at least in fixed assets and real estate development. Data in the table do not include investment in cross-regional projects,nor investment in power transmission and distribution projects as the voltage reach 220KV and above.

27−35 续表 continued

单位：万元 (10000 yuan)

县(市、区、特区)名 称	County (City,District, Special region)	2013	2014	2014年比2013年增长(%) Increase Ratein 2014 over 2013(%)
江口县	Jiangkou	511733	651508	27.3
※玉屏县	Yuping	464836	585552	26.0
石阡县	Shiqian	353791	448443	26.8
思南县	Sinan	1068861	1358292	27.1
※印江县	Yinjiang	622016	788458	26.8
德江县	Dejiang	579909	740747	27.7
※沿河县	Yanhe	921574	1161750	26.1
※松桃县	Songtao	902006	1148705	27.4
兴义市	Xingyi	2433114	3176955	30.6
兴仁县	Xingren	939701	1223457	30.2
普安县	Puan	451381	591309	31.0
晴隆县	Qinglong	489099	638274	30.5
贞丰县	Zhenfeng	617501	805221	30.4
望谟县	Wangmo	293906	400887	36.4
册亨县	Ceheng	225459	307075	36.2
安龙县	Anlong	549948	719882	30.9
凯里市	Kaili	2796497	3538127	26.5
黄平县	Huangping	332861	425063	27.7
施秉县	Shibing	260428	301233	15.7
三穗县	Sansui	325830	421499	29.4
镇远县	Zhenyuan	386347	489115	26.6
岑巩县	Cengong	316647	407624	28.7
天柱县	Tianzhu	599939	758921	26.5
锦屏县	Jinping	220007	282929	28.6
剑河县	Jianhe	277378	350686	26.4
台江县	Taijiang	284791	361115	26.8
黎平县	Liping	555483	699481	25.9
榕江县	Rongjiang	403978	507307	25.6
从江县	Congjiang	463581	589675	27.2
雷山县	Leishan	178677	232362	30.0
麻江县	Majiang	317823	390335	22.8
丹寨县	Danzhai	398319	499101	25.3
都匀市	Duyun	1500000	2393834	59.6
福泉市	Fuquan	863000	1183367	37.1
荔波县	Libo	419375	550482	31.3
贵定县	Guiding	540000	686533	27.1
瓮安县	Wengan	881581	1183367	34.2
独山县	Dushan	401000	596200	48.7
平塘县	Pingtang	392519	532933	35.8
罗甸县	Luodian	501046	652333	30.2
长顺县	Changshun	418408	560067	33.9
龙里县	Longli	840000	1085933	29.3
惠水县	Huishui	770000	975600	26.7
※三都县	Sandu	375892	496833	32.2

27-36 各县(市、区、特区)一般公共预算收入(2014)

General Public Financial Budget Revenue by County (City,District,Special region)

县（市、区、特区）名称	County (City,District, Special region)	一般公共预算收入(万元) General Public Financial Budget Revenue (10000 yuan)	#增值税 Value Added Tax	位次 Order
南明区	Nanming	398313	31607	2
云岩区	Yunyan	326371	33704	5
花溪区	Huaxi	294655	18602	7
乌当区	Wudang	152990	12076	17
白云区	Baiyun	218671	18743	9
观山湖区	Guanshanhu	373388	14145	3
开阳县	Kaiyang	102188	8905	28
息烽县	Xifeng	68771	6903	36
修文县	Xiuwen	70305	7254	35
清镇市	Qingzhen	118960	8116	23
钟山区	Zhongshan	168543	6143	14
六枝特区	Liuzhi	122210	2933	22
水城县	Shuicheng	195076	10807	13
盘　县	Panxian	461446	34160	1
红花岗区	Honghuagang	218478	16896	10
汇川区	Huichuan	133186	13936	20
遵义县	Zunyi	165453	11466	15
桐梓县	Tongzi	65593	4739	38
绥阳县	Suiyang	49165	1951	47
正安县	Zhengan	40078	1354	55
※道真县	Daozhen	31711	1595	65
※务川县	Wuchuan	35800	1789	60
凤冈县	Fenggang	28814	1173	73
湄潭县	Meitan	48938	1738	49
余庆县	Yuqing	34225	1758	63
习水县	Xishui	78017	6708	33
赤水市	Chishui	49049	1791	48
仁怀市	Renhuai	258089	78073	8
西秀区	Xixiu	200665	13947	11
平坝区	Pingba	80368	3267	31
普定县	Puding	60366	2481	40
※镇宁县	Zhenning	56658	2252	42
※关岭县	Guanling	36241	1949	59
※紫云县	Ziyun	37654	939	57
七星关区	Qixingguan	196118	17319	12
大方县	Dafang	134740	7186	19
黔西县	Qianxi	113192	5901	25
金沙县	Jinsha	159142	14881	16
织金县	Zhijin	111618	9161	26
纳雍县	Nayong	64279	6759	39
※威宁县	Weining	79400	3812	32
赫章县	Hezhang	29743	2160	67
碧江区	Bijiang	110893	7586	27
万山区	Wanshan	15087	1409	86

注：资料来源于省财政厅(下表同)。
Note:Data in the table are obtained from Guizhou Provincial Financial Department(the same applies to the next table).

27-36 续表 continued

县（市、区、特区）名 称	County (City,District, Special region)	一般公共预算收入(万元) General Public Financial Budget Revenue (10000 yuan)	#增值税 Value Added Tax	位 次 Order
江口县	Jiangkou	15549	617	85
※玉屏县	Yuping	35784	3107	61
石阡县	Shiqian	28880	870	72
思南县	Sinan	42357	2701	54
※印江县	Yinjiang	26526	1119	77
德江县	Dejiang	42410	1975	53
※沿河县	Yanhe	36681	1998	58
※松桃县	Songtao	45755	3803	51
兴义市	Xingyi	305789	11924	6
兴仁县	Xingren	132546	5554	21
普安县	Puan	71520	2982	34
晴隆县	Qinglong	42889	1939	52
贞丰县	Zhenfeng	95101	5446	30
望谟县	Wangmo	24533	1379	78
册亨县	Ceheng	22016	961	79
安龙县	Anlong	59591	5411	41
凯里市	Kaili	361348	9109	4
黄平县	Huangping	29282	1745	70
施秉县	Shibing	19209	1181	82
三穗县	Sansui	27788	851	74
镇远县	Zhenyuan	49194	3600	46
岑巩县	Cengong	31646	1069	66
天柱县	Tianzhu	48765	2134	50
锦屏县	Jinping	14639	1674	87
剑河县	Jianhe	29584	1274	68
台江县	Taijiang	17297	501	83
黎平县	Liping	37730	1163	56
榕江县	Rongjiang	49967	1107	44
从江县	Congjiang	35374	1109	62
雷山县	Leishan	20333	595	81
麻江县	Majiang	16514	1525	84
丹寨县	Danzhai	11214	680	88
都匀市	Duyun	142256	5708	18
※福泉市	Fuquan	115191	6830	24
荔波县	Libo	27093	1446	76
贵定县	Guiding	49694	4042	45
瓮安县	Wengan	98362	5394	29
独山县	Dushan	33337	1892	64
平塘县	Pingtang	29051	657	71
罗甸县	Luodian	20888	2946	80
长顺县	Changshun	29450	1523	69
龙里县	Longli	67069	5583	37
惠水县	Huishui	50484	3513	43
※三都县	Sandu	27603	870	75

27-37 各县(市、区、特区)一般公共预算支出(2014)

General Public Financial Budget Expenditure by County(City,District,Special region)

县(市、区、特区)名称	County (City,District, Special region)	一般公共预算支出(万元) General Public Financial Budget Expenditures (10000 yuan)	#教育支出 Operating Expenses for Education	位次 Order
南明区	Nanming	434083	112262	9
云岩区	Yunyan	378036	91558	15
花溪区	Huaxi	519977	89696	3
乌当区	Wudang	239058	38118	39
白云区	Baiyun	285387	52573	28
观山湖区	Guanshanhu	383541	28425	14
开阳县	Kaiyang	233000	52728	41
息烽县	Xifeng	207353	35646	52
修文县	Xiuwen	200911	40265	58
清镇市	Qingzhen	282634	79529	29
钟山区	Zhongshan	257602	58364	34
六枝特区	Liuzhi	321911	90648	22
水城县	Shuicheng	443543	93189	7
盘　县	Panxian	795377	149847	1
红花岗区	Honghuagang	350297	80389	17
汇川区	Huichuan	203583	39465	54
遵义县	Zunyi	406495	104850	10
桐梓县	Tongzi	263713	66800	33
绥阳县	Suiyang	212232	49123	49
正安县	Zhengan	233937	60001	40
※道真县	Daozhen	180582	41948	65
※务川县	Wuchuan	204035	52308	53
凤冈县	Fenggang	178317	44231	67
湄潭县	Meitan	217278	53466	47
余庆县	Yuqing	146829	35433	74
习水县	Xishui	327729	78746	20
赤水市	Chishui	193046	37018	61
仁怀市	Renhuai	402661	83856	11
西秀区	Xixiu	438453	82923	8
平坝区	Pingba	249446	54090	35
普定县	Puding	212730	40395	48
※镇宁县	Zhenning	207927	37820	51
※关岭县	Guanling	182485	36952	64
※紫云县	Ziyun	201489	39471	56
七星关区	Qixingguan	480275	153527	5
大方县	Dafang	390927	93391	13
黔西县	Qianxi	351641	72499	16
金沙县	Jinsha	349698	71403	18
织金县	Zhijin	392310	101781	12
纳雍县	Nayong	306990	90887	25
※威宁县	Weining	519197	146333	4
赫章县	Hezhang	310497	81086	24
碧江区	Bijiang	239102	46986	38
万山区	Wanshan	141570	29256	78

27-37 续表 continued

县（市、区、特区）名称	County (City,District, Special region)	一般公共预算支出(万元) General Public Financial Budget Expenditures (10000 yuan)	#教育支出 Operating Expenses for Education	位次 Order
江口县	Jiangkou	131543	28053	82
※玉屏县	Yuping	128747	20572	84
石阡县	Shiqian	243178	53394	36
思南县	Sinan	328926	84906	19
※印江县	Yinjiang	228118	60323	44
德江县	Dejiang	279921	69967	30
※沿河县	Yanhe	296729	70549	26
※松桃县	Songtao	313793	79309	23
兴义市	Xingyi	529207	119727	2
兴仁县	Xingren	322160	71029	21
普安县	Puan	209577	46208	50
晴隆县	Qinglong	169760	37211	71
贞丰县	Zhenfeng	267715	65458	32
望谟县	Wangmo	230898	54906	43
册亨县	Ceheng	148272	31043	73
安龙县	Anlong	222562	56678	45
凯里市	Kaili	476120	86561	6
黄平县	Huangping	171429	34204	70
施秉县	Shibing	103352	22558	88
三穗县	Sansui	133518	26960	81
镇远县	Zhenyuan	145017	30477	76
岑巩县	Cengong	141733	26550	77
天柱县	Tianzhu	191481	49747	63
锦屏县	Jinping	130336	26198	83
剑河县	Jianhe	137362	24556	80
台江县	Taijiang	105115	21940	87
黎平县	Liping	239809	52746	37
榕江县	Rongjiang	201152	45013	57
从江县	Congjiang	201949	43671	55
雷山县	Leishan	127402	26004	85
麻江县	Majiang	120087	25747	86
丹寨县	Danzhai	193659	41415	60
都匀市	Duyun	295615	48299	27
福泉市	Fuquan	231783	43557	42
荔波县	Libo	146231	29454	75
贵定县	Guiding	192303	37675	62
瓮安县	Wengan	271319	59940	31
独山县	Dushan	166906	38343	72
平塘县	Pingtang	176939	37521	68
罗甸县	Luodian	179372	43525	66
长顺县	Changshun	140411	34036	79
龙里县	Longli	176488	34649	69
惠水县	Huishui	219083	58128	46
※三都县	Sandu	200016	46637	59

27-38 各县(市、区、特区)城镇常住居民人均可支配收入(2014)

Per Capita Disposable income of Urban Households by County (City,District,Special region)

单位：元 (yuan)

县(市、区、特区)名称	County (City,District, Special region)	城镇常住居民人均可支配收入 Per Capita Disposable Income of Urban Households	位次 Order	县(市、区、特区)名称	County (City,District, Special region)	城镇常住居民人均可支配收入 Per Capita Disposable Income of Urban Households	位次 Order
南明区	Nanming	25796	2	万山区	Wanshan	20609	39
云岩区	Yunyan	25840	1	江口县	Jiangkou	20099	68
花溪区	Huaxi	24374	8	※玉屏县	※Yuping	20937	34
乌当区	Wudang	24435	7	石阡县	Shiqian	19614	81
白云区	Baiyun	24508	5	思南县	Sinan	19666	79
观山湖区	Guanshanhu	24446	6	※印江县	※Yinjiang	19530	84
开阳县	Kaiyang	23745	11	德江县	Dejiang	19666	80
息烽县	Xifeng	22420	20	※沿河县	※Yanhe	19797	77
修文县	Xiuwen	23601	13	※松桃县	※Songtao	19480	85
清镇市	Qingzhen	23627	12				
				兴义市	Xingyi	23122	15
钟山区	Zhongshan	22759	18	兴仁县	Xingren	20816	35
六枝特区	Liuzhi	19293	87	普安县	Puan	19975	71
水城县	Shuicheng	19603	83	晴隆县	Qinglong	19866	75
盘　县	Panxian	20137	66	贞丰县	Zhenfeng	20113	67
				望谟县	Wangmo	19360	86
红花岗区	Honghuagang	24965	3	册亨县	Ceheng	19714	78
汇川区	Huichuan	24965	3	安龙县	Anlong	20017	70
遵义县	Zunyi	24089	10				
桐梓县	Tongzi	20588	42	凯里市	Kaili	22401	22
绥阳县	Suiyang	20963	33	黄平县	Huangping	20610	38
正安县	Zhengan	19975	72	施秉县	Shibing	20399	54
※道真县	※Daozhen	19947	73	三穗县	Sansui	20677	37
※务川县	※Wuchuan	19898	74	镇远县	Zhenyuan	21000	32
凤冈县	Fenggang	20309	61	岑巩县	Cengong	20570	43
湄潭县	Meitan	22950	17	天柱县	Tianzhu	20441	53
余庆县	Yuqing	20390	56	锦屏县	Jinping	20443	52
习水县	Xishui	20751	36	剑河县	Jianhe	20538	45
赤水市	Chishui	21722	27	台江县	Taijiang	20320	60
仁怀市	Renhuai	24283	9	黎平县	Liping	20484	51
				榕江县	Rongjiang	20358	58
西秀区	Xixiu	22410	21	从江县	Congjiang	20496	48
平坝区	Pingba	20593	41	雷山县	Leishan	20383	57
普定县	Puding	20065	69	麻江县	Majiang	20605	40
※镇宁县	※Zhenning	19801	76	丹寨县	Danzhai	20555	44
※关岭县	※Guanling	19609	82				
※紫云县	※Ziyun	19267	88	都匀市	Duyun	23518	14
				福泉市	Fuquan	22091	23
七星关区	Qixingguan	22727	19	荔波县	Libo	21057	30
大方县	Dafang	20496	49	贵定县	Guiding	20486	50
黔西县	Qianxi	21019	31	瓮安县	Wengan	21891	25
金沙县	Jinsha	23001	16	独山县	Dushan	21068	29
织金县	Zhijin	20498	47	平塘县	Pingtang	20325	59
纳雍县	Nayong	20395	55	罗甸县	Luodian	20502	46
※威宁县	※Weining	20306	62	长顺县	Changshun	20163	65
赫章县	Hezhang	20269	63	龙里县	Longli	21860	26
				惠水县	Huishui	21466	28
碧江区	Bijiang	21957	24	※三都县	※Sandu	20167	64

27−39 各县(市、区、特区)农村常住居民人均可支配收入(2014)

Per Capita Net Income of Rural Households by County(City,District,Special region)

单位：元 (yuan)

县(市、区、特区)名 称	County (City,District, Special region)	农村常住居民人均可支配收入 Per Capita Annual Net Income of Rural Households	位 次 Order
南明区	Nanming	12722	3
云岩区	Yunyan	12839	1
花溪区	Huaxi	11327	6
乌当区	Wudang	11924	5
白云区	Baiyun	12833	2
观山湖区	Guanshanhu	12103	4
开阳县	Kaiyang	10227	9
息烽县	Xifeng	9787	13
修文县	Xiuwen	9807	11
清镇市	Qingzhen	10439	7
钟山区	Zhongshan	9044	15
六枝特区	Liuzhi	6404	47
水城县	Shuicheng	6400	48
盘 县	Panxian	6933	37
红花岗区	Honghuagang	10210	10
汇川区	Huichuan	10228	8
遵义县	Zunyi	9788	12
桐梓县	Tongzi	8155	22
绥阳县	Suiyang	8645	16
正安县	Zhengan	6786	40
※道真县	※Daozhen	6785	41
※务川县	※Wuchuan	6757	44
凤冈县	Fenggang	7711	27
湄潭县	Meitan	9144	14
余庆县	Yuqing	8061	24
习水县	Xishui	7082	35
赤水市	Chishui	8350	20
仁怀市	Renhuai	8548	17
西秀区	Xixiu	8129	23
平坝区	Pingba	6863	39
普定县	Puding	6116	64
※镇宁县	※Zhenning	5969	70
※关岭县	※Guanling	5986	69
※紫云县	※Ziyun	5868	77
七星关区	Qixingguan	6382	49
大方县	Dafang	6260	54
黔西县	Qianxi	6279	53
金沙县	Jinsha	7146	34
织金县	Zhijin	6184	56
纳雍县	Nayong	5873	75
※威宁县	※Weining	6196	55
赫章县	Hezhang	5857	79
碧江区	Bijiang	8458	18
万山区	Wanshan	6119	63
江口县	Jiangkou	6162	58
※玉屏县	※Yuping	7921	25
石阡县	Shiqian	6148	59
思南县	Sinan	5996	68
※印江县	※Yinjiang	6037	67
德江县	Dejiang	5907	74
※沿河县	※Yanhe	5960	71
※松桃县	※Songtao	5915	73
兴义市	Xingyi	8190	21
兴仁县	Xingren	6345	51
普安县	Puan	5729	83
晴隆县	Qinglong	5463	86
贞丰县	Zhenfeng	6134	61
望谟县	Wangmo	5206	88
册亨县	Ceheng	5361	87
安龙县	Anlong	6086	65
凯里市	Kaili	7879	26
黄平县	Huangping	5816	81
施秉县	Shibing	6497	46
三穗县	Sansui	6168	57
镇远县	Zhenyuan	6329	52
岑巩县	Cengong	6144	60
天柱县	Tianzhu	6349	50
锦屏县	Jinping	5705	84
剑河县	Jianhe	5825	80
台江县	Taijiang	5580	85
黎平县	Liping	5945	72
榕江县	Rongjiang	5766	82
从江县	Congjiang	6126	62
雷山县	Leishan	6064	66
麻江县	Majiang	5870	76
丹寨县	Danzhai	5862	78
都匀市	Duyun	8410	19
福泉市	Fuquan	7495	30
荔波县	Libo	6916	38
贵定县	Guiding	7197	32
瓮安县	Wengan	7519	28
独山县	Dushan	7029	36
平塘县	Pingtang	6666	45
罗甸县	Luodian	7160	33
长顺县	Changshun	6768	42
龙里县	Longli	7513	29
惠水县	Huishui	7330	31
※三都县	※Sandu	6758	43

27－40 各县（市、区、特区）乡村从业人员(2014)

Number of Rural Employment by County (City,District,Special region)

单位：人 (person)

县(市、区、特区)名称	County (City,District, Special region)	合计 Total	第一产业 Primary Industry	第二产业 Secondary Industry	第三产业 Tertiary Industry	2014年比2013年增长(%) Increase Rate in 2014 over 2013(%)
南明区	Nanming	39567	13528	6302	19737	-4.6
云岩区	Yunyan	53463	1822	17911	33730	-8.8
花溪区	Huaxi	149608	68648	21070	59890	4.6
乌当区	Wudang	78222	24043	10744	43435	-2.0
白云区	Baiyun	50942	21849	10412	18681	2.2
观山湖区	Guanshanhu	69255	20056	28098	21101	0.0
开阳县	Kaiyang	183247	81324	30023	71900	-2.1
息烽县	Xifeng	120446	51868	17674	50904	-1.7
修文县	Xiuwen	171371	83832	25851	61688	3.6
清镇市	Qingzhen	241543	106917	59597	75029	-2.7
钟山区	Zhongshan	76941	44007	16970	15964	-17.0
六枝特区	Liuzhi	340453	140964	53010	146479	0.7
水城县	Shuicheng	400653	220581	54247	125825	0.5
盘　县	Panxian	611485	341373	75197	194915	0.4
红花岗区	Honghuagang	128113	47946	26457	53710	-6.1
汇川区	Huicuan	121627	40136	37385	44106	1.5
遵义县	Zunyi	743718	231741	150779	361198	0.8
桐梓县	Tongzi	413284	154174	83345	175765	1.5
绥阳县	Suiyang	334255	140431	44089	149735	2.9
正安县	Zhengan	432229	121294	105529	205406	10.1
※道真县	Daozhen	204125	95504	15513	93108	7.0
※务川县	Wuchuan	273993	133743	31511	108739	3.2
凤冈县	Fenggang	251770	122936	25825	103009	-0.4
湄潭县	Meitan	257637	133239	21298	103100	-1.7
余庆县	Yuqing	178499	76660	16514	85325	2.8
习水县	Xishui	378726	161330	61913	155483	-0.8
赤水市	Chishui	140193	75173	12787	52233	-4.9
仁怀市	Renhuai	339319	164645	71081	103593	5.7
西秀区	Xixiu	372826	159014	59031	154781	-2.7
平坝区	Pingba	206596	136567	19472	50557	1.1
普定县	Puding	263272	125703	45698	91871	0.3
※镇宁县	Zhenning	212484	125277	27004	60203	1.3
※关岭县	Guanling	219443	119844	15120	84479	10.7
※紫云县	Ziyun	246039	121751	20294	103994	4.6
七星关区	Qixingguan	889956	368162	123381	398413	0.8
大方县	Dafang	611216	310294	64596	236326	-9.8
黔西县	Qianxi	529380	266773	71632	190975	-4.9
金沙县	Jinsha	282723	122144	34292	126287	-1.4
织金县	Zhijin	552996	281070	75768	196158	0.3
纳雍县	Nayong	571956	242261	90440	239255	4.1
※威宁县	Weining	799568	501496	59486	238586	1.1
赫章县	Hezhang	395077	177888	34000	183189	0.7
碧江区	Bijiang	108536	52910	13725	41901	-3.4
万山区	Wanshan	72404	32743	9819	29842	1.5

27-40 续表 continued

单位：人 (person)

县(市、区、特区)名称	County (City,District, Special region)	合计 Total	第一产业 Primary Industry	第二产业 Secondary Industry	第三产业 Tertiary Industry	2014年比2013年增长(%) Increase Rate in 2014 over 2013(%)
江口县	Jiangkou	125486	68675	9429	47382	0.0
※玉屏县	Yuping	85963	35367	18891	31705	-0.5
石阡县	Shiqian	272312	139699	19910	112703	2.0
思南县	Sinan	389514	176023	82393	131098	-2.3
※印江县	Yinjiang	242017	85088	42574	114355	-1.3
德江县	Dejiang	196649	90108	24512	82029	-15.5
※沿河县	Yanhe	330786	187025	20859	122902	0.6
※松桃县	Songtao	424073	212320	32139	179614	0.5
兴义市	Xingyi	396366	228405	59442	108519	-1.7
兴仁县	Xingren	258485	158041	26196	74248	2.9
普安县	Puan	181757	109670	15772	56315	0.9
晴隆县	Qinglong	175956	111624	13308	51024	-7.3
贞丰县	Zhenfeng	227428	136710	23872	66846	-1.5
望谟县	Wangmo	168942	75904	31949	61089	3.5
册亨县	Ceheng	135402	75688	12014	47700	0.0
安龙县	Anlong	319125	165225	52030	101870	-1.0
凯里市	Kaili	209696	96915	30602	82179	19.0
黄平县	Huangping	203970	127570	32102	44298	-9.9
施秉县	Shibing	62377	45482	4210	12685	0.6
三穗县	Sansui	125995	45562	11994	68439	0.4
镇远县	Zhenyuan	121913	67925	16878	37110	0.1
岑巩县	Cengong	126512	68647	8072	49793	-0.8
天柱县	Tianzhu	223475	98354	7506	117615	0.1
锦屏县	Jinping	124004	60088	15022	48894	0.8
剑河县	Jianhe	146821	75893	17639	53289	0.5
台江县	Taijiang	96369	44685	13741	37943	0.5
黎平县	Liping	284122	142288	27190	114644	-0.1
榕江县	Rongjiang	210888	118871	17214	74803	2.4
从江县	Congjiang	185400	121546	13951	49903	-0.2
雷山县	Leishan	82395	43365	6027	33003	-19.6
麻江县	Majiang	95847	59218	10443	26186	-24.5
丹寨县	Danzhai	98206	38042	8060	52104	1.0
都匀市	Duyun	203107	100107	21002	81998	0.2
福泉市	Fuquan	149866	67292	37494	45080	2.8
荔波县	Libo	102023	52711	10671	38641	1.2
贵定县	Guiding	164597	71162	14378	79057	-0.7
瓮安县	Wengan	282621	117318	36755	128548	-2.6
独山县	Dushan	207972	91497	26119	90356	-2.1
平塘县	Pingtang	198780	114587	12318	71875	0.6
罗甸县	Luodian	176767	94150	12890	69727	0.7
长顺县	Changshun	136570	86164	9253	41153	0.1
龙里县	Longli	116427	67430	9766	39231	0.6
惠水县	Huishui	278555	126254	33976	118325	2.1
※三都县	Sandu	207859	111056	12290	84513	1.1

27-41 各县(市、区、特区)农林牧渔业总产值(2014)

Gross Output Value of Farming,Forestry,Animal Husbandry and Fishery and Its Order by County(City,District,Special region)

单位：万元 (10000 yuan)

县(市、区、特区)名称	County (City,District, Special region)	合计 Total	农业 Agriculture	林业 Forestry	牧业 Animal Husbandry	渔业 Fishery	农林牧渔服务业 Services	位次 Order	2014年比2013年增长(%) Increase Rate in 2014 over 2013(%)
南明区	Nanming	52110	42822		9128		160	86	6.3
云岩区	Yunyan	8406	7077		1303		26	88	2.0
花溪区	Huaxi	231568	171854	430	56309	88	2887	37	6.8
乌当区	Wudang	183006	142884	1702	35690	866	1864	53	6.9
白云区	Baiyun	73771	58696	716	13685	104	570	84	7.2
观山湖区	Guanshanhu	39752	32382	145	5918	1087	220	87	6.2
开阳县	Kaiyang	362960	227694	2225	128660	1876	2505	15	7.3
息烽县	Xifeng	202638	133627	1221	57625	9051	1114	43	7.3
修文县	Xiuwen	253258	182130	840	69059	743	486	35	7.1
清镇市	Qingzhen	299363	200843	3145	86122	8418	835	24	7.0
钟山区	Zhongshan	72616	37031	361	26416	51	8757	85	7.2
六枝特区	Liuzhi	286976	179780	16055	74022	2296	14823	27	7.2
水城县	Shuicheng	331023	227441	9715	89353	147	4368	22	7.0
盘　县	Panxian	531106	292244	42698	180701	1290	14172	4	6.9
红花岗区	Honghuagang	184091	94278	785	80942	2315	5771	51	6.6
汇川区	Huicuan	155928	84446	722	60368	608	9784	66	7.9
遵义县	Zunyi	833457	586305	6864	189406	43201	7681	1	7.1
桐梓县	Tongzi	421931	278472	25316	110059	7172	912	8	6.7
绥阳县	Suiyang	410796	307959	5193	88403	6461	2780	10	6.8
正安县	Zhengan	343402	220675	39825	77693	2180	3029	18	6.8
※道真县	Daozhen	236452	153734	12245	68323	1340	810	36	6.9
※务川县	Wuchuan	258426	176775	11155	66009	2388	2100	34	7.2
凤冈县	Fenggang	286004	177116	29659	75159	1720	2350	28	6.6
湄潭县	Meitan	296439	203578	9194	72410	5328	5928	25	6.9
余庆县	Yuqing	231382	142246	8513	69920	9094	1609	38	6.7
习水县	Xishui	374926	209973	7922	151539	2999	2493	12	6.9
赤水市	Chishui	178295	81050	50047	39317	5429	2452	54	7.0
仁怀市	Renhuai	354090	205857	8800	133388	2856	3189	17	6.2
西秀区	Xixiu	358265	236061	3017	108782	9049	1356	16	7.0
平坝区	Pingba	173819	110712	2783	51642	7709	973	58	6.8
普定县	Puding	193963	124072	2027	58249	8288	1327	48	6.7
※镇宁县	Zhenning	167508	101519	5033	49965	10379	612	60	7.2
※关岭县	Guanling	197291	117934	7061	66854	4769	673	47	6.8
※紫云县	Ziyun	224657	124925	12862	79791	4075	3004	40	6.9
七星关区	Qixingguan	734383	519943	9721	191166	865	12689	3	7.1
大方县	Dafang	453227	309524	7218	128071	2053	6361	7	7.3
黔西县	Qianxi	394796	274379	2802	110124	1873	5618	11	7.4
金沙县	Jinsha	341229	222985	6124	100572	4693	6854	20	7.5
织金县	Zhijin	414447	279271	4513	122174	1248	7240	9	7.1
纳雍县	Nayong	342922	231923	6073	100658	1363	2905	19	6.9
※威宁县	Weining	757032	522129	3815	219236	622	11231	2	5.8
赫章县	Hezhang	454820	326484	8883	115037	490	3926	6	7.1
碧江区	Bijiang	156598	105470	5668	33754	7030	4676	64	7.0
万山区	Wanshan	111841	67952	6759	31597	2607	2925	74	6.9

27-41 续表 continued

单位：万元 (10000 yuan)

县(市、区、特区)名称	County (City,District, Special region)	合计 Total	农业 Agriculture	林业 Forestry	牧业 Animal Husbandry	渔业 Fishery	农林牧渔服务业 Services	位次 Order	2014年比2013年增长(%) Increase Rate in 2014 over 2013(%)
江口县	Jiangkou	164202.5	108322.1	6299.8	38616.7	6158.9	4805	61	7.1
※玉屏县	Yuping	100766.7	60301.1	3426.9	28432.5	4609.2	3997	76	6.6
石阡县	Shiqian	291531.6	190702.6	8375.8	76637.2	9536	6280	26	6.3
思南县	Sinan	368209	210947	6688.4	121541.6	17846	11186	13	6.6
※印江县	Yinjiang	284604.7	179512	8205	80769.9	9564.8	6553	29	7.0
德江县	Dejiang	317771	202535.6	12230	84316	9734.4	8955	23	6.8
※沿河县	Yanhe	331090.7	205663.2	6092.7	93854.8	15455	10025	21	6.5
※松桃县	Songtao	368208	231838.7	9646.3	102784.5	13458.5	10480	14	6.8
兴义市	Xingyi	479852	320848	5546	122034	25548	5876	5	6.9
兴仁县	Xingren	273188	189000	8500	73746	442	1500	33	7.1
普安县	Puan	147484	101312	2733	41248	511	1680	69	7.0
晴隆县	Qinglong	143886	86025	4278	45504	5923	2156	70	6.5
贞丰县	Zhenfeng	228882	150315	3976	71809	784	1998	39	7.2
望谟县	Wangmo	211006	129527	13372	58263	7774	2070	41	6.1
册亨县	Ceheng	131633	80514	29838	40295	7354	3632	71	6.2
安龙县	Anlong	280214	152652	17943	74689	31126	3804	32	7.3
凯里市	Kaili	208448	129659	8588	60384	5729	4088	42	6.4
黄平县	Huangping	187307	115736	15813	46993	4914	3851	49	7.1
施秉县	Shibing	96183	65077	7091	21431	1355	1229	77	7.2
三穗县	Sansui	94197	47432	10991	31004	2990	1780	78	7.8
镇远县	Zhenyuan	153664	93129	19090	36790	3793	862	67	7.2
岑巩县	Cengong	103998	55169	7464	31221	1335	8809	75	7.6
天柱县	Tianzhu	173319	95657	20831	51133	4849	849	59	7.3
锦屏县	Jinping	87754	37575	15738	24428	7961	2052	79	6.8
剑河县	Jianhe	119353	49269	20720	36316	12116	932	72	7.4
台江县	Taijiang	78525	34391	15456	22591	4733	1354	82	7.5
黎平县	Liping	201005	78475	54024	50206	15616	2684	44	6.9
榕江县	Rongjiang	177885	93480	36714	38890	7907	894	55	6.6
从江县	Congjiang	176993	82271	40251	38696	13697	2078	56	7.8
雷山县	Leishan	79691	45683	6062	23795	1801	2350	81	6.7
麻江县	Majiang	84325	47699	3865	24264	1491	7006	80	6.6
丹寨县	Danzhai	78488	39664	10655	24282	1959	1928	83	7.9
都匀市	Duyun	198035	117481	4805	70419	2919	2411	46	6.6
福泉市	Fuquan	174080	121392	4592	45511	2086	499	57	6.6
荔波县	Libo	114487	65348	9344	30353	5843	3599	73	7.2
贵定县	Guiding	152125	108116	6831	28297	4910	3971	68	8.6
瓮安县	Wengan	281076	154249	5599	107833	10365	3030	30	9.1
独山县	Dushan	198590	136236	5252	53652	1951.8	1499	45	6.7
平塘县	Pingtang	185785	135911	6491	39868	1892	1622	50	6.7
罗甸县	Luodian	183928	105351	9522	50505	15289	3261	52	6.7
长顺县	Changshun	161092	100975	8820	44164	1143	5990	62	7.3
龙里县	Longli	156181	116540	1624	33902	1536	2579	65	6.6
惠水县	Huishui	280974	188805	17648	62506	2980	9035	31	6.7
※三都县	Sandu	157376	91488	12126	45869	5128	2765	63	6.5

27-42 各县(市、区、特区)粮食、肉类产量(2014)

Output of Grain, Meat and Its Order by County(City,Section,Special region)

县(市、区、特区)名称	County (City,Section, Special region)	粮食产量(吨) Output of Grain (ton)	位次 Order	2014年比2013年增长(%) Increase Rate in 2014over 2013(%)	人均粮食产量(公斤) Per Capita Output of Grain (kg)	位次 Order	肉类产量(吨) Output of Meat (ton)	位次 Order	2014年比2013年增长(%) Increase Rate in 2014 over 2013(%)
南明区	Nanming	2640	87	0.3	43	87	2857	86	1.2
云岩区	Yunyan	105	88	2.9	1	88	553	88	1.5
花溪区	Huaxi	45888	79	-7.8	179	83	17651	47	0.3
乌当区	Wudang	33746	83	6.2	256	76	10914	70	1.3
白云区	Baiyun	11007	85	1.2	145	84	5407	84	1.1
观山湖区	Guanshanhu	10755	86	2.0	77	86	1198	87	3.3
开阳县	Kaiyang	104590	46	6.8	324	47	45880	8	3.1
息烽县	Xifeng	72818	64	8.0	383	19	16632	52	2.0
修文县	Xiuwen	89891	55	11.5	323	48	19744	44	1.2
清镇市	Qingzhen	87720	56	8.3	219	82	33265	21	0.7
钟山区	Zhongshan	21171	84	-12.6	126	85	7881.2	81	-27.8
六枝特区	Liuzhi	211815	21	-1.7	358	29	25453.1	32	5.6
水城县	Shuicheng	226254	17	-2.7	288	63	32824.5	23	3.6
盘　县	Panxian	354900	4	5.3	334	41	54794.2	5	4.9
红花岗区	Honghuagang	70857	65	8.6	347	32	18224	46	0.3
汇川区	Huicuan	70573	66	10.6	326	43	21983	40	2.0
遵义县	Zunyi	575990	1	8.9	481	8	92261	1	7.6
桐梓县	Tongzi	232984	14	16.2	336	39	42773	10	1.0
绥阳县	Suiyang	242790	12	10.1	471	9	27832	29	0.1
正安县	Zhengan	224845	18	11.7	375	25	24985	34	0.8
※道真县	Daozhen	144025	31	11.7	469	10	21730	41	-0.2
※务川县	Wuchuan	172784	28	10.8	410	16	25415	33	1.4
凤冈县	Fenggang	177334	26	16.3	445	13	29543	27	0.3
湄潭县	Meitan	217885	20	16.4	499	7	30580	25	1.1
余庆县	Yuqing	166104	30	16.1	629	1	30740	24	0.4
习水县	Xishui	254071	9	8.8	378	23	60085	4	-0.7
赤水市	Chishui	138067	33	17.6	583	2	16744	51	2.0
仁怀市	Renhuai	227191	16	14.1	382	21	47053	7	1.0
西秀区	Xixiu	177183	27	16.2	283	65	42602	11	1.8
平坝区	Pingba	106190	43	3.0	342	35	17471	48	2.5
普定县	Puding	104845	45	6.5	237	80	22337	38	2.3
※镇宁县	Zhenning	100583	49	10.0	277	67	12781	65	2.0
※关岭县	Guanling	96270	54	0.6	269	70	19280	45	5.1
※紫云县	Ziyun	97567	52	8.2	261	75	33331	20	0.5
七星关区	Qixingguan	420254	3	8.1	376	24	68479	3	10.6
大方县	Dafang	262018	7	8.9	307	57	41446	13	8.1
黔西县	Qianxi	270850	6	9.3	308	56	38849	16	8.1
金沙县	Jinsha	230705	15	18.0	523	4	35531	18	8.4
织金县	Zhijin	331762	5	7.8	381	22	41788	12	10.1
纳雍县	Nayong	258024	8	14.9	303	58	33901	19	5.9
※威宁县	Weining	478049	2	3.0	372	26	80090	2	2.1
赫章县	Hezhang	249577	10	18.4	337	38	40527	14	15.8
碧江区	Bijiang	82533	59	15.2	503	6	13368	62	2.1
万山区	Wanshan	52483	74	8.1	383	20	11984	68	2.0

注：人均粮食产量指标中人口数为乡村人口。

Note:The population of Per Capite Output of Grain refers to the rural population.

27-42 续表 continued

县(市、区、特区)名 称	County (City,District, Special region)	粮食产量(吨) Output of Grain (ton)	位次 Order	2014年比2013年增长(%) Increase Rate in 2014 over 2013(%)	人均粮食产量(公斤) Per Capita Output of Grain (kg)	位次 Order	肉类产量(吨) Output of Meat (ton)	位次 Order	2014年比2013年增长(%) Increase Rate in 2014 over 2013(%)
江口县	Jiangkou	67169	68	0.4	315	52	15249	55	2.2
※玉屏县	Yuping	40785	82	15.1	314	53	10138	74	2.1
石阡县	Shiqian	129947	35	9.7	325	45	24361	35	2.1
思南县	Sinan	220915	19	14.8	355	30	44687	9	1.8
※印江县	Yinjiang	136203	34	10.8	329	42	29774	26	2.0
德江县	Dejiang	178256	25	33.8	464	11	28251	28	2.0
※沿河县	Yanhe	199214	22	21.9	323	49	33101	22	2.0
※松桃县	Songtao	237097	13	7.9	349	31	37826	17	2.3
兴义市	Xingyi	245236	11	7.8	359	28	49487.8	6	0.1
兴仁县	Xingren	170598	29	7.8	387	18	22582.6	37	1.6
普安县	Puan	83512	58	17.4	248	78	12632.2	66	2.7
晴隆县	Qinglong	86300	57	8.4	280	66	12982.8	64	5.5
贞丰县	Zhenfeng	117100	37	26.0	289	62	15059	57	2.2
望谟县	Wangmo	75644	63	3.8	241	79	17139.1	50	1.8
册亨县	Ceheng	52200	75	6.3	224	81	10656.4	72	2.8
安龙县	Anlong	190400	23	14.2	439	14	27192.1	30	1.2
凯里市	Kaili	99013	50	20.1	268	73	23162.1	36	4.2
黄平县	Huangping	105534	44	20.5	301	59	12294.5	67	2.0
施秉县	Shibing	56473	72	6.0	537	3	7224	82	2.5
三穗县	Sansui	53219	73	9.0	268	71	13470	60	7.5
镇远县	Zhenyuan	80699	61	8.5	462	12	10782	71	5.2
岑巩县	Cengong	63112	69	9.2	325	46	9973	76	5.3
天柱县	Tianzhu	114258	39	7.4	319	50	22205	39	5.9
锦屏县	Jinping	57613	71	9.6	268	72	9300	78	5.4
剑河县	Jianhe	61669	70	4.1	252	77	13439	61	3.1
台江县	Taijiang	41753	81	5.3	274	69	5031.5	85	5.2
黎平县	Liping	126371	36	5.4	274	68	16461	53	1.7
榕江县	Rongjiang	81573	60	8.8	261	74	11828	69	5.3
从江县	Congjiang	108092	42	9.2	346	34	15106	56	4.6
雷山县	Leishan	45533	80	4.6	335	40	6178	83	5.3
麻江县	Majiang	46554	77	-22.2	317	51	9992.4	75	-11.4
丹寨县	Danzhai	46240	78	13.0	293	61	8394.5	80	5.7
都匀市	Duyun	101815	48	1.3	314	54	25703	31	2.3
福泉市	Fuquan	116526	38	12.1	508	5	13782	59	0.8
荔波县	Libo	47415	76	3.8	286	64	9392	77	1.6
贵定县	Guiding	80540	62	6.9	310	55	10295	73	2.5
瓮安县	Wengan	181740	24	13.8	415	15	39946	15	1.8
独山县	Dushan	111527	40	4.5	340	36	17400	49	0.0
平塘县	Pingtang	109037	41	4.6	347	33	14053	58	2.6
罗甸县	Luodian	103960	47	4.6	326	44	21083	42	2.3
长顺县	Changshun	97475	53	4.0	398	17	13043	63	2.6
龙里县	Longli	70360	67	1.0	365	27	9169	79	13.2
惠水县	Huishui	138994	32	6.1	339	37	20060	43	1.3
※三都县	Sandu	97821	51	6.8	297	60	16304	54	2.1

27-43 各县(市、区、特区)油菜籽、烤烟产量(2014)

Output of Rapeseed and Fluecured Tobacco and Its Order by County(City,District,Special region)

县(市、区、特区)名称	County (City,District, Special region)	油菜籽产量(吨) Output of Rapeseed (ton)	位次 Order	2014年比2013年增长(%) Increase Rate in 2014 over 2013(%)	烤烟产量(吨) Output of Fluecured Tobacco (ton)	位次 Order	2014年比2013年增长(%) Increase Rate in 2014 over 2013(%)
南明区	Nanming						
云岩区	Yunyan						
花溪区	Huaxi	4061	64	-15.2	675	60	
乌当区	Wudang	4730	56	2.3			
白云区	Baiyun	642	79	-20.3			
观山湖区	Guanshanhu	916	77	-19.3			
开阳县	Kaiyang	19879	9	1.5	7856	15	-6.3
息烽县	Xifeng	11615	22	2.1	1316	55	-19.4
修文县	Xiuwen	12539	20	17.6	1841	50	-33.2
清镇市	Qingzhen	10741	27	4.4	5653	25	12.4
钟山区	Zhongshan						
六枝特区	Liuzhi	7440	39	1.7	191	65	-46.5
水城县	Shuicheng	167	84	-23.7	6911	19	7.0
盘　县	Panxian	2330	74	22.1	8155	13	-18.8
红花岗区	Honghuagang	6733	46	0.3	55	68	7.8
汇川区	Huicuan	6457	48	6.0	1672	52	-33.0
遵义县	Zunyi	71908	2	1.3	16854	2	-19.4
桐梓县	Tongzi	19655	10	13.2	6717	22	-17.6
绥阳县	Suiyang	31807	4	4.3	8509	11	-14.4
正安县	Zhengan	21694	8	7.2	9659	8	-11.5
※道真县	Daozhen	8749	32	6.2	13342	4	-5.4
※务川县	Wuchuan	9091	31	3.0	14711	3	-5.2
凤冈县	Fenggang	16728	14	2.0	7293	18	-14.2
湄潭县	Meitan	23040	7	8.4	8576	10	-12.7
余庆县	Yuqing	17640	13	0.4	9606	9	-15.7
习水县	Xishui	8246	35	3.1	1999	47	0.2
赤水市	Chishui	318	81	3.9			
仁怀市	Renhuai	14001	18	2.9	2750	40	11.6
西秀区	Xixiu	33851	3	0.6	5522	29	-35.6
平坝区	Pingba	11572	23	-1.1	3632	36	-26.2
普定县	Puding	11918	21	7.2	1983	49	11.3
※镇宁县	Zhenning	10167	28	5.2	459	61	96.2
※关岭县	Guanling	4735	55	5.7	344	63	-5.5
※紫云县	Ziyun	7922	37	1.8	2615	41	-15.5
七星关区	Qixingguan	6976	42	18.4	8494	12	-34.1
大方县	Dafang	7900	38	6.6	12200	6	-32.4
黔西县	Qianxi	76887	1	11.9	7846	16	1.7
金沙县	Jinsha	26419	5	7.4	4149	35	35.8
织金县	Zhijin	14430	16	9.6	3520	38	-14.5
纳雍县	Nayong	224	82	1.8	3521	37	-24.9
※威宁县	Weining	50	85	-36.7	30569	1	-29.9
赫章县	Hezhang	178	83	-1.1	5444	31	-19.4
碧江区	Bijiang	4372	62	-1.8			
万山区	Wanshan	3263	68	-3.0			

27-43 续表 continued

县(市、区、特区)名称	County (City,District, Special region)	油菜籽产量(吨) Output of Rapeseed (ton)	位次 Order	2014年比2013年增长(%) Increase Rate in 2014 over 2013(%)	烤烟产量(吨) Output of Fluecured Tobacco (ton)	位次 Order	2014年比2013年增长(%) Increase Rate in 2014 over 2013(%)
江口县	Jiangkou	4648	58	0.7	1994	48	-23.3
※玉屏县	Yuping	4012	65	7.0	333	64	6.7
石阡县	Shiqian	18710	11	12.0	5963	24	-0.8
思南县	Sinan	24321	6	4.9	4590	34	-3.1
※印江县	Yinjiang	14385	17	2.4	4685	32	-16.0
德江县	Dejiang	14669	15	2.3	6834	20	-14.7
※沿河县	Yanhe	9849	29	5.5	5650	26	-5.4
※松桃县	Songtao	13765	19	1.8	2373	43	-20.9
兴义市	Xingyi	11524	24	15.4	12063	7	-12.2
兴仁县	Xingren	6424	49	8.8	6751	21	-22.5
普安县	Puan	1879	75	33.5	12928	5	-13.2
晴隆县	Qinglong	1630	76	9.2	2546	42	-10.7
贞丰县	Zhenfeng	5314	53	14.5	3426	39	10.5
望谟县	Wangmo	2550	72	10.7			
册亨县	Ceheng	3440	67	52.8			
安龙县	Anlong	4697	57	14.6	8041	14	-5.2
凯里市	Kaili	4189	63	44.1	709	58	-12.6
黄平县	Huangping	6692	47	27.7	2036	46	-12.5
施秉县	Shibing	4640	59	9.3	5508	30	9.1
三穗县	Sansui	3084	69	19.7	182	66	-27.2
镇远县	Zhenyuan	7276	40	0.2	5562	28	-8.4
岑巩县	Cengong	5310	54	2.0	5645	27	-14.5
天柱县	Tianzhu	5680	51	0.9	1472	54	9.1
锦屏县	Jinping	4560	61	8.8	370	62	-24.5
剑河县	Jianhe	2940	70	21.8			
台江县	Taijiang	2422	73	6.7			
黎平县	Liping	8008	36	4.8	18	69	12.5
榕江县	Rongjiang	6777	43	7.5			
从江县	Congjiang	5320	52	3.5			
雷山县	Leishan	566	80	11.4			
麻江县	Majiang	3592	66	-25.5	2273	45	-17.4
丹寨县	Danzhai	792	78	1.5	168	67	-55.9
都匀市	Duyun	8558	33	3.0	707	59	-30.0
福泉市	Fuquan	11280	25	7.2	4600	33	-18.6
荔波县	Libo	4598	60	5.9			
贵定县	Guiding	6980	41	4.2	1558	53	-24.2
瓮安县	Wengan	17960	12	2.5	7587	17	1.5
独山县	Dushan	8500	34	9.0	1155	56	-49.6
平塘县	Pingtang	9833	30	11.7	2312	44	-14.9
罗甸县	Luodian	2717	71	持平			
长顺县	Changshun	6332	50	10.4	6049	23	1.1
龙里县	Longli	6775	44	23.2	825	57	-60.7
惠水县	Huishui	6741	45	38.6	1833	51	-37.4
※三都县	Sandu	10992	26	0.6			

27-44 各县(市、区、特区)规模以上工业增加值(2014)

Value-added of Industry above Designated Size and Its Order by County(City,District,Special region)

单位：万元 (10000 yuan)

县(市、区、特区)名称	County (City,District, Special region)	工业增加值 Value-added of Industry	轻工业 Light Industry	重工业 Heavy Industry	位次 Order
南明区	Nanming	225831	193475	32356	42
云岩区	Yunyan	1004036	633217	370819	6
花溪区	Huaxi	1845602	1272540	573062	3
乌当区	Wudang	461724	307540	154184	19
白云区	Baiyun	793154	264202	528952	11
观山湖区	Guanshanhu	117557	14086	103471	55
开阳县	Kaiyang	716107	41625	674483	12
息烽县	Xifeng	544802	60808	483994	16
修文县	Xiuwen	470223	280350	189873	17
清镇市	Qingzhen	319924	35351	284573	27
钟山区	Zhongshan	906040	23323	882717	9
六枝特区	Liuzhi	231003	6968	224035	40
水城县	Shuicheng	1134345	19054	1115291	5
盘　县	Panxian	2292250	4681	2287569	2
红花岗区	Honghuagang	385671	116363	269308	22
汇川区	Huicuan	974584	758587	215997	7
遵义县	Zunyi	1137448	294558	842890	4
桐梓县	Tongzi	259502	1766	257736	33
绥阳县	Suiyang	166690	55108	111582	48
正安县	Zhengan	61266	34843	26423	69
※道真县	Daozhen	34761	8021	26740	79
※务川县	Wuchuan	32686	6095	26591	80
凤冈县	Fenggang	76022	56967	19055	68
湄潭县	Meitan	150998	124065	26933	51
余庆县	Yuqing	128063	28228	99835	53
习水县	Xishui	566117	410283	155834	15
赤水市	Chishui	251192	210143	41049	36
仁怀市	Renhuai	3963600	3951004	12596	1
西秀区	Xixiu	666490	175482	491008	13
平坝区	Pingba	285561	60538	225024	30
普定县	Puding	234626	15226	219400	38
※镇宁县	Zhenning	47229	24560	22668	73
※关岭县	Guanling	37799		37799	77
※紫云县	Ziyun	21199	2727	18472	87
七星关区	Qixingguan	811266	520034	100407	10
大方县	Dafang	338503	7857	295787	26
黔西县	Qianxi	273504	2984	235661	32
金沙县	Jinsha	636905	151277	485628	14
织金县	Zhijin	242848	12287	230561	37
纳雍县	Nayong	433305	5587	427718	20
※威宁县	Weining	194051	5972	188079	46
赫章县	Hezhang	112675	4548	108127	59
碧江区	Bijiang	255858	134784	121074	35
万山区	Wanshan	113698	17011	96687	57

注：统计口径为年主营业务收入2000万元及以上工业企业。

Note: The Statistical caliber of this table in the table refers to the industries which main business revenue achieve 20 millions yuan and above.

27−44 续表 continued

单位：万元 (10000 yuan)

县(市、区、特区)名 称	County (City,District, Special region)	工业增加值 Value-added of Industry	轻工业 Light Industry	重工业 Heavy Industry	位 次 Order
江口县	Jiangkou	43379	32966	10413	74
※玉屏县	Yuping	283115	56503	226612	31
石阡县	Shiqian	53704	34012	19692	72
思南县	Sinan	164982	42686	122296	49
※印江县	Yinjiang	80351	41771	38580	64
德江县	Dejiang	100288	61295	38993	61
※沿河县	Yanhe	90398	22984	67414	62
※松桃县	Songtao	214142	16912	197230	43
兴义市	Xingyi	960434	85375	875059	8
兴仁县	Xingren	256273	17454	238819	34
普安县	Puan	212555	13259	199296	44
晴隆县	Qinglong	138531	6061	132470	52
贞丰县	Zhenfeng	417384	46775	370609	21
望谟县	Wangmo	32323	4899	27424	81
册亨县	Ceheng	31683	7132	24551	82
安龙县	Anlong	197309	3125	194184	45
凯里市	Kaili	375895	69543	306352	24
黄平县	Huangping	38244	3524	34720	76
施秉县	Shibing	22329	4826	17503	85
三穗县	Sansui	60664	40554	20110	70
镇远县	Zhenyuan	231195	112188	119007	39
岑巩县	Cengong	118510	31663	86847	54
天柱县	Tianzhu	168282	4219	164063	47
锦屏县	Jinping	113566	7147	106419	58
剑河县	Jianhe	34838	7289	27549	78
台江县	Taijiang	55291	15911	39380	71
黎平县	Liping	90102	9790	80312	63
榕江县	Rongjiang	78303		78303	67
从江县	Congjiang	43310		43310	75
雷山县	Leishan	14063	6601	7462	88
麻江县	Majiang	31367		31367	83
丹寨县	Danzhai	78739	12497	66242	66
都匀市	Duyun	293935	92428	201507	29
福泉市	Fuquan	463972	2648	461324	18
荔波县	Libo	112669	5584	107085	60
贵定县	Guiding	377244	296290	80954	23
瓮安县	Wengan	349564	2632	346932	25
独山县	Dushan	162371	21784	140587	50
平塘县	Pingtang	21852	5127	16725	86
罗甸县	Luodian	79532	42260	37272	65
长顺县	Changshun	116466	47460	69006	56
龙里县	Longli	295480	141788	153692	28
惠水县	Huishui	228535	78614	149921	41
※三都县	Sandu	27885	9109	18776	84

27-45 各县(市、区、特区)社会消费品零售总额(2014)

Total Retail Sales of Social Consumer Goods by County (City,District,Special Region)

单位：万元 (10000 yuan)

县(市、区、特区)名称	County (City,District, Special Region)	社会消费品零售总额 Total retail sales of social consumer goods	城镇 Urban	乡村 Rural
南明区	Nanming	3027450	3027450	
云岩区	Yunyan	2758339	2758339	
花溪区	Huaxi	1876264	1227077	649187
乌当区	Wudang	303320	291632	11688
白云区	Baiyun	383962	381895	2067
观山湖区	Guanshanhu	905172	905172	
开阳县	Kaiyang	319386	128713	190673
息烽县	Xifeng	173316	96929	76387
修文县	Xiuwen	201603	84114	117489
清镇市	Qingzhen	359214	308924	50290
钟山区	Zhongshan	1451104	1088328	362776
六枝特区	Liuzhi	323343	242507	80836
水城县	Shuicheng	151600	113700	37900
盘　县	Panxian	687707	515781	171927
红花岗区	Honghuagang	1729113	1323924	405190
汇川区	Huicuan	924245	900759	23486
遵义县	Zunyi	592169	327985	264185
桐梓县	Tongzi	224159	170361	53798
绥阳县	Suiyang	173333	135199	38133
正安县	Zhengan	171962	120373	51589
※道真县	Daozhen	109618	71251	38367
※务川县	Wuchuan	110463	64754	45709
凤冈县	Fenggang	149682	94777	54904
湄潭县	Meitan	227742	148032	79710
余庆县	Yuqing	142118	92377	49741
习水县	Xishui	214884	161163	53721
赤水市	Chishui	208531	135545	72986
仁怀市	Renhuai	726022	642247	83775
西秀区	Xixiu	549648	348139	201509
平坝区	Pingba	206738	109085	97653
普定县	Puding	156686	81012	75674
※镇宁县	Zhenning	166951	100724	66227
※关岭县	Guanling	184652	114213	70439
※紫云县	Ziyun	129061	83069	45992
七星关区	Qixingguan	956662	669664	286999
大方县	Dafang	260683	182478	78205
黔西县	Qianxi	277250	194075	83175
金沙县	Jinsha	278973	195281	83692
织金县	Zhijin	259006	181305	77702
纳雍县	Nayong	213036	149125	63911
※威宁县	Weining	258515	180961	77555
赫章县	Hezhang	189678	132775	56904
碧江区	Bijiang	402774	306109	96666
万山区	Wanshan	48060	36045	12015

27−45 续表 continued

单位：万元 (10000 yuan)

县(市、区、特区)名称	County (City,District, Special Region)	社会消费品零售总额 Total retail sales of social consumer goods	城镇 Urban	乡村 Rural
江口县	Jiangkou	74181	57119	17062
※玉屏县	Yuping	80408	64327	16082
石阡县	Shiqian	85167	64727	20440
思南县	Sinan	200411	146300	54111
※印江县	Yinjiang	107292	83688	23604
德江县	Dejiang	140284	103810	36474
※沿河县	Yanhe	150423	115826	34597
※松桃县	Songtao	191902	136250	55651
兴义市	Xingyi	1192815	1037602	155213
兴仁县	Xingren	154739	101783	52956
普安县	Puan	69263	55622	13641
晴隆县	Qinglong	57074	42158	14916
贞丰县	Zhenfeng	80290	65091	15200
望谟县	Wangmo	39327	28890	10437
册亨县	Ceheng	22288	17420	4869
安龙县	Anlong	102731	92458	10273
凯里市	Kaili	874069	669362	204707
黄平县	Huangping	99015	75826	23189
施秉县	Shibing	67261	51508	15753
三穗县	Sansui	111089	85072	26017
镇远县	Zhenyuan	112776	86364	26412
岑巩县	Cengong	91729	70246	21483
天柱县	Tianzhu	155373	118985	36388
锦屏县	Jinping	82618	63269	19349
剑河县	Jianhe	85869	65758	20111
台江县	Taijiang	50153	38407	11746
黎平县	Liping	168851	129306	39545
榕江县	Rongjiang	114182	87441	26741
从江县	Congjiang	113301	86766	26535
雷山县	Leishan	55220	42288	12933
麻江县	Majiang	61324	46962	14362
丹寨县	Danzhai	49090	37593	11497
都匀市	Duyun	556603	445282	111321
福泉市	Fuquan	186588	149270	37318
荔波县	Libo	88525	70820	17705
贵定县	Guiding	135154	108123	27031
瓮安县	Wengan	168261	134609	33652
独山县	Dushan	146367	117094	29273
平塘县	Pingtang	106890	85512	21378
罗甸县	Luodian	103391	82713	20678
长顺县	Changshun	84763	67811	16953
龙里县	Longli	126196	100957	25239
惠水县	Huishui	150533	120426	30107
※三都县	Sandu	107352	85882	21470

27-46 各县(市、区、特区)金融机构人民币各项存贷款余额(2014)

Urban and Rural Resident Savings Deposit Balance and Loan by County(City,District,Special region)

单位：亿元 (100 million yuan)

县(市、区、特区)名称	County (City,District, Special region)	金融机构人民币各项存款余额 Total Deposits	#个人储蓄蓄存款 Personal Saving Deposits	金融机构人民币各项贷款余额 Total Loans
开阳县	Kaiyang	93.02	55.89	84.13
息烽县	Xifeng	69.85	38.48	63.95
修文县	Xiuwen	57.61	35.85	41.74
清镇市	Qingzhen	142.75	82.36	98.12
六枝特区	Liuzhi	93.73	61.37	79.80
盘　县	Panxian	218.74	133.26	168.87
遵义县	Zunyi	238.26	157.46	172.98
桐梓县	Tongzi	99.96	77.49	55.31
绥阳县	Suiyang	80.87	63.49	44.91
正安县	Zhengan	81.87	60.19	40.56
※道真县	Daozhen	64.71	51.85	29.51
※务川县	Wuchuan	70.02	46.06	35.79
凤冈县	Fenggang	64.68	47.13	37.10
湄潭县	Meitan	98.64	77.84	61.81
余庆县	Yuqing	57.24	43.52	44.66
习水县	Xishui	108.36	68.64	60.44
赤水市	Chishui	89.30	66.19	69.81
仁怀市	Renhuai	451.42	116.48	182.55
平坝区	Pingba	104.28	56.88	84.09
普定县	Puding	47.94	29.72	57.42
※镇宁县	Zhenning	56.76	28.86	63.66
※关岭县	Guanling	49.73	31.33	33.62
※紫云县	Ziyun	44.84	23.24	29.01
七星关区	Qixingguan	329.12	156.96	237.74
大方县	Dafang	95.56	73.12	58.58
黔西县	Qianxi	78.95	57.33	74.65
金沙县	Jinsha	88.13	59.52	78.31
织金县	Zhijin	102.43	70.90	92.91
纳雍县	Nayong	76.28	50.71	57.87
※威宁县	Weining	80.52	54.65	55.83
赫章县	Hezhang	65.80	45.53	33.60
碧江区	Bijiang	246.78	112.13	187.51
万山区	Wanshan	25.25	14.20	13.62

注：资料来源于中国人民银行贵阳中心支行。

Notes:Data in the table are obtained from Guiyang Central Branch of PBC.

27-46 续表 continued

单位：亿元 (100 million yuan)

县(市、区、特区)名 称	County (City,District, Special region)	金融机构人民币各项存款余额 Total Deposits	#个人储蓄存款 Personal Saving Deposits	金融机构人民币各项贷款余额 Total Loans
江口县	Jiangkou	42.81	27.65	39.52
※玉屏县	Yuping	32.87	23.62	42.35
石阡县	Shiqian	52.75	38.09	39.85
思南县	Sinan	91.98	67.37	78.72
※印江县	Yinjiang	61.63	42.39	51.86
德江县	Dejiang	53.42	39.61	49.75
※沿河县	Yanhe	68.49	50.33	40.60
※松桃县	Songtao	78.16	60.38	57.86
兴义市	Xingyi	391.27	162.28	300.78
兴仁县	Xingren	62.74	36.80	66.51
普安县	Puan	40.86	25.20	34.81
晴隆县	Qinglong	37.45	23.08	21.89
贞丰县	Zhenfeng	69.41	37.93	37.57
望谟县	Wangmo	47.19	18.19	23.53
册亨县	Ceheng	41.11	18.13	23.14
安龙县	Anlong	69.30	44.04	31.74
凯里市	Kaili	339.39	162.47	239.70
黄平县	Huangping	46.38	35.04	24.05
施秉县	Shibing	38.70	31.07	17.75
三穗县	Sansui	29.71	24.02	20.46
镇远县	Zhenyuan	40.31	30.20	29.15
岑巩县	Cengong	32.35	25.23	23.87
天柱县	Tianzhu	67.94	49.93	29.40
锦屏县	Jinping	41.73	30.36	17.58
剑河县	Jianhe	33.85	27.09	19.74
台江县	Taijiang	22.28	16.63	29.62
黎平县	Liping	66.71	52.29	46.90
榕江县	Rongjiang	43.86	35.61	37.87
从江县	Congjiang	32.70	24.38	22.49
雷山县	Leishan	26.51	18.00	18.11
麻江县	Majiang	30.86	22.25	20.72
丹寨县	Danzhai	32.52	19.44	16.24
都匀市	Duyun	283.06	139.02	169.76
福泉市	Fuquan	76.04	48.38	76.89
荔波县	Libo	43.16	25.96	31.27
贵定县	Guiding	47.68	35.01	33.54
瓮安县	Wengan	93.03	67.04	62.05
独山县	Dushan	59.79	45.21	37.37
平塘县	Pingtang	38.54	25.99	25.68
罗甸县	Luodian	45.20	25.91	31.48
长顺县	Changshun	30.95	18.07	22.96
龙里县	Longli	57.57	34.15	44.26
惠水县	Huishui	50.67	33.29	39.23
※三都县	Sandu	41.73	27.95	30.04

27-47 各县(市、区、特区)普通中学(2014)

县(市、区、特区)名 称	County (City,Distric, Special Region)	学校数(所) Total Schools (unit)	#初中 Junior Secondary Schools	毕业生数(人) Graduates(person) 初中 Junior Secondary Schools	高中 Senior Secondary Schools
南明区	Nanming	67	57	7654	2776
云岩区	Yunyan	64	50	9923	4880
花溪区	Huaxi	52	39	7889	3682
乌当区	Wudang	15	11	2594	833
白云区	Baiyun	12	8	4368	2539
观山湖区	Guanshanhu	23	16	3682	2167
开阳县	Kaiyang	22	18	6769	3101
息烽县	Xifeng	14	11	3314	1380
修文县	Xiuwen	17	12	3609	1551
清镇市	Qingzhen	25	16	8104	3067
钟山区	Zhongshan	48	38	11488	7922
六枝特区	Liuzhi	40	36	10508	2860
水城县	Shuicheng	61	57	12279	3094
盘　县	Panxian	76	64	22759	7975
红花岗区	Honghuagang	41	29	9859	4872
汇川区	Huicuan	34	25	7302	3194
遵义县	Zunyi	60	51	19712	9512
桐梓县	Tongzi	44	37	10159	3176
绥阳县	Suiyang	32	26	8150	1847
正安县	Zhengan	39	35	9124	2582
※道真县	Daozhen	22	20	5340	2423
※务川县	Wuchuan	28	24	9109	2638
凤冈县	Fenggang	20	16	8204	3172
湄潭县	Meitan	24	21	9089	2769
余庆县	Yuqing	15	13	5221	2340
习水县	Xishui	33	25	9061	3453
赤水市	Chishui	17	14	3532	1443
仁怀市	Renhuai	39	31	11612	3660
西秀区	Xixiu	52	42	13208	5749
平坝区	Pingba	23	18	4599	1744
普定县	Puding	15	13	5585	1344
※镇宁县	Zhenning	21	20	3738	789
※关岭县	Guanling	20	19	3826	1167
※紫云县	Ziyun	21	20	5455	964
七星关区	Qixingguan	114	98	30192	8512
大方县	Dafang	56	42	19943	5668
黔西县	Qianxi	59	51	13620	4413
金沙县	Jinsha	30	27	9698	2815
织金县	Zhijin	47	40	17138	4545
纳雍县	Nayong	40	35	13585	4035
※威宁县	Weining	67	57	30775	5243
赫章县	Hezhang	53	43	15906	3605
碧江区	Bijiang	23	16	5518	5254
万山区	Wanshan	10	8	2250	249

注：资料来源于省教育厅（以下相关表同）。

Regular Secondary Schools by County(City,District,Special region)

招生数(人) New Enrollment(person)		在校学生数(人) Students Enrollment(person)		专任教师(人) Full-time Teachers(person)	
初中 Junior Secondary Schools	高中 Senior Secondary Schools	初中 Junior Secondary Schools	高中 Senior Secondary Schools	初中 Junior Secondary Schools	高中 Senior Secondary Schools
8439	2686	24938	8290	1787	600
9756	5691	30928	16500	2104	1309
7460	4441	24376	12682	1589	804
2956	1186	8054	3160	650	260
4472	2618	13551	7583	813	608
4137	2981	12719	8093	951	555
4162	3067	14995	9992	992	455
2794	1961	9311	5371	589	309
2973	2124	9755	5716	757	363
6279	3692	21140	10951	1340	769
14238	8826	40830	27014	1749	1362
10443	3862	30833	11562	1749	516
12966	5075	38789	13603	2199	909
16426	12052	57525	34120	3269	1781
9231	7258	28573	20369	1792	1143
6742	4120	21231	11650	1308	755
14295	11380	49250	34283	3176	1474
9237	4918	28185	13558	1718	693
7181	3806	23032	9252	1530	497
7704	4139	24119	10675	1716	615
5272	3129	16338	8063	998	422
8416	4424	25023	12563	1182	687
6321	3693	20819	10970	1305	562
7299	4530	23572	11879	1253	646
4115	2627	13404	7760	782	386
10145	5043	29399	12640	1695	763
3141	1765	9535	5199	663	287
10917	5805	34076	16035	2331	905
14253	8300	42099	23173	2455	1099
5113	2227	15258	6290	918	383
6520	2146	19504	5915	1141	330
5023	1525	14139	3608	854	176
4850	1683	14246	4782	872	307
5492	2004	16293	5282	757	263
30658	14313	92509	36176	4940	1734
16616	9233	52371	22261	3313	1246
14302	6358	43352	16733	2565	780
9929	4668	30335	11505	1778	682
19279	8311	60326	20431	2756	1133
17823	6026	52380	15412	2358	695
34722	14806	119020	35532	4754	1663
18679	7653	54618	17991	2868	1125
6477	6405	19364	18810	1247	1011
1857	1006	6394	1968	409	141

Note：Data in the table are provided by the Provincteal of Education(The rclative tables in the chapter are the same).

27-47 续表

县（市、区、特区）名　称	County (City,Distric, Special Region)	学校数(所) Total Schools (unit)	#初中 Junior Secondary Schools	毕业生数(人) Graduates(person) 初中 Junior Secondary Schools	高中 Senior Secondary Schools
江口县	Jiangkou	15	13	3266	1586
※玉屏县	Yuping	9	7	2125	959
石阡县	Shiqian	27	23	6680	2479
思南县	Sinan	39	33	13254	5108
※印江县	Yinjiang	24	18	6663	2499
德江县	Dejiang	29	25	9074	2815
※沿河县	Yanhe	37	33	11231	2512
※松桃县	Songtao	39	35	10381	3461
兴义市	Xingyi	83	60	15093	8638
兴仁县	Xingren	42	38	8662	1654
普安县	Puan	30	28	4906	1019
晴隆县	Qinglong	23	21	4744	1274
贞丰县	Zhenfeng	23	20	4951	1234
望谟县	Wangmo	20	18	5397	1225
册亨县	Ceheng	19	17	3542	837
安龙县	Anlong	26	22	7181	1999
凯里市	Kaili	37	25	8576	5662
黄平县	Huangping	13	11	5377	1722
施秉县	Shibing	10	9	2414	692
三穗县	Sansui	9	6	2635	992
镇远县	Zhenyuan	19	17	3580	1223
岑巩县	Cengong	14	12	3586	1146
天柱县	Tianzhu	20	17	5016	2610
锦屏县	Jinping	18	16	3330	1693
剑河县	Jianhe	15	12	3529	979
台江县	Taijiang	9	8	2189	808
黎平县	Liping	25	21	7611	2311
榕江县	Rongjiang	23	20	4046	1465
从江县	Congjiang	22	20	4643	769
雷山县	Leishan	6	5	2304	890
麻江县	Majiang	10	7	3350	1272
丹寨县	Danzhai	5	4	2287	863
都匀市	Duyun	29	19	6048	3884
福泉市	Fuquan	18	15	4579	1693
荔波县	Libo	8	7	2831	1379
贵定县	Guiding	17	15	3790	1000
瓮安县	Wengan	29	24	6347	3559
独山县	Dushan	7	4	5402	2308
平塘县	Pingtang	19	18	4622	1371
罗甸县	Luodian	22	20	4124	1684
长顺县	Changshun	18	17	3746	1169
龙里县	Longli	16	15	2995	1008
惠水县	Huishui	24	22	7122	2374
※三都县	Sandu	22	20	5353	1666

continued

招生数(人) New Enrollment(person)		在校学生数(人) Students Enrollment(person)		专任教师(人) Full-time Teachers(person)	
初中 Junior Secondary Schools	高中 Senior Secondary Schools	初中 Junior Secondary Schools	高中 Senior Secondary Schools	初中 Junior Secondary Schools	高中 Senior Secondary Schools
2978	2031	9492	5459	674	331
1876	1015	5930	3082	464	218
6698	4065	20607	9806	1136	563
11651	8479	37810	22867	1561	1158
6313	3316	19060	9291	1147	542
9752	4349	29171	11446	1548	657
11658	3441	34390	9160	1768	444
10189	5635	31561	13080	2095	682
16170	10931	47621	30132	3141	1977
9445	2953	27584	7272	1775	481
5317	2199	17494	5415	830	257
4689	2306	15148	5631	678	270
7196	2033	18699	5266	1112	283
6190	2103	17855	5305	1049	285
4086	1554	12670	3425	718	224
4832	3392	20989	9203	1305	476
9253	6878	27775	19171	1624	1223
5952	2605	17676	7263	980	362
2364	982	7374	2848	421	159
2800	1470	8196	4084	435	379
4224	2037	11994	5269	696	295
3660	2008	11547	5044	638	334
3467	2639	12251	7870	1033	400
2507	2023	8038	5671	651	333
4167	2011	12087	4664	652	238
2312	1215	6993	3092	395	178
6464	4193	21915	10800	1268	506
5311	2251	15518	6575	981	374
5004	2279	14674	6167	850	274
2262	1363	6978	3499	416	192
3016	1881	9031	4175	678	242
2501	1368	7578	3297	482	166
5310	4415	17020	12709	1163	736
3342	2401	11244	6971	850	432
2366	1455	7598	4628	458	251
3654	1707	11574	4254	721	273
5442	3718	17504	11343	1098	566
3490	2411	11912	6948	808	453
4583	2203	13527	5469	906	243
5771	2018	15116	6334	921	397
3952	1244	11541	4654	710	259
2875	1066	9011	3262	580	192
7001	3308	22239	8547	1336	460
6102	2533	17826	6806	899	397

27-48 各县(市、区、特区)小学(2014)

Primary Schools by County(City,District,Special region)

县(市、区、特区)名称	County (City,Distric, Special Region)	学校数(个) Schools (unit)	毕业生数(人) Gruaduates (person)	招生数(人) New Enrollment (person)	在校学生数(人) Students Enrollment (person)	专任教师(人) Full-time Teachers (person)	学龄儿童入学率(%) Enrollment Ratio of Primary Schools(%)	学龄女童入学率(%) Enrollment Ratio of School Girls(%)
南明区	Nanming	82	9473	9949	56113	2688	112.1	100.6
云岩区	Yunyan	74	10571	11538	62932	3066	118.4	118.6
花溪区	Huaxi	96	7898	8774	46943	2505	110.8	110.6
乌当区	Wudang	44	2553	3266	16160	1070	142.8	141.9
白云区	Baiyun	50	4096	4602	25260	1338	132.3	132.8
观山湖区	Guanshanhu	40	3322	5728	26649	1525	138.8	137.4
开阳县	Kaiyang	33	4148	3926	20869	1299	96.1	97.6
息烽县	Xifeng	27	2769	2996	16010	1061	99.6	99.6
修文县	Xiuwen	41	2797	3485	16962	973	98.9	98.9
清镇市	Qingzhen	84	6040	6435	32102	1948	100.0	102.6
钟山区	Zhongshan	83	13381	10884	66175	2746	122.3	121.5
六枝特区	Liuzhi	156	10015	10115	58439	3036	96.6	96.5
水城县	Shuicheng	203	13924	10305	66841	3608	85.7	89.4
盘　县	Panxian	231	15740	11068	63880	4344	97.9	98.1
红花岗区	Honghuagang	74	9236	9078	52009	2379	155.2	152.8
汇川区	Huicuan	72	6383	6009	34595	1726	133.2	130.0
遵义县	Zunyi	238	13061	12414	68614	5115	106.2	110.1
桐梓县	Tongzi	152	9098	7819	48084	2636	79.9	73.1
绥阳县	Suiyang	96	7664	4988	31545	1909	86.2	88.5
正安县	Zhengan	113	7171	6171	35910	2330	87.9	86.6
※道真县	Daozhen	68	5100	4108	24479	1526	86.2	87.5
※务川县	Wuchuan	89	7831	4435	32034	1785	75.2	77.1
凤冈县	Fenggang	87	5999	4162	28231	1653	88.2	89.2
湄潭县	Meitan	78	6887	5305	31474	1888	96.9	97.0
余庆县	Yuqing	81	3935	3812	23348	1156	86.5	87.4
习水县	Xishui	87	9916	8933	51238	2786	84.6	86.4
赤水市	Chishui	56	3068	3724	19862	1284	80.8	81.6
仁怀市	Renhuai	78	11025	7776	49159	3064	91.0	84.8
西秀区	Xixiu	152	13119	12226	74798	4417	106.3	107.9
平坝区	Pingba	139	5237	4802	28345	1897	95.3	98.9
普定县	Puding	96	6656	6302	38338	2224	98.9	98.5
※镇宁县	Zhenning	100	5415	4567	31340	1648	90.2	93.0
※关岭县	Guanling	102	4913	5176	29974	1661	93.2	93.6
※紫云县	Ziyun	125	5597	5474	30340	1645	94.3	96.0
七星关区	Qixingguan	341	29561	23426	155148	7979	101.8	101.9
大方县	Dafang	323	17258	13329	88282	5028	96.4	96.0
黔西县	Qianxi	158	14238	11114	65848	3823	102.1	104.4
金沙县	Jinsha	86	10612	10223	61332	3223	90.9	89.5
织金县	Zhijin	310	20088	13952	95145	4449	88.9	89.4
纳雍县	Nayong	240	18461	14498	100189	4472	90.3	92.0
※威宁县	Weining	421	34713	25630	187115	8550	98.2	99.1
赫章县	Hezhang	291	19349	13461	88955	4492	99.3	99.7
碧江区	Bijiang	68	5365	5326	31132	1883	146.2	150.5
万山区	Wanshan	45	1817	1814	10102	687	74.4	76.3

27-48 续表 continued

县(市、区、特区)名称	County (City,Distric, Special Region)	学校数(个) Schools (unit)	毕业生数(人) Gruaduates (person)	招生数(人) New Enrollment (person)	在校学生数(人) Students Enrollment (person)	专任教师(人) Full-time Teachers (person)	学龄儿童入学率(%) Enrollment Ratio of Primary Schools(%)	学龄女童入学率(%) Enrollment Ratio of School Girls(%)
江口县	Jiangkou	37	3298	2480	16282	906	88.4	86.3
※玉屏县	Yuping	34	1885	2000	11137	781	89.0	89.8
石阡县	Shiqian	78	6961	4191	29524	2034	78.1	79.3
思南县	Sinan	171	11168	6954	51236	2850	96.6	98.5
※印江县	Yinjiang	107	7036	4512	34404	2040	99.9	98.9
德江县	Dejiang	168	10470	6210	47826	2322	96.7	97.0
※沿河县	Yanhe	203	11823	7741	62809	3446	99.1	100.2
※松桃县	Songtao	163	10596	7002	49660	3705	99.9	99.8
兴义市	Xingyi	179	13171	12245	75001	4298	106.5	108.1
兴仁县	Xingren	122	9903	8708	54425	2914	99.7	100.3
普安县	Puan	104	5662	4243	30783	1459	99.2	99.2
晴隆县	Qinglong	95	5261	5090	32486	1517	99.3	98.9
贞丰县	Zhenfeng	135	7491	5732	42718	2414	95.3	96.2
望谟县	Wangmo	106	6573	4301	33491	2151	89.5	91.7
册亨县	Ceheng	59	4260	3092	19161	972	99.2	99.1
安龙县	Anlong	51	4812	5745	34843	2085	102.1	103.2
凯里市	Kaili	58	8723	8052	48518	2560	104.7	106.0
黄平县	Huangping	76	5819	3824	27792	1391	99.2	95.0
施秉县	Shibing	42	2661	1967	12855	865	99.5	100.8
三穗县	Sansui	37	2850	2967	16146	885	99.3	99.9
镇远县	Zhenyuan	43	4240	2881	18239	1029	99.8	102.1
岑巩县	Cengong	54	3616	2695	17003	1050	87.8	86.8
天柱县	Tianzhu	48	3495	4264	23416	1505	93.8	98.0
锦屏县	Jinping	39	2477	2338	13557	820	93.4	93.3
剑河县	Jianhe	65	4058	3398	19059	1076	98.9	98.9
台江县	Taijiang	35	2452	2157	13418	835	99.1	98.8
黎平县	Liping	136	6500	5603	32360	2037	99.8	99.8
榕江县	Rongjiang	86	5463	4401	27812	1535	99.6	97.0
从江县	Congjiang	107	5313	4471	27751	1537	92.5	92.7
雷山县	Leishan	30	2197	1767	11019	815	99.1	99.8
麻江县	Majiang	35	3093	2353	14343	1020	99.2	100.6
丹寨县	Danzhai	25	2449	2365	14303	846	99.2	99.7
都匀市	Duyun	76	5170	4898	28244	1834	99.7	101.9
福泉市	Fuquan	76	3372	3678	19068	1232	99.2	99.7
荔波县	Libo	39	2322	1891	12162	728	95.1	96.2
贵定县	Guiding	86	3723	3172	18774	1306	99.9	100.0
瓮安县	Wengan	81	5170	6000	31010	1676	99.2	99.1
独山县	Dushan	41	3256	3362	18985	1279	99.7	102.8
平塘县	Pingtang	96	4528	3318	24498	1203	99.9	99.9
罗甸县	Luodian	85	5884	4186	27591	1501	95.3	95.1
长顺县	Changshun	77	3987	2675	17028	1140	99.0	99.0
龙里县	Longli	61	2928	2841	15579	1019	92.5	91.6
惠水县	Huishui	108	6982	5128	32288	2018	99.8	99.8
※三都县	Sandu	111	6244	4770	32152	1692	99.6	99.4

全国及各省(区、市)资料

28

Main Statistics of Provinces (autonomous regions,municipalities) in the Whole Country

28-1 全国及各省(区、市)人口、地区生产总值(2014)

单位：亿元

地 区	Region	年末总人口(万人) Total Population year-end (10000 persons)	位次 Order	地区生产总值 Gross Domestic Product	位次 Order	第一产业增加值 Primary Industry	位次 Order
全 国	**National Total**	**136782**		**636463**		**58332**	
北 京	Beijing	2152	26	21330.83	13	158.99	29
天 津	Tianjin	1517	27	15726.93	17	199.90	28
河 北	Hebei	7384	6	29421.15	6	3447.46	5
山 西	Shanxi	3648	18	12761.49	24	788.89	25
内蒙古	Inner Mongolia	2505	23	17770.19	15	1627.85	17
辽 宁	Liaoning	4391	14	28626.58	7	2285.75	12
吉 林	Jilin	2752	21	13803.14	22	1524.01	20
黑龙江	Heilongjiang	3833	15	15039.38	20	2611.36	9
上 海	Shanghai	2426	24	23567.70	12	124.26	30
江 苏	Jiangsu	7960	5	65088.32	2	3634.33	3
浙 江	Zhejiang	5508	10	40173.03	4	1777.18	15
安 徽	Anhui	6083	8	20848.75	14	2392.39	11
福 建	Fujian	3806	16	24055.76	11	2014.80	13
江 西	Jiangxi	4542	13	15714.63	18	1683.72	16
山 东	Shandong	9789	2	59426.59	3	4798.36	1
河 南	Henan	9436	3	34938.24	5	4160.01	2
湖 北	Hubei	5816	9	27379.22	9	3176.89	6
湖 南	Hunan	6737	7	27037.32	10	3148.75	8
广 东	Guangdong	10724	1	67809.85	1	3166.82	7
广 西	Guangxi	4754	11	15672.89	19	2413.44	10
海 南	Hainan	903	28	3500.72	28	809.52	24
重 庆	Chongqing	2991	20	14262.60	21	1061.03	22
四 川	Sichuan	8140	4	28536.66	8	3531.05	4
贵 州	**Guizhou**	**3508**	**19**	**9266.39**	**26**	**1280.45**	**21**
云 南	Yunnan	4714	12	12814.59	23	1990.07	14
西 藏	Tibet	318	31	920.83	31	91.64	31
陕 西	Shanxi	3775	17	17689.94	16	1564.94	18
甘 肃	Gansu	2591	22	6836.82	27	900.76	23
青 海	Qinghai	583	30	2303.32	30	215.93	27
宁 夏	Ningxia	662	29	2752.10	29	216.99	26
新 疆	Xinjiang	2298	25	9273.46	25	1538.60	19

The Population and GDP of the Whole Country and All Provinces

(100 million yuan)

第二产业增加值 Secondary Industry	位 次 Order	第三产业增加值 Tertiary Industry	位 次 Order	地区生产总值比上年增长(%) Increase Rate of GDP in 2014 over 2013(%)	位 次 Order	人均地区生产总值(元) Per Capita Gross Domestic Product(yuan)	位 次 Order
271392		**306739**		**7.4**		**46652**	
4544.80	24	16627.04	5	7.3	25	99995	2
7731.85	17	7795.18	14	10.0	4	105231	1
15012.85	6	10960.84	12	6.5	27	39984	18
6293.91	21	5678.69	22	4.9	31	35070	24
9119.79	14	7022.55	16	7.8	22	71044	6
14384.64	7	11956.19	8	5.8	29	65201	7
7286.59	19	4992.54	24	6.5	27	50163	11
5544.41	22	6883.61	17	5.6	30	39226	20
8167.71	16	15275.72	6	7.0	26	97370	3
30854.50	2	30599.49	2	8.7	16	81875	4
19175.06	4	19220.79	4	7.6	24	73002	5
11077.67	12	7378.68	15	9.2	11	34425	26
12515.36	10	9525.60	13	9.9	6	63472	8
8247.93	15	5782.98	21	9.7	7	34674	25
28788.11	3	25840.12	3	8.7	15	60880	10
17816.56	5	12961.67	7	8.9	14	37071	22
12852.40	9	11349.93	10	9.7	9	47145	13
12482.06	11	11406.51	9	9.5	10	40271	17
31419.75	1	33223.28	1	7.8	23	63469	9
7324.96	18	5934.49	20	8.5	17	33090	27
875.97	30	1815.23	28	8.5	18	38924	21
6529.06	20	6672.51	18	10.9	1	47850	12
13962.41	8	11043.20	11	8.5	18	35129	23
3857.44	**26**	**4128.50**	**25**	**10.8**	**2**	**26437**	**30**
5281.82	23	5542.70	23	8.1	20	27263	29
336.84	31	492.35	31	10.8	3	29231	28
9577.24	13	6547.76	19	9.7	7	46928	14
2926.45	27	3009.61	27	8.9	13	26432	31
1234.31	29	853.08	30	9.2	12	39671	19
1341.24	28	1193.87	29	8.0	21	41819	15
3948.96	25	3785.90	26	10.0	5	40653	16

28-2 全国及各省(区、市)固定资产投资(不含农户)、房地产开发情况(2014)

地 区	Region	固定资产投资(亿元) Investment in Fixed Assets(100 million yuan)	位 次 Order	房地产开发投资(亿元) Real Estate Investment (100 million yuan)	位 次 Order
全 国	**National Total**	**502004.90**		**95035.61**	
北 京	Beijing	6873.44	26	3715.33	12
天 津	Tianjin	10490.37	21	1699.65	20
河 北	Hebei	26147.20	4	4059.72	10
山 西	Shanxi	11976.96	18	1403.55	22
内蒙古	Inner Mongolia	17431.05	13	1370.88	23
辽 宁	Liaoning	24426.83	6	5301.31	5
吉 林	Jilin	11254.84	19	1030.13	26
黑龙江	Heilongjiang	9587.09	22	1324.09	24
上 海	Shanghai	6012.97	27	3206.48	14
江 苏	Jiangsu	41552.75	2	8240.22	1
浙 江	Zhejiang	23554.76	7	7262.38	3
安 徽	Anhui	21069.24	10	4338.96	9
福 建	Fujian	17911.71	12	4567.40	6
江 西	Jiangxi	14677.04	15	1322.49	25
山 东	Shandong	41599.13	1	5817.95	4
河 南	Henan	30012.28	3	4375.71	8
湖 北	Hubei	22491.67	9	3983.79	11
湖 南	Hunan	20575.33	11	2883.57	15
广 东	Guangdong	25843.06	5	7638.45	2
广 西	Guangxi	13287.60	16	1838.49	19
海 南	Hainan	3039.46	29	1431.65	21
重 庆	Chongqing	12136.52	17	3630.23	13
四 川	Sichuan	22662.26	8	4380.09	7
贵 州	**Guizhou**	**8778.40**	**24**	**2187.67**	**18**
云 南	Yunnan	11073.86	20	2846.65	16
西 藏	Tibet	1069.23	31	52.91	31
陕 西	Shanxi	16840.44	14	2426.49	17
甘 肃	Gansu	7759.62	25	721.47	28
青 海	Qinghai	2788.91	30	308.27	30
宁 夏	Ningxia	3093.92	28	654.80	29
新 疆	Xinjiang	9058.31	23	1014.81	27

注：1.本表统计口径为计划总投资500万元及以上固定资产项目投资和房地产开发项目投资，分省数据不含跨省项目。

The Investment in Fixed Assets(Excluding Rural Households) and Real Estate Development of the Whole Country and All Province

房地产开发企业房屋施工面积(万平方米) Floor Space under Construction(10000 aq.m)	位 次 Order	房地产开发企业房屋竣工面积(万平方米) Floor Space Completed (10000 aq.m)	位 次 Order	房地产开发企业商品房销售面积(万平方米) Floor Space of Commercial Houses(10000 aq.m)	位 次 Order
726482.34		**107459.05**		**120648.54**	
13588.08	22	3054.12	14	1454.19	26
10652.37	26	2924.82	16	1612.98	23
31628.39	9	4037.56	9	5706.19	8
15476.89	19	2182.48	20	1576.27	25
18474.17	17	2012.08	22	2457.18	20
38616.88	6	6146.96	6	5754.81	7
12268.44	24	1573.86	26	1581.72	24
14218.09	21	3000.90	15	2475.74	19
14690.18	20	2313.29	18	2084.66	21
57637.72	1	9620.47	1	9846.84	1
42144.35	4	6390.17	5	4676.83	12
33479.11	8	5196.37	8	6202.18	6
30051.77	10	3583.57	12	4119.48	13
13332.64	23	1871.79	23	3067.16	18
54508.45	2	7787.31	2	9180.12	3
38857.60	5	7324.34	4	7879.67	4
26321.99	13	3431.18	13	5601.98	9
27747.75	12	4022.89	10	5439.53	10
53977.47	3	7327.99	3	9315.76	2
17472.15	18	1865.98	24	3156.55	16
7557.15	28	1203.90	27	1003.97	29
28623.93	11	3717.78	11	5100.39	11
36499.35	7	5334.45	7	7142.44	5
20369.36	**14**	**2842.32**	**17**	**3178.12**	**15**
20034.58	15	1788.62	25	3194.19	14
273.17	31	52.47	31	59.33	31
19466.10	16	2188.91	19	3093.64	17
7660.30	27	813.22	29	1325.51	27
2545.90	30	559.49	30	415.77	30
7019.37	29	1203.68	28	1129.46	28
11288.65	25	2086.08	21	1815.88	22

Note: The statistic scope in the table refers to those projects planned to invest 5 million yuan at least in investment in fixed assets and real estate development, but provincial data don't include inter-provincial project.

28-3 全国及各省(区、市)内外贸易(2014)

Imports and Exports of the Whole Country and All Provinces

单位：亿美元 (USD 100 million)

地区	Region	社会消费品零售总额(亿元) Total Retail Sales of Consumer Goods (100 million yuan)	位次 Order	进出口总额 Total Exports and Imports	位次 Order	出口额 Exports	位次 Order	进口额 Imports	位次 Order
全国	**National Total**	**271896.1**		**43030.37**		**23427.47**		**19602.90**	
北京	Beijing	9638.0	11	4156.54	4	623.48	8	3533.06	2
天津	Tianjin	4738.7	23	1339.12	8	525.97	10	813.16	7
河北	Hebei	11820.5	9	598.83	13	357.13	13	241.69	13
山西	Shanxi	5717.9	19	162.49	24	89.42	24	73.06	25
内蒙古	Inner Mongolia	5657.6	21	145.54	26	63.94	25	81.59	24
辽宁	Liaoning	11857.0	8	1139.60	9	587.59	9	552.01	9
吉林	Jilin	6080.9	16	263.78	23	57.78	26	206.00	15
黑龙江	Heilongjiang	7015.3	15	389.00	18	173.40	21	215.60	14
上海	Shanghai	9303.5	13	4664.09	3	2101.63	4	2562.45	3
江苏	Jiangsu	23458.1	3	5637.61	2	3418.68	2	2218.93	4
浙江	Zhejiang	17835.3	4	3551.47	5	2733.54	3	817.94	6
安徽	Anhui	7957.0	14	492.73	14	314.93	15	177.80	16
福建	Fujian	9346.7	12	1774.99	7	1134.57	6	640.42	8
江西	Jiangxi	5292.6	22	427.83	16	320.38	14	107.45	23
山东	Shandong	25111.5	2	2771.15	6	1447.45	5	1323.70	5
河南	Henan	14005.0	5	650.33	12	393.84	12	256.49	11
湖北	Hubei	12449.3	6	430.64	15	266.46	16	164.18	17
湖南	Hunan	10723.5	10	310.27	19	200.23	19	110.04	21
广东	Guangdong	28471.1	1	10767.34	1	6462.22	1	4305.12	1
广西	Guangxi	5772.8	18	405.53	17	243.30	17	162.23	18
海南	Hainan	1224.5	28	158.73	25	44.17	28	114.57	20
重庆	Chongqing	5710.7	20	954.50	10	634.09	7	320.41	10
四川	Sichuan	12393.0	7	702.52	11	448.50	11	254.02	12
贵州	**Guizhou**	**2936.9**	25	**107.71**	**27**	**93.97**	**23**	**13.74**	**28**
云南	Yunnan	4632.9	24	296.22	20	188.02	20	108.20	22
西藏	Tibet	364.5	31	22.55	30	21.01	30	1.54	31
陕西	Shanxi	5918.7	17	274.08	22	139.29	22	134.79	19
甘肃	Gansu	2668.3	26	86.49	28	53.31	27	33.18	27
青海	Qinghai	620.8	30	17.19	31	11.28	31	5.91	30
宁夏	Ningxia	737.2	29	54.35	29	43.03	29	11.32	29
新疆	Xinjiang	2436.5	27	276.69	21	234.83	18	41.87	26

注：进出口数据按经营单位所在地分。

Note: The data of import and export are estimated according to the enterprise's location of business activity.

28-4 全国及各省(区、市)主要农产品产量(2014)

The Output of Main Agricultural Products of the Whole Country and All Provinces

单位：万吨 (10000 tons)

地 区	Region	粮食产量 Output of Grain	位 次 Order	油料产量 Oil-bearing Crops	位 次 Order	肉类产量 Output of Pork, Beef and Mutton	位 次 Order	蔬菜产量 Vegetables Products	位 次 Order
全 国	**National**	**60702.61**		**3507.43**		**8706.7**		**76005.48**	
北 京	Beijing	63.94	31	0.67	30	39.3	27	236.16	29
天 津	Tianjin	175.95	27	0.52	31	46.4	26	460.20	27
河 北	Hebei	3360.17	8	150.20	8	468.1	5	8125.69	2
山 西	Shanxi	1330.78	18	17.32	24	87.5	24	1271.40	22
内蒙古	Inner Mongolia	2753.01	10	170.31	7	252.3	15	1472.68	20
辽 宁	Liaoning	1753.90	14	63.69	16	429.2	8	3090.08	9
吉 林	Jilin	3532.84	4	85.70	13	262.0	14	875.95	24
黑龙江	Heilongjiang	6242.19	1	17.15	25	230.2	16	985.61	23
上 海	Shanghai	112.54	28	1.28	29	23.4	31	393.18	28
江 苏	Jiangsu	3490.62	5	146.60	9	379.5	11	5416.97	4
浙 江	Zhejiang	757.41	23	30.66	22	157.1	20	1762.79	14
安 徽	Anhui	3415.83	6	228.80	6	414.0	10	2550.97	11
福 建	Fujian	667.03	24	29.82	23	213.7	18	1801.35	13
江 西	Jiangxi	2143.50	12	121.71	10	339.8	13	1312.44	21
山 东	Shandong	4596.60	3	335.89	3	770.2	1	9973.70	1
河 南	Henan	5772.30	2	584.33	1	719.0	2	7272.46	3
湖 北	Hubei	2584.17	11	341.73	2	440.4	6	3671.52	7
湖 南	Hunan	3001.26	9	233.77	5	546.5	4	3763.51	6
广 东	Guangdong	1357.34	17	105.48	11	429.4	7	3274.75	8
广 西	Guangxi	1534.41	15	61.30	18	420.0	9	2610.08	10
海 南	Hainan	186.60	26	11.57	27	79.5	25	551.46	25
重 庆	Chongqing	1144.54	21	56.94	20	214.2	17	1689.11	18
四 川	Sichuan	3374.90	7	300.79	4	714.7	3	4069.31	5
贵 州	**Guizhou**	**1138.50**	**22**	**98.05**	**12**	**201.8**	**19**	**1625.62**	**19**
云 南	Yunnan	1860.70	13	64.68	15	378.5	12	1735.54	15
西 藏	Tibet	97.97	30	6.38	28	26.4	30	68.21	31
陕 西	Shanxi	1197.78	19	62.30	17	116.7	22	1724.68	16
甘 肃	Gansu	1158.65	20	72.42	14	95.5	23	1705.19	17
青 海	Qinghai	104.81	29	31.51	21	33.4	28	158.58	30
宁 夏	Ningxia	377.90	25	16.52	26	28.5	29	540.83	26
新 疆	Xinjiang	1414.47	16	59.33	19	149.3	21	1815.44	12

28-5 全国及各省(区、市)主要工业产品产量(2014)

The Output of Main Industrial Products of the Whole Country and All Provinces

地 区	Region	成品钢材(万吨) Products Steel (10000 tons)	水泥(万吨) Cement (10000 tons)	农用化肥(万吨) Chemical Fertilizers (10000 tons)	家用电冰箱(万台) Household (10000 sets)	十种有色金属(万吨) Ten Kinds of Nonferrous Metals (10000 tons)	铝(万吨) Electrolyzed Aluminum (10000 tons)	铁合金(万吨) Ferroalloy (ton)
全 国	**National Total**	**112557.2**	**247619.1**	**6933.5**	**9337.1**	**4417.0**	**2438.1**	**3786.0**
北 京	Beijing	195.0	703.1					0.8
天 津	Tianjin	7303.9	957.9	16.4	45.4	7.5		9.2
河 北	Hebei	23995.2	10625.5	214.7		17.3	1.5	23.9
山 西	Shanxi	4701.0	4537.9	461.3		122.4	82.7	195.5
内蒙古	Inner Mongolia	1763.2	6268.3	126.1		329.9	235.9	539.3
辽 宁	Liaoning	6946.0	5790.6	71.8	157.0	67.0	24.4	131.5
吉 林	Jilin	1412.2	4663.7	17.9		0.6		44.0
黑龙江	Heilongjiang	483.5	3672.1	49.0		0.1		
上 海	Shanghai	2309.1	686.0	1.5	154.0	9.7		
江 苏	Jiangsu	13255.2	19402.6	235.0	1284.7	48.5	1.3	155.6
浙 江	Zhejiang	4171.0	12367.5	31.5	757.8	35.6	0.4	24.3
安 徽	Anhui	3265.7	12913.1	299.2	2765.8	137.5		7.3
福 建	Fujian	3019.6	7732.3	48.7		38.8	14.3	37.4
江 西	Jiangxi	2611.1	9803.6	134.7	109.5	165.1		1.9
山 东	Shandong	8939.4	16406.0	568.9	610.1	402.6	283.6	154.5
河 南	Henan	4704.1	16975.3	536.3	335.5	529.8	337.8	181.6
湖 北	Hubei	3429.0	11669.9	1209.0	243.5	106.3	19.8	31.9
湖 南	Hunan	1989.3	12004.6	105.5	69.5	299.4	33.0	286.8
广 东	Guangdong	3447.1	14737.4	57.5	2293.9	39.5		0.1
广 西	Guangxi	3262.6	10645.8	108.6		140.9	51.5	488.4
海 南	Hainan	29.7	2151.6	66.3				
重 庆	Chongqing	1322.0	6666.6	214.0	262.0	62.8	62.6	46.0
四 川	Sichuan	2935.2	14581.0	433.2	80.2	68.3	44.0	226.3
贵 州	**Guizhou**	**552.4**	**9386.9**	**533.5**	**168.2**	**71.9**	**65.2**	**348.2**
云 南	Yunnan	1935.1	9492.6	314.9		320.4	100.0	133.4
西 藏	Tibet	1.1	342.2					
陕 西	Shanxi	1683.9	9083.5	179.3		204.7	66.8	68.8
甘 肃	Gansu	1108.1	4925.5	49.2		347.7	213.9	118.2
青 海	Qinghai	131.4	1843.7	502.9		246.8	233.6	220.6
宁 夏	Ningxia	165.6	1777.9	46.5		151.0	139.0	285.8
新 疆	Xinjiang	1489.5	4804.4	300.1		444.9	426.8	24.7

注：统计口径为年主营业务收入2000万元及以上工业企业。

Note:The Statistical caliber of the table refers to the industry enterprises whose main business revenue are 20 millions yuan and above.

28-5 续表 continued

地区	Region	轮胎外胎（万条） Tires (10000 tires)	磷肥（万吨） Phosphate Fertilizer (10000 tons)	磷矿石（万吨） Phosphorite Mineral (10000 tons)	卷烟（亿支） Cigarettes (100 million pieces)	白酒（万千升） Distilled Spirit (10000 kiloliter)	中成药（万吨） Traditional Chinese Medicine (10000 tons)
全国	**National Total**	**111388.8**	**1669.7**	**12043.8**	**26098.5**	**1256.9**	**367.2**
北京	Beijing	424.1			189.2	29.5	4.4
天津	Tianjin	18090.7	0.4		236.0	2.3	0.8
河北	Hebei	1562.1	3.5	56.7	863.5	29.4	6.2
山西	Shanxi	165.2	8.0		163.5	9.4	1.3
内蒙古	Inner Mongolia		9.2		355.0	61.7	1.0
辽宁	Liaoning	2155.8		8.9	290.4	50.4	3.1
吉林	Jilin	348.3			585.0	59.4	39.9
黑龙江	Heilongjiang	496.3	1.0		450.0	57.0	4.2
上海	Shanghai	1045.5	0.3		971.5	0.1	0.7
江苏	Jiangsu	11078.5	21.5	8.3	1039.0	89.9	2.2
浙江	Zhejiang	8925.9	0.7		931.0	1.9	2.6
安徽	Anhui	3308.9	80.4	71.6	1329.8	43.6	4.4
福建	Fujian	3700.5	17.7	7.4	969.7	4.4	1.7
江西	Jiangxi	293.8	21.0		676.5	16.4	11.1
山东	Shandong	43074.2	54.9		1447.2	118.1	18.3
河南	Henan	2686.4	22.7	102.1	1733.2	107.7	29.3
湖北	Hubei	967.3	562.0	4663.8	1407.7	84.9	86.8
湖南	Hunan	422.1	11.4	16.0	1743.8	21.7	18.5
广东	Guangdong	5063.3	57.5		1408.4	17.1	24.2
广西	Guangxi	196.4	49.3		784.0	9.9	26.0
海南	Hainan				122.5	0.2	0.1
重庆	Chongqing	2916.7	53.8	27.9	576.0	19.8	9.3
四川	Sichuan	3411.8	134.6	1015.5	1003.7	350.0	51.7
贵州	**Guizhou**	**546.5**	**299.1**	**3397.4**	**1291.8**	**38.0**	**7.7**
云南	Yunnan	4.2	217.4	2667.0	3848.1	8.6	4.6
西藏	Tibet					0.1	0.2
陕西	Shanxi	192.8	15.4	1.2	914.5	11.9	4.9
甘肃	Gansu		12.2		500.0	4.4	1.3
青海	Qinghai					1.9	0.2
宁夏	Ningxia	153.8	14.2		77.5	0.9	0.1
新疆	Xinjiang	157.7	1.5		190.0	6.3	0.4

历年资料

29

Historical Statistics

29-1 全省地区生产总值

Gross Domestic Product

单位：亿元 (100 million yuan)

年 份 Year	地 区 生产总值 Gross Domestic Product	第一产业 Primary Industry	第二产业 Secondary Industry	工 业 Industry	建筑业 Construction	第三产业 Tertiary Industry	#交通运输、仓储、邮政业 Transport, Storage and Post	人均地区生产总值(元) Per Capita Gross Domestic Product(yuan)
1978	46.62	19.42	18.73	15.24	3.49	8.47	1.68	175
1979	55.28	23.29	22.41	18.33	4.08	9.58	1.86	204
1980	60.26	24.86	24.00	19.37	4.63	11.40	2.01	219
1981	67.89	29.90	24.95	20.36	4.59	13.04	2.56	242
1982	79.39	37.37	27.44	22.58	4.86	14.58	2.74	278
1983	87.38	37.76	33.14	28.16	4.98	16.48	3.76	302
1984	108.27	45.73	43.51	36.85	6.66	19.03	4.66	371
1985	123.92	50.45	49.88	41.96	7.92	23.59	5.86	420
1986	139.57	56.46	50.96	43.57	7.39	32.15	7.34	467
1987	165.50	66.46	60.11	49.93	10.18	38.93	7.74	546
1988	211.79	85.20	78.63	68.32	10.31	47.96	9.78	683
1989	235.84	92.88	86.74	77.26	9.48	56.22	12.36	750
1990	260.14	100.10	92.83	82.15	10.68	67.21	11.69	810
1991	295.90	115.71	101.54	88.96	12.58	78.65	13.98	896
1992	339.91	121.18	122.08	106.41	15.67	96.65	19.00	1034
1993	417.69	133.41	155.03	135.40	19.63	129.25	25.45	1234
1994	524.46	183.56	194.80	173.03	21.77	146.10	18.02	1527
1995	636.21	227.13	232.52	208.75	23.77	176.56	22.77	1826
1996	723.18	254.53	255.09	225.36	29.73	213.56	26.79	2048
1997	805.79	271.96	288.99	251.10	37.89	244.84	23.51	2250
1998	858.39	265.04	319.40	273.82	45.58	273.95	29.14	2364
1999	937.50	267.75	350.41	294.42	55.99	319.34	59.17	2545
2000	1029.92	271.20	391.20	328.73	62.47	367.52	75.86	2759
2001	1133.27	274.41	433.52	360.73	72.79	425.34	88.47	3000
2002	1243.43	281.10	481.96	395.45	86.51	480.37	102.48	3257
2003	1426.34	298.69	569.37	473.38	95.99	558.28	119.26	3701
2004	1677.80	334.50	681.50	577.40	104.10	661.80	134.90	4317
2005	2005.42	368.94	821.16	707.35	113.81	815.32	138.65	5394
2006	2338.98	382.06	967.54	839.13	128.41	989.38	192.95	6305
2007	2884.11	446.38	1124.79	978.86	145.93	1312.94	282.04	7878
2008	3561.56	539.19	1370.03	1195.30	174.73	1652.34	370.65	9855
2009	3912.68	550.27	1476.62	1252.67	223.95	1885.79	399.77	10971
2010	4602.16	625.03	1800.06	1516.87	283.19	2177.07	480.32	13119
2011	5701.84	726.22	2194.33	1829.20	365.13	2781.29	590.91	16413
2012	6852.20	891.91	2677.54	2217.06	460.48	3282.75	687.45	19710
2013	8086.86	998.47	3276.24	2686.52	590.69	3812.15	772.44	23151
2014	9266.39	1280.45	3857.44	3140.88	717.69	4128.50	828.69	26437

注：1.2013年起，三次产业划分采用新的分类标准，详见2-1表注；2.1978-2004年按老行业分类标准计算，2005年开始按新行业分类标准计算，第三产业中"交通运输、仓储、邮电通信业"从2005年起按新标准分类为"交通运输、仓储和邮政业"。3.2005-2011年人均地区生产总值按人口普查资料修订。4.2005年起人均地区生产总值按常住半年人口计算，以往年份按常住一年人口计算(以下相关表同)。

Note: 1. New standards of classification of three industries started from 2013, details in the 2-1 note. 2.From 1978 to 2004,data in the table were calculated by the Old Industry Classification Standard;from 2005, data in the table were calculated by the New Industry Classification Standard from 2005,acording to the New the Industry Classification Standard, the data of Transportation, Storage,Post and telecommunications refers to data of Transportation, Storage and Post. 3.From 2005 to 2011,the data of per capital GDP have been adjusted according to the result of national population census. 4.Data from 2005 were calculated by permanent resident population in half a year scope,while they were calculated by permanent population in a year scope in the past(the relative tables in the chapte are the same).

29-2 全省地区生产总值增长速度

Indices of Gross Domestic Product

单位：%　　　　(%)

年份 Year	地区生产总值 Gross Domestic Product	第一产业 Primary Industry	第二产业 Secondary Industry	工业 Industry	建筑业 Construction	第三产业 Tertiary Industry	#交通运输、仓储、邮政业 Transport, Storage and Post	人均地区生产总值 Per Capita Gross Domestic Product(yuan)
1978	23.7	6.6	37.3	39.7	23.7	32.7	33.6	21.4
1979	11.0	2.8	17.3	19.1	5.2	11.4	7.2	9.1
1980	4.4	0.4	4.3	6.9	-14.4	11.7	6.5	2.7
1981	6.5	9.9	1.7	-0.9	12.7	9.5	9.8	4.7
1982	15.8	23.0	9.3	11.4	1.3	12.6	3.6	13.8
1983	12.6	4.6	22.9	26.4	8.8	12.3	34.6	11.2
1984	19.8	18.2	23.8	23.8	23.5	14.9	37.6	18.6
1985	7.9	-1.2	12.8	12.0	16.6	17.8	24.3	6.7
1986	5.6	6.1	-2.0	-0.3	-9.5	20.9	8.7	4.3
1987	10.8	2.9	16.2	13.8	28.6	14.8	13.9	9.3
1988	8.6	-1.0	13.2	15.5	3.1	15.0	8.3	6.2
1989	4.5	6.3	3.9	6.8	-10.6	3.3	13.0	3.1
1990	4.3	1.7	6.1	5.6	8.8	4.6	-15.1	2.1
1991	9.2	13.2	3.5	3.5	3.8	11.2	6.8	6.2
1992	8.1	-0.7	15.0	16.0	8.0	12.6	21.2	8.6
1993	10.4	3.9	13.5	15.8	-4.8	14.8	15.1	8.8
1994	8.4	3.7	11.8	12.4	5.8	9.8	11.9	6.9
1995	7.5	2.4	10.5	11.1	4.0	9.3	7.8	5.9
1996	8.9	3.8	12.6	12.1	17.8	9.2	11.1	7.4
1997	9.0	4.2	12.3	11.8	18.0	9.3	12.5	7.5
1998	8.5	1.5	11.8	10.4	26.4	10.5	17.5	6.9
1999	8.8	3.4	13.2	11.8	25.1	7.3	14.5	7.3
2000	8.4	3.6	7.6	7.5	8.3	13.7	17.5	7.0
2001	8.8	1.1	9.4	9.2	10.7	13.6	12.0	7.5
2002	9.1	2.2	13.2	11.0	24.5	9.4	5.4	7.9
2003	10.1	4.6	13.3	13.3	13.5	10.1	10.9	9.1
2004	11.4	5.3	14.2	15.9	6.5	12.0	16.0	10.4
2005	12.7	5.2	12.0	13.0	7.4	17.6	26.5	17.9
2006	12.8	4.6	13.4	13.8	11.2	16.0	29.6	13.1
2007	14.8	3.3	13.2	14.0	7.8	21.1	29.4	16.4
2008	11.3	6.8	8.1	8.6	4.7	15.8	19.4	12.8
2009	11.4	4.3	12.1	10.2	25.6	13.1	5.3	12.9
2010	12.8	4.7	16.6	15.7	22.1	12.1	15.2	14.7
2011	15.0	1.2	17.9	17.8	18.3	16.5	15.3	16.1
2012	13.6	8.6	16.8	15.6	23.3	12.1	13.8	13.5
2013	12.5	5.8	14.1	13.1	19.2	12.5	12.4	11.9
2014	10.8	6.6	12.3	11.1	18.2	10.4	9.3	10.4

29－3 全省地区生产总值指数（1978年=100）

Indices of Gross Domestic Product (year of 1978=100)

年份 Year	地区生产总值 Gross Domestic Product	第一产业 Primary Industry	第二产业 Secondary Industry	工 业 Industry	建筑业 Construction	第三产业 Tertiary Industry	人均地区生产总值 Per Capita Gross Domestic Product
1978	100.0	100.0	100.0	100.0	100.0	100.0	100.0
1979	111.0	102.8	117.3	119.1	105.2	111.4	109.1
1980	115.9	103.2	122.3	127.3	90.1	124.4	112.0
1981	123.4	113.4	124.4	126.2	101.5	136.3	117.3
1982	142.9	139.5	135.9	140.5	102.9	153.4	133.5
1983	160.9	145.9	167.1	177.6	111.9	172.3	148.4
1984	192.8	172.5	206.8	219.9	138.2	198.0	176.0
1985	208.0	170.4	233.4	246.3	161.1	233.2	187.9
1986	219.6	180.8	228.7	245.6	145.8	281.9	195.9
1987	243.4	186.0	265.8	279.4	187.5	323.7	214.1
1988	264.3	184.2	300.9	322.8	193.3	372.2	227.5
1989	276.2	195.8	312.6	344.7	172.8	384.5	234.4
1990	288.1	199.1	331.7	364.1	188.0	402.2	239.4
1991	314.6	225.4	343.3	376.8	195.1	447.2	254.2
1992	340.1	223.8	394.8	437.1	210.8	503.6	276.1
1993	375.3	232.5	448.3	506.1	200.6	578.3	300.5
1994	407.0	241.2	501.1	568.7	212.2	635.2	321.2
1995	437.4	246.8	553.7	632.0	220.6	693.9	340.3
1996	476.1	256.3	623.4	708.7	259.8	757.9	365.3
1997	519.0	267.1	700.3	792.3	306.6	828.6	392.8
1998	562.9	271.0	783.1	874.8	387.6	915.3	420.0
1999	612.4	280.0	886.4	978.4	485.0	982.5	450.5
2000	663.7	290.2	953.4	1051.5	525.1	1117.4	481.8
2001	721.8	293.4	1043.5	1148.3	581.5	1269.5	517.9
2002	787.2	300.0	1181.3	1274.5	724.2	1388.3	558.7
2003	866.6	313.8	1338.4	1443.5	821.8	1528.6	609.4
2004	965.4	330.4	1528.4	1673.0	874.9	1711.4	673.1
2005	1088.0	347.6	1711.8	1890.5	939.6	2012.6	793.6
2006	1227.3	363.6	1941.2	2151.4	1044.8	2334.6	897.6
2007	1408.9	375.6	2197.4	2452.6	1126.3	2827.2	1044.8
2008	1568.1	401.1	2375.4	2663.5	1179.2	3273.9	1178.5
2009	1746.9	418.3	2662.8	2935.2	1481.1	3702.8	1330.5
2010	1970.5	438.0	3104.8	3396.0	1808.4	4150.8	1526.1
2011	2266.1	443.3	3660.6	4000.5	2139.3	4835.7	1771.8
2012	2574.3	481.4	4275.6	4624.6	2637.8	5420.8	2011.0
2013	2896.1	509.3	4878.4	5230.4	3144.2	6098.4	2250.3
2014	3208.9	543.0	5478.5	5811.0	3716.5	6732.7	2484.3

29-4 年末常住人口

Permanent Population at the year-end

单位：万人 (10000 persons)

年 份 Year	合 计 Total	按城镇、乡村分 Grouped by Urban and Rural		按性别分 Grouped by Sex		性别比 Sex Ratio (女=100) (female=100)	年平均人口 Annual Average Population
		城 镇 Urban	乡 村 Rural	男 Male	女 Female		
1978	2686.40	323.97	2362.43	1364.82	1321.58	103.27	2663.27
1979	2730.99	520.82	2210.17	1386.93	1344.06	103.19	2708.70
1980	2776.67	543.18	2233.49	1409.61	1367.06	103.11	2753.83
1981	2826.78	528.41	2298.37	1439.89	1386.89	103.82	2801.73
1982	2875.21	542.13	2333.08	1470.43	1404.78	104.67	2851.00
1983	2901.46	550.96	2350.50	1484.73	1416.73	104.80	2888.33
1984	2931.85	854.14	2077.71	1501.55	1430.30	104.98	2916.65
1985	2972.18	883.18	2089.00	1522.93	1449.25	105.08	2952.02
1986	3025.86	909.55	2116.31	1550.90	1474.96	105.15	2999.02
1987	3072.58	1002.93	2069.65	1576.23	1496.35	105.34	3049.22
1988	3127.27	951.23	2176.04	1599.01	1528.26	104.63	3099.93
1989	3171.00	1000.26	2170.74	1628.85	1542.15	105.62	3149.14
1990	3267.53	1083.67	2183.86	1684.53	1583.00	106.41	3219.27
1991	3314.63	1238.48	2076.15	1709.31	1605.32	106.48	3291.08
1992	3360.96	2256.05	1104.91	1735.46	1625.50	106.76	3337.8
1993	3408.69	2324.92	1083.77	1761.65	1647.04	106.96	3384.83
1994	3458.41	2371.06	1087.35	1789.32	1669.09	107.20	3433.55
1995	3508.08	2408.78	1099.30	1815.63	1692.45	107.28	3483.25
1996	3555.41	2457.33	1098.08	1840.38	1715.03	107.31	3531.75
1997	3605.81	2503.75	1102.06	1866.48	1739.33	107.31	3580.61
1998	3657.60	2539.76	1117.84	1893.29	1764.31	107.31	3631.70
1999	3710.06	2539.80	1170.26	1920.40	1789.66	107.30	3683.83
2000	3755.72	896.49	2859.23	1968.00	1787.72	110.08	3732.89
2001	3798.51	910.12	2888.39	1973.41	1825.10	108.13	3777.12
2002	3837.28	932.11	2905.17	1993.15	1844.13	108.08	3817.90
2003	3869.66	958.52	2911.14	2010.22	1859.44	108.11	3853.47
2004	3903.70	1025.89	2877.81	2022.22	1881.48	107.48	3886.68
2005	3730	1002.25	2727.75	1920.55	1809.45	106.14	3717.61
2006	3690	1013.27	2676.73	1908.85	1781.15	107.17	3710
2007	3632	1025.68	2606.32	1879.70	1752.30	107.27	3661
2008	3596	1046.79	2549.21	1868.73	1727.27	108.19	3614
2009	3537	1057.21	2479.79	1827.56	1709.44	106.91	3567
2010	3479	1176.25	2302.75	1797.43	1681.57	106.89	3508
2011	3469	1212.76	2256.24	1801.21	1667.79	108.00	3474
2012	3484	1268.52	2215.48	1818.61	1665.39	109.20	3476.50
2013	3502.22	1324.89	2177.33	1822.5	1679.72	108.50	3493.15
2014	3508.04	1403.57	2104.47	1817.91	1690.13	107.56	3505.13

注：1. 2000年以后的城镇、乡村人口的划分标准按国家统计局1999年发布的《关于统计上划分城乡的规定》计算，与以前年份数据不可比。2.2005年及以后为常住半年口径。 3.2006—2009年常住总人口数据已根据第六次人口普查资料进行修订（下表同）。

Note:1.Ater 2000,standards of grouping rural and urban residents were calculated on the basis of Statistical Partition Ordain about Urban or Rural that had been issued by National Bureau of Statistial of China, So the data are not comparable with the preceding years. 2.Population cablier have refer to permanent population in half a year scope(the same applies to the next table). 3.Data from 2006 to 2009 had been verified according to the Six National Population Census since 2005(the same applies to the next table).

29-5 人口自然变动
Natural Change of Population

单位：万人 (10000 persons)

年 份 Year	出 生 Birth		死 亡 Death		自然增长 Natural Grouth	
	人 数 Number of Persons	率(‰) Rate(‰)	人 数 Number of Persons	率(‰) Rate(‰)	人 数 Number of Persons	率(‰) Rate(‰)
1978	76.22	28.62	19.65	7.38	56.57	21.24
1979	72.84	26.89	19.23	7.10	53.61	19.79
1980	68.02	24.70	19.39	7.04	48.63	17.66
1981	66.46	23.72	21.07	7.52	45.39	16.20
1982	70.73	24.81	21.67	7.60	49.06	17.21
1983	60.11	20.81	26.46	9.16	33.65	11.65
1984	54.98	18.85	21.29	7.30	33.69	11.55
1985	59.97	20.33	17.43	5.91	42.54	14.42
1986	72.04	24.11	18.08	6.05	53.96	18.06
1987	71.77	23.69	25.87	8.54	45.90	15.15
1988	73.76	23.81	18.62	6.01	55.14	17.80
1989	67.08	21.23	21.58	6.83	45.50	14.40
1990	74.13	23.09	25.36	7.90	48.77	15.19
1991	72.96	22.42	26.39	8.11	46.57	14.31
1992	73.61	22.40	28.00	8.52	45.61	13.88
1993	74.96	22.60	28.19	8.50	46.77	14.10
1994	76.93	22.92	27.32	8.14	49.61	14.78
1995	76.14	21.86	26.47	7.60	49.67	14.26
1996	77.88	22.05	27.16	7.69	50.72	14.36
1997	79.31	22.15	27.46	7.67	51.85	14.48
1998	79.97	22.02	28.18	7.76	51.79	14.26
1999	80.75	21.92	28.29	7.68	52.46	14.24
2000	76.86	20.59	28.11	7.53	48.75	13.06
2001	70.10	18.56	27.31	7.23	42.79	11.33
2002	68.57	17.96	27.53	7.21	41.04	10.75
2003	61.31	15.91	26.47	6.87	34.84	9.04
2004	58.61	15.08	24.68	6.35	33.93	8.73
2005	54.00	14.59	25.00	7.21	29.00	7.38
2006	51.83	13.97	24.89	6.71	26.94	7.26
2007	48.62	13.28	24.16	6.60	24.46	6.68
2008	48.75	13.49	24.47	6.77	24.28	6.72
2009	48.68	13.65	23.86	6.69	24.82	6.96
2010	48.52	13.96	22.76	6.55	25.76	7.41
2011	46.24	13.31	24.07	6.93	22.17	6.38
2012	46.13	13.27	24.20	6.96	21.93	6.31
2013	45.58	13.05	24.97	7.15	20.61	5.90
2014	45.50	12.98	25.17	7.18	20.33	5.80

29－6 户籍人口
Household Registered Population

单位：万人 (10000 persons)

年 份 Year	年末总人口 Total Population at the Year-end	按农业非农业分 Grouped by Agriculture and Non-agriculture		占总人口比重(%) Proportion(%)	
		农 业 Agriculture	非农业 Non-agriculture	农 业 Agriculture	非农业 Non-agriculture
1978	2686.40	2380.52	305.88	88.6	11.4
1979	2730.99	2416.67	314.32	88.5	11.5
1980	2776.67	2456.37	320.30	88.5	11.5
1981	2826.78	2500.74	326.04	88.5	11.5
1982	2875.21	2544.10	331.11	88.5	11.5
1983	2901.46	2564.92	336.54	88.4	11.6
1984	2931.85	2588.11	343.74	88.3	11.7
1985	2967.91	2609.04	358.87	87.9	12.1
1986	3007.99	2643.57	364.42	87.9	12.1
1987	3051.39	2678.60	372.79	87.8	12.2
1988	3143.94	2760.47	383.47	87.8	12.2
1989	3184.05	2793.35	390.70	87.7	12.3
1990	3236.97	2840.21	396.76	87.7	12.3
1991	3271.40	2868.27	403.13	87.7	12.3
1992	3300.97	2887.95	413.02	87.5	12.5
1993	3332.30	2910.71	421.59	87.3	12.7
1994	3380.58	2927.54	453.04	86.6	13.4
1995	3419.54	2957.32	462.22	86.5	13.5
1996	3459.54	2979.85	479.69	86.1	13.9
1997	3495.50	3004.76	490.74	86.0	14.0
1998	3536.54	3032.50	504.04	85.7	14.3
1999	3582.05	3063.23	518.82	85.5	14.5
2000	3676.63	3144.98	531.65	85.5	14.5
2001	3710.20	3156.33	553.87	85.1	14.9
2002	3747.68	3175.17	572.51	84.7	15.3
2003	3786.84	3196.70	590.14	84.4	15.6
2004	3831.19	3224.62	606.57	84.2	15.8
2005	3867.73	3258.05	609.68	84.2	15.8
2006	3921.91	3295.08	626.83	84.0	16.0
2007	3985.04	3346.09	638.95	84.0	16.0
2008	4036.75	3385.66	651.09	83.9	16.1
2009	4090.78	3429.36	661.43	83.8	16.2
2010	4189.00	3512.92	676.07	83.9	16.1
2011	4238.44	3551.18	687.26	83.8	16.2
2012	4249.48	3557.14	692.34	83.7	16.3
2013	4286.15	3584.17	701.98	83.6	16.4
2014	4325.49	3616.27	709.22	83.6	16.4

注：资料来源于省公安厅。1984年及以前为公安、统计共同使用的数据，1985年起为公安户籍人口统计口径。

Note: Data in the table is provided by Provincial Public Security Department. Data after 1985 in the table is obtained from the Public Security Department of Guizhou Province,while data before 1984 are used by Statistics Beaura and Public Security Department of Guizhou Province.

29—7 就业人员
Employed Persons

单位：万人　　(10000 persons)

年份 Year	就业人员 Tutal Employed Persons	第一产业 Primary Industry	第二产业 Secondary Industry	第三产业 Tertiary Industry
1978	1053.67	872.89	108.26	72.52
1979	1060.62	873.88	105.63	81.11
1980	1109.63	919.69	102.01	87.93
1981	1152.95	954.55	102.64	95.76
1982	1207.06	989.78	109.53	107.75
1983	1234.18	1014.15	109.99	110.04
1984	1285.32	1037.71	122.12	125.49
1985	1335.17	1018.38	185.98	130.81
1986	1383.17	1053.26	197.09	132.82
1987	1435.85	1115.35	180.53	139.97
1988	1501.32	1172.51	185.80	143.01
1989	1570.84	1228.64	163.19	179.01
1990	1651.75	1292.30	169.10	190.35
1991	1701.47	1329.56	177.72	194.19
1992	1739.03	1359.00	173.35	206.68
1993	1779.01	1374.00	171.00	234.01
1994	1828.30	1365.00	181.90	281.40
1995	1812.20	1312.80	268.80	230.60
1996	1783.20	1235.60	278.50	269.10
1997	1796.70	1251.10	256.60	289.00
1998	1844.43	1284.72	251.57	308.14
1999	1832.50	1299.90	201.40	331.20
2000	1866.28	1305.28	221.80	339.20
2001	2068.01	1692.33	133.88	241.80
2002	2106.14	1698.39	108.89	298.86
2003	2145.00	1671.20	120.49	353.31
2004	2186.00	1672.29	124.60	389.11
2005	1944.29	1497.26	164.00	283.04
2006	1953.24	1487.40	174.17	291.67
2007	1872.64	1388.02	172.31	312.31
2008	1867.20	1350.32	180.73	336.15
2009	1841.92	1299.29	197.60	345.03
2010	1770.90	1209.55	203.52	357.82
2011	1792.80	1194.39	215.86	382.55
2012	1825.82	1189.04	238.10	398.68
2013	1864.21	1179.76	264.32	420.13
2014	1909.69	1171.02	291.42	447.25

注：就业人员数2010年根据第六次人口普查长表数据推算，2005—2009年根据第六次人口普查结果，采用趋势离差法修订，2011年及以后按同口径进行推算。

Note:Data of employees were estimated according to the 6th National Population Census in 2010,From 2005 to 2009, according to the result of the first National Population Census,the total number of employees were revised by the trend deviation method,and the same to 2011 and after.

29–8 非私营单位在岗职工人数

Number of Employed persons in Non-private Units

单位：万人 (10000 persons)

年份 Year	合计 Total	国有单位 State-owned Units	集体单位 Collective-owned Units	其他单位 Units of Other Types of Owership
1978	171.19	137.66	33.53	
1979	175.56	142.32	33.24	
1980	178.18	146.14	32.04	
1981	185.73	153.50	32.23	
1982	191.03	158.08	32.95	
1983	193.33	160.54	32.79	
1984	197.13	159.53	37.60	
1985	202.33	162.11	40.03	0.19
1986	206.69	167.81	38.78	0.10
1987	211.92	172.58	38.88	0.46
1988	214.43	176.32	37.56	0.55
1989	216.70	180.10	35.90	0.70
1990	225.48	185.35	39.19	0.94
1991	231.88	190.45	40.49	0.94
1992	235.80	193.61	40.94	1.25
1993	233.11	192.83	38.35	1.93
1994	230.88	194.47	34.87	1.54
1995	226.55	193.36	29.63	3.56
1996	231.64	196.60	30.45	4.59
1997	232.80	196.08	31.33	5.39
1998	207.01	167.14	23.98	15.89
1999	197.80	156.86	21.03	19.91
2000	193.96	153.55	19.00	21.41
2001	189.18	148.87	15.73	24.58
2002	188.47	146.96	14.39	27.12
2003	188.70	141.75	13.71	33.24
2004	192.67	139.57	12.77	40.33
2005	202.02	140.50	9.81	51.71
2006	201.87	137.86	8.86	55.15
2007	207.53	141.48	8.10	57.95
2008	199.76	140.97	7.42	51.37
2009	206.44	141.79	6.69	57.96
2010	210.67	146.81	6.41	57.45
2011	225.91	158.26	7.17	60.47
2012	249.67	161.19	6.16	82.32
2013	273.27	152.41	5.49	115.37
2014	278.63	153.30	5.27	120.07

29—9 非私营单位在岗职工平均工资

Average Wages of Employed persons in Non-private Units

单位：元 (yuan)

年 份 Year	在岗职工平均工资 Average Wages of Staff and Workers	国有单位 State-owned Units	集体单位 Collective-owned Units	其他单位 Units of Other Types of Owership
1978	616	642	450	
1979	654	692	448	
1980	755	797	502	
1981	774	804	535	
1982	783	815	562	
1983	801	830	608	
1984	913	949	708	
1985	1066	1132	787	
1986	1216	1297	859	1236
1987	1319	1395	961	1204
1988	1531	1627	1072	1389
1989	1676	1777	1158	1647
1990	1947	2070	1347	2281
1991	2090	2214	1489	2527
1992	2406	2543	1717	3286
1993	2823	2958	2104	3375
1994	3870	4085	2618	4475
1995	4475	4672	3061	5369
1996	4917	5125	3456	5613
1997	5206	5434	3556	6461
1998	5775	5819	4426	7289
1999	6595	6695	5008	7456
2000	7453	7594	5444	8325
2001	8991	9308	6218	8831
2002	9810	10150	6566	9680
2003	11037	11390	7504	10975
2004	12431	12870	8630	12103
2005	14344	14681	10506	14161
2006	16815	17638	12873	15365
2007	20668	22106	16893	17668
2008	24602	25874	20914	21659
2009	28245	29956	22167	24772
2010	31458	32718	24703	29006
2011	37331	38914	31601	33851
2012	42733	45825	40420	36816
2013	49087	52327	50545	44819
2014	54685	56918	59458	51627

29-10 全社会固定资产投资

Total Investment in Fixed Assets in the Whole Province

单位：亿元 (100 million yuan)

年 份 Year	全社会固定资产投资 Total Investment in Fixed Assets in the Whole Province	比上年增长(%) Growth Rate(%)	按经济类型分 Grouped by Ownership		
			国有经济 State-owned Units	集体经济 Collective-Owned Units	其他 Others
1978	10.93		9.73	0.56	0.64
1979	11.94	9.2	10.20	0.61	1.13
1980	13.97	17.0	11.59	0.83	1.55
1981	15.16	8.5	12.06	0.99	2.11
1982	15.52	2.4	11.56	1.08	2.88
1983	17.07	10.0	11.88	1.23	3.96
1984	23.02	34.9	15.02	0.98	7.02
1985	33.14	44.0	21.24	1.76	10.14
1986	35.99	8.6	24.09	1.71	10.19
1987	42.97	19.4	27.10	3.61	12.26
1988	45.42	5.7	33.05	2.74	9.63
1989	44.08	-3.0	32.29	2.73	9.06
1990	51.51	16.9	36.95	2.14	12.42
1991	58.44	13.5	42.97	3.67	11.80
1992	78.82	34.9		3.59	16.41
1993	106.30	34.9	77.84	6.81	21.65
1994	140.95	32.6	93.74	9.77	37.44
1995	173.66	23.2	108.85	12.94	51.87
1996	207.10	19.3	133.19	14.75	59.16
1997	247.23	19.4	149.75	15.09	82.39
1998	304.91	23.3	188.93	19.34	96.64
1999	333.90	9.5	210.80	22.19	100.91
2000	402.50	20.5	259.95	28.45	114.10
2001	533.74	32.6	357.69	22.45	153.60
2002	632.44	18.5	423.88	18.86	189.70
2003	754.13	19.2	457.10	39.26	257.77
2004	869.25	15.3	507.74	38.41	323.10
2005	1018.25	17.1	545.37	12.61	460.27
2006	1197.68	17.6	602.50	12.93	582.25
2007	1488.80	24.3	697.68	17.27	773.85
2008	1864.45	25.2	910.69	25.23	928.53
2009	2450.99	31.5	1250.42	29.70	1170.87
2010	3186.28	30.0	1605.82	29.01	1551.45
2011	5101.55	60.1	2412.97	57.23	2631.36
2012	5717.80	35.0	2530.97	42.55	3144.28
2013	7373.60	29.0	3284.11	27.33	4062.17
2014	9025.75	22.4	4167.03	21.97	4836.76

注：2011年及以前统计口径为计划总投资50万元及以上固定资产项目投资、房地产开发投资及农户投资；2012年起统计口径为计划总投资500万元及以上的固定资产项目投资、房地产开发投资及农村农户投资，增长速度为可比口径速度。

Note: Data before 2011 refers to planing investment 500 thousands at least in fixed asset, real estate and household investment. While the data after 2012 refers to planing investment 5 millions at least in fixed asset, real estate and household investment.and the growth rate is the ration of comparable caliber speed.

29−11 财政收支

Financial Revenue and Expenditure

单位：亿元 (100 million yuan)

年份 Year	财政总收入 Total Government Financial Revenue		一般公共预算收入 General Public Financial Badget Revenue		一般公共预算支出 General Public Financial Badget Expenditure	
	绝对数 Absolute Numbers	比上年增长(%) Growth Rates(%)	绝对数 Absolute Numbers	比上年增长(%) Growth Rates(%)	绝对数 Absolute Numbers	比上年增长(%) Growth Rates(%)
1978	14.20	48.2	6.26	157.6	12.30	39.9
1979	14.26	0.4	6.54	4.5	13.30	8.1
1980	13.23	-7.2	6.69	2.3	12.66	-4.8
1981	13.74	3.9	6.32	-5.5	13.28	4.9
1982	16.00	16.4	7.70	21.8	15.11	13.8
1983	18.26	14.1	9.56	24.2	16.38	8.4
1984	21.81	19.4	11.81	23.5	22.28	36.0
1985	26.71	22.5	15.17	28.5	24.55	10.2
1986	31.38	17.5	17.01	12.1	30.43	24.0
1987	36.80	17.3	21.37	25.6	31.43	3.3
1988	39.55	7.5	25.96	21.5	36.14	15.0
1989	45.37	14.7	32.14	23.8	45.89	27.0
1990	49.36	8.8	35.37	10.0	47.87	4.3
1991	55.71	12.9	42.80	21.0	53.42	11.6
1992	60.98	9.5	47.28	10.5	60.63	13.5
1993	68.43	12.2	56.50	19.5	67.39	11.1
1994	77.30	13.0	31.24	-44.7	74.23	10.1
1995	87.40	13.1	38.80	24.2	85.33	15.0
1996	103.92	18.9	49.46	27.5	99.58	16.7
1997	116.19	11.8	57.90	17.1	113.79	14.3
1998	136.31	17.3	65.34	12.8	133.09	17.0
1999	133.75	-1.9	74.26	13.7	170.72	28.3
2000	153.04	14.4	85.23	14.8	201.57	18.1
2001	177.04	15.7	99.75	17.0	275.20	36.5
2002	203.03	14.7	108.28	8.6	316.67	15.1
2003	236.64	16.6	124.56	15.0	332.35	5.0
2004	296.48	25.3	149.29	19.9	418.42	25.9
2005	366.16	23.5	182.50	22.2	520.73	24.5
2006	448.88	22.6	226.82	24.3	610.64	17.3
2007	556.98	24.1	285.14	25.7	795.40	30.3
2008	674.58	21.1	349.55	22.6	1055.39	32.7
2009	779.59	15.6	416.48	19.1	1372.27	30.0
2010	969.57	24.4	533.73	28.2	1631.48	18.9
2011	1329.99	37.2	773.08	44.8	2249.40	37.9
2012	1644.48	23.6	1014.05	31.2	2755.68	22.5
2013	1918.23	16.7	1206.41	19.0	3082.66	11.9
2014	2130.90	11.1	1366.67	13.3	3542.80	14.9

注：资料来源于省财政厅。

Note:Data in the table are obtained from provincial financial department.

29-12 人民生活

单位：元

年 份 Year	城镇常住居民人均可支配收入 Amual Per Capita Disposable Income of Urban Households	比上年增长 (%) Tear-on year Increase Index (%)	指 数 (1978年=100) Index (year of 1978=100)	城镇常住居民人均消费性支出 Amual Per Capita Consumption of Urban Households	#食 品 #Food
1978	261.26	1.2	100.0	246.53	150.15
1979	279.66	5.2	105.2	273.60	176.64
1980	343.83	11.9	117.7	334.32	202.32
1981	434.10	22.5	144.1	393.24	237.60
1982	459.73	3.8	149.6	403.92	243.96
1983	483.33	3.5	154.8	426.36	258.72
1984	558.00	12.3	173.8	480.36	279.48
1985	682.27	10.9	192.7	617.52	324.24
1986	824.40	13.6	218.8	722.28	381.84
1987	912.26	0.9	220.7	788.76	431.40
1988	1101.84	-0.6	219.4	1050.24	554.52
1989	1275.45	-1.8	215.4	1102.56	640.20
1990	1399.36	8.5	233.8	1163.25	658.19
1991	1593.54	9.6	256.2	1338.86	750.79
1992	1887.51	9.7	281.0	1564.34	886.89
1993	2300.38	5.1	295.4	1876.24	1021.42
1994	3196.06	14.1	337.2	2531.78	1353.13
1995	3916.25	2.2	344.5	3250.55	1752.41
1996	4210.74	-2.9	334.4	3572.78	1923.49
1997	4438.05	1.8	340.4	3555.69	1819.90
1998	4566.17	2.3	348.3	3799.38	1839.64
1999	4935.47	9.0	379.6	3964.35	1683.38
2000	5121.22	5.1	399.0	4278.28	1847.63
2001	5451.91	3.9	414.5	4492.25	1832.26
2002	5944.02	9.8	455.1	4598.30	1788.61
2003	6568.91	9.5	498.4	4947.62	1967.67
2004	7322.04	7.7	536.8	5494.43	2260.46
2005	8147.13	10.6	593.7	6156.27	2457.09
2006	9116.61	10.1	653.7	6848.39	2649.02
2007	10678.40	10.6	723.0	7758.69	3122.46
2008	11758.76	2.9	744.0	8349.21	3597.94
2009	12862.53	10.9	825.1	9048.29	3755.61
2010	14142.74	7.0	882.9	10058.29	4013.67
2011	16495.01	10.8	978.3	11352.88	4565.85
2012	18700.51	10.4	1080.0	12585.70	4992.85
2013	20667.07	7.4	1159.9	13702.87	4915.02
2014	22548.21	7.0	1241.1	15254.64	5319.60

注:1.表中指数已扣除价格因素。2.城镇常住居民2013年及以前为城镇居民，农村常住居民人均可支配收入2013年及以前为农民人均纯收入。3.农村常住居民人均消费性支出2013年及以前为农村居民数据。

People's Living Conditions

(yuan)

农村常住居民人均可支配收入 Amual Per Capita Net Income of Rural Households	比上年增长 (%) Tear-on year Increase Index (%)	指　数 (1978年=100) Index (year of 1978=100)	农村常住居民人均生活消费支出 Amual Per Capita Consumption Expenditures of Rural Households	#食 品 #Food
109.30	3.5	100.0	104.52	72.20
131.09	15.4	115.4	116.23	82.44
161.50	16.6	134.5	139.24	96.45
208.87	27.3	171.2	162.51	105.16
223.13	5.3	180.3	187.02	121.67
224.87	0.5	181.1	185.20	126.01
262.81	15.5	209.1	208.87	144.00
302.14	8.8	227.5	254.58	177.83
303.57	-3.9	218.6	271.60	190.60
341.84	6.4	232.5	304.22	212.90
397.74	-0.8	230.7	359.73	254.32
430.34	-7.3	213.9	407.28	282.92
435.14	-1.3	211.0	403.28	281.92
465.53	3.5	218.4	420.44	286.60
506.13	2.0	222.9	454.47	309.77
579.67	-1.4	219.8	550.11	390.45
786.84	6.6	234.2	684.27	484.41
1086.62	6.6	249.6	930.59	661.85
1276.67	5.5	263.3	1068.09	774.62
1298.54	4.2	274.4	1065.70	742.16
1334.46	4.4	286.5	1094.39	757.55
1363.07	4.7	299.9	1069.81	722.16
1374.16	3.6	310.7	1096.59	687.32
1411.73	3.7	322.2	1098.39	659.37
1489.91	4.3	336.1	1137.56	661.35
1564.66	4.7	353.2	1185.17	674.71
1721.55	5.6	373.0	1296.34	754.39
1876.96	5.2	392.4	1552.39	819.87
1984.62	4.7	410.8	1627.07	838.42
2373.99	11.6	458.5	1913.50	998.39
2796.93	8.9	499.3	2165.70	1119.64
3005.41	9.2	545.2	2421.95	1093.94
3471.93	12.6	613.9	2852.48	1319.43
4145.35	14.0	699.8	3455.76	1646.51
4753.00	11.5	780.3	3901.71	1740.58
5434.00	12.4	877.2	4740.18	2036.22
6671.22	10.3	967.5	5970.25	2488.50

Note: 1.The Indices in the table have been deducting price factors. 2.Befor 2013, The Permaneht Residents in cities and towns refers to urban Residents; Rural Permanent Residents disposable income in 2013 and before was per-capita net income of farms. 3.Rural Permanent Residents Per capita Consum spending in 2013 and before was Rural Residents Data.

29-13 农林牧渔业总产值

Gross Output Value of Farming, Forestry, Animal Husbandry and Fishery

单位：亿元 (100 million yuan)

年份 Year	合计 Total	农业 Farming	林业 Forestry	畜牧业 Animal Husbandry	渔业 Fishery	农林牧渔服务业 Services of Farming, Forestry, Animal Husbandry and Fishery
1978	27.46	21.72	1.07	4.64	0.03	
1979	31.74	24.54	1.27	5.90	0.03	
1980	36.44	28.05	1.46	6.89	0.04	
1981	41.93	32.07	2.08	7.69	0.09	
1982	51.49	38.93	2.49	9.95	0.12	
1983	52.66	38.17	3.48	10.84	0.17	
1984	63.09	45.43	4.44	12.94	0.28	
1985	70.24	47.42	5.37	17.05	0.40	
1986	79.34	53.54	5.27	20.05	0.48	
1987	92.25	61.95	5.50	24.23	0.57	
1988	123.39	78.90	6.13	37.55	0.81	
1989	133.69	85.64	5.90	41.30	0.85	
1990	145.53	95.23	7.95	41.38	0.97	
1991	165.34	112.08	9.44	42.68	1.14	
1992	176.73	116.03	12.22	47.18	1.30	
1993	201.40	126.20	11.85	62.33	1.02	
1994	277.13	180.26	13.61	81.18	2.08	
1995	344.85	224.16	15.29	102.54	2.86	
1996	388.29	265.57	14.99	104.57	3.16	
1997	417.54	289.20	15.39	109.37	3.58	
1998	402.32	274.55	15.48	108.12	4.17	
1999	407.12	278.67	16.02	108.07	4.36	
2000	412.97	279.61	18.04	110.67	4.65	
2001	418.61	279.95	15.08	118.46	5.13	
2002	431.39	278.88	18.17	128.80	5.54	
2003	466.72	275.46	25.87	139.48	6.08	19.83
2004	524.64	317.69	23.25	168.79	7.02	7.89
2005	571.84	335.53	23.91	194.20	9.41	8.79
2006	601.54	347.97	25.85	189.79	7.44	30.49
2007	697.01	392.20	27.77	231.60	9.04	36.40
2008	843.80	464.80	35.63	291.65	10.49	41.23
2009	875.20	501.52	36.92	281.53	11.06	44.17
2010	997.82	587.31	41.01	304.16	13.82	51.52
2011	1165.46	655.30	46.66	381.95	19.90	61.65
2012	1436.61	864.86	54.19	421.55	28.21	67.80
2013	1663.02	997.13	69.87	482.68	38.30	75.04
2014	2118.48	1321.86	99.62	569.29	47.01	80.70

注：1.2006年数据为第二次农业普查修订数(以下相关表同)。2.农林牧渔服务业2004、2005年计算口径有变化(以下相关表同)。

Note:1.Data were adjusted according to the Second National Agricultural Census in 2006(The same applies to the relative tables below).

2.The calculate caliber of Farming,Forestry,Animal Husban-dry and Fishery have changed in the year of 2004 and 2005(The same applies to the relative tables below).

29-14 农林牧渔业总产值增长速度

Indices of Gross Output Value of Farming, Forestry, Animal Husbandry and Fishery

单位：% (%)

年 份 Year	合 计 Total	农 业 Farming	林 业 Forestry	畜牧业 Animal Husbandry	渔 业 Fishery	农林牧渔服务业 Services of Farming, Forestry,Animal Husbandry and Fishery
1978	2.9	0.7	7.7	13.2		
1979	1.0		2.4	11.0	1.4	
1980	4.3	3.7	6.2	6.1	59.3	
1981	6.9	7.3	-13.4	9.9	-3.7	
1982	19.8	20.9	13.8	16.9	4.4	
1983	2.6	-1.4	39.8	8.2	36.9	
1984	11.4	9.0	23.1	15.6	48.9	
1985	0.4	-3.1	0.9	12.6	12.5	
1986	8.4	9.4	-11.6	12.3	2.6	
1987	4.0	3.3	1.1	7.0	2.6	
1988	2.3	1.2	-5.6	7.4	5.2	
1989	4.8	5.9	-2.4	3.5	-2.9	
1990	2.4	2.9	6.4	0.2	6.6	
1991	13.1	16.5	9.2	6.3	9.9	
1992	0.8	-1.6	14.0	3.6	2.4	
1993	4.2	5.9	-9.9	3.9	20.2	
1994	3.7	4.0	0.7	3.6	9.7	
1995	3.0	0.8	0.3	8.9	16.6	
1996	4.5	5.6	-5.5	3.9	7.2	
1997	4.9	5.0	1.4	4.8	20.2	
1998	0.3	-2.7	2.2	7.1	19.2	
1999	3.6	3.6	-0.5	4.0	9.6	
2000	3.8	3.1	11.0	3.7	13.4	
2001	1.2	-0.1	-15.9	6.9	10.2	
2002	2.5	-1.4	16.7	8.5	8.1	
2003	5.4	4.9	1.0	8.8	6.4	
2004	5.5	5.4	-14.4	9.2	8.7	5.2
2005	5.9	4.3	-0.1	9.8	6.7	7.3
2006	4.8	2.4	4.4	8.2	19.8	9.2
2007	3.3	3.4	2.3	2.1	6.5	6.4
2008	6.8	6.1	15.5	7.1	1.5	6.9
2009	4.6	2.8	0.7	8.5	2.6	4.7
2010	5.2	2.7	9.7	8.2	11.6	9.2
2011	1.4	-0.2	7.4	1.2	25.1	10.3
2012	9.3	12.0	7.1	5.3	23.2	3.5
2013	6.0	5.9	7.1	5.1	21.2	4.8
2014	6.6	8.5	7.5	2.0	20.4	3.6

29-15 农林牧渔业总产值指数(1978年=100)

Indices of Gross Output Value of Farming, Forestry, Animal Husbandry and Fishery (year of 1978=100)

年 份 Year	合 计 Total	农 业 Farming	林 业 Forestry	畜牧业 Animal Husbandry	渔 业 Fishery	农林牧渔服务业 Services of Farming, Forestry,Animal Husbandry and Fishery
1978	100.0	100.0	100.0	100.0	100.0	
1979	101.0	98.9	102.4	111.0	101.4	
1980	105.3	102.6	108.7	117.8	161.5	
1981	112.6	110.0	94.2	129.4	155.6	
1982	134.9	133.0	107.2	151.3	162.4	
1983	138.4	131.2	149.8	163.7	222.3	
1984	154.2	143.0	184.4	189.2	331.0	
1985	154.8	138.6	186.1	213.1	372.4	
1986	167.8	151.6	164.5	239.3	382.1	
1987	174.5	156.6	166.3	256.1	392.0	
1988	178.5	158.5	157.0	275.0	412.4	
1989	187.1	167.8	153.2	284.6	400.5	
1990	191.6	172.7	163.0	285.2	426.9	
1991	216.7	201.2	178.0	303.2	469.2	
1992	218.4	198.0	203.0	314.1	480.4	
1993	227.6	209.6	182.9	326.3	577.5	
1994	236.0	218.0	184.2	338.1	633.5	
1995	243.1	219.8	184.7	368.2	738.6	
1996	254.1	232.1	174.6	382.5	791.8	
1997	266.5	243.7	177.0	400.9	951.8	
1998	267.3	237.1	180.9	429.4	1134.5	
1999	276.9	245.6	180.0	446.5	1243.4	
2000	287.5	253.2	199.8	463.0	1410.0	
2001	290.9	253.0	168.0	495.0	1553.8	
2002	298.2	249.4	196.1	537.1	1679.7	
2003	314.3	261.6	198.1	584.4	1787.2	100.0
2004	331.6	275.7	169.5	638.1	1942.7	105.2
2005	351.1	287.6	169.4	700.7	2072.8	112.9
2006	368.0	294.5	176.8	758.1	2483.3	123.3
2007	380.1	305.1	180.9	774.8	2647.2	131.2
2008	406.0	323.7	207.0	829.8	2686.9	140.3
2009	424.6	332.8	208.4	900.3	2756.8	146.9
2010	446.7	341.8	228.6	974.1	3076.6	160.4
2011	453.0	341.1	245.5	985.8	3848.8	176.9
2012	495.1	382.0	262.9	1038.0	4741.7	183.1
2013	524.8	404.6	281.6	1091.0	5747.0	191.9
2014	559.5	439.0	302.7	1112.8	6919.3	198.8

29-16 主要农产品产量
Output of Major Farm Crops

单位：万吨 (10000 tons)

年 份 Year	粮 食 Grain	油 料 Oil-Bearing Crops	烤 烟 Flue-cured Tobacco	水 果 Fruits	肉类总产量 Total Yield of Meat	水产品 Aquatic Products
1978	643.36	9.89	8.11	4.82	12.80	0.37
1979	623.05	10.90	9.54	4.68	22.84	0.38
1980	648.35	15.59	5.56	4.97	26.67	0.55
1981	567.36	34.04	11.93	6.23	31.61	0.58
1982	654.00	48.10	16.41	6.58	35.26	0.60
1983	703.00	28.50	13.62	7.19	38.58	0.81
1984	757.80	30.59	21.48	9.23	44.76	1.22
1985	594.96	31.97	26.55	10.14	50.46	1.35
1986	672.34	41.90	19.24	13.88	57.09	1.40
1987	673.17	46.34	21.19	15.19	62.26	1.80
1988	635.68	39.87	29.15	15.63	68.73	1.86
1989	708.25	32.93	31.58	16.80	71.82	2.01
1990	721.00	43.87	28.66	16.68	74.47	2.24
1991	885.50	61.79	38.53	17.17	81.65	2.29
1992	788.90	53.38	44.90	14.18	85.59	2.36
1993	869.50	43.28	49.66	16.53	88.91	2.55
1994	938.70	47.32	33.04	16.47	95.02	2.80
1995	948.85	58.83	33.53	20.97	105.69	3.27
1996	1002.60	55.62	52.27	19.46	103.65	3.50
1997	1025.90	58.97	68.66	25.14	106.77	4.21
1998	1100.00	62.24	29.19	27.50	113.33	5.02
1999	1125.21	67.31	32.32	32.57	117.09	5.50
2000	1161.30	74.34	31.09	58.33	124.06	6.24
2001	1100.30	71.32	26.38	62.93	131.70	6.89
2002	1034.20	72.48	30.65	71.57	145.02	7.46
2003	1104.30	72.31	28.72	78.75	156.99	7.96
2004	1149.58	82.71	29.98	87.17	171.06	8.85
2005	1152.06	84.89	34.45	95.96	187.01	9.46
2006	1038.00	68.24	30.71	109.19	163.70	6.71
2007	1100.86	69.66	31.22	112.86	150.60	7.68
2008	1158.00	68.39	37.71	114.28	161.46	7.80
2009	1168.27	78.68	36.92	119.74	169.60	8.03
2010	1112.30	60.34	37.02	123.47	179.09	8.79
2011	876.90	78.85	32.50	128.03	179.97	10.88
2012	1079.50	87.38	37.31	147.72	190.27	13.47
2013	1029.99	91.53	41.79	167.75	199.74	16.70
2014	1138.50	98.05	35.34	196.38	201.80	20.99

注：1.肉类总产量1978—1984年为猪牛羊肉产量，1985—1988年为猪牛羊禽肉产量，1989年以后为猪牛羊禽肉产量和其他肉(如：马肉、狗肉、兔肉等)产量。2.2000年以后的水果包含果用瓜。

Note:1.The Data of Total Yield of Meat included output of pock,beef and mutton from 1978 to 1984;it included Output of Pock,Beef,Mutton and Meat of Poultry from 1985 to 1988;after 1989,it includes output of pock,beef,mutton,meat of poultry and other meat(e.g.horse,dog,rabbit meat and so on). 2.After 2000,the data of yield of fruits included output of melon used as fruits.

29-17 工业总产值

Gross Output Value of Industry

单位：亿元 (100 million yuan)

年 份 Year	规模以上工业总产值 Gross Output Value of Industry above Designated Size	轻工业 Light Industry	重工业 Heavy Industry
1996	514.10	191.40	322.70
1997	575.49	211.58	363.91
1998	507.91	185.66	322.25
1999	551.93	187.05	364.88
2000	631.60	206.30	425.30
2001	696.63	220.11	476.52
2002	797.90	253.00	544.90
2003	977.64	279.50	698.14
2004	1394.91	307.81	1087.10
2005	1690.40	380.85	1309.55
2006	2066.77	449.67	1617.10
2007	2520.36	527.16	1993.20
2008	3111.13	641.78	2469.34
2009	3426.69	758.14	2668.55
2010	4206.37	914.19	3292.18
2011	5520.68	1192.92	4327.76
2012	6544.02	1389.71	5154.31
2013	8074.60	1864.15	6210.45
2014	9507.33	2305.15	7202.18

注：本表统计口径1998年以前为乡及乡以上，1998—2010年为年主营业务收入500万元及以上工业企业，2011年及以后为年主营业务收入2000万元及以上工业企业(以下各相关表同)。

Notes: Before 1998, industrial statistics were based on type of industrial enterprises which are township level and above. From 1998 to 2010, industrial statistics referred to the industry enterprises which main business revenue achieve 5 million yuan and above. After 2011, industrial statistics referred to industry enterprises which main business revenue achive 20 million yuan and above. (The relative tables in the chapter are the same).

29-18 工业增加值
Value-added of Industry

单位：亿元 (100 million yuan)

年 份 Year	全部工业增加值 Value-added of Industry	#规模以上工业增加值 Value-added of Industry above Designated Size	轻工业 Light Industry	重工业 Heavy Industry
1996	225.36	188.43	74.71	113.72
1997	251.10	204.72	75.27	129.45
1998	273.82	181.80	76.48	105.32
1999	294.42	196.04	77.46	118.58
2000	328.73	216.99	82.16	134.83
2001	360.73	236.57	87.66	148.91
2002	395.45	271.09	88.20	182.89
2003	473.38	346.49	116.72	229.77
2004	577.40	476.75	147.79	328.96
2005	707.35	585.85	177.19	408.66
2006	839.13	747.38	218.52	528.86
2007	978.86	890.48	267.87	622.61
2008	1195.30	1051.26	302.25	749.01
2009	1252.67	1170.29	352.38	817.91
2010	1516.87	1227.17	413.99	813.18
2011	1829.20	1638.71	545.78	1092.93
2012	2217.06	2055.46	773.04	1282.42
2013	2686.52	2531.92	969.29	1562.63
2014	3140.88	3117.60	1185.13	1932.47

注：规模以上工业增加值统计口径1996—2010年为年主营业务收入500万元及以上的工业企业，2011年起为年主营业务收入2000万元及以上的工业企业（以下相关表同）。

Note:The statistical caliber of value added of industry above designated size referred to the Industry enterprises which main business revenue achieve 5 million yuan and above. After 2011, industrial statistics referred to industry enterprises which main busines revenue achieve 20 million yuan and above. (The relative tables in the chapter are the same)

29-19 工业增加值增长速度
Indices of Value-added of Industry

(%)

年 份 Year	全部工业增加值 Value-added of Industry	#规模以上工业增加值 Value-added of Industry above Designated Size	轻工业 Light Industry	重工业 Heavy Industry
1996	12.1	10.3	11.0	9.8
1997	11.8	9.0	6.0	11.1
1998	10.4	10.2	8.1	11.5
1999	11.8	6.2	0.8	9.3
2000	7.5	13.8	12.2	14.7
2001	9.2	12.6	6.4	13.6
2002	11.0	16.2	13.4	17.6
2003	13.3	16.9	9.8	20.3
2004	15.9	20.1	22.1	19.2
2005	13.0	17.0	25.3	13.3
2006	13.8	17.5	13.1	19.7
2007	14.0	16.8	13.9	18.1
2008	8.6	10.1	14.0	8.4
2009	10.2	10.6	11.6	10.2
2010	15.7	15.8	15.9	15.7
2011	17.8	21.0	22.7	20.1
2012	15.6	16.2	17.6	15.5
2013	13.1	13.6	12.7	14.1
2014	11.1	11.3	11.5	11.2

29-20 规模以上工业主要经济指标

Main Indicators of Industrial Enterprises above Designated Size

单位：亿元 (100 million yuan)

年 份 Year	主营业务收入 Revenue from Principal Business	轻工业 Light Industry	重工业 Heavy Industry	利税总额 Total Profits and Taxes	轻工业 Light Industry	重工业 Heavy Industry
1996	434.00	129.12	304.88	50.61	29.73	20.88
1997	419.82	128.07	291.75	60.82	38.42	22.40
1998	463.24	149.81	313.43	62.25	37.38	24.87
1999	507.55	162.34	345.21	65.81	40.47	25.34
2000	593.80	178.54	415.26	87.44	45.66	41.78
2001	646.01	193.35	452.66	94.30	51.27	43.03
2002	752.97	213.50	539.47	104.43	57.76	46.67
2003	974.30	248.48	725.82	135.87	72.15	63.72
2004	1325.95	274.04	1051.91	201.21	85.43	115.78
2005	1577.16	338.02	1239.14	232.49	113.50	118.99
2006	1948.57	389.38	1559.19	299.09	137.05	162.04
2007	2430.62	486.28	1944.34	403.49	187.27	216.22
2008	2922.35	567.80	2354.55	453.53	233.66	219.87
2009	3234.59	674.36	2560.23	470.60	252.25	218.35
2010	3926.01	807.13	3118.88	671.39	326.72	344.67
2011	5022.11	1091.79	3930.32	901.36	463.03	438.33
2012	5966.52	1299.99	4666.53	1172.15	608.19	563.96
2013	7357.43	1697.41	5660.02	1268.68	722.35	546.33
2014	8655.87	2064.97	6590.89	1310.38	781.12	529.27

29-20 续表 continued

年 份 Year	利润总额 Total Profits	轻工业 Light Industry	重工业 Heavy Industry	资产合计 Total Assets	轻工业 Light Industry	重工业 Heavy Industry
1996	-3.57	-2.47	-1.10	960.79	257.78	703.01
1997	0.76	0.65	0.11	1076.72	294.65	782.07
1998	1.64	-0.65	2.29	1166.76	312.79	853.97
1999	0.65	1.14	-0.49	1328.55	357.12	971.43
2000	12.56	4.48	8.08	1517.13	371.83	1145.30
2001	18.59	6.98	11.61	1698.58	412.57	1286.01
2002	21.41	10.82	10.59	1797.46	404.54	1392.92
2003	37.52	19.00	18.52	1958.57	409.35	1549.22
2004	61.99	18.03	43.96	2441.52	430.64	2010.88
2005	70.79	34.31	36.48	2734.05	458.41	2275.64
2006	110.91	48.52	62.39	3214.39	514.26	2700.13
2007	174.41	81.29	93.12	3521.19	541.49	2979.70
2008	181.83	108.56	73.27	4566.10	700.92	3865.18
2009	191.73	109.42	82.31	5066.17	819.69	4246.48
2010	317.63	149.62	168.01	5960.13	1007.10	4953.03
2011	456.20	220.40	235.80	6990.58	1200.82	5789.76
2012	627.02	307.74	319.28	8302.29	1458.24	6844.05
2013	636.59	370.74	265.85	10339.87	1989.29	8350.58
2014	628.68	397.58	231.10	11747.39	2338.93	9408.46

29-21 主要工业产品产量
Output of Major Industrial Products

年 份 Year	卷 烟 (万箱) Cigarettes (10000 cases)	茅台酒 (吨) Mao-Tai Chiew (ton)	发电量 (亿千瓦小时) Electricity (100 million kwh)	粗钢 (万吨) Crude Steel (10000 tons)	成品钢材 (万吨) Steel Products (10000 tons)	水泥 (万吨) Cement (10000 tons)	农用化肥 (万吨) Chemical Fertilizer (10000 tons)	磷矿石 (万吨) Phosphorite Material (10000 tons)
1978	31.60	1067	41.43	8.73	4.95	130.93	11.57	169.02
1979	34.30	1143	44.90	9.11	6.48	148.38	21.8	124.61
1980	44.00	1200	45.17	8.66	7.75	144.47	30.34	188.02
1981	48.70	1055	43.55	8.60	5.17	145.82	30.22	170.03
1982	56.10	1181	57.86	10.62	9.43	161.07	30.98	207.98
1983	64.40	1189	69.51	11.63	13.73	182.26	32.37	216.72
1984	85.70	1320	76.46	13.87	18.93	206.94	36.85	214.34
1985	106.10	1266	78.07	19.28	20.47	231.26	30.31	92.77
1986	102.10	1267	82.52	26.34	21.45	247.31	34.99	162.58
1987	146.40	1331	84.90	32.67	25.30	258.10	39.32	248.39
1988	188.40	1300	90.12	33.17	23.13	293.38	39.23	281.82
1989	205.10	1727	96.53	37.78	22.96	295.51	43.49	285.46
1990	208.00	1879	103.87	47.11	25.36	278.29	46.73	323.86
1991	194.00	1959	116.03	52.71	31.87	308.13	51.65	342.96
1992	202.90	2089	129.35	64.19	48.83	370.44	51.54	348.42
1993	193.60	2281	146.56	70.67	53.03	406.68	60.06	307.00
1994	204.90	3390	197.21	69.89	56.14	463.10	53.60	341.43
1995	202.90	3978	231.55	65.94	51.69	468.34	61.02	390.81
1996	197.70	4365	248.80	59.47	51.60	522.00	57.50	446.40
1997	205.30	4468	255.75	78.77	57.65	632.00	69.17	509.91
1998	195.80	5072	291.77	100.28	77.28	559.42	72.82	436.51
1999	187.60	5074	334.46	140.09	118.77	710.29	73.12	493.92
2000	187.40	5397	404.70	166.90	150.93	783.88	84.05	588.70
2001	180.80	7317	480.25	146.99	138.61	920.01	86.75	669.91
2002	177.80	9625	547.12	194.65	177.79	1121.11	158.49	729.20
2003	183.19	10869	636.60	206.10	192.97	1324.66	186.89	783.68
2004	194.74	12836	713.04	208.07	203.22	1428.80	213.78	801.98
2005	208.21	8885	786.78	237.83	214.85	1557.97	268.28	878.79
2006	211.73	9719	974.66	332.51	256.57	1799.40	338.76	1034.60
2007	220.71	10789	1166.32	349.36	328.14	1943.10	321.84	1198.83
2008	226.74	11308	1192.08	345.64	337.52	2048.94	262.21	1317.18
2009	232.24	12161	1363.09	343.10	337.62	2664.78	347.28	1360.66
2010	239.24	12911	1358.69	360.48	391.04	3694.84	384.92	1579.21
2011	245.23	13815	1359.01	434.01	462.77	5250.89	360.37	2084.18
2012	249.35	14272	1548.44	531.27	560.22	6100.45	503.82	2281.95
2013	254.29	15729	1620.08	531.44	573.28	8352.95	524.26	2905.44
2014	258.36	18319	1682.27	551.81	552.39	9386.89	533.52	3397.42

注：1.表中工业产品产量1998年以前为全社会口径，1998年及以后为规模以上工业企业数据。2.茅台酒产量从2001年起计量单位为千升，2005年起按包装量统计。

Note: 1.Before 1998, the data of industrial product output from this chart referred to all the industries in society and it refers to the industrial above designated size after 1998.2. The measurement unit of the production of Maotai is Kiloliter from 2001. And, it has measured at packages from 2005.

29-22 建筑业总产值和房屋建筑面积

Gross Output Value of Construction and Floor Space of Building

年份 Year	建筑业总产值(亿元) Gross Output Value of Construction (100 million yuan)	#国有及国有控股 State-owned and State-controlled	施工面积(万平方米) Floor Space Under Construction (10000 sq.m)	竣工面积(万平方米) Floor Space Completed (10000 sq.m)
1978	4.40	3.55	313	164
1979	4.44	3.40	371	185
1980	4.55	3.37	380	198
1981	4.76	3.27	392	213
1982	5.34	3.46	450	236
1983	6.22	3.85	501	258
1984	7.54	4.79	551	293
1985	9.81	6.34	662	342
1986	11.27	7.21	720	368
1987	12.93	8.62	725	378
1988	15.30	10.43	823	326
1989	15.57	11.07	765	305
1990	16.98	11.85	699	328
1991	20.32	14.09	739	335
1992	26.20	18.13	906	393
1993	37.65	26.63	1250	597
1994	48.69	36.65	1119	467
1995	55.40	44.58	1191	477
1996	66.49	52.45	1216	510
1997	76.70	59.78	1278	585
1998	83.20	62.42	1457	592
1999	96.65	70.91	1671	694
2000	109.06	77.04	1792	824
2001	150.20	110.40	1946	892
2002	181.12	133.62	2309	1054
2003	212.29	164.02	2520	980
2004	255.45	191.63	2820	1251
2005	271.23	207.88	3153	1150
2006	312.34	247.90	3369	1108
2007	348.79	271.69	3813	1204
2008	393.88	303.28	4230	1216
2009	523.91	408.00	4953	1244
2010	622.96	496.00	5756	1350
2011	824.72	659.29	6779	1530
2012	1039.95	859.68	8254	1863
2013	1365.00	1103.42	12174	2450
2014	1640.24	1264.19	13890	2801

29-23 交通运输

Transportation

年 份 Year	铁路营业里程(公里) Length of Railways in operation (km)	公路线路里程(公里) Length of Highways(km)	客运量(万人) Passenger Traffic (10000 persons)	铁 路 Railway	公 路 Highway	水 运 Waterway	货运量(万吨) Freight Traffic (10000 tons)	铁 路 Railway	公 路 Highway	水 运 Waterway
1978	1365	25954	3294	977	2260	57	3467	1320	2083	64
1979	1373	26166	4608	1083	3462	63	3599	1314	2209	76
1980	1374	27367	5950	1164	4700	86	3424	1395	1953	76
1981	1373	27422	7175	1224	5873	78	3541	1481	1991	69
1982	1396	27499	8026	1288	6648	90	3825	1581	2164	80
1983	1396	27675	8259	1456	6707	96	4233	1665	2488	80
1984	1411	27872	9915	1620	8184	111	4600	1777	2735	88
1985	1419	27999	10874	1638	9102	134	5717	1874	3758	85
1986	1419	28383	11033	1458	9387	188	6551	1949	4510	92
1987	1420	29823	13512	1461	11854	197	7613	2043	5479	91
1988	1420	30445	14361	1633	12564	164	8570	2074	6413	83
1989	1420	30716	14923	1530	13125	268	9459	2178	7170	111
1990	1420	31157	17048	1256	15682	110	9840	2315	7414	111
1991	1419	31588	19081	1255	17718	108	10008	2365	7551	92
1992	1423	31889	21641	1251	20262	128	11349	2498	8752	99
1993	1423	32092	23494	1366	22010	118	11495	2537	8851	107
1994	1423	32398	27076	1515	25313	248	12189	2599	9453	137
1995	1423	32487	36151	1572	34304	275	12586	2657	9806	123
1996	1423	32700	42429	1843	40245	341	12182	2770	9192	220
1997	1640	33211	46644	1957	44416	271	13077	2739	10117	221
1998	1648	33604	48468	2048	45987	433	13577	3044	10219	314
1999	1654	33973	49457	2194	46807	456	14065	3272	10449	344
2000	1641	34643	53032	2251	50313	468	15615	3577	11684	354
2001	1644	34618	54665	2017	52154	494	16344	3875	12114	355
2002	1893	44220	55980	1947	53478	555	17399	4356	12685	358
2003	1900	45304	55074	1796	52695	583	18224	4971	12886	367
2004	1891	46128	58707	1855	56077	775	19439	5504	13541	394
2005	1986	46893	64450	2191	61414	845	21771	6169	15082	520
2006	2014	113278	69270	2536	65786	948	24709	6826	17284	599
2007	2012	123247	74440	2979	70377	1084	26788	7289	18834	665
2008	1962	125365	80056	3199	75350	1507	33576	6683	26156	737
2009	1983	142561	84981	3204	80044	1733	34844	6997	27031	816
2010	2002	151644	97793	3437	92426	1930	40310	7991	31409	910
2011	2070	157820	120554	3939	114429	2186	44890	7219	36684	987
2012	2058	164542	142809	3902	136454	2453	52765	6665	45000	1100
2013	2093	172564	83435	4322	77358	1755	72700	6458	65100	1142
2014	2373	179079	86572	4409	80231	1932	85673	6319	78017	1337

注：1.资料来源于省交通运输厅、成都铁路分局。2.2006年起，公路线路里程包括村道里程；2008年公路、水路运输量采用全国公路水路运输量专项调查数据(下表同)。3.由于交通运输部对公路、水运运输量统计方案进行调整，2013年相关数据统计口径发生变化，相同指标数据与以往年份不可比(下表同)。

Notes: 1. Data in the table are obtained from provincial transports department and Chengdu Railway Branch. 2.Since 2006, the data of total length has contained the length of village road; the data of highways and waterways freight traffic highways have been adapted to special volume investig data in 2008 (the same applies to the next table). 3.Because the statistics schemes of highway, waterway transport volume are adjusted by the Ministry of Transport of the People's Republic of China, the correlation data statistics caliber changes for 2013, the same indicators can not coı with previous years (the same applies to the next table)

29-24 旅客周转量和货物周转量

Passenger-kilometers and Freight Ton-kilometers

年 份 Year	旅客周转量 (亿人公里) Passenger-kilometers (100 million passenger-km)	铁 路 Railway	公 路 Highway	水 运 Waterway	货物周转量 (亿吨公里) Freight Ton-kilometers (100 million ton.km)	铁 路 Railway	公 路 Highway	水 运 Waterway
1978	25.50	16.04	9.26	0.20	79.60	72.30	6.57	0.73
1979	31.54	19.66	11.68	0.20	93.99	86.49	6.59	0.91
1980	37.69	22.77	14.67	0.25	96.03	88.99	5.91	1.13
1981	43.28	25.32	17.73	0.23	100.43	93.19	6.23	1.01
1982	46.93	26.70	19.99	0.24	109.69	98.99	9.50	1.20
1983	52.35	30.69	21.40	0.26	117.22	104.86	10.97	1.39
1984	61.04	36.21	24.55	0.28	132.72	119.19	11.61	1.92
1985	74.07	45.11	28.64	0.32	151.42	133.22	16.32	1.88
1986	76.45	47.39	28.70	0.36	171.03	148.13	20.44	2.46
1987	93.19	53.22	39.60	0.37	186.09	156.33	26.87	2.89
1988	105.67	61.20	44.14	0.33	196.04	159.75	33.50	2.79
1989	105.73	58.08	47.16	0.49	216.45	174.59	38.96	2.90
1990	102.90	49.20	53.34	0.36	224.31	179.72	41.84	2.75
1991	117.61	54.84	62.52	0.25	232.91	186.96	42.51	3.44
1992	136.77	66.62	69.84	0.31	268.80	214.88	49.84	4.08
1993	156.26	80.86	75.12	0.28	292.96	239.40	49.12	4.44
1994	173.71	88.72	84.53	0.46	298.44	243.87	50.06	4.51
1995	180.09	91.23	88.32	0.54	301.28	245.76	51.34	4.18
1996	185.94	88.32	96.84	0.78	317.70	261.99	51.07	4.64
1997	191.02	97.97	92.52	0.53	336.08	277.95	54.06	4.07
1998	201.77	101.13	99.97	0.67	330.30	270.40	54.84	5.06
1999	229.20	118.37	109.95	0.88	370.03	305.68	60.28	4.07
2000	238.36	120.79	116.54	1.03	404.07	334.11	65.86	4.10
2001	251.06	124.22	125.76	1.08	439.30	364.71	70.36	4.23
2002	250.79	116.10	133.60	1.09	486.03	407.26	74.25	4.52
2003	248.55	112.08	135.31	1.16	547.01	465.92	76.63	4.46
2004	278.21	125.87	150.79	1.55	610.88	520.70	84.27	5.91
2005	312.40	145.71	164.91	1.78	646.55	544.31	94.15	8.09
2006	349.82	160.98	186.91	1.93	680.96	557.70	114.48	8.78
2007	369.20	160.51	206.40	2.29	721.26	583.85	127.99	9.42
2008	407.59	163.00	241.15	3.44	809.93	564.31	234.96	10.66
2009	430.56	162.41	264.06	4.09	897.38	644.41	241.60	11.37
2010	514.41	189.38	320.46	4.57	1012.20	706.45	293.00	12.75
2011	631.74	204.58	422.01	5.15	1060.69	696.36	350.10	14.23
2012	718.22	199.20	513.07	5.95	1177.78	693.68	467.60	16.50
2013	593.62	211.21	377.87	4.54	1292.11	655.85	610.64	25.62
2014	635.50	217.39	412.92	5.19	1442.24	634.35	776.95	30.94

29－25 内外贸易

Domestic Trade,Foreign Trade and Economic Cooperation

年份 Year	社会消费品零售总额(亿元) Total Retail Sales of Consumer Goods (100 million yuan)	进出口总额(万美元) Total Value of Imports and Exports (USD 10000)	#出口额 Exports	实际利用外资额(万美元) Total Amount of Foreign Investment Actually Utilized (USD 10000)	#国外贷款 Foreign Loans	#外商直接投资 Foreign Direct Investments
1978	21.23	1645	285			
1979	23.57	2111	703			
1980	26.73	2797	1641			
1981	30.48	4782	3617			
1982	34.55	5455	4522			
1983	38.43	5238	4186			
1984	43.64	6997	4548	61	61	
1985	52.25	8720	4010	286	12	148
1986	57.25	8605	6361	1276	38	74
1987	66.39	12488	9296	376	127	101
1988	83.40	15527	11586	1408	425	440
1989	83.84	18681	13322	2102	826	747
1990	85.90	21802	15358	2983	1925	463
1991	92.92	24614	18958	2845	1436	1034
1992	106.75	33907	22424	3574	1595	1979
1993	143.09	36470	24491	4922	628	4294
1994	165.01	53595	37346	8363	2000	6363
1995	204.45	68144	43023	9637	3934	5703
1996	241.57	64240	43554	10628	7490	3138
1997	274.68	67660	48239	13834	8857	4977
1998	299.97	62243	38794	18100	13565	4535
1999	324.67	54763	35780	19532	15442	4090
2000	355.58	66002	42060	19545	17044	2501
2001	391.14	64978	42170	14010	11181	2829
2002	430.64	69141	44181	9383	5684	3700
2003	474.57	98477	58834	13191	7565	5626
2004	535.31	151442	86709	13932	7399	6533
2005	615.75	140425	85925	19568	8800	10768
2006	710.00	161745	103874	18413	9029	9384
2007	858.15	227285	146513	15333	2682	12651
2008	1075.24	337037	190084	17379	2475	14904
2009	1265.46	230732	135856	18027	4663	13364
2010	1531.64	314680	192018	34026	4480	29546
2011	1899.92	488758	298509	71674	4353	51541
2012	2266.27	663156	495223	109805	5223	49116
2013	2601.20	829009	688598	157415	4853	57673
2014	2936.85	1077133	939726	213053	8524	46565

注：1.进出口总额1997年及以前数据来源于原省对外贸易经济合作厅，1998年及以后数据来源于贵阳海关。2.实际利用外资额数据来源于省发展改革委、省商务厅。

Note:1.The total amount of import and export were obtained from the former provincial department of foreign trade and economic cooperation in 1997 and before, while After 1998 they obtained from Guiyang Customs.2.Data of foreign capital actually utilized are obtained from Provincial Development and Reform Commission and Department of Commerce.

29-26 旅游

Tourism

年 份 Year	国内旅游人数（万人次） Number of Domestic Visitors (10000 person-times)	国内旅游收入（亿元） Earnings from Domestic Tourism (100 million yuan)	入境旅游人数（万人次） Number of Overseas Visitor Arrivals (10000 person-times)	#外国人 Foreigners	国际旅游外汇收入（万美元） Foreign Exchange Earnings from Intennational Tourism(10000 USD)
1980			0.17	0.07	0.70
1981			0.23	0.06	2.49
1982			0.51	0.18	5.73
1983			0.71	0.19	8.03
1984	204	0.07	1.02	0.27	15.86
1985	244	0.07	1.13	0.29	61.95
1986	248	0.05	1.40	0.46	100.19
1987	261	0.07	1.88	0.77	137.22
1988	296	0.18	2.36	0.75	162.54
1989	397	0.18	1.37	0.47	136.75
1990	399	0.19	2.41	0.74	180.90
1991	630	0.66	3.75	1.04	307.35
1992	1426	2.21	7.63	1.87	686.13
1993	1647	4.29	10.25	4.26	1049.45
1994	1700	4.28	12.08	7.61	2109.63
1995	1750	7.18	13.65	7.78	2897.73
1996	1800	8.53	12.53	6.67	3811.95
1997	1850	30.81	15.02	7.81	4429.10
1998	1880	35.14	15.13	6.77	4831.18
1999	1910	43.75	16.70	6.57	5501.54
2000	1980	57.95	18.39	7.12	6092.23
2001	2100	75.81	20.55	7.85	6873.23
2002	2200	99.86	22.81	8.45	7950.63
2003	1835	114.36	7.70	2.40	2893.91
2004	2480	161.02	23.10	7.63	8020.27
2005	3099	242.83	27.62	9.26	10141.36
2006	4716	377.79	32.14	10.70	11515.66
2007	6220	504.04	43.00	15.48	12917.55
2008	8151	643.82	39.54	18.22	11697.37
2009	10400	797.69	39.95	16.28	11044.40
2010	12863	1052.64	50.01	18.61	12957.88
2011	16961	1420.70	58.51	23.62	13507.18
2012	21331	1849.49	70.50	30.42	16893.60
2013	26684	2358.18	77.70	31.97	20143.41
2014	32049	2882.66	85.50	35.94	21671.23

注：资料来源于省旅游局。
Note:Data in the table is obtained from Provincial Tourism Bureau.

29-27 金融机构人民币各项存贷款余额

Saving Deposits and Loans Balance of Financial Institutions

单位：亿元 (100 million yuan)

年 份 Year	各项存款余额 Total Deposits	#个人储蓄存款 Personal Saving Deposits	人均储蓄余额（元） Per Captia Savings Deposit (yuan)	各项贷款余额 Total Loans
1978	18.05	1.84	6.91	21.62
1979	19.82	2.42	8.93	23.31
1980	24.43	3.73	13.54	24.94
1981	25.75	5.28	18.85	30.10
1982	30.75	7.26	25.46	33.99
1983	35.25	8.86	30.68	36.07
1984	45.33	12.33	42.27	46.22
1985	52.27	16.61	56.27	63.41
1986	69.76	22.21	74.06	89.67
1987	83.79	30.37	99.60	107.76
1988	91.92	34.99	112.87	125.17
1989	107.35	44.54	141.44	142.73
1990	144.39	61.27	190.32	183.91
1991	187.06	80.30	243.99	234.56
1992	232.80	102.07	305.80	290.01
1993	291.22	141.88	419.16	357.00
1994	364.84	181.05	527.30	421.07
1995	478.21	247.62	710.89	513.41
1996	586.26	311.19	881.12	610.51
1997	712.80	362.87	1013.43	761.88
1998	815.43	423.08	1164.96	840.63
1999	945.80	484.51	1315.23	899.83
2000	1106.64	539.49	1445.23	1064.82
2001	1341.11	641.67	1698.83	1212.23
2002	1553.00	759.05	1988.13	1403.92
2003	1898.62	912.84	2368.88	1714.04
2004	2322.27	1094.55	2816.16	2020.04
2005	2777.54	1350.90	3633.79	2303.93
2006	3300.08	1596.86	4304.20	2696.11
2007	3826.37	1790.14	4889.76	3128.63
2008	4736.93	2237.05	6189.96	3569.27
2009	5898.26	2676.09	7503.41	4656.50
2010	7363.92	3244.99	9250.26	5747.53
2011	8742.79	3934.48	11325.50	6841.92
2012	10540.06	4806.09	13824.51	8274.78
2013	13265.01	5919.05	16944.93	10104.30
2014	15263.26	6620.56	18888.19	12368.30

注：1.资料来源于中国人民银行贵阳中心支行。2.2005年及以后各年人均储蓄余额采用按人口普查修订后常住半年的年平均人口计算，以前年份按常住一年口径计算。3.表中储蓄存款及人均储蓄2010年及以前为城乡居民储蓄存款和城乡居民人均储蓄。

Note:1.Data in the table are obtained from Guiyang Central Branch of PBC. 2.Per captia savings deposit are calculated by permanent population in half a year scope since 2005,and by permanent population in one year scope before 2005.3.The year 2010 and before,savings deposit refer to resident savings deposit of urban and rural.

29-28 教 育

年份 Year	在校学生数(万人) Students Enrollment(1 0000 persons)			小学毕业生升学率(%) Percentage of Graduates of Primary Schools Entering into Junior Secondary Schools(%)
	普通高等学校 Regular Institutions of Higher Education	普通中学 Regular Secondary Schools	小学 Primary Schools	
1978	1.33	137.17	423.60	76.1
1979	1.78	126.07	413.71	70.0
1980	1.71	110.24	404.22	62.6
1981	1.81	96.58	403.49	56.7
1982	1.67	89.53	412.30	53.8
1983	1.68	82.39	415.79	51.5
1984	2.03	85.13	436.56	53.1
1985	2.30	91.59	447.68	54.2
1986	2.52	99.00	461.99	53.8
1987	2.60	102.35	458.27	47.7
1988	2.73	98.63	449.70	56.6
1989	2.76	93.31	440.36	67.1
1990	2.70	96.54	435.05	60.8
1991	2.57	100.23	433.85	59.6
1992	2.67	103.99	435.94	59.9
1993	2.93	100.55	439.81	63.9
1994	3.23	103.08	455.30	70.5
1995	3.47	108.43	475.34	72.7
1996	3.57	113.47	489.32	71.5
1997	3.85	121.54	503.82	75.8
1998	4.26	127.10	505.36	75.1
1999	5.65	138.63	500.96	77.8
2000	7.55	157.20	500.21	78.7
2001	10.82	184.60	490.17	84.4
2002	12.27	212.81	484.28	88.2
2003	14.94	235.30	476.87	92.4
2004	17.99	249.34	479.41	96.0
2005	20.68	254.96	473.76	97.4
2006	22.15	256.31	474.38	97.8
2007	24.17	256.00	466.31	95.6
2008	26.75	261.78	469.79	98.7
2009	29.91	269.45	456.87	97.7
2010	32.33	276.75	433.50	96.3
2011	34.41	282.71	408.74	96.5
2012	38.38	287.38	380.08	96.3
2013	41.90	296.01	355.53	99.0
2014	46.04	301.10	346.31	100.0

注：资料来源于省教育厅。

Education

学龄儿童入学率(%) Percentage of School-Aged Children Enrolled(%)	专任教师数(人) Number of Full-time Teachers(person)		
	普通高等学校 Regular Institutions of Higher Education	普通中学 Regular Secondary Schools	小学 Primary Schools
89.5	2753	54227	155930
86.1	3357	55532	151860
80.8	3638	51950	155708
78.5	3606	46892	159494
78.3	3986	44646	152176
81.2	4183	43821	152338
83.6	4555	41879	155715
84.9	4830	45159	157622
86.9	5177	47119	162105
89.2	5559	50216	161689
89.9	5588	51618	163514
88.8	5530	53279	164298
91.3	5469	55528	166662
90.3	5371	57074	168364
92.4	5542	59006	166769
93.8	5550	60453	165276
95.1	5540	63059	168842
96.0	5599	64292	168358
96.7	5600	66842	166526
97.4	5699	69355	168493
97.7	5929	72865	167823
98.2	6050	76654	170680
98.5	7240	81156	174822
98.2	9007	88079	173238
98.2	11079	97641	177920
98.2	11775	107312	179367
97.8	13792	115616	180793
98.3	14353	122721	183679
98.6	15398	128274	188762
98.6	16964	131087	191991
97.2	18037	135360	200024
98.4	19634	139302	199189
97.9	20351	143128	197913
98.6	21855	147396	197094
99.3	22803	156325	197983
99.3	25351	162309	192953
99.1	28144	171988	192850

Note:Data in the table are obtained from Provincial Education Department.

29-29 卫生

Health Care

年 份 Year	卫生机构数(个) Number of Health Institutions (unit)	#医院、卫生院 Hospitals Health Center's	卫生机构床位数(张) Number of Beds in Health Institutions (bed)	#医院、卫生院 Hospitals Health Center's	卫生技术人员数(人) Medical Technical Personnels (person)	#执业(助理)医师 Licensed (Assistant) Doctors	每万人口拥有 Per 10000 person 床位数(张) Number of Beds(bed)	执业(助理)医师数(人) Number of Licensed(Assistant) Doctors(person)
1978	6274	4510	40274	37533	58190	21228	14.0	7.9
1979	6267	4516	42812	40001	60635	21868	14.6	8.0
1980	6246	4529	43627	40835	63766	26491	14.7	9.5
1981	6634	4588	44752	41314	68918	26798	14.6	9.5
1982	6595	4605	46226	42301	70671	27097	14.7	9.4
1983	6605	4602	47555	43292	72988	28433	14.9	9.8
1984	6673	4643	49271	44123	75808	29309	15.0	10.0
1985	6480	3295	49805	45226	76722	29153	15.2	9.8
1986	6760	3358	50893	46259	79776	30475	15.3	10.1
1987	6716	3349	52595	48059	81599	31305	15.6	10.2
1988	7021	3896	54193	49543	84904	35249	15.8	11.3
1989	6926	3620	57428	52063	84891	35646	16.4	11.2
1990	6949	3721	59013	53074	86120	37185	16.2	11.4
1991	6908	3630	59168	53978	87774	37978	16.3	11.5
1992	4734	1624	57767	52405	87927	38537	15.6	11.5
1993	3908	1623	57720	51888	84409	38060	15.2	11.2
1994	3930	1660	59648	53766	88053	40358	15.5	11.7
1995	3934	1692	60295	54475	87005	40260	15.5	11.5
1996	10932	1870	58205	54051	84273	43548	15.2	12.2
1997	8955	1870	57560	53627	84348	43236	14.9	12.0
1998	9113	1877	57844	54492	84400	44138	14.9	12.1
1999	9703	1874	58624	55138	85613	45473	14.9	12.3
2000	8992	1878	58380	55148	85397	45673	14.8	12.2
2001	8791	1872	59120	55876	86103	46412	14.8	12.3
2002	7027	1857	59850	57742	79727	36964	15.1	11.3
2003	6499	1866	59281	56273	77557	36911	14.9	11.2
2004	6664	1850	61313	58113	76699	36911	14.9	12.2
2005	6571	1843	61784	58398	77805	35521	16.6	9.5
2006	6147	1855	66452	62586	82324	41147	17.9	11.1
2007	5907	1939	75806	71400	85298	42100	20.7	11.5
2008	5848	1934	83132	78129	89313	38830	23.0	10.7
2009	5736	1982	97527	91164	95270	40171	27.3	11.3
2010	5637	2005	105277	97490	102527	42158	30.0	12.0
2011	5683	2071	117534	108029	112210	44037	27.7	10.4
2012	27379	2210	136542	129670	152608	49200	32.1	11.2
2013	29182	2429	163332	155848	156557	55877	38.1	13.0
2014	28995	2512	181728	174002	169799	57802	42.0	13.4

注：1.资料来源于省卫生计生委。2.表中数据2011年及以前的数据不含村卫生室,2012年起含村卫生室。3.每万人口指标2011年以前以常住人口数为基数计算，2011年起以户籍人口数为基数计算。

Note:1.Data in the table are provided from the Department of Health and Family Planning. 2.In the year of 2011 and before data in this table exclude health clinics of village, but including health clinics of village in 2012 and after. 3.Before 2011, per ten thousand population indicators were calculated on the number of permanent resident population , but since 2011 they have calculated on the number of household registered population.

中国统计出版社最新图书简目

(仅供参考，以实际出版为准)

统计资料

中国统计年鉴　中国统计摘要　中国发展报告
中国经济普查年鉴2013　国际统计年鉴　金砖国家联合统计手册
中国-东盟国家统计手册　中国区域经济统计年鉴　中国县域统计年鉴
中国城市统计年鉴　中国农村统计年鉴　中国地区经济监测报告
中国贸易外经统计年鉴　中国对外直接投资统计公报　中国商品交易市场统计年鉴
大中型批发零售和住宿餐饮企业统计年鉴　中国零售和餐饮连锁企业统计年鉴　中国住户调查年鉴
中国价格统计年鉴　中国农产品价格调查年鉴　全国农产品成本收益资料汇编
中国环境统计年鉴　中国能源统计年鉴　国外资源、能源和环境统计资料汇编
中国工业统计年鉴　中国建筑业统计年鉴　中国房地产统计年鉴
中国城市建设统计年鉴　中国城乡建设统计年鉴　中国第三产业统计年鉴
中国证券期货统计年鉴　中国科技统计年鉴　中国高技术产业统计年鉴
工业企业科技活动资料　中国劳动统计年鉴　中国人口和就业统计年鉴
中国人才资源统计报告　中国社会统计年鉴　中国文化及相关产业统计年鉴
文化及相关产业统计概览　中国教育经费统计年鉴　中国民政统计年鉴
中国民族统计年鉴　中国工会统计年鉴　中国残疾人事业统计年鉴
中国妇女儿童状况统计资料（英）　中国乡镇街道行政区域简册

省级综合统计年鉴系列

北京 天津 河北 山西 内蒙古 辽宁 吉林 黑龙江 上海 江苏 浙江 安徽 福建 江西 山东 河南 湖北 湖南 广东 广西 海南 重庆 四川 贵州 云南 西藏 陕西 甘肃 青海 宁夏 新疆 新疆生产建设兵团

市(县)级综合统计年鉴系列

天津滨海新区 石家庄 唐山 邯郸 保定 沧州 邢台 廊坊 承德 衡水 秦皇岛 张家口 太原 大同 阳泉 长治 晋城 朔州 晋中 运城 忻州 临汾 呼和浩特 呼和浩特新城区 鄂尔多斯 包头 沈阳 大连 长春 四平 哈尔滨 齐齐哈尔 黑龙江垦区 上海浦东新区 南京 无锡 徐州 常州 苏州 南通 连云港 淮安 盐城 扬州 镇江 泰州 宿迁 江阴 丹阳 杭州 宁波 温州 嘉兴 绍兴 金华 衢州 舟山 台州 丽水 合肥 安庆 马鞍山 福州 厦门 宁德 南昌 九江 上饶 新余 抚州 济南 青岛 枣庄 滕州 郑州 洛阳 平顶山 三门峡 南阳 商丘 济源 武汉 十堰 荆州 宜昌 荆门 咸宁 长沙 广州 深圳 惠州 东莞 南宁 柳州 桂林 来宾 海口 三亚 成都 贵阳 昆明 西安 兰州 庆阳 银川 乌鲁木齐 兵团一师 兵团十师

调查年鉴系列

天津 山西 内蒙古 辽宁 吉林 上海 福建 河南 湖北 湖南 广西 重庆 四川 云南 甘肃 宁夏 新疆

“十二五”规划教材

统计学（经济管理类专业本科适用，单薇 等）　抽样调查理论与方法（冯士雍 等）
贝叶斯统计（茆诗松 等）　统计学（黄良文 等）　试验设计（茆诗松 等）
统计学：从数据到结论（吴喜之）　医学统计学（于浩）　统计学（经济、管理类专业基础教材，张小斐）
概率论与数理统计三十三讲（魏振军）　概率论与数理统计三十三：学习指导与习题解答（魏振军）
非参数统计（吴喜之 等）　统计学：经济与管理中的数据分析（李慧云 等）
卫生管理统计学（新编医学院校基础课教材，尚磊）　医院统计学（新编医学院校基础课教材，徐天和 等）
社会统计学（蒋萍 等）　现代金融投资统计分析（李腊生 等）
国民经济核算初级教程（经济类、统计类、管理类专业适用，蒋萍 等）

重点图书

图解中国经济2015　新编英汉汉英统计大词典　中华医学统计百科全书
挑大学选专业2016—考研择校指南　挑大学选专业2015—高考志愿填报指南